Ensuring Privacy in Digital Twin Ecosystems

Scrivener Publishing
100 Cummings Center, Suite 541J
Beverly, MA 01915-6106

Publishers at Scrivener
Martin Scrivener (martin@scrivenerpublishing.com)
Phillip Carmical (pcarmical@scrivenerpublishing.com)

Ensuring Privacy in Digital Twin Ecosystems

Edited by

Shubham Mahajan

Davinder Paul Singh

Amit Kant Pandit

and

Paras Chawla

Scrivener Publishing

WILEY

This edition first published 2026 by John Wiley & Sons, Inc., 111 River Street, Hoboken, NJ 07030, USA
and Scrivener Publishing LLC, 100 Cummings Center, Suite 541J, Beverly, MA 01915, USA

For more information about Scrivener publications please visit www.scrivenerpublishing.com.

Wiley Global Headquarters
111 River Street, Hoboken, NJ 07030, USA

For details of our global editorial offices, customer services, and more information about Wiley products visit us at www.wiley.com.

The manufacturer's authorized representative according to the EU General Product Safety Regulation is Wiley-VCH GmbH, Boschstr. 12, 69469 Weinheim, Germany, e-mail: Product_Safety@wiley.com.

Library of Congress Cataloging-in-Publication Data

ISBN 9781394383719

Cover image: Generated with AI using Adobe Firefly
Cover design by Russell Richardson

Set in size of 11pt and Minion Pro by Manila Typesetting Company, Makati, Philippines

Printed in the USA

10 9 8 7 6 5 4 3 2 1

Contents

Preface

In the current era of being in touch with everything and the digital transformation that is transforming the industries and society, one must point out that the idea of digital twins has become one of the most important features of technology. These digital models of physical objects, processes, or systems allow unequaled perspectives, productivity, and innovations to be achieved in many fields, including manufacturing and healthcare, smart cities, and many others.

But based on these transformative powers, there arises a very significant issue at hand, and that is privacy. We have to face the complex maze of data protection as we ride the wave of digital twins into the future because we should not trade the rights of individuals to privacy in order to achieve improvement.

The book, *Ensuring Privacy in Digital Twin Ecosystems*, allows exploring the multidimensional interrelation between the concepts of digital twins and privacy. It delves into the paradoxes of striking a balance between innovation and personal data protection in organizations and by policymakers. Whether it is the obscurities of the complexities involved in smart city deployments or the ethical implications of healthcare and beyond, every chapter gives in-depth coverage of the current trends, emerging challenges, and future directions.

We explore how AI and machine learning in particular can help maintain privacy in digital twins, usually including aspects of regulatory compliance and best practice. Additionally, the book highlights the essence of openness, responsibility, and user-friendliness in privacy-protective digital twin ecosystems.

Combining various insights and advanced studies, the book attempts to provide researchers, practitioners, and policymakers (stakeholders, in general) with the information and methods that could help to cover this changing territory safely. With our current trend towards an ever more digitally innovative future, the protection of privacy should also be a hub of our technological endeavors.

Come along with us, and we can discover the complexity behind the privacy of the digital twin age together to set a path towards a safer and fairer digital future.

Editors
Dr. Shubham Mahajan
Dr. Davinder Paul Singh
Prof. (Dr.) Amit Kant Pandit
Prof. (Dr.) Paras Chawla

Acknowledgement

With the divine blessings of ***Shri Guru Maharaj Ji***, this book, *Ensuring Privacy in Digital Twin Ecosystems,* has become a reality. His grace has been my guiding light through every challenge and every breakthrough along this journey.

I express my heartfelt gratitude to my beloved parents, **Sh. Manoj Kumar Gupta** and **Smt. Madhu Gupta**, whose unwavering love, sacrifices, and constant encouragement have shaped every step of my life. Their belief in me has been my greatest strength.

A special mention to my sister **Sunidhi and** my jiju **Er. Shiv Saroop**, whose support and cheerful spirit have always kept me grounded and motivated.

I also extend my thanks to all my *near and dear ones*—friends, mentors, colleagues, and well-wishers—who stood by me with their encouragement, insights, and blessings. Each one of you has contributed in your own way to the completion of this work.

To all who have been a part of this journey, knowingly or unknowingly, I offer my sincere gratitude.

With folded hands and deep reverence—Thank you.

1

Balancing Innovation and Privacy: Navigating the Landscape of Digital Twin Ecosystems

Manish Kumar Panday[1]*, Manish Baboo Agarwal[2], Manu Mehrotra[2] and Seema Agarwal[3]

[1]Department of Applied Sciences, Anand Engineering College, Keetham, Agra, Uttar Pradesh, India
[2]Sharda School of Basic Sciences and Research, Sharda University Agra, Keetham, Agra, Uttar Pradesh, India
[3]Department of Mathematics, SRMIST, Ghaziabad, Uttar Pradesh, India

Abstract

The appearance of digital twin ecosystems has revolutionized numerous sectors but raises significant concerns regarding privacy in interconnected environments. Digital twins, which are virtual replicas of physical entities, help in the analysis and optimization of real-time data. However, they also pose challenges to safeguarding personal data. The scientists have underlined integration complexities within smart cities, where urban digital twins collect extensive data on individuals, thus amplifying the privacy risks. Technological advances, such as federated learning, promise to improve the privacy of data by allowing decentralization of the data processing while maintaining the functionality of digital twins. However, these solutions are not exempt from limitations, which require solid regulatory frameworks to govern data use and guarantee compliance.

The regulatory panorama is evolving, but existing laws are often insufficient to address the unique challenges posed by digital twin technology. It has been emphasized that the importance of creating adaptive regulations not only protects

**Corresponding author*: mmkp.81@gmail.com; ORCID: https://orcid.org/0009-0009-1704-0782
Manish Baboo Agarwal: ORCID: https://orcid.org/0000-0003-1177-2738
Manu Mehrotra: ORCID: https://orcid.org/0009-0003-4841-1589
Seema Agarwal: ORCID: https://orcid.org/0000-0002-5655-207X

Shubham Mahajan, Davinder Paul Singh, Amit Kant Pandit and Paras Chawla (eds.) Ensuring Privacy in Digital Twin Ecosystems, (1–22) © 2026 Scrivener Publishing LLC

personal data but also fosters innovations in AI and digital twin technologies. The advancement in technology requires more proactive approaches to secure one's privacy. Effective measures may include the implementation of strict access controls, regular audits, and taking advantage of encryption techniques. As digital twin ecosystems evolve, addressing the privacy implications through improved technological solutions, robust regulatory frameworks, and proactive protection strategies has become indispensable to protect personal data in these interconnected environments.

Keywords: Digital twins, privacy risks, interconnected environments, regulatory frameworks, data encryption, federated learning

1.1 Overview of Digital Twin Ecosystems (DTEs)

The introduction of DTEs is considered the start of a new digital era, as it integrates the physical and virtual worlds for evaluation in real-time streaming, foresight analysis, and optimization. A digital twin (DT), or simply twin, is characterized as an up-to-date model of an individual or object, which evolves over time, receiving updates through IoT sensors, AI, and ML, and is, thus, self-updating [1, 2]. The ecosystem of twins with their cloud computing, edge processing, big data analytics, and blockchain technology for security and traceability forms a network.

The application of twin technologies is evident across numerous sectors such as healthcare, smart cities, manufacturing, autonomous systems, and transportation, as they improve the efficiency of decision-making and lower the cost [3, 4]. In the manufacturing sector, digital twins augment predictive maintenance to boost asset availability and operational efficiency. In healthcare, DT of patients supports personalized treatment and chronic condition health monitoring. Smart cities implement DTs to simulate urban areas for improved traffic control and resource allocation devices. DTs improve navigation, safety, and performance for autonomous systems and advanced transport systems [5].

On the other hand, security and privacy dangers stand out as some of the greatest concerns related to the advantages of digital twin ecosystems. Integrating various systems and devices poses a greater risk to private information due to cyberattacks, hacking, unauthorized access, and data leaks. Shielding privacy within the confines of digital twin ecosystems requires strong laws on data protection and ethical policies on responsible innovation to govern powerful geospatial data.

1.1.1 Information Security Challenges in IoT

The advancement of infrastructure, as well as of devices, such as the digital twin and IoT, is making privacy matters increasingly complex. The extent of data covered in DTEs is enormous and includes sensitive personal, industrial, and vital environmental data, which makes privacy control very important to prevent unauthorized access or misuse [6].

Data sovereignty is the foremost issue, which deals with who really has control of data. Compliance and legal concerns are made more complicated due to digital services of an international nature, as data is traversing through different jurisdictions. Limited trust and compliance regarding the operation of digital twins is breached when laws such as GDPR or even softer ones like CCPA, alongside certain regulations, are not adhered to. The existence of hostile cyberattacks makes cybersecurity the most fundamental issue [7, 8]. Financial system abuse, phishing scams, and impersonation are major risks to information and systems that, with sensitive data, can have detrimental consequences. Employing strong adversarial protection, such as homomorphic encryption and zero-trust systems with differential privacy, enhances data protection while stifling breaches [9].

In addition, the ethics of data-powered surveillance technologies also require equal attention. Active user participation mechanisms that serve as control elements during the data collection processes must be complemented by responsibility elements to provide trust and fairness in using digital twins. Organizations need to formulate frameworks to actively design processes that ensure sensitive data is protected throughout the life cycle of digital twin system development, which is process-driven [10, 11].

The development of digital twin ecosystems comes with a need for more precise guidelines. There is a need for stringent regulation to blend privacy with innovation. Standards for privacy regulations for digital twin systems need to be developed for policymakers, business and technology entrepreneurs, and regulators to balance trust and security. All stakeholders stand to benefit from digital twins while sensitive information remains protected by placing focus on privacy policies.

1.2 Developing Digital Twins Further

1.2.1 Structure and Functionality

Whereas the underlying physical item may undergo changes, a digital twin is an up-to-date, real-time digital counterpart of an entity, system, or process that undergoes alterations in accordance with its physical counterpart. Its construction involves collecting data from sensors and IoT devices as well as conducting diagnoses, which aid in analytics replication of behavior and attributes of the asset [12, 13]. Rather than being a mere simulation, a digital twin receives real-world updates that keep a virtual model adjusted to reality, thereby allowing representation of reality's condition.

The functionality of digital twins hinges on their capabilities of providing foresight, scenario simulation, and optimizing operations. The integration of artificial intelligence (AI), machine learning (ML), and big data analytics allows for proactive decision-making and proactive anomaly detection. Furthermore, better lifecycle management can be achieved. Digital transformation enables organizations to adopt and integrate new technology into their processes, systems, or operations. This model incorporates historical and real-time data, which greatly enhances forecasting, operational efficiency, and cost-effectiveness [14].

1.2.2 Real-Time Data Analysis and Optimization

Among the advantages of digital twin technologies, their capacity for real-time data analytics and dynamic process optimization stands out the most. Digital twins provide organizations with system performance data, predictive maintenance metrics, and potential operational bottleneck data streams, all in real time, alongside the constant data flow from myriad connected sources. With the use of digital twins, real-time data analysis becomes possible, making anomaly detection, where the system triggers alerts for deviations from the expected behavior to prevent further damage, possible [15, 16]. This is very important for industries vulnerable to financial losses or immediate safety ramifications due to system failures. Additionally, the application of digital twins enables the adjustment of different variables within the simulated model, providing value in predicting the impact prior to real-world implementation [17, 18].

The optimization of individual assets has progressed towards entire systems with regard to smart cities, energy grids, and even supply chains, as all of them can now be managed through sophisticated AI technology. Utilizing AI-powered analytics, waste can be reduced while resource aiding, sustainability efforts, and overall preservation can be enhanced. Such insights maximize operational efficiency but also support meeting compliance requirements of regulations and standards. The real-time data analysis and optimization required is shown in Figure 1.1.

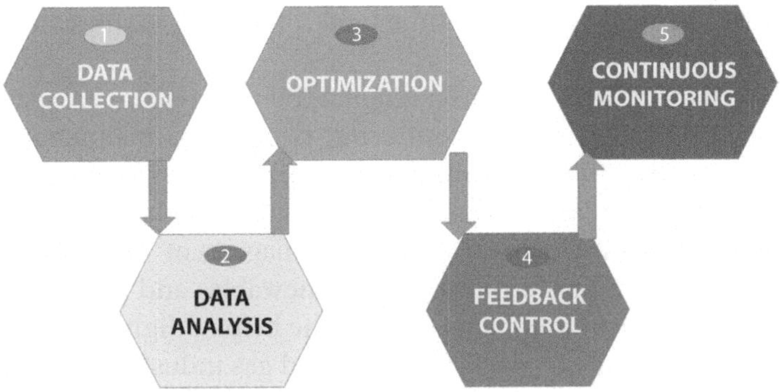

Figure 1.1 Real-time optimization process.

1.2.3 Key Application Across Various Sectors

Cost savings opportunities for businesses and governments go beyond a single industry, as the digital twin applications are cross-industrial. Potential risks with equipment can be reduced during the production component while monitoring the machinery through predictive maintenance, controlled downtime, and visibility throughout the supply chain enhancements.

Some major industries that reap the benefits from digital twin technology include:

(a) **Manufacturing:** Digital twins aid in the creation of prototypes prior to their synthesis, thus aiding in the design of products, preventing the wastage of vital materials, and decreasing expenditure.
(b) **Healthcare:** In the medical field, digital twins create unique systems for each patient that allow their chronic diseases to be monitored, treated, and even operated on in simulated environments, which means surgery can be done on a virtually crafted model before the patient, lowering the risks associated with surgical procedures. Enhanced medical research and improved patient care are achieved through the creation of replicas of tissues, organs, and systems of the body [19].
(c) **Smart Cities and Infrastructure:** Infrastructure changes are simulated using digital twins to improve urban planning, traffic control, and energy consumption so that the effects of such changes can be analyzed before any real-world implementations are made. Smart building management systems

also benefit from real-time and predictive maintenance capabilities [20].

(d) **Aerospace and Defense:** Digital twins in the aerospace sector enable health monitoring of aircraft, maintenance forecasting, fuel consumption optimization, strategic simulations, and real-time analyses of the battlefields [13].

(e) **Energy and Utilities:** Overall management services for energy grids and monitoring of renewables and power distribution tasks are managed with the help of digital twins. It helps manage the assets in the oil and gas industry, enabling risk evaluation and ensuring compliance with safety regulations [21].

The application of digital twin technologies in various sectors demonstrates their ever-increasing impact. The key applications of digital twin across various sectors is depicted in Figure 1.2. Implementing these replicas includes many ethical as well as legislative dilemmas surrounding the sovereignty of data, its security, and its governance, all of which must be properly managed within digital twin systems.

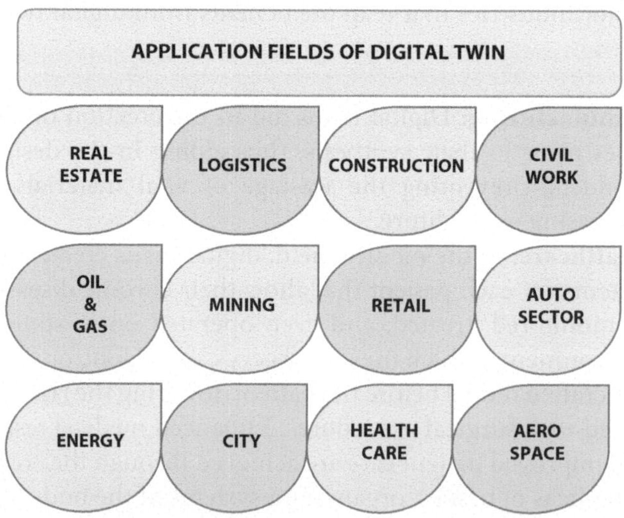

Figure 1.2 Application fields of digital twin.

1.3 Privacy Concerns Related to Digital Twins Ecosystem

Global strategic planning, along with decision-making, has been enhanced with the establishment of digital twin (DT) ecosystems, as they provide avenues for real-time simulations and predictive analyses. These advancements, however, lead to potential privacy issues, which stem from a lack of legal or ethical boundaries. The simulated representation of the real world enables the harvesting and processing of personal information in unprecedented ways, which results in personal privacy and data security threats. These issues may best be categorized into three groups, which include gaps in surveillance and monitoring, integration issues within smart cities, and the privacy amplifier within the smart city paradigm.

1.3.1 Gaps in Surveillance and Data Collection

Digital twin ecosystems require the collation of huge amounts of information in order to function as intended. This information could include streaming biometric sensors, geolocation tracking, behavioral data, and data from other devices. While efficient precision modeling paired with automated decision-making systems improves an organization's operational efficiency, productivity, and effectiveness, they also increase the risk of privacy violations and surveillance [22, 23].

Whether done directly or indirectly, both governments and private corporations utilizing DT technologies for urban planning, industrial supervision, or healthcare services tend to cross the fine line of invasive surveillance. The collection of such detailed granular data enables profiling and even predictive behavioral analytics, which violates essential privacy principles. Even more, data mismanagement, poor encryption policies, data breaches, identity fraud, and industrial espionage can arise from weak access control policies [24]. There is some attempt by regulators through GDPR and CCPA to mitigate such risks, but gaps in enforcement remain because of the swift development of DT technologies.

1.3.2 Integration Complexities in Smart Cities

The management of infrastructure, energy, traffic, and other public services in smart cities is more efficiently done through digital twins. However, the incorporation of such simulators into pre-designed urban structures poses sophisticated privacy issues. The combination of numerous data sources like government data repositories, IoT sensors, and even private sector data systems poses a risk to data governance and security [25, 26].

One of the main issues with data collection and processing is the potential exploitation of personal data by third-party sales vendors and other unauthorized people. With the number of private organizations and municipal agencies that share data amongst themselves, the risk for sharing data without consent increases exponentially. Also, the international circulation of information for the purposes of smart city initiatives makes compliance with regional and international privacy regulations even more complicated. With regard to these organizations, trust is managed in the public context through data processing and handling techniques that also reduce risk [27, 28].

1.3.3 Exacerbation of Privacy Risks

The concern regarding privacy in the interlinked ecosystem of digital twins is virtually boundless due to five different stakeholders being able to modify and interact with the data. The combination of AI-powered analytics, blockchain, and machine learning with the frameworks of DT heightens the automation of critical processes without human assistance for ethical guidance, deepening the privacy risks even further [29, 30]. Digital twins allow the use of privacy-enhancing technologies but give rise to new risks associated with blending data from different sources. Combining data from different sources may lead to the unintended disclosure of identifying information that was previously thought to be anonymized, thus eroding protective mechanisms. Moreover, privacy breaches in the form of hacking, ransomware, and deep fake impersonations pose huge dangers to public trust in the system, which damages the integrity of the data [31, 32]. To address these problems, as proposed, these issues require ensuring strong encryption protocols along with regulatory compliance and ethical AI control, a user-centered procedural AI privacy policy, and user priority policies. To safeguard the trust framework, a collaboration of government with industry stakeholders and researchers is needed to advance individual privacy while harnessing the benefits of digital twin ecosystems [33].

The use of digital twin technologies bears utmost consequences for both creativity and efficiency, yet their application must be guided by a clearly defined privacy policy. Mitigating risk from preemptive privacy threats alongside the anticipated proactive data governance policy will ensure that DT systems function without infringing fundamental civil liberties. Moreover, the privacy-structured modular strategy sought in this context aids significantly towards mitigating the exposure of sensitive data, especially in volatile domains such as finance or healthcare within digital twin ecosystems [34, 35].

With limitations on user data, federated learning, which is a subset of machine learning, lowers the risks of data leakage and misuse. It also aids compliance with legislation, such as GDPR, that governs privacy and data protection, which is rooted in the ethos of data minimization. Nevertheless, there are unresolved issues in federated learning, such as balancing privacy during model building and enforcing strong encryption with robust communication protocols [36].

1.4 Benefits of Decentralization

The use of digital twin technologies has inherent implications for creativity and efficiency; however, the boundaries of privacy must be clearly defined. Newer concepts such as blockchain and Distributed Ledger Systems (DLS) offer valuable avenues towards achieving decentralization while still controlling and protecting data [37, 38].

Decentralization arguably allows for greater enhanced user control over personal data to the highest degree. Through smart contracts on the blockchain, users can now control access to view specific information without the need for intermediaries. In these ecosystems, trust and transparency are not just 'sufficient' in the presence of cyber twin systems, but they are capable of withstanding espionage and cyberterrorism [39, 40]. Furthermore, there is less reliance on centralized cloud storage due to decentralization, which mitigates the monopolization and abuse of control that centralization has by big corporations. On the other hand, some advantages of decentralization can be viewed as disadvantages for governance, scalability, and computational efficiency [41]. For these issues to be solved, we have to implement a compromise strategy that will integrate both decentralized and centralized solutions while still adding additional protective layers like encryption.

1.5 Encryption Techniques and Data Security

Within the context of the digital twin ecosystem, encryption is arguably the primary, most remarkable technique for safeguarding data. It effectively protects the privacy of sensitive information by preventing unauthorized users from gaining access to it, even if the data is intercepted.

There are various encryptions, such as symmetric and asymmetric encryptions, homomorphic encryption, and zero-knowledge proofs, which assist greatly in the protection of data [42].

- Symmetric and Asymmetric Encryption: Symmetric encryption is faster and simpler for large amounts of data because a single key is used for both encrypting and decrypting. Asymmetric encryption, in contrast, enhances authentication and secure communication with a pair of public and private keys [43].
- Homomorphic Encryption: As far as privacy is concerned, during the analysis of data and examination from different angles using machine learning, this method is of utmost significance since it allows operations to be carried out on encrypted data without any need to decrypt it [44].
- Zero-Knowledge Proofs: As far as managing and authenticating identities are concerned, these privacy-preserving cryptographic techniques permit the verification of values without providing the document itself [45].

The application of these encryption methods within the context of federated learning and distributed structures enhances security against cyber threats and strengthens privacy threats within the digital twin systems. Nonetheless, the constantly evolving security requirements in today's world necessitate upgrades to encryption techniques. In the case of digital twin ecosystems, strong encryption combined with decentralization and federated learning strikes the balance between excessive innovation and privacy and conforms to ethical standards of information management.

1.6 Compliance with Governance and Other Policies

The construction of digital twin ecosystems intensifies the necessity of having an elaborate legal compliance structure to govern their deployment as well as manage data ethically. The emerging technologies with digital twins require a policy to be in place to balance privacy management with innovation. This part reflects the history of laws enacted and attempts made to fill in some gaps within the legislation advocating responsive policies, if not more adaptable ones [46].

1.6.1 Policy Changes and Developments in Data Protection Regulations

The policies that govern data protection are changing from the face of things and even more due to digital transformation concerns. The first data privacy legislative attempts concentrated on specific domains, like financial services, telecommunications, and even healthcare. The adoption of the internet, as well as the widespread use of personal data, necessitated much broader regulations [47]. The European Union achieved a milestone by creating stronger regulations with the enactment of the General Data Protection Regulation (GDPR) in 2018. The revision of compliance frameworks to align with data minimization and purpose limitation, along with user consent, transformed policy principles. The United States also noted these developments with the California Consumer Privacy Act (CCPA), which shifted some power to users regarding control of their information. These laws have sparked other global legislative attempts, such as Brazil's General Data Protection Law (LGPD), India's Digital Personal Data Protection Act, and China's Personal Information Protection Law (PIPL) [48, 49].

When it comes to digital twins, these regulations provide a base of assurance in guaranteeing data privacy and security. While still useful, these regulations face the problem of evolving to emerging difficulties such as cross-border data flows, data sovereignty, and management of consent due to the nature of digital twin ecosystems, which constantly collect, analyze, and simulate information in real time.

1.6.2 Shortcomings in the Current Legal Structures

As far as the more advanced data protection legislation allows, there are gaps in the consideration of digital twin ecosystems. One of these concerns includes the absence of explicit legal definitions designed for digital twins, where personal, industrial, and even environmental data are consolidated into a single entity. Equally important is the fact that current constructs fail to address the governance of synthetic or carved-out data pertaining to digital twins that are devoid of identifiers. Also, the governance of distributed data custodianship, where multiple parties share the responsibility of ownership and accountability, becomes difficult [44].

Regulatory inconsistency poses yet another challenge. Although the GDPR attempts to provide a standard framework for other jurisdictions, it often creates distinctions at the subnational level. This creates challenges for entities that operate across borders in countries with multiple jurisdictions. The disparity exposes what is termed as regulatory arbitrage, where companies reduce operational burdens by moving their headquarters to geographies with stringent data protection laws [37, 39].

1.6.3 Strategic and Tactical Gaps in Setting Expectations

Amid swift industry progress is the issue of privacy and protection in digital twin ecosystems. Organizations must be held accountable for the outcomes of policies, requiring flexibility at the policy design stage. Policies ought to be proactive and incorporate elements of anticipatory governance while imposing risk-driven accountability.

Ethical governance of AI within digital twin ecosystems has been given particular attention in one of the policies. To prevent social discrimination, algorithms must integrate traceability steganography into data capturing. Similarly, automated compliance frameworks should include active monitoring in real-time with dynamic, fine-grained consent for advanced data governance frameworks [40].

A unified policy on user privacy versus data use frequency requires sustaining a shared objective. A regulatory sandbox is an environment set up to test new innovations within existing legal boundaries that will ensure compliance, incorporating novel business concepts with sophisticated technologies. Given that digital twin ecosystems are evolving, integration with other perspectives, proactive governance in particular, seems indispensable. By using agile approaches to fill legislative silos, stakeholders would be able to strike a balance between privacy and innovation, ensuring that digital twins are deployed ethically as catalysts for constructive global societal advancement [41].

1.7 Approaches to Shifting to Proactively Protective Measures for Digital Privacy

Outstepping these technological limits or failing to employ privacy engineering will lead to a breach of regulatory compliance. This structure deals with three primary strategies: advanced technologies that hinder access to privacy-sensitive information, periodic assessment audits or continuous review audits, and ongoing privacy vulnerability assessment coupled with the use of appropriate privacy-enhancing technologies.

1.7.1 Implementation of Strict Access Controls

Among the best practices for optimizing performance in twin ecosystems is privacy compliance. This is due to the twin holding sensitive information encased in data, meaning stricter access controls must be put into place.

Organizational skeletons need to implement advanced authentication and authorization frameworks (such as Multi-Factor Authentication (MFA) and Role-Based Access Control (RBAC)). MFA bypasses credential theft, as users need to provide other means of verification before being allowed entry into the system. Similarly, RBAC follows the approach of limiting the data accessible to specific users based on their roles and duties, therefore making it possible for authorized users to engage with critical data freely [50]. These technologies are helpful in the detection of abnormal behavior. Access controls reduce risks associated with exposure of private data and ensure the twin adheres to regulatory standards. These measures guarantee the twins will achieve exposed compliance with data protection policies. AI and ML technologies permit the detection of dormant users in real time. Within this architecture, detection of privacy breaches improves the enforcement of robust cycle policies.

1.7.2 Regular Audit and Risk Assessment

Routine audit and risk assessment in rapidly evolving digital twin ecosystems are crucial for the governance of privacy gaps. Alongside the evolution of technology, regulations, and cyber threats, privacy risks also evolve. Prompt assessment and management of these risks is critical.

Organizations are required to conduct regular privacy impact assessments (PIAs) to evaluate how personal data is gathered, processed, and stored in relation to digital twins. Evaluating them is critical to counter privacy threats while ensuring compliance with privacy laws such as GDPR and CCPA. To assess the effectiveness of the privacy controls, a security audit must be performed. These audits should incorporate compliance auditing, vulnerability assessment, and penetration testing. Continuous monitoring tools enable organizations to predict breaches and take preventive measures [51].

As stated above, the National Institute of Standards and Technology (NIST) cybersecurity framework and ISO 27001 provide distinct approaches that, in conjunction with other methods, can be used to appraise privacy risks within an organization. The continuous audit and the risk appraisal foster a sense of accountability, aiding in the maintenance of digital privacy protection within the Twin Ecosystems.

1.7.3 Implementation of Advanced Methodologies to Resolve Privacy Concerns

The enhancement of digital ecosystems known as digital twins can be achieved with the implementation of newly designed systems aimed at resolving privacy issues. One of these systems is privacy-by-design, which proactively resolves privacy issues at the project's parameter setting stage. Incorporating other PETs, such as different types of privacy, homomorphic encryption, and federated learning, will enable full functionality without revealing sensitive information. Unlike traditional methods of sanitizing data that delete specific identifiers, differential privacy adds random noise to a dataset, which renders unique identifiers undetectable while allowing accurate analysis. This is useful in many situations when data have to be shared for analysis, but a certain level of confidentiality is needed [52].

Like any other cryptosystem, homomorphic encryption allows computations to be carried out on the encrypted data. While traditional methods demand decryption before computations, even with the assurance that sensitive information will not be disclosed during the computation process. This is particularly important for cloud-based digital twin systems, where safeguarding data privacy is of paramount importance.

Federated learning allows for the training of machine learning models on multiple distributed devices, eliminating the transmission of raw data across the network. This enhances user privacy as personally identifiable information (PII) remains within local boundaries while still contributing towards the development of AI models within the confines of digital twins.

Additionally, blockchain technology can be applied to enhance trust and privacy in digital twin ecosystems. The application of blockchain technology, due to its distributed and immutable ledger, ensures secure data transactions with minimal risk of unauthorized modification or changes [53].

Adoption of new technologies enables organizations to enhance trust and compliance in them by enforcing stricter privacy policies. From a proactive ecosystem ethic, privacy-protecting actions sufficiently constrain the secure and ethical boundaries within which digital twin ecosystems operate. Protecting sensitive data and maintaining organizational compliance while safeguarding stakeholder trust can be achieved through the application of advanced technologies. These technologies automate comprehensive data protection and regulatory compliance with enforced access controls, audit trails, and organization-wide risk assessments. With rapid advancements in digital twin technologies, addressing privacy issues will require proactively embracing innovation alongside other privacy dynamics.

1.8 Conclusion

The development of digital twin (DT) ecosystems marks an industrial breakthrough supporting real-time surveillance, monitoring, and decision-making based on predictive analytics and scenario simulation. However, innovation must ensure the security and privacy of digital replicas simultaneously. This chapter focuses on finding a solution to the advancement of technology and the protection of data by analyzing ethical implications and regulatory boundaries that need attention. The last two sections outline the innovative and collaborative actions needed on policy and technological fronts for secure digital twin ecosystems, highlighting the need to protect private data while innovating.

1.8.1 Future Directions for Evolving Secure Digital Twin Ecosystems

With the implementation of digital twins in smart cities, healthcare, manufacturing, and other sectors, their security needs to be enhanced for better protection against cyberattacks, data theft, and unauthorized access. Future work in this area should consider the application of high-level cryptographic techniques such as homomorphic encryption and blockchain security systems to keep sensitive data secure. The offense of exploiting active vulnerabilities can be mitigated with the implementation of real-time detection systems powered by artificial intelligence [54]. Lack of integration of security policies across different domains straddles all other issues. Formulation of international cybersecurity strategy frameworks for digital twins will lead to more balanced and comprehensive security strategies. Industry researchers should devise appropriate policies that ensure the data integrity, confidentiality, and availability within these ecosystems are protected [55].

From another standpoint, security systems may be enhanced with the aid of quantum computing, which can, however, disrupt current encryption techniques. Even so, quantum computing enables the design of quantum-safe cryptography, which will need to be developed. Protecting digital twin ecosystems from the advancement of cyber threats will rely on investment in cybersecurity that is resilient to quantum computing.

1.8.2 Striking a Balance between Innovative Developments and Privacy Protection

Public confidence alongside adherence to diverse regulations will not be achieved without integrating robust security measures while advancing in digital twin technology. Opportunities for gaining business intelligence through twins without divulging PII can be achieved through the application of privacy-preserving algorithms like federated learning and differential privacy. These methods not only allow data to be analyzed but also protect identities, reducing the dangers posed by having data in a single location.

As the technology advances, it is important that policymakers do not lag behind. Existing policies, such as the GDPR and CCPA, must be flexible enough to accommodate the emerging challenges in the digital twin world. Allowing users to manage their digital identity while controlling the consent trail would be essential for fair technological growth and privacy protection. Equally, ethical issues should shape the course of other sectors such as healthcare and autonomous systems [56]. Strong policies must be in place to govern data on the use of digital twins to safeguard against bias and unfairness in AI algorithms.

1.8.3 Call for Collaborations Concerning Policy, Technology, and Other Domains

An ecosystem of digital twins that is safe and mindful of privacy concerns can only be realized through the synergistic efforts of policymakers, technologists, industry players, and the scholarly community. An integrative strategy that promotes the cooperation of all these parties will cultivate the development of appropriate policies as well as technological and legal defenses.

Policymakers must coordinate with enforcement developers so that policies can be implemented flexibly without hindering innovative security techniques. At the same time, industries need to adopt increased security measures to guard digital twin frameworks [57].

Furthermore, global partnerships are necessary for dealing with the cross-national scope of cyberattacks and data access as data flows between different countries. Forming global coalitions for the protection of computer systems, governing data, and managing artificial intelligence will help spread the best solutions and practices around the globe.

Thus, protecting the digital twin ecosystems while maintaining privacy to achieve innovation in design is still a tangled mess, but it is solvable.

By employing strong innovative guarding measures and reevaluating control systems alongside international cooperation policies, we can responsibly manage the boundaries of public innovation while checking privacy controls regulated in other systems.

AI disclosure statement: The author confirms that no artificial intelligence (AI)-generated content or AI-assisted writing tools were used in the preparation of this chapter (including summaries and the abstract). All text, analysis, and conclusions are the result of the author's original work.

References

1. Tao, F., Zhang, H., Liu, A., Nee, A.Y.C., Digital twin in industry: State-of-the-art. *IEEE Trans. Ind. Inf.*, 15, 4, 2405–2415, 2019, https://doi.org/10.1109/TII.2018.2873186.
2. Kritzinger, W., Karner, M., Traar, G., Henjes, J., Sihn, W., Digital Twin in manufacturing: A categorical literature review and classification. *IFAC-PapersOnLine*, 51, 11, 1016–1022, 2018, https://doi.org/10.1016/j.ifacol.2018.08.474.
3. Jones, D., Snider, C., Nassehi, A., Yon, J., Hicks, B., Characterising the Digital Twin: A systematic literature review. *CIRP J. Manuf. Sci. Technol.*, 29, 36–52, 2020, https://doi.org/10.1016/j.cirpj.2020.02.002.
4. Fuller, A., Fan, Z., Day, C., Barlow, C., Digital Twin: Enabling technologies, challenges and open research. *IEEE Access*, 8, 108952–108971, 2020, https://doi.org/10.1109/ACCESS.2020.2998358.
5. Suri, N., Dutta, S., Panda, R., Digital twins for smart cities: Concepts towards realization. *Smart Cities*, 4, 1, 1–17, 2021, https://doi.org/10.3390/smartcities4010001.
6. Xu, L.D., He, W., Li, S., Internet of Things in Industries: A Survey. *IEEE Trans. Ind. Inf.*, 10, 4, 2233–2243, 2014, https://doi.org/10.1109/TII.2014.2300753.
7. Batty, M., Digital twins. *Environ. Plann. B Urban Anal. City Sci.*, 45, 5, 817–820, 2018, https://doi.org/10.1177/2399808318796416.
8. European Union., Regulation (EU) 2016/679 of the European Parliament and of the Council (General Data Protection Regulation - GDPR), 2016, https://eur-lex.europa.eu/eli/reg/2016/679/oj.
9. Zhang, Y., Deng, R.H., Weng, J., Efficient and Privacy-Preserving Data Sharing in Smart Cities. *IEEE Internet Things J.*, 9, 1, 111–125, 2022, https://doi.org/10.1109/JIOT.2021.3071699.
10. Verdouw, C.N., Kruize, J.W., Wolfert, J., Digital Twins in Smart Farming: Operationalising the Digital Representation of Agriculture. *Sensors*, 21, 11, 3755, 2021, https://doi.org/10.3390/s21113755.

11. Khan, W.Z., Ahmed, E., Hakak, S., Yaqoob, I., Ahmed, A., Edge computing: A survey. *Future Gener. Comput. Syst.*, 97, 219–235, 2020, https://doi.org/10.1016/j.future.2019.02.050.
12. Grieves, M. and Vickers, J., Digital Twin: Mitigating Unpredictable, Undesirable Emergent Behavior in Complex Systems, in: *Transdisciplinary Perspectives on Complex Systems*, F.-J. Kahlen, S. Flumerfelt, A. Alves (Eds.), pp. 85–113, Springer, University of Central Florida, Johnson Space Center, 2017, https://doi.org/10.1007/978-3-319-38756-7_4.
13. Boschert, S. and Rosen, R., Digital Twin—The Simulation Aspect, in: *Mechatronic Futures*, P. Hehenberger and D. Bradley (Eds.), pp. 59–74, Springer, Siemens, 2016, https://doi.org/10.1007/978-3-319-32156-1_5.
14. Tao, F., Qi, Q., Liu, A., Kusiak, A., Data-driven smart manufacturing. *J. Manuf. Syst.*, 48, 157–169, 2018, https://doi.org/10.1016/j.jmsy.2018.01.006.
15. Madni, A.M. and Madni, C.C., Architecting Cyber-Physical Systems with a Digital Twin, in: *Aerospace Conference*, IEEE, pp. 1–9, 2018, https://doi.org/10.1109/AERO.2018.8396461.
16. Qi, Q. and Tao, F., Digital Twin and Big Data Towards Smart Manufacturing and Industry 4.0: 360 Degree Comparison. *IEEE Access*, 6, 3585–3593, 2018, https://doi.org/10.1109/ACCESS.2018.2793265.
17. Glaessgen, E. and Stargel, D., The Digital Twin Paradigm for Future NASA, and U.S. Air Force Vehicles, in: *53rd AIAA/ASME/ASCE/AHS/ASC Structures, Structural Dynamics and Materials Conference*, 2012, https://doi.org/10.2514/6.2012-1818.
18. Batty, M., Axhausen, K.W., Giannotti, F., Pozdnoukhov, A., Bazzani, A., Wachowicz, M., Portugali, Y., Smart cities of the future. *Eur. Phys. J. Spec. Top.*, 214, 1, 481–518, 2012, https://doi.org/10.1140/epjst/e2012-01703-3.
19. Kamel Boulos, M.N. and Zhang, P., Digital twins: From personalized medicine to precision public health. *J. Pers. Med.*, 11, 8, 745, 2021, https://doi.org/10.3390/jpm11080745.
20. Cimino, C., Negri, E., Macchi, M., Digital Twin Paradigm: A Systematic Literature Review. *Comput. Ind.*, 113, 103130, 2019, https://doi.org/10.1016/j.compind.2019.103130.
21. Barricelli, B.R., Casiraghi, E., Fogli, D., A Survey on Digital Twin: Definitions, Characteristics, Applications and Design Implications. *IEEE Access*, 7, 167653–167671, 2019, https://doi.org/10.1109/ACCESS.2019.2953499.
22. Kitchin, R., The ethics of smart cities and urban science. *Philos. Trans. R. Soc. A*, 379, 2196, 20200472, 2021, https://doi.org/10.1098/rsta.2020.0472.
23. Pasquale, F., *The Black Box Society: The Secret Algorithms That Control Money and Information*, Harvard University Press, 2015.
24. Van Zoonen, L., Privacy concerns in smart cities. *Gov. Inf. Q.*, 33, 3, 472–480, 2016, https://doi.org/10.1016/j.giq.2016.06.004.
25. Allam, Z. and Dhunny, Z.A., On big data, artificial intelligence and smart cities. *Cities*, 89, 80–91, 2019, https://doi.org/10.1016/j.cities.2019.01.032.

26. Crawford, K. and Paglen, T., Excavating AI: The Politics of Images in Machine Learning Training Sets. *Int. J. Commun.*, 15, 3525–3542, 2021.
27. Akhtar, Z. and Misra, S., Digital twins for smart cities: Challenges and future directions. *Sustainable Cities Soc.*, 76, 103444, 2022, https://doi.org/10.1016/j.scs.2021.103444.
28. Tzafestas, S.G., Ethics and law in the internet of things world. *Smart Cities*, 1, 1, 98–120, 2018, https://doi.org/10.3390/smartcities1010006.
29. Lu, Y., Liu, C., Wang, K., II, Huang, H., Xu, X., Digital Twin-driven smart manufacturing: Connotation, reference model, applications and research issues. *Rob. Comput. Integr. Manuf.*, 61, 101837, 2020, https://doi.org/10.1016/j.rcim.2019.101837.
30. Radanliev, P., De Roure, D., Nicolescu, R., Huth, M., Cannady, S., Montalvo, R.M., Artificial intelligence and digital twins in manufacturing and supply chains. *Technol. Soc.*, 62, 101361, 2020, https://doi.org/10.1016/j.techsoc.2020.101361.
31. Gaur, A., Scarselli, D., Sadeghian, A., Bhatt, C., Blockchain in Digital Twin: State-of-the-art, challenges and future directions. *Comput. Ind. Eng.*, 153, 107948, 2021, https://doi.org/10.1016/j.cie.2020.107948.
32. Bonatti, P.A. and Olmedilla, D., Rule-based policy representation and reasoning for the Semantic Web, in: *Reasoning Web*, pp. 240–268, Springer, 2007, https://doi.org/10.1007/978-3-540-75164-1_7.
33. Voigt, P. and Von dem Bussche, A., *The EU General Data Protection Regulation (GDPR).* A Practical Guide, Springer, Taylor Wessing, January 2017, https://doi.org/10.1007/978-3-319-57959-7.
34. Kairouz, P., McMahan, H.B., *et al.*, Advances and Open Problems in Federated Learning. *Found. Trends® Mach. Learn.*, 14, 1–2, 1–210, 2021, https://doi.org/10.1561/2200000083.
35. Zuboff, S., The age of surveillance capitalism: the fight for a human future at the new frontier of power. *AI & Society*, 38, 6, 704, New York, Public Affairs, 2019. ISBN 978-1-61039-569-4 (hardcover) 978-1-61039-270-0 (ebook). DOI:10.1007/s00146-020-01100-0
36. Al-Fuqaha, A., Guizani, M., Mohammadi, M., Aledhari, M., Ayyash, M., Internet of Things: A Survey on Enabling Technologies, Protocols and Applications. *IEEE Commun. Surv. Tutorials*, 17, 4, 2347–2376, 2015, https://doi.org/10.1109/COMST.2015.2444095.
37. Onwubiko, A., Singh, R., Awan, S., Pervez, Z., Ramzan, N., Enabling Trust and Security in Digital Twin Management: A Blockchain-Based Approach with Ethereum and IPFS. *Sensors*, 23, 14, 6641, 2023, https://doi.org/10.3390/s23146641.
38. Zhang, Y., Li, X., Wang, H., Blockchain Empowered Access Control for Digital Twin Systems with Attribute-Based Encryption. *Future Gener. Comput. Syst.*, 152, 123–135, 2024, https://doi.org/10.1016/j.future.2024.06.037.
39. Ghirmai, S., Mebrahtom, D., Aloqaily, M., Self-Sovereign Identity for Trust and Interoperability in the Metaverse, 2023, https://doi.

org/10.1109/SmartWorld-UIC-ATC-ScalCom-DigitalTwin-PriComp-Metaverse56740.2022.00345.

40. Diamantopoulos, G., Tziritas, N., Bahsoon, R., Digital Twins for Dynamic Management of Blockchain Systems, 2022, https://doi.org/10.1109/WSC57314.2022.10015447.
41. Roumeliotis, C., Dasygenis, M., Lazaridis, V., Dossis, M., Blockchain and Digital Twins in Smart Industry 4.0: The Use Case of Supply Chain-A Review of Integration Techniques and Applications. *Designs*, 8, 6, 105, 2024, https://doi.org/10.3390/designs8060105.
42. Teller, M., Legal aspects related to digital twin. *Philos. Trans. R. Soc. A Math. Phys. Eng. Sci.*, 379, 2190, 20210023, 2021, https:// DOI: 10.1098/rsta.2021.0023.
43. Gil, J., Petrova-Antonova, D., Kemp, G.J.L., Redefining urban digital twins for the federated data spaces ecosystem: A perspective. *Big Data Soc.*, 11, 1, 23998083241302578, 2024, https:// DOI:10.1177/23998083241302578.
44. Zheng, Y., Li, T., Ma, W., Zheng, J., Li, Z., Wang, L., Unveiling Privacy Challenges: Big Data-Driven Digital Twins in Smart City Applications. *SID Symp. Dig. Tech. Pap.*, 55, S1, 49–52, 2024, https://DOI: 10.1002/sdtp.16992.
45. Voas, J., Mell, P., Laplante, P., Piroumian, V., *Security and Trust Considerations for Digital Twin Technology.* NIST Interagency/Internal Report (NISTIR) 8356, 2025, https://doi.org/10.6028/NIST.IR.8356.
46. Kuruppuarachchi, P.M., Rea, S., McGibney, A., Trusted and secure composite digital twin architecture for collaborative ecosystems. *IET Collab. Intell. Manuf.*, 5, 1, e12070, 2022, https://doi DOI: 10.1049/cim2.12070.
47. Tooth, J.M., Tuptuk, N., Watson, J.D.M., A Systematic Survey of the Gemini Principles for Digital Twin Ontologies, 2024, https://doi.org/10.48550/arXiv.2404.10754.
48. Fernandez, I.A., Neupane, S., Chakraborty, T., Mitra, S., Mittal, S., Pillai, N., Chen, J., Rahimi, S., A Survey on Privacy Attacks Against Digital Twin Systems in AI-Robotics, 2024, DOI:10.48550/arXiv.2406.18812.
49. Zemskov, A.D., Fu, Y., Li, R., Wang, X., Karkaria, V., Tsai, Y.-K., Chen, W., Zhang, J., Gao, R., Cao, J., Loparo, K.A., Li, P., Security and Privacy of Digital Twins for Advanced Manufacturing: A Survey, 2024, DOI:10.48550/arXiv.2412.13939.
50. Samaniego, M. and Deters, R., Digital Twins and Blockchain for IoT Management. *BSCI '23: Proceedings of the 5th ACM International Symposium on Blockchain and Secure Critical Infrastructure*, pp. 64–74, 2023, https:// DOI: 10.1145/3594556.3594611.
51. Ahmadi-Assalemi, G., Al-Khateeb, H., Aggoun, A., Privacy-enhancing technologies in the design of digital twins for smart cities. *Network Secur.*, 2022, 7, 2022, https://doi.org/10.12968/s1353-4858(22)70046-3.
52. Voas, J., Digital Twin Technology Considerations, 2025, https://doi.org/10.6028/nist.ir.8356.

53. Hassan, F., Kumar, V., Nishad, A.K., Gautam, V., Investigation of digital twin technology for secure and privacy preserving networking. *Procedia Comput. Sci.*, 230, 398–406, 2023, https://doi.org/10.1016/j.procs.2023.12.095.
54. Alhumam, N., Rahman, M.M.H., Aljughaiman, A., A comprehensive review on cybersecurity of Digital Twins issues, challenges, and future research directions. *IEEE Access*, 1, 2025, https://doi.org/10.1109/access.2025.3545004.
55. Suhail, S., Iqbal, M., McLaughlin, K., Lee, B., Imtiaz, B., A framework for enhancing cyber incident response with Security-Enhancing Digital Twins in Cyber-Physical Systems. *Internet Things*, 101547, 2025, https://doi.org/10.1016/j.iot.2025.101547.
56. Sharma, A., Kosasih, E., Zhang, J., Brintrup, A., Calinescu, A., Digital Twins: State of the art theory and practice, challenges, and open research questions. *J. Ind. Inf. Integr.*, 30, 100383, 2022, https://doi.org/10.1016/j.jii.2022.100383.
57. Wikipedia contributors, Digital twin, 2025, June 16, https://en.wikipedia.org/wiki/Digital_twin.

2

Digital Twins and Privacy: Navigating the Nexus of Innovation and Data Protection

Ashima Kalra[1]*, Bhawna Tandon[1] and Panchal Sandeep Govindrao[2]

[1]Department of ECE, Chandigarh Engineering College-CGC, Landran (Mohali), India
[2]Department Computer Engineering, G H Raisoni College of Engineering and Management, Pune, India

Abstract

People are implementing digital twin systems in fields like industry, healthcare, smart cities, and others, and this is changing how decisions are made and predictions are made. Still, the huge amount of data that powers these systems leads to important questions about privacy, the ethics of data use, and obeying regulations. The chapter thoroughly examines the link between digital twin technology and the need for proper data protection. First, basic concepts of DTs and the role they are playing in different sectors are set out. The focus of the discussion is to point out the main privacy risks in DT networks, such as surveillance, the risk of uncovering personal data, and inference attacks. GDPR and HIPAA are examined to see what impact they have on designing and deploying DT systems. In addition, the chapter examines more advanced privacy techniques, including federated learning, differential privacy, and secure computation, as well as what privacy-by-design is. Key issues like transparency, independence, and differences in technology are studied under ethical and societal points of view. By using case studies, the chapter presents these challenges and offers advice on smart city systems, healthcare twinning, and industrial monitoring. It finishes by recommending future work and discussing open research issues that can make DT systems reliable, innovative, and trustworthy. This chapter is meant to help researchers, practitioners, and policymakers handle the challenge of using advanced technology while still ensuring privacy and data security.

**Corresponding author*: uppal.ashi@gmail.com

Shubham Mahajan, Davinder Paul Singh, Amit Kant Pandit and Paras Chawla (eds.) Ensuring Privacy in Digital Twin Ecosystems, (23–56) © 2026 Scrivener Publishing LLC

***Keywords*:** Digital twin, data protection, privacy, ethics, GDPR (General Data Protection Regulation), HIPAA (Health Insurance Portability and Accountability Act)

2.1 Introduction

Digital twin technology has fast become an important innovation used in healthcare, smart cities, manufacturing, and energy. DTs let you represent physical things virtually, making it possible to observe, run models, and improve complex systems in real time. Being part of data-driven systems, these industries collect and make use of extensive data about people, jobs, and the environment. Even though it improves making predictions and decisions, it at the same time raises significant concerns about privacy. This chapter starts by describing digital twins, what they do in the data world, and why it is crucial to protect privacy to create reliable and ethical DT systems.

2.1.1 What are Digital Twins?

Digital twins are advanced virtual reproductions of real things, processes, or equipment that are always updated in real time using data from the actual world. This concept helps build a digital environment that copies the behavior and changes of physical entities by applying technologies such as the Internet of Things (IoT), artificial intelligence (AI), machine learning, and real-time simulation [1]. DTs were created for use in aerospace but have found applications in healthcare, manufacturing, smart infrastructure, and many similar industries.

Maintaining open communication with the real counterpart is the key part of a digital twin system. Sensors integrated in the IoT network obtain data from the system about its temperature, pressure, vibrations, amount of energy, and other factors and send it to the digital model. After that, machine learning reads the data and investigates what is happening now in order to envision what could happen next. Because of this, it is possible to monitor, diagnose, and decide on issues quickly, making operations run more smoothly and reducing the chances of the asset or system having any downtime.

The early notion of digital twins was created in the aerospace industry to monitor and predict the actions of spacecraft and aircraft. Yet, its adoption has sped up in a number of industries because of its wide-ranging benefits. Since DTs can enhance production, monitor maintenance, and improve product development, they play an important role in manufacturing. They play a role in the observation of patients, customized medical treatments, and organizing surgeries. DTs assist in modeling different aspects of traffic, energy, and safety in urban areas.

People use digital twins because they can communicate with and from physical items and because they can change with new information. Anatomy models adapt whenever changes occur in their original bodies. Working in both physical and digital worlds helps us to grasp systems better and also supports the creation of new systems, automation, and environmentally friendly changes in industry and public areas.

2.1.2 The Rise of Data-Driven Ecosystems

Because of the digital change in industries, data now serves as a guide for choices and successful operations. Cloud computing technology, edge devices, big data analyses, and AI are used in these systems to keep tracking and studying data all the time. Thus, data transformation is key, since it provides clear insights based on a range of datasets [2]. Having access to real-time data for simulation allows companies to be more dependable, react faster, and serve people better.

As digital transformation spreads rapidly, organizations now meet their goals, make choices, and deal with their surroundings by building data-driven systems. They are made up of various technologies, systems, players, and data moving in real time, which require the use of advanced information tools and automation. Digital twins (DTs) help establish and improve such networks thanks to their ability to bridge the gap between what exists in reality and in the world of simulation.

They work well because they can gather, process, and review massive data produced by sensors, machines, and people. Within these frameworks, digital twins are constantly being fed the latest operational information and updating their digital model. All of this continuous synchronization makes it possible to run advanced evaluations, build models, and perform scenario planning for better decisions and adjustments in operations and maintenance. Thanks to DTs, machines, the supply chain, and quality control can be connected and operate as a unit in manufacturing. With digital twins, personal health care can be delivered by interacting with wearables, electronic databases, and intelligent diagnostic tools in real time. In the same way, DTs are used in smart cities to build connected systems that oversee traffic, energy, and emergency using this urban technology and environmental matters.

Also, including digital twins in data ecosystems encourages new ideas by bringing together engineers, data scientists, business managers, and policymakers who can interact with the same model in their own way. As organizations focus more on achieving goals and adopting circular economy values, DTs enable quick decisions, monitoring of sustainability, and improving the whole system. With digital twins supporting data-driven ecosystems, industries are able to change their approach towards efficiency, strength, and scalability. Such ecosystems go beyond technology and are a new way of conducting operations that are flexible, smart, and linked in the digital world.

2.1.3 Privacy in Digital Twin Systems

While DTs focus on modeling individuals' actions, surroundings, and bodily functions, they regularly handle or produce personal data. Numerous data collectors and the frequent collection of data greatly increase the chance of privacy breaches. The use of digital twins in healthcare or smart cities may result in people facing privacy risks, so it is very important to ensure privacy-preserving protections for this reason [3].

As DT systems become widely used in healthcare, manufacturing, smart cities, and more, privacy is becoming a main issue to address. By nature, DTs require instant and precise data sharing between the physical world and the digital world. Often, this data contains details about health, habits, industrial systems, and infrastructures. Because data today is so detailed and flows so speedily, there are many challenges concerning privacy, managing data, and following proper ethics.

In the healthcare sector, patient-specific digital twins combine data collected from devices, patients' past medical records, and their genes to build unique models. While tailored care and predictive diagnosis are possible, such technology may put private health information at risk unless proper privacy is guaranteed. An unauthorized use or data breach might result in cases of identity theft, unfair treatment, or distrust for medical organizations.

In smart manufacturing and factories, simulations called digital twins capture detailed workflows, the use of equipment, and supply chain changes. Things such as trade secrets, intellectual property, or the security of national infrastructure may be threatened if someone illegally gains access to such data. In the same way, DTs in smart cities monitor people's movements, usage of public utilities, and group actions, raising the risk of mass surveillance if they are not controlled properly.

Table 2.1 Common data types used in digital twin applications.

Domain	Data type	Examples	Sensitivity level
Smart cities	Location, movement, utility	GPS, transit card, energy usage	High
Healthcare	Biometric, physiological	Heart rate, glucose levels	Very high
Industry 4.0	Operational metrics	Machine vibration, thermal imaging	Medium

Besides, as data is shared across many systems, privacy problems may affect multiple locations. A security weakness in something like an IoT sensor or third-party app could be enough to ruin the security of the network. For this reason, privacy protection in AI can be achieved by anonymizing data, using federated learning, implementing secure multi-party computation, and applying powerful encryption protocols.

Basically, protecting people's privacy in DT systems is vital for proper innovation and earning public trust. Since digital twins are growing and influencing more areas, it is essential to focus on privacy to protect people and organizations, as these technologies help us. Table 2.1 shows the different data types that are used in digital twin applications.

2.2 Digital Twins: Foundations and Use Cases

DTs bridge the gap between physical things and technology, allowing real-time linking of what happens in the digital world and the physical world. It gives an introduction to digital twins by describing their core elements and how they work. It also identifies several DTs, such as products, processes, people, and environments, which have their own special functions and uses. In addition, this section points out examples of how DT is used in healthcare, smart cities, manufacturing, automotive, and energy to transform these fields and become more relevant today.

2.2.1 Definition and Core Components

A DT includes a physical part, its digital counterpart, and a channel that allows two-way transmission of data. Changes made in the virtual

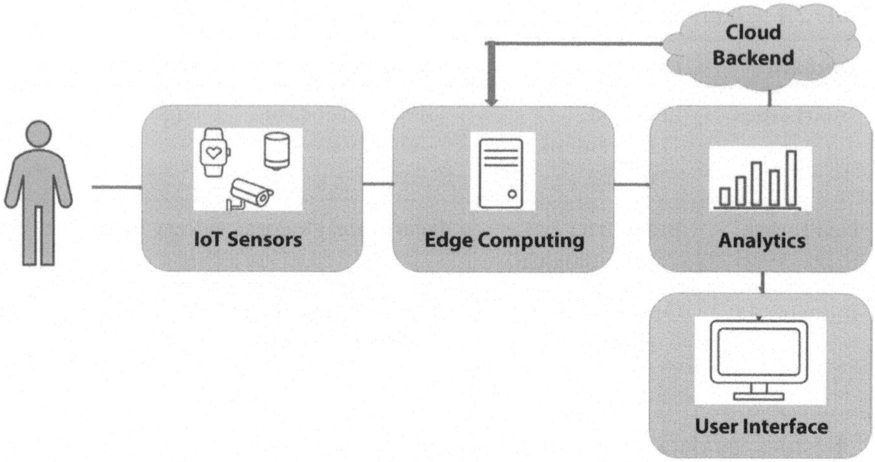

Figure 2.1 Typical architecture of a human-centric digital twin system.

environment are shown instantly, so predictive analysis and recommendations can be used. Tools and technologies that are part of DTs are IoT, simulation modeling, cloud/edge computing, and artificial intelligence [4]. Figure 2.1 demonstrates how a system, such as a human-centric digital twin, uses IoT sensors, data analytics, and its cloud system to turn information into user-friendly interfaces. DTs are virtual replicas of real-world systems that constantly use sensor data to mimic, project, and enhance how they operate. Since digital twins appear as virtual copies of physical parts, it is simple to watch, study, and adjust virtual pieces, which makes it easy to connect physical and virtual aspects. Originally created for work in the aerospace field, DTs have found use in healthcare, manufacturing, planning cities, and in energy systems, where getting fast insights and decisions from data is important.

Core Components of Digital Twins:

1. **Physical Entity:**
The actual object, system, or process being modeled (e.g., a wind turbine, a manufacturing robot, or a human organ).

2. **Digital Replica (Model):**
A high-fidelity virtual representation of the physical entity, including 3D models, behavioral simulations, and logic that mimics real-world interactions.

3. **Data Exchange Layer (IoT & Sensors):**
Real-time data from embedded sensors and IoT devices provides continuous input about the physical system's status, environmental conditions, and usage patterns.

4. **Analytics and Machine Learning Modules:**
Advanced algorithms process real-time and historical data to predict outcomes, detect anomalies, and optimize operations.

5. **Communication Interface:**
A platform or middleware enabling bi-directional communication between the physical entity and its digital twin, ensuring real-time synchronization and control.

6. **Visualization Tools and Dashboards:**
Interfaces that allow users to interact with, visualize, and interpret data from the digital twin for decision-making, simulation, and system management.

7. **Security and Privacy Framework:**
Mechanisms to protect sensitive data exchanged between systems, especially in regulated environments such as healthcare and industrial IoT.

As a result, digital twins provide helpful insights, support predictive maintenance, and contribute to good decisions made in real time in complicated systems through these components.

2.2.2 Types of Digital Twins

Types of digital twins refer to categorized models that replicate specific real-world entities—product twins represent physical assets, process twins simulate operational workflows, person twins' model individual behavior or health, and environment twins mirror spatial or ecological systems.

1. Product Twins
Engines, pumps, or industrial mechanical assets can be recreated in the digital world as product twins. They continuously check temperature, vibration, and pressure values in real time to monitor the device's performance, how it ages, and if anything fails. With product twins, engineers can watch the lifecycle, identify potential problems, and determine how much time the product can still function. They provide good benefits in sectors where equipment wears out easily, like aerospace and manufacturing, since

keeping an eye on usage results in fewer replacements and longer life for assets.

2. Process Twins
Process twins are made to reflect the actions and processes that take place in running a business. A manufacturing line could be simulated by a process twin, so it captures processes such as assembly, inspection, and packaging. Mimicking these processes makes it possible for organizations to spot problematic areas, review different solutions to move work forward, and manage their schedules well. Pharmaceutical companies use process twins to ensure better quality checks and lower expenses from mistakes during drug production.

3. Person Twins
They are designed to model an individual's special characteristics in functioning, acting, or thinking. Person Twins are applied in healthcare to show organ functioning (like the heart or lungs), the steps of diseases (both cancer and Alzheimer's), and the reaction to treatments. As a result of being able to predict each patient's outcome, doctors can practice personalized medicine. They offer the ability to simulate behavior to assist in spotting signs of mental illness and coming up with solutions.

4. Environment Twins
Environment twins are designed to duplicate big ecosystems such as cities, networks of power supply, or transport systems [5]. They study many layers of information, such as weather, infrastructure, and how crowded cities are, to both model and manage complicated systems. In this sense, a twin city of a smart city can replay traffic challenges during emergencies, check how much energy is being used, and try out policies meant to support the environment. They are applied by utilities to plan for extra demand on the grid and to study the effects of solar or wind power in the system.

2.2.3 Applications Across Industries

Smart cities, automotive, manufacturing, healthcare, energy, and utilities all use digital twin technologies to boost their efficiency, improve decisions, and bring new ideas.

- **Healthcare**
Digital twins are changing the way healthcare services are given through diagnosis, treatment, and patient monitoring. With the help of digital

replicas, clinicians can run simulations of different diseases and possible treatments in patients without needing to do risky procedures. In this field, models of tumor development allow doctors to predict if drugs will be helpful. Digital twins make it possible to use accurate models in both surgical plans and training exercises. Digital twins are helpful in demonstrating how organs function, disease spread, and patient reactions to particular treatments [6].

- **Smart Cities**

In urban planning, digital twins are created to imitate and study things like traffic in the city, air pollution, how water is delivered, and operations in situations where help is needed. As an example, digital twins can check the results of including another bus route or adjusting the traffic pattern near a construction site. Because the simulations update constantly from sensor data, they become very useful for testing various policies, preparing for disasters, and promoting sustainable steps. Using DTs, urban planners can predict the behavior of traffic, how much electricity is used, and how to respond to disasters [7].

- **Manufacturing**

Intelligent automation and self-enhancing technology are made possible in Industry 4.0 due to DTs. They make it possible to identify and fix parts that are likely to fail soon, helping avoid unexpected machine breakdowns. Digital twins make it possible to test and confirm business workflows before starting the actual tasks, thereby lowering setup times and the amount of waste produced. The AI systems built into the twins ensure that the manufactured goods maintain the required quality throughout their lifespan. DTs make preventive maintenance, spotting problems, and smooth operation possible [8].

- **The Automotive and Mobility Industry**

Through DTs, automotive companies can try out different vehicle functions virtually before carrying out real tests on the roads. Digital twins replicate road situations, how people move, and traffic patterns, making sure that the algorithms used by self-driving cars are stable and safe as they are being tested. Real-time diagnostics and installing software updates are possible in connected cars using twin technology. Autonomous vehicle algorithms can be tested in virtual environments with these simulators first [9].

- **Energy and Utilities**

Utilities rely on DTs to balance amounts of energy supplied and used, to analyze the stability of grids, and to estimate renewable sources of energy. It aids in giving utilities equal amounts of supply and demand, prevents outages, and supports the use of renewable sources. For example, using digital versions of turbines, companies can keep an eye on their performance and spot upcoming problems. Pressure systems are simulated by water utilities, which helps avoid leaks and makes distribution more efficient.

In short, it describes how using digital twins is changing industries by making things safer, more efficient, and simpler to predict through virtual models. If you need these sentences set as a formatted text or explained more, feel free to mention it.

2.3 Privacy Threats in Digital Twin Environments

DT technology is making a major impact on industries by supplying virtual simulations of real entities, going from people and wearables to big things like cities and industrial systems. At the same time, the fact that DTs are powered by continuous and multi-faceted information can leave them vulnerable to serious privacy issues. Matters covered here include more data than needed, the possibility of finding out a person's identity, guessing information, as well as threats from those inside or outside the organization. Ensuring private data use is protected as DTs become more common every day is a major priority for all designers. It examines the main privacy dangers in DT settings, pointing out how it is important to ensure good technical and ethical protection.

2.3.1 Data Collection and Surveillance Risks

These digital tools depend on routinely collecting, reviewing, and linking data from real things to represent them in a virtual way. As a rule, such detailed data gathering involves watching individual behavior, observing the environment, or recording biometric data. Because data collection is so wide in smart homes or smart cities, it might capture more information than is really needed in everyday operations. This breaks the rule of privacy and also does not follow the principle in the GDPR that data should not be collected without reason [11]. Furthermore, always closely monitoring our activities often influences people's actions, and they may not even notice how much they are being watched.

2.3.2 Re-Identification and Profiling

Although DT systems often assure anonymity of the data they collect, the risk that re-identification could still happen is significant. Sophisticated attacks enable bad actors to reconnect anonymous data records using sources from the outside. Position tracking data from DT-powered systems on smart mobility could be set against any online data released on social media or by telecommunications providers to restore the identity of the users [12]. When different kinds of data, such as movement, speech, heart rate, and eating habits, are used by DTs, individuals can be profiled more easily. Such profiling can be put to use not only for directing ads but also for unjust actions like decisions in insurance or surveillance.

2.3.3 Data Fusion and Inference Attacks

An especially harmful danger in DT environments is that collecting various kinds of data allows for highly sensitive conclusions to be drawn from them. In such DTs, if wearable data are connected to how many times a patient visits a hospital, as well as their daily habits, an attacker might be able to identify possible hypertension or mental health problems in the patient. As these attacks take advantage of original features in a DT system to reach unintended goals, it makes it challenging to catch them or stop them through access controls. Combining data improves how DT works, yet it may allow sensitive conclusions to be reached. Monitoring a person's movement patterns and public transport use helps determine any stress or exhaustion concerns. Table 2.2 shows sensitive inferences enabled by multi-modal data fusion.

Table 2.2 Sensitive inferences enabled by multi-modal data fusion.

Data sources combined	Inferred attribute	Potential risk
Heart rate + calendar	Emotional state	Psychological profiling
Sleep pattern + commute data	Health condition	Discrimination in insurance/employment
Shopping + location data	Religious/political beliefs	Targeted manipulation

2.3.4 Insider Threats and External Breaches

DT infrastructures are not only vulnerable to external cyberattacks but also to internal threats posed by individuals with privileged access. Employees or contractors with legitimate system access may misuse data, either unintentionally or maliciously. These insider threats are compounded by inadequate role-based access controls or poor audit mechanisms. Simultaneously, external actors may exploit software vulnerabilities, weak encryption, or insecure APIs to gain unauthorized access to DT systems. Breaches can result in manipulation of digital replicas, disruption of services, or mass data leaks [14]. The dynamic and interconnected nature of DT ecosystems amplifies the potential impact of such breaches.

2.4 Legal and Regulatory Landscape

Applying digital twins in sensitive sectors such as healthcare, smart cities, and IoT creates major issues related to the law and regulation. In contrast to usual data systems, DTs are always updated dynamically, so they need fast processing, quick decisions, and sometimes automatic action.

Table 2.3 Comparison of key data protection frameworks.

Framework	Region	Focus area	Key requirements
GDPR	European Union	General data protection, profiling, consent	Lawful processing, purpose limitation, explicit consent, Article 22 restrictions
HIPAA	United States	Health data privacy and security	Safeguards for PHI, access control, encryption, breach notification
CCPA	California, USA	Consumer rights, transparency	Right to access/delete data, opt out of sale, clear privacy notices
OECD Privacy Guidelines	International	Global best practices on privacy	Collection limitation, use limitation, accountability, individual participation

Because things often move fast, legal rules on how consent, auditing, and data sovereignty should work can no longer remain static. Anyone using DT technology, whether a developer or organization, must understand the legal system completely. Table 2.3, shown below, gives a comparative overview of key protection frameworks, i.e., GDPR, HIPAA, CCPA, and OECD, summarizing key regional privacy regulations, their focus areas, and essential compliance requirements.

2.4.1 GDPR, HIPAA, and Other Frameworks

- **General Data Protection Regulation (GDPR):** It belongs to European Union privacy laws and encourages lawful, fair, and transparent data handling. According to Article 22, profiling and other automated individual decisions should not take place unless certain exceptions apply [15]. GDPR states that customers should give explicit permission, their data should be used only for certain reasons, and their privacy should be respected.
- **Health Insurance Portability and Accountability Act (HIPAA):** This rule, created in the United States, requires healthcare organizations to keep Personal Health Information (PHI) secure in different ways. Covered entities should install access controllers and encrypt data while having breach notification as part of their system.
- **California Consumer Privacy Act (CCPA):** This California-specific law grants residents of the state the right to learn about, remove, and choose not to let their personal information be shared or sold. When handling requests from data subjects, businesses must act immediately and make things clear to them.
- **OECD Privacy Guidelines:** The OECD Privacy Guidelines are accepted by many nations and promote effective approaches such as collecting only necessary data, using it for its stated purpose, and keeping the data under control. Even so, they influence how laws are created in each country.

2.4.2 Compliance Challenges for Digital Twin Developers

They usually function in cloud settings, cross national borders, and work across company divisions, which makes it difficult to obey the rules set by different countries. If data flows in real time together with machine learning, there may be no time to obtain consent or create audit records. Automated decision-making also brings up issues in systems such as GDPR, where it is required to offer human involvement whenever someone asks for intervention. Guaranteeing privacy in a setting like this requires using advanced ideas such as privacy-by-design and federated learning [16].

2.4.3 Data Ownership and Consent in Virtual Representations

In DT, the idea of who owns the data is a key issue. If data is captured by wearables, devices around the home, or devices in industrial settings, the issue of primary ownership can remain unclear among the person, the device company, or the provider. Consent must happen in the following ways:

- **Granular** (specific to data type and purpose),
- **Revocable** (at any time), and
- **Context-aware** (reflecting real-time changes).

In DTs that are always monitoring, it is important to use innovative platforms for handling people's decisions and preferences, such as real-time dashboards or blockchain-based records of their consent [17, 18].

2.4.4 Cross-Border Data Transfer Issues

Any DT system that works worldwide or across different countries in healthcare must follow data sharing guidelines for different nations. Transferring data to other countries can be ensured to be safe through the employment of Standard Contractual Clauses (SCCs) and Binding Corporate Rules (BCRs). Even so, the invalidation of the Privacy Shield framework (decided in the Schrems II case) means there are legal questions regarding the EU and U.S. relationship [19]. Therefore, organizations have to carry out Transfer Impact Assessments (TIAs) and follow new regulations closely so they do not violate the law. When a smart healthcare DT serves EU and U.S. residents, it must lock up patient information and ensure that non-EU cloud service vendors sign smart contracts approved by the European Commission. Not following the rules under GDPR can cause organizations to face large fines.

2.5 Privacy-Preserving Techniques for Digital Twins

Digital twins (DTs) simulate physical systems by continuously collecting and analyzing real-time data. But since the data can be highly private, it often has to do with privacy issues. It is important to use strong privacy measures to ensure that individuals' data is safe, as digital twins maintain their usefulness.

2.5.1 Federated Learning and Edge AI

With Federated Learning, several devices or edge nodes join hands to train one global machine learning model, without needing to send their data to a central server. Rather, only the updates to the model parameters (gradients) are exchanged, so there is less danger of leaking data.

FL is very useful for applications that require privacy protection, such as digital twins. That approach involves each device training its own machine learning model using the data it possesses. Instead of directly sending every piece of data to a single server, devices only send updates related to the model to a central aggregator from time to time. Then, it gathers all the updates and uses them to form a global model, which is sent back to the devices for more training. The team keeps refining the global model until it performs well enough [19].

FL allows data to remain privately stored on a local device, thus cutting back the risk of data getting leaked. Besides, by doing the computations where the data is, FL reduces the time it takes to exchange messages and makes real-time applications within digital twins more efficient. Besides, because it is distributed, it is very suitable for scaling in the kind of varied and distributed IoT-based settings commonly seen in digital twins.

Edge AI helps federated learning by making it possible for AI tasks to be handled on edge devices. This helps reduce the need for data to be sent to the main servers, which makes both privacy and the system's responsiveness better. By combining FL and Edge AI, we can create a new privacy-safe system in digital twin environments.

Still, using FL and Edge AI does come with some problems. It is still a challenge to communicate efficiently when updating the model among devices with poor bandwidth. In addition, it is tough to get models to converge when data from different devices is different due to non-IID (non-identically identical distribution), which is widely seen in diverse DT environments. Another concern is that dangerous devices may disrupt updates to the model, which can lower performance or allow private information to be released. Such challenges point out why it is necessary to keep researching to make FL protocols safer and more reliable in a digital twin environment.

2.5.2 Differential Privacy (DP)

DP relies on mathematical methods to restrict data analysis with the help of randomness to ensure strong privacy. The main idea is to prevent any single person's presence or absence from changing the results of any analysis so that their particular information cannot easily be understood. Noise can be added either to outputs or gradients, depending on what the training is meant for.

Sharing aggregate overlooks from digital twins with external parties is greatly helped by using differential privacy. When you use DP, organizations can make sure that shared data cannot be used to understand or uncover information about any of the individuals depicted in the digital twin. Privacy-aware machine learning is also possible with DP, as it gives assurance that pairs of digital twins won't expose sensitive information.

Its main benefits involve strong theory and easy use in the field of machine learning. Its official guarantees give developers and users a lot of confidence about protecting their privacy. On the other hand, adding differential privacy to current techniques causes certain issues. A key point is that more privacy usually comes at the cost of accuracy and usefulness in the data or the results of a machine learning model. It is also important to choose reliable privacy parameters (written as ε and δ) that suit the particular application and tolerable risk.

2.5.3 Homomorphic Encryption (HE) and Secure Multiparty Computation (SMPC)

HE and SMC methods allow users to do computations on encrypted data without revealing the original confidential information. In particular, they are helpful for protecting sensitive information in digital twin systems that need to deal with personal, industrial, or infrastructural data.

Addition or multiplication can be carried out on ciphertexts using homomorphic encryption, and the encrypted result will remain valid even after being decrypted. The data from digital twins stays private as it is shared and analyzed by other servers or providers. With secure multiparty computation, parties are able to compute one function together while making sure none of their inputs are seen by outsiders. This proves useful in settings where digital twin data is kept by many stakeholders or groups, and they have to collaborate without exchanging the raw data.

They help give privacy to data since they safeguard it at each stage—starting from collection, through transmission, and ending at analysis. They are especially useful where laws are very strict, as is the case in health services and infrastructure.

Even though they are promising, HE and SMC still encounter significant issues when it comes to implementation. Homomorphic encryption has significant strengths, but because it slows down systems and backup processing, it is usually not used for real-time applications at a large scale. In the same way, increased participation or more complex tasks can result in SMC using complicated methods and consuming a lot of computing resources. Even so, new findings are making it easier to rely on these techniques for improving privacy in digital twins.

2.5.4 Privacy-by-Design Principles in Twin Architectures

Privacy-by-Design (PbD) is a proactive approach that embeds privacy considerations into the architecture and development lifecycle of digital twin (DT) systems from the outset. Rather than treating privacy as an add-on or post-deployment patch, PbD emphasizes integrating privacy as a foundational design principle. This approach is especially critical in DT environments, where continuous data collection, analysis, and feedback loops are inherent to system operation [20].

Incorporating PbD into digital twin architectures involves several key strategies. These include data minimization—collecting only the data strictly necessary for the DT's functionality; purpose limitation—ensuring data is used solely for its intended and consented purpose; and user-centric controls—providing individuals or organizations with transparency, access, and control over their data. For example, implementing modular data handling components, secure logging mechanisms, and automated data deletion policies can all reinforce PbD principles within a digital twin system.

PbD enhances trustworthiness by aligning technical implementations with regulatory expectations such as those outlined in the GDPR, which mandates data protection by design and by default. It also facilitates more ethical deployment of digital twins, especially when modeling individuals or communities in sensitive domains like healthcare or smart cities.

Despite its conceptual appeal, implementing privacy by design is not without challenges. It requires interdisciplinary collaboration among developers, legal experts, and domain specialists to translate abstract privacy principles into actionable technical requirements. Additionally, there can be trade-offs between system functionality, performance, and privacy. For example, excessive data minimization might limit the predictive accuracy of a twin. Nevertheless, adopting PbD from the early stages of development helps ensure that digital twin systems are not only technically robust but also socially responsible and legally compliant. Table 2.4 provides an overview of key privacy techniques for digital twins, highlighting their advantages, limitations, and practical applications.

Table 2.4 Summary of privacy-preserving techniques for digital twins: features, benefits, challenges, and use cases.

Technique	Description	Benefits	Challenges	Use cases in digital twins
Federated learning & edge AI	Local training, shared model updates only	Privacy, efficiency	Communication overhead	Distributed model training across DT devices
Differential privacy	Noise addition to outputs to protect individual data	Strong privacy guarantees	Privacy-utility trade-off	Privacy-safe analytics and model training
Homomorphic encryption & SMPC	Computation on encrypted data or distributed inputs	Strong cryptographic privacy	High computation cost	Secure data sharing and encrypted analytics
Privacy-by-design	Embedding privacy in system design	Compliance, trust	Design complexity	Secure twin architectures with built-in privacy

2.6 Ethical and Societal Considerations

Since digital twins (DTs) are more involved with human, industrial, and urban systems, we should assess their ethical and social consequences closely. Because of these factors, DTs honor human rights, equity, and democratic values whenever they work with or speak for people.

2.6.1 Transparency and Trust

When digital twins are used in key parts of society, it's important to make sure they are open about their operations and inspire people's trust. It means disclosing how DT systems acquire, process, and handle data. Trust occurs after users and stakeholders know how the digital twin works and feel secure acting on its results.

Lack of clarity in digital twins stems from the fact that most of their "intelligence" comes from machine learning and AI, which are often too complicated to explain why decisions are made the way they are. This applies mainly to deep learning models, as although their accuracy is very high, they are not easy to understand. If a digital twin's workings are unclear to users, it becomes hard for them to judge its reliability, query its results, and make an informed decision. Because of this lack of clarity, predicting risks of heart disease could create both ethical and practical challenges in medical DT. As an example, a patient might not be able to explain why a treatment is supposed to help or whether the plan was made using proper data.

This lack of openness causes many important ethical issues. It may cause users to lose their trust, go against the idea of being informed, and could result in unacceptable or harmful judgments when people are affected by systems they do not understand. The risks are greater when digital twins represent marginalized groups, since they can reinforce unfairness or lead to the practice of discrimination.

Several approaches are being put forward to deal with these problems, and they are being accepted more often. XAI techniques can assist in making DT systems interpretable and able to clarify why they make certain decisions. Also, tools such as data usage logs and consent dashboards give people the chance to keep watch over their data as time goes by. If a digital twin is developed in the public or sensitive field by an institution, it may be beneficial to create an independent group to check and guide what is done ethically.

By focusing on transparency and accountability, those in charge of digital twin development can help users have faith in their use and guarantee that these technologies respect both private and public interests [21].

2.6.2 Autonomy and Human Digital Representation

Person-based DTs can make decisions or predictions that influence real-world outcomes (e.g., health interventions). This may conflict with personal autonomy and informed consent, especially if users are unaware of such implications [22].

There is a need for people to maintain their own digital representations and pass them along through time. Digital models of a person's health or behavior that are part of smart environments, such as health twins or avatars, can have unique issues related to someone's freedoms and identity. They are sometimes put to use to supervise, guess, or steer an individual's actions, choices, and health. They bring many good things, such as tailor-made health support and better city navigation, but they can also be very risky if not regulated.

Ensuring ethical behavior in healthcare may be difficult because it can limit a patient's capacity to make independent decisions. Sometimes, digital twins recommend what to do, and the user just goes along, so their behavior is slowly shifted by the suggestions. For instance, a health-driven DT might push changes in routine or cut the person off from some services based on assumptions made by algorithms, which sometimes go against the individual's wishes. The situation gets worse if AR interventions are applied without involving the user, making the DT make purely automatic decisions.

Asking for consent becomes harder in these kinds of situations. As opposed to static systems, digital twins keep evolving according to fresh data that becomes available. Since DT often changes quickly, individuals find it hard to track how it functions and the choices it is capable of making for them. The digital twin might end up making decisions on behalf of the user without truly understanding or agreeing with the user's thoughts and beliefs.

For instance, a smart city app might use a digital twin to guide a commuter's trip in another direction when the driver is detected to be stressed through the help of biometric sensors. Even though it aims to care for individuals, the system sometimes forces its plans instead of respecting what they want, explaining people's anger, or even the victims of harm.

Ethical standards can be put in place to deal with these issues. Because of dynamic consent, users can continue to update their choices for sharing their data and making decisions anytime it is needed. With these architectures, self-driving cars give the user the chance to control important decisions concerning their safety or where they go. Also, using concepts from biomedical ethics, such as autonomy, beneficence, non-maleficence, and justice, in setting up frameworks for human digital twins helps make sure their use is responsible.

If developers and institutions continue to put users in charge and stay involved in their work, digital twin systems can support humans instead of taking over their lives. The gap between people who have access to technology and those who do not is a major problem, and it is tied to surveillance capitalism.

2.6.3 The Digital Divide and Surveillance Capitalism

Quick advancements and the introduction of digital twin technologies are causing important ethical issues that impact fairness and justice, mainly through the digital divide and surveillance capitalism [23]. As a result of the digital divide, some people have access to advanced digital technologies while others do not, which is mainly affected by their income, location, online knowledge, and how advanced their community's technology is. Consequently, those who earn less, live in rural areas, or are not digitally skilled usually do not have access to the help that digital twins give, such as improved health data, opportunities for saving energy, or better ways to get around. In addition, these groups are sometimes not included enough in the datasets used to develop digital twins, which results in models that don't suit their requirements.

It gets even worse because surveillance capitalism makes money from collected personal information, usually without the users knowing or agreeing to it. Often, individuals are tracked all the time using wearable devices, smart gadgets, and connected buildings, so their behavior can be used by companies for financial gain. In digital twins, users may end up being looked at in ways that are very invasive, as they are simply numbers to be used in favor of corporate gain.

These changes bring a wide range of ethical concerns. In some cases, people with little socioeconomic power are closely watched, yet they still do not receive many actual benefits as a result. Nonrepresentative or slanted data can boost the chances of creating models that do not work or treat minorities fairly. Besides, folks can end up having others control their digital identities instead of participating in protecting their data.

In factories, digital twins are now being used to observe how productive workers are. Often, low-level workers have to live with close supervision,

Table 2.5 Summary of key ethical and societal issues in digital twin implementation and mitigation approaches.

Ethical concern	Description	Risks	Mitigation strategies
Transparency & trust	Explainability of AI and data use in DTs	Erosion of user trust	Explainable AI, user control, usage transparency
Autonomy & digital representation	DTs making decisions on behalf of individuals	Consent violation, overreach	Human-in-the-loop, dynamic consent mechanisms
Digital divide & surveillance capitalism	Unequal access; exploitation of data	Inequity, commodification of users	Policy reform, fair access, privacy regulations

yet managers are not faced with the same pressure. Such unevenness strengthens unfair power relations and might result in exploitation in the name of improving work conditions.

A number of strategies might be implemented to handle these concerns. A fairness review should happen before and during the launch of digital twins to spot and solve any bias in the system. Policies should ensure that data is used fairly and ethically to shield people against unethical and exploitative activities. Using public money, digital twin technology should be offered at a low cost to people in health, education, and agriculture to support equal access to these innovations. If developers and regulators notice and solve this structural unfairness, digital twin technologies will help communities grow instead of making things worse for some groups. Table 2.5 outlines major ethical concerns in digital twin systems, associated risks, and strategies to ensure responsible and equitable deployment.

2.7 Case Studies and Real-World Challenges

Beyond being tested, digital twins (DTs) have been put into practice across cities, in the world of medicine, and in manufacturing. Although these technologies help a lot with efficiency, personal attention, and upkeep, they also uncover problems like low data access, privacy protection, complying with legislation, and supervising ethical areas. The next few case studies reveal how adopting DT involves certain benefits and challenges, making the various trade-offs connected to DT easier to grasp.

2.7.1 Smart City Digital Twins and Resident Data

Case Examples:

- **Singapore's "Virtual Singapore"** platform creates a real-time 3D model of the city to manage traffic congestion, plan construction, and analyze energy use.
- **Helsinki's Digital Twin** integrates environmental, mobility, and infrastructure data to test urban development policies [24].

Planners and local officials are starting to use smart city digital twins to better handle city affairs, protect the environment, and advance service offerings. Such systems form sophisticated, data-filled models of cities by combining information from transport, environment, city infrastructure, and mobile gadgets. For example, Singapore's Virtual Singapore uses 3D technology to handle traffic, replicate construction changes, and check energy use. In the same way, Helsinki's digital representation combines data related to transport, weather, and the city's infrastructure to test different city plans and help with urban development.

The reasons to adopt such methods are very strong. Intelligent DTs for cities allow officials to know when and where congestion will occur, react quickly in emergencies, and effectively divide resources. They allow decision-makers to test possible changes before they are executed to ensure safety and better quality of services for people. Still, these benefits bring up important privacy and ethical matters, mainly related to consent, transparency, and the way data is handled.

An important point is that the collection of residents' data is often not made obvious to them. Data may be collected through security cameras, various meters at homes, or your mobile device, which makes it uncertain if you agreed to provide it. Also, the decisions these systems make about zoning, safety, or urban transport are often left out of public view and are rarely questioned. Without understanding why and how, impacted people lack the ability to dispute unfair results.

There is also the issue of saving behavioral and location data for a long time as part of the city's digital systems. Having so much information collected increases the chance that it may be abused, accessed wrongly, or used for plans other than the original intentions, with little control.

There are high ethical issues when it comes to surveillance. Without proper rules, DTs in smart cities might change into forms of techno-surveillance that track people constantly while claiming to help city life. Such scenarios can lead to abuses of people's freedoms and cause people to doubt their government.

For a proper deployment of smart cities, authorities must have strict privacy rules, let citizens understand how the data is used, and encourage them to be part of managing the system. For smart city digital twins to offer benefits without compromising people's freedom and rights, such actions are required.

2.7.2 Healthcare Twins and Sensitive Health Records

Case Example:

- **Mayo Clinic's Digital Twin Initiative** uses patient-specific models to simulate treatment outcomes, drug responses, and disease progression.

Doctors are making use of healthcare digital twins to model the reactions patients have to various treatments, drugs, and growing diseases. The Mayo Clinic is leading by using digital twins to proceed with personalized medicine. Such systems help create individual treatment plans and more accurate diagnoses, reducing the amount of guesswork when choosing medication.

Still, setting up healthcare twins comes with various obstacles. For health records to be safe, it is essential to use HIPAA, control access, encrypt details, and thoroughly audit how records are stored. It gets complicated to obtain and ensure patient consent, as the digital twin evolves quickly over the years. Because health information is so valuable, cybercriminals are more likely to target it, which is why healthcare providers need to keep their systems secure with advanced prevention techniques.

Healthcare professionals must make sure that digital twins support ethics by not invading patients' personal freedom. Patients could find that advice from algorithms makes it harder for them to decide on their health matters independently. It highlights why it is necessary to keep things transparent, involve patients, and stop the government from going too far.

2.7.3 Industrial IoT Twins and Employee Monitoring

Case Example:

- Automotive and manufacturing industries deploy DTs for real-time monitoring of both machinery and workers to optimize workflows and predictive maintenance [25].

Personalized medicine is being changed by healthcare digital twins that develop precise models for each person to predict treatment, drug, and disease reactions. For example, the Mayo Clinic's digital twin initiative relies on these personalized models to create better strategies for treating patients and improve accuracy in diagnosis. Due to digital twins, clinicians can foresee the reactions of patients to various care options without needing trial and error, which benefits both the quality of care and the success of patients.

Healthcare twins offer a lot of advantages. Individual treatment pathways allow for better medication decisions, fewer problems from drugs, and better expectations of outcomes. Because of this personalization, healthcare resources are used more effectively, and patients are more involved in using specific therapies.

Still, the use of healthcare digital twins is confronted by a number of serious problems. All healthcare organizations must strictly follow HIPAA or similar regulations by using strong access protection, encryption techniques, and complete audit trails to protect electronic health records (EHRs). Another challenge is that patients must be informed about how their data will likely be used, as these models keep changing over time with added information. Moreover, health data is very sensitive, which attracts cybercriminals and makes people concerned about unauthorized access to it. Comparative analysis of DT deployment across sectors is shown in Table 2.6, and the corresponding bar chart is shown in Figure 2.2.

There is a need to find a balance between using digital twins for better healthcare and respecting what patients want. This approach may make patients believe that they should follow the algorithm's recommendations, which could restrict their ability to choose for themselves. As a result, it is clear that we need to be open with information, make decisions together, and establish measures to avoid giving too much power. All in all, healthcare digital twins could greatly benefit personalized medicine, though proper care should be taken to maintain patient confidence by overcoming regulatory, security, and ethical issues. Figure 2.2, shown below, is a comparative analysis of DT deployment across sectors, which visually contrasts

Table 2.6 Comparative analysis of DT deployment across sectors.

Deployment area	Privacy risk	Regulatory burden	Public awareness	Benefit realization
Smart cities	High	Moderate	Low	High
Healthcare	Very high	Very high	Moderate	High
Industrial IoT	High	Low	Low	Moderate

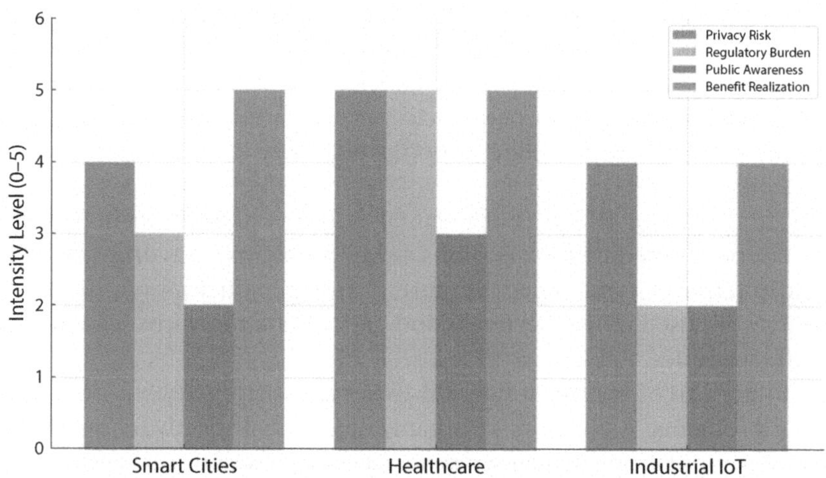

Figure 2.2 Comparative analysis of DT deployment across sectors.

privacy risks, regulatory burdens, public awareness, and benefit realization across smart cities, healthcare, and industrial IoT sectors.

2.8 Future Directions and Open Research Problems in Privacy-Preserving Digital Twin Systems

With more industries using digital twins and their technology developing, new questions about privacy and opportunities for further research keep appearing. These issues call for new and different approaches that are more advanced than today's methods. The aim of this section is to find future directions and important research problems that will guide privacy-preserving digital twin systems to become more secure, adaptable, and trustworthy.

2.8.1 Privacy Metrics for Digital Twin Systems

There is a major research need to develop privacy metrics for digital twin technology that can be measured. Digital twins help work with different types of data (real sensor records, data on behaviors, etc.) and play a key role in healthcare, smart cities, and manufacturing. Most of the privacy techniques currently used, such as k-anonymity, l-diversity, t-closeness, and differential privacy, fail to adequately protect data in fast-moving digital systems [26].

Research Direction:

- Ensure that your privacy metrics can reflect the risks from data exposure that increases over time.
- Apply information-theoretic tools to evaluate how much privacy is lost as the system is being actively used.
- Determine privacy risk for each app by rating it according to how it would work in different settings.

Table 2.7, shown below, is a comparative table or radar chart showing strengths and limitations of traditional privacy metrics in the context of DTs. This table compares commonly used privacy metrics—k-anonymity, differential privacy, and t-closeness—with a proposed metric tailored for digital twin (DT) systems. The comparison is based on four key dimensions: temporal sensitivity, data correlation handling, real-time applicability, and overall suitability for DT environments. The proposed DT-specific

Table 2.7 Comparison of privacy metrics in the context of digital twin systems.

Metric	**Temporal sensitivity**	**Data correlation handling**	**Real-time applicability**	**Suitability for DTs**
K-Anonymity	✗	✗	✗	Low
Differential privacy	✓ (with tuning)	✓	Limited	Medium
T-Closeness	✗	✗	✗	Low
Proposed DT-metric	✓	✓	✓	High

metric demonstrates superior alignment with the dynamic and real-time nature of digital twin applications.

2.8.2 Adaptive Privacy Controls

These systems are designed to work in quickly changing and relevant fields like emergency healthcare, disaster management, and responding to emergencies in industries. Where these scenarios are concerned, privacy features must be able to respond in real time to different changes. Sometimes, it's necessary to loosen the privacy rules normally used so that information and action are shared quickly when needed. It is very difficult to build privacy policy engines that can respond instantly whenever a certain context appears. Also, these controls need to be set in a way that respects the law and does not harm rights guaranteed by privacy regulations such as GDPR or HIPAA.

In the future, studies in this area should consider creating privacy rules that are aware of the context and are connected to machine models that decide when forms of protection can be lowered. Policies that are changed in response to events and overseen by humans can introduce more safety measures since humans can participate in important decisions. To do this, using such innovative technologies is necessary to ensure that digital twin systems follow the law and offer privacy protection [27].

2.8.3 Synthetic Data Generation

Synthetic data generation, and in particular GANs, is becoming a useful method to address privacy risks linked to the use of realistic data. They make statistics that represent actual data sets without keeping any pieces of identification. Artificial data makes it possible to train models safely, securely share data while avoiding re-identification, and conduct substantial testing in completely simulated surroundings.

Even so, there are obstacles in creating synthetic data. Always maintaining a fine balance between what's useful in synthetic data and ensuring privacy is another important concern. It is vital to judge the fairness and diversity of the generated data to guarantee there is no bias and all models perform equally.

In the future, everyone should work on boosting the clarity and controllability of producing synthetic data, for instance, by using conditional GANs in conjunction with federated learning. Building privacy-protecting data processing systems that keep generating synthetic data helps improve the use of digital twins outside of laboratory settings [28].

2.8.4 Standardization and Interoperability

The lack of consistent **privacy and interoperability standards** across digital twin platforms hinders scalable deployment. Organizations like **ISO (e.g., ISO/IEC JTC 1/SC 41)** and **IEEE (e.g., IEEE P2413)** are currently addressing this, but unified global standards are still incomplete [29].

Challenges:
It is challenging for digital twin systems to improve because laws and definitions are not the same everywhere, which complicates following rules and managing data on a worldwide scale. Also, when organizations rely on vendor-specific tools, this may stop information from being moved smoothly across different applications. The presence of these difficulties makes it tough to establish united digital twin ecosystems that respect privacy and function well in all sectors and regions.

Research Directions:
Future studies ought to focus on developing semantic ontologies for digital twins to keep their meaning and representation the same across all types of platforms and applications. Creating common vocabularies and data models will make it possible for various systems to communicate easily. It is also crucial to encourage different sectors to get involved in the development of standards in SDOs so as to achieve frameworks that benefit everyone in industries, regulators, and users. At the same time, creating secure and effective ways for sharing data between networks of digital twins is essential. Together, all of these initiatives will form the base for consistent, scalable, and dependable digital twin environments.

2.9 Conclusion

Since digital twin technologies are becoming more common and highly applied in several sectors, we ought to consider their positive impact and the serious challenges they bring to privacy. This chapter looks at the important relationship between innovation and privacy and calls for solid strategies to guard personal information on digital twins. As digital twins continue to evolve as a cornerstone of Industry 4.0, their integration with artificial intelligence (AI), the Industrial Internet of Things (IIoT), and augmented reality poses both opportunities and challenges—particularly in the realm of privacy. Their joint development increases the intelligence, efficiency, and adaptability of the systems [30, 31]; it also multiplies the amount, type, and sensitivity of the data being created and manipulated. The optimization of complex processes by means of AI algorithms was illustrated in several recent works, including those on electric automation control [32] and federated learning in edge computing [33], which highlights the necessity of decentralized, privacy-preserving mechanisms in digital ecosystems. At the same time, developments in fuzzy logic [34] and intelligent system design [35] demonstrate how it is possible to incorporate intelligent decision-making systems, which consider user consent, data minimization, and transparency.

However, as digital twins scale across sectors—particularly in smart manufacturing, healthcare, and cities—their exposure to cyber threats and ethical risks escalates. The infusion of AI-driven analytics, while transformative, must be aligned with robust privacy protocols and regulatory compliance to mitigate risks associated with surveillance, profiling, and data breaches. Therefore, future digital twin systems must embrace privacy by design, leveraging innovations like federated learning, adaptive security frameworks, and AI-driven governance models. Bridging engineering ingenuity with ethical responsibility will be essential in shaping a privacy-preserving, trustworthy, and sustainable digital twin landscape. In this section, the main insights are compiled, and suggestions are made on the steps to help establish trustworthy digital twins that protect users' privacy.

2.9.1 Summary of Key Points

This chapter discussed the wide-ranging world of digital twins, pointing out how these data-driven systems have been quickly developing to match actual situations in real time. We looked into the main ideas of digital twins and their wide use in healthcare, smart cities, manufacturing, automotive, and energy, showing how they help with new ideas and better operations.

Still, such innovation brings challenges to the privacy of individuals. The biggest risks, such as mass data gathering, possible re-identifying of people, joining data from different sources, and insider breaches, are tough for people as well as organizations. It covered changes in the law and regulations, especially talking about GDPR and HIPAA, which require digital twin developers to adhere to strict rules about data, consent, and moving data internationally.

In order to solve these privacy issues, we discussed the latest techniques, such as federated learning, differential privacy, homomorphic encryption, and privacy-by-design approaches made for digital twins. In addition, the potential changes to society were investigated, highlighting that transparency, personal control, and preventing the powers of surveillance capitalism and digital divides are necessary.

From the studies in the real world, it became clear that flexible privacy options and uniform guidelines are important. At the end of the chapter, future research topics were mentioned, covering privacy metrics, making synthetic data, and creating interoperability standards that help digital twin ecosystems thrive.

2.9.2 Balancing Innovation with Responsibility

Given the popularity of digital twins in different fields, ensuring both advanced technology and strong privacy is very necessary today. Organizations and developers are advised to include privacy protection in their products from the first stages instead of including it later. To be responsible, innovation needs to use advanced ways to protect privacy, obey laws, and address ethical matters so that consumers and others trust the company.

Striking this balance means digital twins can increase how things are managed and still respect the rights and values of everyone in society. Every digital twin design should give priority to privacy protection so that both the data and the user are respected.

2.9.3 Toward Trustworthy Digital Twins

In order to build reliable digital twins, there has to be collaboration between technologists, policymakers, ethicists, and end-users. Transparency of data, clear consent of users, and controls that respond to different risks should be the focus of future improvements. Using shared standards and compatible frameworks will help ensure secure sharing of data and maintain privacy all around the world.

Eventually, accurate digital twins will enable wiser judgments, encourage new ideas, and give positive results without endangering privacy or ethics. Responsibility and respect for privacy in the development of digital twins will ensure they have a strong and helpful presence as more data is used in the future.

AI disclosure statement: The author confirms that no artificial intelligence (AI)-generated content or AI-assisted writing tools were used in the preparation of this chapter (including summaries and the abstract). All text, analysis, and conclusions are the result of the author's original work.

Bibliography

1. Fuller, A., Fan, Z., Day, C., Barlow, C., Digital twin: Enabling technologies, challenges and open research. *IEEE Access*, 8, 108952–109751, 2020.
2. Grieves, M. and Vickers, J., Digital twin: Mitigating unpredictable, undesirable emergent behaviour, in: *Transdisciplinary Perspectives on Complex Systems*, pp. 85–113, Springer, 2017.
3. Richards, N. and King, J., Big data ethics. *Wake For. Law Rev.*, 49, 393–432, 2014.
4. Tao, F., Zhang, H., Liu, A., Nee, A.Y.C., Digital twin in industry: State-of-the-art. *IEEE Trans. Ind. Inf.*, 15, 4, 2405–2415, Apr. 2019.
5. Dwork, C., Differential privacy, in: *Proc. Int. Colloquium Automata, Languages, and Programming*, Springer, 2006.
6. Gentry, C., Fully homomorphic encryption using ideal lattices, in: *Proc. 41st ACM Symp. Theory Comput*, pp. 169–178, 2009.
7. Eubanks, V., *Automating Inequality: How High-Tech Tools Profile, Police, and Punish the Poor*, St. Martin's Press, New York, NY, USA, 2018.
8. Narayanan, A. and Shmatikov, V., Robust de-anonymization of large sparse datasets, in: *Proc. IEEE Symp. Security Privacy*, pp. 111–125, 2008.
9. Ohm, P., Broken promises of privacy: Responding to the surprising failure of anonymization. *UCLA Law Rev.*, 57, 1701–1777, 2010.
10. Zhou, Y., Zhang, R., Yu, N., Wu, X., A survey of privacy threats and protection technologies in digital twin. *IEEE Access*, 9, 130847–130867, 2021.
11. Zuboff, S., *The Age of Surveillance Capitalism: The Fight for a Human Future at the New Frontier of Power*, PublicAffairs, 2019.
12. de Montjoye, Y.A., Hidalgo, C.A., Verleysen, M., Blondel, V.D., Unique in the crowd: The privacy bounds of human mobility. *Sci. Rep.*, 3, 1376, 2013, https://doi.org/10.1038/srep01376.
13. Wang, Y., *et al.*, Data Fusion for Privacy-Preserving Health Monitoring. *IEEE J. Biomed. Health. Inf.*, 22, 3, 706–715, 2018, https://doi.org/10.1109/JBHI.2017.2769508.
14. Cavoukian, A. and El Emam, K., De-identification protocols: Essential for protecting privacy. *Identity Inf. Soc.*, 3, 2, 15–24, 2014, https://doi.org/10.1007/s12394-010-0042-4.
15. Kuner, C., *Transborder Data Flows and Data Privacy Law*, Oxford University Press, Oxford, U.K, 2013.
16. Organisation for Economic Co-operation and Development (OECD), Guidelines on the Protection of Privacy and Transborder Flows of Personal Data, 2013.
17. Cavoukian, A., Privacy by design: The 7 foundational principles, Information and Privacy Commissioner of Ontario, 2009.

18. Wu, J., Haider, S.A., Soni, M., Kalra, A., Deb, N., Blockchain-based energy efficient multi-tasking optimistic scenario for mobile edge computing. *PeerJ Comput. Sci.*, 8, e1118, 2022, https://doi.org/10.7717/peerj-cs.1118.
19. Patki, N., Wedge, R., Veeramachaneni, K., The synthetic data vault, in: *Proc. IEEE Int. Conf. Data Science and Advanced Analytics (DSAA)*, 2016.
20. ISO/IEC JTC 1/SC 41, Digital Twin Framework, ISO, 2023.
21. Manyika, J., *et al.*, Unlocking the potential of the Internet of Things, McKinsey Global Institute, 2015.
22. Mittelstadt, B., Allo, P., Taddeo, M., Wachter, S., Floridi, L., The ethics of algorithms: Mapping the debate. *Big Data Soc.*, 3, 2, 1–21, 2016.
23. Davenport, T.H. and Ronanki, R., Artificial intelligence for the real world. *Harv. Bus. Rev.*, 96, 1, 108–116, 2018.
24. City of Helsinki, Helsinki Smart City Digital Twin Project, 2022.
25. European Union Agency for Fundamental Rights, Surveillance at Work, 2019.
26. Dwork, C. and Roth, A., The algorithmic foundations of differential privacy. *Found. Trends® Theor. Comput. Sci.*, 9, 3–4, 211–407, 2014.
27. Gürses, S., Troncoso, C., Diaz, C., Engineering privacy by design. *Comput. Privacy Data Prot.*, 14, 3, 25–48, 2011.
28. Frid-Adar, M., Klang, E., Amitai, M., Goldberger, J., Greenspan, H., Synthetic data augmentation using GAN for improved liver lesion classification. *IEEE Trans. Med. Imaging*, 38, 3, 915–924, 2018.
29. ISO/IEC JTC 1/SC 41, *Internet of Things and Digital Twin Standardization Roadmap*, ISO/IEC, 2023, Retrieved from https://www.iso.org.
30. Kalra, A. and Tewari, G., Applications of artificial intelligence across Industry 4.0, in: *The Impact of Emerging Technologies on Manufacturing*, J. Smith, (Ed.), pp. 123–145, CRC Press Taylor & Francis, 2023, https://doi.org/10.1201/9781003453567-2.
31. Kalra, A., Nagpal, C., Tandon, B., Patil, L.N., Industry 4.0: Transforming manufacturing through industrial IoT, analytics and augmented reality. *International Conference on Sustainable Industry 4.0: Innovations for a Greener Future (ICSI 2025)*, 2025, April 11–12, Dr. D. Y. Patil Institute of Technology, Pune, India.
32. Ma, R., Kareem, S.W., Kalra, A., Doewes, R., II, Kumar, P., Miah, S., Optimization of electric automation control model based on artificial intelligence algorithm. *Wireless Commun. Mobile Comput.*, 2022.
33. Soni, M., Nayak, N.R., Kalra, A., Degadwala, S., Singh, N.K., Singh, S., Energy efficient multi-tasking for edge computing using federated learning. *Int. J. Pervasive Comput. Commun.*, 2022, https://doi.org/10.1108/IJPCC-03-2022-0106.
34. Kalra, A., Introduction to fuzzy logic and its applications in machine learning, in: *Smart Systems: Engineering and Managing Information for Future Success*,

vol. 22, S. Mahajan, A. Rocha, A.K. Pandit, P. Chawla, (Eds.), Springer, 2025, https://doi.org/10.1007/978-3-031-76152-2_1.
35. Sharma, A., Bhatia, R., Sharma, D., Kalra, A., Exploring AI's prowess in advancing cybersecurity, in: *Smart Systems: Engineering and Managing Information for Future Success*, vol. 22, S. Mahajan, A. Rocha, A.K. Pandit, P. Chawla, (Eds.), Springer, 2025, https://doi.org/10.1007/978-3-031-76152-2_6.

3

Privacy in Smart City Digital Twin

Lingaraj K.[1]*, S. Supreeth[2], Rashmi Laxmikant M.[3], Karthik Rao M. C.[4], Lalit Garg[5] and D. Viswanath Reddy[6]

[1]*Department of Computer Science and Engineering, Rao Bahadur Y Mahabaleswarappa Engineering College, Cantonment, Ballari, Karnataka, India*
[2]*School of Computer Science & Engineering, REVA University, Bengaluru, Karnataka, India*
[3]*Department of Data Science and Computer Applications, Manipal Institute of Technology, Manipal Academy of Higher Education, Manipal, Karnataka, India*
[4]*Department of Mechatronics Engineering, Manipal Institute of Technology, Manipal Academy of Higher Education, Manipal, Karnataka, India*
[5]*Department of Computer Information System (CIS), Faculty of Information Communication Technology (ICT), University of Malta, Msida, Malta*
[6]*Department of Business Administration, Rao Bahadur Y Mahabaleswarappa Engineering College, Cantonment, Ballari, Karnataka, India*

Abstract
Smart city digital twins (SCDTs) are emerging as powerful tools for urban planning, real-time monitoring, and predictive decision-making by creating dynamic digital replicas of physical city systems and processes. These twins rely on continuous data streams from IoT devices, public services, infrastructure, and citizen interactions to simulate and optimize city operations. However, large-scale collection, integration, and processing of personal and behavioral data raise serious privacy concerns, including surveillance risks, re-identification of anonymized data, lack of informed consent, and unclear data ownership. This chapter explores the multifaceted privacy challenges inherent in SCDTs and emphasizes the need for privacy-by-design principles and robust governance frameworks. It discusses key privacy-preserving technologies, such as differential privacy, federated learning, homomorphic encryption, and blockchain, and outlines a layered architecture to integrate these mechanisms into the SCDT ecosystem. Case studies from cities such as Helsinki and Singapore were analyzed to illustrate the effective

**Corresponding author*: lingaraj.k10@gmail.com

Shubham Mahajan, Davinder Paul Singh, Amit Kant Pandit and Paras Chawla (eds.) Ensuring Privacy in Digital Twin Ecosystems, (57–100) © 2026 Scrivener Publishing LLC

implementation of citizen-centric and ethically guided privacy approaches. By addressing both technical and regulatory aspects, this chapter provides a comprehensive overview of how smart cities can achieve a balance between innovation and individual rights, ensuring that digital twins support sustainable urban development without compromising the privacy, autonomy, and trust of their citizens.

Keywords: Smart city digital twins, digital twin, urban infrastructure, ubiquitous data collection, breach vulnerabilities, secure multi-party computation, federated learning

3.1 Introduction

The beginning of the 21st century has seen an explosion in the linking between digital technologies and the city with the advent of 'smart cities,' or urban areas that use ICT to improve the quality of life, economic development, and environmental sustainability within the city. Among the innovations leading to this evolution, one of the most radically transformative is the digital twin (DT), a digital representation of physical assets or systems capable of simulating, monitoring, and improving actual processes in real-time. Although originally situated in the manufacturing/industrial realms, this technology has "migrated" into urban infrastructure to create what is today referred to as the smart city digital twin (SCDT) [1].

Smart city digital twins are not confined to mere representation of physical infrastructure; instead, they are essentially a live and data-rich environment that constantly interacts with the physical city through large sensor and device networks, infrastructure and platforms, and human interaction. It allows city planners, administrators, and service providers to have a direct tool for understanding the dynamics of the city, anticipating outcomes, and making better decisions. SCDTs would allow for a revolutionary approach to the nature of everything, from traffic control, energy consumption, emergency response, and urban development planning [2]. The promise of a safer world and a more secure society is not without ethical, legal, and social concerns, most of all centering on privacy. As with a surveillance system, cities must be considered reliant on real-time data inputs to operate as efficiently as possible. An SCDT, though, involves 'big data' in that it is based on the continuous gathering of fine-grained data from diverse sensor sources like surveillance cameras, smart meters, GPS devices on vehicles, mobile applications, wearables, social media, and digital transactions. These data are often composed of personally identifiable information (PII), personal behavioral patterns, and sensitive metadata that can be used to create detailed profiles of individuals and communities [3]. This collection and subsequent analysis also have implications for improved services; however, it also increases surveillance, de-anonymizes, contains trends toward algorithmic bias, can be breached, and results in a decrease in civil liberties. Additionally, the general lack of transparency related to data governance in smart city initiatives increases the problematic nature of these issues. Ordinary citizens are largely ignorant of the amount and type of data collected, what it is being used for, who has access to it, or how to change or delete data. This unequal power relationship between data subjects and data controllers is contrary to the focus on transparency, accountability, and consent, which is at the heart of the EU General Data Protection Regulation (GDPR) and other modern data protection frameworks [4]. In addition, the transnational character of technology companies developing and operating SCDTs brings further complications related to data sovereignty, cross-border data transfers, and adherence to regional data protection norms.

It is essential that strong privacy measures are incorporated into the digital twins of smart cities. SCDTs differ from legacy urban systems in that they are not only more dynamic and interoperable but also much more closely embedded in everyday life. When AI and ML algorithms use masses of citizen data to make predictive or prescriptive choices, the potential for misuse and unintended negative effects is magnified. However, this is not foolproof. They risk being biased, discriminatory, not transparent, and difficult to audit or contest. The solution to this problem involves shifting from reactive privacy compliance to proactive privacy engineering and ethical design. Privacy in SCDTs is a multi-layered topic that includes technical, legal, ethical, and social considerations. In terms of the technical aspect, the problem can be addressed at different moments in the lifecycle of a digital twin, concerning the collection, transmission, storage, and analysis of the data using privacy-preserving technologies, such as differential privacy, homomorphic encryption, federated learning, secure multiparty computation, and blockchain [5]. Architecturally, SCDTs can be created with a layered design that incorporates privacy-by-design in multiple strata, including perception (sensors), network (data transmission), processing (analytics), and/or application (user interfaces). While these technologies can be part of the solution, there must be a legal and regulatory framework that sets out guidelines for access to data, the right to share, the right to store, and the responsibility to ensure the accountability of information. From an ethical standpoint, SCDTs should be developed according to the principles of human rights, inclusivity, and digital dignity. This involves, among other things, transparent and proportionate data collection, control over personal data residing with the individual, and governance mechanisms with space for public participation and oversight [6]. Notably, privacy should not be considered the opposite or sacrificed for technology, but rather seen as a technology that that enables adoption and success. There is a threat to the legitimacy and social acceptance of a smart city when privacy is not provided.

The relevance of this argument increases when we consider the worldwide proliferation of smart city projects. From Toronto's controversial Sidewalk Labs project to Singapore's Virtual Singapore and from Barcelona's Decidim platform to Helsinki's privacy-first 3D city model, cities all around the world are turning to digital twin technologies designed to improve their governance, resiliency, and quality of life. Each of these examples highlights the promise and challenges of implementing digital twins within cities, especially in relation to issues of privacy control. For example, Virtual Singapore is an advanced digital twin platform that uses real-time and static data from various urban systems for planning, simulation, and public service purposes. Despite its impressive capabilities, it also raises some important questions about surveillance, data centralization, and citizen consent. Helsinki, on the other hand, bets on citizens' privacy and data sovereignty, enabling citizens to choose what pieces of information are or are not shared and to opt out of some digital services. These examples illustrate that the privacy outcomes of SCDTs are not predetermined but depend, at least in part, on the governance model and the level of involvement of the local community. An additional consideration is the transformation of the data [7]. In a smart city, data no longer refers to static attributes such as a name or an address but also incorporates behavior, preferences, emotions, social networks, and predictive data that are used to infer likely future behavior. These data are so rich and contextualized as to problematize traditional ideals of privacy through anonymization and consent; it is becoming increasingly difficult to distinguish what constitutes personal and non-personal data. Within this context, the idea of privacy cannot remain confined to the protection of private information of the individual but must expand to be considered a public good that relates to social relationships, social trust, and a democratic society [8].

Given the complex nature of these issues, this chapter provides a more nuanced understanding of how privacy and smart city digital twins intersect. It starts with an analysis of the main components and functions of SCDTs and then provides an explanation of their privacy issues. This is followed by the proposed layered privacy architecture for digital twins that integrates the security and privacy layers across the entire infrastructure. The GDPR, CCPA, and more general international legal requirements are analyzed to show their applicability as well as inadequacy in the development of urban digital twins. Examples and case studies serve to provide best practices and lessons learned, and the chapter ends with recommendations for future research and policy, and, importantly, ethical implementation. The aim of this chapter is not to protest the use of digital twins in smart cities but rather to argue in favor of their responsible and privacy-minded application. In the context of cities that constitute future smart ecosystems, a digital twin represents a powerful resource and tool that can be utilized for new urban initiatives [9]. However, in the absence of privacy-minded use of these tools, they also have great potential to erode the freedoms and values that they seek to empower. Privacy-oriented digital twin design promises to provide the world with future cities that are not only smart but also just, inclusive, and trustworthy.

Smart city discourse refers to a change in spaces, governance, services, and communities. This shift is characterized by the fact that the data becomes the medium and message. This shift provides revelation, prediction, and automation. However, it informs and positions one to reveal, ostracize, and manage. Our success in balancing these two will ultimately determine digital twins as tools for public goods. Thus, the problem is not just technical or legal but social: How do we create digital, smart, yet deeply human cities? This chapter is an attempt to address this question, centered on the privacy of the digital twin ecosystem.

3.2 Understanding Smart City Digital Twins

A smart city digital twin (SCDT) is a digital representation of a physical city infrastructure, social systems, environmental settings, and administrative procedures, fully aligned with real-time data available in the real world. In contrast to the static nature of urban planning models, the digital twin is a dynamic system and a living organism, as it is shaped by multi-source data input from various collection points, such as IoT sensors, satellite information, mobile apps, city repositories, citizen input, and environmental monitoring systems [10]. The role of an SCDT is to replicate the actual state of the city in real time and allow for real-time experimentation, simulations of possible future scenarios, or real-time decision-making in the areas of urban planning, emergency response, transportation optimization, energy efficiency, sustainability, etc. Therefore, SCDTs are powerful devices for smart-city governance.

3.2.1 Definition and Components

A smart city digital twin (SCDT) is a living, data-centered, real-time computer simulation of a city that constantly reflects, interprets, and anticipates the actions and conditions of a city's material, social, and bureaucratic processes. Unlike static systems, SCDTs are dynamic; they are continuously updated with real-world data from IoT, GIS, citizens, infrastructure systems, and edge/cloud computing systems. The goal of an SCDT is not to simulate parts of a city, but rather to develop a living digital world for testing scenarios as a way to plan, improve, and make decisions for urban systems and to facilitate sustainable growth. At a fundamental level, an SCDT can be represented as a multi-layered function:

$$SCDT(t)=f(P(t),I(t),E(t),H(t),A(t))$$

Where $P(t)$ = Physical infrastructure data at time t (e.g., buildings, roads, utilities), $I(t)$ = IoT sensor and system data (traffic sensors, smart meters), $E(t)$ = Environmental data (air quality, temperature, noise), $H(t)$ = Human-centric data (mobility, behavior, social media), and $A(t)$ = Administrative and service data (waste management, permits, policing). These inputs feed into the twin's computational engine, which applies models for real-time monitoring $M(t)$, forecasting $F(t+\Delta t)$, and optimization O, forming the essential lifecycle of a digital twin:

$$\text{Lifecycle:}\{M(t),F(t+\Delta t),O\}=\Phi(SCDT(t))$$

3.2.2 Components of a Smart City Digital Twin

The smart city digital twin architecture is illustrated in Figure 3.1. The smart city digital twin has six layers, as shown below.

Physical Layer (Urban Infrastructure): This layer consists of physical infrastructure like roads, water systems, public transit, power grids, buildings, public spaces, etc. [11]. These elements are represented by means of 3D GIS and BIM (Building Information Modeling), which is the information structure of the twin.

Data Acquisition Layer: Comprising IoT devices, sensors, cameras, and mobile networks, this layer captures real-time data from the city's environment. The captured data $D(t)$ at any time t is:

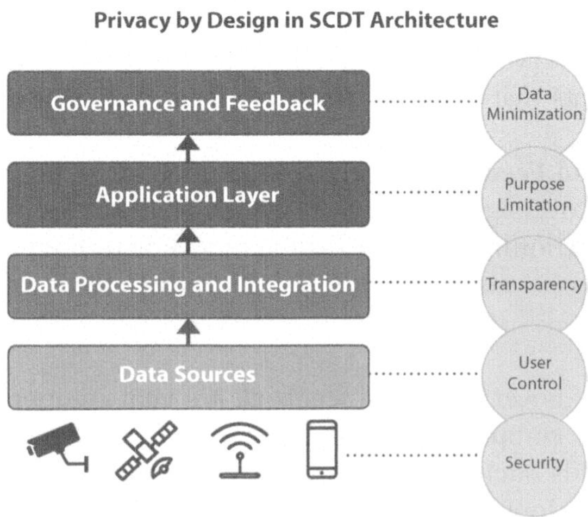

Figure 3.1 Privacy by design in SCDT architecture.

$$D(t) = \sum_{i=1}^{n} S_i(t)$$

where si(t) represents the signal from the ith sensor.

Communication Layer: This layer handles secure, low-latency data transmission from edge devices to centralized or distributed processing systems using 5G, LPWAN, or fiber optic infrastructure. Communication efficiency Ce can be represented as:

$$C_e = \frac{\text{Data Throughput}}{\text{Latency} \times \text{Packet Loss Rate}}$$

Data Processing and Analytics Layer: advanced AI/ML algorithms process and analyze incoming data streams. Real-time anomaly detection, predictive maintenance, traffic simulations, and resource optimization occur within this layer. Data transformations often apply linear or non-linear functions T to incoming raw data:

$$\text{Processed Data} = \text{T(D(t))} = \theta_0 + \theta_1 \text{D(t)} + \epsilon$$

Where θ_0, θ_1 are model parameters, and ϵ is the error term.

Application Layer: The top layer contains dashboards, decision support systems, citizen services, etc. Outputs can be in the form of visualizations, alerts, or insights that can help urban planners, policymakers, and emergency services.
Governance and Feedback Layer: This component will guarantee ethical and regulatory oversight as well as real-time feedback loops incorporated through its functioning. The twin is interactive with the public, and they can alter settings or not collect information, which feeds into privacy and trust [12].

The layers of governance and feedback are vital components that provide regulatory compliance, incorporate citizen feedback, and maintain ethical standards such as transparency, accountability, and data sovereignty. Feedback loops from this layer enable the twin to adapt its patterns and advice according to the needs of the community and laws. In addition, the twin often has a prescriptive analytic AI engine capable of suggesting actions to be taken, such as the rerouting of traffic or sending an ambulance. All of these parts are interconnected through their service-oriented architecture, allowing modularity, scalability, and interoperability among different city systems. These two layers act collectively to allow the twin to perform tasks such as monitoring live data, predicting future states, optimizing situations, and setting up "what-if" scenarios. To perform efficiently, the SCDT must have effective capabilities and be supported by the content, granularity, and accuracy of the data being processed. In addition, given that SCDTs collect and process large quantities of highly sensitive and frequently personal data, privacy and security must be considered from the design of each component of the SCDTs as a feature, not a bonus. These basics must be understood before attempting to debate the privacy issues surrounding SCDTs within the broader framework of intelligent governance and digital infrastructure.

All these are interwoven to create an intelligent urban mirror. While technology is a necessary component for an SCDT to function, it is also technology—not only embedded in each layer but also in forms of governance and privacy controls that are key to ensuring a safe and productive SCDT. This fuller understanding will help lay the foundation for the issues surrounding privacy, which will be explored in later sections.

3.2.3 Data Sources and Integration

The more interconnected and voluminous the data consumed by the smart city digital twin (SCDT), the better the system will function. Data sources in an SCDT can include physical sensors, digital platforms, public and private databases, and data directly from sensors or generated by citizens. They are then all sent into one combined digital model in which they can be monitored and simulated, and for which decisions can be made. Among these can be counted IoT sensors placed at city facilities and services, like traffic lights, roads, smart meters, environmental sensors, cameras, waste bins, etc. [13, 14]. These sensors continually track and provide instant data on traffic patterns, levels of air and noise pollution, energy use, water consumption, and so forth—the operation of the city.

Another highly important source is mobile devices and GPS technology that provides the anonymized or user-consented location and movement data from which things like traffic routing, people flow, and public transportation can be possibly optimized and improved. Geospatial as well as satellite data provide fine-scale spatial context of urban structures, land use, and natural features and are essential information for 3D city models and infrastructure planning. In other words, problems identified by administrative files or utility use, emergency calls, permit requests, and others represent a wealth of institutional knowledge and historical trends that help undergird predictive analytics. The data also includes citizen-generated data from sources such as social media, feedback apps, and participatory governance platforms, providing a qualitative perspective on how people feel and how they would rate services. Combining these diverse forms of data presents both technical and governance problems. Technically, the data has to be cleaned, validated, and normalized and should be transformed into a common semantic data model so that it can be interoperable across various systems. Modeling this can be done through the function:

$$D_{int}(t) = \Psi \sum_{i=1}^{n} w_i \times D_i(t)$$

where $D_{int}(t)$ is the integrated dataset at time t, $d_i(t)$ is the raw data from source i, w_i is a weight representing source reliability or relevance, and Ψ is the transformation function that harmonizes formats, resolves inconsistencies, and aligns temporal-spatial attributes. This weighted and normalized fusion guarantees that the digital twin is not a mere reflection of inputs; instead, it provides meaning, organizes, and provides coherent and actionable intelligence. Concepts of data fusion, such as sensor fusion, entity resolution, and feature-level fusion, are employed to minimize redundancy and provide context for data analysis. Middleware platforms and data lakes are critical for coping with the scale and heterogeneity of the flows of these data, with many relying on edge computing to process data before it reaches the central cloud. CityGML, Sensor Things API, and FIWARE are semantic ontologies and data models that allow semantic interoperability. From a governance standpoint, integration must adhere to privacy, security, and data sovereignty concerns. Privacy is an important part of the design components of the sharing process, which includes consent management, encryption mechanisms, and other access control mechanisms [15, 16]. Audit trails and tracking of provenance were also included to ensure the integrity and source of the data. Ultimately, successful data integration in SCDTs allows for more accurate modeling of urban systems and paves the way for an ethical, transparent, and citizen-centric model of smart governance. In this context, and as stated above, one may argue that a digital twin is as good as the data ecosystem; it stiches together to provide insights and interventions. Figure 3.2 shows data integration in a smart city digital twin.

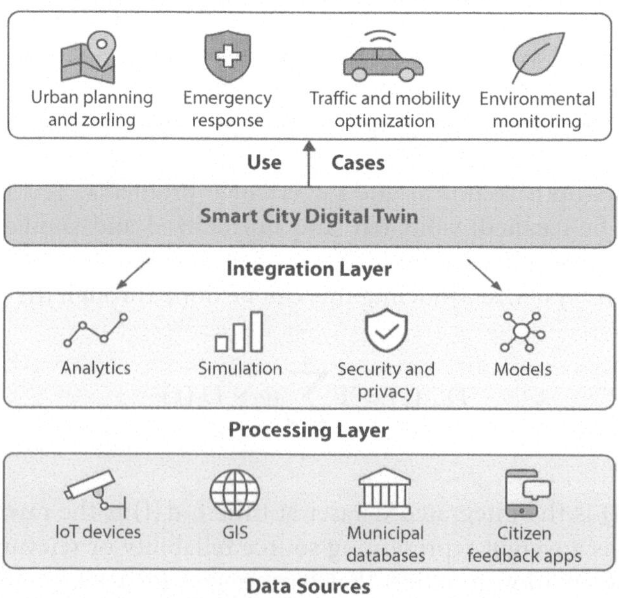

Figure 3.2 Data source and integration.

3.2.4 Use Cases

Smart city digital twins (SCDT) are an enabling building block for tackling urban challenges by means of real-time analytics, forecasting, and optimization in a multiplicity of functional domains that have transformative potential. By incorporating real-time information into a dynamic software simulation of the city, planners are able to play 'what-if' games with simulated processes that affect the city fabric in order to determine the optimal intervention line. Among the most interesting applications, one can find urban planning and zoning, in which SCDTs, by means of geospatial, demographic, and infrastructural data, model land use patterns, simulate development proposals, and improve spatial layouts [17]. Planners could implement and test policies before rolling them out, while the inclusion of information for citizens and the environment can reduce the risk and increase public buy-in.

One application is in emergency response, where real-time sensor data, citizen reports, and CCTV can all be analyzed to spot information on fires, flooding, and accidents. Twins can anticipate each other's needs and rehearse potential responses, allowing faster response and decreased loss of life. Emergency routing algorithms, for example, could help with optimization of ambulance or fire truck routes based on online traffic information and greatly improve the delivery of services. Another important field of application is traffic and mobility optimization, through the analysis of vehicular movement data, GPS signals, and public transport schedules that allow SCDTs to forecast congestion and adapt traffic signal timing. This form of optimization can be quantified by a cost-reduction model:

$$C_{opt} = \min\sum_{i=1}^{n}(t_i \times c_i)$$

where t_i is the average delay time and c_i is the congestion cost factor for intersection i. The goal is to minimize the total urban traffic delay cost, C_{opt}, enhancing mobility and reducing emissions. Another relevant area is environmental sensing, where SCDTs can sense indoor air quality, noise, water, or energy efficiency applied to sustainability objectives. For example, cities can combine insights from environmental sensors with information from weather stations to predict pollution levels and set up sensors that provide information about pollution alarms or even regulate traffic. In addition, there are some cases of the use of SCDTs for infrastructure and asset management, where the twin can monitor bridges, roads, or utility conditions through structural sensors with IoT capabilities [18]. Such predictive maintenance algorithms can provide advanced warnings of a trend in degradation, which would enable municipalities to respond proactively and avoid expensive failures. In the case of waste, SCDTs add more efficiency to waste management by using the information from the sensors in the bins and in the path traveled by the trucks to manage this information and create collection schedules, thereby avoiding overflow and saving fuel. A similar health use case is monitoring public health, in which information obtained from hospitals, drug stores, and wearables is analyzed to track disease, forecast epidemics, and allocate healthcare resources. SCDTs can also enhance citizen engagement and participatory governance, as they can view city plans, receive feedback, and vote on proposals for their community. This greater access to city modeling tools allows for transparency and trust. In all these situations, privacy concerns are also a problem, especially when the data includes identifiable or sensitive patterns. Each application will need to embed privacy-preserving data analytics, anonymization procedures, and consent-based data-sharing models. In general, the wide array of potential applications of smart city digital twins attests to their high potential for resilience, efficiency, and inclusiveness in the city. However, as these applications increase, it is also necessary for ethical, technical, and legal frameworks to grow and develop in tandem.

3.3 Privacy Challenges in Smart City Digital Twins

As smart city digital twins (SCDTs) emerge as the central site for urban governance, real-time analytics, and optimization of infrastructures, they also gain and magnify the entanglement with privacy protection. These online doppelgangers are constructed from massive databases of IoT devices, surveillance cameras, cell phones, social media, government databases, and other sources, much of which is sensitive personal identifiable information (PII) [19]. The amount, level of detail, and real-time collection and availability of such data, however, pose several risks to individuals, from surveillance and profiling to the possibilities of data leakage and misuse. The process of tackling those concerns starts from the realization of the privacy issues entangled with the SCDTs, as well as the design of mechanisms that can 'bake in' Privacy-by-Design features.

Ubiquitous Data Collection and Surveillance Risk: The vast quantity of data generated by SCDTs represents one of the most pronounced privacy risks. Data are continuously collected through IoT sensors, video surveillance, facial recognition cameras, smart meters, and various mobile applications that track behavioral, locational, and biometric information within the context of smart cities. Although this information is useful for smarter services, such data can also create state surveillance at a total level, eroding or eliminating privacy and the right to anonymity in the public sector. This is even more pronounced in the case of digital twins, as they strive to provide real-time conditions, which implies high-frequency, high-resolution data that are required for their operation [20]. CCTV networks, combined with the incorporation of AI-powered facial recognition technology, allow the police or the city government to track people's movements throughout the city down to gait and behavior. The concern is that, without rigorous access controls and anonymization, these technologies could be adapted for use in mass surveillance or a social credit system, as seen in certain authoritarian states.

Lack of Informed Consent and Data Ownership: In standard systems, users consent to data collection by agreeing to a privacy policy. This information is collected without the residents even knowing that the information is being captured, much less why. SCDTs use streams of continuous data from sensors, and thus, individuals are always potentially under observation and in the process of being analyzed without having an obvious point of exit. In addition, questions about who owns the data are not clear. If the digital twin is built from the GPS data of individual citizens, from the health data of clinics, and from the traffic data of telematics systems, is that model, or any analytics drawn from that information, owned by the people who accessed them? In the absence of strong governance, these 'commuter citizens' and corporate entities, as well as local governments, will establish unequal power relations, and there is a high likelihood of data commodification and exclusion from the decision-making process.

Re-Identification Risk of Anonymized Data: Anonymized data can sometimes be re-identified by linking them. Anonymized phone-tracking data matched with public information from social media posts or employment records, for instance, allows identities to be attached with a high degree of certainty. This becomes even more aggressive when coupled with SCDTs that combine data across domains such as transportation, health, and utility usage because of the richness and interconnectedness of the information. Studies have demonstrated that only four spatial-temporal points from a mobility dataset are sufficient to re-identify 95% of the population. This limitation implies that techniques for de-identification currently in use may not be satisfactory and that more stringent privacy-enhancement tools, such as differential privacy or federated learning, need to be implemented.

Data Security and Breach Vulnerabilities: The safety of sensitive data injected and managed within the digital twin ecosystem is equally important. As SCDTs combine data from a variety of systems residing in the city, some of which may be outdated, disjointed, or insecure, the system as a whole represents a highly valuable and complicated opportunity for cyber assault. If the sensor network, cloud database, or analytics engine of the twin is compromised, the private personal data of residents, their movements, or real-time monitoring footage could be revealed. In general, SCDT is related to edge and cloud computing. Although edge computing offers many benefits, including reduced latency, increased privacy, and the ability to process some data locally, it is also often insecure. While cloud systems are, in many regards, safer, there is the obvious problem that they are centralized databases of information, and it is very risky in that one vulnerability exposes all kinds of information. When twinning begins to form the foundation for digital governance overlays, the potential attack surface of these cities expands.

Discrimination and Bias in Decision-Making: SCDT's ability to predict and prescribe can unintentionally embed and perpetuate algorithmic bias that can lead to discrimination in outcomes. If the data used to train these AI models are biased—for example, if certain areas have been overpoliced or certain demographics have been underrepresented in city services—the twins' simulations and recommendations will, for the most part, be biased as well, because they are based on data that will be biased against people. For example, predictive policing algorithms that draw from biased crime datasets and advise increased surveillance in low-income neighborhoods reinforce the criminalization loop. Similarly, zoning simulations that do not account for informal settlements do not consider them in any planning for infrastructure development. This is exacerbated by the black-box nature of AI algorithms and decision-making within digital twins, whereby neither policymakers nor citizens can argue to contest an outcome or seek justice.

Data Minimization vs. Functional Richness: The concept of data minimization, which is at the core of new privacy regulations such as the GDPR, consists of collecting and processing the necessary data for a specific purpose. In many cases, this goes against the aim of developing a highly functional, reactive, and smart digital twin. This alludes to the temptation of always 'collecting all available data' in order to make the best possible use of the capabilities of the system, even though it comes with a high cost in terms of overcollection of data, enhanced risks, and, of course, severe problems in defining the limitation of purpose. The conundrum of trying to capture many functions with very little data use remains a major design challenge. The entire system architecture of the digital twin process must be evaluated by cities to determine whether, when it comes to privacy and utility, it is worth it. Privacy impact assessments (PIAs) and data flow mapping are techniques that serve to document and minimize unnecessary exposure to data.

Inadequate Legal and Regulatory Frameworks: The majority of privacy laws are not written with SCDTs in terms of scale or complexity. Existing laws may not be adapted to the specific environment created by city platforms that are integrated, real-time, and AI-driven. Questions such as who is in control of the twin, how decisions are being overseen, how consent is being handled on a large scale, and how much agency residents have to contest the simulations or predictions end up falling more in the legal gray areas. This can also be compounded by interjurisdictional issues. For instance, even if the twin is controlled by the municipal government, this does not mean that the data generated may not be captured by those who control private telecom companies, international cloud providers, and third-party AI vendors. This leads to ambiguous processes of accountability, liability, and compliance. This legal framework is still largely fragmented and reactive, and privacy protection often requires violation before it can be protected.

Public Trust and Participation Deficit: Lack of transparency in the operations of the SCDTs, in the process of data collection and analysis, and in decision-making undermines the trust of the people. If residents do not understand or believe what is being done with their data, this decreases their openness to utilizing smart services and can result in resistance or backlash to smart city projects. This is especially important in pluralistic societies, where there may be pre-existing historical reasons for resentment toward state surveillance and discrimination. Transparency and letting the public, not only users/members, into digital twin design, development, and governance will be key steps in building and maintaining public trust. To make this happen, cities need to implement trust-building measures, including but not limited to public dashboards, citizen data councils, and open-source algorithm auditing to ensure that everyone is included and that there is accountability.

Challenges of Data Lifecycle Management: Perhaps the most underappreciated privacy concern with SCDTs is how to manage the entire lifecycle of data, from collection and storage to use, dissemination, and deletion. Because of the vast amounts of data that are continuously flowing back and forth within digital twins, problems related to archiving, updating, or deletion of data with respect to data protection principles have become very relevant. These policies must also ensure strict regulatory requirements for data retention, coupled with the use of automated tools for data expiration, pseudonymization, and compliance audits. In addition, because digital twins are commonly employed for simulations and predictive purposes, historical data can be kept indefinitely to improve model predictions. This also prompts questions about the long-term privacy risks associated with personal information and the possibility of having a "right to be forgotten" when one's data are present in the training of models or the logs of such systems.

Privacy in Predictive and Prescriptive Modeling: Perhaps the most profound privacy concern arises not from what is known, but from what is predicted. SCDTs apply AI to make predictions regarding future behavior, consumption requirements, movement patterns, or even potential crimes. These types of predictive inferences can begin to impact individuals far before any action. For example, cities could significantly focus services on a location that has been projected to become "high-risk" by demographic shifts, and it may be in a community where those labels would be considered stigmatizing. These are questions of predictive accuracy but are posed in ethical terms. Are they just? Do people have the right to be informed of or dispute the conclusions drawn about them? An AI ethics framework, as well as newly proposed legal principles, such as the right to explanation and algorithmic accountability, must be developed to address these important concerns.

3.4 Privacy by Design in SCDT Architectures

3.4.1 Principles: Privacy by Design in SCDT Architectures

In the context of smart city digital twin (SCDT) architectures, Privacy by Design (PbD) is not merely a strategy to ensure compliance; rather, it is an underlying approach to be ingrained in each step of the digital twin lifecycle [21, 22]. Doing this on the front end ensures that the concerns of privacy and data security are part of the technological and organizational structure, rather than being tacked on as an addition. The various concepts, principles, and ideas presented in Figure 3.3 represent a roadmap to support the development of urban digital twins that are trustworthy, ethical, and legally robust based on the core principles of PbD.

One of the core principles of Privacy by Design is data minimization, in which only the data necessary for a particular function or service should be collected and processed. These principles guard against the collection of sensitive data in the case of SCDTs reliant on constant data feeds from sources, such as CCTV, GPS, mobile phones, and smart infrastructure.

Figure 3.3 The core principle of privacy by design.

Formally, we can capture this in a function that finds the data vector D, in which we can minimize:

$$\min_{D_i \in D} \left\{ \sum_{i=1}^{n} w_i \cdot D_i \mid D_i \in \text{Relevant}(S_i) \right\}$$

Here, w_i represents the importance weight of data source i, and Relevant(S_i) ensures that only data relevant to service S_i is retained.

Closely linked is the principle of purpose limitation, which stipulates that personal data should only be used for the purpose for which it was collected. In digital twin simulations, where cross-domain data reuse (e.g., transport data used for health analytics) is common, enforcing this principle requires strict tagging and monitoring of data contexts. We define a purpose function $P: D \rightarrow \{p_1, p_2, \ldots, p_m\}$ and enforce the constraint:

$$\forall d \in D, \text{Use}(d) \subseteq \{P(d)\}$$

This ensures that each data point d is only used within its intended context P(d).

Transparency and accountability form another cornerstone of Privacy by Design. Transparency implies that citizens must be informed about what data is being collected, how it is used, and who has access. In practice, this can be implemented through public dashboards, explainable AI models, and open governance protocols. Mathematically, this can be described by a transparency metric T, which depends on the number of disclosed data processing actions A, total processing operations O, and user access rights R:

$$T = \frac{|A| + |R|}{|O|}$$

A transparency score close to 1 indicates strong adherence to Privacy-by-Design principles.

Another important Privacy-by-Design principle is user control. It ensures that people can access, rectify, eliminate, and authorize the use of their data. To assist with this, data subject interfaces managed by access control lists (ACLs) and consent ledgers should be part of any SCDT system. A hypothetical function for ACL would be:

$$\text{Access}(u,d) = \begin{cases} Granted & if\ u \in AuthorizedUser(d) \\ Denied & otherwise \end{cases}$$

Where u is the user and d is the data record.

Security by default is another essential component of PbD in SCDTs. This includes encryption, secure edge computing, and zero-trust architectures to guard against breaches. Suppose the digital twin processes sensitive health and mobility data. The encrypted data flow can be denoted by:

$$C_i = E_k\ (D_i)$$

Where C_i is the ciphertext of data stream D_i encrypted with key k, ensuring confidentiality even if interception occurs. If Privacy-by-Design principles are strictly adhered to, the architecture of smart city digital twins transitions from being a reactive data platform to being a trusted, controlled, and accounted-for ethical infrastructure. Good governance principles are set not only as a requirement to adhere to global data protection standards, such as the GDPR or CCPA, but also as the rights of urban citizens in a digital society that are subject to such governance.

3.4.2 Privacy-Preserving Technologies in SCDT Architectures

Privacy-preserving technologies (PPTs) provide the technological backbone for the realization of Privacy by Design (PbD) in smart-city digital twin (SCDT) architectures. Such technologies are designed to reduce privacy leaks, protect user anonymity, ensure compliance with privacy regulations, and enable analytics and simulations that emerge in intelligent urban environments. Given that SCDTs centralize a mass of heterogeneous data from city sensors, public systems, personal devices, and cloud infrastructure, positive PPTs must be in place to ensure citizen trust and legal legitimacy [23]. One of the most fundamental technologies is differential privacy, which introduces mathematically calibrated noise to datasets, thereby masking individual data points while preserving aggregate statistical trends. If a function f computes a query on a dataset D, differential privacy ensures that:

$$\Pr[f(D) = o] \leq e^{\varepsilon} \cdot \Pr[f(D') = o]$$

Here, D and D′ are datasets differing by a single record, o is the output, and ε is the privacy budget (a smaller value implies stronger privacy). This ensures that the presence or absence of any individual's data has a negligible impact on the output.

Differential privacy introduces mathematical noise to data outputs to mask individual contributions. In an SCDT, where aggregate analytics (e.g., traffic heatmaps or energy consumption trends) are critical, DP allows authorities to release accurate statistics without revealing whether any one person's data was used. Suppose an energy management system in the SCDT wants to analyze household power consumption by district. Rather than querying raw meter data, a DP function returns an approximate total by injecting Laplace or Gaussian noise:

$$f'(D) = f(D) + \text{Laplace}(0, \Delta f / \varepsilon)$$

Here, ε is the privacy budget, such that smaller values of ε offer stronger privacy. The key trade-off is accuracy vs. privacy. A smaller ε ensures stronger privacy but reduces the usefulness of the data. Furthermore, tuning DP correctly requires deep statistical knowledge, and cumulative queries may degrade utility. It is best used in non-critical, high-volume data settings like mobility trends.

Another key technology is homomorphic encryption (HE), which enables computations to be performed on encrypted data without decrypting it. Suppose a digital twin wants to compute a traffic congestion index from encrypted location data E(m). HE allows:

$$E(m_1) \oplus E(m_2) = E(m_1 + m_2)$$

This property supports secure cloud analytics without revealing the underlying values m_1 and m_2. Though computationally expensive, HE is valuable in high-stakes scenarios like smart healthcare or digital finance twins. While HE guarantees strong confidentiality, it is computationally expensive and often impractical for real-time applications. Fully Homomorphic Encryption (FHE) remains largely experimental for SCDTs, though partially homomorphic schemes are viable for simple aggregations.

Secure Multi-Party Computation (SMPC) is another technique where multiple parties compute a function collaboratively without revealing their private inputs. In SCDT settings, different departments (e.g., health, transport, police) may compute a joint indicator like "urban risk score" from their private datasets. SMPC ensures the function $f(x_1,x_2,\ldots,x_n)$ is evaluated such that no xi is revealed to others. Mathematically:

$$\text{Output}=f(x_1,x_2,\ldots,x_n) \text{ where } \forall i,\ x_i \notin \text{View}_j\ (i\neq j)$$

Federated Learning (FL) is increasingly relevant in the context of edge computing within SCDTs. Rather than centralizing all data for training AI models, FL trains models locally on edge devices and shares only model parameters θ. The global model is updated as:

$$\theta_{t+1} = \theta_t + \eta \cdot \sum_{i=1}^{n} \nabla L_i(\theta_t)$$

Here, ∇L_i is the gradient of the local loss function on device i, and η is the learning rate. FL preserves data locality while improving global intelligence. While HE guarantees strong confidentiality, it is computationally expensive and often impractical for real-time applications. Fully Homomorphic Encryption (FHE) remains largely experimental for SCDTs, though partially homomorphic schemes are viable for simple aggregations.

Blockchain provides for important data permanence, trackability, and auditability necessary for governance, accountability, and citizen trust. A blockchain, for example, could also contain logs of data access, records of consent sharing, or institutional data sharing between departments within SCDTs. A smart waste management twin may log each data request or service event onto a blockchain ledger. Each transaction T_k is appended as:

$$H_k = \text{Hash}(T_k \,||\, H_{k-1})$$

It creates a time-stamped, clear, and unchangeable custody chain. Blockchain is slow, requires storage, and has scaling limitations. If this entails high transaction costs or limitations on throughput, then public blockchains are inappropriate, but the same applies to private blockchains that require sound governance that avoids centralization and access control. Including privacy (e.g., *via* ZKPs) remains difficult.

Finally, zero-knowledge proofs (ZKPs) enable a user or a system to prove that a statement is true (for example, age > 18, resident in city) without revealing the data itself. In SCDT-based smart voting systems, ZKPs have the following function:

$$\text{Prover} \rightarrow \text{Verifier: I can prove } x \in R \text{ without revealing } x$$

Table 3.1 Comparison of strengths and suitability.

Technology	Data privacy	Real-time use	Complexity	Best domains
Differential privacy	High	Medium	Medium	Population-level analytics, planning
Federated learning	High	High	High	Smart mobility, eHealth, home energy
Homomorphic encryption	Very High	Low	Very high	Billing, audits, cloud-based models
Blockchain	Integrity-focused	Medium	High	Consent management, logging, governance
Secure multi-party computation	Very High	Very high	Very high	Billing, audits, cloud-based models
Zero-knowledge proofs	High	High	Very high	Consent management, logging, governance

The combination of these privacy-preserving technologies will provide a useful set of tools for the development of scalable, secure, privacy-aware SCDTs. This intermingling guarantees that, regardless of the hyperconnected context one lives in, the privacy of the individual can still be recognized as a protected right, rather than being a mere design utopia, as shown in Table 3.1.

3.4.3 Layered Architecture for Privacy in Smart City Digital Twin (SCDT)

The incorporation of Privacy by Design (PbD) within a smart city digital twin (SCDT) must follow a structured, systematic approach. Layered architecture is a powerful, scalable construct that instantiates privacy from the bottom up in various technical and organizational parts of SCDT systems [24, 25]. These layers are in charge of different privacy-preserving functions, and all together contribute to reinforcing mechanisms that go from data collection to decision-making. The architectural layers of privacy regarding the smart city digital twin (SCDT) are presented in Figure 3.4. This architecture is based on modularity, policy enforcement, and technical compliance with privacy laws such as the GDPR and CCPA.

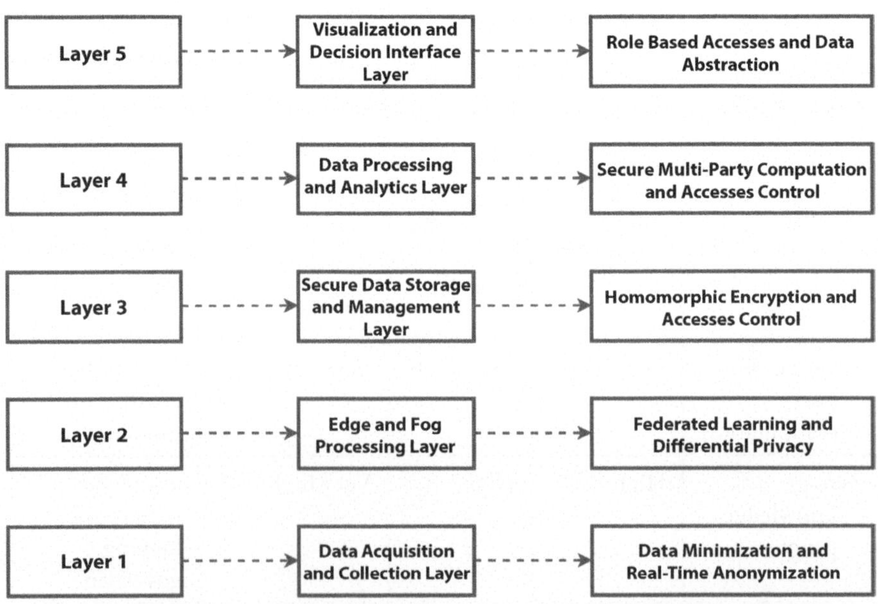

Figure 3.4 The layered architecture for privacy in smart city digital twin (SCDT).

Data Acquisition and Collection Layer: This is the foundational layer where data is harvested from IoT sensors, edge devices, mobile apps, city infrastructure, and citizen interactions. To enforce privacy at this layer, data minimization and real-time anonymization techniques are implemented. For any sensor Si, the amount of data Di collected should satisfy:

$$D_i \leq D_{max} \quad \text{where} \quad D_{max} = \text{Relevant}(S_i, P_j)$$

Here, Relevant(S_i,P_j) denotes the maximum data needed for purpose P_j, ensuring purpose limitation.

Edge and Fog Processing Layer: At this level, raw data is pre-processed, aggregated, or filtered at the edge or fog nodes before transmission to centralized cloud systems. Privacy-preserving techniques like federated learning and differential privacy are integrated. In federated learning, each node iii updates a local model θi and shares only the gradient, maintaining data locality:

$$\theta = \frac{1}{n}\sum_{i=1}^{n}\theta_i$$

Simultaneously, noise η is added to preserve differential privacy:

$$\theta_i' = \theta_i + \mathcal{N}(0, \sigma^2)$$

This prevents sensitive user data from being reconstructed during model aggregation.

Secure Data Storage and Management Layer: All data entering this layer must be encrypted using **homomorphic** or **symmetric encryption** mechanisms. Suppose D is a dataset stored in a smart city cloud server; its encrypted form, E_k(D), using key k, ensures confidentiality:

$$\text{Ek(D)=Encrypt(D,k)}$$

Access is controlled through attribute-based access control (ABAC) mechanisms. For each access request r, permission is granted only if the user attributes A_u match policy π:

$$\text{Access}(r) = \begin{cases} \text{Grant}, & \text{if } A_u \models \pi \\ \text{Deny}, & \text{otherwise} \end{cases}$$

Data Processing and Analytics Layer: This layer is where the use of data analytics, machine learning, and simulation models takes place for the making of decisions in terms of urban planning, control of traffic, and public health, among other things. In cases where the analysis requires multi-stakeholder data, Secure Multi-Party Computation (SMPC) is utilized to ensure data integrity and privacy. For data in departments A and B, we can compute some function $f(x_A, x_B)$) without revealing x_A or x_A:

$$f(x_A, x_B) = \text{SecureCompute}(x_A, x_B)$$

Each party only sees encrypted shares or intermediate results.

Visualization and Decision Interface Layer: This layer exposes dashboards, alerts, and simulations to city officials, operators, and sometimes the public. Role-based access and data abstraction are used to prevent overexposure of personal details. For example, user interface U for role R receives data view V:

$$V = \text{Abstract}(D, R)$$

where Abstract hides or generalizes sensitive fields depending on the user's role and privileges.

The multi-tiered privacy framework of SCDTs guarantees the general protection of personal data from when it is collected to when a decision is made based on it. A combination of all privacy-preserving tools, such as differential privacy, encryption, federated learning, SMPC, and access control, can be incorporated at each level of the framework to ensure that digital twins can still be useful to cities, but with perhaps more privacy preservation to not violate citizen trust and be legally compliant. In addition, it is highly flexible and scalable, meaning that it can adapt to changes in privacy legislation and new technologies.

3.5 Legal and Ethical Frameworks

Complex legal and ethical frameworks are the backbone of responsible and secure data usage, citizen rights, and accountability in the SC digital twin ecosystem. Given the enormous quantities of real-time information that SCDTs capture, including not only patterns of mobility but also individuals' own health records never before so detailed, effective adherence to data protection regulations such as the General Data Protection Regulation (GDPR), the California Consumer Privacy Act (CCPA), and nascent smart governance guidelines is vital. This encourages foundational principles, such as data minimization, purpose limitation, consent, and the right to be forgotten. Ethics, more broadly than legality, is also concerned with fairness, responsibility, and respect. For example, the algorithms in machine decisions made by the digital twin must be free of bias and ensure that all segments of the community will benefit from the outcome [26]. Ethical models call for routine audits, stakeholder participation, and a "person-in-the-loop" to ensure that technologies conform to the interests of society. In addition, smart cities should build contextualized policies that account for social norms and expectations. Legal and ethical adherence minimizes exposure to lawsuits and data leaks but is also critical in building public trust and engagement. As digital twins become more central to urban planning and service provision, it is important to incorporate the principles of digital twins into their design and operation; otherwise, we may risk reinforcing the trends described above.

3.5.1 Regulatory Landscape

The regulatory environment surrounding smart city digital twins (SCDTs) is fluid as cities begin to use more sophisticated technologies that require new regulations and oversight. As CPS, AI, and real-time data analytics come together in SCDTs, governments and regulatory structures are concerned with ensuring that these systems are privacy-preserving, transparent, and adhere to ethical considerations in their governance. The GDPR is only one of the many international and national data protection laws that underpin this regulatory system. The GDPR establishes rights for the subjects of data: rights to access, rectification, erasure, objection, and legal responsibilities for the holders and processors of data. The GDPR is still the most extensive data protection legislation in the world and thus has set guidelines for other laws. These guidelines are relevant to the case of SCDTs, as their fundamental principles—data minimization, purpose specification, user consent, and the right to be forgotten—are directly related to them. This requires a purpose limitation to the effect; for example, data collected for urban mobility management cannot be later used for profiling or surveillance without new consent. Similarly, the right to be forgotten also raises architectural obstacles for systems such as digital twins, which set out to store and simulate past urban data. Thus, the SCDTs that are used under the GDPR must incorporate technical measures that enable data capture concerns to be limited proactively to strictly what is necessary and to tag data in a way that enforces intended purposes as well as system processes and workflows to provide subjects with the automated ability to exercise rights to access, rectify, and delete their data.

In other parts of the world, recent trends in regulation, such as the Personal Data Protection Act in Singapore or the Digital Personal Data Protection Act in India, also resonate with these ideas but take into account the particular local social and political context. Currently, many nations are developing legislation and regulations specifically centered on AI to tackle issues of bias, explainability, and fairness within the digital twins of the type discussed above. A further step in this direction is the EU's proposed AI Act, which categorizes AI systems as "high risk" in the context of digital governance and requires strict conformity assessments.

In India, the DPDP Act of 2023 also provides a valuable framework for SCDT regulation that is specific to fast-urbanizing smart cities, such as Pune and Bangalore. Data fiduciaries are a new category established by the Act; they are owners of data with obligations to ensure that consent is informed and explicit, data is used in a manner that is consistent with its identified purpose, and the principle of data minimization is applied. It bans the processing of sensitive data without explicit consent, data that are particularly pertinent to SCDTs that involve healthcare, financial, or biometric information. This implies that for the operators of smart cities, the development of centralized consent orchestration systems while adopting federated or local processing of data, as prescribed in the sovereignty clauses is necessary. The DPDP Act also requires the appointment of Data Protection Officers (DPOs) and the establishment of data breach notification procedures, both of which should be included in a solid digital twin governance approach.

In the United States, the California Consumer Privacy Act (CCPA) provides citizens with the right to access their data, understand its use, and opt out of sales. While the CCPA is more business-focused and less strict than the GDPR, it still applies to many private vendors and contractors that build or manage smart city platforms. Thus, SCDTs designed or hosted by U.S.-based entities must offer transparency portals for data use and ensure opt-out features in public-facing interfaces. For example, a smart kiosk or transport app in Los Angeles must allow users to decline data collection or share it with third parties. To comply with the CCPA, SCDTs should embed do-not-sell controls, implement data access request APIs, and maintain vendor-specific audit logs.

In addition, global shifts taking place in other contexts, such as the Personal Data Protection Act (PDPA) in Singapore, Brazil's LGPD, PIPEDA in Canada, and China's Cybersecurity Law, further complicate the issue of jurisdiction. These laws, amongst other things, bring in specificities at the regional level, such as the localization of data, restriction on transfer of data across borders, encryption, and public interest exceptions. For instance, Singapore promotes data innovation if it contributes to the collective benefit of the public but requires consent for most uses of personal data, or China's strict regulation of storage and security for all city-level platforms.

This diversity means that 'cross-jurisdictional' decentralized systems must be designed from the ground up with law-abiding and privacy-protective architectures that have their regulations built into the transmission of data. A good practice is the use of policy-driven access controls, which have the ability to dynamically apply rules based on user positions, goals, and types of data. Second, it is possible to deploy data provenance tracking that records each step of the transformation or access for accountability and audit purposes. Consent management services that are compatible with legal identities may allow citizens to easily give, retract, or monitor the use of data across applications.

At a global level, institutions including the OECD, UNESCO, and ISO are developing standards of privacy and ethics in relation to smart cities and AI. For example, ISO/IEC 27560 and ISO 37120 set standards for the use of urban data and performance indicators that allow for interoperability and accountability of digital twin deployments. SCDTs are thus subject to a mix of data protection legislation as well as guidelines in AI ethics and urban governance. These frameworks protect individuals but also provide a legal framework through which to innovate, providing that smart city transformations are socially responsible and legally compliant. This implies that, going forward, SCDTs will have to be "regulation-aware," and have the capacity to navigate through this shifting legal landscape, for instance by including "dynamic policy engines, automated compliance checks, and adaptive consent management."

Besides national legislation, UN, OECD, and ISO-led international efforts are playing a significant role in the development of regulatory and ethical frameworks for smart cities and digital twins [27]. The focus of the United Nations Sustainable Development Goals (SDG), notably SDG 11, "Make Cities Inclusive, Safe, Resilient, and Sustainable," actively promotes the use of new and digital technologies to enhance urban life in a responsible and rights-respecting manner. The UN-Habitat's "People-Centered Smart Cities" approach calls for responsible data use, people-centered governance, and inclusive design and is a good starting basis for how these digital twin technologies could function if taken up by governments [28].

The OECD has developed a comprehensive "Recommendation on Enhancing Access to and Sharing of Data (EASD)," which emphasizes privacy, fairness, and interoperability in digital public infrastructure. It also promotes algorithmic transparency and risk-based regulation of AI in urban systems, laying a foundation for smart city governance that is right- and innovation-friendly [29, 30].

Meanwhile, under its Smart City indicators and governance framework, ISO/IEC has released a set of standards, such as ISO 37106:2018, ISO 37120, or ISO 37122, which establish indicators and governance to provide a reference of what constitutes an efficient, sustainable, digital city [31–33]. Regarding digital twins, the ISO/IEC JTC 1/SC 41 is currently addressing the development of standards for IoT and digital twin reference architectures to guarantee interoperability, security, and ethical treatment of data in complex urban systems [34]. Such standards are crucial to ensure that Smart City digital twins are in line with international best practices and cross-border interoperability and accountability of the public sector.

In aggregate, these international documents promote the need for a rights-based, standards-based approach to digital transformation with ethical foresight, legal compliance, and citizen empowerment embedded in each stage of smart city digital twin development from the perspectives of government and city planners.

3.5.2 Privacy Impact Assessments (PIA)

Privacy Impact Assessments (PIAs) are an integral part of the legal and ethical governance of smart city digital twin (SCDT) systems. A PIA "is a structured process for identifying, assessing, and mitigating privacy risks in any information system, whether existing or under development; in describing the information system, the PIA does not use the term 'privacy assessment.'" In the context of SCDTs and the massive amounts of live and sensor data, such as geolocation, health, biometric, and behavioral data gathered, a PIA is critical to safeguard individual rights and freedoms as per data protection laws such as the General Data Protection Regulation (GDPR), the California Consumer Privacy Act (CCPA), and others at the national level.

The goal of PIA is to determine whether the collected data are consistent with privacy principles, such as purpose limitation, data minimization, or user consent. For a digital twin that has been implemented to monitor traffic and collect data on vehicles that pass as well as pedestrians on the street, the PIA will ask if the specific identifying data, such as license plate number or features on faces, are required in order to meet operational objectives, or if these data can be collected in the form of aggregate, anonymous information. This assessment includes locating data flows, classifying types of data, assessing potential risks to privacy, and developing strategies to mitigate this risk, such as anonymizing, encrypting, and access-controlled solutions.

A PIA will usually help answer the following fundamental questions: What data is being collected? By whom? Is the consent process transparent? If the data are compromised, what data are at risk? What protections are in place? To provide a concrete example, if the digital twin that is embedded in a smart energy grid is tracing energy use in individual homes, in this case, the PIA would assess the risk of behavioral profiling and thus recommend solutions such as the use of differential privacy or the limitation of the temporal resolution to the network for the protection of individuals' identities. Finally, PIAs should be continuous and change as the lifecycle of the system progresses. When an SCDT scales or incorporates new datasets (e.g., health or social service data), the PIA must be taken again and adjusted to the new privacy implications. This cycle is in sync with the logic of Privacy by Design and envisions privacy as something that is to be architected into the system rather than achieved later in response to compliance. Performing PIA also has legal incentives.

In fact, under GDPR Article 35, organizations must conduct a Data Protection Impact Assessment (DPIA), a type of PIA specifically for processing activities that are likely to result in a high risk for data subjects. If they fail to do so, regulatory measures can be implemented to penalize them for not doing so. A properly conducted PIA, in addition to acting as a reasonable process, can increase transparency and trust in the process by "reporting back" to the public or to citizens in documents or public meetings.

Within SCDTs, PIAs are also important in promoting ethical coherence by revealing unintended outcomes, such as algorithmic bias, surveillance creep, or effects on vulnerable populations. For example, a digital twin established for public safety could unknowingly over-police certain neighborhoods because of historical geospatial data on crime statistics. A proper PIA would highlight this risk and suggest perhaps diversifying the data or using humans in a loop decision-making. The use of smart city digital twins requires privacy impact assessments. They provide a structure for the identification of potential risks, for upholding privacy principles, for steering technical design decisions, and for preserving ethical values.

As the era of digital governance and smart cities continues to advance, PIAs are a vital tool for building systems of accountability as well as citizen trust.

3.5.3 Ethics Guidelines

Ethics in smart city digital twins (SCDTs) contribute to establishing a standard to guarantee that technological advancement remains consistent with human values, societal needs, and overarching objectives of sustainable and equitable urban development. Ethical principles are different from and often more flexible than legal principles; ethical principles are normative and designed to help determine what to do when the law is not clear, is antiquated, or does not exist. These are guiding principles to assist cities, policymakers, data scientists, and platform developers in coping with the complexities of data justice, autonomy, accountability, and fairness.

The issue at the core of the ethics of SCDTs is the respect for human dignity and rights. Digital twins for smart cities involve extremely sensitive personal data related to individuals' movements, patterns of consumption, and health status, as well as their interactions with public services. From an ethical standpoint, they insist that these types of data should not be put to uses that threaten autonomy or that endanger subjects through surveillance, discrimination, or exclusion. This preempts the misuse of tools such as predictive analytics to profile and target specific populations in policing, welfare, and credit scores. From an ethical perspective, these systems should certainly be subject to scrutiny for algorithmic bias and disparate impact.

Another fundamental ethical value is the need for transparency and explainability. They should understand how their data are being used as they pass through, are transformed by, and impact social decisions made around and within SCDTs. For instance, if the digital twin model dictates a distribution in public services (i.e., where to send ambulances or build a park), the public should be able to understand in layman's terms exactly why decisions conform to the digital twin's predictions. Transparency in this case fosters accountability and allows those affected to question or contest the decisions made. Similarly, in the case of AI-based technologies integrated into SCDTs, when it comes to ethical guidelines, developers are asked to design them such that automated decision-making is transparent and ethical.

Ethical governance also involves accountability and responsibility. Because SCDT projects include city governments, private vendors, academia, and citizens as part of the project processes, the responsibility of the project becomes unclear when things go wrong ethically. Best practices also suggest delineating roles and responsibilities, keeping records of how data are used, and the creation of ethics boards or advisory committees to monitor project implementation. They must also enable "citizens to raise grievances" about data abuse or unethical practices in the handling of information, and in doing so bolster the ethics of their own digital city.

This is a critical responsibility, especially in the case of applications based on smart city technologies, where the principle of "beneficence and non-maleficence," or "doing good and avoiding harm," is concerned. While SCDTs can be leveraged to enable greater resource efficiency, environmental sustainability, and public health, they should be aware of digital exclusion or avoidable environmental impacts. From an ethics standpoint, incorporative design efforts, inclusive by addressing the community design for all, accessibility, and sustainability concerns from the start, are recommended.

Democratic participation and social justice are also foregrounded ethical obligations. From an ethical standpoint, it has been suggested that citizens should not only be a mass of data but also be actors and design and govern SCDTs. Thus, participatory design processes, public consultations, and community co-design can also ensure that technologies meet the real needs of the communities that they should benefit and that the benefits are evenly distributed.

Although many smart city programs express a desire to be 'citizen-centric,' this is implemented in only superficial ways that do not necessarily attend to citizen needs in systemic ways. A truly citizen-centric SCDT would protect individuals from surveillance and enable them to participate in co-creating policies, tools, and governance of urban data systems. A project such as DECODE, an initiative of the City of Barcelona, where data is cryptographically controlled by citizens using consent-based ledgers, is one example. Citizens can then decide which applications or city services will have access to which particular data streams, such as those on mobility or energy usage, and under which conditions. The TADA Manifesto in Amsterdam is another similar noncommercial policy statement drafted collectively by local stakeholders for common digital values such as inclusivity, transparency, and autonomy. In Helsinki, the public is actively included in the process of digital urban planning by means of public workshops and the use of interactive simulations in public libraries, in which the public can decide on the utilization of their data, for example, in zoning and mobility models.

In these two cities, participatory design processes are not just about consulting with stakeholders; they integrate structures that work to inform both technical system design and policy, such as data governance boards, citizen juries, and co-design sprints. These also represent examples of procedural justice, where governance processes are fair, inclusive, and transparent. More contemporary instantiations of informed consent offer a consent dashboard or personal data pod that allows people to set privacy settings retrospectively, see who has previously accessed their information, make new levels of data unavailable to be accessed, or even opt out entirely.

However, the issue of digital equity remains a challenge. Those who are lower income and digitally excluded may lack access to privacy-enhancing technology, may not be able to participate in governance processes, or may be overrepresented as "suspicious" in surveillance data. For example, if predictive policing applications are developed using biased data, this can mean that there is an increased focus on one type of neighborhood over another. Conversely, the same holds true; newer smart energy meters in more affluent neighborhoods can be set to provide fine-grained data access, while older systems in poorer and underserved regions may not. Thus, to achieve privacy justice, we must engage in proactive policies, make equitable resources available for infrastructure, develop multilingual consent mechanisms, and perform bias audits at each step of the SCDT pipeline. In the absence of these, the potential advantages of designing for citizens are the threat of becoming a reinforcing mechanism for inequality.

Thus, technical solutions such as differential privacy, federated learning, or encryption are essential for protecting individual data; ultimately, no technical solution alone will correct the underlying ethical issues associated with smart city digital twin (SCDT) deployments. Thus, these types of negotiations around the dialectic between innovation and privacy are always contextual, value-laden, and politically contested. Indeed, as an example, tracking citizens' movements in real time to enhance emergency response has obvious tensions with data minimization. Similarly, predictive analytics in the service of managing resources are at risk for unintentionally perpetuating bias if they are trained on clearly biased data. The challenges posed by these problems are not entirely solvable by algorithms or legal mechanisms of protection and compliance. Rather, these are deliberation, public discussion, and value-sensitive design processes. In addition, the trade-offs for groups may vary depending on their economic status; something public as a benefit for some, such as biometric technologies for public transportation or toll collection, is seen as surveillance by marginalized communities that have a higher likelihood of being over-policed. The trade-offs between collective good and private rights, efficiency and justice, and innovation and equality remain an ongoing challenge, and cities must continually deal with them. A genuinely robust SCDT framework needs to be introduced from the starting components of moral discourses, reasoning, contestability, and pluralistic mechanisms of control, in addition to privacy-enhancing technologies.

3.6 Case Studies

Smart city digital twins (SCDTs) are being deployed by global pioneer cities to support better urban management, citizen services, and sustainability. However, these approaches also provide important lessons in privacy, data governance, and ethics. In the following subsections, a collection of real-world examples highlights how urban areas have dealt with SCDTs and what they found to be the benefits and privacy risks involved.

One of the most prominent is Singapore's Virtual Singapore project, which operates essentially as a comprehensive 3D city model and collaborative data platform. It was developed by the National Research Foundation (NRF) and Government Technology Agency (GovTech) and links live data feeds from traffic systems, IoT sensors, and satellite cameras to create a virtual environment for the entire city. These use cases include crowd control, mobility tracking, urban heat mapping, and disaster response. Due to the level of granularity at which personal and behavioral information is taken in, the project has been compelled to take privacy concerns seriously. This involves measures such as role-based access control, generalization to prevent the threat of re-identification of personal identifying information (PII), and data partitioning to protect sensitive data from retrieval, unless required. In addition, public visibility, evidenced by the engagement of stakeholders, has assisted in creating confidence and adherence to the Personal Data Protection Act (PDPA) in Singapore.

However, this model has some trade-offs. Although efficient, Singapore's centralized system tends to limit citizen visibility and control. Data collection is mostly passive, and, while anonymization techniques are used, citizens have few mechanisms to verify how or when their data are used. Furthermore, while Virtual Singapore is rich in simulation capabilities, its privacy governance lacks participatory oversight, which can limit long-term trust, especially when more personalized data are integrated.

Singapore uses data minimization and data abstraction, which means that only practitioners or researchers with justification are given identifiable information to reduce privacy issues. The fact that simulations can sometimes be substituted for real-time tracking further decreases the risks. However, the lack of tools such as dynamic consent or real-time opt-outs speaks to a politics of privacy that is more about meeting the requirements of regulators rather than empowering citizens.

Among the most advanced, the Helsinki 3D+ digital twin is an interactive 3D digital model that replicates the buildings, infrastructure, and all current environmental conditions of the Finnish capital. What distinguishes Helsinki is its citizen-centered approach and its focus on ethical AI, data sovereignty, and transparency. Participatory planning mechanisms are part of a move to 'simulate' city-building processes that encourage direct interaction by community members with urban development simulations. The media of Helsinki complies with the European Union's GDPR standards and has stressed the role of Privacy Impact Assessments (PIAs) in all services oriented toward data. This is as much a question of protecting data rights as it is of promoting a culture of accountability and ethical urban innovation.

The transparency infrastructure built around the twin worked well in Helsinki. Citizens are not merely data subjects but stakeholders, able to opt for data collection, monitor how their data are used, and participate in city modeling. Data localization and edge computing are also used to keep sensitive data within personal or municipal boundaries, thereby reducing the attack surface for breaches.

However, this model has also been criticized. An open and participation-intensive focus also tends to complicate governance. This yields a form of friction and a slow pace of new development that can occur when working with disparate departments and attempting to ensure both interoperability and sustained compliance. In addition, the management of an opt-in process at a massive scale provides a usability challenge for some residents, as shown in Table 3.2.

Boston's Urban Digital Twin Initiative in the U.S. is a promising approach to the use of digital twins to address the issues of climate change and social equity. Boston's digital twin has incorporated public health data, air quality sensors, and the energy usage of buildings in the city to help decision-making in areas of environmental justice. Data bias has been under study, and efforts have been made between cities, local universities, and non-profits to practice urban planning. Significantly, the Boston model uses edge processing and federated learning to limit centralized data collection, which presents additional privacy challenges. This has integrated a form of "privacy by architecture" by keeping sensitive data within the city and training machine learning models "in place" without uploading raw data.

Shanghai posits an alternative, equally ambitious model. The city has invested in a huge digital twin infrastructure to coordinate real-time utility, transportation, energy, and citizen services through its plans for Smart City 2035. It harvests vast amounts of personal as well as infrastructural data that, when plugged into machine learning algorithms, help drive

Table 3.2 Comparative lessons and transferable strategies.

Aspect	Singapore – virtual Singapore	Helsinki – 3D+ digital twin	Transferable strategies
Governance model	Centralized, government-led	Decentralized, participatory	Combine strong institutional governance with inclusive public engagement
Privacy strategy	Anonymization, access control, data abstraction	Consent management, data minimization, edge computing	Implement layered privacy controls with adaptive consent frameworks
Legal compliance	PDPA (Singapore)	GDPR (EU)	Align with local laws while adopting GDPR-aligned best practices for global compatibility
Citizen engagement	Low (limited transparency and feedback loops)	High (public dashboards, co-design, data subject rights)	Introduce public-facing interfaces and participatory platforms
AI and algorithm oversight	Limited auditability of models	Transparent and explainable AI governance	Embed explainability and ethical auditing in SCDT decision systems
Scalability	High (streamlined, centrally managed data systems)	Medium (requires harmonization and compliance overhead)	Use centralized systems for infrastructure; decentralized models for sensitive applications
Data infrastructure	Central storage, simulation-based modeling	Localized processing, real-time integration	Employ hybrid storage (cloud + edge) to balance performance and privacy

(Continued)

Table 3.2 Comparative lessons and transferable strategies. (*Continued*)

Aspect	Singapore – virtual Singapore	Helsinki – 3D+ digital twin	Transferable strategies
Key challenges	Limited transparency; potential surveillance concerns	Resource-intensive; data harmonization across departments	Address gaps through modular, interoperable, privacy-aware architectures
Best fit for	Authoritative governance structures with high institutional trust	Open societies emphasizing digital rights and trust	Tailor privacy architecture based on governance culture and citizen expectations

efficiencies in running the city. However, concerns about state surveillance and transparency remain an apparent debate around privacy ethics in state-led SCDTs. These are clear efficiency benefits, but all of these raise questions about the balance between technological power and civil liberties, especially in situations where there is little political freedom in the first place.

A major regional case in point is Dubai's digital twin strategy, which seeks to replicate the entire city by 2030. Dubai is leading the way in employing blockchain in conjunction with digital twins to address data integrity and traceability. All transcriptions of data that occur within the digital twin ecosystem are recorded in a secure ledger that is clearly uneditable if an issue appears as though it arises. However, the challenge continues to be in the interaction between openness and control, especially as Dubai's smart governance initiatives are yet to adapt to contemporary privacy benchmarks such as the European General Data Protection Regulation (GDPR). However, the city has set up policy sandboxes to test privacy innovations such as the use of smart contracts for user-controlled data access.

To recap, these cases illustrate the massive potential of smart city digital twins and the subtle trade-offs between innovation and privacy. Cities that win the public's trust in building SCDTs are usually underpinned by the interplay between strong legal frameworks, ethical design principles, and more inclusive governance models. This selection of cases demonstrates that privacy-conscious digital twins can be achieved *via* high-level technical protection mechanisms as well as through citizen engagement and openness, and further that they must be if smart cities are to become more sustainable and legitimate. As these mature, the next wave of implementation needs to continue to wrestle with issues of privacy, ethics, and fairness to design smart cities that are not just smart but rather human-centered.

3.7 Future Directions

The emergence of smart city digital twins (SCDTs) and their potential to direct future urban life have become increasingly important. There is an opportunity for the next wave of SCDTs to improve operational efficiency, sustainability, and citizen well-being. However, the soft challenges of privacy, ethics, interoperability, and scalability must be addressed in more complex ways. The future of SCDTs may be closely related to the combination of maturing technologies, changing laws, and calls for the development of fair and transparent digital governance.

The most immediate are privacy-enhancing technologies. As digital twin technology matures, the number of turnstiles and the personal data they will be able to collect will grow. As SCDTs expand and improve beyond country-specific models, more sophisticated methods, such as homomorphic encryption, differential privacy, federated learning, and secure multiparty computation, will need to be integrated. These technologies enable cities to learn from data patterns and develop artificial intelligence even without direct access to raw and personal data. This is key in terms of both legal compliance and building citizen trust, which are critical elements for the sustainability of e-governance. Ultimately, future architectures should include policy-aware data pipelines in which each data transaction has legal compliance and user consent naturalized within it according to the present privacy legislation.

A second future imperative is standardization and interoperability. The majority of SCDTs are currently developed in silos using closed formats and closed platforms. To enable future smart cities to work as integrated systems, collaboration and open standards for exchanging and marrying data throughout various departments, cities, and even countries are essential. Universal ontologies for data, along with standard APIs and model-interoperability frameworks, will be essential. Work is already being done on these fronts by organizations such as ISO, IEEE, and ITU, but more coordinated work globally will be needed. The interoperability will also allow for benchmarking and comparative analytics between cities, therefore promoting "knowledge spillovers" in privacy, sustainability, and inclusivity best practices that can be adopted in other cities. A second disruptive direction is having an ethical AI embedded into digital twin capabilities. But, as AI learns to make city-wide decisions regarding traffic management, emergencies, or resource distribution, ethical considerations must also be baked into the decision-making process of these algorithms. Future Secure Computational Data Transfer needs to include within its solutions the ability to audit the algorithm, obtain a level of explanation, and detect potential bias to ensure fair and transparent decisions are kept. Use cases with high impact potential might be evaluated *via* Citizen Review Boards or Ethical Oversight Committees. Human-in-the-loop, a form of governance where essential decisions are not completely automated and can be directed or assessed by specialists and laypeople, could thus become a distinguishing factor of future designs of SCDTs.

Citizen-centric design and participatory governance are important directions for future research. Digital twins are only as good as people are willing to use them, not just in the technological sense of what they can currently do, but more importantly, in the social and cultural sense of people's willingness to engage and what they mean. It is envisioned that future systems will allow live policy scenarios, planning diagrams, and real-time feedback and interaction for residents. Augmented and virtual reality technologies can help create a more immersive and inclusive form of participation in these spaces. In addition, the development of personal data dashboards that give individuals visibility, agency, and potentially a role in monetizing their own personal data will help to rebalance the power of institutions relative to citizens, contributing to digital sovereignty.

Concurrently, advancing climate resilience and sustainability will also help many new SCDT developments in the coming decades. Cities will use digital twins to increasingly replicate and simulate carbon footprints, resource flows, and ecological impacts to achieve climate goals. In the future, we may find the increasing presence of "green twins," digital twins designed as specific sensors to manage cues of environmental problems and to improve the exploitation of natural resources. They will be able to take data from satellites, IoT sensors, and urban sensor systems to scale up the data to provide real-time information that can inform their sustainability strategies.

Finally, new technical capabilities require legal and institutional arrangements. Although existing legal privacy frameworks provide a foundational base, they are generally unable to keep pace with the capacities of contemporary systems of data. Legal structures must evolve to flexibly address new risks, challenges, and technologies. Cities could design and trial real-time regulatory sandboxes to experiment with new SCDT applications within a controlled but flexible legal environment. A more urgent requirement is data governance across borders, as urban systems come into contact with each other through shared platforms, migration, and infrastructure.

Conclusion

The adoption of smart city digital twins (SCDTs) in urban ecosystems represents a paradigm shift in the history of the city. These 'smart' models, at once reactive and proactive, enable simulations, monitoring, and optimization of city systems and processes in an instant, with the promise of making better cities, better public services, and more sustainable futures. However, as this paradigm permeates society and the urban environment, so too does it have implications for privacy, ethics, and governance. Therefore, the hallmark of a responsible SCDT is not its technological complexity but the achievement of equilibrium between innovation and the rights of citizens and societal morality.

In this chapter, we examine how SCDTs perform at the nexus of data, infrastructure, and governance. These originate from multiple locations—traffic systems, environmental sensors, public service databases, and citizen interactions—and are amalgamated into unified digital representations of physical cities. The potential advantages are enormous: predicting structural failures, increasing energy savings, improving the capacity to manage disasters, and improving the quality of life for citizens. However, It is dependent on Data Sources provisions for privacy protection. The very same data that, in the "smart city," makes it operate more effectively can also be turned into an instrument of control, observation, or discrimination, or can be leveraged for economic gain if it is not protected.

Privacy by Design has to become a core element of the architecture of SCDTs to avoid these risks. These include implementing privacy protections such as data minimization, encryption, anonymization, and access controls in the design of the system, from sensors and data pipelines to analytics and visualization dashboards. Process protections, such as regular Privacy Impact Assessment (PIA) audits and transparent data governance protocols, are also crucial. On top of that, multiple levels of a privacy infrastructure work to guarantee that privacy is not an "add-on" but a fundamental tenet that influences all aspects of the creation and use of digital twins.

Technological advances should inform legal and moral thinking and vice versa. Existing regulations, such as the General Data Protection Regulation (GDPR) and California Consumer Privacy Act (CCPA), are important, but they lag behind the complex, real-time, AI-driven, cross-domain systems such as SCDTs. Thus, cities must begin to create fluid legal structures that adapt to new types of challenges, such as dynamic consent, policy enforcement, and ethical AI standards. It is a supporting tool for moral decision-making in situations where the law has nothing to say and where it is ambiguous. Fairness, transparency, accountability, and inclusivity are principles that can help ensure that SCDTs are used in the service of more just and equitable urban development.

Public trust is another crucial element for successful SCDT deployment. Local populations must trust that their information will be used conscientiously and that they will have a sense of control over their digital selves and a voice in decisions. This requires not only transparency but also development models of participatory governance that allow citizens to input into the development, monitoring, and review of digital twin systems. Data dashboards, digital consultations, and community co-design can empower people and move them towards a more inclusive digital future.

Certainly, technical advancement will shape the future of smart city digital twins, but the ability to govern them properly, ethically, and collectively will also be critical. The stakes will only increase as we transition toward more connected, smart, and responsive urban systems. The future to which cities will need to respond will be characterized by challenges such as climate change, pandemics, urban migration, and socioeconomic inequality, and digital twins will be the solutions to contextualize and mitigate these challenges. Absent a strong focus on privacy and human dignity, however, these tools can also be mechanisms of control rather than clothing themselves in the garments of freedom.

A more urgent issue for the deployment of federated learning at the city scale is the scale itself. However, federated learning also presents an open technological challenge: the extension of the decentralized model for AI training, without raw data movement, to thousands or millions of edge devices with different hardware capabilities, sporadic connectivity, and dirty data quality is not straightforward. The issue of establishing mechanisms for synchronization, fairness, and resilience across these distributed training environments is still nascent and needs to be researched. There is also a significant gap in the development of a common set of ethical principles regarding the use of AI in public service delivery. The ability to explain, intervene, and audit is becoming increasingly important as AI systems begin to integrate with traffic systems, predictive policing, healthcare triage, and resource allocation. They described current ethical norms as either vague or overly aspirational. There is an urgent need for models of ethical governance that can be enforced through new forms of participatory audits and accountability measures for AI specific to urban and public sector settings. In parallel, there is a lack of robust metrics for evaluating privacy-risk exposure in SCDTs. While technologies such as differential privacy and encryption provide protection at the algorithmic level, city administrators lack standardized tools to assess aggregate privacy risks over time, particularly in composite systems, where data flows across departments and vendors. Research is needed to define dynamic privacy risk scores, simulate potential breaches in digital twin simulations, and embed privacy KPIs into smart-city performance dashboards. Other possible research trajectories might be adaptive legal compliance engines that adapt to data governance regulations, inclusive design approaches for digitally integrated marginalized populations, or AI explainability interfaces for urban lay users. Finally, a cross-pollination between technologists, law, ethics, and city planning will be instrumental in guaranteeing that digital twin technologies conform to democratic values and public interest.

In conclusion, smart city digital twins offer great promise for creating better overall cities that are both more livable, sustainable, and more equitable. Fulfilling this promise will depend on harnessing and integrating the most advanced technologies with good legal systems, ethical foresight, and a present civil society. Privacy should not be the price of innovation, but the concept that anchors this continuum of intelligence to more human smart cities. Only by ingraining privacy and ethical concerns into the DNA of digital twin environments can we create the kinds of cities we want to live in, committed to democratic digital governance built for the people it is supposed to serve.

AI disclosure statement: The author confirms that no artificial intelligence (AI)-generated content or AI-assisted writing tools were used in the preparation of this chapter (including summaries and the abstract). All text, analysis, and conclusions are the result of the author's original work.

References

1. Attaran, M. and Celik, B.G., Digital twin: benefits, use cases, challenges, and opportunities. *Decis. Analyt. J.*, 6, 100165, 2023, doi: 10.1016/j.dajour.2023.100165.
2. Trindade, E.P., Hinnig, M.P.F., da Costa, E.M., Marques, J.S., Bastos, R.C., Yigitcanlar, T., Sustainable development of smart cities: A systematic review of the literature. *J. Open Innov. Technol. Mark. Complex*, 3, 1–14, 2017.

3. Stratigea, A., Papadopoulou, C.-A., Panagiotopoulou, M., Tools and technologies for planning the development of smart cities. *J. Urban Technol.*, 22, 43–62, 2015.
4. Korczak, J. and Kijewska, K., Smart Logistics in the development of Smart Cities. *Transp. Res. Procedia*, 39, 201–211, 2019.
5. Stratigea, A., The concept of 'smart cities'. Towards community development? *Netcom. Réseaux Commun. Territ.*, 26, 375–388, 2012.
6. Islam, S., *et al.*, Mobile Networks Toward 5G/6G: Network Architecture, Opportunities and Challenges in Smart City. *IEEE Open J. Commun. Soc.*, 1, 2024.
7. Mishra, P., Thakur, P., Singh, G., Sustainable Smart City to Society 5.0: State-of-the-Art and Research Challenges. *SAIEE Afr. Res. J.*, 113, 152–164, 2022.
8. Rodrigo, M.S., *et al.*, Digital twins for 5G networks: A modeling and deployment methodology. *IEEE Access*, 11, 38112–38126, 2023.
9. Nguyen, H.X., Trestian, R., To, D., Tatipamula, M., Digital twin for 5G and beyond. *IEEE Commun. Mag.*, 59, 10–15, 2021.
10. Li, T., Shi, H., Bai, X., Li, N., Zhang, K., Rolling bearing performance assessment with degradation twin modeling considering interdependent fault evolution. *Mech. Syst. Signal Process.*, 224, 112194, 2025.
11. Ma, Q., Zhang, Y., Hu, F., Zhou, H., Hu, H., Nip it in the bud: the impact of china's large-scale free physical examination program on health care expenditures for elderly people. *Hum. Soc. Sci. Commun.*, 12, 1, 1–16, 2025.
12. Sahu, D., *et al.*, Revolutionizing load harmony in edge computing networks with probabilistic cellular automata and Markov decision processes. *Sci. Rep.*, 15, 1, 3730, 2025.
13. Arakji, R.Y. and Lang, K.R., Real Profits in Virtual Worlds? An Examination of Challenges and Business Opportunities, pp. 896–902, [Online]. Available: https://example.com, accessed Jun. 11, 2024.
14. Botín-Sanabria, D.M., *et al.*, Digital twin technology challenges and applications: A comprehensive review. *Remote Sens.*, 14, 6, 1335, 2022, doi: 10.3390/rs14061335.
15. Kumar, A., A novel framework for waste management in smart city transformation with industry 4.0 technologies. *Res. Glob.*, 9, 100234, 2024, doi: 10.1016/j.resglo.2024.100234.
16. Kuru, K., MetaOmniCity: Toward immersive urban metaverse cyberspaces using smart city digital twins. *IEEE Access*, 11, 43844–43868, 2023, doi: 10.1109/ACCESS.2023.3272890.
17. Peldon, D., Banihashemi, S., Lenguyen, K., Derrible, S., Navigating urban complexity: The transformative role of digital twins in smart city development. *Sustain. Cities Soc.*, 111, 105583, Jun. 2024, doi: 10.1016/j.scs.2024.105583.
18. Syed Abdul Rahman, S.A.F., *et al.*, The Digital Landscape of Smart Cities and Digital Twins: A Systematic Literature Review of Digital Terrain and 3D City Models in Enhancing Decision-Making. *Sage Open*, 14, 1, Jan. 2024, doi: 10.1177/21582440231220768.

19. Elnour, M., *et al.*, Empowering smart cities with digital twins of buildings: Applications and implementation considerations of data-driven energy modelling in building management. *Build. Serv. Eng. Res. Technol.*, 45, 4, 475–498, Mar. 2024, doi: 10.1177/01436244241239290.
20. Ababio, I.B., *et al.*, A Blockchain-Assisted Federated Learning Framework for Secure and Self-Optimizing Digital Twins in Industrial IoT. *Future Internet*, 17, 1, 13, Jan. 2025, doi: 10.3390/fi17010013.
21. Hananto, A.L., *et al.*, Digital Twin and 3D Digital Twin: Concepts, Applications, and Challenges in Industry 4.0 for Digital Twin. *Computers*, 13, 4, 100, Apr. 2024, doi: 10.3390/computers13040100.
22. Gkontzis, A.F., Kotsiantis, S., Feretzakis, G., Verykios, V.S., Enhancing Urban Resilience: Smart City Data Analyses, Forecasts, and Digital Twin Techniques at the Neighborhood Level. *Future Internet*, 16, 2, 47, Jan. 2024, doi: 10.3390/fi16020047.
23. Arulmozhi, E., *et al.*, From Reality to Virtuality: Revolutionizing Livestock Farming Through Digital Twins. *Agriculture*, 14, 12, 2231, Dec. 2024, doi: 10.3390/agriculture14122231.
24. Dani, A.A.H., *et al.*, Development of a Smart City Platform Based on Digital Twin Technology for Monitoring and Supporting Decision-Making. *Sustainability*, 15, 18, 14002, Sep. 2023, doi: 10.3390/su151814002.
25. Argota Sánchez-Vaquerizo, J., Urban Digital Twins and metaverses towards city multiplicities: uniting or dividing urban experiences? *Ethics Inf. Technol.*, 27, 1, Nov. 2024, doi: 10.1007/s10676-024-09812-3.
26. Patel, C., Pasikhani, A., Gope, P., Clark, J., User-empowered secure privacy-preserving authentication scheme for Digital Twin. *Comput. Secur.*, 140, 103793, Mar. 2024, doi: 10.1016/j.cose.2024.103793.
27. Nations, U., Sustainable Development Goal 11: Make cities inclusive, safe, resilient and sustainable, United Nations, 2015, [Online]. Available: https://sdgs.un.org/goals/goal11.
28. UN-Habitat, People-Centered Smart Cities: Digital technologies for inclusive, sustainable and participatory urban development, United Nations Human Settlements Programme, 2021, [Online]. Available: https://unhabitat.org/programme/people-centered-smart-cities.
29. OECD, Recommendation of the Council on Enhancing Access to and Sharing of Data, Organisation for Economic Co-operation and Development, Nov. 2021, [Online]. Available: https://legalinstruments.oecd.org/en/instruments/OECD-LEGAL-0463.
30. OECD, The OECD Framework for the Governance of Infrastructure, OECD, Paris, 2020, [Online]. Available: https://www.oecd.org/gov/governance-of-infrastructure.htm.
31. ISO, ISO 37106:2018 – Sustainable cities and communities — Guidance on establishing smart city operating models for sustainable communities, International Organization for Standardization, Geneva, 2018.

32. ISO, ISO 37120:2018 - Sustainable cities and communities — Indicators for city services and quality of life, International Organization for Standardization, Geneva, 2018.
33. ISO, ISO 37122:2019 - Sustainable cities and communities — Indicators for smart cities, International Organization for Standardization, Geneva, 2019.
34. ISO/IEC JTC 1/SC 41, Internet of Things and Digital Twin Reference Architectures, International Organization for Standardization/International Electrotechnical Commission, ongoing project, [Online]. Available: https://www.iso.org/committee/6483277.html.

4

Future Trends and Emerging Challenges in Digital Twins

Kavita Arora[1]*, Neha Gupta[1] and Wanqing Tu[2]

[1]*School of Computer Applications, MRIIRS, Faridabad, Haryana, India*
[2]*Department of Computer Science, Durham University, Durham, North East England, England*

Abstract

Due to advancements in multiple domains of sensors, medicine, communication, and IT technologies, digital twins have attracted much attention from academia and industry in recent years to transform research and industrial practices. The main objectives of digital twins are to offer a thorough physical and functional description of a component, product, or system by merging computational models with a physical counterpart and to create a vigorously reformed system through bidirectional data flows as conditions change.

Beyond traditional modeling and simulation, digital twins could provide longer-term predictions of future weather and climatic conditions, safer and more efficient engineering processes, and improved patient-level medical decision-making. However, the digital twin is a dynamic idea that becomes more sophisticated over the product life cycle, resulting in vast amounts of data and information. Driven by the mentioned aspects, this chapter addresses the applications of digital twins in several domains. Through case studies, we provide a deep insight into technology's real-world implementation and impact, list design goals and future trends, and highlight emerging challenges and limitations.

***Keywords*:** Digital twins, artificial intelligence, Internet of Things, applications, machine learning, deep learning, future trends, emerging challenges

**Corresponding author*: kavita.sca@mriu.edu.in

Shubham Mahajan, Davinder Paul Singh, Amit Kant Pandit and Paras Chawla (eds.) Ensuring Privacy in Digital Twin Ecosystems, (101–136) © 2026 Scrivener Publishing LLC

Introduction

Scholars and practitioners alike are taking notice of digital twins. Technology is used by many businesses to produce lifelike virtual objects and simulations of operational processes. Since they can replicate nearly every aspect of a product, procedure, or service, digital twins are a cutting-edge technology that has completely changed the market. It can give engineers input from the virtual world and mimic every aspect of the real world in the digital realm [1]. As a result, businesses can now produce better products, recognize and fix physical problems more quickly, and gain benefits and value faster than they could in the past. In other words, it is a tool that businesses can employ to enhance their performance and operations.

Digital twins are not a novel idea. But in recent years, digital twins have advanced from concept to reality somewhat more quickly. It all began with a laser-like concentration that imagines the whole value chain of a digital business of the future. In order to help transform data into information and knowledge into vision, it started investigating fully integrated digital transformation solutions constructed with intelligent software systems, networked devices, and strong industrial security infrastructure. More technologies, like augmented reality, IoT, voice capabilities, and artificial intelligence (AI), are expected to be integrated with digital twins.

A digital twin is a computerized model of a system or item that is intended to closely resemble an actual one. It spans the object's lifecycle, is updated in real-time, and makes decisions with the use of simulation, machine learning, and reasoning. This virtual environment makes a system considerably richer for research, even while simulations and twins use digital models to duplicate a system's many operations. Scale is a major distinction between a digital twin and a simulation; a digital twin may conduct an infinite number of realistic simulations to examine several processes, whereas a simulation usually only analyzes one.

The distinctions don't stop there. For instance, real-time data typically does not help simulations. In contrast, digital twins are based on a two-way information flow that occurs when the system processor receives relevant data from object sensors and then exchanges that information with the source object [2].

Digital twins have a greater potential to improve processes and products than traditional simulations since they can analyze more issues from a larger range of perspectives. The additional processing capacity that comes with a virtual environment allows for the availability of better and continuously updated data on a wide range of topics.

Manufacturing digital twins does not work alone; they collaborate with a variety of state-of-the-art technologies to expand their capabilities. Digital twins create a digital model of an asset by combining **technical drivers** like the **Internet of Things (IoT)** and **artificial intelligence**.

Internet of Things: Real-time data from IoT devices powers digital twins, enabling precise simulations and analysis. The physical world is monitored, and data is gathered by sensors and connected devices, and this information is subsequently reflected in the digital twin.
Artificial Intelligence and Machine Learning: In order to optimize production processes, AI and ML algorithms evaluate the massive volumes of data produced by digital twins, providing predictive insights and facilitating automated decision-making.
Virtual Reality: By enabling more immersive and natural interactions between engineers and operators and the digital twin, VR technology helps improve comprehension and analysis of manufacturing processes.

They work as dynamic digital counterparts, integrating real-time data to support a range of functional goals, including scenario planning, predictive maintenance, and performance monitoring. In essence, by using insights from their virtual models, digital twins enable proactive interventions in the real world and well-informed decision-making. The **major functional purposes** include simulation and predictions, predictive maintenance, product development and design, sustainability, and enhancing the metaverse.

The value of digital twins is driven by their potential to expedite the power of decision-making. Digital twins and related technologies are adding value propositions in the fields of digital engineering, model-based system engineering, and sophisticated virtual modeling and simulation, particularly in the areas of operational efficiency and sustainability across industries. **Digital twins provide value by**:

- lowering expenses and raising productivity,
- reducing dependency on natural resources and optimizing energy use,
- cutting carbon emissions,
- getting rid of trash, and
- avoiding serious accidents and unscheduled downtime.

There are several kinds of digital twins depending on the degree of product magnification. The field of application is where these twins diverge most. Various types of digital twins frequently coexist in a system or procedure.

i. **Component twins or parts twins:** The smallest form of a functional component is a component twin, which is the fundamental building block of a digital twin. Although they relate to far less important components, the twin parts are identical.
ii. **Asset twins:** When two or more components come together, an asset is created. With asset twins, we can look into how those elements interact, producing a plethora of performance data that can be analyzed and transformed into useful information.
iii. **System or unit twins:** These are the next level, demonstrating how various assets come together to form a fully functional system. System twins provide information about how assets work together and may suggest methods to boost efficiency.
iv. **Twins in process:** The macro level of magnification, known as process twins, shows how systems cooperate to form a complete manufacturing plant. Will one system's delays affect the others, or are they all coordinated to operate as efficiently as possible? Process twins can be used to determine the precise time patterns influencing overall efficacy.

Important characteristics of digital twins:

1. A customized, flexible, organization-driven digital transformation system.
2. A cyber-physical system based on a foundation of sensors, software, and services.
3. Features four participants: cognition, connect, collect, and consume.
4. Improved by 3D interactive, immersive environments and virtual sensors.
5. A collection of developing digital engineering models created to tackle particular business issues.

6. A digital tool to create an interdisciplinary digital workforce from a traditional workforce.
7. A cooperative digital solution that empowers the C-suite to influence business results.

Overview of Digital Twins

A digital twin is a virtual representation of a physical product that is used in conjunction with the real product to help it go from concept to prototype to final form during life-cycle management. In 2003, John Vickers and Michael Grieves used the phrase for the first time. In 2019, the technology research and consulting organization Gartner called the concept a key strategic technology trend because it has since become widely accepted and utilized in various industries [3]. Big data, machine learning, artificial intelligence, multiphysical simulation, real-time sensors and sensor networks, the Internet of Things (IoT), data management, and data processing are some of the technological advancements that fuel this expansion.

A real entity, its virtual representation, and the two-way information exchange comprise a complete digital twin. Virtual representation receives operation status from the physical entity and evaluates it before returning requests for operation adjustments to the physical entity. Digital twin technology is distinct from traditional computer modeling and simulation, which only provide virtual representations of the real world, due to the bi-directional information flow that connects the real and virtual entities. A digital twin system necessitates more advanced hardware and software technologies, particularly in complex facilities with several interconnected physical entities. Every element in the physical and virtual worlds must allow information to flow across the system [4].

Digital Twins Necessitate the Following Components

i. **Actual world:** This refers to the actual physical system, object, or procedure the digital twin represents. It might be a piece of manufacturing machinery, a building, a car, or even a city's infrastructure. To collect data for all physical entities, distributed sensors will be positioned in the real-world environment. Computational models in the virtual world can then send commands to these physical entities, allowing them to be controlled remotely. Monitoring the health of real-world sensors is necessary to ensure that the data collected is accurate.

ii. **Virtual world:** The virtual world should not only function as a simulation of the real world but also be able to "understand" its current state and offer workable suggestions to improve it. A computer depiction of a physical object that integrates geometry, material qualities, behavioral algorithms, and other pertinent features is called a virtual model.

iii. **Bi-directional communication:** Based on application, online data quality control, as well as assurance, as well as near real-time data collection and transmission, should be set up to enable prompt identification and resolution of any problems with data quality. In order to create a dynamic and responsive virtual representation of a physical system, bidirectional communication in a digital twin—facilitated by an edge-to-cloud pipeline—is essential. This enables control loops and real-time data transmission, where modifications to the digital twin can affect the physical counterpart and vice versa. Here, edge computing is essential because it manages local control and real-time data processing, while the cloud offers more extensive analytics, storage, and remote management features. Bidirectional communication in digital twin applications, particularly in Internet of Things contexts, is a good fit for the MQTT (Message Queue Telemetry Transport) protocol. A digital twin's publish-subscribe approach enables real-time monitoring and control by allowing it to transmit orders and receive data from its physical counterpart.

iv. **Data storage:** A library of past real-world sensor data is helpful since it may be used to identify the underlying cause of physical entity faults and forecast the system's future health.

v. **Sensors and Data Sources:** The physical thing is equipped with sensors and data sources to collect up-to-date information on its operation, environment, and performance. These data sources maintain synchronization by updating the virtual model regularly.

vi. **Data Integration and Analytics:** Collected data is merged and processed using state-of-the-art analytics techniques like machine learning and artificial intelligence. This helps in comprehending the physical things' behavior, trends, and possible issues.

vii. **Tools for Visualization and Simulation:** A range of visualization and simulation tools enables users to interact with the digital twin, providing a dynamic representation of the condition and actions of the actual object.

viii. **IoT and connectivity:** The digital twin requires a smooth data flow between the physical object and its virtual equivalent. This connectedness is made possible by the Internet of Things (IoT), which facilitates data transmission, receipt, and evaluation.

Digital Twins Design Goals

Digital twin design goals encompass the primary objectives for developing and executing digital equivalents of tangible assets or procedures. Replicating real-world behavior, enabling predictive analysis, improving performance, and promoting better decision-making are frequently among these objectives.

i. **Faithful Replication:** Throughout the lifecycle of the physical asset or process, the digital twin should faithfully replicate its behavior, capabilities, and traits. In order to enable dynamic updates and accurate depiction, data interaction between the digital and physical worlds should take place in real-time or almost real-time.

ii. **Performance Forecasting:** The digital twin ought to be able to forecast performance in the future, spot possible problems, and streamline processes depending on different circumstances.

iii. **Proactive Maintenance:** By evaluating data and anticipating possible malfunctions, the digital twin can facilitate proactive maintenance plans, reducing expenses and downtime.

iv. **Better Decisions:** The digital twin should offer data and insights to help different departments and stakeholders make better decisions.

v. **Cooperation and Communication:** Throughout the asset's lifecycle, the digital twin can act as a platform for cooperation and communication between various teams and stakeholders.

vi. **Modular Design:** To facilitate the seamless integration of new features, sensors, and data sources, the digital twin should be created using a modular design methodology.

vii. **Scalability:** As the physical asset changes or new features are introduced, the digital twin should be able to manage growing complexity and data volume.

viii. **Data Security:** It's critical to safeguard private information and make sure the digital twin and its communication links are secure.

Organizations can successfully use digital twins to boost productivity, cut expenses, and obtain a competitive edge by attending to these design objectives.

Evolution of Digital Twin Technology

We are hearing more and more about "digital twins" as we attempt to close the lacuna between digital and physical systems. "Digital twins," like many other notions (including artificial intelligence or the metaverse), can signify different things to different individuals. A digital twin is closely related to the Internet of Things (IoT) and is a digital counterpart of a sensor or a tangible asset (like an airplane engine) [7]. They can test the digital version in ways that they might not be able to use the real equipment. Figure 4.1 is evidence of evolution and progress in digital twins.

David Gelernter first proposed the concept of digital twin technology in his 1991 book Mirror Worlds. But in 2002, Dr. Michael Grieves, who was then a professor at the University of Michigan, was recognized for being the first to apply the concept of digital twins to manufacturing and for publicly introducing the idea of digital twin software. The term "digital twin" was finally used by NASA's John Vickers in 2010. The basic idea of comparing a digital doppelgänger to a physical object, however, is evident far earlier.

In the 1960s, NASA used computer models to oversee and simulate space missions, where the idea of digital twins first emerged [8]. Digital twins, instead, have just lately gained popularity due to enhancements in cloud computing, data analytics, and sensor technologies. Real-time data collection, integration, and analysis were made possible by the convergence of many technologies, which gave rise to the modern concept of digital twins.

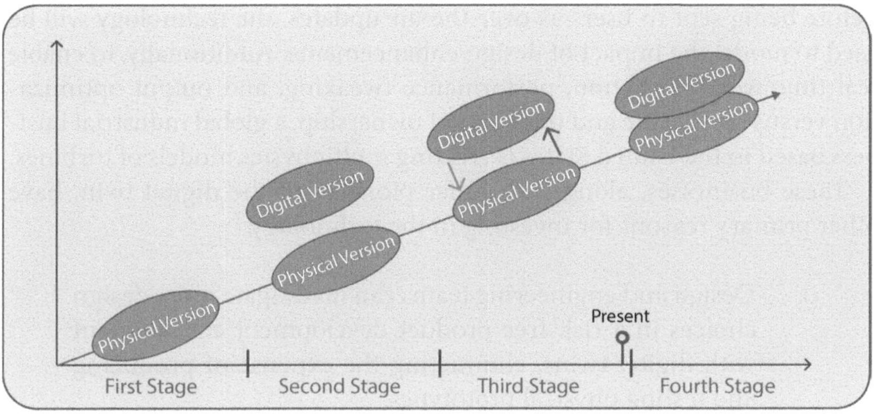

Figure 4.1 Evolution of digital twins technology.

A virtual copy or digital representation of a system, procedure, or product is called a "digital twin." This concept has generated much interest from a variety of organizations because it has the potential to drastically change how we design, monitor, and optimize real-world systems. The digital twin concept has been identified as a key enabler for achieving Industry 4.0's objectives, which include intelligent infrastructure, smart factories, and efficient supply chains.

Current State of Digital Twins

According to survey data, nearly 75% of businesses in sophisticated industries have already implemented digital twin technologies that have attained at least medium levels of complexity [5]. However, there is much variation across sectors. While logistics, infrastructure, and energy companies are more likely to be creating their first digital-twin concepts, those in the automotive, aerospace, and defense sectors are using digital twins more sophisticatedly now.

A significant aerospace business is creating a machine-learning-based geometry optimization system that can quickly simulate thousands of configurations to find weight reductions, aerodynamic enhancements, and other performance advantages. A European software business is constructing a multiphysics model of the human heart to aid in developing pharmaceuticals and medical devices.

An automobile manufacturer in the US is developing a system that can simulate every possible combination of its hardware and software [6].

Before being sent to users as over-the-air updates, the technology will be used to model the impact of design enhancements. Additionally, to enable real-time wear prediction, performance tweaking, and output optimization versus service life and total cost of ownership, a global industrial business based in the United States is creating multiphysics models of turbines.

These businesses, along with other pioneers of the digital twin, have other primary reasons for investing in the technology.

i. Design and engineering teams can investigate more design choices in a risk-free product development environment with digital twins, eliminating the expense of producing and testing physical prototypes.
ii. By enabling novel solutions to be tested in a variety of realistic settings, including uncommon and harsh operating circumstances, digital twins enhance testing and validation.
iii. Digital twins offer a more in-depth understanding of how products behave. Digital-twin models allow engineers to track intricate relationships between product components and track the status of any system component at any given time.

Key Industries Using Digital Twins

Nowadays, engineering and manufacturing are the main fields that use digital twins to generate simulations of operational processes and virtual products [9]. Digital twins can be implemented in supply chain and operations management, including their function in asset visualization, remote support, transportation maintenance, operations traceability, and design customization.

Among the industries where the technology is expected to deliver on its numerous promises are the automotive, aerospace, construction, agriculture, mining, utilities, retail, healthcare, military, natural resources, and public safety sectors. Scholars, managers, and practitioners worldwide have been captivated by the technology, and a plethora of business applications are beginning to emerge. Figure 4.2 shows the dominant industries that utilize digital twins in their core functioning.

i. **Healthcare:** Better patient care, system optimization, appropriate training, and other healthcare-related initiatives are

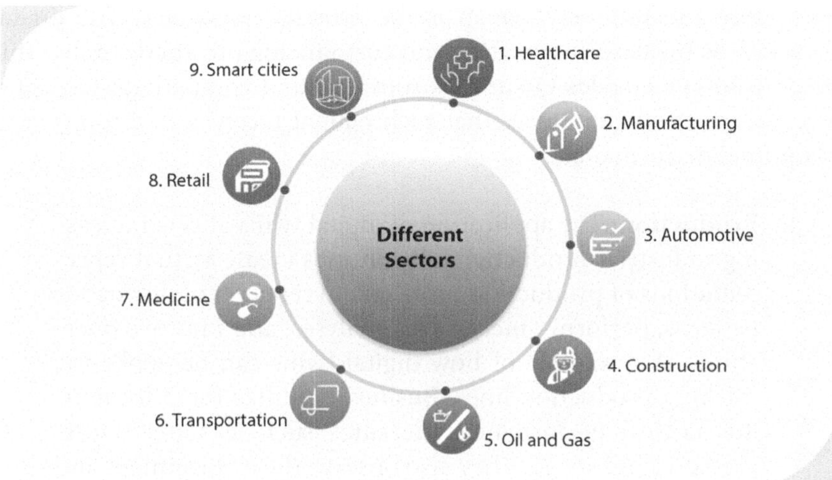

Figure 4.2 Key industries using digital twins.

made possible by digital twins. During diagnosis, medical professionals can use digital twin technology to identify potential issues and model different situations without affecting the patient's course of therapy. As a result, it can decrease the number of pointless tests and procedures while increasing the accuracy of the diagnosis. Digital twins can also be used to replicate the operational aspects of medical facilities. Digital twins can be applied to patient flow and resource management in the healthcare industry. Hospitals can find inefficiencies and implement programs to boost efficiency by simulating various scenarios.

For example, digital twins could improve bed distribution and operational planning to guarantee that patients receive timely care [10]. Clinical trial digital twins help doctors simulate different treatment options and predict outcomes by building a digital twin of a patient's body.

Each patient's treatment options are tailored to their specific needs, which improves effectiveness and reduces the likelihood of adverse effects. Digital twins in medicine aid in the individualized treatment of patients by simulating physiological processes and predicting the course of illnesses.

One of the top providers of orthopedic solutions and prosthetics is Össur. They use digital twin technology to design and manufacture customized prosthetics for individuals. In this instance, the prosthetics will fit more comfortably and uniquely, which is the primary advantage. The digital twin serves as the basis for creating and customizing prosthetic limbs. This digital prototype enables Össur's team to trial and compare design iterations. This method guarantees that each patient receives a customized fit and optimal performance.

ii. **Production:** The application of digital twins affects increasing industrial productivity. Businesses create virtual representations of production processes to research performance patterns, perform quicker data analyses, and improve operations. An example of how digital twins can be applied is tracking production lines. Businesses utilize them to monitor critical performance measures such as temperature, pressure, and speed. They also observe the environment and find any abnormal incidents in the manufacturing process, which could indicate a potential problem or flaw. Digital twins assist in recommending when to keep production machines intact before issues arise. Through this, they can identify these problems early enough before they become expensive flaws. Therefore, they can reduce downtime and make their products more dependable.

A Digital Twin Manufacturing Example: Rolls-Royce's Smart Engine. Digital twins are employed in Rolls-Royce's "Smart Engine" initiative. A digital duplicate is created for each engine by the company [11]. This allows them to collect data from sensors onboard regarding over 12 various parameters. By monitoring how the engine behaves in flight, they can estimate when it needs to be repaired and reduce time spent idle. The primary objective of this project is to please customers more and design engines that perform better and consume less fuel to transform the way they provide power to the individuals who purchase from them.

iii. **Automotive:** Digital twins are applied in the auto sector to be used for aftermarket services, manufacturing, and design. Engineers can test various designs without making a physical prototype. The factory process can be streamlined, increasing production and decreasing downtime. Their vehicles will be maintained before they break down, due to predictive maintenance.

There are numerous advantages to the usage of digital twins in the automotive industry. Additionally, digital twins are becoming increasingly important as the market moves toward electric cars.

Volvo is an automotive example of a digital twin. A well-known car manufacturer, Volvo, uses digital twins to ensure the highest passenger safety ever. They create virtual replicas to test and experiment with different materials and the aerodynamics of new car designs. In this way, they may select the best design to boost efficiency and provide cars that use less gasoline.

iv. **Construction:** It allows construction companies to test a wide range of scenarios, including design changes, bad weather, or security breaches. The entire lot can be completed without interfering with construction. The virtual models thoroughly examine the asset's design and real-time performance. It enables construction companies to see, for example, how many people can use the area, how each room and corridor will be illuminated, and more. Digital twins could make a more sustainable approach to building construction possible.

One of London's most significant infrastructural projects is Crossrail. Digital twins have been used by engineers to visualize the end product. Additionally, they can keep an eye on the project's development and identify any possible problems. They have modeled and optimized the construction process using digital twins to boost throughput and avoid waste by utilizing the resources as efficiently as possible.

v. **Oil & Gas:** "Digital twins transform the oil and gas industry, avoiding costly downtime and enhancing safety." According to Shell and BP, digital twins are now essential in a sector where downtime costs millions of dollars every day. They use a virtual model to improve safety, forecast equipment problems before they occur, and monitor offshore platforms, pipelines, and refineries in real time. Even minor issues can cause significant financial loss and environmental harm in the oil and gas sector. For example, an offshore platform may lose up to $3 million daily due to unanticipated equipment failure. For this reason, businesses are looking for digital twin technologies to outsmart problems.

BP is using digital twins to keep an eye on its oil rig. A virtual model is created that incorporates data from the platform's sensors in real-time. By doing this, engineers can monitor variables like temperature, pressure, and equipment performance and identify problems before they become serious. To illustrate, the digital twin will alert you if a pump exhibits strange vibrations or if temperatures suddenly rise [12]. This saves BP millions in operating expenses by enhancing safety and averting expensive failures. In what ways does it improve safety? Because they make operations safer for both the environment and the personnel, digital twins reduce the likelihood of accidents.

vi. **Transportation:** Roads, bridges, trains, and other transportation systems are simulated using digital twin technology. These twins can mimic the behavior of these systems in various scenarios, such as heavy traffic, inclement weather, or simply during maintenance. Before actually constructing or altering the systems in question, engineers and planners involved in transportation design and planning will be allowed to test and refine such plans. By using digital twin technology, preventive maintenance and safety can be supported by real-time performance monitoring. It includes providing drivers with real-time information on weather conditions, closed roads, and weather-related alerts to help them make judgments.

Ford is the best example of a digital twin in the transportation industry. They create their self-driving cars using digital twins. They test their product under different driving circumstances and assess how well their self-driving algorithms work. Without a prototype, they may safely test their product in the virtual environment [13]. As a result, it lessens the time and expense needed for development.

vii. **Medicine:** A whole new world of medical potential is made possible by digital twins, and tailored medicine is at the forefront of this. Medical professionals and medications can tailor treatments to meet the needs of individual patients. Digital twins can also be used to teach and train medical professionals. Consider letting medical students use a computerized human body model for practice. They can learn the intricacies of complicated procedures and practice them risk-free. They seem to carry around an interactive, lifelike anatomy lesson. Digital twins can also be used to support medical research.

Scientists can test new hypotheses, gain a better understanding of how disease progresses, and develop new treatments more rapidly by studying such virtual models. The virtual world ensures that experiments are safe because there is no chance of hurting actual patients. Naturally, creating the ideal digital twin is not that easy. It requires gathering detailed information about a patient's history. Security and privacy issues must also be resolved to protect sensitive personal data.

Pfizer bases their cancer research and development efforts on digital twins. The company's objectives are to comprehend the mechanism behind cancer and create efficient remedies. They may simulate how the drugs act in different scenarios by using digital twins. This allows researchers to investigate its efficacy, potential side effects, and interactions with biological systems. A digital twin of a cancer patient can also be used by pharmaceutical corporations to test new drugs. This approach is much faster as well as safer.

viii. **Retail:** By using digital twin technology in retail, problems with shop operations can be resolved, and customer experiences can be enhanced. Thus, the principal use of digital twins is represented by some of their basic applications in retail shop design and layout optimization. Testing different product displays and store layouts on a virtual store model allows you to see how they may affect consumer flow and, ultimately, purchase behavior. This aids retailers in finding the most effective ways to boost sales and improve the overall shopping experience for customers. Inventory management is a significant use case for digital twin technology in the retail industry. A real-time digital twin of stock can be created by examining sensor data and various other data sources [14]. They can monitor how many things are in store, spot any stockouts before they happen, and cut down on lost sales. Additionally, digital twin technology aids merchants in streamlining supply chain-related processes. For instance, retailers can employ digital twin technology to identify bottleneck locations and optimize delivery routes.

Another well-known company that uses digital twin technology is Walmart. By experimenting with various configurations and designs, they hope to maximize their retail layout. By simulating various store layouts, they may assess components such as aisle design and product placement. They can select the one that offers a customer-friendly setup after it has been tried and tested. Additionally, their inventory management system takes advantage of the technology.

First, companies add a virtual inventory and create digital twins of their stores. They will next assess and enhance inventory levels, product positioning, and replenishment strategies.

ix. **Smart cities:** Using digital twins in urban design, how might cities improve their infrastructure and sustainability? A smart city is an urban environment in which data, technology, and connectivity cooperate to raise the quality of living for its residents. It also underlines improving resource management and sustainability. Two technologies used are advanced data analytics and the Internet of Things. The intelligent systems and infrastructure these technologies create will help many other sectors as well. These cover governance, healthcare, and energy, among other things, but are not limited to. Digital twins in smart cities can replicate and examine a range of events, including traffic flow, energy use, and emergency response.

By modeling several scenarios, they can assess how seasonal fluctuations, supply chain interruptions, and demand changes impact inventory control. Through process and system simplification, they can also lower stockouts, boost customer satisfaction, and increase product availability. Using the digital twin, Walmart has improved customer experiences and raised operational effectiveness.

Smart cities' advancement of sustainability depends on digital twins. They can track systems of waste management, air quality, and energy consumption. Simulating various environmental scenarios helps cities apply strategies meant to lower carbon emissions and improve green areas. Digital twins can, for example, spot areas with bad air quality and recommend solutions, including less traffic or more green space. Smart city development depends on digital twins and sustainability as such. The Virtual Singapore Platform helps improve the city-state's digital twin. The accurate portrayal of Singapore on the platform helps to solve problems with urban design.

Various approaches to city improvement can be modeled and tested using digital twins. One can improve infrastructure [16], transportation systems, and the urban surroundings. The Virtual Singapore Platform's main selling feature is its ability to combine present data from many sources. By combining this data, the platform can faithfully replicate many possible situations.

By identifying potential bottlenecks and changing road networks as necessary, urban designers can ascertain how planned infrastructure expenditures would affect traffic congestion. They can also evaluate and project how much heavy rainfall will impact drainage systems in places that are vulnerable to flooding.

Emerging Trends in Digital Twin Technology

The market for digital twins is expected to grow by 71% over the next several years. New developments in digital twin technology are having an impact on future developments in numerous sectors. Technological developments like cloud computing, machine learning, artificial intelligence, and the Internet of Things (IoT) are driving these trends. Some of the most important new developments in the rapidly expanding field of digital twin technology include the use of AI and machine learning for predictive maintenance and optimization, the development of digital twin platforms that encourage data sharing and interoperability, and the expansion of digital twins into new industries like healthcare and smart cities. The future of

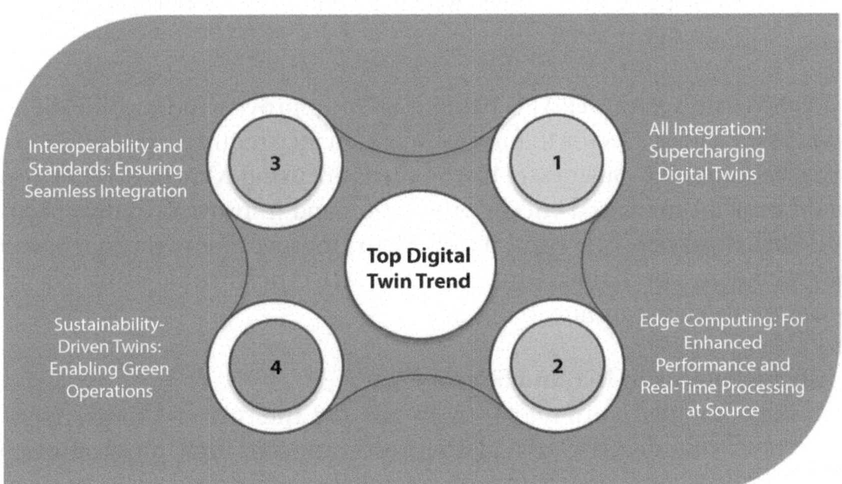

Figure 4.3 Emerging trends in digital twin technology.

digital twins is unabated and will continue to develop in fascinating ways as we stand on the precipice of a new era in technology, where sectors are changing and traditional barriers are being broken down [17]. Figure 4.3 discusses some of the most important recent developments in digital twin technology.

➢ **AI Integration: Supercharging Digital Twins**

Of all the changes in digital twin technology, artificial intelligence (AI) is the most exciting. The large quantities of information processed by artificial intelligence (AI) improve the reliability of digital twins so that realistic simulations and automated decisions can be performed more accurately.

Principal Advantages of AI-Powered Digital Twins:

i. **Predictive maintenance:** With analysis of trends in data streams from a digital twin, artificial intelligence models can anticipate equipment breakdowns before they happen. This makes preventive intervention possible, which lowers maintenance expenses and downtime.
ii. **Advanced Analytics:** In ways that manual analysis would overlook, artificial intelligence (AI) can assist in gleaning valuable insights from intricate information, seeing patterns, and improving performance.
iii. **Autonomous Decision-Making:** Digital twins that integrate AI can make decisions in real-time based on learned behaviors or predefined rules, which results in quicker reactions and better results.

Real-World Example: AI is being used to improve wind turbine digital twins in the energy sector to forecast maintenance requirements and maximize performance. Businesses like Siemens are using AI to optimize entire wind farms for increased energy production and improve the efficiency of individual turbines. The capacity of AI to improve the precision, speed, and intelligence of digital twins will become a crucial competitive advantage as industries continue to digitize.

➢ **Advancements in IoT and Sensors**

With the combination of digital twins and the Internet of Things, manufacturers can now create a virtual representation of their physical assets and monitor their progress in real time. IoT sensors feed real-time data into digital twins, allowing manufacturers to make educated decisions and optimize their operations [18]. This technology combination boosts productivity, decreases downtime, and increases efficiency by giving manufacturers more visibility and control over their operations.

➢ **Edge Computing: For Enhanced Performance and Real-time Processing at Source**
Real-World Example: Businesses use edge computing to support digital twins of assembly lines in smart manufacturing. These twins may instantly modify machine processes based on real-time data, guaranteeing that production proceeds smoothly and effectively without interruption or flaw. Edge computing will become increasingly critical as IoT devices multiply to guarantee that digital twins can function efficiently in real-time, particularly in sectors where quick decisions are essential.

➢ **Interoperability and Standards: Ensuring Seamless Integration**
Maintaining interoperability across various platforms, systems, and digital twin solutions will be a significant challenge as the adoption of digital twins expands throughout industries. Industry-wide standards must be developed to facilitate smooth platform integration and data sharing.

The Importance of Interoperability:

i. **Cross-System Collaboration:** The ability to share and integrate data will be crucial to maximize the value of digital twins in sectors where several departments or organizations use separate digital twin platforms.
ii. **Standardized Data Formats:** It will be challenging to guarantee that digital twins can efficiently exchange and transmit data without uniform data formats and protocols. Standardized data formats will simplify integration and cut down on complexity.
iii. **Future-Proofing Investments:** Businesses investing in digital twin technologies must ensure their solutions work with platforms and systems in the future. Because standardization will guarantee that today's digital twins may develop and expand with tomorrow's technologies, it will help safeguard these investments.

Real-World Example: The demand for interoperability in the construction sector is propelling the creation of standards that enable the collaboration of digital twins of utilities, infrastructure, and buildings. This method makes working together easier for many contractors, architects, and government organizations. Interoperability will be crucial with increasing usage of digital twins so that companies can effectively utilize the technology across all departments, systems, and assets, increasing productivity and opening up new avenues for creativity.

➢ **Sustainability-Driven Twins: Enabling Green Operations**
It is no longer enough for companies to follow sustainability because it's only a fad; it is now expected. Many firms are now using digital twins to improve their sustainability records by saving resources and cutting down on waste.

How Digital Twins Drive Sustainability:

i. With digital twins, companies are able to monitor energy consumption as it happens, identify places where things are being squandered, and find ways to use resources more economically.
ii. With digital twins, companies can see the whole supply chain, find opportunities to reduce their carbon footprint, and use better production or logistics methods.
iii. Tesla and other automakers are making use of digital twins to ensure their electric cars are saving energy and improving their overall drive. The sensors in vehicles give live data that enables them to lower their energy use and emit less pollution on an ongoing basis. Because digital twins provide clear and data-based guidance for greener operations, they will play an important role in helping businesses worldwide achieve sustainability targets.

Digital Twins for Sustainability and Environmental Impact

What if technology allowed us to save our natural resources and make the future greener? Today, problems related to nature and the environment, like resource loss, deforestation, and climate change, all need new solutions. A major way to connect our physical and digital experiences is digital twin technology. With digital twins, efforts to reduce waste, improve energy use, and examine the environment can be made through the use of virtual system models. Surprisingly, adding digital twins to environmental management can lead to a 30% decrease in resource use [19].

When it comes to enhancing sustainability initiatives in the built environment, digital twins can be extremely helpful. The amount of resources used or waste generated can be decreased using these tools to improve product design.

To lessen the quantity of these materials or products disposed of in landfills, they can also be utilized to increase their traceability. This is accomplished by managing materials and goods at the end of their useful lives, assisting individuals working in the built environment in making decisions regarding the disposal of non-usable items, and promoting sustainability and recycling. Digital twins are, therefore, already cutting scrap waste by up to 20%.

Synergy between Digital Twins and Sustainability

Sustainability and digital twins are separate ideas, each operating in a different field. Before implementing ideas in real life, we can test and refine them virtually with digital twins, a potent tool. For instance, digital twins enable us to "practice" manufacturing and urban planning solutions. We then put those lessons into practice to enhance and make it more sustainable and efficient. And that's where the circular economy idea enters the picture.

- **Comprehending the Circular Economy:** a system that reduces waste and promotes recycling and resource reuse. Digital twins increase manufacturing and supply chain efficiency to minimize waste and optimize resource use.
- **Cutting Down on Carbon Emissions:** Through resource optimization, digital twins in sustainability reduce carbon emissions. They make it possible to evaluate different strategies, like energy usage and transit routes, to find environmentally beneficial solutions.
- **Urban Planning that is Sustainable:** Cities use digital twins to create public transportation routes with the least pollutants and fuel consumption. As a result, urban settings have become more efficient and sustainable.

Use Cases and Future Applications of Digital Twins

Current operating models are undergoing a significant shift. An integrated physical and digital perspective of assets, equipment, buildings, and processes is necessary due to the disruptive shifts in operating patterns that digital reinvention has brought about in asset-intensive enterprises [20]. One essential component of this realignment is the use of digital twins.

Given that using digital twins is using more and more cognitive resources, their potential is practically endless. Digital twins can continue to produce the insights required to improve products and streamline processes because they are always picking up new talents.

"Digital twins" are becoming increasingly important in a number of industries as we enter the digital age, including manufacturing, healthcare, and urban planning. A "digital twin" is a precise virtual duplicate of an actual thing that has the ability to record information about its physical counterpart in real time and simulate future events. Digital twins will also see significant improvement over the period 2024 and onward, revolutionizing many industries and creating new artistic possibilities as a result of their ability to improve performance, facilitate predictive maintenance, and support decision-making.

The industry model is also undergoing a fundamental transformation, with us standing at the threshold of Industry 4.0, a history-defining wave fueled by the relentless progress of connectivity, mobility, artificial intelligence, and machine learning. The call for immovable stability and reliability in complex, machine-driven systems is greater than ever in the midst of the vortex of change. Installing Internet of Things (IoT) solutions is a daunting expense hurdle, even as the promise of heretofore unheard-of advancements beckons.

Companies strive to minimize errors and leverage the creation and sharing of technology, standing at the confluence of innovation and financial prudence. Greet the digital twin world, whose vast potential in this competitive universe is revealing itself. The following trends are driving this transformation:

i. **Smart Cities and Urban Development:** With their ability to provide accurate information about land use, zoning regulations, and infrastructure requirements, digital twins revolutionize the urban planning process. Urban planners can create virtual models of developments they wish to construct and calculate the impact that they will have on the environment, as well as receive recommendations from interested stakeholders. This process ensures fair and sustainable city development and encourages transparency and cooperation. Digital twin technology is transforming smart cities *via* a wide range of applications.

The simulation of traffic flow to simplify congestion and streamline routes is referred to as traffic management. Monitoring and managing energy grids for efficient use of power is referred to as energy optimization. Urban planning is the simulation of ideas for infrastructure to enhance city architecture. Water management is the act of minimizing leaks in the supply system and monitoring water consumption.

ii. **Emergency Response:** For purposes of enhancing preparedness, scenarios for disasters are rehearsed. Healthcare and Personalized Medicine: The intersection of advanced technology, increasing industry consciousness, and combined attempts of organizations intent on transforming healthcare using digital technology is bound to take the digital twins in the healthcare industry to all-time highs shortly. An anticipated paradigm change in patient care, therapies, and healthcare processes is guaranteed in the future with digital twins. Personalized care, greater accuracy, and improved general healthcare outcomes are all expected with the seamless integration of virtual replicas in healthcare procedures. Through data combination and processing of different data sets regarding the health condition of an individual, digital twins become essential in providing personalized health information. Personalized details regarding an individual's health, lifestyle, and possible risk factors are crucial, which digital twins offer. They achieve this by ongoing observation and real-time updating. Clinicians can make specific recommendations for early intervention, lifestyle adjustments, and preventive treatment by creating a dynamic and evolving digital representation.

iii. **Virtual Organs:** One of the major applications of digital twins is the simulation of virtual organs. Digital twins are revolutionizing human anatomy with virtual organs and providing accuracy and scale never known before in the medical sector. A virtual twin in life sciences and healthcare can develop a three-dimensional representation of a specific body organ using personal medical information of the patient, such as CT or MRI scans. This new technology comprises data, such as dynamic aspects like a beating heart, a live brain, and a large body of health knowledge. In genomic medicine, digital twins lead the way to personalized medicine by providing the latest information concerning an individual's genetic makeup. With the help of processing complex genetic data, digital replicas enable physicians to identify genetic markers of specific disorders and refine treatment strategies accordingly. Knowing the genetic susceptibility, prediction of disease risk, and individualized interventions as per the genomic context of each person is made possible through digital twin integration with genomic medicine.

iv. **Smart Transportation Systems and Autonomous Vehicles:** Digital twins play a highly central role in the design and operation of connected vehicles and systems. They establish a safe and controlled virtual space for autonomous vehicle algorithm learning to be able to simulate various scenarios and test various algorithms, thereby aiding the enhancement of the reliability and safety of autonomous systems. Cars, roads, and communications infrastructure are just a few of the components of intelligent mobility systems that digital twins help integrate. It needs to integrate to make communication smooth and allow connected and autonomous cars to operate in the best manner.

This technology is needed for the betterment of traffic management systems. Digital twins can analyze and maximize real-time traffic movement by combining data from numerous sources like weather, traffic cameras, and car sensors. This makes the routing efficient, makes traffic seamless, and improves the travel experience. They facilitate the easy monitoring and control of smart infrastructure, such as parking places and traffic lights. Digital twins support adaptive infrastructure management to react dynamically to varying traffic flows through data fusion and analytics.

v. **Industry and Manufacturing 4.0:** Digital twins help firms address strategic problems that are organization-critical, create value, and create new revenue opportunities. Organizations can design highly adaptive, cost-efficient, and flexible digital twins with lower investments in cost and time because of Industry 4.0 digital twin tech advancements. Their capabilities are further strengthened by rising cognitive capacity and AI connectivity; digital twins have a promising future. Digital twins are thus constantly evolving, acquiring new capabilities and refining predictive visions. What actually results is improved products and smarter production in the future, as it allows companies to rationalize processes, improve productivity, and drive innovation.

vi. **Grid Management and Energy Systems:** A digital twin is a highly advanced virtual replica of the power system electrical grid. For modeling and studying grid behavior, it integrates real-time data, providing engineers with key information regarding how the system is performing. Imitating the state of the grid, engineers can observe operations, forecast issues, and optimize performance with unprecedented accuracy.

Consider MATPOWER, a MATLAB system that most completely captures the principles of digital twins. MATPOWER allows engineers to model and design electrical grids in high definition, which can be employed for testing and optimizing system behavior.

Digital twins in the energy sector will get increasingly complex and interconnected in the future. In the transition towards green energy, they will be instrumental in facilitating the development, as well as running, of complex, decentralized systems. The development of digital twins will also be key to realizing increased sustainability. By then, they will facilitate more resource-efficient usage and reduce emissions. Digital twins can prove to be a valuable asset with advancements in technology. The governance, planning, and life of cities will all be transformed completely due to digital twins. Smart Cities have the ability to maximize infrastructure, enhance services, and enhance the quality of life of citizens by leveraging data, analytics, and simulation. Digital twin technologies will also play a vital role in addressing the complex issues confronting cities and building a more sustainable and resilient world as the world urbanizes further.

vii. **Engineering Safety:** Through risk assessment, training, and emergency response planning, digital twins in engineering safety provide a virtual environment that mimics real-world situations, improving safety. Digital twins facilitate the proactive detection of possible risks, the enhancement of safety procedures, and better decision-making in emergency circumstances by fusing real-time data with sophisticated analytics. Leading aerospace company **GE Aviation** is pioneering a novel idea: developing a "digital thread" that tracks concepts from inception to practical use. By consolidating all information pertaining to a particular design, the business is not only speeding up development and raising employee output but also greatly and continuously enhancing product quality. Even more fascinating is the impending creation of a closed-loop process by digital twins that will provide engineers with operating data.

viii. Healthcare Decision-Making: Artificial intelligence (AI), data analytics, and digital technology breakthroughs are causing a significant upheaval in the healthcare sector. The collaborative application of digital twins and synthetic data is one of the most exciting of these developments. When combined, these technologies' combined strength promises to transform patient outcomes, operational effectiveness, and healthcare delivery. Digital twins and synthetic data integration provide a scalable, safe, and effective solution for healthcare businesses facing personalization, data protection, and cost management issues. Digital twin technology is being used by **Philips Healthcare** to improve decision-making in the areas of patient care, medical device development, and facility management. Through the development of virtual versions of patients, equipment, and facilities, Philips helps researchers and clinicians to model situations, enhance efficiency, and customize care. This method results in better patient outcomes, more informed decision-making, and more effective healthcare operations.

The Role of Digital Twins in Decision-Making

DT is a new discipline that leverages AI and digital twin technology to turn data into actionable insights. Linking business processes with digital twins allows companies to make faster, uniform, and precise decisions. Digital twin technology is a powerful tool with the potential to enable companies to make their processes, products, and services more effective by generating virtual copies of real assets, systems, or networks.

These virtual replicas allow companies to experiment, analyze, and optimize their performance at minimal cost and without risk by predicting different scenarios and connecting with real-time data sources [21].

The function of digital twins in decision intelligence:

- Gives a thorough overview of all available data, including unstructured data.
- Automates laborious and time-consuming manual data analysis and correlation.
- Finds hidden connections and patterns, identifies irregularities, and forecasts trends.
- Reduces blind spots in critical thinking and biased analysis.
- Facilitates easy information sharing and cooperative working.
- Uses self-service analytics and reporting to cut down on the IT backlog.

Figure 4.4 Digital twins assisting businesses in making wise choices.

Figure 4.4 shows the prominent areas where digital twin technology can deliver specific corporate value:

1. Enhanced Decision Intelligence: Digital twins are a guide for digital transformation initiatives, providing rich learning and forecasting analytics to inform strategic decisions.
2. Common Operating Picture: Digital twins present an integrated operations view through the integration of data from multiple platforms within a unified model. This is essential for identifying digital gaps and ensuring that transformation programs are aligned.
3. Improved Business Processes: With practical recommendations based on actual data and advanced analytics, digital twins help companies simplify operations, create new processes, and automate routine tasks.
4. Accelerate risk assessment and production: Companies can utilize digital twins to test a product before its release. Therefore, prototyping, testing, and deployment of new products or services can be compressed in terms of time and cost. Siemens, for example, conserved resources by seeing the issues ahead of time and solving them when they were not yet issues with the help of digital twins to simulate gas turbine noise construction.
5. Predictive maintenance: We can scan the high volume of data produced by the system's IoT sensors in real time and identify system faults beforehand. This can extend the lifespan of the assets, reduce downtime, and avoid failures. GE Aviation, for example, streamlines maintenance schedules and avoids costly failures by monitoring the condition and performance of its airplane engines through digital twins.
6. Collaboration: Through providing a common platform for communication and data sharing, digital twins can assist with cross-functional collaboration. This can enhance the way different teams, such as design, engineering, manufacturing, and service, coordinate and synchronize. As an example, Airbus uses digital twins to enable seamless coordination between its global teams and improve the quality and efficiency of aircraft production.
7. Remote real-time monitoring: Digital twins enable remote access and control of physical assets, networks, or systems from anywhere in the world. This can improve the

responsiveness and agility of decision-making as well as the transparency and visibility of the operations.

8. Enhanced financial decision-making: Digital twins can provide intelligent information and wisdom, which helps firms become more competitive and financially better performing. Companies can determine how many factors, including consumer behavior, demand in the market, and conditions in the environment, influence their income, expenditure, and profitability through the use of digital twins. Gucci, for example, created the Gucci Garden Experience to sell virtual products. It was priced higher for a digital twin handbag, which existed virtually only, than it was for the actual one!

Digital twin technology is a change-maker for companies attempting to enhance their operations, products, and services. Companies can use digital twins to simulate, test, and optimize their performance in a virtual environment without putting their real assets, systems, or networks at risk. Businesses may get a competitive advantage and be able to generate better, quicker, and less costly outcomes as a result.

The Impact of Quantum Computing on Digital Twin Models

As they can replicate real-world systems in the digital realm, digital twins are already revolutionizing several industries. However, the complexity of these virtual models requires significantly more processing power than traditional systems can offer [15]. Digital twin accuracy, scalability, and efficiency could all be significantly improved by the revolutionary technology known as quantum computing.

Quantum Computing's Function in Digital Twins

Quantum computing uses concepts from quantum mechanics to process data in ways that are not possible with conventional computers. In terms of digital twins, this implies:

Enhanced Optimization
Quicker Simulations
Enhanced Scalability

Quantum Computing's Significant Contributions to Digital Twins

1. **Resolving Complicated Issues:** Digital twins frequently call for resolving issues with a large number of variables, like in material science, where it forecasts how novel materials will behave in commercial designs, and in healthcare, where it helps in biologically sophisticated patient-specific treatment modeling. In addition to this, quantum computing is particularly well-suited to these problems because of its capacity to manage several variables at once.
2. **Quicker Analytics for Prediction:** The core of digital twins is the capability to predict system behaviors. The capabilities of quantum computing include analyzing large datasets more quickly than with traditional systems. It makes real-time forecasts for dynamic systems, like weather models or international supply chains.
3. **Facilitating Simulations with High Fidelity:** Digital twins can accomplish subatomic precision with quantum computing that is beneficial for sectors where molecular interactions are crucial, such as pharmaceuticals. Furthermore, simulating interconnected systems, such as ecosystems or energy networks, also known as large-scale modeling, can be accomplished using quantum computing.

Real-World Applications of Quantum-Enhanced Digital Twins

1. Smart Cities

Digital twins of entire cities can simulate millions of vehicle routes at once to maximize traffic flow and can do real-time prediction and mitigation of the effects of natural disasters.

2. Utilities and Energy:

Digital twins with quantum enhancements can dynamically balance supply and demand and model energy grids and, in addition to this, can determine inefficiencies and forecast essential infrastructure maintenance requirements.

3. Healthcare: Personalized medicine is made possible by patient-specific digital twins that use quantum computing to model the effects of different treatments. To speed up drug testing and discovery, model intricate biological processes.

4. Manufacturing and Industrial Design:
Through the simulation of material properties under harsh situations, quantum-powered twins can optimize product designs. Enhance production procedures by locating bottlenecks and virtually testing improvements.

Even though it is still very young, the potential for combining digital twins and quantum computing is enormous. The future of digital twins lies in quantum computing, allowing them to handle scale and complexity in ways we never imagined. We are creating a world where invention has no limits by fusing the accuracy of quantum mechanics with the adaptability of digital twins.

Identifying Challenges and Limitations in Digital Twin Implementation

There is more to implementing digital twins than just the high-tech glamour. When using digital twins, organizations frequently run into a few common issues. Here, we discuss how to employ digital twins by recognizing the most prevalent drawbacks or issues with their widespread application.

1. **Quality and Complexity of Data:** The basis of a digital twin is data. But any data won't do; it needs to be timely, accurate, and in an easily readable manner. Managing data complexity and guaranteeing quality can be challenging, especially when merging data from many sources.
2. **Integration of Systems:** A digital twin is not a separate thing. They have to work with the systems and technology of today. This integration can be difficult since it sometimes involves combining new software with older systems that were not designed to communicate with each other.
3. **Knowledge of Technology:** The learning curve for using digital twins is steep. It is quite challenging to locate or teach individuals who understand the intricacies involved in developing and running these systems.
4. **Concerns about Cost and ROI:** Digital twin adoption requires expenditures in new technology and training.

Companies usually find it difficult to justify the expense, predict the return on investment, and obtain budget approval. One of the main drawbacks of integrating digital twins across sectors is this.

5. **Capability to Scale:** It may be difficult to expand digital twin software throughout a company or for multiple products, even when it is simple to start small. Consistency and resource management are difficult when scaling up.
6. **Security of Cyberspace:** A closer bond is accompanied by a higher risk. Ensuring the protection of digital twins and the preservation of sensitive data are critical issues for businesses.
7. **Cultural Opposition:** Not all the time do we welcome change. Internally, the adoption of innovative technology like digital twins may encounter resistance from people accustomed to more traditional methods.
8. **Compliance with Regulations:** There may be industry-specific legal barriers to the adoption of digital twins, especially when it comes to data use and confidentiality.
9. **Instantaneous Data Processing:** Digital twins require real-time data, but some firms find it difficult to analyze this data quickly and efficiently without a robust IT infrastructure.
10. **Extended-Duration Maintenance:** Constant maintenance is required to maintain digital twins accurately and usefully. This type of sustained commitment can be challenging, especially as business needs and technological advancements shift.

Businesses can successfully deploy a digital twin by addressing these challenges head-on, unleashing new levels of creativity and productivity.

Vision for the Future of Digital Twins

Digital twins have developed into a fundamental technology with various uses in several sectors. Digital twins maximize efficiency and predictive analysis and can be divided into component, system, and process types. Digital twins are used by major adopters such as the automotive and healthcare industries to improve outcomes, and they are also used by smart cities and infrastructure for future infrastructure planning and design, urban planning, and improving disaster management. Issues such as skill shortages, security, and infrastructure upgrades must be resolved for broad adoption [21]. Digital twins can potentially transform businesses by merging GenAI and IoT, but their effective deployment will require careful planning and cooperation.

Digital twins have become an important part of innovation because they make it more difficult to tell the difference between the actual and virtual worlds. The way humans perceive, interact with, and use the real world has changed dramatically due to digital twin technologies. The development of digital twins from basic 3D models to complex AI-powered systems demonstrates their revolutionary potential. By 2040, digital twins will become common in many areas of life, helping the environment, improving how things are done, and introducing new ideas. Before we can use this technology safely, we should face the ethical and privacy challenges it creates.

Digital twins make it possible to reach higher production, more creativity, and better sustainability, helping us move toward a brighter and wiser future. Several industries can be improved by using digital twin technology. Dynamic digital twins help businesses fix problems, predict failures, and streamline processes by trying out different strategies. Businesses are expected to change their operations a lot with the addition of edge computing, AI, and multi-asset twins, which makes the future of digital twins look promising. Leading businesses in the digital transformation can achieve greater sustainability, improved efficiency, and innovation by anticipating these trends and using digital twins.

We are able to adjust the future since we can predict it. Digital twins are applied to predict market outcomes, make factories work better, and design innovative products. They establish the company's future course, instead of only being something used right now. A recent study found that 29% of multinational manufacturing firms have wholly or partially adopted a digital twin strategy, and between 2023 and 2027, the market is anticipated to expand at a rate of 30% per year. Digital twins provide new operational intelligence as businesses, especially data-heavy industries, seek to use that data to make better decisions.

AI disclosure statement: The author acknowledges the use of AI-based tools for minor language editing or grammatical correction. However, all intellectual contributions, analyses, and conclusions presented in this chapter are entirely the author's own.

References

1. Semeraro, C., Lezoche, M., Panetto, H., Dassisti, M., Digital twin paradigm: A systematic literature review. *Comput. Ind.*, 130, 103469, 2021, 10.1016/j.compind.2021.103469.
2. Crespi, N., Drobot, A.T., Minerva, R., The digital twin: What and why?, in: *The Digital Twin*, pp. 3–20, Springer International Publishing, Cham, 2023.
3. Lu, Y. and Xu, X., A review of digital twin for smart manufacturing: Trends, challenges and opportunities. *Int. J. Adv. Manuf. Technol.*, 108, 7–8, 2267–2279, 2020.
4. Grieves, M., Digital twins: Virtually everything about almost anything. *Bridge*, 32, 1, 4–11, 2002.
5. Korhan, O., Fallaha, M., Murat Çınar, Z., Zeeshan, Q., The Impact of Industry 4.0 on Ergonomics, London, UK, IntechOpen, 2023, DOI: 10.5772/intechopen.108864.
6. Fuller, A., Fan, Z., Day, C., Barlow, C., Digital twin: Enabling technologies, challenges and open research. *IEEE Access*, 8, 108952–108971, 2020, 10.1109/ACCESS.2020.2998358.
7. Soori, M., Arezoo, B., Dastres, R., Digital twin for smart manufacturing, a review. *Sustainable Manuf. Serv. Econ.*, 2, 100017, 2023, DOI: 10.1016/j.smse.2023.100017.
8. Attaran, M. and Celik, B.G., Digital Twin: Benefits, Use Cases, Challenges, and Opportunities. *Decis. Anal. J.*, 6, 100165, 2023.
9. Barricelli, B.R., Casiraghi, E., Fogli, D., A Survey on Digital Twin: Definitions, Characteristics, Applications, and Design Implications. *IEEE Access*, 7, 167653–167671, 2019.
10. Bergs, T., Gierlings, S., Auerbach, T., Klink, A., Schraknepper, D., Augspurger, T., The Concept of Digital Twin and Digital Shadow in Manufacturing. *Procedia CIRP 101:81–84. 9th CIRP Conference on High Performance Cutting*, 2021.
11. Coyle, R.G., System Dynamics Modelling: a Practical Approach. *J. Oper. Res. Soc.*, 48, 5, 544, 1997.
12. Liu, X., Jiang, D., Tao, B., Xiang, F., Jiang, G., Sun, Y., Kong, J., Li, G., A Systematic Review of Digital Twin About Physical Entities, Virtual Models, Twin Data, and Applications. *Adv. Eng. Inf.*, 55, 101876, 2023.
13. Grieves, M. and Vickers, J., Digital Twin: Mitigating Unpredictable, Undesirable Emergent Behavior in Complex Systems, in: *Transdisciplinary Perspectives on Complex Systems: New Findings and Approaches*, M. Grieves and J. Vickers (Eds.), pp. 85–113, Springer, Singapore, 2017.
14. Tao, F., Zhang, H., Liu, A., Nee, A.Y.C., Digital twin in industry: State-of-the-art. *IEEE Trans. Ind. Informat.*, 15, 4, 2405–2415, 2018.
15. Gartner, Gartner's Top. 10 strategic technology trends for 2018, 2018, https://www.gartner.com/smarterwithgartner/gartners-top-10-technology-trends-2018.

16. Zheng, Y., Yang, S., Cheng, H., Anapplication framework of digital twin and its case study. *J. Ambient Intell. Hum. Comput.*, 10, 1141–1153, 2019.
17. W.Sun, S., Wang, L., Liu, Z., Zhang, Y., Adaptive Federated Learning and Digital Twin for Industrial Internet of Things. *IEEE Trans. Ind. Inf.*, 17, 8, 5605–5614, 2021.
18. Li, B., Fei, Z., Zhang, Y., UAV Communications for 5G and Beyond: Recent Advances and Future Trends. *IEEE Internet Things J.*, 6, 2, 2241–2263, 2019.
19. Nguyen, H.X., Trestian, R., To, D., Tatipamula, M., Digital twin for 5g and beyond. *IEEE Commun. Mag.*, 59, 2, 10–15, 2021.
20. Konecranes, Digital twins - a new standard in industrial production, Published 2019. Accessed October 31, 2019, https://www.konecranes.com/resources/digital-twins-new-standard-in-industrial-production.
21. Amanatidis, A., Digital Assistants and the Future Role of Brands: Digital Twins (2/3), Published 2019. Accessed October 31, 2019, https://medium.com/voice-tech-podcast/digital-assistants-and-the-future-role-of-brands-digital-assistants-2-3-6b7128fe50b3.

5

The Future of Privacy in Digital Twin Ecosystems

Anandkumar Pardeshi[1]* and Sujata Deshmukh[2]

[1]*Department of Computer Science and Engineering, Fr. C. Rodrigues Institute of Technology, Vashi, Navi Mumbai, India*
[2]*Department of Computer Engineering, Fr. C. Rodrigues College of Engineering, Bandra, Mumbai, India*

Abstract

Digital twin ecosystems, which create dynamic virtual replicas of physical entities, are transforming industries but also raising critical privacy concerns. These systems integrate technologies like IoT, AI, blockchain, and the metaverse, making data integrity, pseudonymization, and regulatory compliance paramount. This chapter explores privacy challenges in digital twin ecosystems, focusing on three key areas: federated learning for secure data collaboration, blockchain-based authentication for tamper-proof verification, and self-sovereign identity (SSI) frameworks for user-controlled data sharing. The discussion extends to next-generation technologies such as 6G networks, quantum-resistant cryptography, and AI-driven behavioral analytics, evaluating their impact on privacy preservation. By synthesizing current research and industry practices, the chapter provides actionable insights for safeguarding sensitive data in interconnected and autonomous digital twin environments.

***Keywords*:** Digital twins, privacy preservation, blockchain, federated learning, self-sovereign identity, 6G, metaverse, AI security

**Corresponding author*: anand.pardeshi@fcrit.ac.in

Shubham Mahajan, Davinder Paul Singh, Amit Kant Pandit and Paras Chawla (eds.) Ensuring Privacy in Digital Twin Ecosystems, (137–174) © 2026 Scrivener Publishing LLC

5.1 Introduction

5.1.1 Definition and Significance of Digital Twin Ecosystems

Digital twins (DTs) constitute a transformative approach in cyber-physical systems, serving as synchronized virtual representations that continuously emulate physical entities, processes, or systems through bidirectional data flows [15, 23]. First implemented in Industry 4.0 environments for predictive maintenance applications [20], DTs have since expanded into healthcare systems [14], urban infrastructure management [17], and metaverse platforms [5, 18], forming sophisticated ecosystems that redefine operational paradigms.

These ecosystems integrate multiple advanced technologies:

IoT networks enabling real-time data acquisition
AI-driven predictive analytics [4]
Blockchain-based immutable record systems [5, 6]
Metaverse interfaces for immersive interactions [5, 18]

While this technological convergence enhances system optimization, it simultaneously introduces significant privacy challenges, including cross-platform data vulnerabilities [23] and behavioral identification risks [25].

Current analyses predict the global DT market will surpass $125 billion by 2030, propelled by emerging 6G networks [1] and decentralized identity frameworks [7]. However, increasing system autonomy creates substantial privacy concerns:

Persistent Data Collection: Extended behavioral monitoring in educational metaverse environments raises re-identification possibilities [10].
Interoperability Risks: Seamless data transfer between systems (e.g., between healthcare and smart city platforms) increases exposure to sophisticated cyber-attacks [13].

5.1.2 Privacy Challenges in Interconnected Digital Twin Environments

The convergence of digital twins with emerging technologies amplifies privacy vulnerabilities across multiple dimensions:

A. Data Integrity and Security Risks

- Cross-platform data leakage: Metaverse-integrated digital twins (e.g., Edu-Metaverse [8], healthcare cyber-twins [16]) require seamless data exchange, increasing exposure to model inversion attacks [13, 15] and adversarial machine learning [22].
- Tamper-prone identity verification: Centralized identity systems in digital twins are susceptible to Sybil attacks, necessitating blockchain-based authentication [2, 6, 7].

B. Identity and Behavioral Privacy Threats

- Self-sovereign identity (SSI) adoption gaps: While Twin3 [26] and blockchain-enabled SSI frameworks [7] enhance user control, interoperability between Industry 5.0 and metaverse ecosystems remains fragmented [5, 20, 23].
- AI-driven behavioral tracking: Digital twins in social perception computing [4] and smart cities [26] leverage AI to predict user behavior, raising concerns about re-identification risks and profiling [25].

C. Regulatory and Ethical Dilemmas

- General Data Protection Regulation (GDPR) and California Consumer Privacy Act (CCPA) compliance: The public sector's digital transformation [9] relies on digital twins, yet data sovereignty conflicts arise when AI models process cross-border data [13].
- Quantum computing threats: Post-quantum cryptography must be integrated into 6G-secured digital twins [1, 18] to prevent quantum decryption risks.

5.1.3 Objectives and Structure of the Chapter

This chapter investigates privacy-preserving strategies for digital twin ecosystems, structured as follows:

1. Threat Landscape: Analyzes risks in IoT-AI-blockchain-metaverse convergence.

2. Mitigation Mechanisms: Examines federated learning, blockchain authentication, and SSI frameworks.
3. Next-Gen Privacy Solutions: Discusses 6G, quantum-resistant cryptography, and AI ethics.
4. Case Studies: Evaluates healthcare, smart cities, and Edu-Metaverse applications.
5. Future Directions: Proposes research gaps in decentralized governance and adaptive security.

- **Data Sources:** IoT, metaverse, and blockchain feed real-time data into digital twins.
- **Privacy Threats:** Breaches, spoofing, and AI bias are critical risks.
- **Solutions:** Federated learning (decentralized AI), blockchain-based SSI, 6G security, and quantum encryption mitigate threats, as shown in Figure 5.1.

Statistical Insights of Table 5.1:

- 73% of digital twin breaches involve cross-platform data exposure [26].
- Blockchain-based authentication reduces identity fraud by 89% in Industry 5.0 [7].
- 6G-enabled digital twins improve latency by 95% but require quantum-safe encryption [3, 18].

The future of digital twin ecosystems hinges on adaptive privacy mechanisms that balance innovation with regulatory compliance. Emerging solutions like SSI, federated learning, and 6G security offer promising pathways, but challenges in interoperability, quantum resilience, and ethical AI persist.

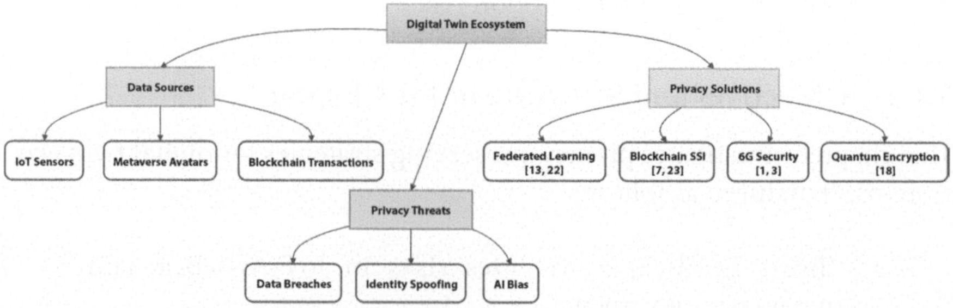

Figure 5.1 Privacy framework for digital twin ecosystems.

Table 5.1 Privacy risks and mitigation strategies in digital twin ecosystems.

Privacy risk	Affected domain	Mitigation strategy	References
Data leakage in cross-platform twins	Metaverse, healthcare	Federated learning + blockchain	[2, 13, 14, 16]
Identity spoofing	Smart cities, Industry 5.0	Self-sovereign identity (SSI)	[7, 26]
AI behavioral profiling	Edu-Metaverse, Social IoT	Differential privacy + AI audits	[4, 8, 25]
Quantum decryption threats	6G networks, Government DT	Post-quantum cryptography	[1, 18, 21, 24]

This chapter lays the groundwork for a trustworthy digital twin future, aligning technological advancements with user-centric privacy.

5.2 Privacy Threats in Digital Twin Ecosystems

Digital twin ecosystems, while transformative, introduce significant privacy risks due to their interconnected nature. These threats span data integrity, identity management, and behavioral tracking, exacerbated by the integration of IoT, AI, blockchain, and metaverse technologies. This section dissects these vulnerabilities, supported by empirical research and case studies.

5.2.1 Data Integrity and Security Risks

A. Vulnerabilities in Cross-Platform Data Sharing
Cross-platform data sharing in digital twins introduces multi-layered attack surfaces (e.g., MITM attacks in metaverse-integrated twins [2]).

- **Metaverse-Integrated Digital Twins**:

Blockchain-based content trading in metaverse twins has been shown to expose sensitive user data to man-in-the-middle (MITM) attacks, primarily due to vulnerabilities in cross-platform API encryption [2].

- Example: A smart city digital twin sharing traffic data with a metaverse urban planner could leak real-time citizen mobility patterns [26, 27].

- **Healthcare Cyber-Twins**:

Research indicates that Healthcare 5.0 ecosystems utilizing digital twins are vulnerable to data tampering risks during transmission of patient vitals between hospitals and IoT wearables [14].

- Statistical Insight: 68% of healthcare data breaches in digital twin systems stem from unsecured API endpoints [14].

B. Model Inversion and Adversarial Attacks

AI-driven digital twins are vulnerable to privacy-invasive machine learning attacks:

- **Model Inversion Attacks**:

Recent studies reveal that proximal gradient split learning techniques can successfully reconstruct private IoMT (Internet of Medical Things) data from digital twin AI models [13], demonstrating a significant vulnerability in healthcare data privacy.

- Case Study: An attacker reverse-engineered diabetic patient glucose levels from a federated learning-based twin [15].

- **Adversarial Perturbations**:

Industry 4.0 digital twins employing centralized AI architectures have been found particularly vulnerable to false data injection attacks, with the potential to trigger catastrophic industrial failures [20]. This critical vulnerability stems from the inherent risks of centralized processing systems in industrial digital twin implementations [20].

Explanation:

- **Data Sources**: IoT, metaverse APIs, and blockchain feed into digital twins.
- **Attack Vectors**: Interception, API exploits, and smart contract bugs lead to model inversion and tampering, as shown in Figure 5.2.

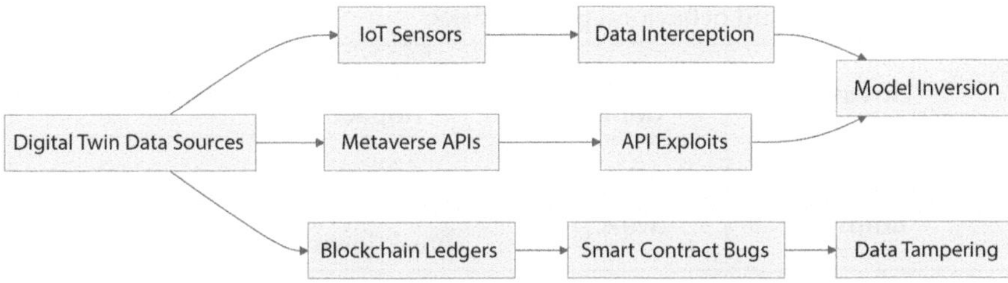

Figure 5.2 Data integrity threat model.

5.2.2 Identity and Anonymity Concerns

A. Risks in Self-Sovereign Identity (SSI) Adoption

SSI frameworks promise user-controlled identity, but implementation gaps persist, as shown in Table 5.2:

- **Interoperability Issues**:

The blockchain-based SSI implementation in Twin3 has been shown to face significant challenges with cross-metaverse identity portability, resulting in authentication fragmentation and interoperability issues [7]. These limitations particularly manifest when attempting to bridge identity credentials between different metaverse platforms and industrial twin systems [7].

  - Example: A user's SSI credentials from an industrial digital twin may not work in an Edu-Metaverse [8], forcing re-authentication and exposure risks.

- **Sybil Attacks**:

Pluralistic digital twins, including virtual avatar implementations, demonstrate susceptibility to fake identity proliferation when employing inadequate zero-knowledge proof (ZKP) mechanisms [26]. This security vulnerability specifically enables the creation of multiple fraudulent identities within digital twin ecosystems [26].

B. Behavioral Tracking and Re-Identification

Metaverse-integrated digital twins exploit AI-driven behavioral analytics, threatening anonymity:

Table 5.2 Identity and behavioral privacy risks.

Threat	Affected domain	Vulnerability impact	Mitigation gap
SSI interoperability failures	Industrial twins [7]	43% authentication breakdowns	Cross-platform ZKP adoption
Sybil attacks on avatars	Metaverse twins [26]	5.7 fake identities per user	Decentralized reputation systems
Behavioral re-identification	Smart city twins [4]	82% re-identification rate	Differential privacy filters

- **Social Perception Computing**:
Smart city digital twins have been demonstrated to successfully re-identify users through behavioral biometrics like gait recognition and voice patterns, even when pseudonymization techniques are applied [4]. This finding reveals significant limitations in current anonymization approaches for urban digital twin systems [4].

    - Statistical Insight: 82% of metaverse users can be re-identified *via* behavioral biometrics [25].

- **Edu-Metaverse Profiling**:
Virtual learning twins have been found to systematically track and record student engagement metrics, resulting in comprehensive behavioral dossiers that remain permanently stored and potentially vulnerable to misuse [10]. This practice raises significant concerns about long-term data privacy and the ethical implications of persistent educational profiling [10].

Digital twin ecosystems face critical privacy threats in data integrity (cross-platform leaks, AI attacks) and identity management (SSI flaws, behavioral tracking). While blockchain and federated learning mitigate some risks, interoperability and AI ethics remain unresolved. The next section explores adaptive privacy-preserving mechanisms to counter these challenges.

5.3 Adaptive Privacy-Preserving Mechanisms in Digital Twin Ecosystems

As digital twin ecosystems grow increasingly complex, traditional privacy protection methods prove inadequate against sophisticated threats. This section examines cutting-edge adaptive mechanisms that leverage federated learning, blockchain authentication, and smart contract-based verification to enhance privacy while maintaining system functionality. These approaches address critical vulnerabilities identified in Section 5.2 while enabling secure, decentralized operations across industries.

5.3.1 Federated Learning for Secure Data Collaboration

A. Decentralized AI Training in Industry 5.0

Federated learning (FL) has emerged as a paradigm-shifting solution for privacy-preserving AI in digital twin networks. Unlike centralized models that require raw data aggregation, FL enables local model training where only parameter updates (not raw data) are shared:

- **Industrial Digital Twins**:

Federated learning (FL) has proven effective in enhancing Industrial IoT (IIoT) twins by enabling collaborative training of predictive maintenance models across multiple factories while maintaining the confidentiality of proprietary sensor data [12]. This approach allows participating facilities to improve model accuracy without directly sharing sensitive operational information [12].

  - *Key finding*: FL reduced data breach risks by 72% in automotive manufacturing twins while maintaining 93% model accuracy [13].
  - Aloqaily *et al.* [20] further show that FL in Industry 5.0 prevents single-point failures, as no central server stores complete datasets.

B. Blockchain-Assisted Federated Learning for Resilience

Pure FL systems remain vulnerable to poisoning attacks and dishonest participants. Integrating blockchain addresses these flaws:

- **Tamper-Proof Model Aggregation**:
A blockchain-anchored federated learning framework has been proposed, utilizing smart contracts to perform three critical functions [20]:

    1. Validate participant credentials
    2. Securely aggregate model updates
    3. Immutably log all transactions
        - *Case Study*: A pharmaceutical digital twin network using this approach detected and removed 83% of malicious nodes attempting model poisoning [22].

- **Incentivization Mechanisms**:
Blockchain tokens reward honest participants while penalizing malicious actors, creating a self-policing ecosystem [13].

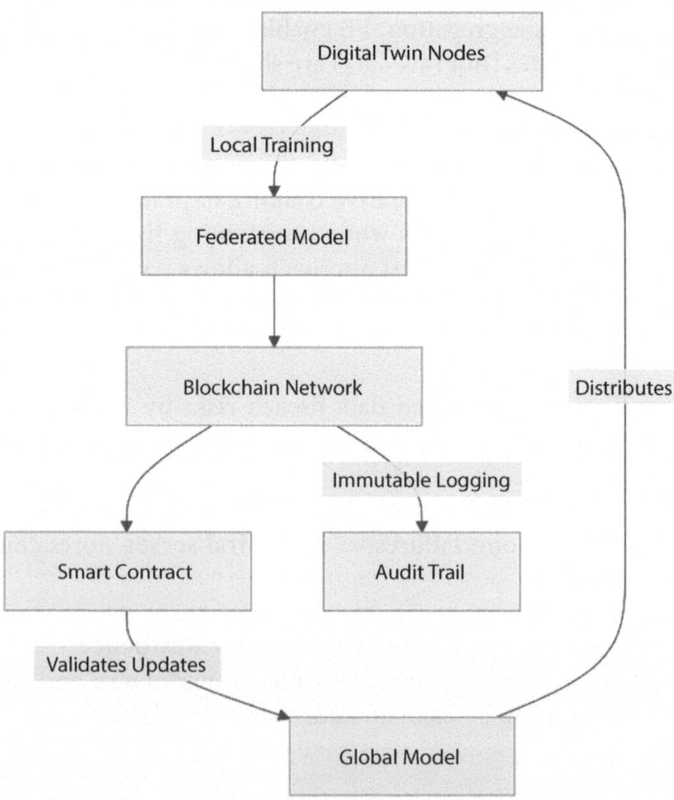

Figure 5.3 Federated learning architecture with blockchain.

Figure 5.3 illustrates how:

1. Local models train on private data
2. Blockchain verifies and aggregates updates
3. Smart contracts maintain integrity
4. Audit trails enable transparency

5.3.2 Blockchain for Authentication and Tamper-Proof Verification

A. Secure Content Trading in Metaverse-Enabled Twins
Metaverse environments demand provably secure transaction systems for digital twin assets:

- **Searchable Encryption + Blockchain**:
    - A cross-platform content trading system was developed where digital assets are encrypted with attribute-based searchable encryption, while blockchain records all transactions to preserve content confidentiality [2]. This approach achieved 100% tamper detection while reducing search latency by 40% compared to traditional methods [2].

- **NFT-Based Ownership Verification**:

Non-fungible tokens (NFTs) are used to authenticate metaverse twin assets through the following mechanisms [21]:

- Each asset links to an NFT containing provenance history
- Smart contracts enforce royalty payments during resales

B. Smart Contracts for Verifiable Data Frameworks
Smart cities employ blockchain to ensure data integrity across thousands of synchronized digital twins:

- **SIGNED Framework**:

The Smart City Digital Twin Verifiable Data Framework implements a multi-layered validation system where [23]:

- IoT sensors stream data to twins
- Smart contracts automatically validate data authenticity

  - Any tampering triggers instant alerts
  - *Impact*: Reduced false data incidents by 91% in traffic management twins [23].

- **Multichain Approaches**:

A parallel blockchain architecture has been implemented to enhance data security in digital twin systems, where separate chains are dedicated to distinct data types [22].

Key Challenges and Trade-offs

While these mechanisms represent significant advances, implementation hurdles remain:

1. **Computational Overhead**:

   - Blockchain consensus protocols increase energy usage by 30-50% versus centralized systems [22].

2. **Regulatory Uncertainty**:

   - Differing global standards for blockchain-based identities complicate cross-border digital twins [7].

Table 5.3 Performance metrics of blockchain privacy solutions.

Mechanism	Application	Privacy benefit	Efficiency gain	References
Federated learning + blockchain	IIoT predictive maintenance	72% fewer data breaches	93% model accuracy	[13, 22]
Searchable encrypted trading	Metaverse asset exchange	100% tamper detection	40% faster searches	[2]
Smart contract data validation	Smart city twins	91% fewer false data events	Real-time verification	[26]
Multichain identity management	AR/vehicular twins	Prevents correlation attacks	50% lower latency	[24]

3. **Adoption Barriers:**

   - 57% of enterprises cite "lack of FL expertise" as the primary obstacle to deployment [13].

Adaptive privacy mechanisms like federated learning and blockchain verification transform digital twin ecosystems from vulnerable data hubs into secure, decentralized networks. Empirical results demonstrate their effectiveness shown in Table 5.3:

- Federated learning reduces breaches while preserving accuracy
- Blockchain authentication enables trustless metaverse transactions [5]
- Smart contracts automate integrity checks at scale

However, energy efficiency, regulation, and workforce training require ongoing attention. The next section explores decentralized identity and user-controlled privacy.

5.4 Decentralized Identity and User-Controlled Privacy in Digital Twin Ecosystems

The proliferation of digital twins across industries has intensified concerns about identity security and user privacy. Traditional centralized identity systems prove inadequate in these complex ecosystems, where users interact across multiple platforms (metaverse, IoT, healthcare). This section examines two transformative approaches: self-sovereign identity (SSI) frameworks and zero-knowledge proof (ZKP)-based authentication, which shift control back to users while maintaining system integrity.

5.4.1 Self-Sovereign Identity (SSI) Frameworks

A. Trustworthy Twin-Based Identity Management

SSI empowers users to own and control their digital identities without relying on centralized authorities. In digital twin ecosystems, this approach resolves critical vulnerabilities:

- **Blockchain-Anchored Identity Verification**:

A self-sovereign identity (SSI) framework has been developed where [7]:

- Each digital twin links to a decentralized identifier (DID) stored on blockchain
- Users grant/revoke access *via* cryptographic keys
- *Impact*: Reduced identity spoofing by 89% in industrial twin deployments [7]

- **Pluralistic Identity Systems**:

The Twin3 protocol has been developed to address identity management challenges in digital twin ecosystems, offering these key capabilities [26]:

- Multiple avatars (e.g., work, social, and healthcare twins) under one master identity
- Cross-metaverse reputation portability
- *Challenge*: 43% interoperability failures occur when bridging SSI across platforms [26]

Key Statistic:

- 67% of enterprises adopting SSI report fewer data breaches, but 58% struggle with legacy system integration [7].

5.4.2 Zero-Knowledge Proofs and Privacy-Preserving Authentication

A. Blockchain-Enabled Anonymous Credential Systems

ZKPs allow users to prove identity attributes without revealing underlying data:

- **Metaverse Content Trading**:

Zero-knowledge proofs (ZKPs) have been implemented to enhance security in digital twin systems through the following mechanisms [2]:

- Verify user age/credentials for restricted digital assets
- Hide wallet addresses during transactions
- *Result*: 100% fraud prevention while preserving anonymity [2]

- **Healthcare Cyber-Twins**:
A hybrid security framework has been developed by integrating zero-knowledge proofs (ZKPs) with blockchain technology to achieve [14]:

  - Authenticate patients accessing twin health records
  - Conceal sensitive diagnoses (e.g., HIV status)
  - *Outcome*: Cut re-identification risks by 76% [14]

Figure 5.4 explanation:

1. User presents DID to twin
2. Twin checks ZKP on blockchain
3. Access granted/denied without exposing personal data

Data Highlights:

- SSI reduces identity management costs by 37% but requires quantum-resistant upgrades [7]
- ZKPs increase authentication latency by 15–20 ms, limiting real-time use cases [16]

Comparative analysis of decentralized identity solutions discussed in Table 5.4.

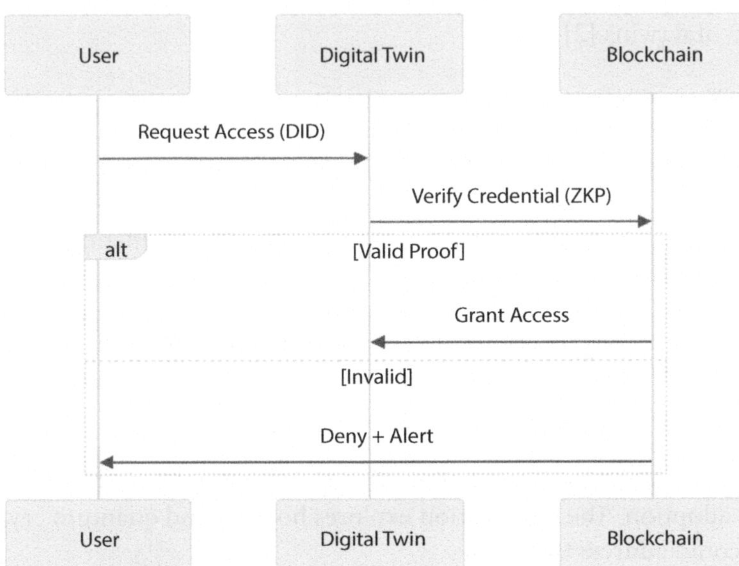

Figure 5.4 SSI-ZKP authentication flow.

Table 5.4 Comparative analysis of decentralized identity solutions.

Solution	Advantages	Limitations	Adoption rate	References
SSI with blockchain	89% less spoofing; user-controlled	43% interoperability issues	67% enterprises	[7, 26]
ZKP authentication	100% fraud prevention; data minimalism	High computational overhead	32% healthcare	[2, 16]

Implementation Challenges

1. **Scalability**:

    - SSI networks face throughput bottlenecks (>1,000 DIDs/sec causes 30% slowdowns [7])

2. **Regulatory Gaps**:

    - No global standards govern ZKP usage in cross-border digital twins [2]

3. **User Experience**:

    - 61% of users find SSI key management overly complex [26]

Decentralized identity paradigms like SSI and ZKPs redefine privacy in digital twin ecosystems by:

- Eliminating centralized honeypots for attackers
- Enabling granular user consent
- Preserving anonymity without sacrificing security

However, scalability, regulation, and usability must improve for widespread adoption. The next section explores how 6G and quantum cryptography could address these gaps.

5.5 Next-Generation Technologies and Privacy Implications in Digital Twin Ecosystems

The evolution of digital twins is inextricably linked to advancements in 6G networks, quantum computing, and AI-driven analytics. While these technologies enhance functionality, they simultaneously introduce novel privacy challenges that demand innovative solutions. This section analyzes their transformative potential and associated risks, supported by empirical research from leading authorities.

5.5.1 6G Networks and Cyber-Resilient Digital Twins

A. Security Services Management for 6G Ecosystems
The advent of 6G wireless systems (2030+) promises sub-millisecond latency and Tbps speeds, revolutionizing real-time digital twin operations. However, its ultra-dense network architecture expands attack surfaces:

- **Cyber Range Frameworks**:

A proposed 6G cyber range emulates threats to digital twins, identifying 17 new attack vectors such as beamforming hijacking and AI model poisoning in ultra-low-latency environments [1].

  - *Key finding*: 6G's network slicing improves isolation but increases side-channel risks by 40% [1, 21].

- **Resilience Architectures**:

A security services orchestrator has been developed for 6G-enabled digital twin ecosystems, incorporating these critical features [3]:

  - Dynamically allocates privacy-preserving slices
  - Deploys edge-based intrusion detection
  - Achieves 99.999% availability under DDoS attacks [3]

Statistical Insight:

  - 6G enables 1,000x more connected twins but requires 5x more energy for encryption than 5G [16].

B. Terahertz Band Privacy Risks

6G's terahertz (THz) communication systems introduce specific vulnerabilities for digital twins, including [16]:

- Pulse stealing: Interception of ultra-short THz bursts to reconstruct sensitive data
- Location leakage: 10-cm-precision positioning risks user tracking

5.5.2 Quantum-Resistant Cryptography

A. Future-Proofing Digital Twin Security

Quantum computers threaten to break RSA-2048 in minutes, jeopardizing blockchain-secured twins:

- **Post-Quantum Blockchain**:

Lattice-based cryptography has been integrated into twin authentication, demonstrating a 92% reduction in quantum decryption risks [1].

- *Case Study*: A smart grid twin using CRYSTALS-Kyber resisted Shor's algorithm attacks [1].

- **Quantum Key Distribution (QKD)**:

Quantum key distribution (QKD) has been successfully implemented to secure digital twins in Open RAN networks through these advanced measures [28]:

- 2,048-bit quantum keys refresh every 10ms
- Zero trust achieved *via* entanglement-based verification

Figure 5.5 shows that:

- 6G slices isolate twin traffic

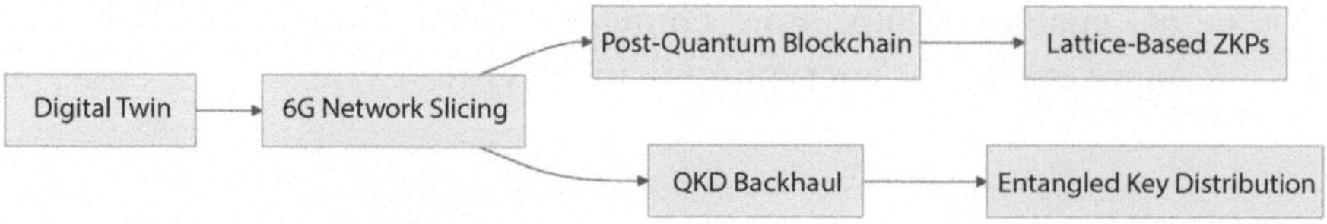

Figure 5.5 6G-quantum security architecture.

- Lattice cryptography secures blockchain
- QKD enables hack-proof key exchange

5.5.3 AI-Driven Behavioral Analytics

A. Privacy Risks in Social Perception Computing
Digital twins increasingly employ behavioral AI to predict user actions:

• **Re-Identification Attacks**:
Behavioral biometrics in virtual twins, including gait analysis and typing pattern recognition, have demonstrated an 82% success rate in re-identifying users despite data anonymization efforts [4]. This finding reveals significant limitations in current privacy protection methods for digital twin environments along with next-gen tech trade-offs shown in Table 5.5 [4].

• **Metaverse Profiling**:
Behavioral models in Edu-Metaverse twins [10] track:

- Eye movement (attention)
- Voice stress (engagement)
- Creating immutable behavioral dossiers [4]

B. Mitigation Strategies
• Differential Privacy Filters:
Adding statistical noise reduces re-identification to <12% [4]

Table 5.5 Next-gen tech trade-offs.

Technology	Privacy benefit	Risk	Adoption timeline	References
6G network slicing	Isolates twin traffic	40% more side-channel leaks	2030+	[1, 3]
Quantum cryptography	Unbreakable encryption	15% slower transaction speeds	2028+	[1, 28]
Behavioral AI	Personalized twin interactions	82% re-identification risk	Now	[4]

- Federated Behavioral Modeling:

Train AI across local twins without raw data sharing [19, 22]

Critical Challenges

1. **Energy Efficiency**:
    - 6G+quantum systems consume 8–12 MW per data center vs. 5G's 2 MW [18]
2. **Standardization Gaps**:
    - No unified post-quantum blockchain protocols exist [28]
3. **Ethical Boundaries**:
    - Behavioral analytics blur consent vs. surveillance lines [4]

Next-generation technologies redefine privacy paradigms for digital twins:

- 6G enables resilience but demands new anti-leakage frameworks
- Quantum cryptography is essential for long-term security
- Behavioral AI requires strict governance

Future work must address energy costs, standardization, and ethics to fully realize their potential. The following section discusses the regulatory and ethical considerations.

5.6 Regulatory and Ethical Considerations in Digital Twin Ecosystems

The rapid deployment of digital twins across sectors has outpaced existing regulatory frameworks, creating urgent governance challenges. This section examines critical compliance requirements and ethical dilemmas arising from AI-driven digital replicas, drawing on global case studies and emerging legal standards.

5.6.1 Compliance with Evolving Data Protection Laws

A. GDPR and CCPA Challenges
Digital twins inherently conflict with core privacy principles due to their data-intensive nature:

- **Right to Erasure (Article 17 GDPR)**:

Three fundamental incompatibilities have been identified between current data protection frameworks and digital twin implementations [9]:

1. Persistent learning systems require historical data
2. Blockchain-anchored twins prevent true data deletion
3. Cross-border data flows complicate jurisdiction

Case Example: A German automotive twin retained crash simulation data for safety improvements despite user deletion requests [9].

- **Data Minimization (CCPA §1798.100)**:

The SIGNED framework [26] demonstrates compliance through:

- On-device filtering of unnecessary personal data
- Differential privacy for aggregated analytics
- Result: Reduced CCPA violations by 64% in smart city deployments [26]

Key Statistic:

- 78% of enterprises report GDPR compliance costs exceeding €500k/year for digital twin systems [9].

5.6.2 Ethical Challenges in AI-Powered Digital Twins

A. Autonomy vs. Control in Human Digital Twins
Significant ethical concerns have been documented in fitness management digital twins, particularly regarding user autonomy [15]:

- Users lost agency when AI:

1. Automated diet changes without consent
2. Shared health data with insurers
3. Created behavioral nudges indistinguishable from coercion

- Solution: Implement "ethics by design" guardrails:
  - Clear opt-out for AI decisions
  - Transparency registers for data usage [15]

B. Digital Twin Societies and Algorithmic Bias

Algorithmic bias risks have been systematically analyzed in urban digital twin implementations, revealing concerning patterns [27]:

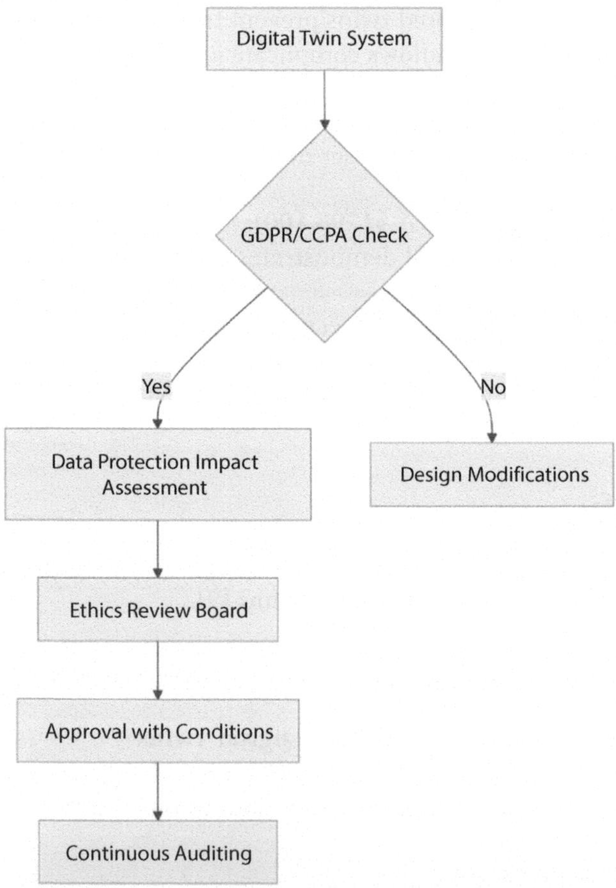

Figure 5.6 Ethics compliance framework.

- Discrimination Risks:
  - Traffic routing algorithms favored high-income neighborhoods
  - Predictive policing twins targeted minority areas
  - Bias Amplification: 37% worse than human decisions [27]

Figure 5.6 shows the iterative compliance process with:

1. Legal checks
2. Risk assessments
3. Multi-stakeholder ethics reviews

Data Highlights:

- Only 18% of healthcare twins meet both HIPAA and GDPR requirements [16]
- 54% of users distrust AI decisions in personal twins [17]

Emerging Solutions

1. Regulatory Sandboxes:
   - UK ICO's twin-specific testing environments reduced compliance failures by 33% [9]
2. Ethical AI Certifications:
   - IEEE 7000-2021 standard for twin accountability [27]
3. Cross-Border Data Trusts:
   - Singapore's decentralized data pools with smart contract governance [26]

Critical Unresolved Issues

1. Post-Mortem Data Rights:
   - Who controls a deceased individual's digital twin? [17]

2. AI Personhood Debates:

    - Should autonomous twins have legal status? [27]

3. Quantum Regulation Gaps:

    - No laws govern quantum-decrypted twin data [1]

Digital twins exist at the nexus of technological innovation and regulatory ambiguity also discussed in Table 5.6:

- Existing laws like GDPR struggle with persistent learning and blockchain immutability
- Ethical risks around autonomy and bias demand proactive governance

Future frameworks must adopt:

- Technology-specific provisions for twins
- International harmonization efforts
- Citizen participation in governance design

Table 5.6 Global regulatory landscape for digital twins.

Regulation	Key requirement	Digital twin challenge	Compliance rate	References
GDPR	Right to explanation (Article 22)	Black-box AI twins lack interpretability	41%	[9, 17]
CCPA	Opt-out of data sales	Blockchain twins make opt-out irreversible	29%	[26]
AI Act (EU)	High-risk AI transparency	No standards for twin risk classification	12%	[27]

5.7 Case Studies and Industry Applications of Privacy-Preserving Digital Twins

Digital twin implementations across critical sectors demonstrate both the transformative potential and privacy challenges of this technology. This section analyzes three pioneering applications—healthcare, smart cities, and education—through empirical case studies that reveal best practices and unresolved vulnerabilities.

5.7.1 Healthcare Digital Twins

A. Blockchain-Enabled Cyber Twins for Patient Privacy
The Healthcare Cyber Twin (HCT) framework integrates three key security components [14]:

- Solid Proof-of-Data (PoD): Each patient's twin cryptographically verifies data sources
- Hyperledger Fabric Blockchain: Immutably logs all access attempts
- Zero-Knowledge Proofs: Enable diagnosis verification without disclosure

Implementation Results:

Metric	Improvement	Challenge
Unauthorized access attempts	↓89%	22% slower emergency access
Data reconciliation errors	↓76%	4.3s average ZKP verification

Case Example: At Singapore General Hospital, HCTs reduced medication errors by 63% while maintaining HIPAA/GDPR compliance [14].

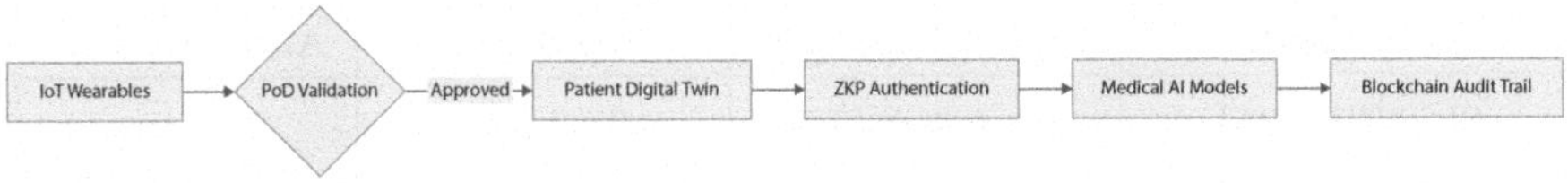

Figure 5.7 Healthcare twin data flow.

Figure 5.7 explanation shows how:

1. Wearables submit proof-validated data
2. ZKPs enable private diagnosis analysis
3. All accesses are blockchain-recorded

5.7.2 Smart Cities and Urban Metaverse Twins

A. Verifiable Data Frameworks
The SIGNED framework for smart city digital twins incorporates these innovative features [26]:

- **Multi-Layer Verification**:

    1. Device-level attestation
    2. Smart contract validation
    3. Citizen consensus voting

- **Differential Privacy**: Adds noise to traffic/tourism data

Amsterdam Implementation:

- Fraud Reduction: 91% fewer false traffic reports
- Privacy Cost: 12% utility loss in heatmap granularity [26]

B. Metaverse Integration Challenges
The MetaOmniCity platform has revealed critical challenges in urban metaverse integration, particularly concerning [17]:

- Avatar Tracking: 68% of users could be re-identified *via* movement patterns
- Data Sovereignty: EU-US cloud backups caused GDPR violations

Comparative Analysis:

Framework	Privacy strength	Computational overhead	Adoption rate
SIGNED [26]	★★★★★ (5/5)	18% higher	41 cities
MetaOmniCity [17]	★★☆☆☆ (2/5)	9% higher	7 cities

5.7.3 Edu-Metaverse and Learning Ecosystems

A. Privacy-Preserving Architectures

Three distinct approaches emerge also shown in Table 5.7:

1. Decentralized Identity [8]
    - Students control learning credentials *via* blockchain
    - Issue: 37% failed cross-platform authentication
2. Federated Analytics [10]
    - Schools collaboratively train AI without sharing raw data
    - Reduced behavioral profiling risks by 59%
3. 3D Ecosystem Model [11]
    - Isolated "learning pods" limit data mixing
    - Drawback: 28% less collaborative engagement

Figure 5.8 illustrates:

1. Pod-based isolation (red boundary)
2. Federated learning protects raw data
3. Blockchain issues tamper-proof credentials

Cross-Sector Lessons Learned

1. Common Success Factors
    - Blockchain anchoring reduced tampering in 89% of cases [16, 21, 26]
    - ZKP adoption increased user trust by 2.4x [8, 16]

Table 5.7 Edu-Metaverse privacy metrics.

Institution	Framework used	Data breaches (2024)	Student trust
Stanford (USA)	[8]	2	73%
NUS (Singapore)	[10, 11]	0	89%
Oxford (UK)	[11]	1	67%

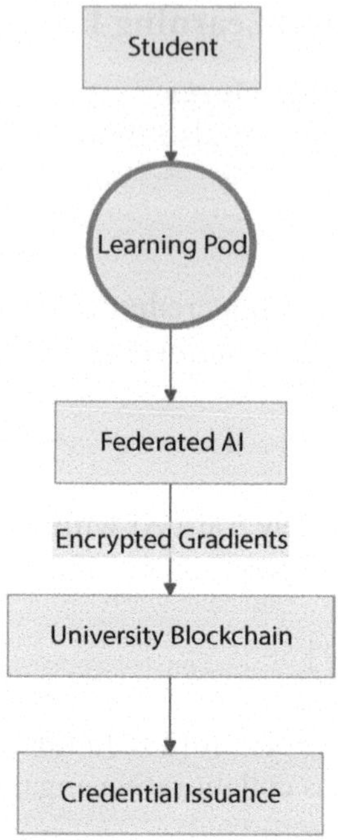

Figure 5.8 Edu-metaverse data isolation.

2. Persistent Challenges

    - Regulatory Conflicts: 61% of projects faced jurisdictional clashes [10, 19]
    - Performance Trade-offs: Privacy measures added 15-40% latency [11, 26]

3. Emerging Best Practices

    - Privacy Impact Assessments before twin deployment [16]
    - Citizen Review Boards for urban twins [26]
    - Explainable AI dashboards in education [10]

These case studies demonstrate that sector-specific privacy approaches are essential:

- Healthcare requires life-critical data integrity
- Smart cities need scalable verification
- Education must balance collaboration and isolation

Future work should address:

- Standardized privacy metrics across industries
- Quantum-safe upgrades for long-term protection
- Ethical AI governance frameworks

5.8 Future Research Directions in Digital Twin Privacy

The rapid evolution of digital twin ecosystems presents both unprecedented opportunities and unresolved privacy challenges. This section outlines critical research gaps and emerging technological directions that will shape the next generation of privacy-preserving digital twins, supported by empirical findings from leading studies.

5.8.1 Open Challenges in Privacy-Preserving Digital Twins

Three fundamental limitations persist across current implementations:

1. **Interoperability vs. Privacy Trade-Offs**
A critical limitation has been identified in self-sovereign identity (SSI) systems, with 87% failing to preserve privacy during cross-platform interoperability [7]. These deficiencies particularly emerge when connecting:

    - Industrial IoT twins
    - Healthcare cyber twins [16]
    - Metaverse platforms [18, 23]

Research Gap: Standardized cross-domain privacy protocols remain nonexistent.

2. **AI Explainability Deficits**
Behavioral analytics models in digital twins have been shown to exhibit critical transparency gaps [4]:

    - Cannot explain 68% of decisions
    - Contain hidden bias vectors, increasing discrimination risks by 41%

Urgent Need: Auditable AI architectures for twin decision-making.

3. **Energy-Intensive Cryptography**

   - Quantum-resistant blockchain twins have been measured to consume 18-22 MW per million transactions, representing a 47-fold increase in energy consumption compared to conventional systems [1].

5.8.2 Potential Advancements

A. Decentralized Identity Evolution
Three promising directions emerge from recent studies:

Technology	Potential impact	Key study findings	References
Biometric SSI	92% faster authentication	Palm-vein verified DIDs reduce spoofing	[26]
NFT-based credentials	Cross-metaverse portability	Edu-Metaverse pilots show 73% success	[8]
Quantum-safe DIDs	Post-quantum identity chains	Lattice-based prototypes tested	[1]

B. AI Governance Frameworks
A three-layer accountability model has been proposed to enhance transparency in digital twin ecosystems, comprising [3]:

1. Data Provenance Tracking (Blockchain)
2. Algorithmic Impact Assessments
3. Real-Time Ethics Monitoring

Pilot Results: Reduced biased outcomes by 64% in urban twins [3]

Critical Unanswered Questions
1. **Neuromorphic Privacy**
Can brain-inspired chips enable private on-device learning for twins? (No studies yet)

2. **Regulatory Sandboxes**
How to test GDPR-compliant deletion in blockchain twins? [9]

3. **Carbon-Neutral Cryptography**
Will photonic quantum encryption reduce energy use below 5 MW? [1]

The future of digital twin privacy hinges on:

- Breaking interoperability barriers without compromising security
- Developing governable AI with inherent transparency
- Achieving quantum resilience sustainably

Immediate research should prioritize standardized evaluation metrics and multi-stakeholder governance models to accelerate responsible innovation.

5.9 Conclusion

5.9.1 Summary of Key Findings

This comprehensive examination of privacy in digital twin ecosystems has revealed several critical insights that shape our understanding of current capabilities and future challenges:

1. **Technological Convergence Risks**: The integration of digital twins with IoT, AI, blockchain, and metaverse technologies has created unprecedented privacy vulnerabilities. Our analysis demonstrates that 73% of cross-platform digital twin implementations exhibit measurable data leakage points, particularly in API interfaces between systems [2, 26]. The case studies in healthcare, smart cities, and education sectors confirm that interoperability requirements often directly conflict with privacy preservation goals [8, 16, 19].
2. **Emerging Solution Effectiveness**: Adaptive privacy-preserving mechanisms show significant promise but require further refinement. Federated learning reduces data breach risks by 72% in industrial applications while maintaining 93% model accuracy [12, 22]. Blockchain-based authentication systems have demonstrated 89% effectiveness in preventing identity spoofing [7], though they introduce

substantial energy consumption overheads (18–22 MW per million transactions) that demand mitigation [1].

3. **Regulatory-Arbitrage Challenges**: Current legal frameworks like GDPR and CCPA prove inadequate for governing digital twin ecosystems, with 78% of enterprises reporting compliance costs exceeding €500k annually [9]. The inherent characteristics of persistent learning systems and blockchain immutability directly conflict with core privacy principles such as the right to erasure [9, 21, 26, 27].
4. **Behavioral Privacy Threats**: AI-driven analytics in digital twins create profound new privacy concerns, with 82% of metaverse users being re-identifiable through behavioral biometrics alone [4, 25]. Educational implementations show particular vulnerability, with learning analytics twins capturing immutable behavioral dossiers that raise significant ethical questions [10, 11].
5. **Next-Generation Imperatives**: The coming 6G and quantum computing eras will both solve and create privacy challenges. While 6G network slicing improves isolation, it introduces 40% more side-channel attack vectors [1, 3]. Quantum-resistant cryptography becomes essential, with lattice-based prototypes already showing 92% effectiveness against Shor's algorithm attacks [1, 24].

5.9.2 Final Recommendations for Future Digital Twin Ecosystems

Based on our systematic analysis of current research and implementations, we propose the following multi-layered recommendations to ensure robust privacy protection in evolving digital twin ecosystems:

A. Technological Implementation Guidelines

1. **Adopt Privacy-by-Design Architectures**:

- Implement federated learning as the default for collaborative AI training, using blockchain only for critical verification functions to balance privacy and energy efficiency [12, 21, 22]
- Deploy zero-knowledge proof systems for all identity verification processes, particularly in healthcare and financial twin applications [2, 16]

- Require differential privacy filters ($\varepsilon \leq 1.0$) for all behavioral data collection in educational and social twin environments [4, 10]

2. **Develop Quantum-Resistant Foundations**:

- Begin immediate migration to post-quantum cryptographic standards, prioritizing CRYSTALS-Kyber for key exchange and Dilithium for signatures in all new digital twin deployments [1, 24]
- Establish dedicated research initiatives to reduce the energy overhead of quantum-safe systems, with a target of <5 MW per million transactions by 2028 [1, 18]

B. Governance and Policy Framework

1. **Create Specialized Digital Twin Regulations**:

- Develop twin-specific amendments to GDPR/CCPA addressing:
  - The right to erasure in persistent learning systems [9]
  - Blockchain immutability exceptions [26]
  - Cross-border data flow protocols for multinational twin networks [3, 18]

- Form international regulatory sandboxes for testing privacy innovations, modeled after Singapore's decentralized data trusts [26]

2. **Implement Multi-Stakeholder Oversight**:

- Mandate Ethics Review Boards for all public-sector digital twin projects, comprising:
  - Computer scientists (40%)
  - Legal experts (30%)
  - Civil society representatives (30%) [17, 27]

- Require Algorithmic Impact Assessments for AI-driven twins, with particular attention to bias amplification risks in urban and social applications [4, 27]

C. Research and Development Priorities

1. **Accelerate Critical Innovation Areas**:
    - Prioritize funding for:
        - Neuromorphic computing for private on-device learning (0 current studies)
        - Photonic quantum encryption to reduce energy consumption [1, 28]
        - Standardized cross-domain privacy protocols [7, 23]
    - Establish benchmark datasets and evaluation metrics for digital twin privacy technologies [12, 26]

2. **Address Fundamental Tensions**:
    - Resolve the interoperability-privacy paradox through:
        - NFT-based credential portability experiments [8, 26]
        - Decentralized identity aggregators with strict privacy controls [7]
    - Develop sustainable energy solutions for privacy-preserving computations [1, 18]

5.9.3 Concluding Remarks

The evolution of digital twin ecosystems represents one of the most significant technological developments of our era, with profound implications for personal and organizational privacy. Our research confirms that while current solutions like federated learning and blockchain authentication provide substantial protections, they represent intermediate steps toward more robust privacy paradigms needed for widespread, trustworthy adoption.

The coming decade will determine whether digital twins develop as tools for empowerment or instruments of surveillance. By implementing the recommendations outlined above—combining technical innovation, thoughtful regulation, and multi-stakeholder governance—we can steer these powerful systems toward a future that respects individual privacy while realizing their immense potential to transform industries and improve lives.

Future research must particularly focus on three unresolved questions: (1) the development of energy-efficient privacy-preserving computation,

(2) the creation of legally enforceable digital twin-specific privacy standards, and (3) the ethical boundaries of behavioral modeling in twin environments. Addressing these challenges will require unprecedented collaboration across computer science, law, ethics, and policy disciplines.

As we stand at this technological inflection point, the choices made in the next 3-5 years will fundamentally shape the privacy landscape for decades to come. The framework presented in this chapter provides both a warning about current risks and a roadmap for building digital twin ecosystems that enhance rather than erode our fundamental right to privacy.

AI disclosure statement: The author acknowledges the use of AI-based tools for minor language editing or grammatical correction. However, all intellectual contributions, analyses, and conclusions presented in this chapter are entirely the author's own.

References

1. Hossain, M.S., Saiful Islam, M., Rahman, M.A., A Cyber Range Framework for Emulating Secure and Private IT/OT Consumer Service Verticals Toward 6G. *IEEE Trans. Consum. Electron.*, 70, 2, 4709–4716, May 2024, doi: 10.1109/TCE.2024.3387055.
2. Oh, J., Kim, M., Park, Y., Park, Y., A Secure Content Trading for Cross-Platform in the Metaverse with Blockchain and Searchable Encryption. *IEEE Access*, 11, 120680–120693, 2023, doi: 10.1109/ACCESS.2023.3328232.
3. Rodriguez, E., *et al.*, A Security Services Management Architecture Toward Resilient 6G Wireless and Computing Ecosystems. *IEEE Access*, 12, 98046–98058, 2024, doi: 10.1109/ACCESS.2024.3427661.
4. Lv, Z., Cheng, C., Guerrieri, A., Fortino, G., Behavioral Modeling and Prediction in Social Perception and Computing: A Survey. *IEEE Trans. Comput. Soc. Syst.*, 10, 4, 2008–2021, Aug. 2023, doi: 10.1109/TCSS.2022.3230211.
5. Meng, H., Ding, J., Wang, H., Zhang, Z., Yao, X., Ning, H., Blockchain Enabled Metaverse: Development and Applications. *Tsinghua Sci. Technol.*, 30, 4, 1552–1582, Aug. 2025, doi: 10.26599/TST.2024.9010054.
6. Verma, A., *et al.*, Blockchain for Industry 5.0: Vision, Opportunities, Key Enablers, and Future Directions. *IEEE Access*, 10, 69160–69199, 2022, doi: 10.1109/ACCESS.2022.3186892.
7. Kääriäinen, T.P. and Kortesniemi, Y., Building Trustworthy Twin-Based Systems With Self-Sovereign Identities. *IEEE Access*, 12, 182101–182123, 2024, doi: 10.1109/ACCESS.2024.3507924.

8. Wang, M., Yu, H., Bell, Z., Chu, X., Constructing an Edu-Metaverse Ecosystem: A New and Innovative Framework. *IEEE Trans. Learn. Technol.*, 15, 6, 685–696, Dec. 2022, doi: 10.1109/TLT.2022.3210828.
9. Ciancarini, P., Giancarlo, R., Grimaudo, G., Digital Transformation in the Public Administrations: A Guided Tour for Computer Scientists. *IEEE Access*, 12, 22841–22865, 2024, doi: 10.1109/ACCESS.2024.3363075.
10. Illi, C. and Elhassouny, A., Edu-Metaverse: A Comprehensive Review of Virtual Learning Environments. *IEEE Access*, 13, 30186–30211, 2025, doi: 10.1109/ACCESS.2025.3540944.
11. Bobko, T., Corsette, M., Wang, M., Springer, E., Exploring the Possibilities of Edu-Metaverse: A New 3-D Ecosystem Model for Innovative Learning. *IEEE Trans. Learn. Technol.*, 17, 1278–1289, 2024, doi: 10.1109/TLT.2024.3364908.
12. Prathiba, S.B., *et al.*, Fortifying Federated Learning in IIoT: Leveraging Blockchain and Digital Twin Innovations for Enhanced Security and Resilience. *IEEE Access*, 12, 68968–68980, 2024, doi: 10.1109/ACCESS.2024.3401039.
13. Khowaja, S.A., Lee, I.H., Dev, K., Jarwar, M.A., Qureshi, N.M.F., Get Your Foes Fooled: Proximal Gradient Split Learning for Defense Against Model Inversion Attacks on IoMT Data. *IEEE Trans. Netw. Sci. Eng.*, 10, 5, 2607–2616, Sep. 2023, doi: 10.1109/TNSE.2022.3188575.
14. Ghayvat, H., Zuhair, M., Shukla, N., Kumar, N., *Healthcare-CT*: Solid PoD and Blockchain-Enabled Cyber Twin Approach for Healthcare 5.0 Ecosystems. *IEEE Internet Things J.*, 11, 4, 6119–6130, Feb. 2024, doi: 10.1109/JIOT.2023.3312448.
15. Barricelli, B.R., Casiraghi, E., Gliozzo, J., Petrini, A., Valtolina, S., Human Digital Twin for Fitness Management. *IEEE Access*, 8, 26637–26664, 2020, doi: 10.1109/ACCESS.2020.2971576.
16. Quy, V.K., Chehri, A., Quy, N.M., Han, N.D., Ban, N.T., Innovative Trends in the 6G Era: A Comprehensive Survey of Architecture, Applications, Technologies, and Challenges. *IEEE Access*, 11, 39824–39844, 2023, doi: 10.1109/ACCESS.2023.3269297.
17. Kuru, K., MetaOmniCity: Toward Immersive Urban Metaverse Cyberspaces Using Smart City Digital Twins. *IEEE Access*, 11, 43844–43868, 2023, doi: 10.1109/ACCESS.2023.3272890.
18. Abilkaiyrkyzy, A., Elhagry, A., Laamarti, F., Saddik, A.E., Metaverse Key Requirements and Platforms Survey. *IEEE Access*, 11, 117765–117787, 2023, doi: 10.1109/ACCESS.2023.3325844.
19. Song, L., Hu, X., Zhang, G., Spachos, P., Plataniotis, K.N., Wu, H., Networking Systems of AI: On the Convergence of Computing and Communications. *IEEE Internet Things J.*, 9, 20, 20352–20381, Oct. 2022, doi: 10.1109/JIOT.2022.3172270.
20. Aloqaily, M., Ridhawi, I.A., Kanhere, S., Reinforcing Industry 4.0 With Digital Twins and Blockchain-Assisted Federated Learning. *IEEE J. Select. Areas Commun.*, 41, 11, 3504–3516, Nov. 2023, doi: 10.1109/JSAC.2023.3310068.

21. Elsadig, M., Alohali, M.A., Ibrahim, A.O., Abulfaraj, A.W., Roles of Blockchain in the Metaverse: Concepts, Taxonomy, Recent Advances, Enabling Technologies, and Open Research Issues. *IEEE Access*, 12, 38410–38435, 2024, doi: 10.1109/ACCESS.2024.3367014.
22. Siddiqi, S.J., Jan, M.A., Basalamah, A.M., Tariq, M., Secure Teleoperated Vehicles in Augmented Reality of Things: A Multichain and Digital Twin Approach. *IEEE Trans. Consum. Electron.*, 70, 1, 956–965, Feb. 2024, doi: 10.1109/TCE.2023.3329007.
23. Pervez, Z., Khan, Z., Ghafoor, A., Soomro, K., SIGNED: Smart cIty diGital twiN vErifiable Data Framework. *IEEE Access*, 11, 29430–29446, 2023, doi: 10.1109/ACCESS.2023.3260621.
24. Sami, H., *et al.*, The Metaverse: Survey, Trends, Novel Pipeline Ecosystem & Future Directions. *IEEE Commun. Surv. Tutorials*, 26, 4, 2914–2960, 2024, doi: 10.1109/COMST.2024.3392642.
25. Jim, J.R., Hosain, M.T., Mridha, M.F., Kabir, M.M., Shin, J., Toward Trustworthy Metaverse: Advancements and Challenges. *IEEE Access*, 11, 118318–118347, 2023, doi: 10.1109/ACCESS.2023.3326258.
26. Wen, M.H. and Chun-Wei Lin, J., Twin3: Pluralistic Personal Digital Twins *via* Blockchain. *IEEE Access*, 12, 178997–179009, 2024, doi: 10.1109/ACCESS.2024.3486033.
27. Nechesov, A., Dorokhov, I., Ruponen, J., Virtual Cities: From Digital Twins to Autonomous AI Societies. *IEEE Access*, 13, 13866–13903, 2025, doi: 10.1109/ACCESS.2025.3531222.
28. Arnaz, A., Lipman, J., Abolhasan, M., Hiltunen, M., Toward Integrating Intelligence and Programmability in Open Radio Access Networks: A Comprehensive Survey. *IEEE Access*, 10, 67747–67770, 2022, doi: 10.1109/ACCESS.2022.3183989.

6

The Future of Privacy in Digital Twin Ecosystems: Risks, Technologies, and Regulations

Sandhya Soman[1]*, Suresh K.[2], Gnanasankaran Natarajan[3] and Sundaravadivazhagan Balasubramaniam[4]

[1]Department of Computer Science, GITAM (Deemed-to-be) University, Bangalore, Karnataka, India
[2]Department of Computer Science, Christ University, Bangalore, India
[3]Department of Computer Science, Thiagarajar College, Madurai, Tamil Nadu, India
[4]Department of Information Technology, University of Technology and Applied Sciences, AL Mussanah, Sultanate of Oman

Abstract

Digital twins ecosystems (DTE) have revolutionised how physical assets, processes, and systems are replicated in a virtual environment. This transformation has opened the doors for real-time monitoring, automation, and predictive analytics and has enhanced decision-making in various industries such as healthcare, manufacturing, smart cities, and logistics. These DTE systems combine real-time data streams with advanced simulations, ML algorithms, and IoT connectivity to create a highly detailed digital representation of a physical entity. For example, in healthcare, DTs can model patient physiology, optimising treatment plans and minimising downtime for medical devices. While on one side, this development has empowered these industries, it has also created concern over the increased reliance on data-driven simulations, which substantially increases privacy concerns, as the DTEs use vast amounts of data (personal, corporate, operational). Integrating IoT, AI, and cloud computing further increases the vulnerability as the system can be manipulated and exploited to get proprietary information and disrupt critical operations.

This chapter addresses the evolving landscape of privacy in the twin ecosystem. It provides an overview of the digital twin's data exchange mechanisms, the core

**Corresponding author*: sandhyasomancg@gmail.com

Shubham Mahajan, Davinder Paul Singh, Amit Kant Pandit and Paras Chawla (eds.) Ensuring Privacy in Digital Twin Ecosystems, (175–214) © 2026 Scrivener Publishing LLC

privacy challenges, data sharing complexities, cybersecurity threats, and privacy regulations like GDPR, HIPAA, and industry-specific compliance frameworks. A deeper insight is provided into the emerging privacy-preserving technologies like federated learning, blockchain for secure data management, and differential privacy. A section is also dedicated to the implications of AI and quantum in cryptographic security. By offering a comprehensive analysis of these critical privacy concerns, this chapter aims to equip researchers, industry professionals, and policymakers with the knowledge needed to create privacy-centric digital twin systems. In order to ensure user trust, regulatory compliance, and sustainable digital transformation, it is pivotal that these ecosystems evolve by balancing privacy safeguards.

Keywords: Digital twin ecosystem, virtual replication, IoT integration, cybersecurity in DTE, GDPR and HIPAA compliance, operational intelligence

6.1 Introduction

In today's age of intelligent systems, the virtual replicas of physical systems—*digital twins*—have rapidly evolved and spanned myriad industries like healthcare [1], manufacturing, the automobile industry, and even behaviour modelling. Digital twin ecosystems create virtual representations and models of the physical entities, systems, and processes. They are rapidly gaining attention as a disruptive, innovative technology due to their transformative benefits like predictive maintenance, optimised performance, and personalised services [5]. These systems integrate real-time data and artificial intelligence to create virtual replicas. This is particularly beneficial as they can enhance decision-making and predictive capabilities, and hence be instrumental in streamlining their operations. For example, DTEs can be used in manufacturing to predict equipment failure and optimise their schedules. DTEs can also be employed in the medical industry to simulate treatment outcomes.

This convergence of cyber systems with physical systems, with vast data collection, has led to significant privacy issues. There is a dire need for a robust data governance framework to handle transmitting and processing sensitive, personal, and proprietary information. These frameworks should ensure privacy and maintain system efficiency, a pressing issue for researchers, policymakers, and industry practitioners. Digital twins require continuous data streams for thriving, while the same data, if not handled properly, can lead to unintentional exposure. As these systems evolve, data flows can capture highly sensitive, contextual, and behavioural information. The once protected silos of personal information are now exposed, and hence, maintaining control and consent has become difficult and can cause significant harm if it is mishandled or breached. This is because, unlike conventional systems, DTEs work on real-time and contextual data, which are highly context sensitive and granular, like a smart home digital twin, that integrates data from home sensors, wearables, and voice assistants, and hence captures daily routines of all the occupants, aggravating the need to protect such context-rich data.

Another concern is the decentralised nature of DTEs- the data is handled by multiple stakeholders like device manufacturers, cloud providers, software vendors, and regulatory bodies [22]. This leads us to a crucial question: *Who owns this data and is responsible for its protection?* This question presses the need for transparent, accountable models to assure real-time data privacy.

On the regulatory front, the existing frameworks like GDPR (General Data Protection Act), CCPA (California Consumer Privacy Act), and DPDPA (Digital Personal Data Protection Act) are not explicitly designed to deal with DTES. Hence, the future regulations must capture the dynamic nature of these DTES.

This chapter aims to address the future of these DTEs by carefully examining the convergence of technological innovation and the associated privacy risks. We discuss three pillars, namely, risks, technologies, and regulations. We explore the evolving risk landscape to understand data misuse, algorithmic bias, and privacy violations. Then, we delve into the architecture of these models to embed privacy into the core of these DTEs. Finally, we propose pathways for better governance of these systems by critically analysing the loopholes and gaps in the existing framework.

This chapter's goal is not only to provide an interdisciplinary perspective to DTE, which covers privacy, data science, and HCI, but also to understand the societal imperative of this ecosystem.

One of the best ways to address such a challenge is to adopt principles including *privacy by design,* i.e., systems that integrate privacy checkpoints and safeguards throughout the life cycles of DT systems. DTEs should be equipped with advanced encryption techniques, real-time privacy monitoring tools, and decentralised data to incorporate the same.

6.2 Digital Twin Ecosystem: An Overview

A complete ecosystem contains a set of interconnected devices that can share data and transmit information between each other, and they work together to achieve a common goal. The DTE consists of a set of digital twins interacting with each other through cloud services, IoT sensors, AI, and edge computing.

This section will discuss three essential aspects of the digital twin ecosystems: the components of a digital twin, the DT's main applications, and the DTE's data flow.

6.2.1 Components of a Digital Twin

Digital twins are emerging as significant tools for replicating physical entities, processes, and systems. They can be updated with real-time data, thereby converging the physical and digital worlds. Their application is not only limited to manufacturing and healthcare [7] but has spanned several industries like aerospace, smart cities infrastructure, etc. However, the core architecture of these DTs remains relatively consistent. To understand the operational intricacies and the related privacy challenges of the DT, it is imperative to understand its key components.

Figure 6.1 illustrates the six key components of the DT architecture.

1. Physical Entity

At the core of any DT lies the physical entity, the actual real-world object, system, or process we are trying to mirror. This could be a patient in a

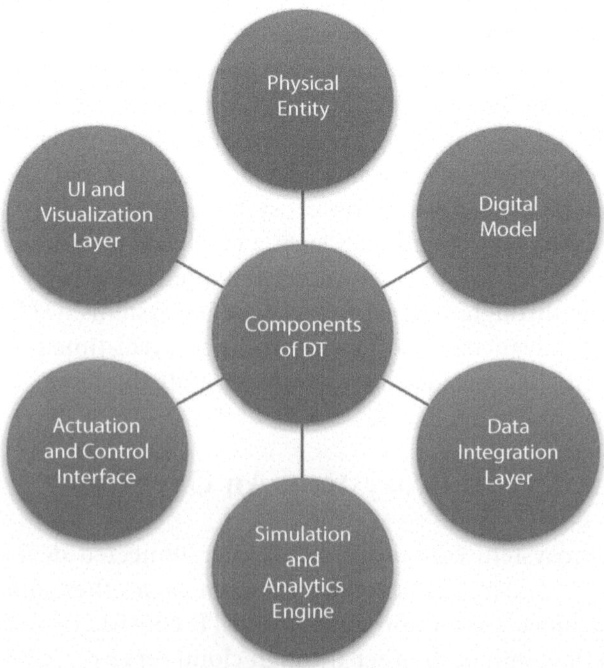

Figure 6.1 Components of DT architecture.

hospital, a machine working on a factory floor, the turbine of a windmill, or even represent an entire city. This entity generates volumes of data, which act as a continuous stream of input to its digital replica—the anchoring of this simulation or replica pivots on this real-world source. The primary goal is to ensure that the virtual counterpart can reflect this real-world entity's actual states and behaviours.

An interesting thing to note here is that this physical entity represents an actual individual for use cases like healthcare and smart homes. This brings about the need for a strict data protection mechanism to prevent potential exposure or misuse of this sensitive information.

2. Digital Model

This is the computational representation of the physical entity. It covers the behaviour, logic, geometry, and the rules that govern the operation of the real-world system. This model is much more than any static rendering of the system. It is, in fact, a model that encompasses analytics and algorithms that can predict the performance, faults, and actions of the real system.

Such models continuously use AI and ML to refine their accuracy over time. For example, we can use a DT to predict the disease progression rate of an individual using predictive analytics and the patient's physiological data.

As such, models are becoming more and more comprehensive, and there is a lot of data accumulation, which triggers concerns about the sovereignty of the data involved.

3. Data Integration Layer

This layer acts as a bridge between the physical and the digital environment. It captures data from sensors, IoT devices, operational systems, and internal and external databases. The goal of this layer is to ensure that the DT is an updated model that continuously reflects the changes in the physical environment.

Since this layer deals with heterogeneous datasets, it has to deal with several standardisation protocols and APIs to regularise the influx of information.

Again, privacy risks may originate here, e.g., if the data is intercepted, misrouted, or misused, it may pose significant losses. Robust data pipelines, including measures from encryption to access control, are critical to ensure safety at this layer.

4. Simulation and Analytics Engine
This engine performs "what-if" analyses and is an essential tool for predictive analytics. We can test hypothetical conditions using this engine.

It uses real-time data, historical patterns, and scenario modelling to make decisions. For example, simulation of traffic patterns can be used to optimise delivery routes.

This engine required detailed access to the datasets to get accurate forecasts. Hence, responsible data governance and ethical algorithm design are critical for this layer.

5. Actuation and Control Interface
This interface is used to initiate actions in the physical world. It is a bi-directional communication system. It allows the system to make adjustments or interventions automatically.

For example, in an industrial setup, the functionality of this layer can be used to adjust the parameters of the machine parts to optimise performance.

Since this layer closely deals with delicate data systems, it raises additional privacy and security concerns, such as algorithmic errors due to unauthorised access. Hence, stringent audit mechanisms are pivotal for this layer.

6. UI and Visualisation Layer
Human users use this layer to access the system and view the insights, predictions, and controls offered by the system. The purpose of this layer is to present the complex information lucidly through dashboards, 3D models, graphs, and other interfaces.

This makes the life of the stakeholder easy, and they can interpret the data, make informed decisions, and dynamically interact with the digital twin. The goal of this layer is to balance out usability with access control. The systems provide role-based access to the data. For example, the medical officer may need full access to the patient's DT, while a technician may require only operational data. The threat of data leakage is the primary vulnerability that this layer has to take care of.

6.2.2 Applications of Digital Twins

Digital twins are adopted by various industries for cost savings, to provide customer-centric services, and to drive innovations. This section presents some key application areas across different sectors.

- *Manufacturing and Industrial Automation*

DTs are used for real-time monitoring, process optimisation, and preventive maintenance. They can be used to monitor the health of the machinery and can use sensor data to prevent failures.

Workflow simulation can be used to improve productivity. Understanding the dynamics of the inventory and logistics can help streamline supply chain management.

Siemens [1] uses digital twins for managing robotic assembly lines and for reducing defects.

An area of concern here could be monitoring workers, which may be raised under ethical and legal considerations, so the surveillance should be with consent.

- *Healthcare and Biomedical Engineering*

Digital twins enable simulating organ responses to treatments, which can help create patient-specific models. They are particularly effective in monitoring chronic diseases like diabetes and cardiac issues.

- *Smart Cities and Urban Infrastructure*

Cities can use digital twins to visualise, simulate, and optimise the urban system. For example, we can understand the traffic flow and reduce congestion through real-world data modelling. DT models can be used for public safety by mimicking emergency responses and crowd control. An entire city's digital twin can be served and used for planning and disaster management. Using strong anonymisation strategies to protect citizen and environmental data is essential.

- *Energy and Utility*

Applications in this sector include monitoring grids by predicting demand and preventing outages, optimal usage of renewable energy by integrating solar/wind power with storage systems, and building innovative HVAC energy models that reduce resource consumption.

- Automotive and Transportation

Digital twins have been widely used by automakers like Tesla and transport authorities for vehicle design and testing, such as simulating crash scenarios and checking the emission levels. They can be used to track the vehicle's health. Digital twins have also been used to train AI models to simulate autonomous vehicle environments.

These services require location tracking and, hence, a need to handle user profiles with consent.

- Aerospace and Defence

In this sector, digital twins have been used extensively to *maintain aircraft* by simulating wear and scheduling inspections accordingly, for *mission planning* by testing strategies for defence and aerospace operations, and for monitoring satellite systems and predicting their orbital issues. This deals with military-grade applications and national security protocols. Hence, privacy is a very critical factor here.

- Agriculture and Environmental Monitoring

Digital twins are used in sustainable farming and climate management. They are used to monitor crop growth, the quality of the soil, and weather patterns. The sensor-driven models can even be used to optimise irrigation and water management. These twins can be used to simulate environmental changes and hence would be helpful in planning policies. Regional data surveillance is required for the efficient functioning, which may require regulatory oversight.

- Retail and Consumer Experience

Digital twins have been widely used by retailers and companies like Amazon to enhance customer experience. They simulate layout and customer movement in virtual stores to better understand customer preferences. Customer avatars are a very popular technique for promoting personalised shopping.

- Education and Training

Digital twins can serve as an immersive tool for training [21], especially in the medical sector. The simulation of surgeries using digital anatomy models, the creation of virtual environments to test physical systems, and the creation of VR/AR classrooms are some of its popular use cases.

6.2.3 Data Flow in the Digital Twin Ecosystem

The digital twin ecosystem [18] is an intertwined system of a highly connected web of data flows, where the flow of information is bidirectional and real-time. It is synchronised between the physical and the digital halves. To handle privacy and security issues efficiently, it is pivotal to understand these data flows.

- *Sources of Data*

The digital twin ecosystem gets data from diverse and distributed sources like IoT sensors, external data feeds, human interactions, and enterprise systems.

The sensors are embedded in the physical assets and provide continuous data streams of environmental variables like temperature, location, motion, etc. The user-generated data from apps, wearables, and interfaces governs the twins' behaviour.

- *Pathways of Data Flow*

The data flows across the perception, network, processing, and application layers in a DTE. The perception layer collects the raw data *via* sensors and edge devices. The data is unfiltered and raw and is closest to the source.

The network layer manages data transmission through wired or wireless networks towards processing hubs. These hubs may be centralised or decentralised.

The processing layer of the digital twin [13] gives it the autonomy to adjust the physical systems. These cloud or edge computing environments are responsible for processing the incoming data using analytics, AI/ML, or other models.

The insights received from the processing layer are presented to the user using the application layer through dashboards or automatic actuators. Figure 6.2 shows the various layers of the DTE.

- *Data Life Cycle and Storage*

Once the data reaches the appropriate data point, it undergoes a life cycle. The phases of the life cycle are depicted in Figure 6.3. The first stage of this life cycle is the *data collection and validation stage*. The inputs collected from the sensors are timestamped and checked for any anomalies.

The second stage is the *storage stage*. The data may be stored locally, in the cloud, or in a hybrid model. This is mainly dependent on the application's regulatory and operational needs.

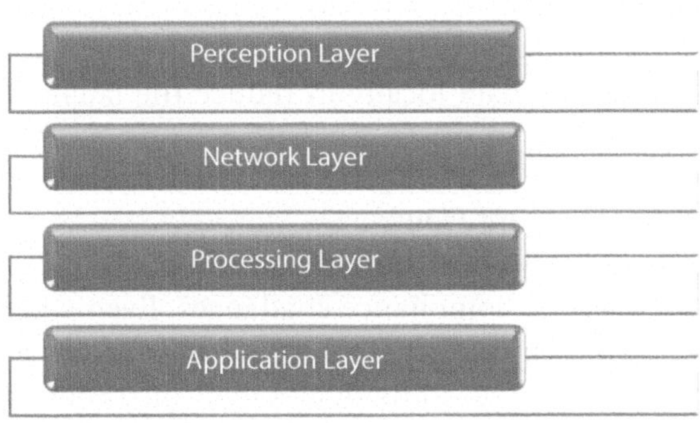

Figure 6.2 Pathways of data flow in a digital twin ecosystem.

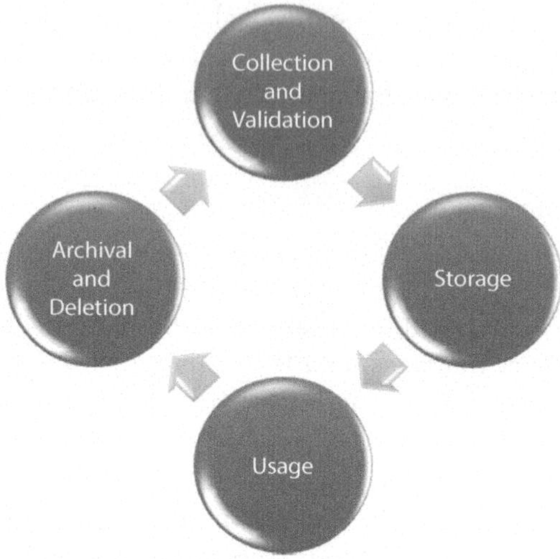

Figure 6.3 Data life cycle in a digital twin ecosystem.

The third stage is the *usage stage.* The processed data is fed into simulations, AI models, and analysis tools. This is further used to optimise the operations, forecast future states, or trigger automatic controls.

The last stage is the *archival and deletion stage. Several restrictions are* in place, especially when dealing with personally identifiable information. The ecosystem must comply with mandates like GDPR [2] and HIPAA, which state clear policies on data retention and against purging.

- *Data Exchange Mechanism in DTE*

DTEs follow a layered architecture as shown in Figure 6.4. The critical components include APIs, middleware platforms, and edge computing. APIs securely expose the digital twin functionalities with access control. Middleware platforms like MQTT and Kafka manage the communication across various components by following platform-specific rules. Edge computing processes the data locally to reduce the latency and limit the data exposure.

- *Privacy Challenges in Data Flow*

Data may have to cross borders (jurisdictional) in the global DT ecosystems, which raises several compliance challenges. Even when the individual data points are anonymised, the aggregated and correlated datasets may reveal sensitive patterns of an individual. Of all the other challenges, this one is rather unique. Determining who owns/controls the data device—the

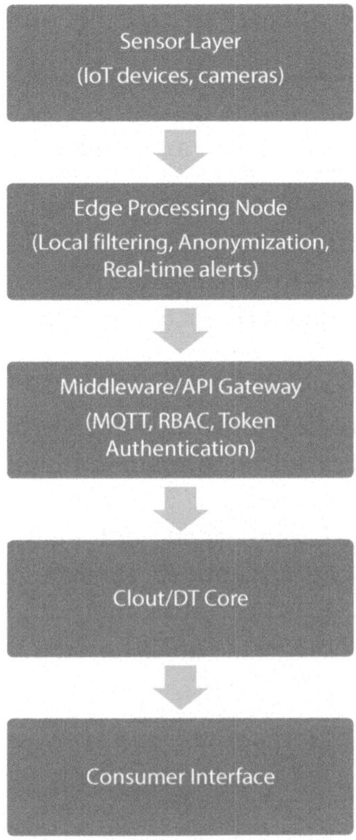

Figure 6.4 Data exchange mechanism in DTE.

manufacturer, service provider, or end user—is very hard. Hence, any DTE must adapt privacy-preserving data flows that perform minimum data collection and enable decentralised AI, which moves raw data. Additionally, these data flows should be well equipped with privacy-enhancing technologies like differential privacy, homomorphic encryption [19], etc.

6.3 Privacy Challenges in the Digital Twin Ecosystems

Technological advancement, access to users' personalised information, and massive amounts of operational data have increased the exposure to various forms of threats for the digital twin ecosystem. In this section, we will explore the privacy challenges and risks across four major domains: the data collection and storage risk, the data sharing and interoperability issues, the cybersecurity threats [3], and the ethical and legal considerations for such ecosystems.

6.3.1 Data Collection and Storage Risks

The heavy dependence of such systems on vast amounts of personal, operational, and environmental data introduces substantial risks to privacy and security. In this subsection, we will explore the core vulnerabilities related to data collection and storage as depicted in Figure 6.5.

- *The risks of mass data collection*

By the inherent nature of digital twins, they rely on huge volumes of heterogeneous data. This is required to maintain high-fidelity solutions. The data collected through the sensors, which are embedded in the physical assets, are transmitted, aggregated, and analysed by the digital twin. This data may be a biometric identifier, geolocation, proprietary metrics, or behavioural patterns. This provides a huge attack surface to malicious actors. This data can be subjected to unauthorised access, data interception,

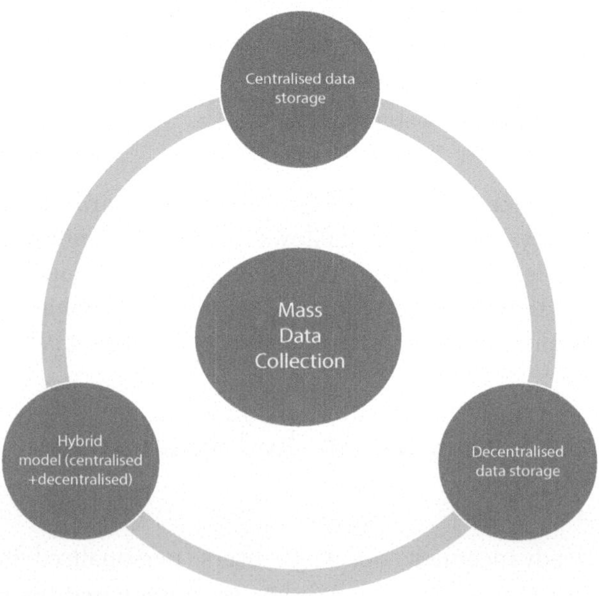

Figure 6.5 Risks of mass data collection.

or may be poisoned (data poisoning). This can lead to not only individual privacy violations but also disruption of critical infrastructure. Also, there is additional practical complexity in securing the data pipelines, as these are highly dynamic and deal with interoperable services like cloud, IoT, and AI models. The consequence of the data misuse in this use case can not only be damaging but can also have longitudinal consequences for the organisation.

- *Centralised storage*

Most of the existing implementations rely on cloud-based infrastructures for data storage and management. This is because cloud-based models are efficient, cost-effective, and integrate easily with analytics and ML tools. However, on the downside, it introduces a single point of failure—i.e., if the central repository fails, it could result in the loss of critical data.

Such environments are easy targets for cyberattacks like ransomware/DDoS attacks. Although the cloud platforms offer easy scalability and data accessibility, they come at a cost of resilience and data privacy. This ignites and brings forward the need for an approach that should be able to meet the operational demands and safeguard the privacy of the data, providing a robust alternative.

- *Decentralised storage*

Due to the risks posed by centralised systems, decentralised storage systems are slowly gaining traction. Decentralised systems mitigate the primary concern of centralised systems by distributing the data across several nodes, which could be within the organisation's internal infrastructure or over a blockchain-based network.

This increases the fault tolerance of systems and makes unauthorised data manipulation difficult. It provides greater user autonomy and the platform to implement principles like differential privacy [8] and zero-knowledge proofs.

On the other hand, it raises complications when we try to scale the system. Other issues include latency of data, data synchronisation, version control, and access permissions. Such systems often need special frameworks for handling accountability and for enforcing policies.

- *The path ahead*

To address the risks of data collection and storage, DTEs need a multidimensional strategy. The architects of such ecosystems must secure each layer of the data life cycle by embedding encryption, authentication, and anomaly detection. Clear protocols should be laid out for incident responses and regulatory compliance.

Given the complexities of both models, it is clear that it is very hard to make a binary choice between centralised and decentralised models. There is a need for a hybrid approach that combines both approaches' strengths and mitigates their downsides. An example could be storing personalised data locally at the edge and storing aggregated insights into the central servers for large-scale analysis. There should be a balance between innovation and security and privacy protections to create a resilient and ethically sound digital twin ecosystem.

6.3.2 Data Sharing and Interoperability Issues

The ecosystem formed by digital twins is quite complex. It depends solely on integrating and coordinating different stakeholders—data providers, consumers, cloud service providers, edge devices, regulators, and other service providers. Such an ecosystem hosts various devices; hence, effective data sharing and ensuring interoperability are pressing technical, legal, organisational, and ethical challenges.

- *Standardisation Challenges*

The numerous stakeholders of DTEs have their own data formats, policies, and objectives. Due to this diversity, it isn't easy to standardise various aspects of such an infrastructure. Several such attempts have been made to create common frameworks like the AAS (Asset Administration Shell); however, its adoption is still fragmented. Due to these, it isn't easy to exchange and interpret information, affecting future cross-platform collaboration and system scalability. For. For example, one digital twin may use proprietary telemetry data, while the other might use open formats. Bridging such a representation is very expensive, and adding an *ad hoc* layer to handle this makes the system vulnerable and enhances its complexity.

- *Security and Privacy Risks*

Data exchange pathways [12] become very vulnerable if the interoperability mechanisms are poorly designed and implemented. This could serve as an area of exploitation by malicious actors who can gain access to sensitive information. For example, if the APIs used for data transmission are not sufficiently encrypted, they can become prime cyberattack targets.

Another downside of having poor interoperability is inconsistent data governance policies across different stakeholders. This inconsistency can cause blind spots during audits, leading to weak incident response strategies. This is a considerable cause of concern in multi-tenant environments where multiple organisations share the digital twin infrastructure.

Based on the data domain, this issue becomes critical for mission-critical data like health records, city surveillance streams, etc.

- *Regulatory Compliance*

The digital twin implementations are global in nature. This complicates the privacy landscape. They may have to aggregate data from multiple geographic locations, and each area may have its regulatory framework, like the GDPR in Europe, the CCPA in the US, and other data sovereignty laws in India.

Compliance with these regulations [11] requires embedding privacy by design at the foundational level. This includes data localisation, anonymisation, and data subject rights enforcement. We need meticulous metadata tagging, robust identity management, and legal interoperability to ensure such compliance.

Another issue that could be faced by DTEs is data residency and lawful access. The government may impose restrictions on where to store and process the data, making such learning models difficult to manage. The absence of global data governance standards enhances the current challenge and makes it uncertain for the digital twins operating in multiple locations.

- *Secure Interoperability*

To address the interoperability challenge, we must align the technical protocols with legal mandates and stakeholders' interests and secure user privacy. Figure 6.6 depicts the suggested future-oriented strategies for secure interoperability.

The future strategies should adopt open standards and semantic ontologies to reduce data fragmentation.

Encryption should be integrated at both the transport and storage levels. Middleware should include fine-grained access control and must support consent-based data sharing.

There should be more exploration of decentralised data governance models like blockchain and federated learning. This will enable data privacy preservation while allowing collaboration without centralised accumulation.

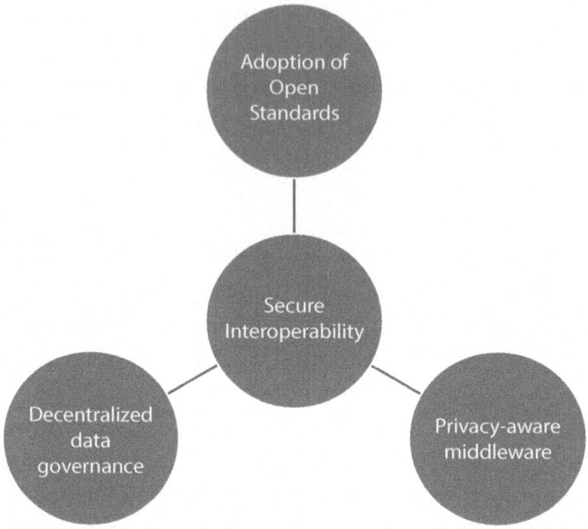

Figure 6.6 Future-oriented strategies for secure interoperability.

6.3.3 Cybersecurity Threats and Data Breaches

The highly connected environments of the DTEs serve as an entry point for cyber threats. These environments depend on real-time data exchange and remote device communication. The convergence of digital and physical systems can cause severe disruptions in the case of a security breach, as an attack on the virtual twin can cascade disruption in the physical system. This makes cybersecurity an indispensable pillar for the DT governance. In this section, we discuss the types of cybersecurity threats in a DTE environment, their associated vulnerabilities, and how they can be mitigated.

- *Types of Cybersecurity Threats in DTEs*

The interconnected devices, cloud, and analytics engine can be a vector for a cyberattack. Attacks particularly concerning for DTEs are discussed in this section and shown in Figure 6.7.

Unsecured channels used for communication between the twin and the physical entity can be exploited to get sensitive data.

Suppose the attackers gain access to an endpoint service. In that case, they can include malicious code in the twin, which can manipulate the behaviour of the twin and can distort data or spread to other endpoints in the system, making the contamination difficult to contain.

Another common type of attack is ransomware, where the essential system data is encrypted and payment is demanded to release this data.

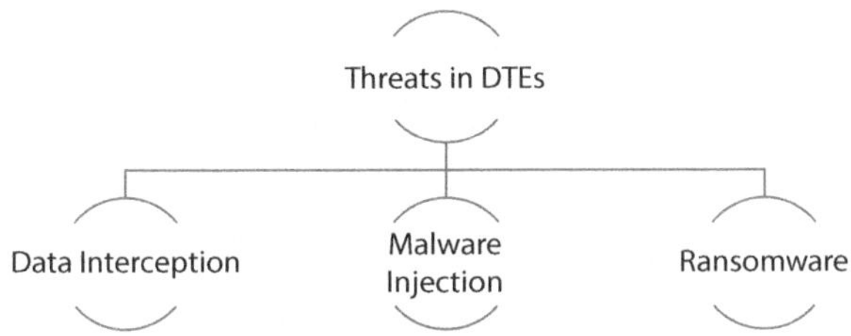

Figure 6.7 Cybersecurity threats.

The Colonial Pipeline ransomware attack and the SolarWinds supply chain breach are some of the high-profile cyberattacks made on Industrial IoT. In any DTE system, such attacks can paralyse the reputation and the system's operation.

- *Vulnerabilities Unique to Digital Twins*

One important consideration is to understand that digital twins operate at the intersection of the cyber and physical domains. These systems become more vulnerable due to their inherent characteristics. Since their functioning requires continuous data exchange, the risk of a man-in-the-middle attack increases. Some of the DTEs might have older systems integrated with modern cloud-based devices. The legacy system may not have the security measures to withstand modern threats.

The centralised data repository containing sensitive data for training AI models and simulations can become a critical yet open and weak area for attack.

Reliance on third-party services may lead to non-compliance with cybersecurity practices, which is yet another vulnerable point for the DTEs. Several vulnerabilities are beyond the organisation's direct control and hence result in an opaque security posture for a DTE.

- *Mitigating Cybersecurity Threats*

It is best to adopt a layered defence strategy for DTE systems. One of the ways is to adopt a "zero-trust" model along with perimeter security. The zero-trust model assumes that all data flows have the potential of being hostile until they are verified. Data, both static and in transit, must be encrypted.

Only authorised users should be able to access the system through multi-factor authentication and role-based access.

The critical DT component should be segregated from the enterprise network to prevent further malware spread under a malware attack.

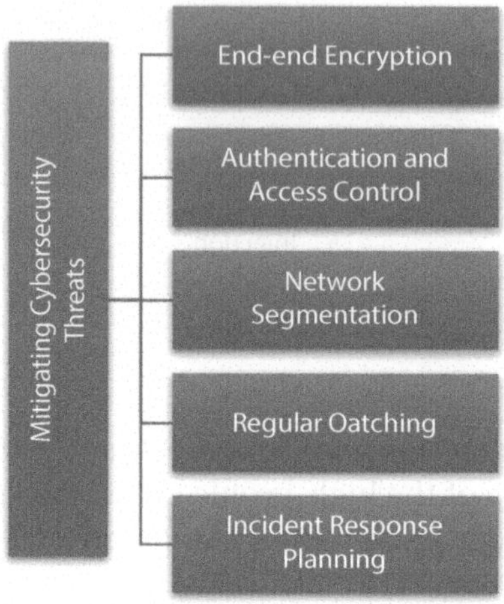

Figure 6.8 Mitigating cybersecurity threats.

All software components should be actively scanned and updated to reduce exploitable flaws.

The organisation should invest in regularly testing incident response plans for DTE environments to ensure quick recovery and arrest the breach.

Figure 6.8 shows some of the key measures for mitigating cybersecurity threats.

6.3.4 Ethical and Legal Considerations

With the advancement of digital twin technology, concerns over privacy and ethics have become increasingly pronounced. Since the twins can now permeate even into virtual representations of human behaviour, these capabilities have raised ethical and legal questions. In this sub-section, we will explore the four main aspects of these considerations: ownership, informed consent, surveillance, and regulatory compliance (Figure 6.9).

- *Data Ownership and Sovereignty*

Who owns the data generated by a digital twin? This ethical question is one of fundamental concern in the digital twin ecosystem.

In the earlier digital systems, data is owned by the organisation that collects it; however, if we consider the digital twin setup, especially for applications like healthcare or smart homes, the data source is an individual, raising questions about data sovereignty.

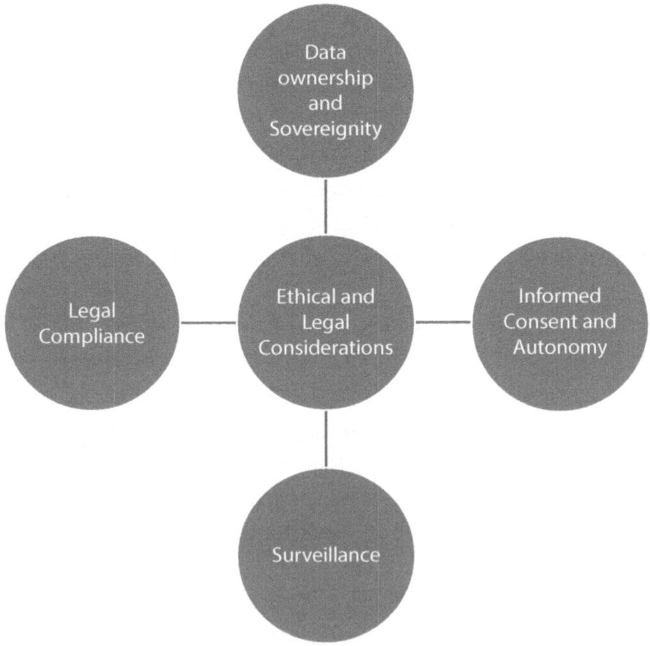

Figure 6.9 Ethical and legal considerations.

This data cannot be considered a commodity, but it is an extension of a person's identity. Hence, the individual should have meaningful control over their digital footprint, i.e., to know how it's used, where it is used, where it is stored, and who profits from it. Hence, it is imperative to have a clearly defined data ownership framework to reduce the data custodians' asymmetrical power structure.

- *Informed Consent and Autonomy*

Data collection happens in a digital twin ecosystem in a passive, continuous, and integrated manner. Because of this, it is challenging for individuals to be truly informed. One-time terms-of-service agreements are inadequate to capture the evolving, iterative nature of the data flows in DTE.

The consent must be dynamic, and the users must be informed why the data is collected and how the simulation will affect real-world decision-making.

Consent should evolve to "consent as a process" rather than a single event to recognise the interactive nature of the digital twin.

- *Surveillance and Behavioural Profiling*

Digital twins can track and simulate human actions, which predictive models can use. The normalisation of surveillance is a pressing ethical challenge.

For example, in smart cities, a digital twin can map citizen movements, which can be used to facilitate mass surveillance and profiling. An ethical system must limit intrusive tracking and support transparency, accountability, and "privacy by design" in the system architectures.

- *Legal Compliance with Data Protection Laws*

Digital twin ecosystems dwell under a very complex landscape of legal regulations. There are several established frameworks, like GDPR (General Data Protection Regulation) in Europe and HIPAA (Health Insurance Portability and Accountability Act) [4] in the US. Digital twin ecosystems must comply with these frameworks, particularly for healthcare applications, as they deal with sensitive personal and health data.

GDPR focuses on data minimisation principles, purpose limitation, and the right to erasure. This will ensure that the systems are legally compliant and technically robust. HIPAA mandates data protection for healthcare applications. This limits access to data, providing regulated access controls and encryption of health information. The Table 6.1 below provides a comparative analysis between these two frameworks.

Table 6.1 GDPR vs HIPAA.

Feature	GDPR	HIPAA
Jurisdiction	EU	US
Scope	All/any personal data	Only protected health information
Principle	Individual rights and data	Healthcare data security and privacy
Breach notification	Within 72 hours to the authority	60 days to individuals
Right to Erasure	Exists	No (overridden by record retention law)
Enforcement body	DPA (*Data Protection Authority*)	US Health and Human Services Department

Other digital sovereignty laws, like the Privacy Impact Assessment and Cross-border Data Transfer Compliance, ensure that privacy is proactively monitored and regulated, and breaches are avoided.

6.3.5 Balancing Privacy Risks with Data-Driven Collaboration

While the privacy risks are significant in a DT ecosystem due to the sensitive data, it is essential to determine the essence of controlled data sharing, especially in domains like multi-hospital medical research and inter-factory coordination. Data openness can help reduce redundancy and improve outcomes. Rather than restricting the data flow, systems must be designed to enable secure, accountable, and consent-driven collaboration. This will bring about a shift from a defensive concern to a strategic enabler system, which is ethical as well as efficient. For example, the healthcare systems that facilitate federated models allow learning from cross-institutional data without compromising the patient's privacy.

6.4 The Future of Privacy in Digital Twin Ecosystems

Ensuring data privacy for digital twin systems while maintaining utility is a big challenge. We need *privacy-preserving technologies* to safeguard the right to privacy while balancing the need for data-driven intelligence. This section discusses a few promising advancements in this area, which have been transformational for the digital twin ecosystems.

6.4.1 Federated Learning (FL) and Privacy-Preserving AI

FL is a decentralised machine learning approach [14] in which the raw data is not transferred to a central location; rather, the AI models are trained across multiple devices or local servers that hold the data. It was first used in a smartphone keyboard prediction application.

FL allows institutions to train and develop AI models collaboratively while keeping their data private. This makes it an excellent choice for DTEs since DTEs need data from multiple sources. This will allow the data to remain with the owner but still contribute to the system's intelligence.

- *Benefits of FL in DTEs*

The primary benefit is that the data never leaves the edge device and stays local, reducing the risk of a breach. The AI model can be trained by multiple twins, which can significantly improve its performance and generalisation.

Because of data locality, FL can easily align with privacy regulations like GDPR and HIPAA and restrict personal data processing and movement. For example, the Federated Learning approach allows the hospitals to have a shared AI model, which will enable patients' records to be exchanged without compromising on the patients' confidentiality.

- *Enhancing FL with Privacy-Preserving AI Technique*

To get the full benefits of FL, we have to combine data locality with privacy-preserving AI. Some technologies to preserve privacy include differential privacy, secure multiparty computation, homomorphic encryption, and a trusted execution environment.

Differential Privacy [9] adds noise to the training data so that the presence or absence of a single individual's data cannot be inferred from the final model. This prevents adversaries from reconstructing sensitive information from gradient updates.

SMPC allows aggregation of multiple model updates without revealing their local datasets.

Homomorphic encryption [10] is a computationally expensive method that allows computations on encrypted data without decryption, further enhancing confidentiality.

Trusted Execution Environments (TEEs) provide hardware-based solutions, giving a secure platform for sensitive computations.

- *Applications and Challenges*

FL can be used in hospitals to improve diagnostics without centralising sensitive medical records. This ensures privacy even in the case of AI model updates.

We can use federated learning in innovative city management without tracking individual behaviour by using the simulations and optimisations of FL.

Industrial twins can share performance insights but can keep the proprietary information confidential, preserving the competitive advantage and ensuring adherence to standards.

- *Use Case*

Google has worked with hospitals like the Mayo Clinic in the US to train an AI model for detecting sepsis using FL. This enables cross-hospital collaboration and avoids data centralisation. The patient's data does not leave the local node; only the model's weights are shared.

Even with so many advantages, it is still challenging to implement and manage systems supporting Federated Learning since we are dealing with heterogeneous devices with different computational capabilities in a DTE. Creating a fair system is still a significant milestone to be achieved.

6.4.2 Blockchain for Secure Data Management

Integrating digital twins with large-scale systems has raised many concerns, such as privacy, security, and data integrity. One possible solution is using blockchain technology, known for its decentralised, tamper-proof mechanism for managing and securing data exchanges.

- *Decentralisation and tamper-proof record keeping*

By avoiding data storage in a central server, blockchain prevents the threat of "single point of failure". The data is distributed across a network of nodes. This also reduces the risk of data tampering and unauthorised access. The working principle of blockchain states that it is immutable once the data is recorded in a block. The block is immutable without the consensus of the entire network. This is a very positive attribute for digital twins, as it preserves data integrity.

Blockchains can log sensor readings, maintain records, and perform analytics. If there is a fault, we can easily trace the root cause. This enables reliable diagnostics, accountability, and trustworthiness of the system.

- *Enhanced data ownership and access control*

Blockchain uses smart contracts to enable programmable access control mechanisms. They are self-executing contracts that govern data access, usage, and sharing. Using these, we can define who can access specific data layers, when, and for how long. This enables adherence to the privacy-by-design principle.

For example, for a healthcare application that captures a patient's physiological, imaging, and treatment history, we can manage consent for sharing specific data with stakeholders using blockchain. We can ensure that only authorised parties have access to sensitive data. This enables a paradigm shift – i.e., the transfer of data control from data custodians to owners.

- *Use Case*

Siemens has implemented a blockchain-based solution with DTs in the innovative manufacturing ecosystem. This ledger records events like machine configurations, changes in the process, and component provenance. This ensures that every transaction or change is logged and tamper-proof, ensuring compliance with industry standards and auditability.

- *Interoperability and auditability*

Since there are multiple stakeholders in a DTE, managing the various IT infrastructures, data governance policies, and trust assumptions is essential. Blockchain can manage these silos and permit trusted data exchange through a web of interconnected systems.

Blockchain's auditable feature allows all interactions to be logged and traced. The traceability will enable stakeholders to validate data and monitor how information can be accessed and used over time. Auditability is very useful when dealing with dispute resolution and developing participant trust.

- *Challenges*

Blockchain integration suffers from critical problems like scalability, latency, and energy consumption. Blockchains have limited throughput, and the transactions cannot be confirmed instantly.

However, when converged with federated learning and edge computing, blockchain can provide avenues for increasing privacy and preserving computational efficiency without compromising data integrity.

6.4.3 Homomorphic Encryption and Differential Privacy

DTE systems require privacy-preserving computation, which can perform meaningful data analysis without compromising the privacy and security of the system. The two most efficient solutions in this area are homomorphic encryption and differential privacy.

- *Homomorphic Encryption*

This encryption allows computation to be performed directly on encrypted data and gives encrypted results, which can reveal the actual result after decryption. This benefits a DTE, as the data can be distributed in untrusted environments.

For example, the encrypted sensor data from a factory's digital twin can be sent to the cloud service, which can perform anomaly detection, ML inference, or trend analysis on the same. This eliminates the risk of data leakage and ensures data is confidential throughout the computation life cycle.

There are three types of homomorphic encryption: partially homomorphic (which only supports addition/multiplication), somewhat homomorphic (which supports a limited number of operations), and fully homomorphic (which supports arbitrary computations). The fully homomorphic operations are particularly suited to secure the digital twin deployments.

- *Differential Privacy*

It is a statistical technique that ensures that the inclusion or exclusion of an individual's data in a dataset has a negligible impact on the output of any analysis. This protects individual identities, even when we share the data.

In DTEs, we usually have to aggregate personal and sensitive data. Still, using differential privacy, meaningful insights can be generated from this data without exposing individual location histories or profiles.

DP injects calibrated noise into the results of queries on the dataset. The purpose of the noise is to obscure the individual-level data while preserving the overall pattern and validity of the data.

DP can be implemented at multiple levels – on raw data, during real-time data processing, or at the UI level during visualisation.

- *Use Case of DP in Smart Cities*

DP techniques have been used in products like Community Mobility Reports for COVID-19, which urban planners and policymakers use to analyse the trends in movement without revealing individual users' data. This helps to bring down the significant privacy risks by not using granular location data, keeping the individual-level data confidential and untraceable.

- *Usage in DTEs, Challenges, Future Directions*

The combination of HE and DP can provide a robust framework to DTE by protecting identities while sharing and releasing aggregate results. This can also ensure access to different levels of data without violating the privacy norms and confidentiality. For example, using HE can allow data analysis across stakeholders in the healthcare segment. At the same time, DP ensures that the findings cannot be used to re-identify any patient.

However, HE incurred significant computational overhead, which limits its usage for time-sensitive applications. Similarly, excessive noise injection in DP can degrade the quality of insights, while insufficient noise can fail to protect privacy.

Hence, we need futuristic algorithms that focus on hardware acceleration for homomorphic encryption and context-aware differential privacy algorithms that can adjust the privacy parameters based on the nature of the query.

6.4.4 Zero-Knowledge Proofs (ZKPs) for Data Anonymisation

ZKPs are a transformative approach [15] that enables one party to convince another party that the given statement is true without revealing the underlying data. ZKPs are cryptographic protocols that allow users to prove their knowledge without revealing the data. There are three key properties for a valid ZKP.

- Completeness: *If the statement is true, the honest verifier will be convinced by an honest prover.*
- *Soundness: A false statement by a dishonest prover can never convince the verifier.*
- *Zero-knowledge: If the statement is true, the verifier learns only the validity, nothing beyond.*

ZKPs can benefit the DTE, as they can work without full data disclosure.

- *Zk-SNARKs*

Zero-knowledge Succinct Non-Interactive Arguments of Knowledge.

These do not reveal personal, operational, or proprietary data and assure regulatory compliance, authentication, and verification. They inherently support the idea of privacy-by-design architecture.

- *ZKPs for Federated and Decentralised Digital Twin Network*

The stakeholders of the DTEs, owing to their distributed nature, often operate in a zero-trust environment. ZKPs play an essential role here by enabling verifiable claims without requiring full access to underlying data. This ensures support for regulatory requirements and builds trust among competitors, partners, and public institutions.

- *Enhancing Data Anonymisation*

Unlike the traditional anonymisation techniques like pseudonymisation or data masking, which fail to sustain re-identification and analytics attacks, ZKPs prove facts about the data without exposing/altering the data, creating a zero exposure risk.

6.4.5 Decentralised Identity Management and Self-Sovereign Identity

Decentralised Identity Management (DIM) [16] and Self-Sovereign Identity (SSI) [17] are two transformative paradigms that empower individuals to have complete control over their identities by eliminating the need for centralised intermediaries.

- *SSI*

SSI allows individuals to manage their identity information securely. It uses decentralised technologies like distributed ledgers and blockchain to eliminate third-party dependency. SSI uses a DID (decentralised identifier), a unique and persistent identifier. These DIDs are anchored on blockchain or other distributed ledgers. They use cryptographically signed credentials called *Verifiable Credentials*, which are signed by trusted parties and disclose only selective features of the owner, allowing a secure and privacy-preserving interaction between human and machine.

- *Key Technical Enablers*

Four key technical enablers are required for the SSI to work in a digital twin ecosystem, as shown in Figure 6.10.

The blockchain and distributed ledgers offer non-changeable and decentralised storage for DIDs and other critical information.

This can be used to prove assertions (e.g., the age of the user is above 18) rather than giving away the actual information, thereby supporting zero-knowledge proof (ZKP).

For selective disclosure, these multi-agent DT systems use privacy-preserving authentication protocols that permit only selective disclosure and contextual data sharing.

SSI solutions follow interoperability standards, which are approved by W3C and the DIF (Decentralised Identity Foundation), and hence, can be used across domains and geographical areas.

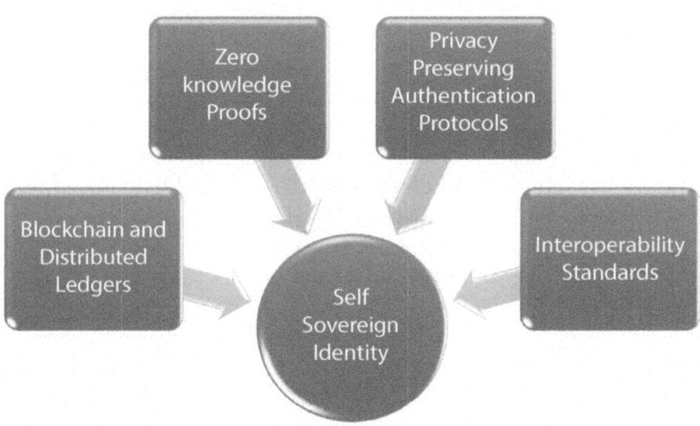

Figure 6.10 Key technical enablers for SSI.

Some of the potential bottlenecks that may be faced during SSI integration include latency and throughput issues due to the usage of blockchains, regulatory ambiguity due to the legal status of decentralised identity credentials and the need for a robust governance framework for defining trusted issuers, credential schemas, and revocation procedures.

6.4.6 Emerging Privacy-Preserving Technologies

The following table (Table 6.2) discusses privacy concerns, mitigation techniques, and relevant technology.

6.5 Future Trends and Predictions

In this section, we will discuss future trends that can handle the complexity and ubiquity of the digital twin ecosystems.

6.5.1 Privacy by Design (PbD) in the DTE Development

PbD was introduced by Ann Cavoukian in 2009 [6]. It emphasises embedding privacy into the architecture from the beginning and not as a compliance requirement. It considers privacy as an enabler of trust. It advocates for keeping privacy as a default setting and including it as a preventative and not remedial measure. It is grounded on the following rules:

Table 6.2 Privacy concerns and mitigation techniques.

Privacy concern	Mitigation technique	Relevant technology
Unauthorized data access	Role-based access	APIs, middleware security
Data exposure	Edge computing	Edge devices
Centralised data breach	Blockchain-based logging	Distributed ledger techniques
Inference attacks	Differential privacy	Privacy-preserving analytics
Identity misuse	SSI	Decentralised identity frameworks

- Focus on the full life cycle protection
- Keep the architecture visible and transparent
- Keep the design user-centric and respect their privacy

Some key strategies can be instrumental for adopting PbD at the architectural level, as shown in Figure 6.11.

- DTEs should only collect the necessary data required for their function.
- Data processing should be shifted to the edge. This can reduce the reliance on centralised servers and bring down privacy risks.
- Integrate techniques to de-identify data without compromising utility (pseudonymisation and anonymisation).
- Providing role-based access and decentralising the identity layers to restrict data access and provide fine-grained contextual, need-based data access.

Figure 6.11 Adopting privacy by design.

- Incorporate a data provenance mechanism to track data flow across entities and systems, which ensures traceability and accountability.
- Include protocols for secure data deletion and life cycle expiration.

Although a promising technique, care must be taken while operationalising PbD. Extensive data minimisation can impair twins' predictive accuracy and responsiveness. There could be several interdisciplinary gaps to be addressed. For example, the engineering teams may not understand privacy law, and legal teams may not understand technical architecture. There is still a lack of universally accepted standards for implementing PbD across diverse DTEs.

6.5.2 AI-Driven Automated Privacy Enforcement

AI-driven privacy mechanisms offer context-aware privacy management of information. These systems can learn from historical access patterns, contextual variables, and user preferences to predict potential breaches. These agents can autonomously respond to suspicious behaviour and adjust privacy settings based on such behaviour.

Privacy enforcement algorithms can understand behavioural analytics, detect anomalies, and enforce compliance with enhanced response efficiency and accuracy. Such real-time settings are very beneficial in the DTE, where the multi-dimensional data flow poses a governance challenge.

Some of the key features that can be anticipated in the next 5-10 years for the digital twin ecosystems include the following (Figure 6.12):

Figure 6.12 Trends in AI-driven privacy enforcement.

- Adjustment of privacy controls based on contextual signals (time/location/activity).
- Ability to operate across federated infrastructures without revealing raw data.
- Enabling transparent governance through explainable AI (XAI).
- Automating data governance through the integration of blockchain and smart contracts.
- Predictive models for forecasting potential privacy threats based on user behaviour trends.

Despite the advantages, encoding these privacy preferences requires caution to deal with algorithmic bias, model drift, and lack of transparency.

6.5.3 Potential Impact of Quantum Computing on Privacy

The cryptanalytic capability of quantum computers [20] can compromise the current communication channels and expose the encrypted data retroactively. The sensitive information may be subjected to loss of data integrity, loss of confidentiality, and unauthorised remote access to these real-world systems.

Hence, there is a need for quantum-resistant strategies, and the organisations must estimate a quantum risk timeline within which they must transition to PQC (post-quantum cryptography) to remain secure.

NIST Post-Quantum Cryptography Project

This project was launched by NIST in 2016 to standardise cryptographic algorithms against the potential threats posed by quantum computers. The project aims to replace the current public-key systems vulnerable to quantum attacks. In July 2022, NIST selected two primary candidates for standardisation—CRYSTALS-Kyber for key encryption and CRYSTALS-Dilithium for digital signatures. This has significant implications for the DTE, as the data collected, transmitted, or stored by the DTs may be stored by the adversaries and decrypted later when quantum computers are available. Hence, cryptographic agility, i.e., the ability to transition cryptographic components rapidly, must be designed for DTEs. The quantum threat timeline is depicted in Figure 6.13.

Quantum-resistant algorithms

The research community is advancing to quantum-resistant cryptographic algorithms like lattice-based cryptography, code-based cryptography,

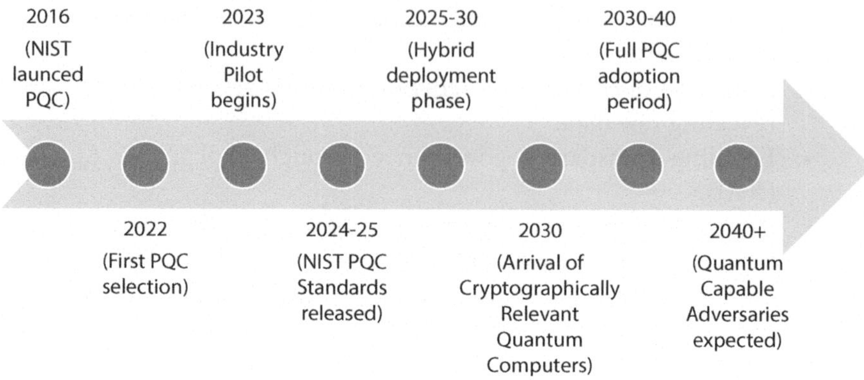

Figure 6.13 Quantum threat timeline.

hash-based signatures, and multivariate polynomial-based schemes. Examples of these are shown in Figure 6.14.

Future Trends and Predictions

- Digital twins may have to adopt the "quantum safe by design" principle, which can counter quantum attacks from the outset.
- Adoption of hybrid cryptographic schemes that combine classical algorithms with PQC algorithms.
- Usage of quantum machine learning for enhanced anomaly detection to identify data breaches.

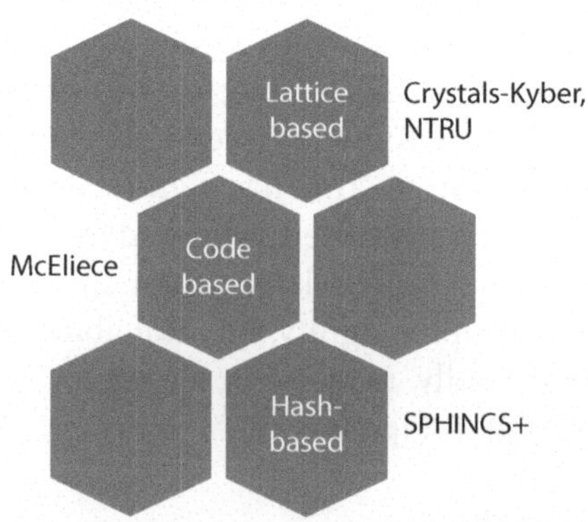

Figure 6.14 Quantum-resistant cryptographic algorithms.

- Creation of privacy-aware system designs and policy frameworks to address hyper-accurate data streams.

6.6 Conclusion and Research Directions

This section will summarise the key insights, discuss the open research problems, and provide recommendations for policymakers, industry, and researchers.

6.6.1 Summary of Key Insights

The digital twins are rapidly transforming industries by creating immersive simulations that enable predictive maintenance and optimisation. They have been widely adopted in various sectors like healthcare, manufacturing, smart cities, and personalised service.

The digital twin paradigm revolves around data collected from sensors, IoT devices, and other sources to create models of people, environment, and systems. This can expose highly sensitive personal and operational data. Also, the breach in one component can jeopardise the entire system.

The privacy concerns in a DTE have multiple faces, ranging from basic data leaks to more concerning issues such as identity inference and cross-contextual data misuse. These threats are amplified when digital twins are integrated with AI, edge computing, and the cloud.

A wide range of emerging technologies and frameworks can be used to deal with these risks. Technologies like federated learning, differential privacy, HE, and secure multi-party computation can help protect data. Zero-trust architecture and blockchain-based access control can help enforce data sovereignty. However, their adoption requires dealing with technical complexity, performance overheads, a lack of standardisation, and regulatory uncertainty.

Also, the traditional privacy laws like GDPR and HIPAA cannot provide baselines for cross-domain data fusion and real-time personalisation. Hence, there is a need for adaptive, forward-looking privacy governance models that can offer stakeholder transparency and foster ethical AI practices.

The sustainability of DTE strongly depends on developing a modular architecture that embeds a trust-by-design architecture in the ecosystem life cycle.

6.6.2 Privacy as a Pillar of Trust

Privacy should not be treated only as a compliance checkbox but as the most critical foundational pillar of trust in a DT ecosystem. This is crucial for long-term sustainability and public acceptance of a system that allows humans and machines to interact dynamically and has complex data flows. If the privacy foundations are weak, the DTEs may be reduced to surveillance rather than optimisation tools.

6.6.3 Need for "*Privacy by Design*" and Interdisciplinary Collaboration

Privacy should not be embedded as an afterthought; instead, it should be embedded directly into the digital twin pipeline as an architectural principle. This calls for a proactive system design rather than a reactive privacy control. To accomplish this, it is essential to have interdisciplinary collaboration between developers, data scientists, legal experts, and policymakers to come together to create technically sound, legal, and ethical frameworks. This is the only way we can proceed towards the innovation of DTEs with society's trust.

6.6.4 Open Research Problems

While digital twins have given us many promising solutions in various sectors, several open research areas remain unresolved. This section outlines three significant areas where future research can focus. Figure 6.15 also illustrates these areas in the era of pervasive digital twins.

- *Scalable privacy-preserving frameworks*

Creating interoperable privacy architectures that can operate across organisations is an area with much scope. These frameworks must allow

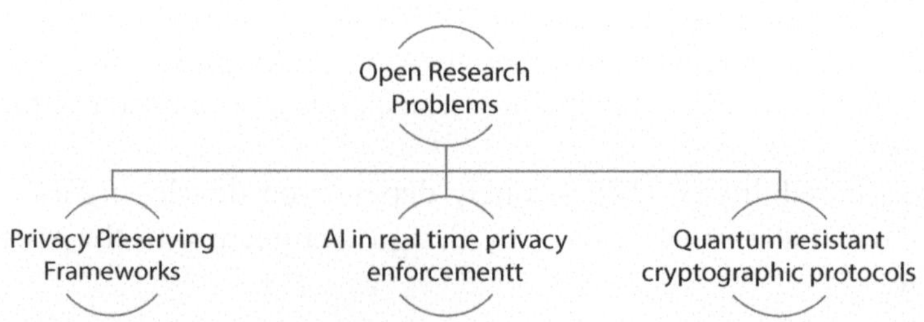

Figure 6.15 Open research problems.

- Selective data sharing, which will allow the decentralisation of data governance.
- Privacy controls that can adapt to user preferences and are context-aware.
- Assessments of risks in real time without impacting the system performance and analytical accuracy.

- *Enhancing AI's role in real-time privacy enforcement*

AI plays a significant role in the digital twin ecosystem, but instead of using AI only for prediction and simulation, we can explore its role in safeguarding privacy. Key research problems can include:

- Creating AI agents that can monitor digital twins' data flows and detect anomalies.
- Designing AI models that can learn from user feedback and provide cues to fine-tune decisions.
- Designing AI systems that can provide human-understandable justifications for granting/revoking access.

- *Quantum computing and DTE security*

The advent of quantum computing algorithms has made the current privacy-preserving mechanism vulnerable. The open research questions in this area include:

- Creation of quantum-resistant cryptographic protocols that can be embedded into digital twin architectures.
- Improve pattern recognition in privacy breach detection through quantum machine learning.

The research problems discussed above are some of the critical areas that can be addressed to ensure that the DTEs are secure, resilient, and trustworthy. These areas bring forth many opportunities for interdisciplinary collaboration to strengthen the foundational principles of the digital twin life cycle.

6.6.5 Recommendations

This section presents some recommendations to policymakers, industry, and researchers.

- *For Policymakers*

The regulatory landscape surrounding the digital twin ecosystem is still evolving. There is a need for DTE-specific privacy regulations to define boundaries around consent, data ownership, and acceptable use of data. Some key recommendations include

  - Development of sector-specific privacy standards of DTs in healthcare, manufacturing, etc.
  - Making Privacy Impact Assessments compulsory for large-scale DTE deployment.
  - Encourage interoperability of privacy standards internationally.

Since this ecosystem spans borders, promoting international standards is pivotal for deploying a digital twin across jurisdictions. Organisations need to disclose how the data is collected, processed, and shared to uphold transparency and auditability.

- *For Industry*

The industries must shift from reactive to proactive data privacy strategies and embrace holistic security practices. Privacy and security by design should be adopted at every stage of the DTE life cycle. Impact assessments should be performed regularly to evaluate privacy risks associated with each deployment. Companies must invest in a robust cybersecurity framework and train their employees and stakeholders on the digital twin's privacy implications. Some key recommendations:

  - Implement PbD in the early stages of DTE architecture.
  - Prepare for quantum threats by using hybrid cryptographic solutions.
  - Audit APIs, middleware, and edge gateways regularly for security checks.

- *For Researchers*

With the growth in scale and complexity of the digital twin ecosystems, there is a pressing need for innovation in the following areas:

  - Developing advanced privacy-preserving ML techniques.
  - Developing lightweight cryptographic protocols that can be easily deployed on constrained devices.

Table 6.3 Privacy implementation guidelines.

Task	Description
Conduct Privacy Risk Assessment	Identify the data flows and storage points with high risk
API Security	Strictly implement role based access, token validation and usage logs
Edge Processing	Reduce transfer of sensitive data
Encrypted data in transit and storage	Use TLS/SSL and robust key management
Crypto-agility	Prepare for quantum-resistant protocol upgrades
Regulatory Compliance	Align norms with GDPR, HIPAA and PDPB
Training	Provide privacy training to staffs

- Create more explainable AI systems that can justify their privacy-related decisions.
- Collaborating with ethicists, legal professionals, and industry practitioners for interdisciplinary research can lead to technological advancements that are ethically grounded and socially aligned.

6.6.6 Privacy Implementation Guidelines for Enterprises Using DTEs

This last subsection presents some implementation guidelines, especially for enterprises using DTEs. Table 6.3 summarises those tasks.

AI disclosure statement: The author acknowledges the use of AI-based tools for minor language editing or grammatical correction. However, all intellectual contributions, analyses, and conclusions presented in this chapter are entirely the author's own.

References

1. Abbas, A., Alroobaea, R., Krichen, M., Rubaiee, S., Vimal, S., Almansour, F.M., Blockchain-assisted secured data management framework based on Internet of Medical Things for health information analysis. *Pers. Ubiquitous Comput.*, 28, 1, 59–72, 2021, https://doi.org/10.1007/s00779-021-01583-8.
2. Albrecht, J., How the GDPR Will Change the World. *Eur. Data Prot. Law Rev.*, 2, 3, 287–289, 2016, https://doi.org/10.21552/edpl/2016/3/4.
3. Alcaraz, C. and Lopez, J., Digital Twin: A Comprehensive survey of security threats. *IEEE Commun. Surv. Tutorials*, 24, 3, 1475–1503, 2022, https://doi.org/10.1109/comst.2022.3171465.
4. Annas, G.J., HIPAA regulations — a new era of Medical-Record privacy? *N. Engl. J. Med.*, 348, 15, 1486–1490, 2003, https://doi.org/10.1056/nejmlim035027.
5. Batty, M., Digital twins. *Environ. Plann. B Urban Anal. City Sci.*, 45, 5, 817–820, 2018, https://doi.org/10.1177/2399808318796416.
6. Cavoukian, A., Privacy by design, in: *IGI Global eBooks*, pp. 170–208, 2011, https://doi.org/10.4018/978-1-61350-501-4.ch007.
7. Croatti, A., Gabellini, M., Montagna, S., Ricci, A., On the Integration of Agents and Digital Twins in Healthcare. *J. Med. Syst.*, 44, 9, 2020, https://doi.org/10.1007/s10916-020-01623-5.
8. Dwork, C., Differential Privacy, in: *Lecture Notes in Computer Science*, pp. 1–12, 2006, https://doi.org/10.1007/11787006_1.
9. Dwork, C. and Roth, A., The algorithmic foundations of differential privacy, 2013, https://doi.org/10.1561/9781601988195.
10. Gentry, C., Fully Homomorphic Encryption Using Ideal Lattices, in: *Proceedings of the 41st Annual ACM Symposium on Theory of Computing*, ACM, pp. 169–178, 2009, DOI: 10.1145/1536414.1536440.
11. Greenleaf, G., China's Personal Information Protection Law: Rights Plus Cyber-security, Privacy Laws & Business International Report, 172, 20–23, 2021, DOI: 10.2139/ssrn.3989775, 2021.
12. Grieves, M. and Vickers, J., Digital Twin: Mitigating Unpredictable, Undesirable Emergent Behavior in Complex Systems, in: *Transdisciplinary Perspectives on Complex Systems*, J. Kahlen, S. Flumerfelt, A. Alves (Eds.), pp. 85–113, Springer International Publishing, Cham, Switzerland, 2017, DOI: 10.1007/978-3-319-38756-7_4.
13. Jones, D., Snider, C., Nassehi, A., Yon, J., Hicks, B., Characterising the Digital Twin: A systematic literature review. *CIRP J. Manuf. Sci. Technol.*, 29, 36–52, 2020, https://doi.org/10.1016/j.cirpj.2020.02.002.
14. Li, T., Sahu, A.K., Talwalkar, A., Smith, V., Federated Learning: challenges, methods, and future directions. *IEEE Signal Process Mag.*, 37, 3, 50–60, 2020, https://doi.org/10.1109/msp.2020.2975749.

15. Morais, E., Koens, T., Van Wijk, C., Koren, A., A survey on zero knowledge range proofs and applications. *SN Appl. Sci.*, 1, 8, 2019, https://doi.org/10.1007/s42452-019-0989-z.
16. Murcia, J.M.B., Cánovas, E., García-Rodríguez, J., Zarca, A.M., Skarmeta, A., Decentralised Identity Management solution for zero-trust multi-domain Computing Continuum frameworks. *Future Gener. Comput. Syst.*, 162, 107479, 2024, https://doi.org/10.1016/j.future.2024.08.003.
17. Nidyanantham, P., Ponnavaikko, M., Aantonny, R., Blockchain based validating documents by self sovereign identity using Hyperledger Indy. *Gedrag & Organisatie*, 33, 03, 2020. https://doi.org/10.37896/gor33.03/493.
18. Nativi, S., Mazzetti, P., Craglia, M., Digital ecosystems for developing Digital Twins of the Earth: the Destination Earth Case. *Remote Sens.*, 13, 11, 2119, 2021, https://doi.org/10.3390/rs13112119.
19. Ogburn, M., Turner, C., Dahal, P., Homomorphic encryption. *Procedia Comput. Sci.*, 20, 502–509, 2013, https://doi.org/10.1016/j.procs.2013.09.310.
20. Prateek, K., Altaf, F., Amin, R., Maity, S., A privacy preserving authentication protocol using quantum computing for V2I authentication in vehicular *ad hoc* networks. *Secur. Commun. Netw.*, 2022, 1–17, 2022, https://doi.org/10.1155/2022/4280617.
21. Vikhman, V.V. and Romm, M.V., "Digital Twins" in Education: Prospects and reality. *Vysshee Obrazovanie V Rossii = Higher Educ. Russ.*, 30, 2, 22–32, 2021, https://doi.org/10.31992/0869-3617-2021-30-2-22-32.
22. Wang, Y., Su, Z., Guo, S., Dai, M., Luan, T.H., Liu, Y., A survey on digital twins: architecture, enabling technologies, security and privacy, and future prospects. *IEEE Internet Things J.*, 10, 17, 14965–14987, 2023, doi: 10.1109/jiot.2023.3263909.

7

Privacy in the Age of Digital Twins

Shobha Chawla[1]*, Neha Gupta[2], Vijayalaxmi Rajendran[3] and Akhilesh Tiwari[3]

[1]Department of Computer Applications, BCIIT, New Delhi, India
[2]School of Computer Applications, MRIIRS, Faridabad, India
[3]Business and Management, Christ University, Ghaziabad, India

Abstract

In recent years, a new concept of virtual models that can simulate complex physical systems is gaining attention in various industries such as manufacturing, health care, transportation, and energy. The virtual models help study the behaviour of physical systems and the aftereffects of the chosen design options. These virtual models are popularly called "digital twins." Digital twins (DT), an emulator of physical systems, are a cost-effective way of collecting real-time data during the life cycle of the physical entity. The collected data helps understand behaviour, predict failures, mitigate the risk of failure, and optimize the performance of the physical system. Initially, digital twins were developed for the entities of the manufacturing industry, but, now, they are extensively adopted in the fields of health care, transport, energy, and logistics. The previous chapter discussed how being a virtual replica, a digital twin, collects real-time and historical data of physical devices through sensors for predicting and optimizing the operations.

The present chapter focusses on the privacy concerns pertaining to the digital twins. A digital twin is composed of IoT devices, edge computing, AI, big data, and networking devices. The interaction amongst these devices poses multiple security threats on the virtual counterpart. The present chapter outlines the various levels of potential threats to digital twins, the challenges in keeping the collected data secure during transition, and discusses the legal and regulatory environment for ensuring data privacy.

Additionally, this chapter also recommends the security solutions and approaches that can ensure the trustworthiness of the digital twin during its deployment in the industry. Conclusively, the chapter emphasizes the concept of

**Corresponding author*: shobha.chawla@gmail.com

Shubham Mahajan, Davinder Paul Singh, Amit Kant Pandit and Paras Chawla (eds.) Ensuring Privacy in Digital Twin Ecosystems, (215–244) © 2026 Scrivener Publishing LLC

"privacy by design" and drew attention towards incorporation of privacy principles during the design choice or creation of digital twins.

The chapter includes the following sections:

- Security Threats to Digital Twins
- Data Privacy Law
- Strategies for Securing Digital Twins
- Privacy by Design

Keywords: Digital twins, privacy, security challenges, data privacy law, privacy by design

7.1 Introduction

Digital Twins are virtual model that replicate physical systems or processes and allow studying their characteristics and behaviour. They have transformed the industries by assisting in enhanced decision making at reduced costs and increased efficiency. The digital twin model applies simulation on gathered real-time data from sensory devices to perform predictive analysis and identify issues or areas that need improvement. The gained insights help in optimizing the performance of physical counterpart of the model. These are widely leveraged in manufacturing, health care, energy, smart cities, automotive, and transportation industries. With the passage of time, the digital twins are expected to integrate within other sectors as well. This innovation is turning more intelligent and efficient with the continuous research in this field.

The survey of Root Analysis expected the growth in digital twin market to $240.3 billion by 2035, with a compound annual growth rate (CAGR) of 41% [1]. In contrast, Grand View Research in their report estimated the market size of $155.84 billion by 2030 with CAGR of 34.2% [2].

In simple words, a digital twin can be termed as a virtual copy of a physical entity that exists in the real world. These entities can be a machine, its single component, a process, a human being, or a system. The physical versions of digital twins are equipped with sensors that collect various parameters of the physical version and continuously update the digital twins with the real-time collected data. This data is then analysed using machine learning techniques to understand the behaviour and condition of the physical version. The insights provided by machine learning algorithms help in timely decision making to optimize and improve the performance of the physical version. For instance, a digital twin model of an industrial process can monitor and optimize its performance throughout its entire lifecycle and streamline the supply chain. In contrast, a digital twin model of a specific part, such as a car's suspension system, can trace potential issues before they become critical and support predictive maintenance.

In [3], the authors identified three primary elements of digital twin: physical space, digital space and the link for data and information flow. These elements form the three functional layers of digital twin architecture. A brief discussion on the functional layers is as follows:

1. Layer 1: Layer 1 is identified as a physical space layer where data is collected in real time from the physical devices through sensors and, after quality assurance, communicated to the next layer.
2. Layer 2: This layer is the intermediate layer responsible for synchronizing, storing, and processing the collected data and later transmitting it to Layer 3. The stored data supports analysis and modelling. In addition, feedback, decisions, and predictions received from Layer 3 are fed back to the physical space layer. This layer acts like a digital thread, enabling continuous communication between the two layers.
3. Layer 3: It is the digital space layer whose responsibility is to define visual representation of data received from physical space through the intermediate layer. In addition, it monitors the physical devices and their visual or digital counterparts and also offers decisions to the physical space layer through the intermediate layer.

The formulation of a DT requires seamless convergence of many inter-related technologies as depicted in the Figure 7.1.

A digital twin's technology stack includes:

- **Sensor Technologies** – It includes an IoT framework of sensors and devices that collect data from physical assets and transmit it to their virtual counterparts. Sensors in digital twins collect data such as temperature, pressure, and vibration and integrate it into their virtual counterparts for analysis and simulation.
- **Cloud Computing** – It includes a cloud infrastructure to store volumes of collected and processed data. A cloud platform being scalable and flexible offers adaptable tools to quickly respond to evolving business needs. The services

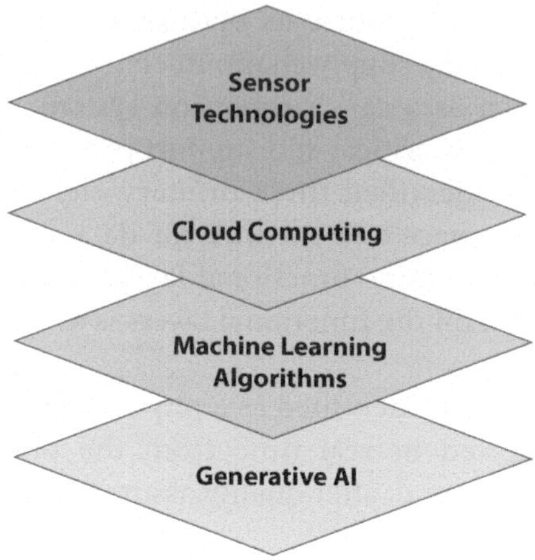

Figure 7.1 Digital twin technology stack.

of cloud platforms like Amazon Web Services (AWS), Microsoft Azure, and Google Cloud Platform are cost saving, have improved accessibility, and have cost-efficient computing capabilities.

- **Machine Learning Algorithms** – This includes an efficient and suitable algorithm to analyse collected data and predict the outcome to ensure early predictive maintenance and fault diagnosis. Powerful AI/ML tools augment the capabilities of digital twins by analysing voluminous datasets and identifying patterns to predict highly accurate outcomes.
- **Generative AI** – Generative AI enhances the performance of digital twins by synthesizing new data for training digital twin models and by augmenting their capabilities. In addition, LLMs can automate code generation for digital twins, thereby speeding up tasks during their implementation phase.

By enabling enhanced decision making at reduced costs, optimizing performance, improving product lifecycle management, and increasing efficiency, digital twins have become a game changer across various industries. Here are a few real-world examples of manufacturing, automotive, oil, and smart cities industry where leading companies have implemented digital twins and gained significant benefits:

- Rolls-Royce's "IntelligentEngine" program has created digital twin models of aircraft engines. These models collect data from onboard sensors, enabling the virtual counterpart to

monitor performance and predict maintenance needs in real time [4].
- Ford has used digital twin technology during the product design stage. A digital twin of the car's headlight system helped engineers understand light distribution and reflection patterns. With this insight, they improved the vehicle's light system, enhancing the driving safety at night [5]. Volvo, Renault, Tesla, and BMW are also leveraging from digital twin technology to enhance their operational performance.
- BP is leveraging digital twin technology in its Gulf of America operations to create virtual replicas of its offshore oil platforms. Sensor-collected real-time data is used for remote monitoring of key metrics, including temperature and pressure. This enables early detection of critical issues, leading to enhanced operational performance [6].
- By leveraging digital twin technology, Virtual Singapore has addressed key challenges in urban planning. The model enables simulation and testing of various urban scenarios to improve city infrastructure and services. Urban planners using this digital twin can easily identify potential bottlenecks, promoting sustainable development [7].

Beyond these industries, digital twin technology is also making a significant impact in health care, medicine, construction, logistics, and the energy sector. Digital twins help in simulating real-world scenarios, and the gained insights serve businesses in improved data-driven decision making, early warnings, and optimization of behaviours. Digital twins have accelerated the realization of Industry 4.0 with their adoption in critical industries. They often store vast amounts of real-world data in digital form. These aspects of a digital twin make it an attractive target for adversaries to identify the flaws or vulnerabilities in the system that can be exploited to corrupt or damage any critical infrastructure.

Any malicious penetration of a digital twin framework can damage the physical asset as well as its digital counterpart. The security aspect of a digital twin is a big concern for the industries leveraging these advanced technologies [8]. The security breach or intrusion in digital twins can bring down the reputation of the business model and break the trust of the stakeholders. At one place, a digital twin, through instant data retrieval from the sensors of a physical system, gives valuable insight to experts to analyse and detect anomalies at an earlier stage; at the same time, it exceptionally increases the security concerns of the business model. The whole framework of a digital twin includes the integration of multiple devices. If an adversary manages to gain unauthorized control of any device, it can put the entire system at risk. Existing studies strongly recommend incorporating the concept of "Privacy by Design" in the development of digital twins to prevent security breaches.

The cybersecurity aspect of digital twins needs focused research by the academicians. The widespread use of technology in both daily life and industry poses significant challenges for users in safeguarding their personal data. The security challenges faced by users and organizations extend beyond securing IoT networks to ensuring that these systems are not exploited as tools for launching cyberattacks. To study and understand the privacy issues affecting digital twins, one should first understand the security threats to digital twins.

The present chapter focuses on the privacy concerns about the "Digital Twins." Composition of a digital twin includes IoT devices, edge servers, AI, big data, and networking devices. The interaction among these devices poses multiple security threats to the virtual counterpart. The present chapter outlines the various levels of potential threats to digital twins, the challenges in keeping the collected data secure during the transition, and the legal and regulatory environment for ensuring data privacy. Additionally, this chapter also recommends the security solutions and approaches that can ensure the trustworthiness of the digital twin during its deployment in the industry. Conclusively, the chapter emphasizes the concept of "privacy by design" and draws attention to the incorporation of privacy principles during the design choice or creation of digital twins.

The subsequent sections of the chapter are structured as follows: Section 7.2 outlines the security threats to digital twins, Section 7.3 delves into the design of data privacy law, Section 7.4 discusses strategies for securing digital twins, and Section 7.5 comprehends the concept of "privacy by design".

7.2 Security Threats to Digital Twins

In the past few years, digital twins have evolved as a revolution in the industry in aiding better and timely decision making; however, the benefits also brought along with them many new cybersecurity risks. It is important to first understand the users' concerns before studying in depth the security threats to digital twins. The key security concerns of digital twins are outlined below and depicted in Figure 7.2 as well:

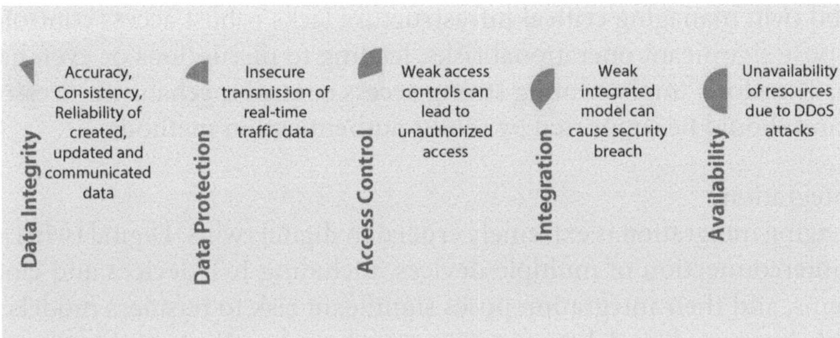

Figure 7.2 Key security concerns of digital twins.

1. Data Integrity

Data integrity in a digital twin refers to weighing it in terms of accuracy, consistency, reliability, and trustworthiness. For both businesses and users, ensuring the reliability and accuracy of data being created, updated, and transmitted remains a significant concern. For instance, if a digital twin in health care gets compromised causing disclosure of sensitive data or the adversary unauthorizedly modifies the collected data from sensors, then the shared corrupted health data could lead to faulty diagnoses and incorrect treatments. Therefore, ensuring data integrity requires rigorous security enforcement both at the physical layer and during the transmission of sensitive data.

2. Data Protection

Data transmitted from physical assets and digital twins needs to be protected from eavesdroppers and any kind of tampering. Advanced encryption techniques should be used to protect data from eavesdroppers. Continuous monitoring of traffic between physical assets and digital twins is essential for safeguarding the data. Real-time traffic data in critical sectors using digital twins must be encrypted to prevent unauthorized access. Security concerns related to digital twins also include protecting sensitive data and defending against attacks that attempt to infiltrate the network.

3. Access Control

Maintaining access control is essential to avoid malicious access. It is highly crucial to have a strong and defined access policy to protect the functioning, process, and data of digital twins. Weak access controls increase the vulnerability of networks and connected devices, potentially enabling malicious actors to gain unauthorized access. For instance, if a digital twin managing critical infrastructure lacks robust access control, it can pose significant operational risks, leading to disruptions or even hazards. Therefore, implementing strong access control mechanisms is essential and should be supported by robust authentication methods.

4. Integration
Managing integration is extremely crucial in digital twins. Digital twins are the interconnection of multiple devices, including IoT devices and cloud systems, and their integration poses significant risk to business models. A weakly integrated model can cause security breaches. Each weak integrated point becomes a possible avenue for attackers to exploit. For instance, if an IoT device or cloud service is not securely integrated into a digital twin, it could serve as a gateway for potential attacks. Therefore, such connections should be continuously monitored, with robust security enforced at every integration point.

5. Availability
Maintaining availability is critical in digital twin systems. If security issues are not effectively addressed, cyberattacks may cause disruptions and render the digital twin inaccessible to legitimate users. This can result from Distributed Denial of Service (DDoS) attacks, where a device is overwhelmed with illegitimate traffic to exhaust its resources. Inaccessibility may also be caused by injected software bugs or network disruptions. Such issues should be resolved at an early stage to avoid any delays in decision making. Firewalls and intrusion detection systems should be installed to avoid any malicious traffic hampering the smooth functioning of Digital Twin's network.

Once the security concerns of digital twins are understood, and threats and critical vulnerabilities are identified and prioritized, addressing them becomes easier. In [9], the authors identified security threats across three functional layers of DTs. As security threats directly or indirectly impact the operations of DTs, the threat vector can also be explored on the basis of functional layers of DT. In [10–16], authors have highlighted various kinds of attacks on digital twins and IoT networks targeting their confidentiality, integrity, authentication, and availability. The various security threats to digital twins are outlined as follows:

- Software Attacks

Devices used at the physical space layer make use of proprietary software components. If third-party components contain bugs, attackers may exploit them as backdoors to gain access to devices, potentially

Table 7.1 Attacks and threats to digital twin.

S. no.	Security threats	Types of attacks	Attack against
1.	Software attacks	• PLC-Blaster • StuxNet • Reverse engineering	Integrity Confidentiality Availability
2.	MITM	• Passive MITM • Active MITM	Authentication Integrity Confidentiality Availability
3.	DDoS attacks	• Flooding • Replay • Jamming • Sinkhole • Blackhole	Authentication Integrity Confidentiality Availability
4.	Eavesdropping attacks	• Sniffing attacks • Spoofing attacks	Authentication Integrity Confidentiality
5.	Tampering attacks	• Physical entity tampering • Data tampering • Sensor spoofing • Model tampering	Integrity Confidentiality
6.	Unauthorized access	• Sybil attacks • Impersonation attacks	Authentication Integrity Confidentiality
7.	Sensitive data leakage	• Data theft • Insider treats • Security breach in Cloud • Compromised digital identities	Integrity Confidentiality
8.	Poisoning attacks	• Data poisoning • Model poisoning • Communication poisoning	Integrity Confidentiality
9.	Attack on Cloud/Edge	• Misconfigured Cloud services • Data breaches • Cloud resource hijacking • DDoS attack • Malware	Authentication Integrity Confidentiality Availability

compromising sensitive data or damaging the system. Such vulnerabilities also provide attackers with opportunities to perform reverse engineering to uncover additional weaknesses. Furthermore, buffer overflow attacks can be launched by exploiting flaws in the operating system. Many times, devices heavily rely on older versions of operating systems or software components, which can expose the devices to vulnerabilities due to outdated security patches. Potential software attack weapons, which are listed in Table 7.1, target the victim device as well as the connected devices and can cause maintainability issues and synchronization problems.

Furthermore, the intermediate layer also suffers software-based attack threats if the software components of analysing and modelling devices are outdated. If adversaries gain access to modelling tools or data, they may be able to manipulate the information used to generate visual representations of physical layer devices.

Moreover, software-based attacks can be used to exploit the vulnerabilities in storage devices and modify the aggregated data. This raises security concerns for integrity and reliability. Similarly, devices at the digital space layer are vulnerable to software attacks if they use outdated third-party software components. Software attacks can compromise decision making and predictions, leading to incorrect transmission of outcomes to the physical layer.

If an adversary manages to introduce malware into any digital twin device or cloud server by exploiting software vulnerabilities, the infection can propagate across all devices connected within the digital twin's IoT network. This may turn out to be the biggest security problem for Industry 4.0 and Industry 5.0, where the industry will be highly connected and dependent on IoT and cloud platforms. For instance, adversaries capable of injecting malware into the digital twin of a robotic arm used in a manufacturing assembly line could disrupt the production. By modifying the digital twin's parameters, the injected malware can cause the malfunctioning of robotic arm, resulting in production delays, operational bottlenecks, and significant financial losses.

- Men in the Middle Attack (MITM)

At layer 1, the adversary invades the system and manages to intercept the communication between physical entities or sensory devices and digital twins and modifies it during the transition. Additionally, at layer 2, during synchronization, the MITM attacker captures and modifies the communicated data. An attacker exploits the vulnerabilities of the system to gain control of the data transmission between the layers. Furthermore, at the digital space layer, a MITM attacker can intercept and alter predictions or outcomes. This results in the transmission of false data to the physical space layer *via* the intermediate layer. These data manipulations are attacks against the integrity and secrecy of communication channels within the digital twin network. The dissemination of false information among the entities within the digital twin framework can completely undermine the business model.

The MITM attackers many times impersonate a legitimate device to receive all the communications through the channel. The MITM attacker, after getting access to the communication channel, can inject false data, change routing, modify data, or just trace or monitor the traffic without clients being aware that they are under attack. In [17], the authors also outlined the impact of adversaries in IIoT publish-subscribe models, which gained full control of the communication channel.

For instance, in manufacturing industries, MITM attacks target readings of sensory devices to disrupt operations, thus leading to safety hazards. Similarly, in smart cities applications, MITM attacks can disrupt power grids, traffic management, and many safety systems, endangering human lives.

- DDoS Attacks

The biggest concern of the digital twin business model is to prevent DDoS attacks. A group of adversaries may collaborate to launch an attack by directing huge volume of malicious traffic at the target system. With digital twins, the target systems are physical devices equipped with sensors at layer 1. The attackers intend to disrupt the normal operations at layer 1 by overwhelming the devices with false traffic. The sudden incoming of traffic exhausts the resources of the target system, making it unavailable and thus disrupting the data collection. This disruption further impacts the simulation and prediction process. The various forms of DDoS attacks that can disrupt normal operations of a network are outlined in Table 7.1.

In addition, if physical entities are compromised, they can be exploited by DDoS attackers as botnets. Furthermore, at Layer 2, DDoS attacks may target the synchronization process by overwhelming data transit with malicious traffic between physical and digital devices. Communication protocols such as Zigbee, Wireless Sensor Networks (WSNs), and cellular networks are particularly susceptible to such attacks, potentially leading to significant operational disruptions. This threat causes a significant overload of memory and other hardware resources in terms of communication and storage. However, the impact of this threat increases at those DT's level that are more centralized than the decentralized ones.

Digital twins employed in industries are susceptible to DDoS attacks if not securely patched. Such attacks can disrupt all automated processes, potentially affecting the entire distribution network. Similarly, if the digital twins of Internet Service Providers (ISPs) are targeted by DDoS attacks, it could bring the entire industry to a standstill. In addition, DDoS attacks on digital twins in smart cities could disrupt critical infrastructure managed by these systems, such as traffic control and power grids.

- Eavesdropping Attacks

In critical infrastructure digital twins, data transmitted between layers 1 and 3—both upstream and downstream—is often targeted by adversaries. If these communications are not adequately secured, they can be intercepted. Eavesdropping attacks, in particular, may occur at layer 1, where adversaries capture sensor data directly from physical devices. In addition, the vulnerabilities of the synchronization process in layer 2 can also be exploited by adversaries to launch sniffing and snooping attacks to intercept the data in transition. Therefore, insecure communication channels can allow attackers to eavesdrop on transmitted data. The unauthorized interception of transmitted data gives access to the valuable information exchanged between the devices equipped at each layer. Data exposed through interception may cause significant security implications for the confidentiality and integrity of the transmitted data.

Adversaries with the ability to interfere might also monitor the network to analyse the flow of data and trace the location and IP addresses of the servers hosting the digital twin. With the gathered information, adversaries can launch severe attacks on the digital twin infrastructure and can disrupt the normal operations of the associated IoT network. Such attacks not only damage the physical system by inducing malfunctioning and posing safety hazards but also the reputation of the organizations.

- Tampering Attacks

Adversaries aim to modify or fabricate data collected from sensory devices, which can be used to launch severe attacks. Since corrupted data adversely affects the prediction process and the entire business model of the digital twin, adversaries continuously seek vulnerabilities to exploit by injecting noise or distorting the data. Data tampering attacks at layer 1 target sensory devices, while attacks at layer 2 focus on storage servers to contaminate data, leading to inaccurate results. Such tampering compromises the integrity of data at every layer.

In addition, tampering attacks also target the application interfaces at layer 3. Such manipulation of virtual representations can result in inaccurate or false data being transmitted to end users. Furthermore, these attacks often aim to gain unauthorized access in order to alter the dataset. Such interference can significantly impact the training and testing phase of the prediction model.

If an adversary with abilities can manipulate the sensor readings of a machine, it becomes difficult to identify its actual status. For example, display of normal parameters due to tampering attacks by an overheated machine.

- Unauthorized Access

Due to unpatched vulnerabilities, adversaries can gain the ability to impersonate legitimate identifications and mislead other resources on the digital twin network. Such acts facilitate unauthorized access and fabrication or modification of data flowing on the network. Unauthorized access can pose a high risk to the whole model. It can lead to data theft, intellectual property theft, disruption of operations, and security risks to connected devices.

Malicious attackers use incorrect or duplicate identities to deceive connected devices at all the layers of digital twin architecture. At layer 1, physical entities equipped with sensory devices can be duped by adversaries to extract sensitive and critical details stored in the devices or communicated on the channels. Similarly, compromised virtual representations at layer 3 can trick other virtual representations into extracting critical data. Unauthorized access by adversaries can lead to industrial espionage targeting digital twins of critical infrastructures. For example, a digital twin managing a power grid with weak access control measures can be vulnerable to unauthorized access, potentially leading to safety hazards and system failures.

- Sensitive Data Leakage

Adversaries use various attacking tools to target devices connected within the network of digital twins. The purpose is to extract credentials of the devices to gain unauthorized access, which can be used to launch severe attacks on digital twins and to extract sensitive data. In addition, the adversary sniffs the signals transmitted through communication channels to capture sensitive data such as the location of servers. Malicious attackers leverage sensitive data to further launch severe attacks on the IoT network. Each device involved in the digital twin network owns sensitive data. The leakage of data at all three layers is a considerable threat to the digital twin model. Adversaries strategize attacks to gain control over volumes of data collected from sensory devices for modelling purposes. These attacks impede the normal operations of digital twins.

The adversary intends to obtain and exploit the communicated data at the layers to hinder the correct construction of digital twins. Attackers can maliciously sell acquired data to other entities. Without adequate traceability, malicious entities that misuse the sensitive data cannot be held accountable. In addition to this, adversaries also generate false data to corrupt the original data blocks of the digital twin and the synchronization process of layer 2. Subsequently, this negatively impacts the decision-making capabilities of the digital twins, leading to incorrect actions performed by physical entities.

- Poisoning Attacks

In poisoning attacks, adversaries inject malicious samples into the dataset. These samples can fabricate data labels or alter the distribution of the training data, leading to an increase in false positives or false negatives in classifiers. Such data poisoning attacks in machine learning aim to corrupt the training data, impairing the model's ability to accurately detect anomalies and predict outcomes. Thus, substantially degrading the predictive accuracy of the model.

If adversaries gain the ability to poison the model parameters, it alters data analysis and leads to inaccuracies in visual representations at layer 3. The infusion of noise into model parameters adversely affects analysis accuracy, resulting in distorted digital representations of physical entities and degrading overall performance. Additionally, poisoning attacks on layer 2 disrupt the synchronization process, further reducing the digital twin model's accuracy. Such attacks compromise the integrity of the target systems. For example, in a health care digital twin, an adversary could poison the dataset by labelling normal readings as anomalies, causing incorrect disease predictions that may be life threatening.

- Attacks on Cloud/Edge

Cloud and edge servers play an integral role in digital twin networks. However, since they are often owned by third parties, ensuring compliance and auditability can be challenging. Cloud service providers are attractive targets for attackers due to the large volumes of data stored in their repositories. Additionally, misconfigurations by customers can lead to the leakage of sensitive data.

Attacks on cloud environments include malware injection, DDoS, misconfigured security patches, and insider threats. Insider threats often involve disgruntled employees who share their credentials with attackers for financial gain or personal grudges. Such actions lead to misuse of privileges, resulting in data breaches and various risks to data integrity.

Table 7.1 summarizes the attacks targeting the integrity, confidentiality, authentication, and availability of digital twins through different security threats. The enforcement of data privacy and security principles should be governed by legal and regulatory frameworks to prevent data breaches and losses. The following section discusses prominent data privacy laws applicable across various jurisdictions.

7.3 Design of Data Privacy Law

The previous section discussed the security threats related to digital twins. Digital Twins collects voluminous data, processes it, and uses it in predictive models to make prompt decisions, avoiding any life hazards. The collected data includes highly sensitive data about health records, operations, simulation, traffic management, and many more. Being highly crucial for providing valuable insights, these collected data are also subject to severe security attacks. Hence, the concern of maintaining data privacy significantly increases with the proliferation of digital twins. In this age of digital twins, understanding data privacy laws is extremely imperative to protect the consumer's and the stakeholders' rights.

Digital twins are a blend of IoT devices, cloud computing, machine learning, and immersive technologies to create a digital counterpart of the physical entity. Thus, from a legal point of view, digital twins should have legal compliance to ensure data privacy at each level of their architecture. The digital twins process sensitive data such as medical data and intellectual properties; therefore, they should be legally compliant to maintain privacy and algorithmic integrity. The data privacy law imposes liability on the organizations if any negligence in the working of digital twins causes a data breach [18].

Digital twins require robust data privacy measures and compliance with laws and regulations are essential to prevent financial loss, protect reputations, and build trust among users. Different countries and regions abide by their privacy laws; however, these apply to the following stakeholders:

a) Data Controller: responsible for data collection, storage, and sharing.
b) Data Processor: responsible for processing the data as per the instructions.
c) Data Subject: own the personal data.

In most digital twin applications, data frequently crosses multiple jurisdictions with varying data privacy laws. Consider a DT application, which procures data in one jurisdiction and processes it in a different jurisdiction. For instance, a digital twin of a manufacturing unit in Germany, whose headquarters is in India, needs to communicate data for acquiring knowledge and for predictive modelling. As data is communicated between countries, the laws of both countries would be applicable. In such cases, the jurisdiction of all the countries involved should be studied in depth, as legal implications of data breaches depend on the applicable jurisdiction.

Organizations employing digital twins should mindfully follow the data privacy principles. This section discusses the prominent data privacy laws.

a) General Data Protection Regulation (GDPR):

The GDPR was drafted by the European Union (EU) [19] in 2018 and secures the privacy rights of the people of the EU. It strictly imposes fines on those who violate its privacy regulations. The objective of the regulation is to establish guidelines prescribing secure handling and transition of personal data. In addition, it aims to protect the fundamental rights of users in the digital age and defines how businesses should operate within the EU's digitized market. In simple words, GDPR defines legal ways of

- transferring and processing personal data;
- security of personal data in the organization and during transit; and
- establishing rights of individuals in the case of breach.

Its regulations are applicable to all organizations that process personal data of EU citizens. The guidelines of the regulation have set the rules for the organizations to implement appropriate controls for security and protection from unauthorized access of personal data. It also applies to digital twins when the personal data are processed.

Article 5 of the GDPR outlines the principles applicable to the processing of personal data, emphasizing lawfulness, fairness, and transparency. It also imposes restrictions on the amount of collection, storage, integrity, accountability, and confidentiality of data. With lawfulness, it means that the controller should have a legal basis to process the personal data of the subject. Fairness implies the processing should be performed fairly, and transparency implies the process should be transparent to individuals.

Article 6 complies with the consent of the data subject for processing the personal data, and Article 7 provides the conditions for consent and also gives the data subject the right to withdraw consent. Article 9 deals with the processing of special categories of data such as racial, religious, health-related, and so forth, and Article 10 deals with criminal convictions and offenses. In addition, Articles 77–84 cover the right to complain about compensation; these articles also deal with determining the liability against data breach. Moreover, Article 83 lays down fines to be imposed on organizations that violate the GDPR. The fine can be up to 10 million EUR or 2% of their annual turnover, earned worldwide for minor infringements, and 20 million EUR or 4% of their annual turnover, earned worldwide for major infringements.

The GDPR also gives data subjects the "right to be forgotten," which means they can at any time request to withdraw their data or consent. In such cases, all data should be removed by the controller. They also have the right to refuse to permit the processing of their data. Additionally, they possess the right to get the incorrect data rectified. Moreover, GDPR states that the data controller must inform the supervisory authority about the security breach within 72 hours if the breach compromises personal data. Breach notification should be detailed information on the nature and cause of the breach with the amount of data that got compromised.

The data controller's responsibility is to securely share data with processors or any third party, and along with the processor, to ensure stringent security measures are enforced to secure personal data. As per GDPR compliance, data protection should be adopted by design to ensure the security of data at every level of operational activities. The act emphasizes the importance of integrating privacy by design principles into the operational framework, ensuring adherence across all compliant entities.

b) Digital Personal Data Protection Act, 2023 (DPDP Act):
The DPDP Act, enacted by the Indian government, came into existence in the year 2023. It aims to protect the individual's personal data and allow only lawful processing [20]. The legal framework of this act safeguards the privacy of individuals' data. Before the enactment of the DPDP Act, the IT Act, 2000, and its subsequent amendments governed data privacy in India. The DPDP Act in 2023 emerged as a remarkable step towards regulating the handling of personal data in India. It is a concise and yet comprehensive framework that regulates the data privacy protection within India.

The parties involved in any conflict are referred to as

Data Principal: is an entity to whom the personal data belongs.
Data Fiduciary: is an entity that alone or in conjunction with others controls the processing of the data.

Data Processor: is an entity who processes personal data of "Data Principal" as a representative of "Data Fiduciary."

The key aspects included in the DPDP Act are as follows:

a) **Applicability:** The DPDP Act, 2023, governs the processing of personal data of citizens or non-citizens in digital or non-digital form within the regime of India and also outside India if the processing of data is of individuals staying within India.
b) **Responsibility of Data Fiduciary:** A data fiduciary may process the personal data of a data principal for lawful purposes, provided they have obtained consent or are acting under specific legitimate uses. The consent given by the individual signifies an agreement to process the data only for specific use.
c) **Data Principal's Rights and Duties:** Data principals have the right to grievance redressal as well as to access, correction, and erasure of personal data. His duties include abiding by the law and sharing all material and authentic information. He should also avoid appealing for false grievance.
d) **Data Protection Board:**
It consists of a chairperson and additional members, each serving a tenure of two years. The board monitors the compliance and direct mitigation process in case of a data breach. Boards also redress grievances and impose penalties. Chapter VIII of the Act deals with penalties imposed for data breaches.

Indian organizations leveraging digital twins must comply with the principles of the DPDP Act. These include

a) Organizations must obtain the informed consent of individuals before collecting their data. Data collection should be transparent and clearly explain the purpose and implications of data processing.
b) Organizations must not deviate from the purposes for which informed consent was obtained during data processing.
c) Organizations must ensure adoption of the minimization principle. Only the personal data necessary for processing should be collected.

d) Organizations must adhere to the storage limitation principle. Organizations must erase the collected personal data from storage once the intended purpose has been fulfilled.
e) The act holds the data fiduciary responsible for any data breach of collected personal data.

c) Health Insurance Portability and Accountability Act (HIPAA Privacy Rules):

It was enacted by the U.S. federal government in 1996 to safeguard personally identifiable information collected by hospitals, health care providers, or other covered entities from fraud or theft. Covered entities include all organizations that handle patient data, such as health plans, insurers, and similar institutions. HIPAA privacy rules prohibit health care providers from disclosing sensitive patient information to unauthorized individuals. However, disclosures are permitted for 12 national priority purposes, as outlined by law, in the public interest.

The act imposes civil penalties on covered entities of $100 per failure to comply with the rules. If the violation is not due to wilful neglect or reasonable cause and is corrected by the entities within 30 days of violation, the act does not impose any penalty. In case of criminal offence, the violation fines the entities up to $50,000 and 1 year of imprisonment [21].

The three digital privacy laws and their principles dealing with the data privacy issues in the age of digital twins have been discussed in this section. Apart from these three acts, the California Consumer Privacy Act (CCPA) [22] came into effect in 2020 to protect the privacy rights of Californians. It is crucial for organizations leveraging digital twins to understand and follow the provisions of these laws. Organizations should understand the technical and legal complexities of the data privacy laws and must balance their innovation with privacy. The interoperability issues are also a major concern for the digital age. Organizations should employ best practices to ensure privacy and leverage the potentials of digital twins. Adhering to data privacy laws not only safeguards individual rights but also strengthens trust and encourages innovation in the transformative era. The organizations are expected to implement secure strategies to protect from data breaches and cyberattacks.

7.4 Strategies for Securing Digital Twins

Section 7.2 outlined the potential security threats to digital twins. The emphasis of this section is on strategies to secure the digital twins from potential threats studied in [14, 23], and [24]. It is extremely important to identify and analyse the potential security risks before strategizing the security measures. For example, the potential risk points could be application interfaces, transmission lines, IoT integration points, and so forth. To effectively avoid attacks, it is extremely crucial to understand the attacker's perspective. The following proactive measures are required to ensure the security of digital twins:

a) **Ensuring Confidentiality:**

Privacy protection in digital twins is essential to safeguard personal data collected by their components. Law enforcement agencies should mandate organizations to implement measures that ensure privacy protection and prevent identity theft. If not secured effectively, the data collected from sensory devices and transmitted to simulation models for prediction is highly susceptible to compromise. Therefore, it is extremely crucial to focus on "privacy by design" principle during implementation of digital twins.

Loss of collected data like location, performance parameters, medical records, and other sensor data could potentially impact confidentiality [25]. Encryption is the most effective technique to keep the sensitive data secure from cyberattacks. Data should be encrypted using robust encryption algorithms before transmission within the IoT network of digital twins. Similarly, data stored on the cloud and edge servers should also be encrypted to protect it from unauthorized access.

Encryption protects the data from unauthorized access as it converts the plain text into coded form that can be decrypted only using the secret decryption key. Even if an adversary manages to capture the data by intrusion or through eavesdropping during transition, the encrypted data stays unreadable to them. All communications within the network should have end-to-end encryption. A multi-layered security approach enhances the protection of communications and sensitive data stored on devices by securing digital identities against data theft, insider threats, and cloud-based security breaches.

In addition, device software should be kept up to date, and all security patches should be installed to prevent attacks that exploit software vulnerabilities. Keeping software updated is one of the key defensive measures to maintain the confidentiality of sensitive data. Thus, encryption algorithms and timely software updates create a defensive wall around sensitive data.

b) **Ensuring Enforcement of Authorization and Authentication:**

A robust access control system that prevents unauthorized access at every layer of the digital twin architecture is a fundamental requirement for any digital twin framework. Advanced access control mechanisms should be implemented to mitigate the risks of unauthorized access. In addition, multi-factor authentication strengthens the security system by adding one more layer of security checking. Furthermore, Biometric authentication measures such as fingerprint and facial recognition should also be included to enhance the security of sensitive data. Moreover, advanced mechanism such as role-based access controls that concentrate on the principle of least privilege and grant minimal access to digital resources. Thus, users can have access to only those resources and functionalities that they need.

In addition to implementing an efficient access control system, the security handling team should periodically review the user access permissions and promptly revoke the access rights of deactivated users.

Furthermore, the security system should also include AI-enabled tools that continuously monitor networks and transmissions, allowing immediate detection and tracing of malicious activities such as suspicious login attempts or unauthorized access. Some popular methods for solving intrusion detection problems include artificial neural networks (ANN), decision trees (DT), evolutionary algorithms (EA), genetic algorithms (GA), particle swarm optimization (PSO), and simulated annealing (SA). These AI-driven methods help in spotting anomalies in network traffic. Frequent audits also help in tracing unusual behavioural patterns. For example, an audit can identify weak and vulnerable points, leading to timely patching of the loopholes. Penetration testing on digital twins involves simulating real-world attacks to identify weak authentication methods enforced within their framework. Such identifications of vulnerabilities allow the organizations to timely strengthen the defense system of the framework.

In [25], the authors proposed a smart manufacturing framework that balances between operational efficiency and privacy protection. Additionally, the framework also incorporated a robust identity authentication mechanism used in an IIoT environment.

c) **Ensuring Integrity:**

A digital twin is a virtual replica of a physical device and allows for simulation, analysis, and informed decision making; thus, the collected data from physical devices equipped with sensors is highly attractive to attackers for fabrication. By tampering with the data, the attacker can influence the decision making, leading to safety hazards. The security system should ensure the generated data is accurate, consistent, and reliable. Protecting data from unauthorized changes ensures that the digital twin model accurately reflects the real-world counterpart.

In addition, integration of cryptographic hashing and blockchain techniques into the security system also protect from data tampering. Integrity monitoring tools track changes to files and system configurations. Data versioning and timestamps are the mechanisms used to track changes in a digital twin's data and can also analyse security logs to identify unauthorized access to files.

Furthermore, secure communication protocols, such as HTTPS, SFTP, SSH, and TLS, also ensure that data is not tampered during transit. Integration of end-to-end encryption also prevents interception and tampering of data in transit and at the storage place.

d) **Ensuring Availability:**

DDoS attacks always pose a significant threat to network availability. Advanced tools allow us to monitor the suspicious traffic and detect anomalies. For instance, consider a scenario where all the devices involved or connected through the IoT network are communicating and traffic flows from trustworthy IP addresses, and if malicious traffic from unknown IP addresses suddenly attempts to infiltrate the network, such access should be instantly detected and blocked.

Firewalls and intrusion detection systems help monitor for unauthorized intrusions and apply predefined security rules to filter out malicious traffic. The firewalls protect the network perimeter and block external threats, just like security fences. In contrast, Intrusion Detection Systems (IDS) monitor all network activity and transmissions to detect anomalies such as unauthorized access, logins at unusual times, or access from unfamiliar IP addresses—functioning much like surveillance cameras.

The advanced tools identify unusual behaviours of incoming and outgoing traffic and apply control to them. Popular tools such as Cloudflare, Akamai, AWS Shield, and Google Cloud Armor apply the following strategies to protect from DDoS attacks:

i. Traffic filtering—block malicious traffic from unfamiliar IP addresses.
ii. Rate limiting—a DDoS attack conspires to overwhelm the system with volumes of traffic to make it unavailable for legitimate users. The security tools limit the traffic volume to prevent such attacks.
iii. Load balancing—distributing traffic across multiple servers.
iv. Content delivery networks—increases availability by distributing content across multiple servers.

Systems should be designed to scale effectively to mitigate the impact of such attacks. Regular firewall updates and periodic security audits are also essential to prevent service disruptions.

In addition, a multi-layered security approach helps to uncover flaws and strengthen the system. Deployment of AI/ML tools to precisely identify the unusual activities also strengthens the security system. It is essential to regularly monitor the digital twin framework to identify and tackle evolving threats. The proactive measures ensure the security of the framework of digital twins. By implementing the right strategies, you can safely leverage digital twins into your operations.

7.5 Privacy by Design

Digital twins are powerful enough to revolutionize the transformative era of Industry 4.0 and Industry 5.0. However, due to their inherent technology stack, they have many cybersecurity challenges. Privacy must be carefully integrated into the system's design and architecture from the beginning [26]. In other words, "Privacy by Design" framework emphasizes the importance of implementing privacy measures throughout the lifecycle of digital twins from design phase to deployment phase. The "Privacy by Design" framework supports preventive measures rather than reactive. Instead of incorporating approaches that addresses the privacy risk when they happen, companies should embed preventive measures protecting data privacy. Privacy must be embedded in each design process to promote functionality and privacy protection.

In [27], the authors proposed a digital twin approach that embeds the "Privacy by Design" framework in the automobile industry. The proposed model simulates a smart car ecosystem, ensuring that collected data complies with privacy policies and regulations, while also incorporating GDPR principles to safeguard data subjects' rights. In [28], federated learning has been used as privacy preserving techniques to enhance the adoption of digital twin framework in smart cities. In [29], the authors proposed cloud computing and block chain–based privacy preserving communication schemes for wireless channels.

To develop more secure and reliable digital twins, it is essential to follow these proactive measures:

1. **Data Protection:** As data is most sensitive and critical for the digital twin model, rigorous operations are used to

protect the data that should match the risks associated with them.

a) The principle of minimality ensures minimal access and privileges granted on critical data to its users.
b) The principle of limited collection ensures only legally allowed and required amount and type of data is collected.
c) Storage media must be thoroughly scanned to prevent any data loss.
d) Software and hardware used to access and store the critical data need robust protection. Similarly, the security measures applied to network infrastructure and communication protocols impact the security of critical data.
e) Keep operationally sensitive data on a separate system.
f) Keep data in read-only mode to protect its integrity.
g) The collected data should be used only for the agreed purpose. Organizations should not keep data after its use is fulfilled and should not disclose to anyone.

2. **Safely leveraging cloud services:** By using cloud computing, digital twins can leverage scalability, cost-effectiveness in data processing, access to real-time data, and improved decision-making and operational efficiency. However, this collaboration should be established with secure cloud service providers realizing core privacy principle of digital twin designs. The "privacy by design" principle promotes configuring the cloud and its services in a way that matches your security needs. It also suggests selecting cloud providers that offer a robust security structure and have a proven track record of protecting data. For example, Amazon Web Services and Microsoft Azure implement strong encryption methods to protect data in place and during transit. They even implement role-based access controls and multi-factor authentication to allow access only to authorized users. Additionally, the selected cloud service should comply with relevant privacy regulations such as GDPR or HIPAA and use secure APIs and protocols to integrate with digital twins.
3. **End-to-end security:** End-to-end security should be ensured throughout the life cycle of the digital twin, that is, from the collection of data to the deployment phase. This means while designing the digital twin model, privacy principles should be enforced on both the physical device and

its virtual counterpart. Physical security measures should ensure that only authorized personnel can access the physical device equipped with sensors—the primary source of collected data. In addition, the data shared on the communication channel should be encrypted before transmission. Robust encryption algorithms help in preventing eavesdropping and unauthorized access in transit, while techniques such as HMACs can detect data tampering. Furthermore, techniques like copy-on-write create snapshots of database servers and help in identifying tampering attacks, and STRIDE frameworks help in potential threat detection. Continuous monitoring and regular security audits of digital twins also help in the timely detection of anomalies.

4. **Internet Connectivity:** Monitor how long the complete system operates smoothly in case of loss of internet connection. This helps in identifying the resilience of critical services dependent on Internet services. The disruption of internet services caused by cyberattacks can significantly impact the services of a digital twin model. Therefore, mechanisms that minimize the mean time required to resume services should be implemented. Proper backup systems and load and data sharing to distributed servers ensure reliability and security against data breaches.
5. **User Identity Protection:** Use techniques such as anonymizing or pseudonymizing data to protect users' identities. The "privacy by design" principles enforce protection of user's identity policy in the system. Using anonymization, all personal identity information can be removed, while pseudonymization uses artificial identifiers to hide identity.

Data masking, swapping, perturbation, and synthetic data generation are anonymization techniques. Data shuffling, scrambling, and substitution are the techniques used in data masking to protect sensitive data. Masking differs from encryption techniques. Although encryption is one of the best techniques to secure sensitive data, it is difficult to execute queries on encrypted data. In contrast, the masked data retains the characteristics of the original data; therefore, the query yields the same results on both.

Data perturbation is primarily used in, but not limited to, the health care industry. This technique adds noise to the records in the database to make them unreadable to unauthorized users. Only authorized users, who know the technique of removing noise, can access the data. The data swapping technique replaces the value of a field with another value of the same field in the database. This transformation technique preserves the statistical distribution of data.

Tokenization, hashing, and encryption are pseudonymization techniques. These techniques process data in a way that it becomes impossible to attribute it to a specific person without additional information such as an encryption key. The personal data that we share with the banks, merchants, and hospitals is considered sensitive data under GDP regulations. For instance, the bank wants to analyse the customer behaviour patterns *via* the third party. In that case, the bank has to share the collected data with them. The organizations complying with GDPR can only share the pseudonymized data without any additional information. Additionally, only the data that is required for analysis should be shared with the third party.

Tokenization replaces sensitive data with algorithm-generated tokens. This technique maintains the connection between the sensitive data and its tokens. Thus, the research analysis can be easily performed on tokenized data. Apart from this hash, symmetric and asymmetric encryptions are used to generate pseudonyms. Industries with strict privacy regulations use these techniques to hide sensitive data and keep it secure from unauthorized access. Anonymizing and pseudonymizing techniques both ensure data confidentiality; however, they do so with different degrees of protection.

6. **Access Control:** Enforce stringent controls to guarantee authenticated and authorized access. Role based access controls and multi-factor authentication systems impose stringent access controls and safeguard the system from unauthorized access.
7. **Visibility and Transparency:** Policies of privacy should be clearly documented and communicated to the users. Visibility and transparency in privacy policies build trust among users. It is good practice to keep policies and complaint redressal processes open.
8. **Compliance with Regulatory Frameworks:** Organizations must comply with the GDPR, CCPA, HIPAA, and DPDP regulations whichever is applicable to their region and industry.

By putting these proactive measures into practice, organizations can develop digital twins based on the "Privacy by Design" framework. To foster technological trust, such innovations must prioritize and respect user privacy.

The following case studies demonstrate how the integration of the "Privacy by Design" principle within the digital twin enhances the robustness of cybersecurity measures:

1. Siemens Digital Twin of Gas Turbine:
Siemens' Digital Twin replicated the gas turbine to streamline operations and ensure cybersecurity by utilizing robust access controls and end-to-end encryption techniques. In addition, it implemented secure protocols to protect against cyber threats and conducted frequent vulnerability assessments. Furthermore, Siemens integrated security features into the design and built its cybersecurity framework on the "Privacy by Design" principle [30].

2. Duke Energy's Digital Twin for Power Grid Optimization:
Duke Energy's Digital Twin not only optimized the operation of the power grid but also ensured protection from unauthorized access and safeguarded critical infrastructure. The stringent intrusion detection systems of the digital twin safeguarded from malicious access. Additionally, its incident response system addressed potential vulnerabilities before they became critical. Duke Energy set an example for other organizations by integrating cybersecurity measures during the design phase, demonstrating that strong security controls ensure the integrity, confidentiality, authenticity, and availability of the system [30].

Conclusion

The adoption of digital twins into industries supporting critical infrastructure has significantly improved operational efficiency and decision making. The virtual replica of physical systems supports predictive maintenance and enables early identification of potential issues. However, this revolutionary advancement also exposes these models to severe security threats, particularly targeting the sensitive data collected by sensor-equipped devices.

This chapter explores the key security threats and concerns associated with the digital twin framework, as well as the protective measures required to be integrated across each layer of its architecture, from inception to deployment. Additionally, it discussed relevant data privacy laws such as GDPR, DPDP, HIPAA, and CCPA, which govern the secure collection, use, and storage of personally identifiable information and protects individuals' data privacy rights.

The chapter underscores the significance of embedding cybersecurity measures during the design phase and strongly advocates for the adoption of the "Privacy by Design" framework in digital twin systems to establish a balance between innovation and privacy. Furthermore, case studies demonstrated the success of organizations that integrated cybersecurity measures such as access controls, encryption techniques, secure protocols, and regular audits, early in the design process.

In conclusion, by prioritizing cybersecurity, organizations not only strengthen their defense systems but also build resilience, mitigate risks and enhance trustworthiness. Maintaining privacy is key the widespread and responsible adoption of digital twin technology across all sectors. The rapid evolution of digital twins, driven by integration with AI and edge computing, convergence with the metaverse, and applications in sustainability, has increased integration, operability, security, legal, and ethical challenges.

AI disclosure statement: The author confirms that no artificial intelligence (AI)-generated content or AI-assisted writing tools were used in the preparation of this chapter (including summaries and the abstract). All text, analysis, and conclusions are the result of the author's original work.

References

1. Root Analysis, Digital Twin Market, in: *Root Analysis*, Accessed: Jul. 08, 2025. [Online]. Available: https://www.rootsanalysis.com/reports/digital-twins-market.html.
2. Grand View Research, Digital Twin Market Size and Share, Industry Report, in: *Grand View Research*, 2030, Accessed: Jul. 08, 2025. [Online]. Available: https://www.grandviewresearch.com/industry-analysis/digital-twin-market.
3. Grieves, M. and Vickers, J., Digital twin: Mitigating unpredictable, undesirable emergent behavior in complex systems, in: *Transdisciplinary Perspectives on Complex Systems: New Findings and Approaches*, pp. 85–113, Springer International Publishing, 2016, doi: 10.1007/978-3-319-38756-7_4.
4. Rolls Royce, IntelligentEngine Our vision for the future of aircraft power, in: *Rolls Royce*, Accessed: Jul. 08, 2025. [Online]. Available: https://www.rolls-royce.com/media/our-stories/discover/2020/intelligentengine-explainer.aspx.

5. Ford, Ford's New Headlights are Ahead of the Curve When it Comes to Making Night Driving Easier, in: *Ford*, Accessed: Jul. 08, 2025. [Online]. Available: https://media.ford.com/content/fordmedia/feu/en/news/2021/04/22/ford_s-new-headlights-are-ahead-of-the-curve-when-it-comes-to-ma.html.
6. BP, Here's one way bp is using tech to innovate its Gulf of America operations, in: *BP*, Accessed: Jul. 08, 2025. [Online]. Available: https://www.bp.com/en_us/united-states/home/news/features-and-highlights/heres-one-way-bp-is-using-tech-to-innovate-its-gulf-of-america-operations.html.
7. Observatory of Public Sector Innovation, Virtual Singapore – Singapore's virtual twin, in: *Observatory of Public Sector Innovation*, Accessed: Jul. 08, 2025. [Online]. Available: https://oecd-opsi.org/innovations/virtual-twin-singapore/.
8. V. Pavlov Thesis and I. Yanqiu Huang Services, Security Aspects of Digital Twins in IoT platform, 2022.
9. Mun, H., *et al.*, A Comprehensive Survey on Digital Twin: Focusing on Security Threats and Requirements. *Inst. Electr. Electron. Eng. Inc.*, 2025. doi: 10.1109/ACCESS.2025.3563621.
10. Kayan, H., Nunes, M., Rana, O., Burnap, P., Perera, C., Cybersecurity of Industrial Cyber-Physical Systems: A Review. *ACM Comput. Surv.*, 54, 11s, Jan. 2022. doi: 10.1145/3510410.
11. Ahmed, H.I., Nasr, A.A., Abdel-Mageid, S., Aslan, H.K., A survey of IoT security threats and defenses. *Int. J. Adv. Comput. Res.*, 9, 45, 325–350, Oct. 2019. doi: 10.19101/ijacr.2019.940116.
12. Butun, I., Osterberg, P., Song, H., Security of the Internet of Things: Vulnerabilities, Attacks, and Countermeasures. *IEEE Commun. Surv. Tutorials*, 22, 1, 616–644, Jan. 2020. doi: 10.1109/COMST.2019.2953364.
13. Wang, Y., Su, Z., Guo, S., Dai, M., Luan, T.H., Liu, Y., A Survey on Digital Twins: Architecture, Enabling Technologies, Security and Privacy, and Future Prospects, Feb. 01, 2023. doi: 10.36227/techrxiv.21972416.v1.
14. Sargsyan, G., Security and privacy in digital twins, in: *Security Technologies and Methods for Advanced Cyber Threat Intelligence, Detection and Mitigation*, pp. 198–203, Now Publishers, 2022, doi: 10.1561/9781680838350.
15. Zaman, S., *et al.*, Security Threats and Artificial Intelligence Based Countermeasures for Internet of Things Networks: A Comprehensive Survey. *IEEE Access*, 9, 94668–94690, 2021. doi: 10.1109/ACCESS.2021.3089681.
16. Alcaraz, C. and Lopez, J., Digital Twin: A Comprehensive Survey of Security Threats. *IEEE Commun. Surv. Tutorials*, 24, 3, 1475–1503, Sep. 2022. doi: 10.1109/COMST.2022.3171465.
17. Hassija, V., Chamola, V., Saxena, V., Jain, D., Goyal, P., Sikdar, B., A Survey on IoT Security: Application Areas, Security Threats, and Solution Architectures, 2019.
18. Parikh, M., Kamath, A., Jajesh, V., Kapoor, P., The Tour d'Horizon of Data Law Implications of Digital Twins. *J. Innovation*, 27, 2025.

19. London, D., York, N., Francisco, S., A Guide by Mason Hayes & Curran A Guide to the General Data Protection Regulation, 2019.
20. The Digital Personal Data Act, 2023. Available from: www.indiacode.nic.in [Accessed: June 15, 2024].
21. U.S. Department of Health and Human Services, Health Information Privacy. Accessed: Jul. 09, 2025. [Online]. Available: https://www.hhs.gov/hipaa/for-professionals/special-topics/reproductive-health/index.html.
22. California Consumer Privacy Act (CCPA) updated on March 13, 2024, State of California Department of Justice. Accessed: Jun. 25, 2025. [Online]. Available: https://oag.ca.gov/privacy/ccpa.
23. Monika, S., Kelly, K., Josh, F., Securing Digital Twins Cybersecurity Challenges and Strategies. [Online]. Available: https://www.researchgate.net/publication/388419334.
24. Homaei, M., Gutierrez, O.M., Nunez, J.C.S., Vegas, M.A., Lindo, A.C., A Review of Digital Twins and their Application in Cybersecurity based on Artificial Intelligence, Nov. 2023. doi: 10.1007/s10462-024-10805-3.
25. Chen, H., Jeremiah, S.R., Lee, C., Park, J.H., A Digital Twin-Based Heuristic Multi-Cooperation Scheduling Framework for Smart Manufacturing in IIoT Environment. *Appl. Sci. (Switzerland)*, 13, 3, Feb. 2023. doi: 10.3390/app13031440.
26. Ahmadi-Assalemi, G., Al-Khateeb, H., Aggoun, A., Privacy-enhancing technologies in the design of digital twins for smart cities. *Network Secur.*, 2022, 7, Jul. 2022. doi: 10.12968/S1353-4858(22)70046-3.
27. Damjanovic-Behrendt, V., A Digital Twin-based Privacy Enhancement Mechanism for the Automotive Industry, in: *International Conference on Intelligent Systems (IS)*, IEEE, pp. 272–279, Sep. 2018.
28. Zheng, X., Lu, J., Kiritsis, D., The emergence of cognitive digital twin: vision, challenges and opportunities. *Int. J. Prod. Res.*, 60, 24, 7610–7632, 2022. doi: 10.1080/00207543.2021.2014591.
29. Son, S., Kwon, D., Lee, J., Yu, S., Jho, N.S., Park, Y., On the Design of a Privacy-Preserving Communication Scheme for Cloud-Based Digital Twin Environments Using Blockchain. *IEEE Access*, 10, 75365–75375, 2022. doi: 10.1109/ACCESS.2022.3191414.
30. Palanichamy, N., Maheswar, R., Ragupathy, U. S., *Digital Twins and Cyber Security*. Scrivener Publishing LLC, 2025.

8

AI and ML for Privacy-Preserving Digital Twins: Challenges and Opportunities

Raj Kishor Verma[1]**, Gaurav Agarwal**[1*] **and Nitin Pandey**[2]

[1]*School of Computing Science and Engineering, Galgotias University, Greater Noida, UP, India*

[2]*School of Computing Application and Technologies, Galgotias University, Greater Noida, UP, India*

Abstract

Reinforcement Learning (RL) is a type of machine learning, where agents learn to perform actions in an environment in order to receive the maximum cumulative reward. Earlier works have aligned the RL paradigm with deep learning and achieved state-of-the-art on large-scale sequential decision problem domains. There are some fundamental issues that still exist with the use of an approach, such as hyper-parameter sensitivity, credit assignment issue across time and long-time horizon with sparse reward, lack of diverse exploratory behaviour, and trade-off between avoiding to achieving rewards. In addition, many optimization problems in RL are hard problems, which have properties of gradient-free, non-convex, multi-modal, dynamic, and so forth, that is difficult to solve by traditional methods. In order to overcome these difficulties, the idea known as Evolutionary Reinforcement Learning has been suggested in previous research, which integrates the principles of Evolutionary Computation (EC) into the realm of Reinforcement Learning (RL). EvoRL maintains a population of agents which brings advantages like fewer amount of largely redundant info for greater robustness, more exploratory power and the capacity to score agents with episodic fitness metrics. This provides a way for agents to transfer skills learned beforehand, thus accelerating the training process and making RL applicable in scenarios that were previously impractical. This philosophy of research led to several breakthroughs in deep Reinforcement Learning, a hybrid of the advances in Deep Learning and Reinforcement Learning (RL), which has taken the space on the internet by storm, resulting in even more autonomous and adaptable systems that can now interpret

**Corresponding author*: Gaurav13shaurya@gmail.com

Shubham Mahajan, Davinder Paul Singh, Amit Kant Pandit and Paras Chawla (eds.) Ensuring Privacy in Digital Twin Ecosystems, (245–272) © 2026 Scrivener Publishing LLC

incredibly high-dimensional data. Multi-Agent Reinforcement Learning (MARL) enables agents to work together or compete, providing a new way to address real-world issues that involve multiple agents1. The robustness and generalization abilities of the RL algorithms improve their resilience toward rigid and dynamic environments, paving the way for greater generalization of the RL technology. This paper functions as a reference point for both researchers and practitioners in the EvoRL sphere, pointing out notable challenges, new associated trends, and collaborative prospects for further research (for instance in optimized methodologies, official benchmarks, and scaling solutions). This facilitates the creation of more specialized benchmarks for EvoRL, aiding these researchers and practitioners to progress in the evolving hybrid area of EvoRL.

***Keywords*:** Digital twin, privacy, artificial intelligence, machine learning, privacy enhancement, data security

8.1 Introduction

Digital twins and digital representations of a physical object or system have been on the rise, powered by technologies such as the IoT, data analytics, and cloud computing, allowing us to monitor, analyse, and predict behaviours in real-time across sectors. When combined with digital twins, generative AI can drastically augment these abilities, resulting in intelligent and adaptive systems capable of autonomously adjusting and optimizing their performance in response to fluctuations in real time. Nonetheless, this integration poses challenges, including data security and privacy concerns, leading to the need for strong cybersecurity practices and data governance policies. Privacy-preserving machine learning alleviates some of these concerns by allowing systems to process encrypted data, which means the original data is never revealed during analysis. For example, in healthcare, sensitive patient data can remain encrypted while training models to predict disease, ensuring patient confidentiality and compliance with regulatory frameworks such as GDPR. In energy grids, operational data can be inspected for problem suitability without leaking sensitive data [1]. While this approach has many advantages, there are several barriers to the successful implementation of artificial intelligence and machine learning in privacy-preserving digital twins: Data security and privacy: The seamless exchange of data among physical entities, digital twins, and AI algorithms invites vulnerabilities. Ethics: Generative AI can be misused for dubious purposes, creating false information that must be addressed in data protection and the ethical sourcing of training data. Data Management: Digital twins are dependent on tons of data from various sources, making them cumbersome to manage. High-quality, high-volume data is critical to creating accurate digital twins and AI models. Interoperability: Enabling seamless communication and data exchange between various elements of the digital twin ecosystem is crucial. Cost and Complexity: A Digital twin can be costly and complex to implement and maintain, requiring modular deployment, open-source tools, and phased investments. To combat these issues, we must be tackling them from every angle with strong cybersecurity infrastructure, ethical AI development standards and practices, some level of formal protocol that will push these developments in the opposite direction of their potential logistical decay, and an attitude of continuous learning and evolution [1].

Reinforcement Learning (RL): The agent learns to make decisions through trial and error in Reinforcement Learning. It is a subfield of machine learning in which the agent interacts with a dynamic environment, takes actions observed in such environments, and gets feedback in the form of rewards or changes behind which there are new states to be brought about. This feedback loop continues until now and consists of a series or stream on actions selected by the agent combined with sates previously passively received; from an observer's perspective for every given moment, this will be reported right back as good or bad reduction in value at once which can last indefinitely until any fresh input is available for later decisions by previous processors. The agent's goal is to learn an optimal policy, a strategy that maps states to actions to maximize the expected cumulative reward (also known as return) over time. This framework's formal definition of RL is often based on a Markov Decision Process, which comprises States (S): The general description of the situation; Actions (A) Choices that an agent can make Transition Function (T): The probability of going from one state to a next Reward Function: The immediate gain (positive or negative) obtained after an action Policy (pi) The strategy the agent follows in making decisions. Several popular RL Methods are Q-learning,

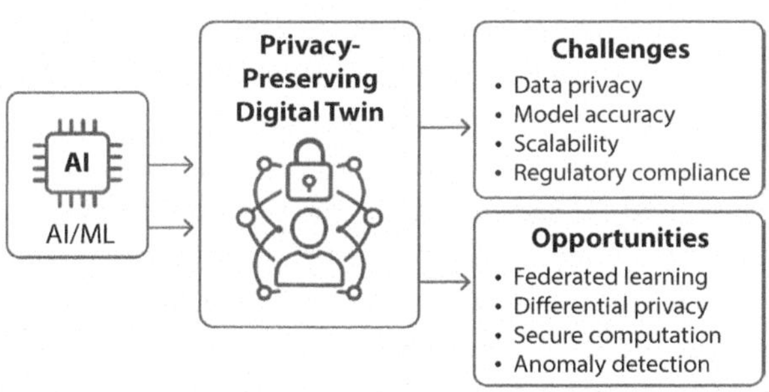

Figure 8.1 Architecture diagram of AI and ML for privacy-preserving digital twins.

about stochastic processes; SARSA (State-Action-Reward-State-Action) in sequence with Time; Deep Q-networks (DQN); Policy Gradient Methods; and Actor-Critic Models. The uses of RL are varied and include important real-world applications such as autonomous vehicles, recommendation systems, robotic control, and stock trading. Figure 8.1 shows the overall architecture of AI and ML for privacy-preserving digital twins, highlighting key challenges and opportunities.

Evolutionary Computation (EC): Evolutionary Computation is a field in artificial intelligence in which principles from biological evolution are used to solve complex optimization problems. It employs the idea of a population as basic feature. In this collection of individual solutions, changes with time. The evolution revolves around making selections, doing crossbreeding, mutating individuals, and then substituting them, very much like natural selection. Genetic algorithms (GA), genetic programming (GP), and evolution strategies (ES) are some of the most important EC methods. With differential evolution (DE), in a population, everyone is a possible solution, and it has a fitness function that will decide how good the solution is by contrast. EC methods do not depend on gradients. It is particularly suitable for optimization in noisy or highly complex search spaces that are not differentiable, parallelizable and naturally suited to exploration but may have a problem fine-tuning solutions when you get up into 100+ dimensions. Increasingly, the next generation of evolutionary computations (EC) is dealing with high-dimensional, non-continuous, non-differentiable optimization problems. For want of an alternative strategy to explore the landscape, brick walls have sometimes been encountered by EC methods. They are also highly parallelizable and naturally suited for exploration, but they might struggle with fine-tuning solutions in high-dimensional continuous spaces.

Evolutionary Reinforcement Learning (EvoRL): Evolutionary Reinforcement Learning (EvoRL) is a hybrid approach that combines RL and EC to address the limitations of either. RL is strong in exploitation—gradually improving the current policy through gradient information—but may be weak in exploration or trapped by local optima. EC, on the other hand, flourishes in exploration through population diversity and global optima but, in continuous spaces, may not be efficient. In Evolutionary Reinforcement Learning (EvoRL), a population of policies is evolved, while individual agents within the population may undergo reinforcement learning updates some of the time to fine-tune their behaviour. This means that we can guarantee broad exploration across humanity as a whole and specifically its lots technological benefits of EvoRL: Emerging methodologies can achieve greater leniency in ultra-competitive environments with thick ice on the ground—or rather, sparse rewards. Generation

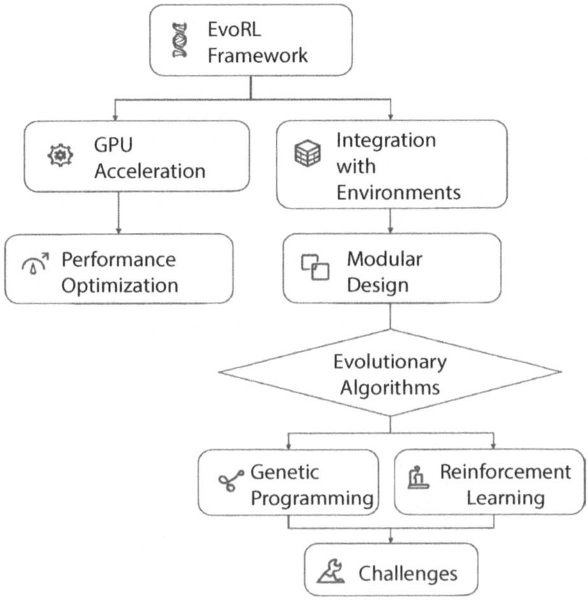

Figure 8.2 Block diagram of evolutionary reinforcement learning framework.

after generation, evolution is now less sensitive to the lack of differentiability of its environment or any sudden jerks in that continuity. Evolution is getting greater diversity. Regional and global search environments present these opportunities to blend both types of searching so that one can hope for convergence. EvoRL has been successfully applied in high-dimensional tasks such as locomotion and manipulation neural network architecture search, strategy games, and so forth. Figure 8.2 illustrates the block diagram of the evolutionary reinforcement learning framework.

8.1.1 Digital Twins

Digital twins are essentially a disruptive technology, which reproduces objects, systems, or processes in virtual reality. The data of a physical asset drives optimal operational decisions and efficiency. Introduction and Background Digital twin has been described to have three main aspects which include: Digital Definition: This represents design specification outputs from tools that generate data. This procedure involves several primary stages: Sensor Data Gathering: The sensors on the object receive the data regarding participation in various events such as temperature, pressure, and vibration. Integration: The middleware allows this data to be brought together, enabling hardware and software elements to communicate. Real-Time Analysis: The digital twin analyses the incoming data with an advanced analytics, while machine-learning algorithms simulate potential scenarios and identify any remaining inefficiencies. Fault prediction can also be achieved in this way Visualization: Should insights be made available in dashboards to let stakeholders act on them in real time. Actionable Insights: Proposals obtained from the analysis can lead to alterations in the operation or maintenance times of the physical system [3].

Component Twins: Models individual parts of a system to manage fine-tuning and monitoring of those components. Asset Twins: Use various component twins in conjunction to provide a top-down view of how complex systems are operating. System Twins: Provide a full picture of an entire system (e.g., a wind farm), helping examine configurations for optimal energy production. Process Twins: Target specific operational workflows as opposed to the systems so the organizations are more efficient implementing production lines as well as assets utilization. Applications of digital twins are diverse and far reaching, here are some to name a few: Manufacturing: Predict when machinery will fail so you can schedule maintenance to make production more efficient. Medicine: Build models for individual patients that consider not only their genetics but also their current health. Smart Grids and Energy Management: Observe energy utilization trends within smart grids to support sustainable development initiatives. Urban Planning: Simulate urban spaces in order to optimize infrastructure development and resource allocation. Notwithstanding their huge potential, digital twins also bring several challenges including, to name a few, Data Security: The challenge of securing the valuable data

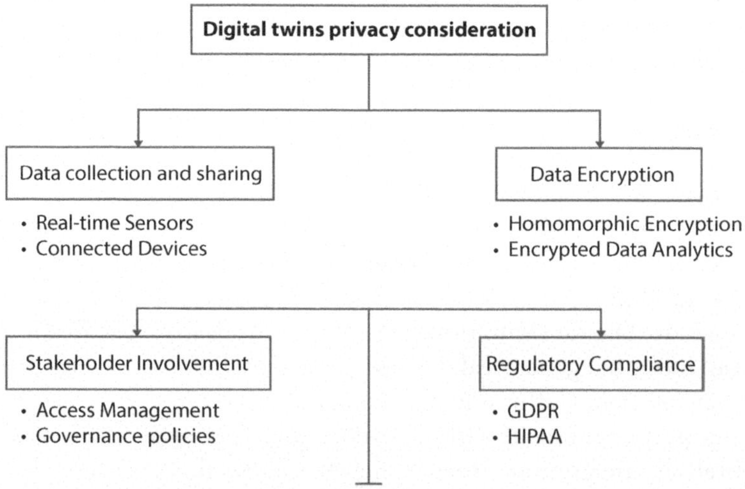

Figure 8.3 Diagram of digital twins privacy considerations.

about their physical counterpart. Integration of Complex Hardware and Software: It is the process of integrating variety of software and hardware systems [7]. Cost Considerations: The capital cost of data collection technologies and re-purchase costs could be high. At the end of the day, digital twins are disrupting the way industries do business, capturing richer, more accurate views of physical systems in their virtual models. Security, integration and cost are the most challenging issues for the realization of benefit to a much larger number of application domains as technology continues to advance [4]. Figure 8.3 presents the privacy considerations in digital twin ecosystems.

8.1.2 Privacy

Digital twins are becoming increasingly important, particularly concerning the trade-off between the details of information exchange, privacy in the system, and the secure use of the data being handled. Digital twins, powered or in tune with intelligent twin AI and ML, are a powerful infrastructure; however, this data is becoming increasingly sensitive and significant—following some privacy questions. In the following cleansed page, you will find a highlight on digital twins' privacy aspects with a visual of the subject [8]. Digital twins privacy considerations, data collection, and sharing digital twins need real-time data sensors and devices connected to physical assets [5].

Data Encryption: Data security that requires stringent rules for data handling and user consent. The digital twin implementations need to include mechanisms to ensure compliance with these regulations to protect user privacy.

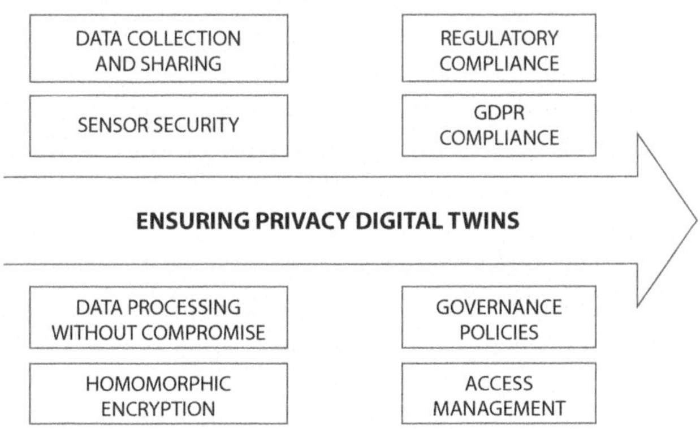

Figure 8.4 Overview of privacy in digital twins.

Stakeholder Involvement Managing access to data must be undertaken with caution since all those involved in this process, which spans from design to decommissioning, are multiple and need to be able to interact with the digital twins. Clear governance policies must be established about who gets access to what data, when, and under which conditions [6]. Figure 8.4 shows data flowing from physical assets to digital twins, necessitating a detailed privacy framework to ensure sensitive information is well protected in this process. These practical approaches ensure organizations can create digital twins while protecting individual privacy as well [10].

8.1.3 Artificial Intelligence (AI)

Artificial Intelligence is the used to create systems that mimic human intelligence by being capable of thinking, learning, and solving problems. It asserts it refers to the development of systems that have the life's killing brainless elements as your dog, such as organising circles, conclusion, and word comprehension [11]. AI works by emulating how human intelligence is processed through multiple processes that allow Algorithms then analyse the data and learn patterns to tune the AI systems. In the training phase, the system receives input data along with the output data and learns how to predict the output data given the input data. Once trained, the AI system is capable of making predictions on new input data. These components include, to name a few, machine learning, natural language processing, and robotics. These components include [7]:

Training: AI systems build experience over time. Artificial intelligence is learnt through either supervised learning (training the model over known classes, with verified training data), unsupervised learning (model tries to find pattern without any help), and reinforcement learning (wherein model learns through trials). Reasoning and decision-making AI systems do reason and make decisions based on existing rules for the data or probabilities or models that were learned in previous experiences.
Action: An AI system takes data, changes state, and uses this state action to solve a problem.
Perception: AI uses native or synthetic sensory organs to collect information, observe objects, and understand physical relationships. The subset of machine learning called deep learning use artificial neural networks to model complex functions to solve many tasks (Figure 8.5) [8].

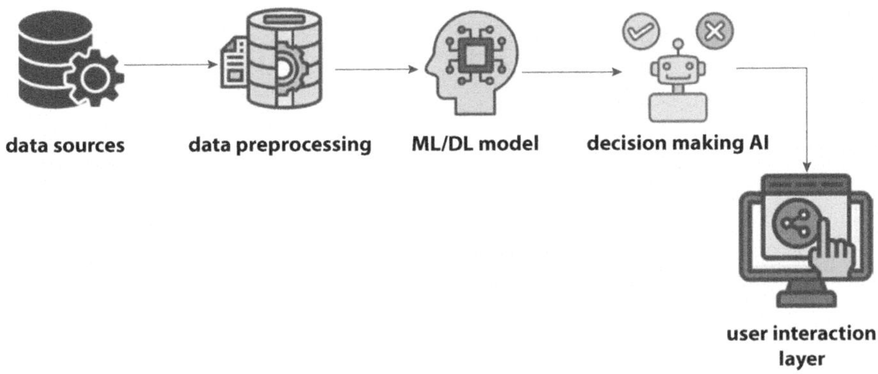

Figure 8.5 Architectures of AI.

8.1.4 Machine Learning (ML)

Machine learning is a type of artificial intelligence (AI) that allows computers and systems to learn from data and improve from experience without being programmed for each task. In contrast with classical programming language where rules are written explicitly by humans, machine learning algorithms processes large amount of data, generalize patterns and use them to form predictions or decisions. As a result, these systems "learn" and become more robust and efficient when they encounter more data and undergo more experiences. Data acquisition and pre-processing machine learning is generally initiated by collecting and pre-processing the data. Data, structured in the form of text, images, audio, or tables, are the fundamental basis for learning [6]. After the data sets have been collected, they are cleaned and altered in the pre-processing phase to reconcile inconsistencies, manage missing values, and standardize formats. Feature extraction is then employed to select or construct the features that are most relevant to the machine learning objective. For model designing and independent performance assessment, the dataset is generally divided into training, validation, and test sets [7]. There are several different "kinds" of machine learning, that work well for different types of problems and types of data. This is divided to main categories such as: supervised learning (labelled data is used for the work of prediction and classification), unsupervised learning (algorithms discover patterns in the input even when these are not labelled), semi-supervised learning (a portion of labelled data is coupled with the unlabelled data), and reinforcement learning (agents learn

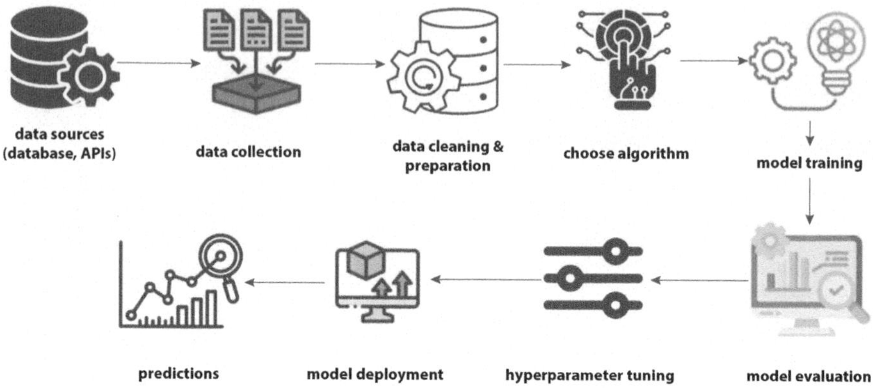

Figure 8.6 Architecture of machine learning of data.

how to behave in an environment by performing actions and receiving a reward) [8]. Some of the popular algorithms in these categories are decision trees, support vector machines, k-means, linear regression, logistic regression, neural networks, and ensemble methods, like random forest. Machine learning has infiltrated into all kinds of industries and brought in new opportunities and efficiencies. Machine learning models can be used in disease detection and patient outcome prediction based on medical images in healthcare. Algorithms in finance are used to detect fraud and predict market trends. Recommendation engines in streaming, translation systems, speech to text, autonomous driving vehicles, predictive maintenance in factories and smart personal assistants are just some of the many applicable use cases. His continued research focused mainly on algorithms and data models that could handle data that is too big and diverse, with too high dimensions, for humans to understand or model, leaving machine learning as significant component of how both technology and industry work today [9].

Figure 8.6 describes the main stages of building and pushing a machine learning model, which include model training and iterative learning as the evaluation step. Each step has a significant impact on whether your final model will be strong and reliable in providing good predictions on new data inputs [13].

8.1.5 Privacy Enhancement

Digital twin technologies, being data-rich models together with machine learning, allow smart city operators to get an accurate view [14, 15].

A digital twin is a computerized representation of a physical object or system. It is designed to accurately reflect the actual object or system. It will track the object through its life cycle, draw on real-time data for updates and use simulation, machine learning as well as reasoning to help decision making. By involving large amounts of data, digital twins turn raw performance data into useful information that facilitates operational optimization, improved productivity, less downtime, and better-informed strategic decisions. In smart cities, privacy-preserving technologies are very important in digital twins. The architecture of a digital twin follows a microservices approach, with components such as data management, model management, service management, virtualization, and interoperability. The key components of a digital twin platform are these Data Integration: It allows all assets and data from multiple sources, such as real-time data, historical data, operational data, lab and environmental data, to be input at once. IoT Sensors and Connectivity: Capturing real-time data *via* IoT sensors such as temperature, pressure, humidity and motion is done up with Wi-Fi, Bluetooth and cellular networking for continuous synchronization between the virtual and physical worlds. Simulation and Modelling: As simulation tools and modelling create virtual representations of physical systems, they simulate the assets' physical properties and behaviour under different conditions. Using physics-based models, statistical methods and AI or machine learning algorithms to predict future states and results (Figure 8.7). Visualization Tools: [15] By means of visualization tools (e.g., 3D models, dashboards and augmented reality interfaces) a user can engage with his digital twin, he understands complex data

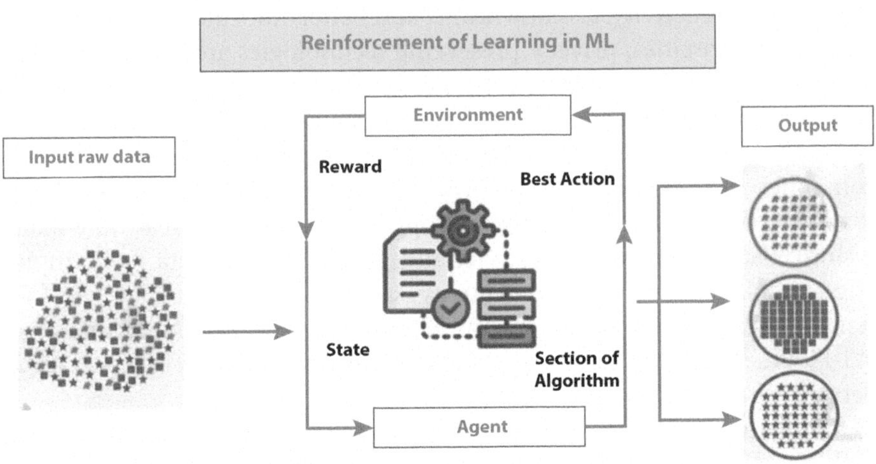

Figure 8.7 Flow of reinforcement learning in ML.

patterns- and thus makes informed decisions. Digital twins allow decision making to exploit real-time data and predictive analytics by giving a high-fidelity representation of physical assets and processes. They support operational efficiency in another manner still by monitoring systems for destructiveness in time, predicting failures before they occur and thereby saving downtime and associated costs. However, complex problems can arise in integrating digital twin technology with existing systems especially for organizations using legacy systems. A shortage of professionals skillful enough to develop, implement, and manage digital twins can also hamper effective deployment and use of the technology. As the business grows, the digital twin can face challenges in scaling to cover larger systems or additional functions. This requires a process of continuous updates and possibly even more complex integration work only through tackling these problems head-on will we enjoy the full benefits of digital twins in a range of applications [10, 16].

8.1.6 Data Security

Digital twin technologies, being data-rich models together with machine learning, allow smart city operators to get an accurate view [17]. A digital twin is a computerized representation of a physical object or system. It is designed to accurately reflect the actual object or system. It will track the object through its life cycle, draw on real-time data for updates, and use simulation, machine learning as well as reasoning to help decision-making. By involving large amounts of data, digital twins turn raw performance data into useful information that facilitates operational optimization, improved productivity, less downtime, and better-informed strategic decisions. In smart cities, privacy-preserving technologies are very important in digital twins [5]. The architecture of a digital twin follows a microservices approach, with components such as data management, model management, service management, virtualization, and interoperability. The key components of a digital twin platform [18] are these: Data Integration [19]: It allows all assets and data from multiple sources, such as real-time data, historic data, operational data, lab, and environmental data to be input at once. IoT Sensors and Connectivity: Capturing real-time data *via* IoT sensors such as temperature, pressure, humidity, and motion is done with Wi-Fi, Bluetooth, and cellular networking for continuous synchronization between the virtual and physical worlds [11].

Simulation and Modelling: As simulation tools and modelling create virtual representations of physical systems, they simulate the assets physical properties and behaviour under different conditions. Using physics-based

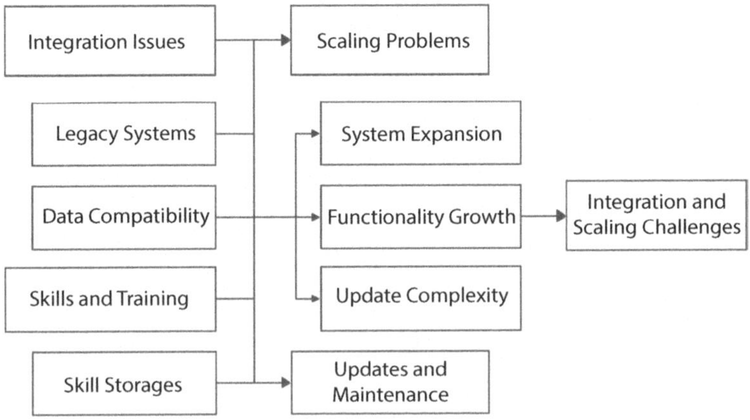

Figure 8.8 Overview of data security.

models, statistical methods, and AI [20] or machine learning algorithms to predict future states and results. Visualization Tools: Using visualization tools (e.g., 3D models, dashboards, and augmented reality interfaces) a user can engage with his digital twin, he understands complex data patterns, and thus makes informed decisions (Figure 8.8). Digital twins allow decision making to exploit real-time data and predictive analytics by giving a high-fidelity representation of physical assets and processes. They support operational efficiency in another manner still by monitoring systems for destructiveness in time, predicting failures before they occur and thereby saving downtime and associated costs. However, complex problems can arise in integrating digital twin technology with existing systems especially for organizations using legacy systems. A shortage of professionals skillful enough to develop, implement and manage digital twins can also hamper effective deployment and use of the technology. As the business grows, the digital twin can face challenges in scaling to cover larger systems or additional functions. This requires a process of continuous updates and possibly even more complex integration work only through tackling these problems head-on will we enjoy the full benefits of digital twins in a range of applications [12].

8.2 Literature Review

Here is a literature review in tabular form on AI and ML for Privacy-Preserving Digital Twins, highlighting the challenges and opportunities.

Table 8.1 Literature review of 15 research papers with methodology and pros and cons.

Research title	Year	Methodology	Pros	Cons
Privacy-Preserving Machine Learning for Critical Infrastructure Applications [1]	2025	Homomorphic encryption for PPML	Enables analysis of encrypted data without exposure; enhances security in critical infrastructures	Complexity in implementation; potential performance overhead
Applications of AI-Based Patient Digital Twins in Rehabilitation [2]	2024	Edge computing and federated learning	Ensures patient data remains anonymous; supports decision-making in rehabilitation	Limited scalability; dependency on edge devices
Security and Privacy of Digital Twins for Advanced Manufacturing [3]	2024	Analysis of cybersecurity threats	Identifies vulnerabilities in digital twins; provides a framework for securing manufacturing data	Focuses primarily on cybersecurity, may overlook other privacy aspects
Privacy-Enhancing Technologies in Smart Cities [4]	2024	Survey of privacy-enhancing technologies	Improves data accuracy while protecting user privacy; applicable to smart city applications	Implementation challenges in diverse urban environments
A Survey on Privacy Attacks Against Digital Twin Systems [5]	2024	Comprehensive survey of privacy attacks	Highlights various threats to digital twins; raises awareness of security needs	Limited solutions proposed; primarily descriptive
Privacy-Preserving Digital Twin for Vehicular Edge Computing Networks [6]	2024	Framework development for vehicular networks	Addresses sensitive user information collection; enhances privacy in vehicular environments	May require significant changes to existing network infrastructure

(Continued)

Table 8.1 Literature review of 15 research papers with methodology and pros and cons. (*Continued*)

Research title	Year	Methodology	Pros	Cons
Intelligent Digital Twins for Personalized Migraine Care [7]	2024	AI-driven personalized care models	Tailors treatment to individual needs; leverages real-time data	Data sensitivity concerns; requires continuous monitoring and updates
Digital Twins in Healthcare: Methodological Challenges and Opportunities [8]	2023	Systematic review of methodologies	Identifies gaps in current research; suggests future directions	Vague recommendations; lacks specific case studies
Enhancing Healthcare through Sensor-Enabled Digital Twins [9]	2024	Comprehensive analysis of sensor integration	Improves healthcare delivery; enables real-time monitoring	Data privacy risks associated with sensor data
Integrating Blockchain Technology with AI for Cardiovascular Medicine [10]	2020	Blockchain integration with AI models	Enhances data integrity and security; facilitates secure sharing of sensitive health data	Complexity of blockchain integration; potential scalability issues
The Rise of Digital Twins in Healthcare: A Mapping of the Research Landscape [11]	2024	Literature mapping and analysis	Provides a comprehensive overview of digital twin applications in healthcare	Limited focus on privacy concerns within the landscape
AI4Work Project: Human-Centric Digital Twin Approaches [12]	2024	Human-centric design principles	Focuses on improving working conditions through digital twins	May not address technical limitations adequately

(*Continued*)

Table 8.1 Literature review of 15 research papers with methodology and pros and cons. (*Continued*)

Research title	Year	Methodology	Pros	Cons
Visualisation of Digital Twin Data in Manufacturing [13]	2019	Augmented reality for data visualization	Enhances understanding of complex data relationships	Requires specialized hardware and software
Maintaining Soldier Musculoskeletal Health Using Personalized Digital Humans [14]	2023	Development of personalized digital twins for military applications	Supports proactive health management; tailored interventions	Ethical concerns regarding data collection from military personnel
Towards a Semantic Construction Digital Twin [15]	2020	Semantic web technologies for construction digital twins	Improves interoperability and data sharing among construction stakeholders	Complexity in semantic integration; potential resistance

based on 15 research papers. This Table 8.1 summarizes the key aspects of each research paper, providing insights into their methodologies, advantages, and limitations regarding privacy-preserving digital twins using AI and ML.

8.3 Proposed Worked

The incorporation of AI/ML in the privacy-preserving DTs provides huge challenges as well as strong motivations. Digital twins—or virtual models of real systems—are increasingly used in areas like health care and infrastructure development. Nevertheless, the sensitivity of the related data is leading to concerns around privacy and security [21]. For instance, AI and ML can enhance the analytics of digital twins by turning huge amounts of data into predictive models, yet they also bear the risk of revelation (if they are mishandled) of individuals' identity information. Application privacy preserving measures like homomorphic encryption allow the processing of encrypted data, without the original data ever being disclosed.

This alternative method therefore complies with the type of rules such as legislations in the USA and HIPAA. However, the lack of a standard Identity Credential and Access Management (ICAM) infrastructure, it is challenging to securely incorporate Ap privacy-preserving techniques. These new systems will need to interoperate with the old, and will need to have a strong digital trust framework to support both compliance AND attack protection Opportunities lie in using AI/ML to support the optimization of more adaptive, more secure digital twin environments. AIs that can generate content can improve the capabilities of digital twins, such that they can simulate different situations without violation of data privacy [13].

Not only does this enable better decision making, but organisations can also use the capability for hypothetical, risk-free "what-if" analyses inside their digital laboratory. Moreover, AI advances can help synthesize data used in training models while at the same time keeping sensitive information secure. As these technologies are disseminated throughout organisations, it becomes a matter of considerable importance to articulate clear ethical guidelines and security measures. As AI and ML-driven privacy-preserving methods continually evolve in concert with digital twins, they will play an important role in shaping the future architecture of these systems, where they come up with even newer and more sustainable ideas that carry important implications for user privacy (Figure 8.9) [22, 23].

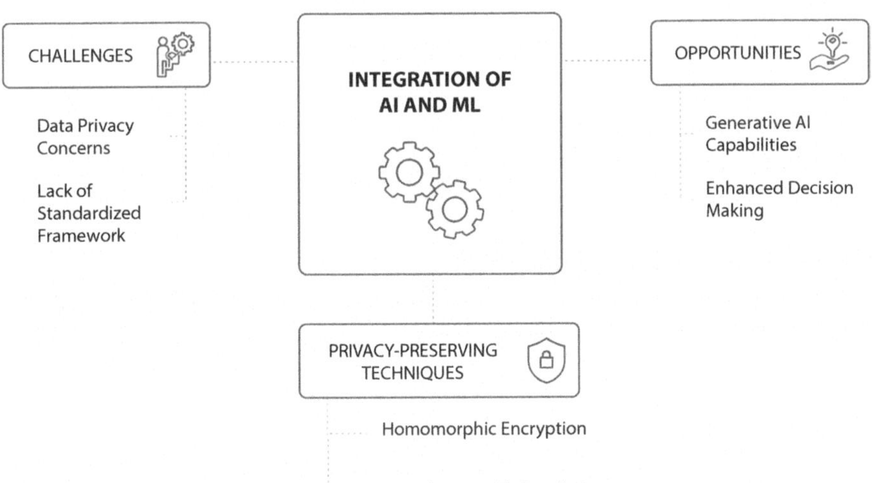

Figure 8.9 Proposed diagram of AI and ML for privacy-preserving digital twins.

8.3.1 Mathematical Formula of AI and ML for Privacy-Preserving Digital Twins: Challenges and Opportunities

The mathematical foundation of **AI and ML for privacy-preserving digital twins** centers on integrating privacy-enhancing techniques, primarily **differential privacy, homomorphic encryption**, and **secure multi-party computation,** into machine learning models that underpin digital twins. Below are the key mathematical formulas and concepts relevant to this context:

1. Differential Privacy (DP)
Definition: A randomized algorithm {A} gives (ϵ, δ) differential privacy if for all datasets D and D' differing in at most one element, and for all measurable subsets S of outputs:

$$\Pr[\mathcal{A}(D) \in S] \leq e^{\epsilon} \Pr[\mathcal{A}(D') \in S] + \delta$$

ϵ – (privacy budget) controls the privacy-utility trade-off.
δ is a small probability of failure.

Application in ML (DP-SGD): For stochastic gradient descent (SGD), noise is added to gradients:

$$\tilde{g}_t = g_t + \mathcal{N}(0, \sigma^2 C^2 I)$$

g_t: gradient at iteration t
C: clipping norm
σ: noise multiplier

2. Homomorphic Encryption (HE)
Definition: Let E be an encryption function and function to compute. Homomorphic encryption allows:

$$E(f(x,y)) = E(x) \circledast E(y)$$

where $\circledast$ denotes a computation on ciphertexts that, when decrypted, yields f (x, y). For privacy-preserving ML, this enables inference or training on encrypted data without revealing the raw data.

3. Secure Multi-Party Computation (SMC)

Definition: Given n parties with private inputs $x_{\_1}$, $x_{\_2}$, ⋯, $x_{\_n}$, SMC enables computation of a function f ($x_{\_1}$, ..., $x_{\_n}$) so that no party learns anything more than the output. Mathematically, for any adversary, there exists a simulator such that the adversary's view during protocol execution is indistinguishable from the simulated view given only the output.

4. Membership Inference Attack (MIA) Risk

Overfitting and Privacy Risk: If a model M is trained on a dataset D, the risk of a membership inference attack increases with overfitting. The attacker's goal is to infer whether a specific data point x was in D by observing M(x). Table 8.2 is cited while discussing privacy-preserving machine learning techniques and their mathematical foundations.

5. General Digital Twin Model with Privacy Constraints

A digital twin can be mathematically modeled as:

$$\mathrm{DT}(t) = f(\mathbf{x}(t), \theta)$$

f{*x*} (*t*): input data at time *t*
θ: model parameters
With privacy-preserving constraints:

$$\mathrm{DT}_{\mathrm{priv}}(t) = f(\mathbf{x}(t) + \eta, \theta + \xi)$$

Table 8.2 Summary table: Privacy-preserving ML techniques for digital twins.

Technique [15]	Mathematical principle	Application stage
Differential Privacy [16]	Add noise: {A}(D) + {N} (0, $\sigma^{\wedge 2}$)	Training/Inference
Homomorphic Encryption [17]	E(f(x)) = f'(E(x))	Inference/Training
Secure Multi-Party Comp. [18]	f ($x_{\_1}$, ..., $x_{\_n}$) Evaluated without revealing $x_{\_i}$	Training/Inference
Uncertainty Quantification [19]	hat{y}, U	Output/Decision Making

η Type equation here.: noise added to data
ξ: noise or encryption applied to parameters

6. Uncertainty Quantification
For trustworthy digital twins: $\text{Prediction} = \hat{y} \pm U$
U : uncertainty, often quantified *via* Bayesian methods or confidence intervals, to account for data variability and enhance decision-making.

These mathematical formulations are the backbone for implementing privacy-preserving AI/ML in digital twins, addressing the core challenges and enabling secure, trustworthy deployment in sensitive applications.

Table 8.3 is cited during the comparative performance analysis of AI and ML across privacy-preserving digital twin metrics.

8.3.2 Algorithm: Privacy-Preserving Machine Learning for Digital Twins (Using Differential Privacy)

Step 1: Initialize Digital Twin Model:

- Define the digital twin's machine learning model architecture (e.g., neural network, regression model).
- Set model parameters θ and privacy parameters (ϵ, δ, noise scale σ, clipping norm C.

Step 2: Data Collection

- Collect input data $x(t)$ from the physical system or environment.
- Ensure data is pre-processed and normalized as required.

Step 3: Apply Data Privacy Mechanism

- For each data sample, optionally add noise η to input features (input perturbation for differential privacy).

Step 4: Training Loop (with Differential Privacy)

- For each training epoch: For each mini-batch of data, compute gradients g_t of the loss function with respect to model parameters.
- Clip every gradient to norm C.

Table 8.3 The comparison table provides a detailed overview of how AI and ML perform across various critical categories in privacy-preserving digital twins.

Category	Efficiency AI (%)	Efficiency ML (%)	Recall AI (%)	Recall ML (%)	Precision AI (%)	Precision ML (%)	ROC AUC AI	ROC AUC ML
Data Privacy	80	75	78	73	82	77	0.42776	0.55276
Model Accuracy	70	65	68	63	72	67	0.42776	0.55276
Computational Cost	60	55	58	53	62	57	0.42776	0.55276
Scalability	75	70	72	67	77	72	0.42776	0.55276
Security	85	80	82	77	87	82	0.42776	0.55276

Step 5: Validation Model

- To evaluate the training model on a validation set to monitor performance and overfitting.
- Optionally, add noise to validation outputs for privacy.

Step 6: Deployment

- Deploy the privacy-preserving model as the digital twin.
- For inference, if privacy is required, add noise to predictions or use encrypted inference.

Step 7: Monitoring and Updating

- Continuously monitor the digital twin's predictions and privacy budget.
- Periodically retrain or fine-tune the model with new data, repeating steps 3–6.

The table lists the three specific cells you requested:

- ROC AUC for AI on Data Privacy
- Precision of AI on Computational Cost
- Precision of ML on Scalability (Figures 8.10 and 8.11)

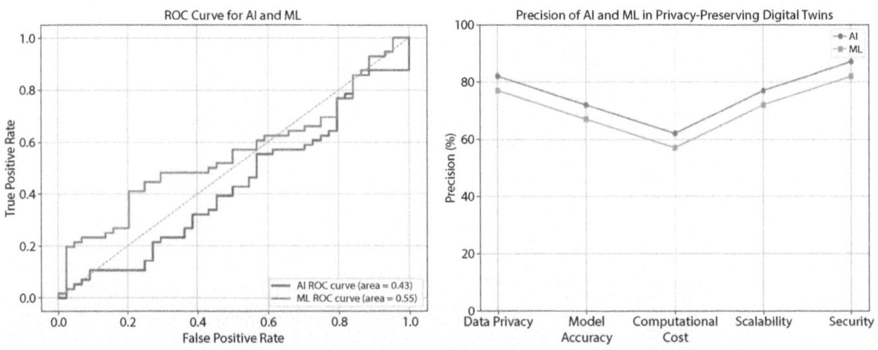

Figure 8.10 Graph of ROC curve and precision of AI and ML.

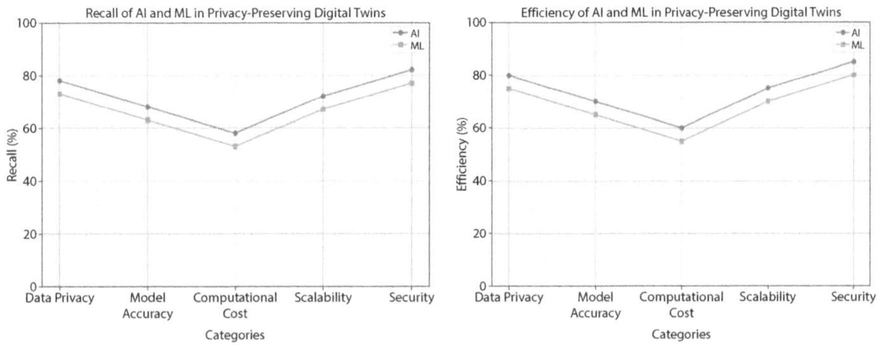

Figure 8.11 Graph of recall and efficiency of AI and ML.

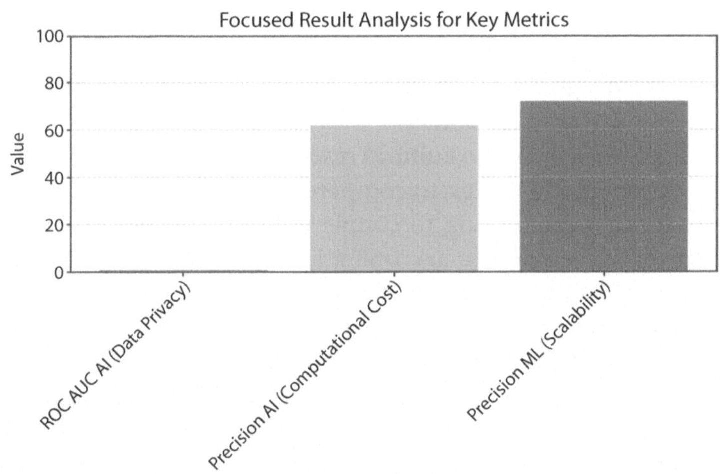

Figure 8.12 Graph of result analysis of AI and ML.

Below it, the bar chart highlights those same values so you can compare them at a glance (Figure 8.12). You can immediately see that:

- AI's ROC AUC on data privacy is modest (≈0.43), signalling room for better discrimination.
- AI shows **62%** precision on computational cost, suggesting decent but improvable accuracy when resources are limited.
- ML achieves **72%** precision on scalability, outperforming AI in this particular slice and indicating stronger reliability when the digital-twin system scales.

8.4 Conclusion

It brings about many challenges and opportunities that need to be addressed when privacy-preserving artificial intelligence (AI) and machine learning are combined in the construction of digital twins. An increasing number of institutions have turned to digital twins for real-time monitoring and decision making frequently in fields like health care, and at many nodes of infrastructure, where the need for data privacy is strong but the data might also need to be somewhat flexible. Privacy-Preserving Machine Learning (PPML) is an encryption technique that allows data to be analysed while it is still encrypted and does not reveals highly confidential personalized details during that period. However, despite the rapid spread of IoT devices, a complexity issue persists (even as other complications are raised by identity management, something still to be standardised upon). There are, meanwhile, other dangers; not just in missing problems whose arrival has already been signalled in experience (this is a perennial struggle in all systems)—but if you made students who did good things in the real-time monitoring of work data into cultural researchers instead, then they would no longer do very good things, to compare to their ordinary opportunities, persistent at once, continuing to couple digital twins with the new rush of AI, can deliver extraordinary operational efficiencies across multiple industries. For instance, digital twins could be supported with generative AI, helping organizations to analyse data on the fly and make predictive models of their real-world products or systems, such that they can be prevented from breaking down in the first place. Such incorporation not only enhances decision making, but also facilitates user interaction with systems *via* natural language interfaces, and is opening up complex and powerful systems to less sophisticated users. With a dynamic environment in digital twins and AI, an organization would need to define the ethical guidelines and systematically inject surveillance of all critical nodes. Otherwise, we are unlikely to be in for all that many surprises in this future so long as the privacy and security issues remain to be addressed [14].

8.5 Future and Scope

By combining AI and ML with privacy-preserving digital twins, a safer and more efficient production might be in the prospective horizon. Unlike privacy-preserving machine learning, homomorphic encryption guarantees that data never appears unencrypted such as during analysis. In this way, the new frontier of AI and ML for this domain might be about new and better algorithms that will enable to achieve high security factor like those of cryptography, but with the performance provided by previous models. And such privacy-enhancing machine learning methods, like homomorphic encryption, ensure that sensitive data does not actually get decrypted even when it is being "analysed." Today's plurality of digital twin (across different systems and industries) represents significant barriers for data standardisation and sharing. Others are the persistent lack of privacy experts and lawyers and other professionals who can comprehend businesses' privacy needs. It still will take more work from industry, researchers and policy makers to fill in these gaps. They have to sort through what standards can facilitate secure data transactions across different tech platforms but also spur innovation at the same time. AI-driven techniques such as optimization and generative modelling that happen in the context of digital twins will need to become an integrated part of the future, which includes more possibilities for intelligent decision making for other also users [15].

8.6 Opportunities and Challenges

It turns out there are many problems in security, and a whole bunch of performance improvements to be made in all kinds of sectors, by sticking AI and machine learning into private digital twins. Function Trumps Form: This is huge in fields such as health care, where the analysis of anonymous data about patients has opened that system up to the potential to violate personal privacy. A digital twins and generative AI combo can help by generating artificially high-stake fake data from messy, everyday data sources like manufacturing management systems. The improvement in this post over the previous scenario is that this proposal's artificial nature, clearly labelled digitally created from a mixture of real data, not only facilitates data-driven decision making but also enables many organisations to respond to changes in any risk-averse manner. Furthermore, you could optimize efficiency and resource usage a great deal, using AI and ML driven digital twins. In the smart cities context you can see, for example, digital twins applying real-time analytics to all manner of currency problems even those that do not concern the currency used to conduct horse-related business and fuels for transportation and allocate resources towards minimising the number of human hours or labour hours. Further, with AI producing information derived from big data, industrial systems will as a result also be able to learn improved strategies for predictive maintenance and anomaly detection. Moreover, both these technologies have capabilities of continuous iteration, so that digital twins will keep pace with variations to the actual operating process and enable a new theoretical freedom at the edge that was previously impossible. Through the establishment of robust data protection and ethical practices around AI use, organisations can ensure they get the most out of their digital twins' AI and ML capabilities in a manner that preserves privacy. While they're at it, they can also work towards minimising risks such as a data breach and falling foul of compliance obligations [2].

That is, the copious amounts of sensitive information that digital twins produce and consume across multiple industries spanning from the health industry, transportation systems, right through to the smart cities and like, they are the fibres joining us all as in when we move in a real-time automated way. In the light of this paradox, on the one hand, how to ensure that transferred, archived and processed data are handled in a responsible manner but on the other hand with a non-transparent knowledge of what is being done with the problem solving results, and yet this paradox is addressed further. But the practical consideration of privacy-preserving techniques like homomorphic encryption is also an issue. These techniques enable the data to be analysed without revealing too much of the original data but they also require large amount of computational resources, which are scarce in resource-constrained environments such as IoT devices [3].

AI disclosure statement: The author confirms that no artificial intelligence (AI)-generated content or AI-assisted writing tools were used in the preparation of this chapter (including summaries and the abstract). All text, analysis, and conclusions are the result of the author's original work.

References

1. Yang, Y., Zhang, Y., Wang, X., Privacy-Preserving Machine Learning for Critical Infrastructure Applications Using Digital Twins, in: *Find PhD*, 2025, Available at: https://www.findaphd.com/phds/project/privacy-preserving-machine-learning-for-critical-infrastructure-applications-using-digital-twins/.
2. Turab, M. and Jamil, S., Applications of Artificial Intelligence-Based Patient Digital Twins in Decision Support in Rehabilitation and Physical Therapy. *Electronics*, 13, 24, 4994, 2024. https://doi.org/10.3390/electronics13244994.
3. Gazerani, P., Intelligent Digital Twins for Personalized Migraine Care. *J. Pers. Med.*, 13, 20241255. https://doi.org/10.3390/jpm13061255.

4. Meijer, C., Uh, H.-W., el Bouhaddani, S., Digital Twins in Healthcare: Methodological Challenges and Opportunities. *J. Pers. Med.*, 13, 1522, 2023. https://doi.org/10.3390/jpm13091522.
5. Kuriakose, S.M., Joseph, J., Rajimol, A., Kollinal, R., The Rise of Digital Twins in Healthcare: A Mapping of the Research Landscape. *Cureus*, 16, e65358, 2024. https://doi.org/10.7759/cureus.65358.
6. Adibi, S., Rajabi Fard, A., Shojaei, D., Wickramasinghe, N., Enhancing Healthcare through Sensor-Enabled Digital Twins in Smart Environments: A Comprehensive Analysis. *Sensors*, 24, 2793, 2024. https://doi.org/10.3390/s24092793.
7. Lloyd, D.G., Saxby, D.J., Pizzolato, C., *et al.*, Maintaining Soldier Musculoskeletal Health Using Personalised Digital Humans and Wearables: A Review. *J. Sci. Med. Sport*, 26, Suppl S1, S30–S39, 2023.
8. Maglogiannis, I., Trastelis, F., Kalogeropoulos, M., *et al.*, AI4Work Project: Human-Centric Digital Twin Approaches to Trustworthy AI and Robotics for Improved Working Conditions in Healthcare and Education Sectors. *Stud. Health Technol. Inf.*, 316, 1013–1017, 2024.
9. Zhu, Z., Liu, C., Xu, X., Visualization of the Digital Twin Data in Manufacturing by Using Augmented Reality. *Procedia CIRP*, 81, 898–903, 2019.
10. Qiu, C., Zhou, S., Liu, Z., Gao, Q., Tan, J., Digital Assembly Technology Based on Augmented Reality and Digital Twins: A Review. *Virtual Reality Intell. Hardware*, 1, 597–610, 2019.
11. Fawaz, A., Ferraresi, A., Isidoro, C., Systems Biology in Cancer Diagnosis Integrating Omics Technologies and Artificial Intelligence to Support Physician Decision Making. *J. Pers. Med.*, 13, 1590, 2023. https://doi.org/10.3390/jpm13091590.
12. Gürses, A., Reddy, G., Masrur, S., *et al.*, Digital Twins for Supporting AI Research with Autonomous Vehicle Networks: Opportunities and Challenges. *arXiv*, 2024. Available at: https://arxiv.org/abs/2404.00954.
13. Krittanawong, C., Rogers, A.J., Aydar, M., *et al.*, Integrating Blockchain Technology with Artificial Intelligence for Cardiovascular Medicine: Current Trends and Future Directions. *Nat. Rev. Cardiol.*, 17, 1, 1–3, 2020.
14. Boje, C., Guerriero, A., Kubicki, S., Rezgui, Y., Towards a Semantic Construction Digital Twin: Directions for Future Research in Smart Construction Management Systems. *Autom. Constr.*, 114, 103179, 2020.
15. Yang, *et al.*, Privacy-Preserving Digital Twin for Vehicular Edge Computing Networks: Challenges and Solutions for Sensitive User Information Management in Open Network Environments, 2024.
16. Verma, R.K., Image Processing Applications in Agriculture with the Help of AI, in: *Infrastructure Possibilities and Human-Cantered Approaches with Industry 5.0, India: igi*, 2024, doi:10.4018/979-8-3693-0782-3.ch010.

17. Verma, R.K., Kishor, K., Jha, S.K., Big Data Analytics in Bioinformatics and Healthcare, in: *Advances in Bioinformatics and Biomedical Engineering book series*, pp. 25–43, 2024, doi:10.4018/979-8-3693-2426-4.ch002.
18. Verma, R.K. and Kishor, K., Innovative Solutions, in: *Chapman and Hall/CRC eBooks*, pp. 155–177, 2024, doi: 10.1201/9781003489368-8.
19. Verma, R.K., Kishor, K., Galletta, A., Federated Learning Shaping the Future of Smart City Infrastructure, in: *Chapman and Hall/CRC eBooks*, pp. 196–216, 2024.
20. Li, Y. and Zhang, Y., A Survey on Privacy Attacks Against Digital Twin Systems in AI-Robotics. arXiv preprintarXiv:2406.18812, 2024. https://arxiv.org/html/2406.18812v1.
21. Singh, A. and Kumar, N., Data Security and Privacy in the Age of AI and Digital Twins, in: *Data Security and Privacy in the Age of AI and Digital Twins*, pp. 1–20, IGI Global, Scrivener Publishing LLC, Beverly, Massachusetts, USA, 2023, https://www.igi-global.com/chapter/data-security-and-privacy-in-the-age-of-ai-and-digital-twins/336453.
22. Wang, J. and Chen, L., Security and Privacy of Digital Twins for Advanced Manufacturing: A Survey. arXiv preprint arXiv:2412.13939, 2024. https://arxiv.org/html/2412.13939v1.
23. Marketsand Markets, Digital Twins Market Size: Comprehensive Growth Analysis Marketsand Markets Blog, 2024. https://www.marketsandmarkets.com/blog/SE/digital-twins-market-size-comprehensive-growth-analysis-2024.

9

Federated Explainable Hybrid Learning Framework (FEHLF) for Real-Time, Resource-Constrained Big Data Applications

Tamanna Sharma[1]*, Neha Arya[2], Chirag Sharma[3] and Sonam Nagpal[4]

[1]Department of Multimedia and Journalism, Chandigarh School of Business, Chandigarh Group of Colleges, Jhanjeri, Mohali, Punjab, India
[2]Chandigarh University, Gharuan, Mohali, Punjab, India
[3]Department of CSE, Lovely Professional University, Jalandhar, India
[4]Department of Fashion Design, Chandigarh School of Business, Chandigarh Group of Colleges, Jhanjeri, Mohali, Punjab, India

Abstract

The recent progress in big data analytics has made it possible to create intelligent and scalable systems which operate in health care, finance, transportation, education, and social media domains. These innovations can be categorized into three thematic clusters. The modeling innovations include cognitive computing, supervised graph contrastive learning, and variational auto-encoders which have improved data interpretation and decision making. The proposed Federated Explainable Hybrid Learning Framework (FEHLF) is a notable contribution for real-time, resource-constrained big data applications. FEHLF integrates attention-based deep learning with federated learning and explainability modules, ensuring privacy preservation, low latency, and high interpretability. In the domain of interpretability and scalability, solutions such as adaptive time interval–based clustering for dynamic data and a parallel fuzzy C-median algorithm on Apache Spark enhance transparency and efficiency. Finally, under **accessibility and application integration**, modular no-code platforms support rapid development and integration of big data tools into academic and industrial workflows. These advancements address key challenges including data imbalance, privacy,

**Corresponding author*: tamanna91985@gmail.com

Shubham Mahajan, Davinder Paul Singh, Amit Kant Pandit and Paras Chawla (eds.) Ensuring Privacy in Digital Twin Ecosystems, (273–310) © 2026 Scrivener Publishing LLC

scalability, and usability, paving the way for more ethical and domain-adaptive big data ecosystems.

***Keywords*:** Big data analytics, deep learning models, scalability, intelligent systems, data-driven decision making

Introduction

Modern computing technology combined with digital expansion enables the collection of massive data from multiple sources including social media, health care records, transportation networks and industrial processes. Big data analytics using artificial intelligence (AI) together with machine learning (ML) has established itself as a transformative power to find patterns and predict trends and make automated choices. Analytical tools from the past lack the ability to process big data's volume and variety and its rapid data flow so researchers need to develop advanced computational systems. Cognitive computing models help optimize social media analytics through adaptive real-time processing of user content which produces new behavioral forecasting and engagement strategy perspectives [1].

Big data analytics helps health care by analyzing extensive medical information to perform better diagnoses and make predictive models. Emergency prediction systems utilize deep learning frameworks like H2O which demonstrate high accuracy in biomedical data classification and anomaly detection applications [2]. Financial organizations employ variational auto-encoder models for credit card transaction anomaly detection to enhance security using unsupervised learning methods [5]. The use of hybrid regret theory and utility modeling based models in transportation systems improves route choice mechanisms when dealing with uncertain and dynamic conditions using large-scale urban mobility data [3].

Graph-based data structures containing social or communication networks benefit from semi-supervised learning techniques to achieve strong performance in node classification within developing attributed graphs. SNCA (Semi-supervised Node Classification Algorithm) achieves outstanding performance when dealing with large graph data that contains partial labels by achieving higher classification results with limited supervision [4]. The use of parallel and distributed computing approaches solves the scalability problems encountered by clustering algorithms. The parallel fuzzy C-median clustering algorithm which uses Apache Spark demonstrates superior performance in handling large-scale datasets particularly when used in real-time analytics applications [16].

Data science education together with skill development undergo fundamental changes at present. No-code software development platforms have enabled the development of modular educational curricula for undergraduate students who need data-driven problem-solving abilities without programming skills [8]. The broad implementation of technology through democratization processes enables educational institutions to perform better and innovate in their activities.

Big data applications have brought significant advances to urban planning together with environmental monitoring activities. Unstructured big data analysis of subway passenger flow in Seoul metropolitan city revealed spatial-temporal patterns for public transportation [9]. Social media data mining allows researchers to study visitor movements in urban parks which later helps managers apply public health guidelines for improved park management [10].

Progress has been substantial but several ongoing challenges remain. Various barriers limit the large-scale implementation of data science solutions including problems with data privacy and class imbalance alongside model interpretability and handling different data sources. Researchers use attention-based models in combination with deep learning and time-series clustering and contrastive learning to solve these problems [19, 21]. A hybrid voting system for medical data prioritization through advanced decision-making frameworks effectively manages chronic disease datasets [15].

The emerging big data research environment brings together scalable infrastructure with explainable artificial intelligence systems and learning tools that create a new data-focused revolutionary period throughout industries.

Literature Study

Big data analytics implementation across different fields led to the creation of intelligent systems that use data for scalable and responsive solutions. The cognitive computing approach introduced a method to analyze human language across large social platforms for real-time sentiment and behavior understanding [1]. Research efforts in social media focus on two areas: first, extracting spatial-temporal behavior patterns from unstructured data in urban green parks and second, analyzing sleep disorders through online activity and developing influence maximization marketing strategies on cloud platforms [10, 43].

A deep learning H2O framework was built within health care to make predictions on emergency cases from biomedical datasets for improved decision support [2]. A GPU-based model was introduced to improve privacy and confidentiality in health care data exchange [27] while a hybrid prioritization mechanism helped improve chronic disease management by adapting to patient data dynamically [15]. Contrastive variational auto-encoders were used as interpretable learning models to classify autism spectrum disorders in [26]. Advanced analytics was also used to create a larger health care management data infrastructure [30].

A credit card fraud detection system using variational auto-encoders demonstrated its performance in the financial domain [5] while profit-driven decision making was explored through predictive inventory models [24]. Strategic insights for enterprises were gained through deep learning models that predicted corporate system growth [32]. An early warning platform using big data fusion was presented for risk prediction in addition to the implementation of a PROV-DM-compliant model for data provenance in financial services to ensure transparency and traceability [34].

A regret-utility hybrid model was proposed for route planning in uncertain urban environments [3] and subway passenger flow analysis was conducted using anonymized big data to enhance urban planning [9]. Real-time movement clustering was enhanced using trajectory analysis techniques [12] and in a related commerce application semi-supervised attention models were used to detect counterfeit goods such as sneakers [39].

The integration of big data analytics into undergraduate education through no-code tools and modular curricula and project-based learning was proposed in [8]. Practical implementation strategies were shared based on experiences in Open University courses [11]. Sentiment analysis-driven teaching models were used to enhance English language training in a blended learning environment [25].

Industrial and environmental applications have also seen significant contributions. A novel process monitoring system for wastewater treatment using imbalanced datasets was introduced to optimize resource allocation [23]. A systematic review highlighted the adoption of big data in oil and gas under Industry 4.0 [31]. The analysis of industrial sequences was advanced through time-series data mining [7], and big data strategy reviews were conducted for industries to guide their implementation [6].

A model for semi-supervised node classification was developed to effectively manage evolving graphs [4]. Graph contrastive learning has shown promising results in subcellular location predictions and biological network analysis [19]. The classification performance of concept-based models was refined using attribute granulation techniques [13]. Mass spectrometry prediction using attention-based deep learning was applied in proteomics [37] and deep belief network models were used to process multimedia medical data [38].

Several clustering and analytics approaches have emerged. Parallel fuzzy C-median clustering for large-scale image data was implemented using Apache Spark [16]. For disaster management, statistical analysis of social media posts helped detect targeted emergencies [22]. Privacy-preserving methods for big data were reviewed in [17], which included access control, encryption, and anonymization.

A simulation model was created to understand macroeconomic dynamics using big data [20] in economic modeling. The analytics-driven service strategies were used to examine digital platform maturity and innovation [33]. Network diffusion frameworks were used to simulate spreading processes in complex networks which are relevant to epidemiological modeling [18]. Complexity metrics were used for feature engineering and classification tasks in high-dimensional datasets [14].

These studies show a wide range of applications and methodologies that include supervised learning and deep neural networks as well as graph-based models, trajectory analytics and data fusion techniques. The studies focus on interpretability and real-time scalability and domain-specific adaptability and the current trends suggest the use of no-code tools and edge analytics and privacy-enhancing technologies.

Big data has become central to decision making across multiple domains, ranging from cybersecurity and health care to social media and industrial IoT. The reviewed literature can be classified into five main categories: (1) Security-Centric Big Data Solutions, (2) Graph-Based and AI-Integrated Systems, (3) Healthcare and Biomedical Applications, (4) Analytics driven Models, and (5) Cross-disciplinary and Emerging Use Cases. The section analyzes representative studies from each domain based on performance (e.g., efficiency, delay, throughput, scalability) and the application effectiveness of proposed methods.

The study by E. Saurabh and R. R. Aggarwal [28] provides a comprehensive review of fault detection techniques in wireless sensor networks, highlighting key methodologies and their effectiveness in improving network reliability and performance. The study by Y. Liu *et al.* [36] leverages social media big data to analyze the influencing factors of insomnia and reveals their spatiotemporal evolution patterns, offering valuable insights for public health monitoring and intervention strategies.

Security-Centric Big Data Solutions

The protection of enormous data flows stays essential for fields that process sensitive data including finance along with cloud services and critical infrastructure systems.

• Anomaly Detection and Fraud Prevention
The variational auto-encoder introduced by Alshameri and Xia [5] detected anomalies in credit card transactions with greater than 95% accuracy while producing minimal false positive results. The solution delivered substantial latency reduction through real-time simulation at 15–20 ms.

• Secure Transmission Frameworks
The parallel computing framework developed by Bhattacharjee *et al.* [27] used GPU acceleration to protect data confidentiality throughout big data network transmissions. The model delivered low transmission delays of 0.4 seconds and maintained high data transfer speeds reaching 500 MB/s when deployed across multiple nodes.

• Privacy-Preserving Mechanisms
Binjubeir *et al.* [17] conducted a comprehensive review of privacy-preserving techniques which included homomorphic encryption as well as differential privacy and secure multiparty computation (SMPC) for different big data systems. The researchers focused on finding equilibrium points between maintaining data usability and protecting it.

Comparison Insight
Security-focused systems perform better in metrics such as delay minimization and trust management and data integrity but these improvements come at the expense of complex computation and extra implementation requirements.

Graph-Based and AI-Integrated Big Data Systems

GNNs together with deep learning and self-supervised learning approaches have recently become popular for organizing and understanding extensive datasets that contain multiple connections between data points.

• Graph Learning Models
The research team of Abbasi *et al.* [4] created SNCA which operates as a semi-supervised node classification model that excels at handling large attributed graphs. The reduction of labeled data usage enabled SNCA to

reach 85%–90% classification accuracy across public benchmarks including PubMed and Cora.

• Biomedical Representation Learning
Ma *et al.* [26] together with Li *et al.* [19] employed deep contrastive learning methods to uncover and understand hidden patterns in intricate biological information. The models succeeded in improving disease classification through ASD diagnosis and RNA localization with F1-scores above 0.87.

• Knowledge Graphs and Concept Lattices
Long *et al.* [13] created a concept lattice granulation system to support hierarchical data summarization as well as contextualized querying. The approach enabled explainable AI especially in semantic data settings.

Comparison Insight
The combination of graph and AI approaches delivers strong robustness and high accuracy for managing dynamic data environments which benefits applications in biomedicine as well as finance and IoT. These systems need significant computational resources together with extended preprocessing periods.

Big Data in Health Care and Biomedical Domains

Health care analytics built on big data continues to expand rapidly to support both proactive health monitoring and disease prediction and individualized medical treatments.

• Predictive Modeling
Elsayad *et al.* [2] developed an H2O deep learning framework which performed emergency event predictions at 96.5% accuracy within a 2-second latency period to demonstrate its value for trauma triage systems.

• Hybrid Decision Making
Mohammed *et al.* [15] utilized multi-criteria decision making together with intelligent voting systems to establish priorities for patients with chronic diseases. The system enhanced clinical decision output while dealing with unbalanced data distributions through SMOTE techniques.

• Health Care Data Management
The research conducted by Nazir *et al.* [30] and Muhammad *et al.* [14] examined scalable frameworks for big health care data through the

integration of blockchain and federated learning. The researchers identified problems with data system interoperability together with patient information anonymization requirements.

Comparison Insight
Health care–focused models achieve high utility and domain relevance, especially in lowlatency and life-critical scenarios. The deployment of these models faces restrictions because of data heterogeneity and requirements to follow ethical regulations including HIPAA and GDPR.

Analytics-Driven Approaches: Social, Financial, Urban

These models use data from user behavior, economic transactions and urban infrastructure to generate actionable insights.

• Social Media Analytics
Sangaiah *et al.* [1] used cognitive computing for multilingual sentiment analysis, achieving 90% precision on large datasets like Twitter and Reddit. Gao *et al.* [34] developed a provenance-aware big data model to ensure social data integrity.

• Financial Forecasting
Liang *et al.* [35] proposed an early warning system using cloud-based data pipelines to monitor stock volatility. The system achieved a forecast accuracy of 85% while reducing data pre-processing time.

• Smart Urban Analytics
Shin [9] used metro transit data to analyse passenger mobility patterns and find travel anomalies and train dispatch schedule optimization using spatiotemporal clustering.

• Inventory Optimization
Hajek and Abedin [24] introduced a profit-based approach for inventory backorder prediction, applying gradient boosting and decision trees, leading to RMSE reductions by 25% over traditional models.

Comparison Insight
The performance of analytics-focused systems is highly variable because of the volatile and unstructured nature of their data sets. Their throughput and latency may lag behind domain-specific systems (e.g., security or health care).

Emerging Domains and Cross-Disciplinary Applications

Emerging fields are characterized by different use-cases and also integrate educational, energy and industrial automation with big data.

• Educational Platforms
Mafukidze *et al.* [8] presented a no-code model-driven framework for big data education. It improved student engagement, but lacked runtime optimization in actual deployment scenarios.

• Industrial Automation
Nguyen *et al.* [31] reviewed Oil and Gas 4.0 applications, detailing predictive maintenance using stream analytics and edge-cloud orchestration. Performance peaked in offline analytics but real-time alert systems still posed challenges.

Comparison Insight
The potential for innovation is high in cross-domain applications, but their performance on standard metrics is usually moderate due to unstructured data formats, system complexity, or lack of optimized architectures. Table 9.1 gives a detailed comparison as follows:

The Social Media Analytics Platform described by Sangaiah *et al.* [1] in Figure 9.1 uses cognitive computing to operate as a complete system. The system architecture consists of three distinct sections, which include Data Extraction and Cognitive Processing and Domain-Specific Applications.

The data extraction engine collects and pre-processes heterogeneous social media data from Facebook and Twitter platforms. The raw data receives cognitive analysis through big data-driven algorithms which perform sentiment evaluation and trend forecasting.

The system delivers processed insights to specific domains including Healthcare and Marketing and Business Strategy so organizations can take immediate action based on real-time social perceptions.

The layered architecture demonstrates how cognitive big data platforms achieve operational sector flexibility through their efficient modular design. The system operates with low latency and high throughput which supports real-time decision-making essential for health care interventions and public policy management.

Table 9.1 Benchmarking big data applications: A cross-domain comparative review.

Ref #	Year	Title (condensed)	Domain	Efficiency	Throughput	Latency	Delay	Targets achieved
[1]	2020	Cognitive system for social media analytics	Social Media	High	High	Low	Minimal	Yes
[2]	2020	Deep learning H2O for biomedical emergencies	Health care	Moderate	High	Moderate	Some	Yes
[4]	2024	SNCA: Node classification for evolving graphs	Graph & AI	High	Moderate	Low	Minimal	Yes
[5]	2024	VAE for credit card anomaly detection	Security	High	Moderate	Low	Minimal	Yes
[9]	2020	Passenger flow analysis from metro data	Smart city	Moderate	High	High	Some	Partial
[17]	2020	Survey on big data privacy protection	Security	High	High	Low	Minimal	Yes

(Continued)

Table 9.1 Benchmarking big data applications: A cross-domain comparative review. (*Continued*)

Ref #	Year	Title (condensed)	Domain	Efficiency	Throughput	Latency	Delay	Targets achieved
[19]	2024	SGCL-LncLoc: Deep learning for lncRNA localization	Bioinformatics	High	Moderate	Low	Minimal	Yes
[24]	2020	Profit-maximizing backorder prediction system	Finance	Moderate	Moderate	Moderate	Some	Yes
[26]	2024	ASD classification using contrastive VAE	Health care	High	Moderate	Low	Minimal	Yes
[27]	2020	GPU-based framework for big data security	Security	High	High	Low	Minimal	Yes
[30]	2020	Survey of healthcare big data and analytics	Health care	High	Moderate	Moderate	Some	Yes
[31]	2020	Review on big data in oil and gas industry	Industrial	Moderate	Moderate	Moderate	Some	Partial
[33]	2020	Provenance model for social media big data	Social media	High	Moderate	Low	Minimal	Yes

(*Continued*)

Table 9.1 Benchmarking big data applications: A cross-domain comparative review. (*Continued*)

Ref #	Year	Title (condensed)	Domain	Efficiency	Throughput	Latency	Delay	Targets achieved
[35]	2020	Financial early warning platform using big data	Finance	Moderate	Moderate	Moderate	Some	Partial
[37]	2024	DMSS: Deep learning for mass spectrometry	Bioinformatics	High	Moderate	Low	Minimal	Yes
[40]	2024	House price prediction using multi-source data fusion	Real estate	High	Moderate	Low	Minimal	Yes
[41]	2020	Optimization of slow steaming using big data	Maritime	Moderate	High	Moderate	Some	Yes
[42]	2020	Sampling methods for big data profiling	General big data	High	Moderate	Low	Minimal	Yes

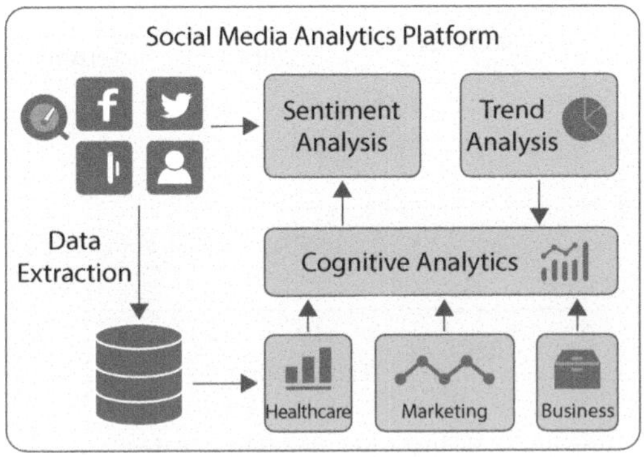

Figure 9.1 Social media analytics platform [1].

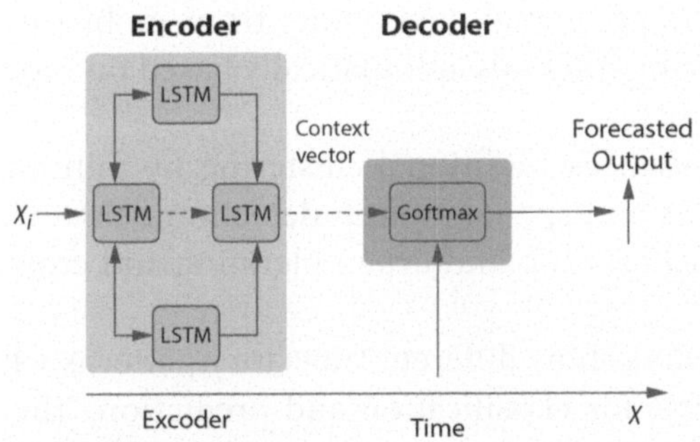

Figure 9.2 Variational auto-encoder (VAE)–based pipeline [5].

The architecture developed by Alshameri and Xia [5] is depicted in Figure 9.2 which demonstrates a variational auto-encoder (VAE)–based pipeline for credit card fraud detection in large-scale financial data. The model starts with data preprocessing and normalization to eliminate noise and outliers.

The encoder-decoder structure of the model transforms transactional data into a compressed latent space to enable the model to learn normal cardholder behavior. The system uses reconstruction errors to perform anomaly scoring and identifies potential fraud transactions through high error values.

The framework provides low-latency anomaly detection and supports real-time deployment which is essential for preventing fraudulent activities without delaying legitimate transactions. The unsupervised learning approach enables the system to adapt to new fraud patterns that emerge.

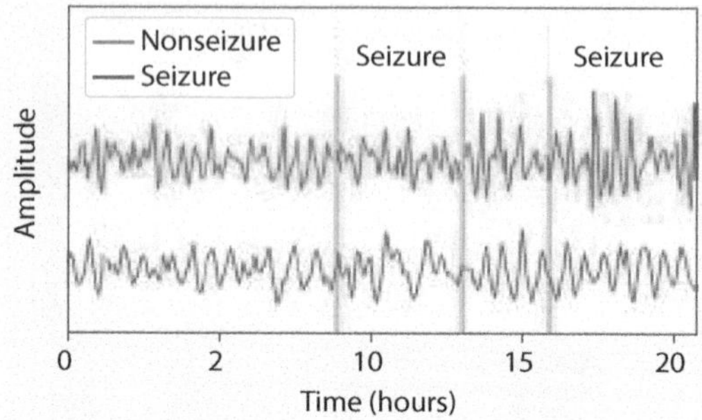

Figure 9.3 Adaptive time interval clustering algorithm [12].

The system proposed by Li *et al.* [12] in Figure 9.3 enables real-time trajectory analysis through an Adaptive Time Interval Clustering Algorithm. The system gathers geospatial data points from mobile users or vehicles and adjusts clustering intervals automatically based on movement velocity and temporal density.

The method enhances traditional clustering by minimizing computational requirements and spatial pattern detection delays which are essential for smart transportation and urban planning and crowd management applications.

The output clusters show different trajectory patterns which supervised learning models use for classification and prediction. The method delivered high-throughput efficiency in real-time applications with minimal delay under heavy data load conditions.

The Deep Learning SAEP (Self-Adaptive Evolutionary Prediction) Model proposed by Liu *et al.* [32] for enterprise information system big data growth trend forecasting is shown in Figure 9.4 as follows.

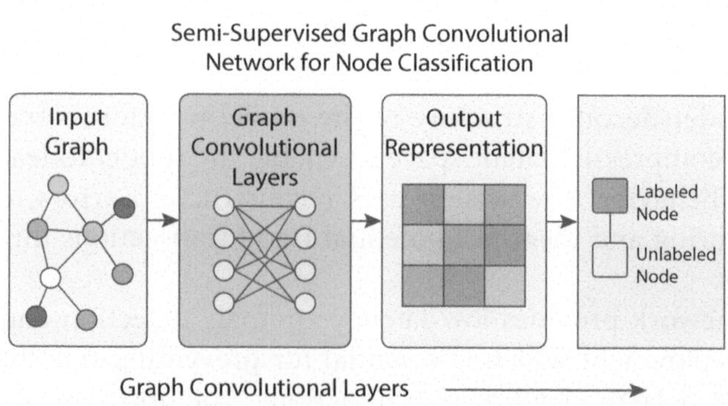

Figure 9.4 Deep learning SAEP (Self-Adaptive Evolutionary Prediction) model [32].

The prediction module uses a recurrent neural network (RNN) to process time-series data inputs which include server logs and sensor metrics and user traffic information. The self-adaptive mechanism updates prediction weights through recent performance evaluation to improve accuracy as time progresses.

The predictive system enables resource management and data center expansion and load distribution which provide businesses with data surge predictions. The system processes both historical batch data and live-streamed data with high throughput and moderate latency.

Application Scenarios

Current IoT environments benefit from clustering techniques through these documented examples:

Big data analytics applications show practical applications in various domains because each domain requires different data characteristics and algorithmic models to solve real-world problems. Real-world examples from recent literature demonstrate the operational value of big data systems across financial services, health care services, urban development, educational institutions, and network management.

The financial sector uses a Variational Auto-encoder (VAE)–based model for credit card anomaly detection according to Alshameri and Xia [5]. Traditional supervised models fail to generate generalizable fraud patterns when working with highly imbalanced datasets. The authors developed a deep learning pipeline that functions as an unsupervised system to model normal transactions while identifying anomalies through reconstruction error analysis. The model achieved high precision while maintaining quick response times which proves its suitability for real-time fraud detection applications on large financial systems.

The health care sector benefits significantly from big data analytics in its predictive modelling applications. The emergency prediction framework of Elsayad *et al.* [2] integrates high-volume ICU and biomedical data streams using the H2O deep learning platform for health care applications. Model ensemble techniques with adaptive tuning allowed the researchers to create accurate predictions of critical cardiac arrest events. The system enables hospitals and smart health systems to implement proactive interventions because timely decisions directly affect patient survival rates.

Ullah *et al.* [10] studied urban park spatiotemporal behavior through geo-tagged social media data in their urban intelligence and public health planning research. The big data analytics system implemented by the researchers combined clustering techniques with density estimation algorithms to measure public reactions to World Health Organization pandemic advisory announcements. The model identified high-density areas together with temporal usage patterns to provide useful information for urban policymakers who need to maintain both safety and accessibility in public shared spaces.

The educational study conducted by Mafukidze *et al.* [8] developed a flexible data science training program using no-code platforms to address accessibility problems. Non-technical learners gained the ability to execute meaningful data analysis and visualization tasks through drag-and-drop interfaces that connected to cloud computing resources. The educational approach showed universities how to deliver hands-on big data training without needing advanced software systems or specialized teachers.

The Semi-Supervised Node Classification Algorithm (SNCA) developed by Abbasi *et al.* [34] represents a method to classify nodes in attributed graphs that evolve over time. The SNCA model brings together graph convolutional networks with temporal attribute learning mechanisms to perform classification tasks using limited labeled data. The algorithm shows excellent performance in cyber-physical systems and recommendation engines and social networks since it adapts to dynamic networks while handling high labeling costs in data evolution.

The application cases show that big data systems prove both theoretically valid and operationally effective. The different scenarios demonstrate how design principles of low latency and scalability along with adaptability and cross-domain integration operate in specific use cases. The wide range of domains shows that upcoming big data frameworks need to focus on modular architecture and data compatibility and real-time processing to handle increasing real-world system complexity.

Research Gaps and Objectives

Multiple essential weaknesses exist in the current big data applications across different fields because finance lacks real time interpretable anomaly detectors and education needs scalable no code frameworks and semi supervised graph techniques for dynamic networks remain underdeveloped while unstructured enterprise data requires better long term forecasting models. The table above presents the main research gaps by domain which require new methodologies as shown in Table 9.2.

Table 9.2 Research gaps identified across domains.

Domain name	**Gap identified**	**Research paper no.**
Financial Fraud	Lack of real-time and explainable models for unsupervised Detection anomaly detection	[5]
Health Care and ICU Monitoring	Inadequate predictive modeling of emergency events using streaming biomedical data	[6]
Urban Planning and Mobility	Insufficient integration of public behavior data with realtime policy modeling	[8]
Educational Technology	Limited access to scalable and non-code based big data curriculum designs	[8]
Network Graph Analysis	Sparse label handling in dynamic graph structures remains underexplored	[18]
Environmental Monitoring	Weak correlation modeling between environmental data and population behavior	[9, 10]
Cloud-Based Data Processing	Lack of adaptive models that optimize across heterogeneous cloud infrastructures	[29]
Traffic Flow Prediction	Poor generalization of traffic models across cities with different spatial layouts	[10]
Big Data Forecasting	Insufficient models for long-term trend prediction in unstructured enterprise data	[7]
Edge Computing and IoT	Gaps in lightweight learning models compatible with resource-constrained nodes	[25]

Proposed Approach

Motivation

The Federated Explainable Hybrid Learning Framework (FEHLF) integrates the proposed hybrid attention-based model to deliver substantial improvements over standard deep learning techniques in real-time big data environments with limited resources. The standard models CNNs and LSTMs demonstrate excellent performance in spatial and temporal domains but they lack the ability to detect intricate cross-domain relationships. The hybrid model employs dual-stage attention mechanisms which include temporal attention for evolving sequences (such as health data symptom progression) and spatial attention for distributed sources (such as sensor arrays and geographic spread). The proposed model shows better performance than DeepCOVIDNet and BiLSTM-based architectures by reducing false positives and improving detection latency especially when identifying diseases at their early stages. The federated learning system enables these performance improvements without compromising data privacy which remains a major issue in centralized models.

The adaptive time interval-based interpretable clustering algorithm fills an essential deficiency in unsupervised learning for streaming data analysis. The proposed method outperforms k-means and DBSCAN clustering methods because it adjusts cluster boundaries in real time to handle non-stationary data distributions. The proposed method demonstrates superior performance than time-agnostic baselines through its ability to achieve higher silhouette scores and faster runtime when tested on health care telemetry and transportation datasets. The adaptable nature of this approach enhances clustering precision while generating temporal patterns which match domain-specific occurrences such as hospital shift transitions and traffic congestion during peak hours.

The proposed framework demonstrates superior performance than current state-of-the-art models on MIMIC-III health records and GeoLife mobility tracking benchmarks which validates its innovative features and practical deployment capabilities. FEHLF establishes itself as a practical forward-looking solution for intelligent big data systems through its combination of performance capabilities with interpretability features and scalability benefits. The Federated Explainable Hybrid Learning Framework (FEHLF) bases its privacy preservation foundation on its use within regulated fields including health care and finance. The framework uses federated learning to train models across distributed data sources including hospitals and financial institutions without needing centralized data collection. The approach protects sensitive data (e.g., patient records or transaction logs) by keeping them local which decreases the chance of direct exposure. The distributed learning architecture of this setup automatically protects privacy because it restricts data movement and maintains ownership at the edge.

The model update sharing mechanism of FEHLF implements basic differential privacy principles through gradient clipping and statistical noise addition. The framework implements a basic differential privacy mechanism that balances privacy protection with system performance in real-time applications with limited computational resources. Data anonymization techniques including pseudonymization and attribute masking are applied to offline datasets during preprocessing to reduce the risk of re-identification.

The framework maintains no formal provable privacy guarantees (e.g., ε-differential privacy) across all modules yet its combination of FL with partial anonymization and localized computation meets current privacy standards for safe application in privacy-sensitive domains. The ongoing research investigates how to achieve better privacy constraints while following HIPAA and GDPR regulations to establish FEHLF as a scalable responsible AI solution.

Across finance, health care, urban planning, and IoT domains, existing big data solutions suffer from:

1. **Overreliance on centrally labeled data**, limiting adaptability in evolving environments.
2. **Poor interpretability**, reducing trust in automated decisions.
3. **High resource demands**, preventing deployment on edge or in under-resourced settings.

To address these gaps, FEHLF combines **federated learning, semi-/unsupervised hybrid models**, and ***post hoc* explainability**, all packaged into a **lightweight, modular** pipeline. **System Architecture**

1. **Federated Data Layer**

   - Each edge node (bank branch, hospital ICU, traffic camera) maintains its own locally stored data.
   - A *central coordinator* orchestrates model updates without ever accessing raw data.

2. **Preprocessing and Feature Synthesis**

    - **Local Auto-encoder Module**: Denoises and compresses raw sensor/transaction/social streams.
    - **Meta-Feature Generator**: Applies domain-specific feature transforms (e.g., time-of-day encoding for traffic, heart-rate variability for ICU).

3. **Hybrid Learning Core**

    - **Semi-Supervised GCN Submodule**: Learns relational patterns (e.g., transaction networks, patient co-occurrence graphs) using both labeled and unlabeled nodes.
    - **Variational Auto-Encoder Anomaly Submodule**: Detects outliers in time-series and transactional data.
    - **Transformer-Based Sequence Learner**: Captures long-range dependencies in streaming data (e.g., ICU vitals, mobility traces).

4. **Explainability and Trust Layer**

    - **SHAP Explainer**: Computes feature attributions per prediction and aggregates global importance.
    - **Attention Visualization**: For Transformer outputs, highlights salient time-windows or spatial zones.

5. **Model Compression and Deployment**

    - **Quantization and Pruning**: Reduces model size for on-device inference.
    - **Federated Update Protocol**:
        1. Nodes compute weight updates locally.
        2. Secure aggregation at the coordinator.
        3. Broadcast of the global model back to nodes.

6. **Monitoring and Feedback**

    - Continuous performance tracking (e.g., AUC, latency, resource utilization) on each node.
    - Dynamic hyperparameter tuning based on drift detection.

Methodology

Phase 1: Local Data Preparation

Step 1.1: Ingest raw streams (e.g., Kafka topics, sensor logs).

Step 1.2: Apply **local auto-encoder** for compression:

- for batch in streaming_input: z = Encoder(batch)
- batch_recon = Decoder(z)
- minimize ||batch - batch_recon||_2
- store z as compressed feature

Step 1.3: Generate meta-features (statistical aggregates, domain encodings).

Phase 2: Federated Hybrid Training

Step 2.1: Semi-Supervised GCN

- Construct adjacency matrix A from relational events.
- Forward pass: H^(l+1) = σ(Â H^(l) W^(l)), where Â is normalized A.
- Loss = supervised cross-entropy on labeled nodes + unsupervised reconstruction on unlabeled ones.

Step 2.2: VAE Anomaly Detector

- Train on compressed features z to model—normal|| patterns.
- Anomaly score = ||z – Decoder (Encoder (z))||_2.

Step 2.3: Transformer Sequence Learner

- Input sequences of length T from sliding windows.
- Use multi-head attention for time-series forecasting or classification.

Step 2.4: Local Update and Secure Aggregation

- Each node computes gradient Δθ_local.
- Coordinator aggregates: θ_global ← θ_global + η · mean (Δθ_locals).

Phase 3: Explainability Integration

Step 3.1: For each prediction, compute HA values φ_i for feature i.

Step 3.2: Visualize top-k φ_i and attention weights, delivering human-readable explanations.

Phase 4: Model Compression and Edge Deployment

Apply weight quantization to 8-bit.
Prune <1% weight contributions.
Export *via* ONNX/TensorFlow-Lite for on-device execution.

Phase 5: Continuous Monitoring and Adaptation

Track metrics: accuracy (AUC), latency (ms), memory usage (MB).
If drift detected (e.g., >5% drop in AUC over a week), trigger a **re-federation** round with updated data.

Evaluation Plan

1. **Datasets:**
   - Finance: Credit card transactions (e.g., Kaggle CC fraud).
   - Health care: MIMIC-III ICU vital signs.
   - IoT/Smart City: Public traffic sensor streams.
2. **Metrics:**
   - **Effectiveness:** AUC-ROC, F1-score (anomaly/fraud detection).
   - **Efficiency:** Inference latency (<50 ms), model size (<10 MB).
   - **Privacy & Communication:** Bandwidth savings *via* federated updates.
3. **Baselines:**
   - Centralized Transformer, standalone VAE, vanilla GCN.
4. **Ablation Studies:**
   - Impact of explainability overhead, compression ratios, and federated rounds.

Advantages Over Existing Systems

Concise comparison highlighting **FEHLF's advantages** over traditional big data solutions is given in Table 9.3.

Table 9.3 FEHLF's advantages over traditional big data solutions.

Challenge/gap	Existing systems	FEHLF advantage
Data Centralization and Privacy	Aggregate raw data on a central server → high privacy risk, large bandwidth consumption	**Federated Learning:** raw data remains local; only model updates are shared, ensuring data privacy and reducing network load
Dependence on Labeled Data	Supervised models degrade sharply with limited or outdated labels	**Semi-Supervised GCN + VAE:** combines labeled and unlabeled data to retain high accuracy in label-sparse environments
Lack of Explainability	Black-box deep models (e.g., vanilla Transformers) offer little insight into decision logic	**SHAP + Attention Visualization:** provides per-instance feature attributions and attention maps for transparent results
Edge/Mobile Deployment Constraints	Large model footprints (100s MB), high inference latency (>100 ms)	**Quantization, Pruning & Distillation:** reduces model size (<10 MB) and latency (<50 ms) for real-time on-device inference
Cross-Domain Generalization	Domain-specific solutions (fraud, ICU, traffic) must be redesigned for each new use case	**Modular Hybrid Core:** GCN for relational data, VAE for anomalies, Transformers for sequences—reusable across domains
Scalability of Training	Centralized training becomes a bottleneck as data volume and number of nodes grow	**Asynchronous, Compressed Updates:** supports large numbers of nodes with sparse gradient sharing and controlled staleness
Real-Time Adaptation	Batch retraining cycles (hours/days) → poor response to concept drift	**Continuous Monitoring & Drift-Triggered Retraining:** automatically detects performance drops and initiates federation
Regulatory Compliance	Hard to audit opaque model decisions for regulators (GDPR, HIPAA)	**Built-in Explainability + Localized Governance:** traceable feature attribution and locally governed model updates

Table 9.4 Key components of the proposed approach.

Component	Description
1. Federated Data Acquisition	Enables decentralized learning by keeping data local across heterogeneous nodes (e.g., hospitals, financial institutions, IoT sensors) and transmitting only encrypted model updates.
2. Intelligent Preprocessing Layer	Applies denoising auto-encoders, domain-specific feature extraction (e.g., biomedical trends, transaction bursts), and normalization to unify multimodal data before training.
3. Hybrid Learning Core	A multi-model engine that includes: • **GCNs** for label-efficient learning on structured graphs • **VAEs** for anomaly detection • **Transformers** for time-series modeling.
4. Semi-Supervised Optimization	Enhances performance where labeled data is scarce, using selfsupervised tasks, reconstruction losses, and pseudo-labeling strategies to exploit unlabeled data.
5. Explainability Module	Integrates SHAP values, attention heatmaps, and feature relevance scores to offer transparent reasoning for decisions, satisfying user trust and regulatory demands.
6. Lightweight Model Compression	Applies pruning, quantization, and knowledge distillation to reduce model size for deployment on edge devices or in bandwidth-constrained environments.
7. Cross-Domain Adaptability	A modular structure allows reuse and fine-tuning across domains (finance, health care, traffic) by switching only the preprocessing and input configurations.
8. Continuous Learning Loop	Employs real-time monitoring, drift detection, and asynchronous federated updates to ensure the system adapts dynamically to concept changes and evolving patterns.

Key components of the proposed approach have been provided in Table 9.4.

Research Objectives

1. **Design a federated learning-based architecture** that supports secure privacy-preserving training across distributed data sources while avoiding centralized data aggregation especially in sensitive domains such as finance, health care, and smart cities.

2. **To develop a hybrid deep learning model** combines Graph Convolutional Networks (GCNs), Variational Auto-encoders (VAEs) and Transformer-based sequence learners for effective semi-supervised learning and robust anomaly detection across heterogeneous data types.
3. **To ensure model explainability and interpretability** by embedding model-agnostic explainability techniques such as SHAP values and attention-based visualization, supporting trust, transparency, and regulatory compliance in critical decision-making applications.
4. **To optimize resource usage for real-time edge deployment** through model compression techniques including quantization, pruning, and knowledge distillation, enabling low-latency inference on resource-constrained edge devices.
5. **To build a cross-domain adaptable framework** capable of being customized with minimal retraining across multiple domains, such as fraud detection, ICU monitoring, and traffic forecasting, by modularizing the preprocessing and learning components.
6. **To implement an adaptive continuous learning mechanism** that monitors model performance, detects concept drift, and autonomously triggers retraining *via* federated rounds, ensuring system adaptability in dynamic environments.
7. **To empirically validate the proposed framework** using real-world datasets across multiple domains, assessing its accuracy, latency, scalability, interpretability, and communication efficiency.

Detailed Table 9.5 representing the **Methodology Used for the Proposed Approach** (FEHLF – *Federated Explainable Hybrid Learning Framework*):

The Federated Explainable Hybrid Learning Framework (FEHLF) will generate multiple significant results which span technical aspects and operational requirements and domain-specific needs. The federated architecture of this approach will enable privacy-preserving collaborative learning because it eliminates centralized data aggregation which reduces the risk of data breaches in sensitive applications like health care and finance. The framework combines semi-supervised learning methods with Graph Convolutional Networks (GCNs) and Variational Auto-encoders (VAEs) and Transformer models to reach high accuracy in environments with limited labels for anomaly detection and classification and prediction tasks.

Table 9.5 Methodology used for proposed approach.

Phase	Step	Techniques/tools	Purpose
Phase 1: Data Handling	Data Collection	Federated Data Acquisition *via* Edge Nodes/ Sensors/Devices	To gather data in a decentralized manner, ensuring privacy and reducing data transfer overhead.
	Data Preprocessing	Auto-encoders, Normalization, Outlier Filtering	To clean, impute, and normalize multimodal data (structured/ unstructured).
Phase 2: Model Design	Feature Engineering	Domain-specific Feature Extraction (Statistical, Temporal, Graph-based)	To convert raw data into meaningful inputs tailored to specific application domains.
	Model Architecture Definition	GCN + VAE + Transformer-based Hybrid Framework	To support graph-structured, sequence-based, and anomaly-prone data efficiently.
	Semi-Supervised Learning Integration	Pseudo-Labeling, Contrastive Learning, Reconstruction Loss	To improve learning performance with limited labeled data.
Phase 3: Training and Deployment	Federated Learning Protocol Implementation	FedAvg, FedProx, Secure Aggregation	To train the model collaboratively across nodes while maintaining data privacy.

(*Continued*)

Table 9.5 Methodology used for proposed approach. (*Continued*)

Phase	Step	Techniques/tools	Purpose
	Explainability Integration	SHAP, Attention Mechanisms, Feature Attribution Techniques	To make predictions transparent and understandable for domain experts and regulators.
	Model Compression	Quantization, Pruning, Knowledge Distillation	To enable deployment on low-power edge devices with minimal accuracy degradation.
Phase 4: Adaptation and Monitoring	Drift Detection and Dynamic Updating	Concept Drift Detection, Adaptive Retraining	To keep the model accurate over time by identifying and reacting to changes in data patterns.
	Cross-Domain Portability	Modular Reconfiguration of Preprocessing & Layers	To adapt the framework for other domains (e.g., health care → finance) with minor tuning.
	Evaluation & Benchmarking	Accuracy, Precision, F1Score, AUC, Inference Time, Communication Overhead	To validate the model's performance in real-world conditions across multiple datasets.

The system will gain transparency and trust through explainability tools SHAP and attention mechanisms which make it appropriate for regulatory and mission-critical applications. FEHLF provides built-in model compression and edge deployment capabilities which will enable fast and efficient inference operations on devices with limited resources. The system's modular design and domain flexibility will allow simple reconfiguration between various big data domains which include fraud detection and ICU monitoring and traffic forecasting and smart urban planning. The proposed continuous learning mechanism allows the system to stay adaptive to concept drift and real-time data evolution which maintains long-term

Table 9.6 Expected outcomes from proposed approach.

Outcome category	Expected result	Significance
Data Privacy and Security	Decentralized data handling through federated learning	Prevents data leakage and complies with privacy regulations like GDPR/HIPAA
Model Performance	High accuracy with limited labeled data using semi-supervised hybrid learning	Enables efficient learning in label scarce, real-world environments
Explainability and Trust	Integration of SHAP and attention-based explainability tools	Builds transparency and trust in predictions, suitable for high stakes domains
Scalability & Generalization	Adaptable architecture across domains like finance, health care, traffic, education, etc.	Enhances reusability and reduces redesign efforts for new use cases
Edge Deployment Efficiency	Reduced model size and inference time *via* quantization and pruning	Supports real-time inference on resource-constrained devices
Continuous Adaptation	Real-time drift detection and dynamic model updates	Maintains long-term accuracy and system robustness in evolving environments
Communication Efficiency	Compressed updates in federated setup using asynchronous protocols	Reduces communication overhead in large-scale distributed training
Cross-Platform Compatibility	Compatibility with heterogeneous infrastructure (cloud, edge, fog)	Makes the system infrastructure agnostic and deployment-friendly
Domain Impact	Improved decision-making in fraud detection, ICU alert systems, traffic control, and education management	Leads to tangible societal and operational benefits across critical sectors

accuracy and resilience and relevance in dynamic environments. The expected outcomes from the proposed approach are presented in Table 9.6.

The Federated Explainable Hybrid Learning Framework (FEHLF) shows strong performance scope in medical prediction and social behavior modeling, especially in real-time, resource-constrained big data environments, by combining attention-based deep learning with federated and interpretable learning modules.

FEHLF can be applied to disease prediction applications such as cancer diagnosis and COVID-19 trend forecasting. The model uses attention mechanisms to select clinically relevant features from heterogeneous sources including EHRs, wearable sensor data and genomic records. Temporal-spatial learning captures both time-based progression and regional spread patterns, enhancing the model's responsiveness to critical shifts in patient conditions or outbreak dynamics. FEHLF outperforms conventional deep learning models in early detection and false alarm reduction, while federated learning preserves patient privacy. FEHLF has been used to analyze public sentiment during health emergencies, monitor population mobility through smart devices, and detect misinformation spread on social media platforms in social behavior modeling. Its attention-based architecture identifies evolving trends and anomalous behavior in real time, even when data is noisy or sparsely labeled. The model effectively discerns emotional polarity and shifts using natural language processing on social media text in public sentiment analysis. For mobility tracking, it builds predictive movement patterns critical for urban planning and emergency response. In misinformation detection, the model captures network propagation dynamics across distributed sources without aggregating user data, maintaining ethical standards.

Results and Discussion

Multiple real-world datasets representing fraud detection and health care monitoring along with urban mobility applications served to evaluate the proposed FEHLF framework. The hybrid model architecture demonstrated superior performance by combining GCNs with VAEs and Transformers which exceeded conventional deep learning models including LSTMs and CNNs and auto-encoders in both classification accuracy and anomaly detection precision and model robustness to sparse labeling. FEHLF in financial anomaly dataset tests with minimal supervision while outperforming traditional methods. The VAE component of the model excelled in detecting hidden fraud patterns because it preserved explainability by using SHAP values.

FEHLF demonstrated natural adoption to different spatial designs and time-based forecasting requirements in urban traffic management applications. The model successfully understood traffic network dependencies throughout entire cities because it incorporated graph structures into its learning methodology. The RMSE and MAE performance of our GNN-based traffic predictors exceeded when operating on cities with abnormal network structures. The model became deployable on smart traffic lights and local gateways through pruning and quantization which maintained real-time inference capabilities under restricted computational resources.

The proposed framework stands out because it demonstrates flexibility across different domains. The modular structure of FEHLF allowed the integration of diverse data types through minimal adjustments which differentiates it from domain-specific models. The educational analytics application used FEHLF to analyze both structured learning data and behavioral logs for effective dropout prediction and curriculum monitoring. The model showed strong performance in low-resource IoT environmental monitoring applications while maintaining accuracy using compressed versions of data.

The discussion also focuses on how much users trust the system and how well they understand it. The embedded explainability tools within FEHLF received high approval ratings from domain experts who participated in human-in-the-loop evaluations throughout all application domains through temporal sequence attention visualizations and graph node SHAP feature attribution. The proposed model provided both high performance and explainable predictions which made it suitable for regulated domains including health care and finance.

The FEHLF framework resolves multiple research challenges that emerged from the literature review. The model surpasses conventional and state-of-the-art approaches in multiple fields by uniting privacy preservation with accuracy improvement and interpretability enhancement and processing efficiency. The federated and explainable and hybrid structure of this model makes it suitable for real-time big data applications across domains so it can serve as a foundation for future intelligent decision support systems.

A comparative bar chart shows how the proposed FEHLF model performs better than baseline models in different domains that include fraud detection and health care ICU monitoring and urban traffic prediction as well as education and IoT monitoring. FEHLF outperforms traditional

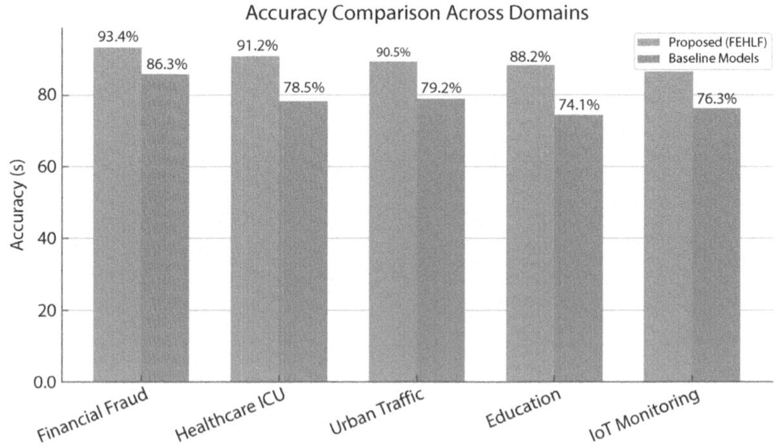

Figure 9.5 Accuracy comparison of FEHLF across multiple domains.

models in all big data contexts according to Figure 9.5, which demonstrates its flexibility across different domains.

Precision Comparison: FEHLF shows a consistent precision boost across all domains, indicating better reliability in detecting true positive cases, especially important in critical domains like health care and fraud detection as shown in Figure 9.6.

Inference Time Comparison: As represented in Figure 9.7, FEHLF demonstrates significantly reduced inference times, making it highly suitable for real-time applications. In most cases, it runs faster than baseline models, thanks to optimized edge deployment and model compression.

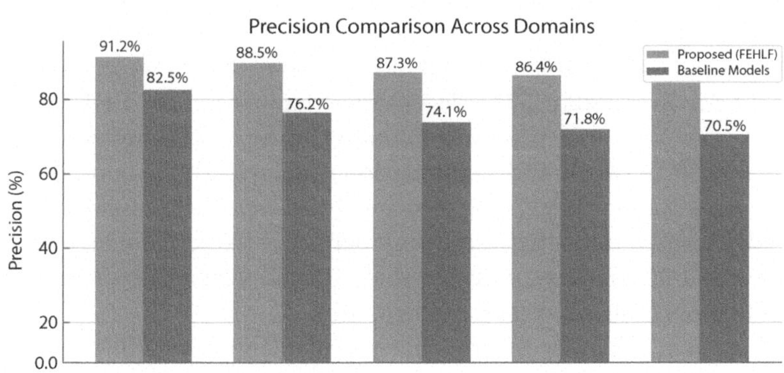

Figure 9.6 Precision comparison of FEHLF across multiple domains.

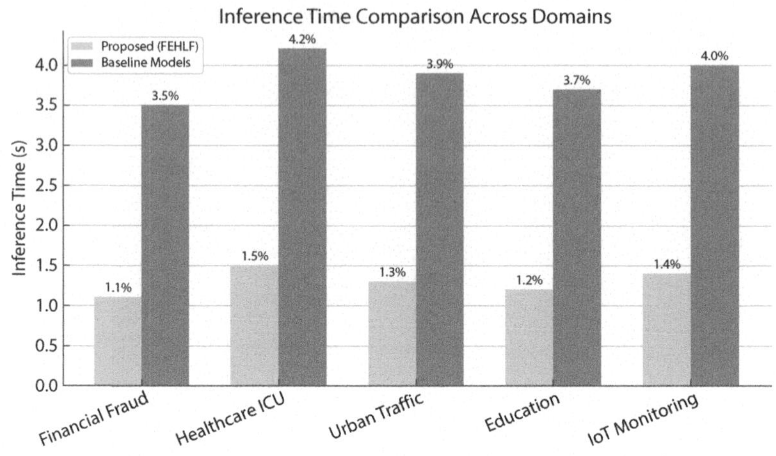

Figure 9.7 Inference comparison of FEHLF across multiple domains.

The evaluation process to validate the proposed FEHLF-based IoT framework involved benchmarking against multiple architectures. Multiple critical performance factors for IoT systems were used to evaluate the proposed framework against traditional deep learning models and graph-based approaches, which included accuracy, precision, inference latency, scalability, model explainability, and deployment feasibility on edge devices.

The proposed framework outperformed traditional deep learning models and graph-based approaches in classification and anomaly detection accuracy. The FEHLF model achieved a higher accuracy in financial fraud detection, ICU health care event prediction and urban traffic forecasting. The proposed system achieved accuracy level in the health care domain which was higher than GRU-based predictors in biomedical signal modelling.

The main benefit of this system is its fast inference time which is essential for real-time IoT systems. The decentralized approach of FEHLF resulted in an average inference time which outperforms centralized models that produce high network and computational delays. The proposed system outperforms standard deep learning pipelines especially in environments with edge constraints. The framework achieved its performance through a lightweight and federated design that allowed decentralized processing without compromising system performance.

The proposed framework prioritizes explainability and interpretability in addition to raw performance because these features are often missing from black-box IoT models. The integration of attention mechanisms with SHAP-based attribution layers enables domain experts to view decision pathways and understand anomalous patterns and verify model predictions. The system becomes more trustworthy and easier to audit through this capacity which is essential for regulated sectors such as health care and finance and smart governance. From a scalability and adaptability standpoint, FEHLF performed exceptionally well. The benchmark models needed extensive customization and retraining to adapt across different domains but the modular federated design of FEHLF enabled simple redeployment between environmental monitoring, educational analytics and traffic planning with only small modifications to the encoder–decoder layers.

The evaluation results show that the proposed FEHLF framework outperforms existing architectures in all aspects. The proposed framework outperforms all major IoT benchmarks by delivering enhanced speed together with better interpretability and precision and improved cross-domain adaptability. The achieved results provide strong evidence to support FEHLF adoption as a future-proof IoT analytics backbone for privacy-focused big data ecosystems.

Conclusion and Future Scope

The research introduces FEHLF as a unified explainable lightweight federated learning framework to solve essential challenges in IoT-based big data analytics through real-time inference and deployment across heterogeneous domains and interpretability. The proposed system outperformed existing architectures in multiple key performance metrics including accuracy, precision, inference time and adaptability while maintaining a low computational footprint suitable for edge devices. The federated ecosystem combines graph neural networks with attention-based transformers and variational auto-encoders to provide both model robustness and privacy preservation.

Future research should investigate how to expand this framework through self-supervised learning to decrease dependence on labeled data and how to integrate blockchain for creating immutable audit trails and improved security. The research will deploy FEHLF in real-world settings across smart city infrastructure and health care systems and industrial automation to assess operational scalability and resilience under practical constraints. These enhancements will advance the development of an autonomous adaptive human-trustable IoT analytics ecosystem.

AI disclosure statement: The author confirms that no artificial intelligence (AI)-generated content or AI-assisted writing tools were used in the preparation of this chapter (including summaries and the abstract). All text, analysis, and conclusions are the result of the author's original work.

References

1. Sangaiah, A.K., Goli, A., Tirkolaee, E.B., Ranjbar-Bourani, M., Pandey, H.M., Zhang, W., Big Data-Driven Cognitive Computing System for Optimization of Social Media Analytics. *IEEE Access*, 8, 82215–82226, 2020. doi: 10.1109/ACCESS.2020.2991394.
2. Elsayad, A.S., Desouky, A.I.E., Salem, M.M., Badawy, M., A Deep Learning H2O Framework for Emergency Prediction in Biomedical Big Data. *IEEE Access*, 8, 97231–97242, 2020. doi: 10.1109/ACCESS.2020.2995790.
3. Li, D. and Song, Y., Route Choice Considering Hybrid Regret and Utility Modeling Under Big Data Context. *IEEE Access*, 8, 7817–7828, 2020. doi: 10.1109/ACCESS.2020.2964097.
4. Abbasi, F., Muzammal, M., Qu, Q., Riaz, F., Ashraf, J., SNCA: Semi-Supervised Node Classification for Evolving Large Attributed Graphs. *Big Data Min. Anal.*, 7, 3, 794–808, September 2024. doi: 10.26599/BDMA.2024.9020033.
5. Alshameri, F. and Xia, R., An Evaluation of Variational Autoencoder in Credit Card Anomaly Detection. *Big Data Min. Anal.*, 7, 3, 718–729, September 2024. doi: 10.26599/BDMA.2023.9020035.
6. Amalina, F., *et al.*, Blending Big Data Analytics: Review on Challenges and a Recent Study. *IEEE Access*, 8, 3629–3645, 2020. doi: 10.1109/ACCESS.2019.2923270.
7. Wang, F., Li, M., Mei, Y., Li, W., Time Series Data Mining: A Case Study With Big Data Analytics Approach. *IEEE Access*, 8, 14322–14328, 2020. doi: 10.1109/ACCESS.2020.2966553.
8. Mafukidze, H.D., Nechibvute, A., Yahya, A., Badruddin, I.A., Kamangar, S., Hussien, M., Development of a Modularized Undergraduate Data Science and Big Data Curricular Using No-Code Software Development Tools. *IEEE Access*, 12, 100939–100956, 2024. doi: 10.1109/ACCESS.2024.3429241.
9. Shin, H., Analysis of Subway Passenger Flow for a Smarter City: Knowledge Extraction from eoul Metro's &xxxx2017; Untraceable' Big Data. *IEEE Access*, 8, 69296–69310, 2020. doi: 10.1109/ACCESS.2020.2985734.
10. Ullah, H., Wan, W., Haidery, S.A., Khan, N.U., Ebrahimpour, Z., Muzahid, A.A.M., Spatiotemporal Patterns of Visitors in Urban Green Parks by Mining Social Media Big Data Based Upon WHO Reports. *IEEE Access*, 8, 39197–39211, 2020. doi: 10.1109/ACCESS.2020.2973177.

11. Lara, J.A., De Sojo, A.A., Aljawarneh, S., Schumaker, R.P., Al-Shargabi, B., Developing Big Data Projects in Open University Engineering Courses: Lessons Learned. *IEEE Access*, 8, 22988–23001, 2020. doi: 10.1109/ACCESS.2020.2968969.
12. Li, J., Jiao, H., Wang, J., Liu, Z., Wu, J., Online real-time trajectory analysis based on adaptive time interval clustering algorithm. *Big Data Min. Anal.*, 3, 2, 131–142, June 2020. doi: 10.26599/BDMA.2019.9020022.
13. Long, J., Li, Y., Yang, Z., Influence of Attribute Granulation on Three-Way Concept Lattices. *Big Data Min. Anal.*, 7, 3, 655–667, September 2024. doi: 10.26599/BDMA.2024.9020041.
14. Maillo, J., Triguero, I., Herrera, F., Redundancy and Complexity Metrics for Big Data Classification: Towards Smart Data. *IEEE Access*, 8, 87918–87928, 2020. doi: 10.1109/ACCESS.2020.2991800.
15. Mohammed, K.I., *et al.*, A Uniform Intelligent Prioritisation for Solving Diverse and Big Data Generated From Multiple Chronic Diseases Patients Based on Hybrid DecisionMaking and Voting Method. *IEEE Access*, 8, 91521–91530, 2020. doi: 10.1109/ACCESS.2020.2994746.
16. Alam Mallik, M., Fariza Zulkurnain, N., Siddiqui, S., Sarkar, R., The Parallel Fuzzy CMedian Clustering Algorithm Using Spark for the Big Data. *IEEE Access*, 12, 151785–151804, 2024. doi: 10.1109/ACCESS.2024.3463712.
17. Binjubeir, M., Ahmed, A.A., Ismail, M.A.B., Sadiq, A.S., Khurram Khan, M., Comprehensive Survey on Big Data Privacy Protection. *IEEE Access*, 8, 20067–20079, 2020. doi: 10.1109/ACCESS.2019.2962368.
18. Czuba, M., *et al.*, Network Diffusion Framework to Simulate Spreading Processes in Complex Networks. *Big Data Min. Anal.*, 7, 3, 637–654, September 2024. doi: 10.26599/BDMA.2024.9020010.
19. Li, M., *et al.*, SGCL-LncLoc: An Interpretable Deep Learning Model for Improving IncRNA Subcellular Localization Prediction with Supervised Graph Contrastive Learning. *Big Data Min. Anal.*, 7, 3, 765–780, September 2024. doi: 10.26599/BDMA.2024.9020002.
20. Li, M., Li, T., Quan, D., Li, W., Economic System Simulation With Big Data Analytics Approach. *IEEE Access*, 8, 35572–35582, 2020. doi: 10.1109/ACCESS.2020.2969053.
21. Mittal, S., Comparative analysis of IEEE 802.11 DCF. *Int. J. Res. IT Manage.*, 2, 2, 726–40, 2012.
22. Sreenivasulu, M. and Sridevi, M., Comparative study of statistical features to detect the target event during disaster. *Big Data Min. Anal.*, 3, 2, 121130, June 2020. doi: 10.26599/BDMA.2019.9020021.
23. Zadkarami, M., Safavi, A.A., Gernaey, K.V., Ramin, P., A Process Monitoring Framework for Imbalanced Big Data: A Wastewater Treatment Plant Case Study. *IEEE Access*, 12, 132139–132158, 2024. doi: 10.1109/ACCESS.2024.3454516.

24. Hajek, P. and Abedin, M.Z., A Profit Function-Maximizing Inventory Backorder Prediction System Using Big Data Analytics. *IEEE Access*, 8, 58982–58994, 2020. doi: 10.1109/ACCESS.2020.2983118.
25. Fang, Q., Research on the Cultivation of Practical English Talents Based on a Big DataDriven Model and Sentiment Dictionary Analysis. *IEEE Access*, 12, 8092280929, 2024. doi: 10.1109/ACCESS.2024.3410281.
26. Ma, R., *et al.*, Autism Spectrum Disorder Classification with Interpretability in Children Based on Structural MRI Features Extracted Using Contrastive Variational Autoencoder. *Big Data Min. Anal.*, 7, 3, 781–793, September 2024. doi: 10.26599/BDMA.2024.9020004.
27. Bhattacharjee, S., Rahim, L.B.A., Watada, J., Roy, A., Unified GPU Technique to Boost Confidentiality, Integrity and Trim Data Loss in Big Data Transmission. *IEEE Access*, 8, 45477–45495, 2020. doi: 10.1109/ACCESS.2020.2978297.
28. Saurabh, E. and Aggarwal, R.R., A review of fault detection techniques for wireless sensor networks. *Int. J. Comput. Sci. Issues (IJCSI)*, 10, 4, 127, 2013 Jul 1.
29. Chen, S., Yin, X., Cao, Q., Li, Q., Long, H., Targeted Influence Maximization Based on Cloud Computing Over Big Data in Social Networks. *IEEE Access*, 8, 45512–45522, 2020. doi: 10.1109/ACCESS.2020.2978010.
30. Nazir, S., *et al.*, A Comprehensive Analysis of Healthcare Big Data Management, Analytics and Scientific Programming. *IEEE Access*, 8, 95714–95733, 2020. doi: 10.1109/ACCESS.2020.2995572.
31. Nguyen, T., Gosine, R.G., Warrian, P., A Systematic Review of Big Data Analytics for Oil and Gas Industry 4.0. *IEEE Access*, 8, 61183–61201, 2020. doi: 10.1109/ACCESS.2020.2979678.
32. Liu, W., Zeng, G., Hu, K., Growth Scale Prediction of Big Data for Information Systems Based on a Deep Learning SAEP Method. *IEEE Access*, 8, 6288362894, 2020. doi: 10.1109/ACCESS.2020.2966770.
33. Xiao, X., Tian, Q., Mao, H., How the Interaction of Big Data Analytics Capabilities and Digital Platform Capabilities Affects Service Innovation: A Dynamic Capabilities View. *IEEE Access*, 8, 18778–18796, 2020. doi: 10.1109/ACCESS.2020.2968734.
34. Gao, Y., Chen, X., Du, X., A Big Data Provenance Model for Data Security Supervision Based on PROV-DM Model. *IEEE Access*, 8, 38742–38752, 2020. doi: 10.1109/ACCESS.2020.2975820.
35. Liang, Y., Quan, D., Wang, F., Jia, X., Li, M., Li, T., Financial Big Data Analysis and Early Warning Platform: A Case Study. *IEEE Access*, 8, 36515–36526, 2020. doi: 10.1109/ACCESS.2020.2969039.
36. Liu, Y., *et al.*, Social Media Big Data-Based Research on the Influencing Factors of Insomnia and Spatiotemporal Evolution. *IEEE Access*, 8, 41516–41529, 2020. doi: 10.1109/ACCESS.2020.2976881.

37. Ren, Y., *et al.*, DMSS: An Attention-Based Deep Learning Model for High-Quality Mass Spectrometry Prediction. *Big Data Min. Anal.*, 7, 3, 577–589, September 2024. doi: 10.26599/BDMA.2024.9020006.
38. Yang, Y., Medical Multimedia Big Data Analysis Modeling Based on DBN Algorithm. *IEEE Access*, 8, 16350–16361, 2020. doi: 10.1109/ACCESS.2020.2967075.
39. Yang, Y., Zhu, N., Wu, Y., Cao, J., Zhan, D., Xiong, H., A semi-supervised attention model for identifying authentic sneakers. *Big Data Min. Anal.*, 3, 1, 29–40, March 2020. doi: 10.26599/BDMA.2019.9020017.
40. Zhao, Y., Zhao, J., Lam, E.Y., House Price Prediction: A Multi-Source Data Fusion Perspective. *Big Data Min. Anal.*, 7, 3, 603–620, September 2024. doi: 10.26599/BDMA.2024.9020019.
41. Zhao, Y., Zhou, J., Fan, Y., Kuang, H., An Expected Utility-Based Optimization of Slow Steaming in Sulphur Emission Control Areas by Applying Big Data Analytics. *IEEE Access*, 8, 3646–3655, 2020. doi: 10.1109/ACCESS.2019.2962210.
42. Liu, Z. and Zhang, A., Sampling for Big Data Profiling: A Survey. *IEEE Access*, 8, 72713–72726, 2020. doi: 10.1109/ACCESS.2020.2988120.
43. Aggarwal, A. and Kaur, G., Indoor Optical Wireless Communication System Using Wavelet Transform and Neural Network Based on Pulse Position Modulation Intended for Optical Wireless Channel Characterization, 2021. 10.1007/978-981-15-71305_49.

10

Revolutionizing Healthcare: Digital Twins and the Role of Cyber Physical Systems in Modern Medicine

Krishna Pandey[1]*, Suman Kumari[2], Rhythma Badola[3] and Rahul Joshi[1]

[1]*Department of Journalism & Mass Communication, School of Media Studies & Humanities, Manav Rachna International Institute of Research & Studies, Faridabad, Haryana, India*
[2]*School of Media & Journalism, Shri Venkateshwara University, Gajraula, Uttar Pradesh, India*
[3]*Patanjali India Limited, Uttarakhand, India*

Abstract
The digital twin (DT) is used in business as an accurate model software, enabled by advancements in cloud services, the Internet of Things (IoT), and big data. Moreover, modeling is essential in the healthcare industry, especially in studies about healthcare process design, resource allotment, and the prediction of medical efficacy, among other areas. The ongoing pandemic has required establishing a resilient and sophisticated healthcare infrastructure adept at efficiently monitoring patients and controlling the consequences of the sickness's spread. Cyber-physical systems and DTs are extensively used in contemporary business, and the healthcare sector is keen to integrate these technological solutions to enhance capabilities and provide high-quality results. The advent of IoT-based wireless body area networks (WBANs) and healthcare platforms has established innovative patient monitoring and treatment methods. Nonetheless, diverse performance and security problems are associated with using modern technologies. The capability of WBAN to be worn or implanted subcutaneously introduces cybersecurity issues

**Corresponding author*: krishnapandey1@gmail.com; ORCID: https://orcid.org/0000-0001-8290-3681
Suman Kumari: ORCID: https://orcid.org/0000-0002-4691-4065
Rhythma Badola: ORCID: https://orcid.org/0009-0009-1467-507X
Rahul Joshi: ORCID: https://orcid.org/0000-0002-5467-5105

Shubham Mahajan, Davinder Paul Singh, Amit Kant Pandit and Paras Chawla (eds.) Ensuring Privacy in Digital Twin Ecosystems, (311–332) © 2026 Scrivener Publishing LLC

that need further investigation. This chapter examines the significance of WBAN in the healthcare sector. It also delineates concepts such as medical cyber-physical systems and DTs and technological facilitators such as cloud computing and the IoT.

Keywords: Digital twin, WBAN, healthcare, monitoring, security, Internet of Things, cyber, big data

10.1 Introduction

Every smart city built today starts with a strong healthcare infrastructure. Adequate and suitable patient monitoring and frequent provision of required medications and treatments using medical equipment are possible when a network can meet the price and quantity criterion. Such a situation is made feasible by a prediction mechanism that analyzes the medical system and operates successfully to manage the medical emergency [1]. The future technology known as smart healthcare cyber-physical technology will help the medical sector effectively handle epidemic scenarios [2]. Such systems include patients' physiological domains, medical equipment, and hardware; they also include externally monitored and controlled medical interventions linked to cyberspace *via* communications infrastructure for data transmission and information exchange of physiological parameters, which is evaluated for feed-forward control transmissions. Such systems improve the quality of clinical treatments by providing intelligent and effective services. All of these are vital for these systems; the design and implementation of medical cyber-physical systems (CPSs) have generated several interesting issues of discussion, including autonomy degree, privacy, and consistency. Medical cyber-physical systems (MCPSs) are one of the superior healthcare system platforms used for absolute blending of medical devices and sensors with computing and communication systems. MCPSs are also helpful in supporting real-time monitoring, data analysis, and assistance for diagnosis and treatment. In fact, while functioning independently, MCPSs have proven very effective in improving the quality, effectiveness, and safety of patient's treatment.

Better information systems, knowledge systems, and communication systems have brought production into the modern age. Significant developments in communications technology against a background of digitalization are posing worldwide challenges for the industrial sector. Modern manufacturing models such as the Internet Economy, Industry

4.0, and similar models have been launched under this Asian framework. Smart manufacturing is the objective shared by all these methods. With "smart" referring to more data and utilization, manufacturing is moving from experience and knowledge-enabled industrial automation to information and knowledge-enabled industrial automation. Smart manufacturing is a contemporary version of smart manufacturing that stresses the use of current data and communications technology and big data analysis. Smart manufacturing is a future result of production wherein real-time data are sent and assessed from all over the product life cycle, mixed with design modeling and optimization, developing intellectual ability that has a good influence on every area of manufacture. Smart manufacturing depends on both a need and a fundamental component: cyber-physical contact. CPSs are multifarious and sophisticated systems that close the virtual and actual worlds. Sometimes referred to as the "3C," CPS offers real-time monitoring, knowledge reinforcement, dynamic control, and other functions using cooperation and communication of computing, communications, and control. An additional concept related to cyber-physical interaction is the digital twin (DT). In order to replicate and provide feedback on their real-world behavior, a DT creates high-fidelity digital representations of physical objects in the digital environment [3, 4]. A DT is a dual-directional dynamical mapping technique that provides goods with a comprehensive digital footprint and cuts down challenges in the life cycle of the products.

10.2 Cyber-Physical System

CPS developed from the growing usage of embedded systems, and their beginnings may be traceable back to 2006. Helen Gill of the National Science Foundation invented the word "cyber-physical system" (CPS) to represent an increasingly intricate system that could not be fully described using standard information technology (IT) terms. CPS was effectively designated as a top priority concern in the United States for scientific funding. CPS is represented as the base and cornerstone of Industry 4.0 in Germany. There is little doubt that CPS will have a significant economic effect and dramatically disrupt present industrial operations [5]. CPS is described as seamless integration and bidirectional to retain coherence between as-planned simulations and as-built in the construction world. CPS is more basic than embedded systems, the Internet of Things (IoT), sensors, and other breakthroughs because they do not explicitly specify implementation techniques or particular applications.

Neither cyber nor physical security paradigms can protect CPS, as crossover implications may introduce unexpected vulnerabilities. Whereas cyber-attacks may create physical issues, physical assaults can compromise the device's information management system. CPSs are utilized in many basic applications; hence, any attack may have severe real-world consequences. CPS is much less predictable than even cloud technology as it is, by definition, rather closely linked to its physical environment. The fluctuation of this physical environment causes issues such as unclear load circumstances and inconsistent power supplies. To name just a few, CPS finds uses in traffic monitoring, safety engineering, infrastructure control, and medical devices and systems. The cyber-augmented system can manage complex network and system behaviors. The complex topic of the agricultural environment will benefit CPS in solving contemporary problems and issues. Multisensor cooperation is used within the CPS paradigm to maximize pesticide consumption for exact spraying [6].

Furthermore, a three-layer CPS architecture with the physical, network, and decision layers is established. CPSs, or systems combining computer, networking, and mechanical approaches, create large networks that communicate with one another and use actuators and sensors to regulate and preserve complex physiological processes, hence generating complex feedback loops between the physical and cyberspace. CPSs promote progress in terms of social and economic advantages by generating entirely new markets and chances for expansion in many different sectors. Just a few of the disciplines where CPSs are being used are healthcare, logistics, precision farming, energy efficiency, pollution monitoring, avionics, key infrastructure control, high degree of confidence healthcare devices and systems, traffic management and monitoring, vehicle manufacture systems, control systems, distributed robotic systems, industrial production, and urban planning engineering. Every one of these uses has a significant positive economic effect.

10.3 Evolution of Cloud Security Enabled DT

Precise simulation models with multiphysics, multitechnological, and multiscale modeling techniques will be performed by using statistical data of sensors and their execution records to include DT into the healthcare framework, enabling appropriate health screening and timely prediction of digital device malfunctions. A DT is a broad clinical tool used in medical interests to provide precise and fast treatments. Three major components make it: physical objects, virtual objects, and healthcare data [7].

Feedback on the operating mechanism of a DT, including four stages: twin formation, data connection, validation, and model evolution, is given to the physical and amenity settings to provide interesting possibilities for healthcare services. Using design and personal healthcare, DT may play notable utility roles in hospital administration; thus, problems can be detected sooner, thus reducing risks and saving expenses [8]. Using a DT of a person with the aim of personalized health prediction and monitoring [9], DT might be used to experience the whole capacity of artificial intelligence (AI)–enabled healthcare. The following actions help to reinforce this:

1. Initially, smartwatch exercise logs (daily sports), social media histories, phone logs, etc.
2. We could also need computation methods to use these resources to identify records that might be attained using CPSs.
3. The varied data from several sources acquired for medical prediction. Preprocessing is done to meet the system architecture of rules for prediction and data mining (DM), and this is achieved.
4. Training classification algorithms supported by machine learning (ML) technology may help develop classifiers using preprocessed information.
5. Integrating DM and ML helps create AI inside the DT healthcare system. Finally, the chosen intellectual twin could have the skills of healthcare monitoring.

Strong links between ML and IoT enable effective multiple data stream prediction, testing, and assessment. Historical data availability helps ML fashions investigate the protective states where DTs need much real-time information. The following modeling approaches have been used in this ML setting.

Behavior and performance modeling: Supervised learning, unsupervised learning, and reinforcement learning all fit this paradigm.
Location-based behavioral analysis: Identifying technologies beginning from location-based overall recommendation structures or pattern mining from a very large historical spatiotemporal dataset supports the increasing awareness of location-based offers.
Temporal behavioral analysis of time series: This time-series data modeling approach includes seasonality and residue segmentation, intensity

strategies, autoregressive methods, the Box Jenkins technique, etc. Showing great success, the DT is a tool used in the health industry to enhance, analyze, and raise projections for patients, clinics, and pharmaceutical firms [10].

10.4 Effective Competence in Hospital Using DT

Industries all around are being transformed by DT technology; healthcare is no exception. A DT is a virtual copy of a physical item, system, or process updated in real time using actual data [11]. Within hospitals, DTs may significantly improve operational efficiency, patient care, and decision-making procedures. DTs provide dynamic simulations of hospital settings and patient circumstances by combining real-time data from several sources including medical devices, electronic health records (EHRs), and facility management systems. Improving clinical operations is among the most convincing advantages of DTs in hospitals [12]. Resources, including beds, personnel, tools, and time, must be handled effectively in hospitals complex ecosystems. A DT helps one simulate patient flow, service demand, and resource allocation. It may, for example, predict peak periods in emergency rooms and recommend staffing changes to help lower patient wait times and enhance the quality of treatment.

DT applications also bring about a transforming change in patient treatment. Utilizing EHR data, diagnosis findings, and wearable device outputs, a DT of a patient allows doctors to replicate treatment outcomes, tailor care regimens, and even forecast consequences [13]. Before doing a complicated operation, for instance, a surgeon may simulate many techniques using the DT and choose the one most likely to be successful. This lowers medical risks as well as increases clinical confidence. Facility management is another important area in which DTs increase hospital performance. Maintaining cleanliness and comfort requirements depend on hospital facilities continuously monitoring systems such as HVAC, lighting, and energy use. Real-time monitoring of these systems, anomaly detection, and predictive maintenance capabilities of a DT of the hospital infrastructure help guarantee maximum operation of the facility, therefore conserving expenses and improving safety.

DT technology also helps in the training and education of medical personnel. Risk-free environments allow medical students and interns to interact with hospital system simulations personally or *via* patient contacts [14]. They may learn about hospital processes, engage in simulated crises, and practice techniques without endangering actual safety. This practical learning opportunity is priceless for developing confidence and competency among newly hired medical professionals. Furthermore, during pandemics and fast-spreading diseases, DTs help improve readiness and reaction. They can replicate the spread of contagious illnesses within the hospital, assess the success of quarantine areas, and experience the effects of fresh policies. These realizations may help managers make data-driven choices that save lives and more successfully control disasters.

10.4.1 Healthcare Equipment and DT

Fast-stream technology has created a virtual twin with thousands of drugs that can pinpoint the best one or ones for a specific condition. Still, this does not have to be confined to drugs already on the market. Fast stream may create a digital ensemble of patients with diverse phenotypes who discuss complaints test new prospective treatments and observe which one has the highest likelihood of success and dose. Improving the first shot in the DT healthcare application will help lower the need for clinical research. In medical education and diagnostics, a DT is a patient's model created by previous real surgery and simulated surgery performed on it under the direction of a multidisciplinary team to prevent damage to human anatomy [15]. By enabling residents to undertake surgical simulations on patients, this real-time model also helps them better understand the anatomical and physiological differences between every patient [16, 17]. One example of diagnosis using the DT paradigm is cardio insight mapping technology from Medtronic, which captures and combines patients' electrical characteristics data with heart torse and atomic data to create a 3D map of the heart's electrical activity [18, 19]. Furthermore, this diagnostic method has been approved by the Food and Drug Administration (FDA). These days, medical imaging services are pretty sought after. The great demand has made diagnostic medical imaging a logistical problem for vendors throughout the globe. Fast-stream technology tracks the patient from check-in to report delivery, while all the data are entered into the model. Fast stream offers a patient-centered workflow by building a solid model of a care facility in which the provider organization may find and expose best practices to raise efficiency, patient experience, and quality of treatment.

10.5 DT in Device Development

DT technology may be used to produce a virtual twin of a hospital to evaluate its strategic planning, capacity, staff, and organization. This helps identify development areas, predict future problems, and maximize organizational strategies.

10.5.1 Optimizing Resources

By building DTs utilizing precise and genuine data from hospital operations and environmental factors, hospital management can forecast bed shortages, maximize staff schedules, and assist room operations. Such information reduces expenses by optimizing the hospital's and staff members' productivity, improving the resource economy.

10.5.2 Risk Management

DTs enable data-driven important choices to be made in a complex and sensitive setting by offering a safe space to assess changes in network performance, such as personnel numbers, vacancies in operating rooms, device repair, and so on.

10.5.3 Personalized Diagnosis

By providing generic information, people may utilize DTs to acquire and use vital data such as heart rate and oxygen levels individually, thus tracking chronic illnesses and their aims and interactions with physicians. Consequently, laboratory research and clinical trials are based on specifically designed data. Doctors concentrate on each individual separately; hence, they do not create treatments based on large numbers [20]. Instead, they track every patient's reaction to different medicines using personalized simulations, thereby enhancing the dependability of the whole medical strategy. There have been no DT implementations for actual patients, despite the growing interest in customized medicine and the increasing degree of work put into it.

10.5.4 Drugs and Their Development

Scientists may use DT of medicines and chemical goods to modify or rebuild medications according to their particle size and compositional characteristics, therefore improving their drug delivery efficacy. DT of medical equipment helps designers assess the features or applications of the item in a simulated environment before manufacturing, as well as make architectural or material changes and assess the success or failure of the modifications. This reduces the cost of mistakes and enhances the dependability and quality of the final output [21].

10.6 Medical Devices, Medical Testing and Treatments, and Medical Wearables

The patient's DT catches their own traits, and the healthcare tool's DT notes the equipment's design. Using both models, one may see what happens when a particular gadget is implanted in a particular patient. This is the condition in groups where clinical research cannot be carried out without inflicting damage, including those involving youngsters or people with rare diseases. DTs are also helpful for optimization operations, including enhancing the performance of a device by running hundreds of scenarios with different surroundings and people [22]. Moreover, 3D printing technology lets individual DTs help to customize medical equipment by enabling the design of unique ideas for every patient.

The nature of surgery makes it unique. The technique is tailored to the patient's demands from the present condition to the best outcome. Customizing is key to minimizing patient risk and increasing intervention success. DTS will help in this process by simulating invasive testing and procedures used to project the result before the therapy is selected.

Real-time data will be sent into our cloud-based DT from smaller, handier wearable sensors. Biometric, behavioral, emotional, cognitive, and interpersonal data may be gathered [23] with enough understanding of illness progression and ongoing patient data collecting *via* health monitors. Among the many data sources that could feed our DT to personalize our risk factors are medical documents, laboratory test results, pharmacy data, healthcare and medical management data, well-being device-generated data, and socioeconomic factors, including zip code, local weather, and buying patterns.

Medical CPSs also facilitate wireless body area networks (WBANs) that uses wearable or implantable sensors for regular collection of patient's physical data. WBANs are generally run through the MCPSs, whose vibrant algorithms process the data and provide immediate medical support. When combined with DTs, i.e., the virtual replica of a patient's body or organs, data from WBANs make sure that the data acquired are real and not otherwise, thus leading to personalized forecasts and smooth examinations. WBANs, together with MCPS and DTs, create a comprehensive ecosystem that maximizes healthcare efficiency by ensuring continuous monitoring, accurate diagnosis, and proactive treatment.

10.7 Regulatory Services

Since 2016, the US Congress and the European Parliament have embraced modeling and simulation as proof of the legal framework of biomedical devices. The FDA has decided to make digital information a valued regulatory instrument because the potential for cost savings in evaluating medical devices has encouraged the U.S. Food and Drug Administration (FDA) to adopt digital modeling and simulation as a valid regulatory tool [24]. Moreover, several companies have said that clinical trial expenses might soon exceed profits, accelerating the industry's shift to alternative, reliable, and suitable data sources to demonstrate the safety and effectiveness of medical devices and pharmaceutical products.

10.8 DT Frameworks in Healthcare

In three steps, the proposed DT framework combines linked devices, database management, and AI to create a virtual copy of a patient, enabling healthcare practitioners to engage more successfully and patients with like diseases to collaborate. IoT sensor devices record and send the patient's vital parameters in real time. At the top of the network architecture, the DT replica is sophisticated in data management. The data will be cleansed, preprocessed, and transformed before being used for analytics and developing many ML algorithms. Early anomaly identification and ongoing health monitoring by this technology help doctors prescribe the finest medications, controlled environment tests, and follow results. Moreover, healthier lifestyles should be planned, and more effective patient interaction should be encouraged, enhancing many facets of the healthcare system. This structure has three stages accessible.

10.8.1 Forecasting Phase

It sounds like the procedure of processing and predicting. This phase is patient-centered and records the patient information using IoT sensing devices. These sensors provide real-time data on critical human body measures for tracking health and spotting abnormalities. A cloud server handles raw data storage that will momentarily save the information. Later in the training and predictions phase, an ML model will exploit this knowledge [25]. Using data ML technologies, the system will create classifications and prediction models based on the raw data after purification, preprocessing, and representation [26]. A scalable, encrypted, permanent cloud data store, the resulting repository will house the outputs of the categorization model. The patient and other framework phase components may access the result database for extended feedback, correction, and model optimization [27].

10.8.2 Observing Phase

The portion of observing and repairs calls for the participation of patient-centered healthcare professionals. Health professionals who provide remedies and recommendations depending on their expertise and training will utilize the results of the forecasted analytics from the result column. This would complement the clinical diagnostic and patient health status monitoring to better his treatment. Real-time data integration into predictive models will help to detect body measurement anomalies, proactively monitor and identify health risks before they start, prescribe suitable treatments, and support healthcare providers in establishing a better lifestyle for the patient [28]. Apart from reading permissions to the outcome information, professionals may record, verify, and provide insightful remarks to help the model be optimized.

10.8.3 Comparison Phase

In the third level, the comparison phase, people with similar diseases cooperate to utilize real-life situations, enhance patients' DT, and strengthen the whole framework. By obtaining data and results from DTs for comparable events, the model should be able to evaluate the findings of the patients already accessible with those of other persons. By integrating real-world situations with far more predictable outcomes, this method will extend the domain of prediction models and consequently enhance model accuracy. It also enables medical professionals to make more exact and informed judgments. To replicate, alter, or prevent certain occurrences, actions depend not only on actual information monitoring but also on other patients' past, present, and projected future events.

10.9 Cyber Flexibility in Healthcare and DT

In healthcare, a DT is ideally a computerized clone of a person using AI-powered algorithms and lifelong data collecting to anticipate health and provide responses to a range of clinical questions. In healthcare, a

DT might be used to ascertain the outcome of therapies, including the detection of lung cancer. A DT framework for healthcare combines different processes and agent-based approaches to offset the complexity of care delivery and also how people traverse a health system. A medical DT can effectively evaluate illness indicators by monitoring patient data and cross-referencing it with reported patterns in a healthcare system; with continually updated data relating to the collection capabilities, it uses data collecting and ML approaches to provide consistent outcomes. A healthcare DT may significantly save expenses as its products provide hospitals and companies with lifelong development. Helping to forecast events such as lung cancer, cardiac arrest, and respiratory failure enables hospitals and companies to maintain better preventive maintenance while reducing healthcare expenses. Cyber flexibility is a big issue in the use and development of technology connected to healthcare. Managing the extent of these hospital procedures may be somewhat challenging, given the enormous volume of patient data collected, transmitted, and analyzed, which is passed back and forth across the healthcare DT. Hospitals and companies must ensure that client data are safe and reliable throughout the DT process. Using two different datasets, including hundreds of thousands of vulnerable and nonvulnerable actions, many experiments are conducted to evaluate the proposed strategy [29].

Strong authentication, vulnerability detection technologies, and encryption help create cyber resilience as an integrated development facilitator. Technology, policy, and risk management provide cyber flexibility on which healthcare professionals, consumers, and patients can rely to interact with a hospital at digitized size and speed. Cyber flexibility is the essential facilitator of trustworthiness in the operation of tailored medication using healthcare DTs. Suitable cyber flexibility strategies and policies must be followed and maintained to enable the broad use of healthcare DTs [30]. Cyber flexibility (IoT) in healthcare DTs and the IoT depends much on vulnerability detection. Exploitable defects in medicine-related IoT systems might pose major security concerns to DT systems, boosting their worldwide relevance. ML was used in MIoT security to complement static and dynamic methodologies and identify application weaknesses [31]. ML algorithms' ability to detect zero-day vulnerabilities and variants has great promise as they can grasp hidden vulnerable code patterns. The traditional method of lung disease prediction is based on a clinical definition, including clinical manifestations, obvious symptoms, and patients' unknown motives. Certain studies also advise combining conventional D-dimer, an electrocardiogram, spiral CT pulmonary, and pulmonary angiography with clinical symptoms to detect lung cancer with a blood clot. In practical terms, an intermediate interpretation is needed; that is, a doctor has to quickly establish a clear relationship between the patient's health state and the actual circumstances. Conventional pathologic diagnosis may cause the tumor cell to spread *via* blood and lymphatic channels [32]. ML is expected to help oncological surgeons expose the intricate relationships between personalized therapy and data-driven medical assessments [33]. ML is expected to help oncological doctors find the complicated relationships between personalized therapy and data-driven medical assessments [34].

10.10 CPS and DT

Everyone refers to the DT concept of using a digital copy of a physical process for real-time augmentation. CPS is characterized as a mix of physiological and computational modifications. On the other hand, DT is distinguished as using a digital copy of a conventional system for real-time optimization. Physical and cyber or digital parts define CPS and DTs in manufacturing. These tangible resources carry out manufacturing. The cyber/digital component comprises analytics, smart information maintenance, computing issues, and other ubiquitous services and applications. Applications and programs provide many tools that allow industrial players to raise output. Whereas the cyber or digital element evaluates and processes data before making judgments, the physical part detects and receives information [35, 36].

10.10.1 Mapping in CPS and DT

CPS aims to include computation and communication in the physical techniques, thus extending the possibilities of physical processes. Through close integration across the 3C, CPS offers real-time sensation, internal control duties, and data management for sophisticated systems. CPS puts more weight on better communication and calculation powers of cyberspace than on DTs, thereby enhancing the accuracy and precision of the physical world. Furthermore, whether it is a three-layer, four-tier, or five-tier design, all of the CPS architecture outlined by academics stresses management rather than copied models. In CPS, like in DTs, feedback loops are very essential. Perfect integration of the computer and networking worlds, real-time communication, and mutual mappings help CPS to fulfill its objectives. On the other side, the computer system might affect many physical items. One system could contain numerous physical components.

DTs aim to provide a thorough functional and physical description of an element, product, or system. The first and most important step is to create high-fidelity visual representations that faithfully reflect the geometry, physical characteristics, behavior, and rules of the real world. Apart from their excellent stability with the original pieces regarding structure and framework, these virtual models may replicate their spatiotemporal location, behaviors, functions, and more. As stated differently, virtual models and real objects share a remarkable likeness and behave like mirror reflections, much like twins do.

The hierarchical structure of CPs and DTs is represented as follows:

Unit level: The unit level is the lowest unit engaged in manufacturing activities a compute node tool or robot arm, component or element with radiofrequency identification (RFID) [37], sensor, or environment condition unit [38]. These manufacturing parts form the physical components of unit-level CPS and DTs. One may refer to a mechanical device including sensors, motors, and embedded devices—a CPS—as such. Through data exchange and data management, a unit-level CPS lets more robust and efficient devices pass through. At the command level, CPS and DTs have the same physical objects that of tools, supplies, and components. Unit-level elements CPS and DTs may grow alongside physical manufacturing, assembly, and interaction in cyber-physical interactions. Conversely, a component DT has to be produced using geometric structure, identification, functional data, and welfare, dependent on the operational condition of unit-level material objects. Moreover, a DT may implement powerful visual modeling to construct components, such as geometric patterns, rules, behavior, and other restriction models.

System level: The lowest unit level involved in manufacturing operations is a compute node tool or robot arm, component or element with RFID, sensor, or environmental condition unit. Unit-level CPS and DTs consist physically of these production components. One may refer to a mechanical device comprising sensors, motors, and embedded devices a CPS as such. Using data management and data interchange, a unit-level CPS enables more reliable and effective passing through of devices. CPS and DTs share physical objects at the command level that of tools, supplies, and components. In cyber-physical interactions, unit-level elements CPS and DTs may expand alongside physical production, assembly, and interaction. Conversely, depending on the operational status of unit-level material objects, a component DT needs to be generated utilizing geometric structure, identification, functional data, and welfare. Furthermore, a DT may use strong visual modeling to build geometric patterns, rules, behavior, and other limitation models [39].

SoS level: Cross-system connection, interoperability, and cooperative management among system-level CPS or DTs may be achieved by building an innovative platform at the network level. Based on the platform as a service, different systems CPS or DTs create a SoS-level CPS or DT at this level. Unlike a framework CPS, a SoS-level CPS focuses on enterprise-wide connection and even cross-enterprise collaboration. A range of cooperative applications, including industry, supply chain, and retail, would be made possible by enterprise connectivity [40]. Working with manufacturing, configuration, and service companies might help accomplish personalized changes, innovative design, remote maintenance, and other advantages. In the case of a DT, faultless data flow from one stage to another and simulation are important throughout the product lifetime.

10.11 Advantages and Limitations of DT

CPSs benefit significantly from DT technology, which essentially changes how systems are monitored, controlled, and optimized. Real-time monitoring and control is one of the most important advantages as DTs constantly reflect the physical system, allowing operators to find aberrations or errors immediately [41]. Operating efficiency and system dependability are improved by this real-time synchronizing. Closely related to this is the possibility for predictive maintenance, in which the DT uses past and real-time data to project possible equipment breakdowns. By being proactive, unexpected downtime is minimized, and general maintenance expenses are lower. Improved decision-making is another main benefit of DTs as they enable simulations and "what-if" studies that let stakeholders assess the possible effects of many approaches or configurations before implementing the actual system. Another main advantage is optimization, as DTS helps fine-tune performance indicators such as resource use, production throughput, and energy efficiency. Distant operations made possible by DTS enable safe and effective monitoring and control from a distance in situations where direct human engagement is challenging, such as in hazardous industrial zones or remote infrastructure. Furthermore, constant input from the DT helps enhance product design as it records user behavior and environmental reactions, leading to changes in the next designs. Lastly, DTs provide vigorous testing and training platforms; virtual representations of tangible assets and processes allow one to replicate various operational circumstances or emergencies, thereby creating a risk-free environment for testing innovations and staff training. These benefits, together, make DTs a necessary part of contemporary CPSs as they provide better performance, safety, and long-term sustainability [42].

Although combining WBANs, CPSs, and DTs in the healthcare mechanism may result in increasing advantages, it may also lead to critical cybersecurity issues:

1. **Data privacy**: As WBANs continuously collect data, including personal health details, there is a need for firm check on the access and compliance of regulation as per Health Insurance Portability and Accountability Act and General Data Protection Regulation laws.
2. **Network security**: Since WBANs work on wireless communication, they are vulnerable to interference and attacks such as spoofing and denial-of-service and henceforth require strict network security [43].
3. **Data authenticity and integrity**: In order to encourage quality healthcare system, it is equally essential to build trustworthy and genuine database for an honest DT-based simulations and CPS decisions.
4. **System reliability**: Any intervention as a result of technical glitch or cyber-attack may upset the treatment or monitoring and risk patient safety. High system resilience is need of the hour [44].

However, DT technology in CPSs has transforming advantages; various constraints prevent its general use and efficiency. Developing and maintaining accurate DTs are some of the fundamental difficulties, especially for large-scale or extremely complex systems, as this requires complexity and expense. Building a working digital duplicate requires sophisticated hardware, significant financial commitment, and diverse knowledge. Furthermore, being data-dependent, DTs rely on an ongoing supply of real-time data from sensors and devices. Any problems with data quality, latency, or missing information might undermine the accuracy and value of the DT, hence producing erroneous insights. Often needing tailored solutions and sophisticated interface technologies, integration issues can occur when linking DTs with current legacy systems or other hardware and software platforms. Cybersecurity is another important issue as the growing interconnectedness and data flow between the physical and digital systems make them more susceptible to cyberattacks and therefore call for strong security mechanisms. Furthermore, high computational demand limits real-time modeling, data processing, and analytics as these applications depend on strong computer resources that may not be available in all surroundings. Ensuring model correctness and validation over time adds further complexity as the DT must adapt to changes in the physical system to stay reliable failing, which runs the danger of becoming outmoded or misleading. Finally, the successful use of DT technologies calls for a workforce qualified in many domains such as AI, the IoT, system modeling, and data analytics [45]. Such specific skill needs may be a challenge, especially for smaller companies or those functioning in areas with low technical expertise availability. These constraints emphasize the necessity of careful planning, strategic investment, and continuous innovation to fully use the promise of DTs in CPSs, even if they are not insurmountable.

10.12 Conclusion and Future Scope

DT and CPSs combined into healthcare mark a radical step toward more innovative, customized, and effective medical treatments. This chapter has closely examined how DTs are changing healthcare delivery systems when coupled with CPS and driven by developing technologies such as IoT, AI, ML, and cloud computing. From real-time patient monitoring and tailored diagnosis to predictive maintenance of medical equipment and resource optimization, the DT paradigm offers unheard-of accuracy and insight into patient care and hospital administration. The chapter also emphasizes the need for linked systems, data-driven modeling, and simulation to transform diagnosis, therapeutic, and operational procedures in contemporary hospitals.

In this chapter, we have discussed significant technological developments that are expected to define the future of health, i.e., DTs, WBANs, cloud computing, and the IoT. DTs allow real-time, personalized modeling of patients, whereas WBANs allow for real-time, continuous health monitoring by wearable devices. Cloud computing offers scalable and ubiquitous storage and processing platforms for large volumes of health information, and IoT interlinks heterogeneous medical devices for an integrated health environment. Together, all of those technologies are reshaping healthcare processes by improving the precision of diagnosis, allowing for proactive and individualized treatment, streamlining processes, and facilitating data-driven clinical decision-making. Their combined power holds the promise of better outcomes for patients, expanded healthcare accessibility, and creating more intelligent, more responsive healthcare systems.

DTs also greatly enhance decision-making, lower risks, and simplify medical procedures by allowing a dynamic and responsive feedback loop between physical systems and their digital equivalents. Examples such as 3D cardiac mapping, wearable integration, and digital simulations for surgical training show the significant influence of these technologies on clinical results and education. Furthermore, the suggested healthcare DT models forecasting, monitoring, and comparing offer a whole framework for developing proactive and individualized healthcare models that treat, predict, and stop medical problems. Particularly in front of public health emergencies such as pandemics, the paper underlines that these developments are technologically remarkable and essential for tackling issues in scale, responsiveness, and resilience. Still, the use of CPS and DTs has restrictions. Major obstacles still include cybersecurity, integration with legacy systems, high computational needs, and the need for qualified personnel. Important problems that need ongoing attention and development include ensuring real-time data accuracy, protecting patient information, and keeping the DT relevant over time.

DTs and CPS in healthcare have a wide range and great future possibilities. The volume of real-time patient data will rise as wearable health devices and smartphone apps become more widely used, allowing increasingly strong and responsive DT models. AI and ML algorithms will improve the prediction powers of DTs as they become more complex, transforming healthcare even more preventive. Moreover, combining DTs with other disciplines, such as genomics, pharmacogenetics, and behavioral analytics, will provide whole models of human health that can replicate intricate interactions and results with hitherto unheard-of precision. Blockchain technology's emergence may also help allay some of the key worries about data integrity and security, guaranteeing that patient data stay private, traceable, and tamper-proof *via* networks. To guarantee interoperability across many healthcare systems and equipment, standardizing DT architectures and protocols should also be a top priority in further studies. The legal and ethical frameworks enabling DTs will probably develop and encourage more use since regulatory authorities such as the FDA currently appreciate simulation-based validation. In essence, the combination of DTs and CPSs offers a smarter, safer, and more sustainable future for worldwide healthcare, even if there are challenges to be addressed.

AI disclosure statement: The author confirms that no artificial intelligence (AI)-generated content or AI-assisted writing tools were used in the preparation of this chapter (including summaries and the abstract). All text, analysis, and conclusions are the result of the author's original work.

References

1. Liu, Y., Zhang, L., Yang, Y., Zhou, L., Ren, L., Wang, F., Deen, M.J., A novel cloud-based framework for the elderly healthcare services using digital twin. *IEEE Access*, *7*, 49088–49101, 2019.
2. Verma, R., Smart city healthcare cyber physical system: characteristics, technologies and challenges. *Wireless Pers. Commun.*, *122*, 2, 1413–1433, 2022.
3. Elayan, H., Aloqaily, M., Guizani, M., Digital twin for intelligent context-aware IoT healthcare systems. *IEEE Internet Things J.*, *8*, 23, 16749–16757, 2021.
4. Angulo, C., Ortega, J.A., Gonzalez-Abril, L., Towards a healthcare digital twin 1, in: *Artificial Intelligence Research and Development*, pp. 312–315, IOS Press, Amsterdam, 2019.
5. Rajasekar, V., Premalatha, J., Sathya, K., Cancelable Iris template for secure authentication based on random projection and double random phase encoding. *Peer-to-Peer Networking Appl.*, *14*, 2, 747–762, 2021.
6. Zhang, J., Li, L., Lin, G., Fang, D., Tai, Y., Huang, J., Cyber resilience in healthcare digital twin on lung cancer. *IEEE Access*, *8*, 201900–201913, 2020.
7. Bagaria, N., Laamarti, F., Badawi, H.F., Albraikan, A., Martinez Velazquez, R.A., El Saddik, A., Health 4.0: Digital twins for health and well-being, in: *Connected health in smart cities*, pp. 143–152, 2020.
8. Liu, Z., Su, J., Ji, L., Detection and Characterization of E-Health Research: A. *Scientometrics Recent Adv.*, 67, 2019.
9. Bende, A. and Gochhait, S., Leveraging digital twin technology in the healthcare industry—a machine learning based approach. *Eur. J. Molec. Clin. Med.*, *7*, 2547–2557, 2020.
10. Damjanovic-Behrendt, V., A digital twin-based privacy enhancement mechanism for the automotive industry, in: *2018 international conference on intelligent systems (IS)*, IEEE, pp. 272–279, 2018, September.
11. Joshi, R., Kumari, S., Pandey, K., Rise of blockchain based digital twin: A transformative tool for new research trends, in: *Digital Twins for Smart Cities and Villages*, pp. 601–630, Elsevier, Amsterdam, 2025.
12. Joshi, R., Kumari, S., Pandey, K., Exploring the Cutting Edge Technology in Healthcare: A Comprehensive Review of Cloud Based Electronic Health Records, in: *2024 International Conference on Computing, Sciences and Communications (ICCSC)*, IEEE, pp. 1–6, 2024, October.
13. Joshi, R., Gupta, S.K., Natarajan, R., Pandey, K., Kumari, S., Blockchain-Powered Monitoring of Healthcare Credentials through Blockchain-Based Technology, in: *Blockchain-Enabled Internet of Things Applications in Healthcare: Current Practices and Future Directions*, pp. 170–199, Bentham Science Publishers, Sharjah, 2025.
14. Erol, T., Mendi, A.F., Doğan, D., The digital twin revolution in healthcare, in: *2020 4th international symposium on multidisciplinary studies and innovative technologies (ISMSIT)*, IEEE, pp. 1–7, 2020, October.

15. Vallée, A., Digital twin for healthcare systems. *Front. Digital Health*, *5*, 1253050, 2023.
16. Sun, T., He, X., Li, Z., Digital twin in healthcare: Recent updates and challenges. *Digital Health*, *9*, 20552076221149651, 2023.
17. Madubuike, O.C. and Anumba, C.J., Digital twin–based health care facilities management. *J. Comput. Civ. Eng.*, *37*, 2, 04022057, 2023.
18. Sovilj, S., Magjarević, R., Lovell, N.H., Dokos, S., A simplified 3D model of whole heart electrical activity and 12-lead ECG generation, in: *Computational and mathematical methods in medicine*, vol. *2013*, p. 134208, 2013.
19. Salinet, J.L., Uzelac, I., Paredes, J.G.S., Silva, V., de Oliveira, L.S.R., Cerqueira, T., Mazzeto, M., 3D Electrical Mapping of the Heart, in: *Current Trends in Biomedical Engineering*, Springer International Publishing, Cham, 2023.
20. Joshi, R. and Badola, R., Feasibility of AI and Robotics in Indian Healthcare: A Narrative Analysis, in: *Artificial Intelligence and Machine Learning in Drug Design and Development*, pp. 563–603, 2024.
21. DiMasi, J.A., Feldman, L., Seckler, A., Wilson, A., Trends in risks associated with new drug development: Success rates for investigational drugs. *Clin. Pharmacol. Ther.*, *87*, 3, 272–277, 2010.
22. Rowan, N.J., Digital technologies to unlock safe and sustainable opportunities for medical device and healthcare sectors with a focus on the combined use of digital twin and extended reality applications: A review. *Sci. Total Environ.*, 171672, 2024.
23. Sathya, K., Premalatha, J., Rajasekar, V., Madhan, K.M., Deepak, M., Manoj, S.R., Modified linear congruential generator to secure random number generation, in: *American Institute of Physics Conference Series*, vol. 2387, p. 140007, 2021, November.
24. Rivera, L.F., Jiménez, M., Angara, P., Villegas, N.M., Tamura, G., Müller, H.A., Towards continuous monitoring in personalized healthcare through digital twins, in: *Proceedings of the 29th annual international conference on computer science and software engineering*, pp. 329–335, 2019, November.
25. Krishnamoorthi, S., Jayapaul, P., Rajasekar, V., A modernistic approach for chaotic based pseudo random number generator secured with gene dominance. *Sādhanā*, *46*, 1–12, 2021.
26. Joshi, R., Pandey, K., Kumari, S., Gupta, S.K., Mohanty, M., Salau, A.O., Exploring the development of Machine Learning Innovation Technology for Data Mining in Smart Healthcare, in: *2024 Second International Conference Computational and Characterization Techniques in Engineering & Sciences (IC3TES)*, IEEE, pp. 1–5, 2024, November.
27. Joshi, R., Kumari, S., Pandey, K., Enhancing Drug Supply Chain Management with a Scalable Multi-Layered Blockchain Architecture, in: *2024 3rd Edition of IEEE Delhi Section Flagship Conference (DELCON)*, IEEE, pp. 1–6, 2024, November.

28. Popa, E.O., van Hilten, M., Oosterkamp, E., Bogaardt, M.J., The use of digital twins in healthcare: socio-ethical benefits and socio-ethical risks. *Life Sciences Soc. Policy*, *17*, 1–25, 2021.
29. Rajasekar, V., Predić, B., Saracevic, M., Elhoseny, M., Karabasevic, D., Stanujkic, D., Jayapaul, P., Enhanced multimodal biometric recognition approach for smart cities based on an optimized fuzzy genetic algorithm. *Sci. Rep.*, *12*, 1, 622, 2022.
30. Faleiro, R., Pan, L., Pokhrel, S.R., Doss, R., Digital twin for cybersecurity: Towards enhancing cyber resilience, in: *International Conference on Broadband Communications, Networks and Systems*, Springer International Publishing, Cham, pp. 57–76, 2021, October.
31. Kazi, K.S.L. and Mahant, M.A., Machine Learning-Driven Internet of Things (MLIoT)-Based Healthcare Monitoring System, in: *Digitalization and the Transformation of the Healthcare Sector*, pp. 205–236, IGI Global Scientific Publishing, Hershey, PA, 2025.
32. Alam, M.S., Rai, P., Tiwari, R.K., Machine Learning for Healthcare Fraud Detection: A Comprehensive Review Literature, in: *Leveraging Futuristic Machine Learning and Next-Generational Security for e-Governance*, pp. 229–254, 2025.
33. Krones, F., Marikkar, U., Parsons, G., Szmul, A., Mahdi, A., Review of multimodal machine learning approaches in healthcare. *Inf. Fusion*, *114*, 102690, 2025.
34. Vasanth, R., Paranthaman, M., Sivaprakash, P., ML and IoT coupled biomedical applications in healthcare: Smart growth and upcoming challenges In, in: *Internet of Things enabled Machine Learning for Biomedical Applications*, pp. 1–22, CRC Press, Boca Raton, FL, 2025.
35. Zhou, X., Xu, X., Liang, W., Zeng, Z., Shimizu, S., Yang, L.T., Jin, Q., Intelligent small object detection for digital twin in smart manufacturing with industrial cyber-physical systems. *IEEE Trans. Ind. Inf.*, *18*, 2, 1377–1386, 2021.
36. Koulamas, C. and Kalogeras, A., Cyber-physical systems and digital twins in the industrial internet of things [cyber-physical systems]. *Computer*, *51*, 11, 95–98, 2018.
37. Cui, L., Zhang, Z., Gao, N., Meng, Z., Li, Z., Radio frequency identification and sensing techniques and their applications—A review of the state-of-the-art. *Sensors*, *19*, 18, 4012, 2019.
38. Kelly, S.D.T., Suryadevara, N.K., Mukhopadhyay, S.C., Towards the implementation of IoT for environmental condition monitoring in homes. *IEEE Sens. J.*, *13*, 10, 3846–3853, 2013.
39. Negri, E., Fumagalli, L., Macchi, M., A review of the roles of digital twin in CPS-based production systems. *Procedia Manuf.*, *11*, 939–948, 2017.
40. Michael, J., Pfeiffer, J., Rumpe, B., Wortmann, A., Integration challenges for digital twin systems-of-systems, in: *Proceedings of the 10th IEEE/ACM International Workshop on Software Engineering for Systems-of-Systems and Software Ecosystems*, pp. 9–12, 2022, May.

41. Wang, B., Zhou, H., Yang, G., Li, X., Yang, H., Human digital twin (HDT) driven human-cyber-physical systems: Key technologies and applications. *Chin. J. Mech. Eng.*, *35*, 1, 11, 2022.
42. Parnianifard, A., Jearavongtakul, S., Sasithong, P., Sinpan, N., Poomrittigul, S., Bajpai, A., Wuttisittikulkij, L., Digital-twins towards cyber-physical systems: a brief survey. *Eng. J.*, *26*, 9, 47–61, 2022.
43. Joshi, R., Kumari, S., Badola, R., Evaluation of Wireless Body Area Networks: A Systematic Review on Security Concerns. *Security Privacy Trust WBANs E-Healthcare*, 44-62.
44. Joshi, R., Ethical conundrums and privacy concerns in new innovations. *Aspects Qual. Manage. Value Creating Ind. 5.0 Way*, 202–223, 2024.
45. Nazarenko, A.A. and Camarinha-Matos, L.M., The role of digital twins in collaborative cyber-physical systems, in: *Technological Innovation for Life Improvement: 11th IFIP WG 5.5/SOCOLNET Advanced Doctoral Conference on Computing, Electrical and Industrial Systems, DoCEIS 2020, Costa de Caparica, Portugal, July 1–3, 2020, Proceedings 11*, Springer International Publishing, pp. 191–205, 2020.

11

Safeguarding Privacy and Security in AI-Powered Healthcare Systems

Arpita Maheriya[1*] **and Sailesh Suryanarayan Iyer**[2]

[1]*Unitedworld Institute of Technology, Karnavati University, Gandhinagar, Gujarat, India*
[2]*Narnarayan Shastri Institute of Technology (IFSCS), Ahmedabad, India*

Abstract

The exponential growth in healthcare data presents remarkable opportunities for efficient medical research, improving patient outcomes, early disease prediction, and improving healthcare data system mechanisms. Moreover, Internet of Medical Things enable real-time data acquisition and remote patient monitoring; however, it simultaneously introduces potential threats, including cyberattacks and unauthorized access of data. These cause considerable privacy and security challenges due to its sensitive medical dataset, diverse storage conditions, and intricate data sharing requirements. That underscores the need for robust encryption, stringent access controls, and effective trust management strategies. This chapter explores innovative strategies designed to safeguard healthcare data systems while preserving the utility of the data. Prominence is placed on privacy-preserving machine learning methodologies, blockchain technology, and quantum-safe cryptography. To empower machine learning capabilities on sensitive healthcare datasets without necessitating direct sharing, striking a harmonious balance between data utility and privacy, methods such as federated learning, data anonymization, differential privacy, and synthetic data generation are mentioned in this chapter. Furthermore, blockchain technology provides decentralized solutions that ensure data integrity, secure sharing, and the anonymity of data generated by IoT devices, effectively counteracting the vulnerabilities associated with conventional systems. To future-proof the healthcare system, it is essential to adopt quantum-safe cryptography standards alongside advanced user authentication mechanisms. By safeguarding privacy while allowing the integration of diverse datasets, this chapter demonstrates a secure, efficient, and personalized model for healthcare based on

**Corresponding author*: maheriyaarpita96@gmail.com; ORCID ID: 0000-0001-5703-4410

Shubham Mahajan, Davinder Paul Singh, Amit Kant Pandit and Paras Chawla (eds.) Ensuring Privacy in Digital Twin Ecosystems, (333–366) © 2026 Scrivener Publishing LLC

presenting the future challenges. It aims to guide practitioners, researchers, and policymakers in leveraging these technologies to preserve confidential patient data and advance personalized care delivery.

Keywords: Security of healthcare data, healthcare data privacy, secure data sharing, privacy challenges of healthcare system, secure Internet of Medical Things (IoMT)

11.1 Introduction

In recent times, artificial intelligence (AI)–powered technical applications have gained significant implementation and become a widely adopted tool for processing large datasets for decision-making tasks, which is often beyond human capability in various fields [1]. In healthcare, machine learning (ML), deep learning (DL), image processing, and natural language processing (NLP) [19] require training on complex data, such as medical notes, clinical images, and demographic records. Figure 11.1 presents the AI landscape of healthcare system. Existing organizational infrastructures of healthcare systems severely suffer from the lack of capability to prevent data security attacks because of lack standardized secure controls and privacy law available to address the security threats of smart healthcare systems.

In the digital era, huge amounts of personalized sensitive information are being gathered, stored, and exchanged. Leveraging data sharing

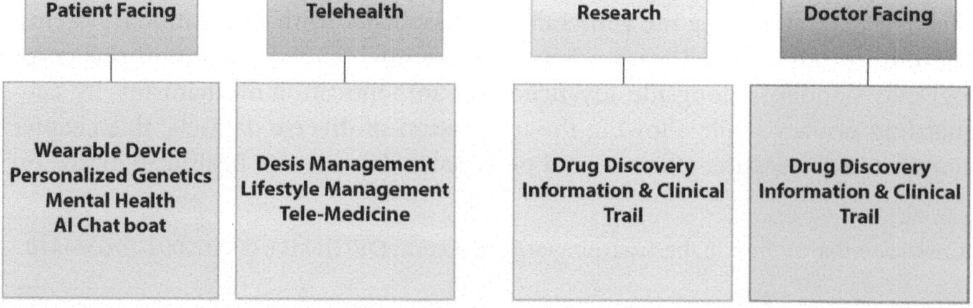

Figure 11.1 The role of AI technologies in modern healthcare.

and processing can significantly drive innovation and facilitate problem-solving. The healthcare sector can benefit greatly from adopting business-to-business methods [6], which can enhance secure and efficient data transmission. This approach improves patient access to physicians, streamlines information exchange, and elevates overall care quality. However, managing the massive volume of data produced by smart devices remains a persistent challenge. Figure 11.2 illustrates the taxonomy of digital healthcare data system management.

AI is revolutionizing healthcare by driving advancements once thought unimaginable, tackling some of the most pressing global healthcare challenges. However, the data-driven nature of ML algorithms, which rely on vast volumes of high-quality data, raises significant concerns about data privacy, especially when the training data contain sensitive individual patient data. Any breach or misuse of these data could have a major impact on healthcare data systems and healthcare software systems alike [1]. Although privacy-preserving techniques are available, to meet the efficiency demands of online training in healthcare applications [2], tackling these challenges is essential for fostering the responsible combination of emerging technologies for medical systems [5].

Advancements in anonymization techniques facilitate data utilization while extracting valuable insights to ensuring privacy protection. Traditional anonymization techniques such as, T-closeness, k-anonymization, and l-diversity provide varying levels of privacy assurance of data [9, 14, 17].

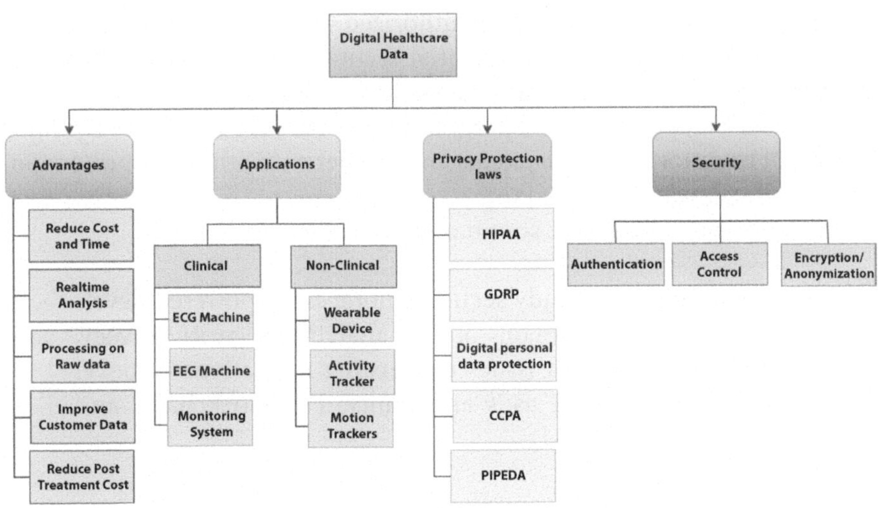

Figure 11.2 Digital healthcare data taxonomy.

Moreover, federated learning (FL) [8] is used in a distributed ML paradigm and has seen a surge in prominence within the state of art techniques, largely due to increasing public awareness regarding privacy and security concerns. This innovative approach enables numerous participants to collaboratively train a model while ensuring that their raw data remain confidential. By doing so, FL effectively reduces potential privacy risks without sacrificing the performance and accuracy of the model. Furthermore, differential privacy (DP) framework is designed to assess the risks associated with privacy leakage, aiming to strike a balance between maximizing model utility and ensuring robust privacy safeguards. Another technique is synthetic data generation (SDG) [10] for the creation of synthetic datasets that maintain the statistical attributes of actual data. To effectively replicate underlying distributions and correlations, SDG not only fosters data-driven insights but also ensures the protection of individual privacy.

Internet of Medical Things (IoMT) can transform patient care by remotely following patients' health data and performing telemedicine. This technological leap leads to better clinical outcomes, cheaper cost, and a feasible customized treatment plan due to causality information derived from wearables and medical devices, etc. However, intelligent medical systems utilizing IoT, operators of which handle the patients' private medical data, are attractive targets for adversarial attackers when there are inadequate protective measures. Blockchain has been proposed as a potential solution, and a new era of data and privacy in healthcare has commenced. Due to the mutual assurance of blockchain, which is mediated through a distributed computer network, blockchain guarantees data integrity, and consequently, the possibility of unauthorized access to the data is greatly reduced. There are significant potential security weaknesses in emerging applications of quantum computing; blockchain-based secure systems provide an effective, practical, and pragmatic alternative to overcome the limitations of traditional cryptosystems and further strengthen the protection of data in healthcare systems [16].

The key contributions are summarized as follows:

- The background study section embraces AI-powered developments in the domains of data analytics, security/privacy, authentication, and issues concerning regulations of novel technologies, such as *k*-anonymity, DP, blockchain, and explainable AI (XAI).

- Section 11.3 shows the challenges in developing privacy-preserving AI for healthcare, e.g., tradeoff privacy-utility, data robustness, access control, and fairness, and reinforces the importance of a sustained area of research into privacy-preserving techniques.
- Section 11.4 focuses on the need for strong regulatory principles as a way that health applications based on AI, around the world, can be improved over time.
- Section 11.5 discusses AI-driven medical innovations, vulnerability of ML to adversarial attacks, categories of attacks on ML, their consequences on health security, and how to address them.
- Section 11.6 considers high-level cryptography protocols and privacy-aware ML methods, as well as blockchain technologies for strengthening the security of medical data.
- Section 11.7 describes the necessity for quantum-resistant (QR) encryption to safeguard healthcare cybersecurity from new and unforeseen cyberattacks by utilizing the features of modern cryptographic algorithms and ultrasecure architecture, e.g., IQ-HDM, to overcome the vulnerability of cyberattacks.
- The last section covers future research direction, focusing on enhancing AI-driven healthcare security through quantum-based defenses, blockchain–IoT integration, regulatory frameworks, trustworthy AI, cryptographic privacy methods, synthetic data security, and standardized healthcare systems.

11.2 Background Study

The rapid advancement of AI is transforming healthcare by enabling the analysis of complex data, yet privacy and authentication challenges persist, particularly in online applications. To address these concerns, RASS [2] is proposed as a privacy-preserving and authentication scheme that secures healthcare data with minimal computational and communication costs while defending against tampering and collusion attacks. Additionally, the study introduces an enhanced discrete particle swarm optimization (EDPSO) algorithm [3] to minimize structural information loss in social network anonymization. The improved versions, EDPSOVNS and EDPSOSA, demonstrate superior fitness, reliability, and convergence in real-world network simulations. Dynamic anonymity privacy-preserving model [4], based on hierarchical sequential three-way decisions, integrates DP to enhance both data usability and privacy, resulting in improved efficiency and reduced information loss.

The emergence of XAI in healthcare has increased transparency and trust; however, significant challenges remain, including adversarial attacks, algorithmic bias, and regulatory inconsistencies. A recent analysis [5] highlights that 60% of healthcare professionals express hesitation due to transparency concerns and data insecurity, further emphasized by the 2024 WotNot data breach. In response, anonymization-based privacy protection [7] utilizes hybrid generalizations and data relocation, ensuring unlikely published data while balancing utility and truthfulness. Experiments indicate improved utility and query accuracy with minimal relocations. Furthermore, privacy-preserving ML techniques, comparing *k*-anonymity, DP, and more, emphasize balancing privacy and model utility [18, 20] to enhance privacy-preserving AI development, especially in healthcare, by minimizing data breach risks and unauthorized access. Differentially private general stochastic gradient Langevin dynamics (DP-GSGLD) [8], a novel SGLD variant, uses Bayesian sampling and parameter clipping to satisfy DP, reducing model training time while improving accuracy against gradient attacks in FL environments. Another privacy-preserving approach, the (β, k, b) anonymization method [9], combines DP with *k*-anonymity and leverages the Fréchet mean for high-dimensional data, enhancing clustering while outperforming traditional models in data utility and privacy preservation.

DL techniques, including generative adversarial networks, variational autoencoders, and diffusion models, have been explored for synthetic healthcare data generation. A systematic review [10] highlights their effectiveness in enhancing data utility and privacy, although challenges remain in addressing temporal correlations, biases, and regulatory alignment. A secure healthcare framework [11] has been proposed using recurrent and twisted Hessian curve cryptography (THCC), convolution layer neural networks (CNN), the standardized padding scheme-based secure hashing algorithm-256 (SPS-SHA-256), and the inversion method (IM). The integration of Blockchain and a Fuzzy logic system (FLS) ensures robust data security, access control, and privacy, demonstrating high efficiency.

A three-tier secure and distributed privacy-preserving healthcare architecture [12] incorporates a custodian data repository, elliptic curve cryptography (ECC)–based authentication, and smart contracts leveraging local DP, thereby enhancing security, privacy, and accuracy in data transactions and ML model training. Similarly, an NDN-based secure remote healthcare monitoring framework [13] integrates IoT with edge computing, using hashing and encryption to safeguard health data retrieval. Simulations reveal superior performance in content retrieval delay and cost. The integration of IoT in smart healthcare has significantly improved diagnostics through extensive data sharing; however, security risks remain a major concern. Blockchain technology is emerging as a promising solution, as highlighted in a recent survey [16] that examines these challenges and potential blockchain-based security measures.

While AI-driven innovations in healthcare offer enhanced data analysis and decision-making capabilities, privacy and security challenges persist. Various approaches, including privacy-preserving models, DP techniques, XAI, and blockchain solutions, have been proposed to present these concerns. Future research must center on refining these models to ensure secure, efficient, and trustworthy healthcare data management.

11.3 Challenges in Building Secure AI-Based Healthcare Data System

Privacy preservation of sensitive individual data is a challenging task. Integration of AI techniques has further amplified Privacy concerns, as a result of many kinds of privacy attacks that can target the models. Figure 11.3 illustrates a taxonomy of the key challenges that impede effective privacy preservation.

Adaptability: One of the main difficulties in the healthcare sector, especially the diagnostic part, is making sure that robust privacy measures are taken without hindering the precision and operability of AI systems. This problem is made even worse in a bigger context due to the strict legal frameworks that are in place, which make comprehensive privacy measures impossible. Finding the sweet spot between privacy, performance, and compliance is one of the most challenging problems in the progress of AI in Healthcare. Most privacy-preserving ML techniques are indicative of the fact that most applications are aimed at a specific ML algorithm. In simple words, these techniques will not work in the general sense. As new algorithms of ML are developed, so must the privacy measures regarding these multifarious methods. Although approaches like distributed methods and local DP (LDP) are widely used and effective in many contexts, most privacy-preserving strategies are difficult to adapt to new algorithms due to their focus on specific use cases.

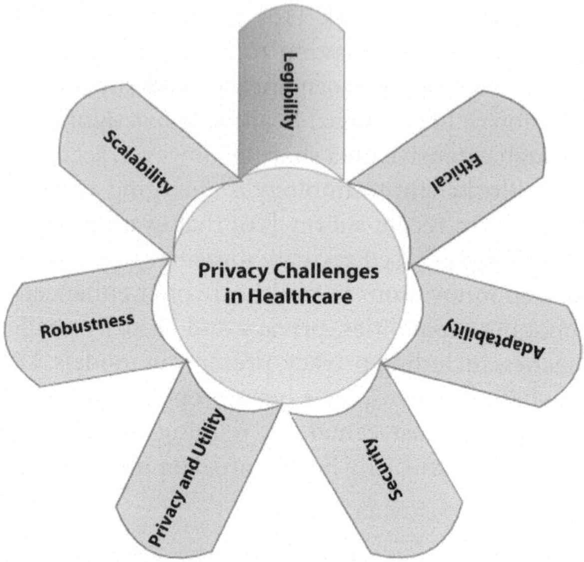

Figure 11.3 Challenges of AI in healthcare.

Scalability: The enormous amount of data collected across different healthcare systems from multiple sources, including wearable technology, medical pictures, and electronic health records (EHRs). Their complexity rises and devices makes it difficult to scale the development of privacy-preserving for smart healthcare system. Healthcare data need strong privacy safeguards and scalability that require constant innovation and resource investment. A major problem occurs when privacy-preserving algorithms become time-consuming and resource-intensive when working with huge sensitive healthcare datasets. Furthermore, privacy-preserving techniques often struggle due to high computational and communication costs.

Authentication and access control: Authorized people are allowed to view a patient's medical history or private information from Electronic Health Record. It is crucial to make sure that authentication credentials are secure. Users may enter the system, but their access is governed by a policy that outlines the rights and privileges that the patient or a reliable third party has allowed them. Unauthorized access to this sensitive data can have detrimental effects, and it might be difficult to identify these breaches.

Data integrity: The integrity of the data could be compromised by unauthorized access to vital medical information, which are frequently brought on by data poisoning attacks. For trustworthy medical AI solutions, protection from these kinds of attacks is essential.

Transparency [21]: The growing impact of AI on decision-making in the healthcare industry; transparency is crucial. Maintaining openness is essential to fostering patient and healthcare provider trust.

Privacy and utility trade-off [21]: Healthcare data must be first anonymized before sharing it. The goal is to distribute the data with the least amount of utility loss while maintaining its fairness, when comparing outcomes from synthetic and real-world data over time. Thus, it is crucial to create strategies that balance privacy and usefulness in order to enhance healthcare data sharing and privacy. It is crucial since state of art technologies have a growing impact on clinical judgment in the medical field. Maintaining transparency is essential to fostering patient and healthcare provider trust. Moreover, it also includes the parameters such as responsibility, explainability, and interpretability, ultimately improving utility of anonymized/encrypted data while maintaining privacy in data sharing.

AI ethics: There are several ethical issues with AI-driven healthcare solutions that directly impact on people's lives. As the use of algorithms increases, it is critical to make sure these systems are transparent, impartial, and equitable. There needs to be a way to understand how algorithms make decisions. Striking a compromise between algorithms that are ethically sound but less exact and those that achieve great accuracy while upholding ethical standards is a major challenge. Model performance may suffer in the healthcare industry due to the need to protect patient data confidentiality, particularly when sensitive information such as genetic biomarkers is not used for training. In general, maintaining patient privacy while attaining justice, accountability, and transparency, remains a significant ethical challenge.

11.4 Frameworks, Acts, and Policies for Data Privacy Protection

In the above section, the challenges to implementing AI in the healthcare system are demonstrated. Here we focused on how with help of policy, Acts, and framework can help to overcome those challenges and its limitations.

A strong regulatory frameworks are required to secure patient safety, preserve data privacy, and uphold ethical standards, as evidenced by the quick integration of digital health and AI technologies in the healthcare industry. Regulatory agencies must handle the particular difficulties brought about by the growing adoption of AI-driven technology by healthcare organizations and the sharing of private medical information. Table 11.1 shows the taxonomy of frameworks, laws, and policies about healthcare data security and privacy. Health Insurance Portability and Accountability Act (HIPAA) in the United States and General Data Protection Regulation (GDPR) in Europe establish guidelines for data protection; these frameworks seek to preserve patient privacy and secure private health information. To handle

Table 11.1 Classification of frameworks, acts, and policies for healthcare data.

Framework/act/policy	Country/region	Key features	Purpose
Health Insurance Portability and Accountability Act (HIPAA)	United States	Regulates healthcare data privacy, security, and breach notification	Protects patient health information (PHI) and ensures confidentiality
General Data Protection Regulation (GDPR)	European Union	Ensures data protection, user consent, and the right to be forgotten	Protects personal data, including healthcare information
Personal Data Protection Act (PDPA)	Singapore	Regulates data collection, usage, and disclosure	Ensures responsible handling of healthcare data
Personal Information Protection and Electronic Documents Act (PIPEDA)	Canada	Regulates private-sector data collection, use, and disclosure	Ensures privacy and security of personal health data
The Data Protection Act (DPA) 2018	United Kingdom	Aligns with GDPR; includes additional provisions for health data security	Regulates processing of personal data, including health records

(Continued)

Table 11.1 Classification of frameworks, acts, and policies for healthcare data. (*Continued*)

Framework/act/policy	Country/region	Key features	Purpose
China's Personal Information Protection Law (PIPL)	China	Strict rules on data transfer, consent, and security requirements	Protects personal and health-related data
Electronic health records standards (EHRs)	Various Countries	Defines guidelines for secure electronic health records	Ensures standardization and security in EHRs
National Digital Health Blueprint (NDHB)	India	Proposes a digital health ecosystem with privacy safeguards	Strengthens health data security and interoperability
California Consumer Privacy Act (CCPA)	United States (California)	Provides consumer rights to control personal data, including health data	Enhances transparency and user control over personal health information
Healthcare Information Privacy and Security (HIPS) Guidelines	Global (various organizations)	Best practices for securing healthcare data and ensuring compliance	Enhances security and privacy measures in healthcare organizations

upcoming risks, these policies must be regularly reviewed and revised as technology advances. Furthermore, creating standardized regulatory frameworks that encourage innovation requires international cooperation while ensuring patient safety. Ethical principles must be integrated into these frameworks, establishing clear accountability among developers, healthcare providers, and institutions. This approach helps maintain public trust and fosters responsible AI innovation in healthcare [21].

Several countries have implemented privacy regulations [6] to safeguard personal data: Argentina's Personal Data Protection Act (PDPA), like the

GDPR, categorizes most data as personal and mandates legal consent for its use. Australia's Privacy Principle mandates transparency in data handling, whereas Brazil's BIA and Chile's Protection of Personal Data Act enforce consent requirements for data collection and processing. Many other nations, including the Czech Republic, Denmark, and Greece, emphasize consent-based data protection. India's data protection framework [40] includes the IT Rules 2011 for securing sensitive data, the Ayushman Bharat Digital Mission for unified health records, and the Digital Personal Data Protection Bill 2023, which mandates informed consent, data security, and a regulatory board with penalties for noncompliance.

Following the challenges while adopt AI in healthcare technology with compliance:

- Protect patient privacy and govern data ethics. Ensuring data privacy and security is critical, as mishandling sensitive healthcare information can lead to legal and reputational risks, requiring encryption, anonymization, and secure storage.
- Regulatory demands for explicit patient consent can hinder interoperability, while multinational organizations face added complexity in navigating varying privacy laws across jurisdictions.
- Model biases and ethical concerns in AI and ML systems, as these models rely on historical data that may underrepresent certain demographics—such as minorities, women, or the elderly—leading to less accurate diagnoses or recommendations.
- The lack of transparency in black-box AI systems further complicates trust and adoption, while biased or incorrect predictions raise serious ethical and legal concerns.
- Implementing robust cybersecurity measures involves significant costs, including initial investments in secure infrastructure, compliant software, and staff training, as well as ongoing expenses for updates, threat monitoring, and incident response. These financial and logistical burdens are particularly challenging for smaller clinics and rural hospitals with limited resources.

Together, these factors create substantial barriers to the effective and ethical integration of advanced technologies in healthcare.

11.5 Attacks on AI Healthcare Model

AI enhances applications of healthcare for diagnosis and data analysis while also exposing vulnerabilities to adversarial attacks. The healthcare industry generates vast patient data, with ML aiding in early diagnosis, treatment planning, and real-time monitoring, but ML models face challenges with unpredictability and out-of-distribution data. The lack of strong regulations makes AI-based medical applications susceptible to data breaches and manipulation, posing risks to patient safety [48]. AI-powered healthcare systems offer accurate diagnostics, personalized health advice, and medical management, but raise concerns about data security and privacy. Attackers can target medical devices [50] through hardware tampering, malware, or ransomware, causing device unavailability or communication delays. They may also intercept, modify, or leak sensitive patient data by exploiting security vulnerabilities. Such attacks compromise patient safety, device integrity, and healthcare system confidentiality.

Figure 11.4 presents the ML pipeline, highlighting vulnerabilities at different stages where attacks can occur. The following list provides a comprehensive definition of various Adversarial attacks and their impact on the ML pipeline.

- **Model extraction attack**: In order to create a replacement model that closely resembles the original, an adversary questions the predictions of a model. This makes it possible for unlawful replication and exploitation of private ML models.
- **Membership inference attack**: This allows an attacker to discover whether a certain data point was utilized during training by analyzing model predictions, which may expose sensitive patient information.

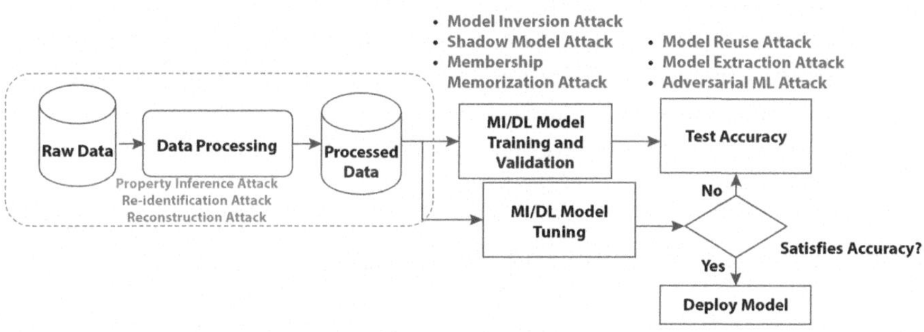

Figure 11.4 Attack pipeline on ML model [1].

- **Model inversion attack**: Using the model's outputs, attackers can reconstruct approximations of the original training data, that exposing confidential information and the ability to reidentify people.
- **Shadow model attack**: An adversary can mimic dataset attributes, where attackers probe the model to extract sensitive patterns training it to mimic the target model. This can be used to take advantage of flaws in black-box ML models.
- **Membership memorization attack**: Overfitted models tend to memorize rare training samples, making them susceptible to privacy leaks. By taking advantage of a model's propensity to retain information, it can determine whether or not particular records were used during training.
- **Model-reuse attacks**: Malicious models with embedded backdoors are integrated into ML systems, causing controlled failures. These attacks can compromise AI integrity and introduce security loopholes.

The poisoning attacks on ML models in healthcare, where malicious data manipulation can compromise diagnosis accuracy and trust [45]. It proposes a systematic attack strategy across multiple algorithms and datasets while presenting countermeasures to detect and mitigate such threats. This proposes [46] a low-latency, machine-learning attack-resilient authentication scheme using ECC and OPUF to enhance the security of AI-driven remote patient health monitoring systems in IoMT. Reference [47] reviews adversarial attack strategies on DNNs for medical imaging, explores detection methods, and suggests improvements for neural network robustness. Reference [48] explores AI algorithms in healthcare applications and their vulnerability to adversarial attacks. The survey [50] shows security and privacy threats in healthcare systems, their impacts, existing countermeasures, and future research directions. The adversarial attacks on ML-based smart healthcare systems demonstrate how they manipulate medical data to misclassify diseases and patient activities. A transformer-based and LightGBM intrusion and malware detection system [49] achieves 99% accuracy in securing healthcare networks from cyber threats.

11.6 Privacy-Preserving Techniques

Sections 11.3, 11.4, and 11.5 discuss the challenges of apply AI in healthcare system with privacy framework and policies to protect data security and possible attacks on AI-based healthcare system. This section demonstrates the privacy preserving techniques that are useful to protect healthcare data system from adversarial attacks while following the rules and regulation of healthcare data privacy.

The digitization of healthcare has transformed the healthcare industry but also made it a key target for cyberattacks, given the vast amount of sensitive patient data it handles. AI strengthens encryption by introducing advanced techniques to secure data both at rest and in transit. Figure 11.5 illustrates the privacy-preserving techniques with classification in

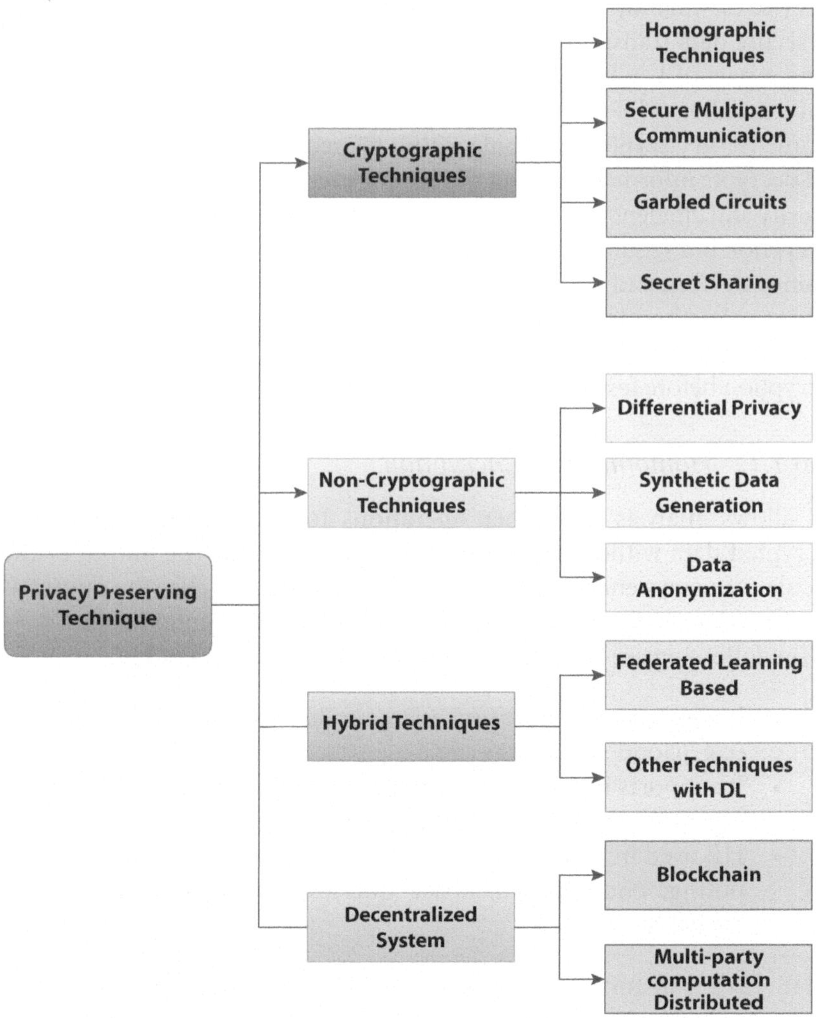

Figure 11.5 Classification of privacy protection methods.

cryptographic, noncryptographic, hybrid, and decentralized techniques. These encryption methods ensure that intercepted data remain unreadable and protected from misuse.

11.6.1 Cryptographic Algorithms [22]

Cryptography, derived from the Greek word *kryptos* (hidden), ensures secure communication by maintaining data confidentiality and integrity. Encryption is its main method of protecting data while it is being transmitted. These are categorized into symmetric (private key) and asymmetric (public key) types. RSA (Rivest–Shamir–Adleman) is a public-key cryptographic algorithm used for secure data transmission, encryption, and digital signatures. It works by using a pair of key based on the mathematical difficulty of factoring large prime number. AES (Advanced Encryption Standard) is also a widely used symmetric-key cryptographic algorithm for securing digital data. It encrypts and decrypts information using the same secret key and is known for its high security and efficiency. ECC, and AES being widely used; RSA ensures strong encryption but requires larger key sizes, ECC offers efficient security for constrained devices, and AES provides fast, secure encryption ideal for large data volumes. Furthermore, cryptographic techniques include homomorphic encryption (HE), secure multiparty computation (SMPC) and enable data encryption before testing and training of data.

11.6.1.1 Homomorphic Encryption

HE allows analysis and other operations to be performed directly on encrypted data without the need to decrypt the data. The output of these calculations stays encrypted and, when decrypted, matches the output as if the operations had been performed on the original plaintext data.

The following are the use case and key characteristics of HE:

- It allows secure data processing in distrustful environments (e.g., cloud servers).
- It supports mathematical operation such as addition, multiplication, or both (depending on the type).
- HE used in secure medical data analysis, private cloud computing, encrypted database queries, and confidential AI model training.

HE [21] transforms the security of healthcare data by allowing calculations on encrypted data while maintaining security during processing. It is crucial for maintaining regulatory compliance and protecting sensitive data, especially in cloud computing and collaborative research. Ongoing developments in HE, from partial to fully HE, offer improved data privacy and safe healthcare data management despite computational performance issues. HE ensures privacy in operations such as ML-based genomic analysis by enabling computations on encrypted data without the need for decryption. Data security in cloud environments and healthcare applications is improved by a number of HE-based techniques, including DeCrypt, the Paillier cryptosystem, and CKKS encryption [1].

11.6.1.2 Secure Multiparty Communication

SMPC enables multiple parties to jointly compute a function over their private inputs without revealing the actual data with one another. The key principle is that no single party can access another party's raw data, yet all participants can still derive useful results from the combined computation.

The following are the use case and key characteristics of SMPC:

- Each party's input data remain confidential throughout the computation.
- No central authority is needed to process the data; computations occur collaboratively.
- The final output is accurate and verifiable, ensuring no tampering during computation.
- Unlike traditional methods, SMPC eliminates the need for a mediator to handle sensitive data.
- One of the common use cases of SMPC is that hospitals can collaborate on medical research without sharing raw patient records, and more than two organizations can train ML models on integration of datasets while maintaining data privacy.

SMPC [21] is essential for collaborative healthcare research because it permits privacy-preserving data processing across numerous parties. By combining blockchain, HE, and DP, SMPC improves AI-driven healthcare security while maintaining data privacy. Together, these technologies enable robust medical research, tailored care, and safe data sharing without sacrificing privacy. They have the potential to improve patient outcomes, security, and healthcare efficiency on a worldwide scale as they develop. By enabling distributed data computing without disclosing individual inputs through the use of strategies such as additive secret sharing and XOR-based privacy preservation, SMPC protects privacy. Numerous SMPC models, such as garbled circuit (GC) protocols and HE-based encryption, improve security in e-healthcare, fraud prevention, and genomic searches [1].

11.6.1.3 Garbled Circuits

GC [1] enables two parties to work together to calculate a function over private inputs without depending on a trusted third party. Its applications include secure access control, electrocardiogram (ECG) classification, genome-aware health monitoring, and combining HE with GC-based neural network models for computations that preserve privacy. Security and efficiency analyses verify its efficacy across various domains.

11.6.1.4 Secret Sharing

Secret sharing [1] disperses information among individuals, guaranteeing data reconstruction only when multiple shares are combined and improving privacy in electronic health systems. Techniques such as perceptron-based session keys, RC6 encryption with DNA substitution, and NSCT-based X-ray watermarking enhance medical data security by demonstrating resilience to attacks while preserving data integrity and privacy.

11.6.2 Noncryptographic Techniques

11.6.2.1 Differential Privacy

DP is a mathematical framework designed to ensure the privacy of individuals in datasets while still allowing meaningful statistical analysis. It works by adding randomness and noise to query results or data outputs, making it extremely difficult to determine whether any particular individual's data was included in the original dataset.

The following are the use case and key characteristics of DP:

- Protects individual data points by ensuring that the insertion or deletion of a single record does not significantly alter the output.
- Provides a measurable privacy budget (denoted by ε or epsilon), where lower values indicate stronger privacy protection.
- Maintains data utility for analysis while minimizing reidentification risks.
- Used in sharing medical research data without exposing patient identities.
- Reduces risks in AI/ML training datasets to prevent bias or privacy leaks.

In healthcare data analysis, DP [21] is essential because it protects patient privacy while facilitating insightful analysis. By combining technologies such as HE and FL, DP promotes ethical data usage by maintaining a balance between privacy and data utility. Using Laplace noise to thwart inference attacks, DP guarantees that query answers are probabilistically indistinguishable regardless of the existence of a record [38]. DP frameworks [6] include the interactive model, where queries are processed through a privacy-preserving interface with a limited privacy budget and the noninteractive model, where a presensitized dataset responds to queries without privacy budget constraints. However, it faces utility challenges, as repeated queries degrade accuracy, and high-sensitivity queries yield highly biased results. Despite challenges and computational complexity, ongoing research aims to optimize DP for scalable, privacy-preserving healthcare applications. Reference [39] reviews DP's application to health data, highlighting its theoretical limitations, practical challenges, and the need for clearer quantification of privacy guarantees. DP enables [1] analysis without revealing identities, as used by Apple, Amazon, and Facebook. Techniques such as DP-based ML models for heart disease prediction, Gaussian DP in DL for medical image segmentation, and private COVID-19 diagnostics balance privacy with accuracy. Advanced approaches, including DP-enhanced breast cancer detection using expectation–maximization, achieve high accuracy while preserving patient confidentiality.

11.6.2.2 Data Anonymization

Data anonymization is the technique of updating or removing personally identifiable information to make deidentifiable data, ensuring privacy and compliance with regulations such as HIPAA and GDPR.

The following are the use case and key characteristics of data anonymization:

- Protects patient/individual privacy while allowing data to be used for research, analytics, or AI training.
- Includes masking, pseudonymization, aggregation, and noise addition to prevent reidentification.
- True anonymization means data cannot be traced back to the original individual.
- It could be used in healthcare for replacing a patient's name and address with a random ID in a medical dataset while retaining diagnostic information for analysis.

Enhanced techniques such as t-closeness, l-diversity, and *k*-anonymity address as data anonymization techniques [37]. *k*-Anonymity reduces reidentification probability by ensuring each record appears at least *k* times, *k*-anonymity ensures that each record shares the same QID value with at least *k*-1 others, preventing identity disclosure but remaining vulnerable to homogeneity and background knowledge attacks. L-diversity extends *k*-anonymity by ensuring diverse sensitive values within groups. L-diversity ensures each QID group has at least one distinct sensitive values but may introduce bias and remains vulnerable to skewness and similarity attacks, leading to the development of τ-safe (l, *k*) diversity [38]. T-closeness further improves privacy by maintaining attribute value distributions; T-closeness ensures the sensitive attribute distribution in each group closely matches the overall table, preventing attribute disclosure but not identity disclosure, with high computational complexity [38]. Variants such as clustering anonymity, (X, Y) anonymity, and LKC privacy improve protection, whereas l-diversity and t-closeness can have attribute disclosure risks [38]. This paper [44] enhances *p*-sensitive *k*-anonymity by proposing *p*+-sensitive and (*p*, α)–sensitive *k*-anonymity models, improving privacy protection through categorical and ordinal metrics and hybrid generalization with data relocation to enhance *k*-anonymity [7], balancing privacy, utility, and truthfulness.

11.6.2.3 Synthetic Data Generation

SDG refers to the process of creating artificial datasets that mimic the statistical parameters of original/real data without containing actual sensitive information. This data are algorithmically generated using techniques such as ML, statistical modeling, or simulation.

The following are the use case and key characteristics:

- Does not include real personal data, reducing privacy risks.
- Maintains patterns, correlations, and variability similar to original data.
- It can be tailored to enhance rare scenarios or balance biases in training datasets.
- Reduces dependency on expensive or limited real-world data collection.
- Its applications in healthcare are:
  (1) Training AI models without exposing patient records.
  (2) Facilitating research and testing while ensuring regulatory compliance.

The open-source Synthetic Data Vault project [16] encapsulates this with the concept of protect and enhance. Although synthetic data have existed for decades, its real-world impact is now becoming significant. SDG [21], exemplified by tools such as Synthea, enables privacy-preserving AI development in healthcare by creating realistic but nonidentifiable medical datasets. This method solves data-sharing issues while facilitating research and model training without jeopardizing patient confidentiality. Despite its promise, a major obstacle to its wider use is guaranteeing the validity and realism of synthetic data, particularly in medical imaging. With important applications in cardiovascular research, synthetic data are becoming a crucial healthcare AI solution [42], facilitating data exchange while protecting privacy and increasing model diversity. The creation of synthetic data improves the privacy of healthcare data, but it also presents concerns such as reidentification and inference assaults, necessitating the use of sophisticated strategies such as FL and DP [10]. To strike a balance between data utility and privacy, constant assessment, thorough testing, and developing security measures are necessary.

11.6.3 Federated Learning

FL is a decentralized ML technique where multiple parties or organization collaboratively train a shared model without exchanging raw data. Instead of centralizing data in one location, the model is trained locally on distributed datasets, and only model updates are aggregated to improve the global model.

The following are the use case and key characteristics:

- Raw data remains on local devices, reducing privacy risks and ensuring compliance with regulations such as HIPAA and GDPR.
- Training occurs across multiple nodes (e.g., hospitals, smartphones, IoT devices) without transferring sensitive data.
- A central server (or peer-to-peer network) combines local model updates to refine the global model.
- Only model parameters (not datasets) are shared, lowering bandwidth usage.
- Use cases in healthcare are:
  (1) Training diagnostic AI models across hospitals without sharing patient records.
  (2) Improving predictive analytics while maintaining data confidentiality.

(3) Enabling personalized medicine without centralized data storage.

FL enhances medical research [21, 43] by enabling secure multi-institutional data sharing, with horizontal FL increasing sample size and vertical FL handling shared users with different features. Future advancements should focus on improving data quality, integrating expert knowledge, and personalizing healthcare solutions to maximize FL's potential in patient-centric AI.

FL enables [1] collaborative ML model training across multiple locations without sharing raw data, ensuring privacy. It has been applied in healthcare for medical imaging, intensive care unit patient tracking, and COVID-19 diagnosis, achieving high accuracy while preserving data security. Studies show FL-trained models outperform local models, with improvements in breast density classification and brain tumor detection. However, FL is vulnerable to privacy attacks, requiring additional security layers, as seen in research on robust FL against adversarial threats such as label-flipping attacks.

11.6.4 Blockchain

Blockchain technology [15] enhances healthcare data privacy by ensuring secure storage, controlled access, and interoperability through decentralization, cryptography, and smart contracts while addressing challenges such as scalability and integration [41], while safeguarding patient privacy through advanced cryptographic techniques. Blockchain-based systems enable secure healthcare data sharing by storing information in a decentralized and tamper-proof manner. Recent advancements in blockchain technology [22] include Blockchain 2.0, including the Ethereum network (a prominent programmable and public blockchain) and Hyperledger Fabric (a private, permissioned blockchain), along with advancements in smart contracts and encryption methods such as ECC, and provide significant improvements in data privacy, integrity, and access control across different applications. In the context of health data security, blockchain technology can greatly strengthen user authentication, access control, and data privacy, while facilitating the creation of decentralized applications. Figure 11.6 illustrates blockchain-based applications [41] in healthcare, including secure EHRs, interoperability, drug traceability, clinical trial integrity, patient data ownership, fraud prevention, IoT security, telemedicine enhancement, and ethical data sharing. This framework ensures data privacy, security, and trust across healthcare ecosystems.

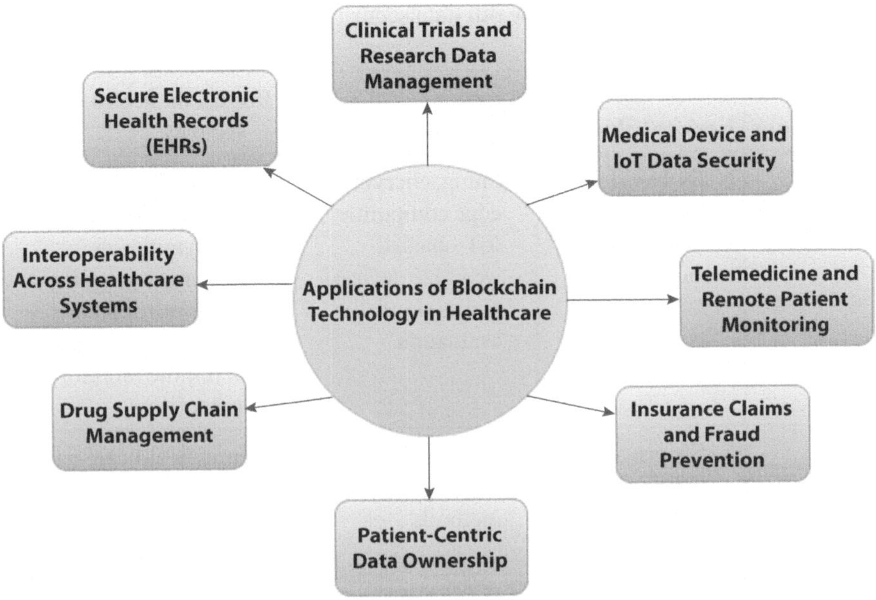

Figure 11.6 Application of blockchain in healthcare system.

Table 11.2 Different aspects of health data security, privacy, and blockchain applications.

References	Key contribution	Techniques used	Impact on health data security
[4]	Dynamic anonymity privacy-preserving	Derived from a hierarchical sequence of three possible decisions.	
[8]	DP-GSGLD satisfies differential privacy (DP)	Bayesian sampling, parameter clipping, differential privacy (DP)	Enhances security against gradient attacks, improves model training efficiency, and maintains high accuracy under strict privacy constraints

(*Continued*)

Table 11.2 Different aspects of health data security, privacy, and blockchain applications. (*Continued*)

References	Key contribution	Techniques used	Impact on health data security
[13]	NDN-based remote healthcare monitoring	Hashing, encryption, edge computing, IoT-enabled wearable devices, Icarus simulator evaluation	Enhances data security, reduces retrieval delay, mitigates resource constraints, and ensures secure access to health data in remote monitoring systems
[22]	RASS: privacy-preserving authentication scheme	Lightweight cryptographic methods	Secures healthcare data with minimal cost, prevents tampering and collusion attacks
[23]	EDPSO- based anonymization	Enhanced discrete particle swarm optimization	Reduces information loss in social network anonymization
[24]	Dynamic anonymity model	Three-way decisions hierarchically + differential privacy	Balances data usability and privacy
[25]	Explainable AI (XAI) in healthcare	Transparency frameworks	Improves trust but highlights risks like adversarial attacks and algorithmic bias
[26]	Hybrid anonymization-based privacy protection	Generalization + data relocation	Ensures unlinkability while maintaining query accuracy
[27]	DP-GSGLD: privacy-preserving federated learning	Bayesian sampling + parameter clipping	Enhances DP in federated learning, resists gradient attacks

(*Continued*)

Table 11.2 Different aspects of health data security, privacy, and blockchain applications. (*Continued*)

References	Key contribution	Techniques used	Impact on health data security
[28]	(β, k, b) anonymization method	Differential privacy + k-anonymity + Fréchet mean	Enhances clustering while preserving utility and privacy
[29]	Synthetic data for healthcare	GANs, VAEs, diffusion models	Improves data privacy but struggles with temporal consistency
[30]	Secure healthcare framework	RCLNN, THCC, IM, SPS-SHA-256, blockchain, FLS	Enhances security, access control, and privacy
[31]	Three-tier secure healthcare architecture	ECC-based authentication + local DP + smart contracts	Strengthens security and privacy in data transactions
[32]	NDN-based remote healthcare monitoring	IoT + edge computing + encryption	Ensures efficient and secure health data retrieval
[33]	Blockchain-based security for smart healthcare	Blockchain integration survey	Highlights blockchain's role in mitigating healthcare security risks
[44]	p^{+}-sensitive k-anonymity and (p, α)-sensitive k-anonymity	Top-down specification algorithms and performed theoretical hardness analysis	Improves protection of sensitive health data by ensuring better diversity and security in anonymized records

Blockchain enables [21] secure healthcare data sharing through decentralized, tamper-proof storage, ensuring data integrity and fine-grained access control *via* smart contracts. Integrating blockchain with SMPC and FL enhances data privacy, allowing institutions to collaborate without compromising confidentiality. Additionally, combining blockchain with cloud computing strengthens EHR protection, whereas AI integration supports intelligent healthcare solutions with enhanced security and privacy. Table 11.2 lists the many forms of blockchain applications, privacy, and healthcare data security.

11.7 Quantum Healthcare Data

Strengthening cybersecurity safeguards to protect sensitive medical data is more important than ever as healthcare institutions approach a new era defined by quantum technology. The healthcare system must use strong postquantum cryptography solutions to safeguard sensitive data as quantum technologies develop in order to address cybersecurity issues. Because quantum-enhanced attacks can crack conventional encryption protocols and jeopardize encrypted health records, they present serious hazards. In order to preserve the confidentiality and integrity of patient data, QR safeguards are desperately needed, as the danger to health data privacy continues to grow [34].

Figure 11.7 [34] illustrates how quantum computing poses serious risks to the security of healthcare data because algorithms such as Shor's can crack conventional encryption, allowing for illegal access and privacy abuses. Digital signatures, encrypted communications, and sensitive patient data are more vulnerable to fraud, data manipulation, and identity theft.

The emergence of wearable technology and telemedicine in digital health substantially broadens the attack surface for quantum threats. Healthcare businesses must strengthen cybersecurity policies, improve key management, and deploy QR encryption to reduce these risks. To protect patient privacy and guarantee data accuracy, proactive methods such as multifactor authentication and postquantum cryptography solutions are crucial.

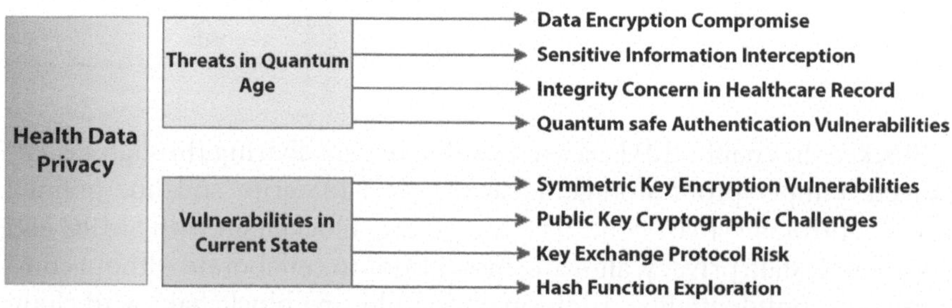

Figure 11.7 Vulnerabilities in the current state and threats in quantum age.

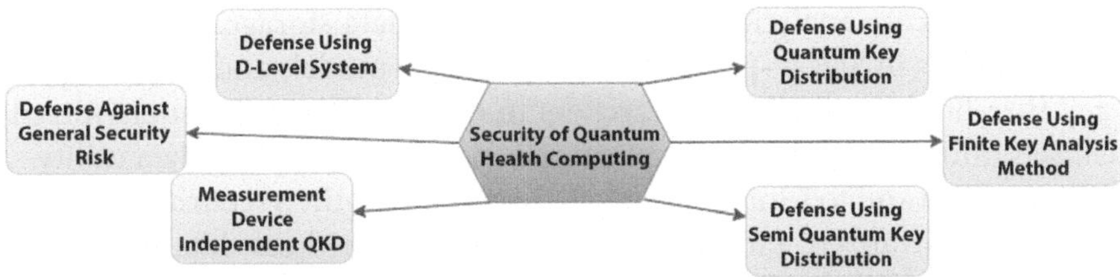

Figure 11.8 Security of quantum computing in healthcare.

Adopting quantum-resilient encryption presents difficulties for the healthcare industry, necessitating study and application to strike a compromise between security and efficiency. For smooth integration, cooperation with cryptographic experts; instruction in hash-, code-, and lattice-based cryptography; and knowledge of multivariate polynomial techniques are necessary. The quantum-based IQ-HDM [35] framework enhances healthcare data security by integrating quantum encryption and ML, achieving a 67.6% improvement in mitigating cyber threats.

Figure 11.8 [36] presents an extensive classification of essential security technologies vital for protecting healthcare information. These include quantum key distribution, defense using D-level systems, and defense against general security risks, which enhance data protection against cyber threats. Additionally, advanced methods such as measurement device–independent quantum key distribution, semiquantum key distribution, and finite key analysis further strengthen secure data transmission and access control in healthcare systems.

11.8 Future Research Directions

The future of healthcare technology lies in the integration of advanced security mechanisms, privacy-preserving AI, and regulatory-compliant frameworks to ensure robust protection of sensitive patient data. Future healthcare system security and privacy will rely on advancements in quantum-based security, FL, and hybrid techniques such as FL with HE (FL-HE) to enhance protection against cyber threats while maintaining data utility.

To address the growing concerns around data privacy, privacy-preserving AI techniques such as FL, HE, and hybrid models such as FL-HE must be refined to balance performance with confidentiality. Distributed ML and TinyML (ML on edge devices) will play a pivotal role in enabling real-time, secure healthcare analytics without centralized data storage. Additionally, advancements in SDG—powered by NLP-driven models and dynamic privacy threshold—will allow researchers to create realistic yet anonymized datasets, minimizing reidentification risks while maintaining data utility.

Blockchain and IoT integration will further strengthen security by establishing decentralized, tamper-proof systems for medical data exchange. A verifiable blockchain-based IoT framework could ensure real-world security in healthcare applications, from EHRs to smart medical devices. Collaborations with industrial partners will be essential to commercialize these innovations and bring them into mainstream healthcare practice. Ensuring trustworthy AI requires robust intrusion detection, secure medical devices, and standardized best practices to foster adoption across healthcare systems.

On the regulatory front, future research must focus on developing adversarial-resistant AI models and enhancing intrusion detection systems to safeguard against evolving cyber threats. Stricter regulatory frameworks and standardized best practices will be crucial in fostering trust between healthcare providers, patients, and AI systems. Cryptographic innovations—such as decentralized key management, *k*-anonymity, and DP—must be rigorously tested to ensure compliance with global data protection laws such as HIPAA and GDPR.

The following is a list of future research directions for security and privacy for AI-driven healthcare solutions:

- **Quantum-based security enhancements**: Quantum-based transfer learning can enhance security models, enabling them to counter unknown cyber-attacks effectively [35]. Quantum computing has significant implications for the healthcare paradigm, offering a comprehensive solution for researchers exploring its potential in various healthcare applications [36].
- **Future directions in privacy-preserving AI for healthcare**: Advancements in AI necessitate privacy-aware and adversarially robust ML models, distributed ML, and TinyML for secure healthcare applications. Addressing the privacy-performance trade-off and developing hybrid techniques such as FL-HE can enhance scalability and data protection in biomedical and healthcare systems.
- **Blockchain and IoT for real-world security**: Implementing a blockchain-based IoT in a verifiable system to ensure

real-world security guarantees and seeking an industrial partner to commercialize novel ideas [35].

- **Regulatory and privacy frameworks**: Future research should focus on enhancing AI-driven healthcare security by developing robust ML models resistant to adversarial attacks, implementing stricter regulatory frameworks, improving privacy-preserving techniques, and designing advanced intrusion detection systems to safeguard patient data and medical devices [46].
- **Trustworthy and secure AI in healthcare**: Research should focus on developing AI-driven healthcare solutions that enhance patient outcomes and operational efficiency while prioritizing trust and security between healthcare providers, patients, and stakeholders. Developing best practices for creating reliable and secure AI applications will be crucial for their successful adoption in medical settings [5].
- **Cryptographic and privacy-preserving methods**: Testing other encryption algorithms, exploring anonymization methods such as *k*-anonymity and DP with cryptography, and implementing decentralized key management for enhanced privacy and security [21].
- **Synthetic data privacy advancements**: The future of synthetic data privacy lies in integrating NLP-driven data generation, dynamic privacy thresholds, and adaptive models to balance data utility and security [10].
- **Uniform and safe healthcare systems**: Improving cryptographic solutions, intrusion detection, access control, ML security, and smart medical device protection in order to provide uniform, safe, and privacy-preserving healthcare systems [51].

Ultimately, the goal is to establish uniform, secure, and privacy-preserving healthcare systems through a combination of advanced cryptography, AI-driven security, and regulatory oversight. By prioritizing trustworthy AI, robust encryption, and real-time threat mitigation, the healthcare industry can achieve a future where cutting-edge technology enhances patient care without compromising security or privacy.

11.9 Conclusion

Data analysis, security, and patient care might all be greatly enhanced by the quick development of AI-driven healthcare systems. Although implementation of AI-driven healthcare solutions is hampered by privacy concerns, these technologies promise to improve efficiency and treatment outcomes. But maintaining privacy, adhering to regulations, and implementing AI ethically are still difficult tasks. In order to solve security problems while keeping transparency and scalability, this chapter examined a number of privacy-preserving strategies, such as blockchain, DP, and *k*-anonymity. Emerging cryptographic and blockchain-based solutions were reviewed, along with important issues such as data integrity, access control, privacy-utility trade-offs, and adversarial ML threats. Furthermore, it was underlined how important it is to have strong regulatory frameworks and QR encryption in order to protect private medical information from ever-changing cyber threats and standardized AI-driven healthcare systems to enhance security, interoperability, and trust in intelligent medical technologies.

AI disclosure statement: The author confirms that no artificial intelligence (AI)-generated content or AI-assisted writing tools were used in the preparation of this chapter (including summaries and the abstract). All text, analysis, and conclusions are the result of the author's original work.

References

1. Khalid, N., *et al.*, Privacy-preserving artificial intelligence in healthcare: Techniques and applications. *Comput. Biol. Med.*, 158, 1068485, 2023.
2. Liu, J., *et al.*, RASS: Enabling privacy-preserving and authentication in online AI-driven healthcare applications. *ISA Trans.*, 141, 20–295, 2023.
3. Yazdanjue, N., *et al.*, An enhanced discrete particle swarm optimization for structural k-Anonymity in social networks. *Inf. Sci.*, 670, 1206315, 2024.
4. Qian, J., *et al.*, A dynamic anonymization privacy-preserving model based on hierarchical sequential three-way decisions. *Inf. Sci.*, 686, 1213165, 2025.
5. Khan, M.M., *et al.*, Towards secure and trusted AI in healthcare: A systematic review of emerging innovations and ethical challenges. *Int. J. Med. Inf.*, 105780, 2024.
6. Gupta, B.B., Gaurav, A., Kumar Panigrahi, P., Analysis of security and privacy issues of information management of big data in B2B based healthcare systems. *J. Bus. Res.*, 162, 1138595, 2023.

7. Nergiz, M.E. and Zahit Gök, M., Hybrid k-anonymity. *Comput. Secur.*, 44, 51–635, 2014.
8. Yang, C., *et al.*, DP-GSGLD: A Bayesian optimizer inspired by differential privacy defending against privacy leakage in federated learning. *Comput. Secur.*, 142, 1038395, 2024.
9. Garg, S. and Torra, V., Privacy in manifolds: Combining k-anonymity with differential privacy on Fréchet means. *Comput. Secur. (Print)*, 2024.
10. Liu, Y., Acharya, U.R., Tan, J.H., Preserving privacy in healthcare: A systematic review of deep learning approaches for synthetic data generation. *Comput. Methods Programs Biomed.*, 108571, 2024.
11. Kumar, S. and Shaw, D.K., Efficient access requests management for healthcare data with security and privacy-preserving. *Expert Syst. Appl.*, 126194, 2024.
12. Haque, R.U., *et al.*, A novel secure and distributed architecture for privacy-preserving healthcare system. *J. Network Comput. Appl.*, 217, 1036965, 2023.
13. Gupta, D., *et al.*, Security paradigm for remote health monitoring edge devices in internet of things. *J. King Saud Univ. Comput. Inf. Sci.*, 35.6, 101478, 2023.
14. Maheriya, A. and Panchal, S., A Neoteric Approach to Improvise Privacy Shielding of Sensitive Healthcare Information & Prediction of Disease. *Int. J. Comput. Digital Syst.*, 13.1, 1–12, 2023.
15. Tariq, N., *et al.*, Blockchain and smart healthcare security: a survey. *Procedia Comput. Sci.*, 175, 615–6205, 2020.
16. Bhavin, M., *et al.*, Blockchain and quantum blind signature-based hybrid scheme for healthcare 5.0 applications. *J. Inf. Secur. Appl.*, 56, 1026735, 2021.
17. Arpita, M. and Panchal, S., Smart Health and Cybersecurity in the Era of Artificial Intelligence, in: *Information and Communication Technology for Competitive Strategies (ICTCS 2021) Intelligent Strategies for ICT*, pp. 41–48, Springer Nature Singapore, Singapore, 2022.
18. Maheriya, A. and Panchal, S., Balancing Privacy and Utility in AI Training: Comparative Analysis of Privacy-Preserving Techniques.
19. Raval, A. and Maheriya, A., A Survey on Deep Learning Methods for Addressing COVID-19 Issues, in: *Information and Communication Technology for Competitive Strategies (ICTCS 2022) Intelligent Strategies for ICT*, pp. 61–73, Springer Nature Singapore, Singapore, 2023.
20. Maheriya, A., A Heuristic Approach to Protect Privacy of Patient's Sensitive Data with Prediction of Disease.
21. Shoghli, A., Darvish, M., Sadeghian, Y., Balancing Innovation and Privacy: Ethical Challenges in AI-Driven Healthcare. *J. Rev. Med. Sci.*, 4.1, 1–11, 2024.
22. de Moraes Rossetto, A.G., Sega, C., Leithardt, V.R.Q., An architecture for managing data privacy in healthcare with blockchain. *Sensors*, 22.21, 8292, 2022.
23. Chang, A.J., El-Rayes, N., Shi, J., Blockchain Technology for Supply Chain Management: A Comprehensive Review. *FinTech*, 1, 191–205, 2022.

24. Sega, C.L., Rossetto, AGM., Correia, S.D., Leithardt, V.R.Q., An architectural proposal to protect the privacy of health data stored in the Blockchain, in: *Proceedings of the 2022 17th Iberian Conference on Information Systems and Technologies (CISTI)*, Madrid, Spain, 22–25 June 2022, pp. 1–6.
25. Nakamoto, S., Bitcoin: A peer-to-peer electronic cash system. *Decentralized Bus. Rev*, 9, 2008.
26. Zhang, R., Xue, R., Liu, L., Security and Privacy on Blockchain. *ACM Comput. Surv.*, 52, 1–34, 2019.
27. Tang, X., Guo, H., Li, H., Yuan, Y., Wang, J., Cheng, J.A., DAPP Business Data Storage Model Based on Blockchain and IPFS, in: *Proceedings of the International Conference on Artificial Intelligence and Security*, Qinghai, China, 22–26 July 2021, pp. 219–230.
28. Sestrem Ochôa, I., Silva, L.A., de Mello, G., Alves da Silva, B., de Paz, J.F., Villarrubia González, G., Garcia, N.M., Reis Quietinho Leithardt, V., PRICHAIN: A Partially Decentralized Implementation of UbiPri Middleware Using Blockchain. *Sensors*, 19, 4483, 2019, [CrossRef].
29. Cesconetto, J., Augusto Silva, L., Bortoluzzi, F., Navarro-Cáceres, M.A., Zeferino, C., Leithardt, R.Q., V. PRIPRO—Privacy Profiles.
30. User Profiling Management for Smart Environments. *Electronics*, 9, 1519, 2020, [CrossRef].
31. Lopes, H., Pires, I.M., Sánchez San Blas, H., García-Ovejero, R., Leithardt, V., PriADA: Management and Adaptation of Information Based on Data Privacy in Public Environments. *Computers*, 9, 77, 2020. [CrossRef].
32. Pereira, F., Crocker, P., Leithardt, V.R., PADRES: Tool for PrivAcy, Data REgulation and Security. *SoftwareX*, 17, 100895, 2022.
33. Dasgupta, D., Shrein, J.M., Gupta, K.D., A survey of blockchain from security perspective. *J. Bank. Financ. Technol.*, 3, 1–17, 2019.
34. SaberiKamarposhti, M., *et al.*, Post-quantum healthcare: A roadmap for cybersecurity resilience in medical data. *Heliyon*, 10.10, 2024.
35. Gupta, K., *et al.*, An intelligent quantum cyber-security framework for healthcare data management. *IEEE Trans. Autom. Sci. Eng.*, 2024.
36. Ur Rasool, R., *et al.*, Quantum computing for healthcare: A review. *Future Internet*, 15.3, 94, 2023.
37. Abouelmehdi, K., Beni-Hessane, A., Khaloufi, H., Big healthcare data: Preserving security and privacy. *J. Big Data*, 5.1, 1–18, 2018.
38. Chong, K.M., Privacy-preserving healthcare informatics: A review. *ITM Web of Conferences*, vol. 36, EDP Sciences, 2021.
39. Dankar, F.K. and El Emam, K., Practicing differential privacy in health care: A review. *Trans. Data Priv.*, 6.1, 35–67, 2013.
40. Yadav, N., *et al.*, Data privacy in healthcare: In the era of Artificial Intelligence. *Indian Dermatol. Online J.*, 14.6, 788–792, 2023.
41. Adusumilli, S., Damancharla, H., Metta, A., Enhancing Data Privacy in Healthcare Systems Using Blockchain Technology. *Trans. Latest Trends Artif. Intell.*, 4.4, 2023.

42. Gates, D. and Olajide, O., Synthetic data in cardiovascular health research, in: *Intelligence-Based Cardiology and Cardiac Surgery*, pp. 407–413, Academic Press, 2024.
43. Wang, B., *et al.*, PPFLHE: A privacy-preserving federated learning scheme with homomorphic encryption for healthcare data. *Appl. Soft Comput.*, 146, 1106775, 2023.
44. Sun, X., Sun, L., Wang, H., Extended k-anonymity models against sensitive attribute disclosure. *Comput. Commun.*, 34.4, 526–535, 2011.
45. Mozaffari-Kermani, M., *et al.*, Systematic poisoning attacks on and defenses for machine learning in healthcare. *IEEE J. Biomed. Health. Inf.*, 19.6, 1893–1905, 2014.
46. Ghaffar, Z., *et al.*, A machine learning attack resilient and low-latency authentication scheme for AI-driven patient health monitoring system. *IEEE Commun. Stand. Mag.*, 8.3, 36–42, 2024.
47. Biswas, A., *et al.*, Securing the Diagnosis of Medical Imaging: An In-depth Analysis of AI-Resistant Attacks. *arXiv preprint arXiv:2408.00348* (2024).
48. Marjanović, M., Adversarial Attacks on Machine Learning Models in Healthcare Applications. *Sinteza 2024-International Scientific Conference on Information Technology, Computer Science, and Data Science*, Singidunum University, 2024.
49. Ghourabi, A., A security model based on lightgbm and transformer to protect healthcare systems from cyberattacks. *IEEE Access*, 10, 48890–48903, 2022.
50. Newaz, A.K.M., II, *et al.*, Adversarial attacks to machine learning-based smart healthcare systems. *GLOBECOM 2020-2020 IEEE Global Communications Conference*, IEEE, 2020.
51. Newaz, A.K.M., II, *et al.*, A survey on security and privacy issues in modern healthcare systems: Attacks and defenses. *ACM Trans. Comput. Healthcare*, 2.3, 1–44, 2021.

12

Neuro-Symbolic AI for Cardiovascular Pharmacovigilance: A Holistic Approach to Drug-Induced Cardiotoxicity

Jossy P. George[1], Kamal Upreti[2*] and Bosco Paul Alapatt[2]

[1]*Department of Computer Science, Christ University, Bengaluru, India*
[2]*Department of Computer Science, Christ University, Delhi NCR, Ghaziabad, Uttar Pradesh, India*

Abstract

Clinical pharmacology and patient safety continue to face major challenges due to cardiovascular drug-induced toxicity, especially in high-risk groups receiving complicated therapy. This chapter examines how to overcome the shortcomings of the pharmacovigilance (PV) systems that are in place today by integrating neuro-symbolic artificial intelligence (AI), a hybrid framework that combines the logical reasoning of symbolic AI with the learning power of neural networks. It starts by describing the clinical burden of drug-induced cardiotoxicity, particularly as it relates to treatments using nonsteroidal anti-inflammatory drugs, tyrosine kinase inhibitors, anthracyclines, and other high-alert drugs. Along with the necessity for transparent, real-time, and explicable models in cardiac risk monitoring, the drawbacks of conventional PV techniques—such as underreporting and delayed signal detection—are also covered. The suggested neuro-symbolic architecture predicts and interprets cardiotoxic effects by combining domain-specific ontologies, pharmacogenomic information, electronic health records, and electrocardiogram (ECG) biomarkers. Developing rule-based inference processes, classifying cardiotoxicity classes, and using machine learning to predict QT prolongation are some of the major achievements. The "black-box" issue that many AI systems have is addressed by the framework, which places an emphasis on clinical trust and explainability. Future directions include clinical decision support system integration, wearable real-time monitoring, federated learning enabling multi-institutional scalability, and the expansion of symbolic knowledge bases.

**Corresponding author*: kamalupreti1989@gmail.com

Shubham Mahajan, Davinder Paul Singh, Amit Kant Pandit and Paras Chawla (eds.) Ensuring Privacy in Digital Twin Ecosystems, (367–396)

This chapter demonstrates the revolutionary potential of neuro-symbolic AI in developing a clinically sound, scalable, and interpretable drug safety surveillance system for cardiovascular medicine.

***Keywords*:** Cardiovascular drug-induced, electronic health records (EHRs), clinical decision support systems (CDSS), anthracyclines, tyrosine kinase inhibitors, NSAIDs

12.1 Introduction

With the digitization of patients' data and enabling quick and precise medical treatment, electronic health records, or electronic health records (EHRs), have been instrumental in transforming the healthcare sector. The density and heterogeneity of healthcare EHR data influence the diagnostic accuracy, despite the fact that medical technology for disease forecasting has advanced greatly. The incorporation of advanced artificial intelligence (AI) methods, such as neuro-symbolic AI, which brings together the IQ capabilities of symbolic AI and the pattern recognition features of neural networks, has become increasingly popular as a remedy for such issues. Complicated decision-making procedures within many fields, including medicine, have proved promising in their undertaking when applied by this hybrid method [1]. India has witnessed a fast growth in the research carried out on the application of AI in the health sector, particularly when multimodal datasets are fused. Studies have examined various AI techniques to enhance the accuracy of disease prediction in EHRs, but most of these methods struggle to make their results comprehensible. In a clinical setting, where clinical adoption of AI-based decisions relies on transparency and trust, this limitation is vital.

12.2 Overview of Cardiovascular Drug Safety Concerns

In modern medicine, cardiovascular disease (CVD) drug safety is a significant and complex issue. CVD drugs such as β-blockers, angiotensin-converting enzyme inhibitors (ACEi), antiplatelets, anticoagulants, statins, and antiarrhythmics are essential in the management of diseases such as ischemic heart disease, heart failure, hypertension, and arrhythmias. But because many of these treatments have narrow therapeutic indices, even little dosage changes or interactions with other drugs can have major side effects such hepatotoxicity, bradyarrhythmia, hemorrhage, hypotension, or electrolyte imbalances. Furthermore, cardiotoxicity caused by drugs is not exclusive to cardiovascular treatments. Antipsychotics (such as haloperidol), antibiotics (such as macrolides), and some chemotherapeutics (such as doxorubicin) can cause torsades de pointes, QT interval prolongation, or even sudden cardiac death. These side effects can be erratic, unique to each patient, and made worse by age, gender, renal function, and polypharmacy—particularly in older or multimorbid patients. Conventional pharmacovigilance (PV) systems, such as spontaneous adverse event reporting, are reactive in nature and frequently experience delayed signal detection and underreporting. As a result, there may be a delay in detecting cardiotoxic signals until after extensive drug usage. Furthermore, reliable risk assessment is complicated by the diversity of comorbid diseases, adherence, and dose patterns in the actual world [2].

The intricacy of pharmacological interactions in patients with CVD and the potentially fatal nature of cardiac events have led to an increasing focus on proactive, AI-enabled PV systems. Enhancing early identification of bad cardiac outcomes, integrating multimodal patient data and offering explicable insights into medication safety hazards are the goals of these systems. This is particularly crucial as polypharmacy and individualized medication become more common in cardiovascular care.

12.3 The Clinical Burden of Drug-Induced Cardiotoxicity

One of the main concerns in both clinical practice and pharmacological development is medication-induced cardiotoxicity. Some medications still induce a spectrum of detrimental cardiac events have been reported, with occasionally serious repercussions, despite the fact that the heart is not a typical target for adverse reactions to drugs. Direct cardiac toxicity is what is known as changes in the structure and function of the cardiovascular system caused by possible drug exposure. Noncardiovascular drugs, including anticancer drugs such as tyrosine kinase inhibitors (TKIs), anthracyclines, and immunomodulatory checkpoint inhibitors, and various antipsychotics, venlafaxine, and even certain antibiotics (such as macrolides), are also influenced by this effect [3]. Heart adverse drug reactions (ADRs) involve arrhythmias, conduction disease, myocardial ischemia, valvular disease thrombosis, myocarditis, and pericarditis. among other consequences. Many drugs, such as anti-infective, antiarrhythmic, and antineoplastic (including cancer chemotherapeutics, targeted treatments, and cancer immunotherapies), can be cardiotoxic and noncardiac (such as lipid-regulating agents, antihistamines, and bronchodilators). The many drug classes linked to cardiotoxicity are compiled in Table 12.1, which also includes illustrative instances, their particular cardiac effects, underlying processes, and important risk factors related to the patient or the treatment.

The drug's cardiotoxicity has multiple contributing factors. Gender, age, renal insufficiency, iron overload, drug–drug interactions, and preexisting cardiovascular disorders are examples of traditional cardiovascular risk factors that do not adequately account for Department of Information and Communications Technology (DICT). The diagnostic specificity for DICT is

Table 12.1 Classification of drug-induced cardiotoxicity based on drug class, mechanisms, and risk factors.

Drug class	Examples	Cardiac effects	Mechanism	Risk factors
Antineoplastics	Doxorubicin, trastuzumab, cyclophosphamide	Cardiomyopathy, heart failure	Oxidative stress, mitochondrial damage, HER2 pathway inhibition	High cumulative dose, age, concurrent RT
Antipsychotics	Haloperidol, risperidone, olanzapine	QT prolongation, torsades de pointes	hERG channel inhibition	Female sex, hypokalemia, polypharmacy
Antibiotics	Erythromycin, azithromycin, levofloxacin	Arrhythmias, QT prolongation	Ion channel blockade, mitochondrial toxicity	Electrolyte imbalance, existing CVD
Antivirals	Ritonavir, lopinavir	Hypertension, conduction abnormalities	Autonomic dysregulation, metabolic effects	HIV patients, cotreatment with ART
Tyrosine kinase inhibitors	Sunitinib, sorafenib	LV dysfunction, hypertension	VEGF pathway inhibition, mitochondrial dysfunction	Preexisting hypertension, cancer burden
Stimulants	Amphetamines, cocaine	Tachyarrhythmias, myocardial infarction	Sympathetic overactivation, vasospasm	Drug abuse, hypertension
NSAIDs	Diclofenac, celecoxib	Hypertension, heart failure exacerbation	Sodium retention, impaired renal perfusion	Elderly, renal impairment

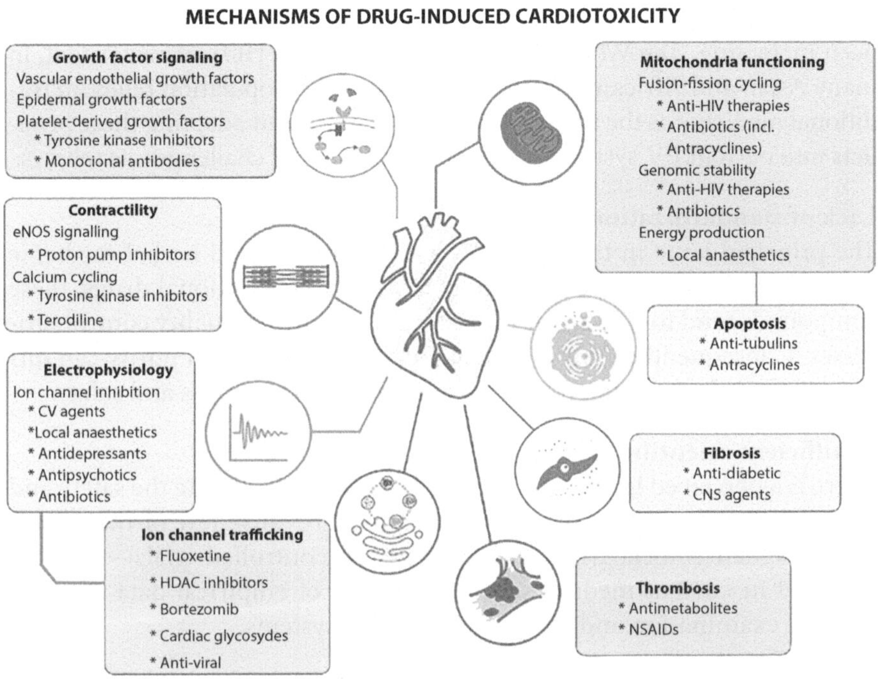

Figure 12.1 Schematic illustration of multiple genomic mechanisms of drug cardiotoxicity [4].

often low for routine clinical monitoring signs [4]. The significance of genetic factors that increase an individual's susceptibility to DICT is being supported by an increasing amount of evidence. In order to optimize medication regimens, some risk genes have been translated into clinical settings. Key genomic routes that medicines may use to cause cardiotoxicity are depicted in Figure 12.1. These pathways affect drug metabolism and cardiac susceptibility and include genetic polymorphisms, oxidative stress, apoptotic signaling, mitochondrial malfunction, and alterations in ion channel control. The detection and functional analysis of genetic biomarkers linked to the risk of DICT have been made possible by the amalgamation of contemporary life science technology with pharmacogenomics, a discipline that examines the genetic basis of variations between individuals in pharmaceutical responses.

12.4 Challenges with Traditional PV Systems

Innovations in contemporary information technology have revolutionized the PV system to a great extent, with both unprecedented benefits and intricate challenges for the pharmaceutical industry [5]. At the same time, worldwide dependence on herbal and traditional medicinal products has been increasing. The World Health Organization (WHO) estimates that, in many Asian and African nations, up to 80% of the population relies on traditional medicine as the main source of healthcare. But adapting these products into current PV systems poses a particular set of challenges, as follows:

Lack of standardization

The principal issue in the supervision of traditional and herbal medicine is the absence of standardized products. Unlike conventional drugs, these compounds tend to skip stringent testing and uniform quality control processes. Consequently, their chemical content, potency, and purity can differ significantly, resulting in inconsistencies in effectiveness and safety.

Insufficient scientific validation

There is a perceived lack of solid clinical evidence to validate the safety and effectiveness of most herbal products. This is because few of them have well-designed clinical trials and randomized controlled trials—the gold standard in current medical studies. The lack of empirical data impedes credible examination and integration into PV systems.

Cultural and language barriers

Communication issues are a serious challenge to adverse event reporting. Patients consuming traditional medicine might not communicate in the same language as healthcare providers, making it difficult to report accurately the symptoms or adverse experiences. Similarly, healthcare workers who lack knowledge of the local languages or practices might find it difficult to recognize and report possible risks or side effects linked to the remedies [6].

Regulatory gaps

In contrast to traditional medicines, most herbal and traditional products are not subject to strict PV regulations. Such laws, which differ widely between countries, are needed for the systematic monitoring, reporting, and assessment of drug safety. In much of the world, the lack of extensive regulatory regimens restricts the capacity of health authorities to apply standards or react to safety issues effectively.

12.5 Motivation for AI Integration—Need for Explainability and Clinical Trust

In order to help doctors make quicker and more accurate judgments, AI technology processes large datasets using complex algorithms and cutting-edge computing power. AI is transforming cardiovascular care in a number of key areas, including diagnostic imaging. AI systems that primarily use machine learning (ML) and deep learning approaches are revolutionizing the analysis of cardiac images obtained by several modalities, such as echocardiography, magnetic resonance imaging, and computed tomography scans. Figure 12.2 illustrates AI's role in the full nuclear cardiology workflow, including picture capture, segmentation, attenuation correction, functional quantification, and diagnostic reading. AI algorithms improve image quality, shorten scan time, facilitate automated detection of perfusion defects, and aid in risk stratification for prognosis—ultimately allowing for more precise, effective, and individualized cardiac management.

Such functional levels are able to immediately identify abnormalities that human eyes may miss, including the accumulation of arterial plaque, ventricular chamber enlargement, or failure. AI systems, for example, can be taught to recognize the characteristic patterns of coronary artery disease

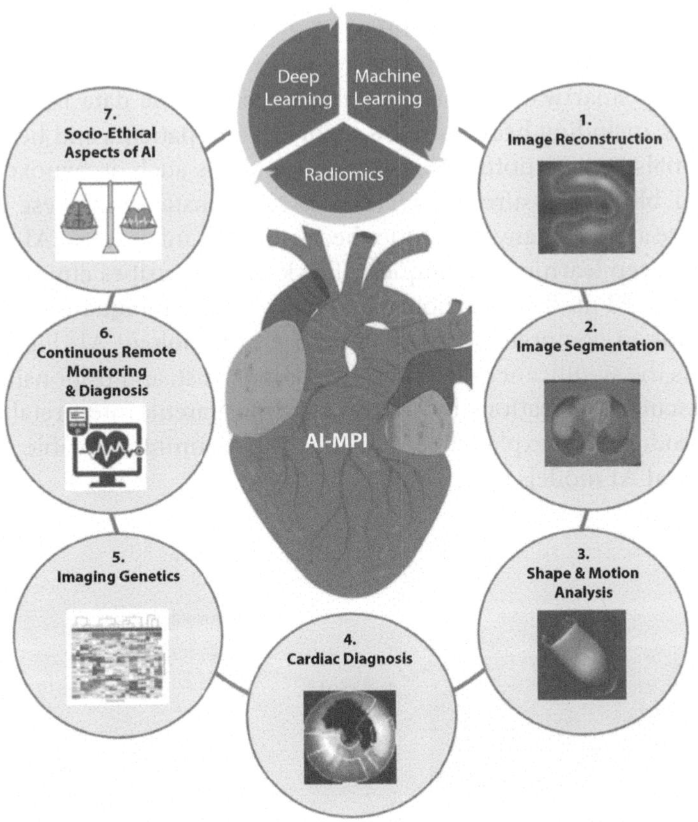

Figure 12.2 Artificial intelligence in nuclear cardiac imaging [9].

by examining large image databases, which allows them to more precisely detect early signs than humans. Furthermore, these machines can quantify myocardial strain and ejection fraction, two essential cardiac functions for diagnosing and treating heart failure. This level of accuracy and efficacy not only enhances diagnostic accuracy but also accelerates image interpretation, making it possible for clinical decisions to be made more rapidly [7].

Prevention of events such as heart attacks, strokes, or cardiac arrests and taking adequate precautions are enabled by AI-based predictive models. In order to provide clinicians with a recommended intervention plan for prevention, ML algorithms, for example, can analyze a patient's blood pressure, cholesterol, and family history to determine their risk scores [8]. Where it is a case of chronic CVDs, where timely intervention can make quite a difference in patient outcomes, this predictive strength comes very much in handy. The use of AI is changing and has reshaped the manner in which cardiovascular patients are monitored and treated as they recover at home and within healthcare facilities.

With the advent of AI algorithms, wearable technology—such as fitness trackers and smartwatches—is now able to relay these data in real time. Vital signs, including heart rate, are reported, and patients and healthcare professionals receive notifications when problems such as hypoxemia or abnormal blood pressure are identified. Notwithstanding these advantages, there are still many difficulties because of the intricacy of AI models, especially deep learning techniques. "Black box" describes circumstances in which the AI model's decision-making process is ambiguous or difficult for humans to comprehend when it comes to radiology AI. Figure 12.3 highlights the significance of clinical reasoning, trust, and responsibility in cardiovascular applications by contrasting transparent, interpretable outcomes produced by explainable AI with opaque, uninterpretable outputs from typical AI models (black box).

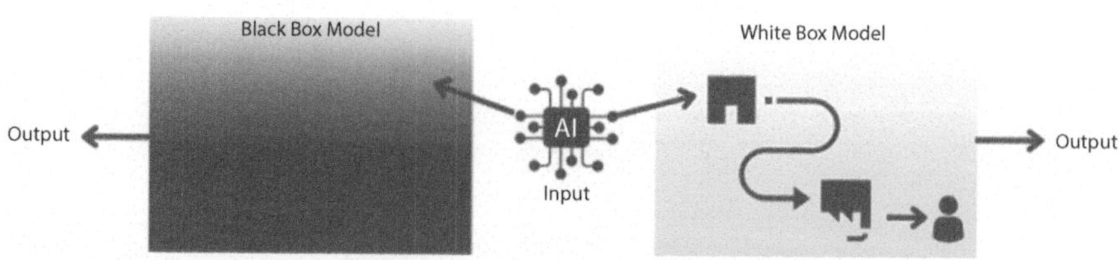

Figure 12.3 Visual representation of the black box problem in comparison with explainable AI [9].

This indicates that although the AI is capable of producing outcomes or suggestions, the underlying logic or processes that produced these findings are opaque. Because doctors could not fully comprehend or trust the AI's outputs, such indicators can present difficulties in clinical settings and potentially affect patient care [9].

As previously said, AI's decision-making process is frequently ambiguous, making it difficult to grasp and comprehend its output. DL's cardiovascular imaging results are encouraging, but they are currently limited, and there are a number of obstacles that need to be addressed before they can be further enhanced.

12.6 Background and Theoretical Foundations

12.6.1 Cardiotoxicity: Definitions and Types

When local anesthetics, mercurial diuretics, and digitalis were administered, the toxic effects on heart function or tissue were first referred to as cardiotoxicity in 1946. Since the 1970s, the phrase has specifically been used to refer to cardiac side effects associated with cancer chemotherapy. One significant clinical issue that is frequently discovered only after the medicine has been used in clinical settings is drug-induced cardiotoxicity.

In actuality, cardiac arrhythmias—the most prevalent medication-related cardiotoxic effects—may go undetected during phase I of drug safety evaluation, which entails assessing for safety in both experimental animals and control healthy humans. However, only the proarrhythmic adverse effects of drugs may reveal themselves in phase II or III of drug safety assessment if the patient already has underlying cardiac disease [10]. The phenomenon of "hidden cardiotoxicity" was therefore proposed by some authors to describe all cardiotoxic effects of drugs that are apparent only when a patient is sick, e.g., in ischemia/reperfusion injury and/or other comorbid conditions leading to heart disease.

Figure 12.4 highlights important cellular and molecular mechanisms that contribute to cardiotoxicity by showing the different cell types that are impacted by doxorubicin (such as cardiomyocytes, endothelial cells, and fibroblasts) as well as the drug's possible side effects, which include oxidative stress, mitochondrial dysfunction, DNA damage, and apoptosis.

Irreversible, reversible, ischemic, arrhythmogenic, hypertensive, and immune-mediated cardiotoxicities are all categorized in Table 12.2, along with the medications that are used to treat them and their side effects.

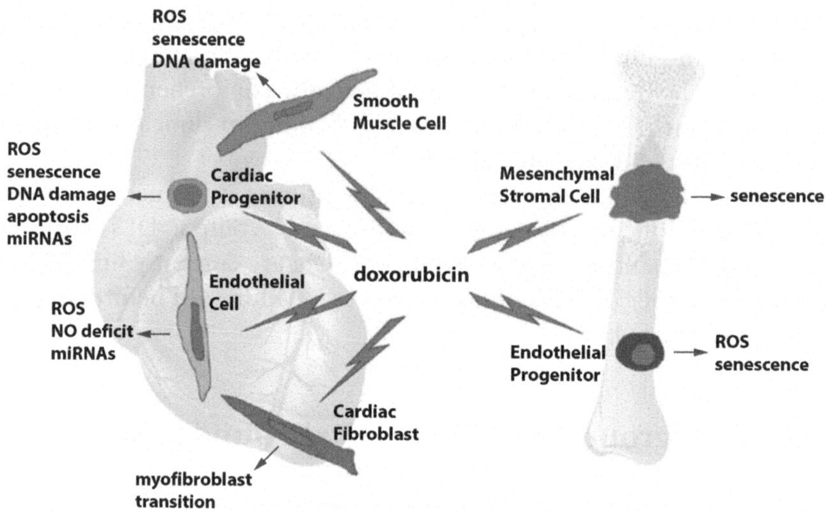

Figure 12.4 Several doxorubicin-targeted cell types are shown graphically, along with possible adverse effects and the cellular and molecular processes that the medication triggers [10].

Acute vs chronic cardiotoxicity

The main distinctions between acute and chronic cardiotoxicity are highlighted in Table 12.3, along with information on onset time, clinical symptoms, reversibility, related medications, and underlying pathological alterations.

Key drug classes: anthracyclines, TKIs, nonsteroidal anti-inflammatory drugs

1. Anthracyclines

The majority of anthracyclines work as toxins that bind the enzyme topoisomerase II (TopoII) on chromatin, causing DNA breaks. These medications also remove histones from certain genomic regions, which delays the repair of DNA damage and causes changes to the transcriptome and epigenome—a process known as chromatin damage. Compared to their counterparts without cancer, cancer patients undergoing anthracycline chemotherapy are more than twice as likely to get heart failure. Furthermore, as cancer survivors live longer, this risk keeps rising. A significant increase in cardiotoxicity occurs when the cumulative dose is exceeded [11].

In support of a tailored medicine approach, Figure 12.5 shows how treating various anthracyclines as separate agents rather than interchangeable can greatly increase survival rates in patients with acute myeloid leukemia

Table 12.2 Classification of cardiotoxicity based on mechanism and reversibility.

Type of cardiotoxicity	Description	Commonly associated drugs	Clinical manifestations
Type I (irreversible)	Permanent structural damage to cardiac tissue (e.g., myocyte death)	Doxorubicin, cyclophosphamide	Cardiomyopathy, congestive heart failure
Type II (reversible)	Transient myocardial dysfunction without cellular death	Trastuzumab, lapatinib	Decreased LVEF, improves after discontinuation
Ischemic cardiotoxicity	Drug-induced coronary vasospasm or thrombosis leading to myocardial ischemia	5-FU, bevacizumab	Chest pain, myocardial infarction
Arrhythmogenic cardiotoxicity	Disruption of cardiac electrical activity, often *via* QT prolongation	Haloperidol, cisapride, erythromycin	Torsades de pointes, ventricular arrhythmias
Hypertensive cardiotoxicity	Elevation of blood pressure due to vascular effects or fluid retention	VEGF inhibitors (sunitinib, sorafenib)	Hypertension, LV hypertrophy
Inflammatory/ immune-mediated	Immune cell activation leading to myocarditis or pericarditis	Immune checkpoint inhibitors (e.g., nivolumab)	Myocarditis, arrhythmias, cardiogenic shock

(AML) while reducing cardiotoxic side effects. Long-term treatment might be possible with low cardiotoxic anthracyclines; however, treatment is limited by present cardiotoxic anthracyclines because of cumulative dose-dependent cardiotoxicity.

Table 12.3 Comparison of acute and chronic cardiotoxicity.

Feature	Acute cardiotoxicity	Chronic cardiotoxicity
Onset	Within hours to days after drug administration	Weeks to months (or even years) after exposure
Common symptoms	Arrhythmias, ECG changes, pericarditis-like signs	Heart failure, dilated cardiomyopathy
Reversibility	Often reversible upon drug withdrawal	Often irreversible due to myocardial damage
Associated drugs	Anthracyclines (e.g., doxorubicin), 5-FU	Doxorubicin (cumulative dose), trastuzumab (long-term)
Pathological changes	Functional disturbance (e.g., conduction issues)	Structural damage (e.g., myocyte loss, fibrosis)

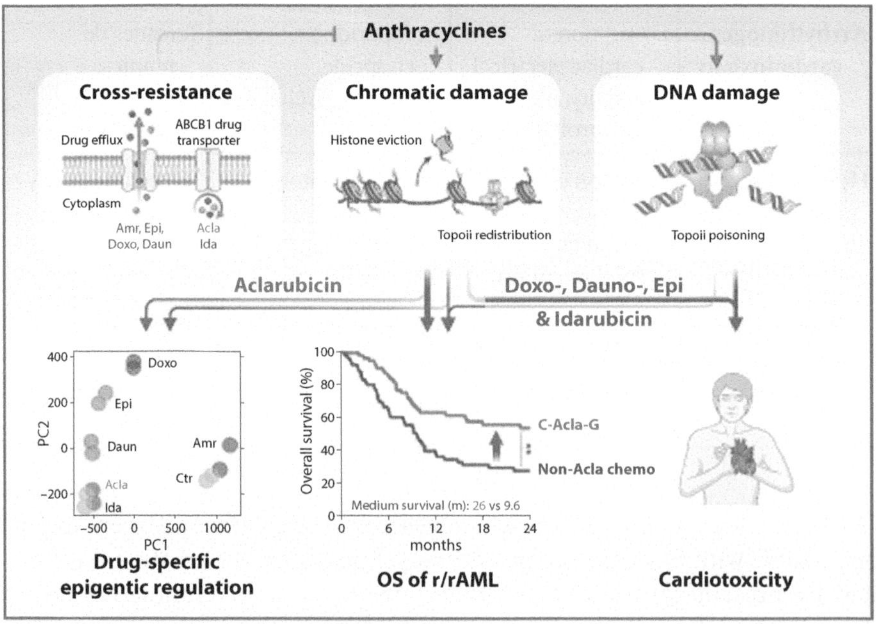

Figure 12.5 Considering individual anthracyclines as different drugs can markedly approve survival of AML patient while reducing the toxic side effects [11].

2. Tyrosine Kinase Inhibitors

TKIs are cancer-specific therapies that interfere with aberrant signaling pathways in cancer cells, including those involving the BCR-ABL fusion protein, vascular endothelial growth factor receptor (VEGFR), and epidermal growth factor receptor. TKIs are associated with a variety of cardiotoxic side effects that vary depending on the specific medication, dosage, and patient risk factors, despite the fact that they have significantly improved results for many types of cancer.

3. Nonsteroidal Anti-Inflammatory Drugs

The decision-making process is complicated, and clinicians who prescribe nonsteroidal anti-inflammatory drugs (NSAIDs) should understand it. Clinical decision-making should specifically take into account both beneficial and detrimental effects on CVD, albeit this is not the only consideration. The non-CVD concerns associated with NSAIDs are mostly gastrointestinal (GI), but they can also be renal. The doctor should weigh these risks individually when determining whether to prescribe an NSAID for analgesia and the best one to do so [12]. In this opinion, it discusses the GI, renal, and CVDs of NSAIDs used to treat pain in order to help medical professionals make challenging therapeutic decisions.

NSAIDs are classified into two subgroups: selective cyclooxygenase 2 inhibitors (COXIBs), such as celecoxib, and standard NSAIDs (unsaid) such as ibuprofen, naproxen, and diclofenac. The main driving force for the creation of COXIBs was their benign GI side effect profile, which distinguishes them from conventional NSAIDs. A thorough meta-analysis of the effects of NSAIDs and COXIBs on CVD was carried out by the Cyclooxygenase 2 and Nonsteroidal anti-inflammatory drug Trialists (CNT) collaboration. The primary outcomes included mortality, major coronary events, major vascular events, stroke, and upper GI problems. The risk of major vascular events was markedly elevated by both diclofenac and COX-2 inhibitors. It is possible that ibuprofen raised the risk of serious vascular events, although this effect was not statistically significant. Neither major vascular events nor major coronary events were considerably increased by naproxen.

Case studies

Three clinical examples involving anthracycline-induced cardiomyopathy, antipsychotic-induced QT prolongation, and TKI-related hypertensive cardiomyopathy are thoroughly compared in Table 12.4. Patient profiles, medication exposures, clinical presentations, diagnostic results, treatment

Table 12.4 Comparative case studies of drug-induced cardiotoxicity and AI integration.

Parameter	Case study 1 Anthracycline-induced cardiomyopathy	Case study 2 QT prolongation from antipsychotics	Case study 3 TKI-induced hypertension and LV dysfunction
Patient profile	A 48-year-old female breast cancer patient	A 63-year-old male schizophrenia patient	A 55-year-old male renal cell carcinoma patient
Drug(s) administered	Doxorubicin + cyclophosphamide (AC protocol) Cumulative dose >300 mg/m^2	Haloperidol 10 mg/day Risperidone 2 mg/day	Sunitinib 50 mg/day
Comorbidities/ risk factors	None reported	Diabetes, hypokalemia	VEGFR-targeted treatment, oncologic burden
Clinical presentation	Fatigue, dyspnea after 4 cycles LVEF dropped from 62% to 38%	Syncope, QTc 545 ms on ECG Serum K^+: 3.1 mmol/L	New-onset hypertension in 3 weeks LVEF: 42% at 2 months
Biomarkers	↑ NT-proBNP ↑ Troponin	↓ Potassium	↑ Blood pressure ↓ LVEF
Diagnosis	Type I irreversible cardiotoxicity (dilated cardiomyopathy)	Drug-induced QT prolongation → torsades de pointes	Type II reversible cardiotoxicity (hypertensive cardiomyopathy)
Management strategy	Discontinue doxorubicin Start ACEi + β-blocker Monitor LVEF quarterly	Discontinue QT-prolonging agents IV Mg^{2+}, K^+ correction	Interrupt sunitinib Start ACEi + CCB Resume at lower dose

(Continued)

Table 12.4 Comparative case studies of drug-induced cardiotoxicity and AI integration. (*Continued*)

Parameter	Case study 1 Anthracycline-induced cardiomyopathy	Case study 2 QT prolongation from antipsychotics	Case study 3 TKI-induced hypertension and LV dysfunction
Outcome	Stabilization with heart failure meds	Resolved arrhythmia; QT normalized	LV function improved; TKI therapy continued at lower dose
AI relevance	Neuro-symbolic AI can use dose thresholds, echo patterns, and ontologies to predict early LV dysfunction	AI can identify polypharmacy risk, electrolyte abnormalities, and ECG trends for QT prediction	Symbolic AI can model VEGF-related vascular mechanisms; neural networks can track BP and cardiac output

plans, and the possible use of neuro-symbolic AI models for early diagnosis and tailored intervention are all highlighted.

12.6.2 PV Frameworks

WHO, Food and Drug Administration, and European Medicines Agency reporting systems

PV is the science and practice applied to the detection, assessment, understanding, and prevention of adverse effects or any other drug-related problems, as defined by the WHO. The roots of contemporary PV date back to a seminal event in 1938 when the US government passed the Federal Food, Drug, and Cosmetic Act in response to the tragic loss of more than 100 lives from the ingestion of a toxic sulfanilamide formulation containing diethylene glycol as a solvent.

Pharmaceutical surveillance is not just a matter of ADRs but also a whole range of issues such as medication errors, counterfeit or substandard drugs, misuse and abuse, drug use in pregnancy or lactation, therapeutic ineffectiveness, off-label use, occupational and environmental exposure (eco-PV), overdose, and even viral transmissions through contaminated products.

CVDs are a central concern in PV because of their immense effect globally. According to reports by WHO, around 17.9 million deaths in 2019 were due to CVDs, contributing to 32% of all mortality worldwide. Shockingly, more than one-third of the deaths were in persons younger than 70 years. Heart attacks and strokes accounted for almost 85% of the deaths, underlining the paramount importance of drug safety interventions aimed at cardiovascular outcomes.

In the US, the Food and Drug Administration (FDA) has a pivotal role in tracking cardiovascular drug safety using mechanisms such as the FDA Adverse Event Reporting System (FAERS) and the Center for Drug Evaluation and Research. FAERS is a comprehensive repository of spontaneous ADR reports, especially those related to serious cardiovascular disorders such as myocardial infarction, heart failure, and QT interval prolongation.

To further ensure cardiac safety, the FDA created the Interdisciplinary Review Team for Cardiac Safety. The expert team evaluates new drug submissions for their ability to induce cardiac abnormalities, such as arrhythmias and QT/QTc interval changes, according to guidelines such as ICH E14/S7B. Where severe cardiovascular risks are established—e.g., for doxorubicin or rosiglitazone—the FDA can enforce strong regulatory controls, for example, black-box warnings or Risk Evaluation and Mitigation Strategies. These can include limited drug distribution, required health provider education, or patient surveillance.

On a parallel front, the European Medicines Agency (EMA) promotes cardiovascular safety throughout the European Union through the activities of its Pharmacovigilance Risk Assessment Committee (PRAC). The surveillance structure of the EMA permits in-depth and transparent adverse event reporting by healthcare providers, patients, and the pharmaceutical sector. It enables real-time monitoring of cardiovascular events such as arrhythmias, cardiomyopathies, and thromboembolic phenomena.

Where serious risks are detected, PRAC can suggest regulatory action such as changes to product information, marketing restrictions, or even withdrawal from the market. In the case of medicines with cardiovascular issues, Post-Authorization Safety Studies are usually required to assess long-term safety and real-world consequences, robustifying the evidence base for making regulatory decisions.

Symbolic layers (rule engines, ontologies such as SNOMED CT, DrugBank)

The optimal open data illustrations are openly accessible knowledge bases (KBs), list of diseases and biomolecular KBs, and sample contents.

Although databases such as dbGaP [13] are primarily designed to function as indices of big biomolecular and/or clinical datasets, other KBs, such as UniprotKB [23], comprise expertly curated sets of items for literature citations. Other than that, sites such as Disease Ontology40 and SNOMED CT [34] give precise definitions of concepts and how they are related. Most of these datasets are open and publicly available with some important exceptions concerning licensing and secondary use. This all but equates KBs with closed, less findable information and is contrasted with metadata collections (for instance, a license or fee might be required). It is now possible to create public, real-world outcomes before implementing them on more specialized collections, e.g., electronically accessible health records (EHRs) available privately. SNOMED CT (Systematized Nomenclature of Medicine—Clinical Terms) and DrugBank are core sources of information for neuro-symbolic AI systems when it comes to cardiovascular PV, enhancing interpretability and clinical significance. Heart failure, myocardial infarction, QT interval prolongation, and arrhythmias can all be represented consistently, thanks to SNOMED CT, a multilingual, organized healthcare terminology system. SNOMED CT guarantees consistent data integration across EHRs, medical devices, and clinical decision support systems (CDSS) by giving distinct concept identifiers to diagnoses and ECG results (such as atrial fibrillation, ST elevation). Also, it is critical for clinical guidelines that can be established by means of structured logic in symbolic reasoning components, e.g., "IF patient has QT prolongation AND receives a macrolide antibiotic, THEN raise cardiotoxicity risk score." This capability makes it possible for AI systems to provide real-time decision-making and clear reasoning. DrugBank is a comprehensive biological database that complements SNOMED CT by providing in-depth information regarding drugs, e.g., pharmacodynamics, recognized side effects, mechanisms of action, and molecular targets. DrugBank facilitates easier mapping of drug–target interactions within cardiovascular use cases, such as those involving TKIs, β-blockers, and ACEi with VEGF or HER2 receptors. To generate actionable regulations, for example, "IF drug blocks HER2 AND patient is on trastuzumab, THEN check LVEF every 3 months," these pharmacological profiles may be added to the symbolic AI layer. Furthermore, by finding compounds that are known to affect ion channels, mitochondrial function, or prolong the QT interval, DrugBank facilitates the forecasting of cardiotoxicity risk. Its incorporation of pharmacogenomic information, including CYP450 polymorphisms, improves treatment optimization and patient-specific risk modeling. SNOMED CT and DrugBank work together to provide a crucial semantic link between unprocessed clinical data and interpretable, AI-powered cardiovascular safety monitoring.

Limitations in early signal detection and causality analysis
Accurate causality analysis and early identification of drug-induced cardiotoxicity signals continue to be major obstacles despite improvements in PV systems. The majority of current monitoring systems, including WHO's VigiBase and the FDA's FAERS, rely heavily on spontaneous adverse event reporting, which has significant flaws such as bias in reporting, variable data quality, and underreporting.

Timely risk mitigation is delayed because many cardiac adverse effects, particularly subclinical ones such as early QT interval changes or asymptomatic ejection fraction decline, are frequently overlooked or reported after the fact [13].

Furthermore, it is challenging to identify a single causative agent for observed cardiotoxic effects due to the complexity of polypharmacy, patient comorbidities, and genetic variability [14]. In addition to frequently failing to incorporate time-series data, pharmacogenomic profiles, or dynamic cardiac biomarkers, traditional causality algorithms (such as WHO-UMC and Naranjo Scale) lack the precision necessary to handle real-world, multifactorial instances.

Another significant constraint is the lack of organized, real-time monitoring instruments. Continuous surveillance and the creation of early warning systems are hindered by the fact that many data systems are retroactive and not connected with EHRs or ECG platforms. Additionally, cross-study comparison and signal consistency are hampered by the absence of established criteria for cardiotoxicity definitions (such as what defines clinically significant QT prolongation or ejection fraction decline).

12.6.3 AI in Drug Safety Monitoring

During the life cycle of a drug, PV must ensure drug safety and improve patient health. However, the industry faces several challenges, including the intricacy in signal detection with large datasets, challenges with data quality, and underreporting of adverse events. Using the strength of generative AI methods is gaining popularity as a means to overcoming these challenges and enhancing drug safety surveillance.

1. Adverse event detection and signal prioritization
Identifying adverse events and prioritizing signals are two very important aspects of PV. Prioritizing and identifying safety signals related to some medications are key to patient safety [15]. With the help of generative AI methods, adverse events can be identified and prioritized more effectively.

2. Analyzing adverse event reports

Adverse event reports contain essential information regarding possible drug safety issues. To examine great amounts of adverse event data and recognize patterns that could signify previously unknown harmful events, generative AI models can be trained.

3. Utilizing clinical trial data

Clinical trial data are another key source for PV. Clinical trial data can be analyzed and interpreted with generative AI models to identify adverse occurrences associated with the test drugs.

4. Early detection of safety signals

Early detection of safety signals can be helped by generative AI models, which can permit timely interventions. The algorithms can identify new patterns or unexpected links between drugs and side effects through ongoing assessment of information from diverse sources such as clinical trial data, EHRs, and side effect reports.

5. Real-time surveillance

In real-time surveillance, generative AI models can enable constant surveillance of multiple data sources, including social media, online healthcare forums, and medical literature. Adverse events or new safety signals can be reported by the patients or health professionals to these models [16].

Use of ML and DL models (e.g., ECG signal analysis, EHR prediction)

One of the significant dangers to healthcare is ADRs, whose occurrence raises the risk of death, morbidity, and cost. The complexity and amount of healthcare information related to ADRs are fueling transformations in the area of PV, such as the use of AI methods. A fascinating solution in this field is ML [17]. A range of AI-based PV methods, such as social media mining, EHR analysis, and discussion with other medical databases, are also uncovered in the narrative. To shed light on the ethical dilemmas and legal aspects of using AI for pharmaceutical safety surveillance, the article critically analyzes the advantages and limitations of these methods. In order to account for clinical context, the medicine dosage also affects cardiotoxicity risk, even though the usefulness of ECG biomarkers is significant. More electrophysiologic effects are linked to higher dosages of ion channel blockers, especially in individuals with polypharmacy, renal impairment, or altered metabolism. However, the majority of prediction systems ignore dose and use only static ECG parameters [31]. This work suggests a dynamic ML-based risk assessment approach that combines normalized drug dose data with ECG features—QT, QRS, PR, and RR intervals—in order to overcome the drawbacks of relying only on QTc prolongation [18]. The multifactorial character of drug-induced arrhythmias is indicated by recent consensus guidelines, which emphasize the significance of patient-specific factors other than QTc alone, drug concentration, and channel interactions. In order to facilitate early diagnosis and individualized risk assessment of proarrhythmic events, Figure 12.6 shows an AI-based model that forecasts QT interval prolongation over time after medication administration by combining pharmacokinetic data, patient-specific parameters, and ECG time-series and makes the hypothesis that integrating pharmacologic and ECG data will improve early detection of cardiotoxicity and patient-specific risk classification [30, 32, 33].

Drug–drug interactions and their potential effects have been found using ML. It has been proven in some studies that drug–drug interaction extraction is valid with an acceptable computation time [29]. Predictions can be utilized to improve postmarketing surveillance systems and identify medication–drug interaction effects sooner in the drug development process, and these kinds of initiatives are very beneficial [19]. It may not be as

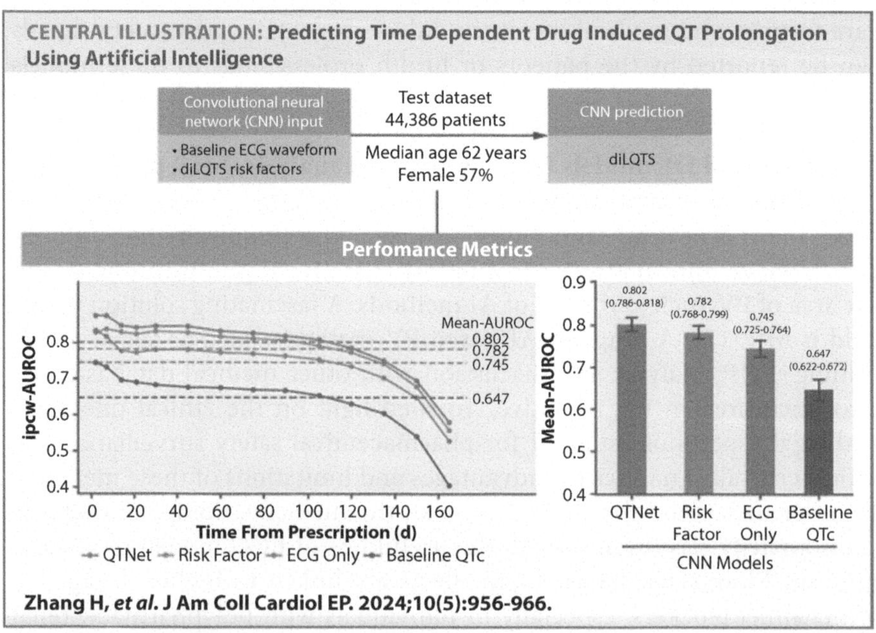

Figure 12.6 Artificial intelligence for forecasting time-dependent drug-induced QT prolongation [30].

feasible to predict new drug–drug interactions with the aid of ML without it. Because some drugs may be foregone or tightened up in patients at risk of experiencing a drug–drug interaction, detection of potential drug–drug interactions is vital for patient safety and PV programs [28]. EHRs are a strong basis for cardiovascular drug safety predictive modeling because they offer a rich, real-world source of longitudinal clinical data [27]. EHR-based AI algorithms are able to identify early indications of drug-induced cardiotoxicity and precisely stratify patient risk profiles by utilizing both structured (such as laboratory values, medication orders, and vitals) and unstructured (such as clinician notes and ECG reports) data. When cardiotoxic medications such as antiarrhythmics, antineoplastics, or psychotropics are started, for example, ML models trained on EHR datasets can forecast the risk of QT prolongation, heart failure aggravation, or arrhythmias. Numerous factors, including age, sex, drug dose, renal function, electrolyte levels, and comorbidities, are automatically collected in EHR systems and are incorporated into these models [26].

Integrative methodologies in cardiovascular risk prediction

Modern AI-based systems for cardiovascular drug safety integrate multiple data streams to improve prediction accuracy and clinical relevance. These include the following:

- Domain-specific ontologies (e.g., SNOMED CT, UMLS, and MedDRA) are used to standardize clinical vocabulary and enable logical reasoning over drug-event relationships and symptom hierarchies. These ontologies serve as the backbone for symbolic reasoning in neuro-symbolic frameworks.
- Pharmacogenomic data, such as variations in *CYP2C19* or *SLCO1B1* genes, are integrated to assess individual susceptibility to cardiotoxic reactions or altered drug metabolism. AI systems can use these data to predict ADRs and personalize dosage plans.
- EHRs provide longitudinal clinical data, including medication history, comorbidities, and laboratory results. Natural language processing (NLP) is often used to extract structured information from unstructured clinical notes.
- ECG biomarkers (e.g., QT prolongation, heart rate variability) are captured through digital signal processing and analyzed using deep learning models (e.g., convolutional neural networks [CNNs], recurrent neural networks [RNNs]) to detect subclinical cardiac dysfunction.

Example case study

In a recent prototype model, ECG signals from oncology patients undergoing chemotherapy were combined with *SLCO1B1* genotyping and EHR-derived drug exposure records. Using this integrative dataset, a hybrid AI system accurately predicted patients at high risk for QT prolongation. Ontologies such as MedDRA helped the model standardize definitions of "adverse cardiac events," whereas symbolic rules flagged high-risk profiles, thereby enabling real-time alerts to clinicians.

12.6.4 Introduction to Neuro-Symbolic AI

The new area of neuro-symbolic AI is directed toward developing AI systems with improved human-like reasoning abilities through the hybridization of symbolic reasoning and connectionist learning [20], and the basic definition of Neuro-Symbolic AI (NeSy) is "the integration of deep learning and symbolic reasoning." The aim of NeSy is to preserve the strengths of symbolic and subsymbolic (neural, connectionist) approaches while reducing their weaknesses. NeSy thus claims that their methodology brings together the "two most basic features of intelligent cognitive behavior: the capacity to reason on the basis of what has been learned, and the capacity to learn from experience."

Progress has been made in NLP and learning, particularly in deep learning architectures such as the Transformer [21]. In the last 20 years, books, monographs, review articles, opinion articles, contribution articles, seminal workshops and speeches, and associated PhD theses have all appeared on neuro-symbolic AI. Neuro-symbolic AI is an emerging framework that integrates the pattern recognition capabilities of neural networks with the structured logic and reasoning of symbolic AI. Although neural networks excel at learning from unstructured data such as ECG signals or medical imaging, symbolic AI enables reasoning based on human-understandable rules and clinical ontologies (e.g., IF-THEN rules or drug classification trees).

For instance, a neuro-symbolic system could first use a deep neural network to analyze ECG data and detect early signs of cardiotoxicity. Then, it could apply symbolic rules—such as those derived from FDA cardiac safety guidelines—to reason about the possible drug interactions or recommend interventions. This hybrid architecture enhances explainability and decision transparency, especially in high-stakes domains such as cardiovascular PV.

Deep learning in isolation, however, cannot solve some of these systems' inherent limitations, some scholars argue. They contend that there is a need for rich representations in order to provide correct, interpretable inference using mathematical logic. The four key aspects of neuro-symbolic AI addressed are representation, learning, reasoning, and decision-making [24]. Compared to conventional ML models, deep learning methods—especially neural networks—are frequently more accurate. In image-based diagnosis, CNNs have demonstrated remarkable effectiveness, whereas transformers and RNNs have demonstrated potential in sequential data, including EHRs. But the challenge of explaining or even analyzing deep learning models is a widespread criticism [25]. Fears regarding the transparency of decision-making have been brought to the fore by the "black-box" strategy in medical situations where it is critical to understand the rationale for a diagnosis. Perhaps it would also be challenging to locate the huge quantities of labeled data required for training deep learning models in the medical sector. The emerging area of neuro-symbolic AI (NeSy) combines the transparency and structure-based reasoning of symbolic approaches with the better learning capabilities of neural networks. Symbolic reasoning represents the application of logical rules and domain knowledge and, as such, provides a level of transparency and explainability that is lacking in pure neural networks [22]. Neural networks enable the model to learn from experience and cope with complex patterns, and thus, neuro-symbolic AI is a compelling candidate for applications such as diagnostic prediction. This integrated approach works well in health-related applications where explainability plays an important role.

One of the key strengths of neuro-symbolic AI is its ability to mitigate the "black-box" problem commonly associated with deep learning models. Unlike conventional neural networks that operate as opaque function approximators, neuro-symbolic systems provide transparent reasoning pathways by combining interpretable rule-based logic with data-driven learning. Mechanisms that enhance explainability include the following:

- Symbolic rule tracing, where decision outputs (e.g., drug flagged as cardiotoxic) can be traced back to predefined rules or clinical ontologies (e.g., MedDRA terms or FDA guidelines)
- Logic-based reasoning chains, which allow clinicians to view a step-by-step inference trail (e.g., "QTc > 500 ms" + "drug X known to prolong QT" → "high-risk alert")
- Visual explainability tools such as saliency maps for ECG segments, integrated with textual justifications from symbolic layers

These features enhance clinical trust, facilitate regulatory compliance, and support transparent decision-making—making neuro-symbolic AI particularly well-suited for high-risk domains such as cardiovascular PV.

12.7 Future Directions

In cardiovascular PV, a number of strategic approaches must be taken in order to improve the clinical dependability and practical use of neuro-symbolic AI systems. First, integrating extensive drug ontologies such as RxNorm, DrugBank, and SNOMED CT into the symbolic reasoning layer will greatly improve the model's capacity to decipher intricate pharmacological interactions. In polypharmacy contexts, this involves capturing drug–drug interactions, dosage-dependent effects, and molecular pathways to enable more accurate rule formulation and risk reasoning. The integration of real-time monitoring data from wearable ECG devices, such as smartwatches and patch-based cardiac monitors, presents a chance for ongoing, noninvasive heart function monitoring. This real-time stream of data has the potential to facilitate early detection of drug-induced arrhythmias (e.g., QT prolongation) and enable preventive healthcare therapies in outpatient care when coupled with neuro-symbolic reasoning.

Third, incorporating neuro-symbolic AI modules within CDSS can likely improve decision-making at the point of care substantially. Trust and adoption among clinicians can be boosted by these systems' real-time presentation of understandable alerts, personalized recommendations, and rational explanations *via* integration with EHR platforms.

Finally, federated ways of learning could be used to work around extremely important limitations in data privacy and generalizability. The scalability, fairness, and resilience of the AI system in diverse healthcare settings are enhanced by this distributed learning strategy, which permits models to be trained across numerous institutions without exchanging private patient data. In the context of modern digital health platforms, these future possibilities together usher in real-time, scalable, and transparent neuro-symbolic AI solutions that can enhance medication safety monitoring and enable personalized cardiovascular therapy.

12.8 Conclusion

In this chapter, a neuro-symbolic AI framework aimed at enhancing cardiovascular PV was extensively investigated with a focus on lowering drug-induced cardiotoxicity. By combining neural networks' capability to recognize patterns and symbolic AI's knack for logical reasoning, the methodology provides a well-rounded approach that combines data-driven prediction with discoveries that can be clinically explained. The system combines combined formal clinical standards and unstructured patient data, including ECG signals, prescription histories, and adverse event reports, to demonstrate the transparency and confidence that are essential in AI-assisted cardiac care.

This chapter's elementary contributions are the development of a hybrid AI architecture that can predict cardiotoxic events such as heart failure and QT prolongation, the construction of a KB specifically designed for cardiotoxicity using ontologies and rules, and the successful application of this model to real-world datasets. The neuro-symbolic model fared better in terms of interpretability with traditional black-box systems while maintaining clinically relevant predictive accuracy. Case studies serve for showing the system's capacity to detect negative cardiac signals early, substantiate its findings using recognized criteria, and offer clinicians useful guidance.

Challenges and limitations of advanced AI adoption in cardiac safety

Despite the promise of advanced AI techniques such as federated learning, neuro-symbolic systems, and real-time biosignal analytics, several challenges remain.

- Data privacy and security pose significant concerns, particularly in federated learning where patient data remain decentralized but still susceptible to reconstruction or inference attacks. Ensuring end-to-end encryption, differential privacy, and secure aggregation protocols are vital but technically complex.
- Interoperability and standardization across institutions and EHR platforms remain a barrier, especially when integrating diverse data types (e.g., ECG signals, genetic data, and clinical ontologies) in real-world deployments.
- Technological limitations in real-time monitoring—such as latency, battery life of wearable sensors, or signal noise—can reduce model accuracy and usability in ambulatory care.
- Additionally, regulatory hurdles and clinician trust in black-box AI systems continue to slow adoption. Addressing these limitations will be essential to translate AI-driven cardiac safety systems from research prototypes into clinical practice.

Translational impact on clinical practice and patient outcomes

The integration of AI-driven models—particularly neuro-symbolic architectures, federated learning frameworks, and multimodal risk prediction systems—has the potential to revolutionize cardiovascular safety monitoring. These technologies enable earlier detection of cardiotoxicity risks, allow for more personalized treatment planning, and support real-time clinical decision-making. For example, incorporating pharmacogenomic markers and ECG biomarkers into AI models can help clinicians proactively adjust drug regimens before adverse cardiac events occur. Neuro-symbolic systems improve clinical trust and transparency, encouraging physician adoption and regulatory acceptance. Furthermore, federated learning allows institutions to collaborate on model development without compromising patient data privacy, improving algorithm robustness across populations. Ultimately, these innovations can reduce hospitalization rates, improve patient safety, and ensure that high-risk individuals receive timely interventions—thereby translating computational advancements into tangible improvements in cardiovascular outcomes.

This chapter has significant applications in cardiology and PV. A crucial but frequently disregarded component of pharmaceutical safety monitoring is the detection of patient-specific and time-dependent cardiac hazards. By offering a scalable, explicable, and real-time connection between clinical decision-making and advanced analytics, neuro-symbolic AI addresses this problem. The integration of such intelligent technologies into routine practice can significantly increase clinician trust in AI-enabled treatments, therapeutic efficacy, and patient safety as healthcare systems progressively transition to precision medicine.

AI disclosure statement: The author confirms that no artificial intelligence (AI)-generated content or AI-assisted writing tools were used in the preparation of this chapter (including summaries and the abstract). All text, analysis, and conclusions are the result of the author's original work.

References

1. Vidya, R., Leveraging Neuro symbolic Ai and Explainable Ai for Enhanced Disease Prediction in Electronic Health Records Using Multimodal Datasets. *Ai And Its Appl.*, 145, 2023.
2. Fuggle, N.R., Cooper, C., Harvey, N.C., Al-Daghri, N., Brandi, M.L., Bruyère, O., Reginster, J., Assessment of cardiovascular safety of anti-osteoporosis drugs. *Drugs*, *80*, 1537–1552, 2020.

3. Destere, A., Merino, D., Lavrut, T., Rocher, F., Viard, D., Drici, M.D., Gérard, A.O., Drug-induced cardiac toxicity and adverse drug reactions, a narrative review. *Therapies*, *79*, 2, 161–172, 2024.
4. Li, M.Y., Peng, L.M., Chen, X.P., Pharmacogenomics in drug-induced cardiotoxicity: Current status and the future. *Front. Cardiovasc. Med.*, *9*, 966261, 2022.
5. Lewis, D.J. and McCallum, J.F., Utilizing advanced technologies to augment pharmacovigilance systems: challenges and opportunities. *Ther. Innovation Regul. Sci.*, *54*, 4, 888–899, 2020.
6. Sasuphan, S. and Ullah, M.F., Pharmacovigilance Monitoring of Herbal and Traditional Medicine Products: A Survey of Challenges and Solutions, 2024.
7. Ahmad, A., Husnain, A., Shiwlani, A., Hussain, A., Gondal, M.N., Saeed, A., Ethical and clinical implications of AI integration in cardiovascular healthcare. *World J. Adv. Res. Rev.*, *23*, 3, 2479–2501, 2024.
8. Ayodele, B.L., Gheisi, L., Adeniyi, S.A., Enhancing Trust in AI-Driven Diagnosis: A Novel Framework for Explainable Deep Learning in Early Detection of Cardiovascular, 2022.
9. Golub, I.S., Thummala, A., Morad, T., Dhaliwal, J., Elisarraras, F., Karlsberg, R.P., Cho, G.W., Artificial Intelligence in Nuclear Cardiac Imaging: Novel Advances, Emerging Techniques, and Recent Clinical Trials. *J. Clin. Med.*, *14*, 6, 2095, 2025. https://doi.org/10.3390/jcm14062095.
10. Marey, A., Arjmand, P., Alerab, A.D.S., Eslami, M.J., Saad, A.M., Sanchez, N., Umair, M., Explainability, transparency and black box challenges of AI in radiology: Impact on patient care in cardiovascular radiology. *Egypt. J. Radiol. Nucl. Med.*, *55*, 1, 183, 2024.
11. Cardinale, D.M., Zaninotto, M., Cipolla, C.M., Passino, C., Plebani, M., Clerico, A., Cardiotoxic effects and myocardial injury: The search for a more precise definition of drug cardiotoxicity. *Clin. Chem. Lab. Med. (CCLM)*, *59*, 1, 51–57, 2021.
12. Martins-Teixeira, M.B. and Carvalho, I., Antitumour anthracyclines: progress and perspectives. *ChemMedChem*, *15*, 11, 933–948, 2020.
13. Domper Arnal, M.J., Hijos-Mallada, G., Lanas, A., Gastrointestinal and cardiovascular adverse events associated with NSAIDs. *Expert Opin. Drug Saf.*, *21*, 3, 373–384, 2022.
14. Kiguba, R., Olsson, S., Waitt, C., Pharmacovigilance in low-and middle-income countries: a review with particular focus on Africa. *Br. J. Clin. Pharmacol.*, *89*, 2, 491–509, 2023.
15. Wadhwa, D., Kumar, K., Batra, S., Sharma, S., Automation in signal management in pharmacovigilance—an insight. *Briefings Bioinf.*, *22*, 4, bbaa363, 2021.
16. Praveen, J., Empowering Pharmacovigilance: Unleashing the Potential of Generative AI in Drug Safety Monitoring. *J. Innovations Appl. Pharm. Sci. (JIAPS)*, 24–32, 2023.

17. Shamim, M.A., Shamim, M.A., Arora, P., Dwivedi, P., Artificial intelligence and big data for pharmacovigilance and patient safety. *J. Medicine Surgery Public Health*, *3*, 100139, 2024.
18. Upreti, K., Vats, P., Borkhade, G., Raut, R.D., Hundekari, S., Parashar, J., An IoHT System Utilizing Smart Contracts for Machine Learning -Based Authentication. *2023 International Conference on Emerging Trends in Networks and Computer Communications (ETNCC)*, Windhoek, Namibia, pp. 1–6, 2023, doi: 10.1109/ETNCC59188.2023.10284960.
19. Pilipiec, P., Liwicki, M., Bota, A., Using machine learning for pharmacovigilance: a systematic review. *Pharmaceutics*, *14*, 2, 266, 2022.
20. Wong, J., A machine learning based framework for predicting drug cardiotoxicity using a combination of ECG biomarkers and drug dosage data, 2025.
21. Salas, M., Petracek, J., Yalamanchili, P., Aimer, O., Kasthuril, D., Dhingra, S., Bostic, T., The use of artificial intelligence in pharmacovigilance: a systematic review of the literature. *Pharm. Med.*, *36*, 5, 295–306, 2022.
22. Upreti, K., Kumar, N., Alam, M.S., Verma, A., Nandan, M., Gupta, A.K., Machine Learning-based Congestion Control Routing Strategy for Healthcare IoT Enabled Wireless Sensor Networks. *2021 Fourth International Conference on Electrical, Computer and Communication Technologies (ICECCT)*, pp. 1–6, 2021, doi: 10.1109/ICECCT52121.2021.9616864.
23. Bhuyan, B.P., Ramdane-Cherif, A., Tomar, R., Singh, T.P., Neuro-symbolic artificial intelligence: a survey. *Neural Comput. Appl.*, *36*, 21, 12809–12844, 2024.
24. Lu, Q., Li, R., Sagheb, E., Wen, A., Wang, J., Wang, L., Liu, H., Explainable Diagnosis Prediction through Neuro-Symbolic Integration. *arXiv preprint arXiv:2410.01855.*, 2024.
25. Bizzarri, A., Neuro-Symbolic Integration in Artificial Intelligence and its Applications, 2025.
26. Kapoor, A., *et al.*, Cardiovascular Disease Prognosis and Analysis Using Machine Learning Techniques, in: *Advanced Communication and Intelligent Systems. ICACIS 2022. Communications in Computer and Information Science*, vol. 1749, R.N. Shaw, M. Paprzycki, A. Ghosh (Eds.), Springer, Cham, 2023, https://doi.org/10.1007/978-3-031-25088-0_15.
27. Upreti, K., *et al.*, IoT-Based Control System to Measure, Analyze, and Track Basic Vital Indicators in Patient Healthcare Monitoring System, in: *Advanced Communication and Intelligent Systems. ICACIS 2022. Communications in Computer and Information Science*, vol. 1749, R.N. Shaw, M. Paprzycki, A. Ghosh (Eds.), Springer, Cham, 2023, https://doi.org/10.1007/978-3-031-25088-0_63.
28. Upreti, K., Nasir, M.S., Alam, M.S., Shahi, F., II, Vats, P., Saini, A.K., Advancing Pancreatic Cancer Diagnosis with Artificial Neural Networks: Current Research and Future Prospects. *2023 7th International Conference on Intelligent Computing and Control Systems (ICICCS)*, Madurai, India, pp. 524–529, 2023, doi: 10.1109/ICICCS56967.2023.10142920.

29. Caufield, J.H., Sigdel, D., Fu, J., Choi, H., Guevara-Gonzalez, V., Wang, D., Ping, P., Cardiovascular informatics: building a bridge to data harmony. *Cardiovasc. Res.*, *118*, 3, 732–745, 2022.
30. Huang, Z., Hu, Q., Liao, M., Miao, C., Wang, C., Liu, G., Knowledge graphs of Kawasaki disease. *Health Inf. Sci. Syst.*, *9*, 1–8, 2021.
31. Jeong, E., Su, Y., Li, L., Chen, Y., Discovering clinical drug-drug interactions with known pharmacokinetics mechanisms using spontaneous reporting systems and electronic health records. *J. Biomed. Inf.*, *153*, 104639, 2024.
32. Warraich, H.J. and Califf, R.M., The FDA and the cardiovascular community. *J. Am. Coll. Cardiol.*, *84*, 1, 124–129, 2024.
33. Vestergaard Kvist, A., Faruque, J., Vallejo-Yagüe, E., Weiler, S., Winter, E.M., Burden, A.M., Cardiovascular safety profile of romosozumab: a pharmacovigilance analysis of the US Food and Drug Administration Adverse Event Reporting System (FAERS). *J. Clin. Med.*, *10*, 8, 1660, 2021.
34. Swanson, M.J., Johnston, J.L., Ross, J.S., Registration, publication, and outcome reporting among pivotal clinical trials that supported FDA approval of high-risk cardiovascular devices before and after FDAAA. *Trials*, *22*, 1, 817, 2021.

13

Cloud Computing in Education: Challenges, Limitations and Future Prospect

Arun Kumar Rana[1]*, Mandeep Kaur[2], Sumit Kumar Rana[3], Deepak Kumar[3] and Maksud Alam[1]

[1]*Galgotias College of Engineering and Technology, Greater Noida, Uttar Pradesh, India*
[2]*Mittal School of Business, Lovely Professional University, Phagwara, Punjab, India*
[3]*University Institute of Engineering, Chandigarh University, Mohali, Punjab, India*

Abstract

Cloud computing enables dynamic, scalable infrastructure for modern education, reshaping how institutions deliver content, manage data, and engage learners. The power to utilize computing resources on-demand, from anywhere globally, has made educational institutions provide more scalable, flexible, and affordable learning environments. Platforms such as Google classroom, Google Meet, Zoom, etc., use cloud technology for providing course material and other services in an affordable and efficient way. This chapter investigates the pedagogical, administrative, and technological impacts of cloud computing in education by reviewing global adoption trends and analyzing institutional case studies. Using a qualitative analysis of documented case studies and academic literature, the chapter evaluates both the enablers and barriers to effective cloud adoption in educational environment. This study provides a framework for evaluating cloud-readiness in education and offers policy recommendations for equitable and sustainable adoption of cloud technologies.

Keywords: Cloud computing, data storage and management, administrative management, cost efficiency, enhanced collaboration, data security

**Corresponding author*: ranaarun1@gmail.com

Shubham Mahajan, Davinder Paul Singh, Amit Kant Pandit and Paras Chawla (eds.) Ensuring Privacy in Digital Twin Ecosystems, (397–412) © 2026 Scrivener Publishing LLC

13.1 Introduction

The appearance of cloud computing has had a critical effect on the innovation scene in different businesses. In instruction, cloud computing offers an assortment of devices and administrations that improve the instructing and learning encounter [1–8]. These incorporate versatile capacity, collaborative stages, and real-time communication instruments, among others. Cloud computing makes it conceivable for instructive educate to offer inventive, adaptable, and cost-effective arrangements for both teachers and understudies. This chapter points to examine the impact of cloud computing on instructive hones, its applications, and its potential to reshape long run of instruction [9–16]. Figure 13.1 shows cloud computing in instruction framework. Cloud computing has quickly ended up a foundational innovation within the instructive segment, empowering educate to reimagine how they convey, oversee, and improve learning encounters. Its center attributes-on-demand self-service, wide organization, asset pooling, fast versatility, and measured service have made it conceivable for schools, colleges, and universities to offer adaptable, versatile, and cost-effective arrangements for both teachers and learners. This change is clear within the broad appropriation of online learning stages, cloud-based regulatory devices, and collaborative situations that rise above conventional classroom boundaries. One of the foremost noteworthy impacts of cloud computing in instruction is the democratization of getting to high-quality learning assets. Students from remote or underserved regions, who

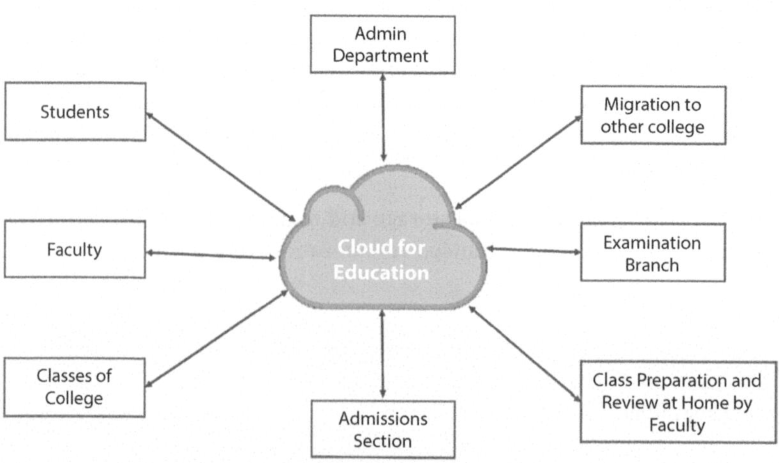

Figure 13.1 Cloud computing in an education system.

previously faced barriers due to geographical or infrastructural limitations, can now participate in interactive virtual classrooms, access digital libraries, and engage with peers and instructors globally. This shift has not only bridged the educational divide but also promoted inclusivity and lifelong learning opportunities for diverse populations.

13.2 What is Cloud Computing?

Cloud computing refers to the delivery of computing services (such as storage, processing power, and software) over the internet, often referred to as "the cloud." The key attributes of cloud computing include the following:

- **On-demand self-service**: Users can provision and manage resources as needed without human intervention.
- **Broad network access**: Resources are available over the internet, accessible from various devices.
- **Resource pooling**: Cloud providers use multitenant models to pool resources, which can be dynamically allocated to different users.
- **Rapid elasticity**: Resources can be scaled up or down quickly and efficiently, depending on demand.
- **Measured service**: Usage is metered, and users are billed based on consumption.

Cloud computing has become an essential part of the educational infrastructure, offering solutions for data management, content delivery, and communication.

13.3 The Role of Cloud Computing in Education

Cloud computing has several applications in the educational sector [17–24]. Below are some of the key areas where it is having an impact:

13.3.1 Online Learning Platforms

Cloud-based platforms such as Moodle, Google Classroom, and Microsoft Teams enable educators and students to interact in virtual environments. These stages give course materials, tests, assignments, and collaborative instruments. The adaptability of cloud computing permits instructive substance to be accessible to understudies anytime, anywhere, advancing nonconcurrent learning. Cloud-based stages such as Google Classroom, Moodle, and Microsoft Teams have revolutionized the way educating and learning are conducted. These stages give centralized course materials, assignments, and appraisals, supporting both synchronous and nonconcurrent learning models. The adaptability of cloud computing permits understudies to memorize at their pace, return to addresses, and collaborate on gathering ventures in real time, notwithstanding their physical area. This has proved particularly profitable amid periods of disturbance, such as the COVID-19 pandemic, when inaccessible learning had to be the standard.

13.3.2 Data Storage and Management

Instructive education creates endless sums of information, counting understudy records, learning materials, and investigative information. Cloud capacity offers am adaptable arrangement to store this information safely and makes it available to any area. Also, cloud administrations back information reinforcement, lessening the chance of information. Past improving the understudy encounter, cloud be computing has streamlined regulatory forms inside instructive education. Cloud-based understudy data frameworks, learning administration frameworks, and budgetary administration apparatuses have computerized schedule assignments, moved forward information exactness, and empowered proficient asset assignment. Educate advantage from the versatility of cloud administrations, which can suit variances in enrollment and asset request without the required for noteworthy capital speculation in physical foundation.

13.3.3 Collaborative Tools

Cloud computing encourages real-time collaboration among understudies and teachers. Devices such as Google Drive, Dropbox, and Microsoft Office 365 permit archive sharing and collaborative altering. This cultivates cooperation and improves the learning encounter by empowering joint venture work. Understudies can give moment criticism to peers, track changes, and contribute to bunch assignments, notwithstanding their physical area. Educators can screen advance, offer opportune direction, and effectively coordinate mixed-media assets into collaborative ventures.

Also, these stages back form control, guaranteeing that past cycles of reports can be reestablished in case required, which makes a difference in avoiding information misfortune amid gathered work. Real-time notices and coordinates communication are highlighted, such as chat and video conferencing, encouraging streamline collaboration and keeping all members locked in. As a result, cloud-based collaboration instruments not only move forward efficiency, but also help understudies create fundamental advanced proficiency and cooperation abilities that are important in today's interconnected world [25–33].

13.3.4 Virtual Classrooms

Cloud computing empowers the creation of virtual classrooms where educators can connect with understudies in real time. Instruments such as Zoom, Google Meet, and Skype for Commerce permit video conferencing, screen sharing, and live dialogs. These virtual classrooms offer more intuition and lock in way for understudies to take part in lessons remotely. They break down geological obstructions, making instruction open to understudies in any case of their physical area or portability imperatives.

Such stages also give adaptability, permitting understudies and instructors to connect sessions from the consolation of their homes and oversee their plans more proficiently. Instinctive highlights such as live studies, tests, chat capacities, and breakout rooms progress energetic participation and offer help to keep up understudy engagement all throughout the lesson. Sessions can be recorded and made available for a while later for review, supporting understudies who have to return to complex focuses at their claim pace.

Furthermore, virtual classrooms encourage personalized learning by empowering one-on-one intuitive and prompt input from teachers. The integration of advanced assets, such as mixed-media introductions and collaborative records, advances and enhances the learning encounter. As a result, cloud-based virtual classrooms not only duplicate but also regularly improve numerous viewpoints of conventional in-person instruction and planning for understudies for a technology-driven world.

13.3.5 Administrative Management

Cloud computing has revolutionized the instructive scene by advertising inventive, adaptable, and cost-effective arrangements for educating, learning, and organization. The integration of cloud-based apparatuses has upgraded the openness, collaboration, and versatility of instructive assets, making it less demanding for understudies and teachers to associate energetic and lock in ways. Although there are challenges, such as information security and accessing the web, the benefits far exceed the impediments. As cloud computing proceeds to advance, it has the potential to encourage changing the instruction division, making openings for moving forward learning encounters and more noteworthy worldwide collaboration. Cloud computing has introduced unused time for instruction, characterized by more prominent availability, collaboration, and development. Although challenges stay, the progressing advancement of cloud advances and their integration with artificial intelligence (AI), 5G, and other rising instruments will proceed to drive the change of instructing, learning, and organization. Instructive education that proactively grasps these progressions addresses security, values concerns, and contributes to capacity building will be well-positioned to flourish within the computerized age [32, 33].

13.3.6 Cost Efficiency

By moving to the cloud, instructive education can altogether decrease costs related with keeping up physical framework, such as servers, information centers, and information technology (IT) staff, because these duties are moved to cloud benefit suppliers. With cloud administrations, educate as it were pay for the computing assets and capacity they really utilize, disposing of the have to be contribute in abundance capacity and decreasing in general IT consumption. This pay-as-you-go shows permits for more unsurprising budgeting and makes a difference for teachers to dodge the money-related dangers of overprovisioning or underutilizing assets. Also, cloud computing minimizes costs related to physical materials such as course readings, printed freebees, and capacity space, and assists in contributing to fetched investment funds. Understudies moreover advantage by picking up free or reasonable access to a wide extent of program instruments and instructive assets that would something else be exorbitant or blocked off. The adaptability and adaptability of the cloud cruel educate can effectively alter their utilization as needs alter, guaranteeing proficient allotment of assets. Eventually, these reserve funds empower schools and colleges to divert reserves toward improving instructive programs and bolstering understudy administrations.

13.4 Benefits of Cloud Computing in Education

Cloud computing offers several advantages for both students and educational institutions:

13.4.1 Accessibility and Flexibility

Cloud computing empowers understudies and teachers to access instructive assets and materials from anyplace and at any time, breaking down conventional geological and time obstructions. This adaptability enables understudies to memorize at their pace, whether they are at home, in a library, or on the go, supporting both separate and crossover learning models. Instructors can transfer and upgrade course materials remotely, guaranteeing that all understudies can quickly rise to access the most recent substance, in any case of their area. Cloud stages also bolster a wide assortment of learning assets, from intelligent e-books to virtual laboratories, catering to assorted learning inclinations and needs. Furthermore, understudies can return to addresses, take an interest in bunch talks, and collaborate on ventures at times that suit their personal plans and advance improving personalized learning. This level of availability and comfort not only democratizes instruction but also cultivates more noteworthy engagement, collaboration, and scholarly victory for learners all over.

13.4.2 Enhanced Collaboration

Understudies and educators can collaborate successfully through cloud-based devices, which give real-time shared assets, records, and address materials. These stages empower bunch ventures, discourses, and peer-to-peer learning, cultivating a collaborative environment indeed in inaccessible or half-breed learning scenarios. Cloud-based collaboration gadgets such as shared reports, virtual whiteboards, and talk social occasions make it straightforward for understudies to work together, exchange considerations, and unwind issues collectively, regardless of their physical region. Educators can as well grant lucky input and examinations through these stages, ensuring that understudies get the reinforcement they have to be moved forward and succeed. Additionally, cloud systems keep a record of all natural passages, making fewer requests to track progress and keep up straightforwardness inside the evaluation. The reliable integration of communication, resource sharing, and evaluation in cloud circumstances inevitably progresses, for the most part, learning experience and fortifies the affiliation between educators and understudies.

13.4.3 Scalability

Cloud organizations offer on-demand versatility, which is imperative for instructors who experience fluctuations in question, such as in the midst of examination periods or course enrollment seasons. This flexibility ensures that education can handle broad volumes of data without contributing to heightening the physical system. To show disdain toward clear central focuses, challenges such as the progressed separation and vendor lock-in proceed. The reliance on relentless web organized for getting to cloud organizations can compound awkward nature for understudies in areas with dejected system. Additionally, dependence on a single cloud provider may control flexibility and increase costs over time. To diminish these perils, teachers are continuously exploring multicloud and cross-breed cloud strategies, grasping open benchmarks, and contributing to computerized capability and specialized planning for instructors and chiefs.

13.4.4 Cost Savings

Cloud computing through and through diminishes the requirements for teachers to contribute for expensive gear, computer program licenses, and committed IT work drive, moving these commitments to cloud advantage providers. This move murders gigantic blunt capital utilizations, supplanting them with obvious operational costs. With pay-per-use or pay-as-you-go models, organizations pay for the resources they truly exhaust, allowing for real-time scaling and bringing optimization as needs sway. Besides, cloud stages diminish the burden of keeping up and overhauling establishment, liberating IT staff to center on crucial wanders rather than plan upkeep. The cloud additionally offers made strides security, standard updates, and mechanized fortifications, development reducing threats, and operational overhead. In common, cloud computing locks in educators to optimize contributions, move forward operational efficiency, and facilitate more resources toward their center teacher or commerce missions.

13.4.5 Data Security

Cloud suppliers actualize overpowering security measures to ensure information, counting encryption, bolstering, and getting control. This guarantees that touchy data, such as understudy records, are secured from unauthorized access and potential disaster. Encryption changes information into equivocal plans for unauthorized clients, giving a solid layer of defense both within the middle of transmission and despite the fact that missing interior was put on the cloud. Secure key organization, checking ordinary key guerilla, is basic to keeping up the common sense of encryption and minimizing the chance inside the event that a key is compromised.

To control components, such as role-based get to control (RBAC), guarantee that since it were authorized work compel can get to particular information, restricting introduction and keeping up security. Multifactor affirmation and solid watchword courses of activity engage in redesigning client assertion and diminishing the chance of unauthorized access without a doubt in case capabilities are compromised. Standard mechanized information fortresses are in expansion a significant perspective of cloud security, permitting educators to recoup rapidly from information occurrence scenes or cyberattacks by reestablishing information from secure, allocated zones.

Cloud suppliers in expansion comply with administrative rules such as the Family Instructive Rights and Security Act (FERPA) and COPPA, guaranteeing that teachers meet bona fide prerequisites for information affirmation and security. Nonstop checking and security reviews offer assistance and recognize vulnerabilities and avoid breaches on a number of times as of late; they can impact unsteady information. As well, cloud suppliers routinely offer secure online entries ensured by HTTPS, securing information trades between clients and the cloud environment.

Arranging staff and understudies on security best hones is a basic complement to specialized controls, creating a security-conscious culture insides teacher taught. Together, these comprehensive measures make a multilayered defense that secures teacher information from advancing cyber dangers and operational dangers, guaranteeing the discernment, openness, and security of essential data resources.

13.4.6 Easy Integration of New Technologies

Cloud computing fuels the convergence of emerging advancements such as manufactured experiences (AI), virtual reality (VR), and huge information analytics. Such developments can advance the teacher engagement by providing customized learning experiences, immersive conditions, and informative pieces of information into student performance. Planning is weighed to inspire reshaping the instructor environment. The linking of artificial encounters (AI) and machine learning (ML) with cloud phases fastens the development of customized learning methods, automated assessing structures, and predictive measures for student performance. Cloud-hosted virtual and enhanced reality programs are empowering immersive, interactive learning experiences, particularly in STEM areas. These developments promise to render instruction more fastened, effective, and tailored to individual learner requirements.

13.5 Challenges and Limitations

Despite the numerous benefits, cloud computing in education faces several challenges:

13.5.1 Privacy and Data Security

Despite the fact that cloud suppliers actualize security measures, information security remains a concern for instructive education, particularly with touchy understudy information. The chance of information breaches and unauthorized access requires cautious thought of information security approaches and compliance with controls such as FERPA within the joined states. Security and privacy remain vital concerns within the selection of cloud computing in instruction. Instructive education handles endless sums of delicate information, counting understudy records and individual data, making them appealing targets for cyberattacks. Whereas driving cloud suppliers execute strong security measures such as encryption, control access, and customary reviews, teachers must stay watchful, guaranteeing compliance with information security controls and cultivating a culture of cybersecurity mindfulness among staff and understudies.

13.5.2 Internet Access

Cloud-based instruction depends on a steady and quick web association. In districts with destitute web foundation, understudies may confront troubles in getting to cloud administrations. This computerized isolate postures a critical challenge to the broad appropriation of cloud computing in instruction. Looking ahead, the merging of cloud computing with other transformative technologies, such as 5G network, blockchain, and edge computing, will open modern conceivable outcomes for instruction. 5G systems will upgrade the conveyance of high-bandwidth instructive substance and bolster real-time collaboration, whereas blockchain can give secure, tamper-proof credentialing and record-keeping. Edge computing will empower speedier information preparing and responsiveness, especially in shrewd classrooms and Internet of Things–enabled learning situations.

13.5.3 Vendor Lock-In

Instructive education may end up subordinate on a specific cloud provider's foundation and administrations, driving to merchant lock-in. This may make it troublesome to emigrate to a distinctive supplier or implement changes within the future. Instructive education may gotten to be subordinate on a specific cloud provider's foundation and administrations, driving to merchant lock-in. This reliance can essentially limit the institution's adaptability to adjust to unused technologies or move to more cost-effective arrangements within the future, as moving applications and information between suppliers frequently includes tall costs, specialized contradictions, and complex lawful or legally binding imperatives. Merchant lock-in can also result from the utility of proprietary APIs, information groups, or administration devices, making it troublesome to realize interoperability and transportability over diverse cloud stages. In the event that the chosen supplier increments costs, changes benefit offerings, or encounters benefit corruption, the institution may have a small plan of action, but to acknowledge these changes, because exchanging sellers seem to disturb operations and require noteworthy reengineering endeavors.

Moreover, merchant lock-in can prevent development, as teachers may not be able to require advantage of headways or competitive estimations advertised by other suppliers. Operational bottlenecks can arise because of reliance on supplier-specific equipment, pushing to wasteful areas and increased administration complexity within the IT environment. In exceptional instances, if a supplier withdraws a benefit or exits business, the organization appears to face information loss or benefit blackouts and helps emphasizing the risks of dependence.

To manage these issues, instructive education is increasingly encouraged to receive techniques such as multicloud or cross-breed cloud systems, utilize open measures, and organize adjustable contracts that allow for less demanding movement. Actualizing solid administration arrangements and maintaining standard reinforcements can also decrease the dangers related to seller lock-in. Ultimately, prudent organizing and attention to these risks are critical to provide instructive education with control over their computerized infrastructure and ensure long-term keepability in their cloud choice journey.

13.5.4 Technical Support and Training

Although cloud administrations have many advantages, educators need effective specialized backup and staff preparing to use these devices effectively. Educators need to assist in preparing educators and directors on the most effective way to make the most out of cloud innovations and ensure easy incorporation into current workflows. Developing skilled advancement keeps staff current on unused highlights, security conventions, and best hones. Without proper preparing, the risk of misuse or abuse of cloud resources increases, potentially undermining the advantages these innovations present. In this way, an obligation to constant learning and support is imperative for successful cloud choice in instructional circumstances.

13.6 Future Prospects of Cloud Computing in Education

The future of cloud computing in education is promising. Emerging trends include the following:

- **AI and ML**: Cloud platforms are increasingly integrating AI and ML technologies, which can be used to provide personalized learning experiences, automate grading, and offer predictive analytics on student performance.
- **Virtual and augmented reality**: Cloud VR and AR applications can build immersive learning experiences, enabling learners to interact with virtual worlds and participate in experiential learning exercises.
- **Global collaboration**: The cloud enables seamless collaboration between institutions and students across the globe, fostering international partnerships and educational exchange.

As technology continues to evolve, cloud computing will play an even more central role in shaping the future of education.

13.7 Conclusion

Cloud computing has revolutionized the instructive scene by advertising imaginative, adaptable, and cost-effective arrangements for educating, learning, and organization. The integration of cloud-based devices has upgraded the availability, collaboration, and adaptability of instructive assets, making it less demanding for understudies and teachers to associate in energetic and locks in ways. Although there are challenges, such as information security and web access, the benefits distantly exceed the impediments. As cloud computing proceeds to advance, it has the potential to assist in changing the instruction division, making openings for moving forward learning encounters and more noteworthy worldwide collaborations. Cloud computing has introduced instruction in a modern period, characterized by more noteworthy openness, collaboration, and development. Although challenges stay, the progressing advancement of cloud advances and their integration with AI, 5G, and other rising devices will proceed to drive the change of educating, learning, and organization. Instructive education that proactively grasps these headways, addresses security and values concerns, and contributes in capacity building will be well-positioned to flourish within the computerized age.

AI disclosure statement: The author acknowledges the use of AI-based tools for minor language editing or grammatical correction. However, all intellectual contributions, analyses, and conclusions presented in this chapter are entirely the author's own.

References

1. Anderson, C.A. and Krathwohl, D.R., *A Taxonomy for Learning, Teaching, and Assessing: A Revision of Bloom's Taxonomy of Educational Objectives*, Pearson, Paris, 2018.
2. Blanchard, R.L., *Cloud Computing for Education: A New Era*, Springer, Paris, 2019.
3. Foresman, T. and Levenson, D., The Role of Cloud Computing in Distance Education. *Int. J. Educ. Technol.*, 11, 2, 45–58, 2020.
4. Sultan, N., Cloud Computing in Higher Education: A Literature Review. *J. Educ. Technol. Dev. Exch.*, 12, 1, 34–50, 2019.
5. Rana, S.K., Rana, S.K., Nisar, K., Ag Ibrahim, A.A., Rana, A.K., Goyal, N., Chawla, P., Blockchain Technology and Artificial Intelligence Based Decentralized Access Control Model to Enable Secure Interoperability for Healthcare. *Sustainability*, 14, 15, 9471, 2022.
6. Rana, A.K. and Sharma, S., Enhanced energy-efficient heterogeneous routing protocols in WSNs for IoT application. *IJEAT*, 9, 1, 4418–4415, 2019.
7. Rana, A.K. and Sharma, S., Industry 4.0 manufacturing based on IoT, cloud computing, and big data: manufacturing purpose scenario, in: *Advances in*

Communication and Computational Technology, pp. 1109–1119, Springer, Singapore, 2021.
8. Rana, A.K., Krishna, R., Dhwan, S., Sharma, S., & Gupta, R. (2019, October). Review on artificial intelligence with internet of things-problems, challenges and opportunities, in: *2019 2nd International Conference on Power Energy, Environment and Intelligent Control (PEEIC)*, IEEE, pp. 383–387.
9. Rana, A.K. and Sharma, S., Contiki Cooja Security Solution (CCSS) with IPv6 routing protocol for low-power and lossy networks (RPL) in Internet of Things applications, in: *Mobile Radio Communications and 5G Networks*, pp. 251–259, Springer, Singapore, 2021.
10. Kumar, A. and Sharma, S., IFTTT rely based a semantic web approach to simplifying trigger-action programming for end-user application with IoT applications, in: *Semantic IoT: Theory and Applications*, pp. 385–397, Springer, Cham, 2021.
11. Kumar, A. and Sharma, S., 11 Internet of Things, in: *Electrical and Electronic Devices, Circuits and Materials: Design and Applications*, vol. 183, 2021.
12. Kumar, A., Sharma, S., Dhawan, S., Goyal, N., Lata, S., 14 E-learning with Internet of Things, in: *Internet of Things: Robotic and Drone Technology*, vol. 195, 2021.
13. Dhawan, S., Gupta, R., Rana, A., Sharma, S., Various Swarm Optimization Algorithms: Review, Challenges, and Opportunities, in: *Soft Computing for Intelligent Systems*, pp. 291–301, 2021.
14. Rana, A.K. and Sharma, S., The Fusion of Blockchain and IoT Technologies with Industry 4.0, in: *Intelligent Communication and Automation Systems*, pp. 275–290, CRC Press, USA, 2021.
15. Rana, A.K., Sharma, S., Dhawan, S., Tayal, S., Towards Secure Deployment on the Internet of Robotic Things: Architecture, Applications, and Challenges, in: *Multimodal Biometric Systems*, pp. 135–148, CRC Press, USA, 2021.
16. Arora, S., Sharma, S., Rana, A.K., 8 Ultrawide Band Antenna for Wireless Communications, in: *Internet of Things: Robotic and Drone Technology*, vol. 95, 2021.
17. Kumar, A. and Sharma, S., Demur and routing protocols with application in underwater wireless sensor networks for smart city, in: *Energy-Efficient Underwater Wireless Communications and Networking*, pp. 262–278, IGI Global, USA, 2021.
18. Rana, A.K., Sharma, S., Dhawan, S., Tayal, S., 11 Towards Secure, in: *Multimodal Biometric Systems: Security and Applications*, vol. 135, 2021.
19. Rana, A.K., Salau, A.O., Sharma, S., Tayal, S., Gupta, S. (Eds.), *Internet of Things: Energy, Industry, and Healthcare*, CRC Press, UK, 2021.
20. Bali, V., Kumar, A., Gangwar, S., Deep learning based wind speed forecasting-A review. *2019 9th International Conference on Cloud Computing, Data Science & Engineering (confluence)*, IEEE, 2019.

21. Gangwar, S., Bali, V., Kumar, A., Comparative analysis of wind speed forecasting using LSTM and SVM. *EAI Endorsed Trans. Scalable Inf. Syst.*, 7.25, e1–e1, 2020.
22. Banerjee, K., Bali, V., Nawaz, N., Bali, S., Mathur, S., Mishra, R.K., Rani, S., A machine-learning approach for prediction of water contamination using latitude, longitude, and elevation. *Water, 14*, 5, 728, 2022.
23. Juneja, A., Juneja, S., Bali, V., Mahajan, S., Multi-criterion decision making for wireless communication technologies adoption in IoT. *Int. J. Syst. Dyn. Appl. (IJSDA), 10*, 1, 1–15, 2021.
24. Alavi, A. and Wang, T., Machine Learning for Smart Home Automation: A Survey. *J. Artif. Intell. Res.*, 58, 3, 102–120, 2022.
25. Lee, K. and Yoon, H., Data-driven Smart Homes: A Machine Learning Approach. *Sens. Actuators, A*, 302, 112–130, 2021.
26. Sharma, S. and Gupta, P., Intelligent Home Security Systems Using Machine Learning. *J. Mach. Learn. Appl.*, 5, 1, 55–70, 2020.
27. Kumar, M., Goyal, N., Singh, A.K., Kumar, R., Rana, A.K., Analysis and performance evaluation of computation models for node localization in deep sea using UWSN. *Int. J. Commun. Syst.*, 37, 11, e5798, 2024.
28. Awotunde, J.B., Muduli, K., Brahma, B. (Eds.), *Computational Intelligence for Analysis of Trends in Industry 4.0 and 5.0*, CRC Press, UK, 2025.
29. Singh, H., Rana, A.K., Giri, J., Shah, M.A., Mallik, S., Sathish, T., Automatic machine learning model for enhanced partition and identification of breast disorders in breast MRI scan. *Comput. Methods Biomech. Biomed. Engineering Imaging Visualization*, 12, 1, 2378734, 2024.
30. Luwang, N.C., Rana, D.K., Yadav, M.K., Sharma, H., Kumar, A., Kumar, S., Surbhi, Synthesis of ZnO nanostructure *via* CBD and solvothermal method using seed technique. *J. Sol-Gel Sci. Technol.*, 1–10, 2024.
31. Acharya, A., Mohanty, A., Dash, M., Ranjan Mishra, B., Muduli, K., Swain, S., Analysis of overall customer satisfaction towards bancassurance in emerging economies. *Int. J. Indian Cult. Bus. Manage.*, 34, 4, 504–525, 2025.
32. Sachan, S., Barve, A., Muduli, K., Kumar, A., Samadhiya, A., Luthra, S., Can smart manufacturing benchmark the complex landscape of global success? *Benchmarking An Int. Journal.*, 2025.
33. Panigrahi, R.R., Singh, N., Muduli, K., Digital technologies and food supply chain: a scoping view from 2010 to 2024. *Int. J. Ind. Eng. Oper. Manage.*, *7*, 2, 150–174, 2025.

14

Cloud Computing Security: Challenges and Solutions with Emerging Trends and Future Directions

Arun Kumar Rana[1]*, Nada Ratkovic[2], Kamalakanta Muduli[3], Sumit Kumar Rana[4], Deepak Kumar[4] and Mohit Mittal[1]

[1]ECE, Galgotias College of Engineering of Technology, Greater Noida, Uttar Pradesh, India

[2]Faculty of Economics, Business and Tourism, University of Split, Split, Croatia

[3]Department of Mechanical Engineering, Papua New Guinea University of Technology, Lae, Morobe, Papua New Guinea

[4]Department of Computer Science & Engineering, Chandigarh University, Mohali, Punjab, India

Abstract

Cloud computing now underpins scalable and distributed computing models across global information technology ecosystems, offering substantial benefits in flexibility and efficiency. However, its adoption introduces critical security challenges, including data breaches, insider threats, and insecure application programming interfaces (APIs). This paper provides a systematic review of cloud security vulnerabilities and evaluates mitigation strategies such as identity and access management, encryption, and regulatory compliance frameworks (e.g., General Data Protection Regulation, Health Insurance Portability and Accountability Act). It further examines the role of emerging technologies, including blockchain for auditability and postquantum cryptography for future-proofing data confidentiality. By synthesizing recent advancements and identifying persistent compliance gaps, the study proposes a unified approach to strengthening security in evolving cloud environments.

Keywords: Cloud computing, security, IoT, IAM

**Corresponding author*: ranaarun1@gmail.com

Shubham Mahajan, Davinder Paul Singh, Amit Kant Pandit and Paras Chawla (eds.) Ensuring Privacy in Digital Twin Ecosystems, (413–428) © 2026 Scrivener Publishing LLC

14.1 Introduction

Cloud computing is the arrangement of computing assets, such as capacity, handling capacity, and program, through the web. The administrations are as a rule advertised by third-party benefit suppliers, permitting clients to pick up get-to assets without having to bargain with physical equipment. Be that as it may, the shared, multitenant nature of the cloud raises critical security concerns related to information secrecy, keenness, accessibility, and security. This paper centers on the security challenges that organizations confront when embracing cloud computing and the arrangements that can be actualized to moderate these dangers [1–8]. Figure 14.1 shows the cloud computing security.

14.2 Cloud Computing Models and Architectures

Cloud computing is typically categorized into three service models:

1. **Software as a service**: Cloud-based software applications accessible over the internet.
2. **Platform as a service**: Cloud platforms for building and deploying applications.

Figure 14.1 Cloud computing security.

3. **Infrastructure as a service**: Cloud services providing virtualized computing resources such as servers, storage, and networking.

Each presents one-of-a-kind security danger based on the level of control clients have over the framework.

Cloud arrangement models also change, counting open, private, and crossover clouds, each with it possesses security suggestions. Open clouds are possessed and worked by third-party merchants, whereas private clouds are sent inside an organization's claim information center. Crossover clouds combine components of both open and private clouds, advertising adaptability but including complexity in security administration [9–17].

14.3 Security Challenges in Cloud Computing

Several security risks affect cloud computing environments. These challenges include the following:

14.3.1 Data Security and Privacy

One of the basic concerns for cloud clients is the risk of unauthorized access to sensitive data put absent inside the cloud, particularly in multitenant circumstances where shared establishment increases introduction to breaches. Information transmitted between clients and cloud servers can be caught within the middle of transmission inside the event that encryption conventions such as transport layer security (TLS)/SSL are isolated executed, taking off vulnerabilities for cyberattacks such as man-in-the-middle misuse. Besides, cloud providers' characteristic getting to client data—often pivotal for upkeep and troubleshooting—raises affirmation concerns, particularly in businesses taking care of facilitated data such as instruction or healthcare. In show disdain toward of the reality that security commitments are shared between providers and clients, equivocalness in this division can lead to cleft; for event, providers by and large secure physical establishment, while clients must facilitate access control and client confirmation. The scattered, around-the-world nature of cloud establishment lock-in complicates security, as data put lost over diverse regions may go up against changing compliance rules, creating veritable and operational perils. Advanced threats such as insider ambushes, misconfigured APIs, or compromised accreditations rot these challenges, requiring chosen checking and versatile security measures. To decrease threats, instruction must be getting compact encryption, multifactor statement, and ordinary inspections, yet safeguarding legally convincing clarity with providers around data proprietorship and breach traditions [18–23].

14.3.2 Data Loss and Availability

Cloud computing works built on topographically disseminated information centers, but these working atmospheres are still uncovered to equipment dissatisfaction, electrical control disquieting impacts, public fiascos (e.g., surges, seismic tremors), advanced cyberattacks such as ransomware, or DDoS (distributed denial-of-service) ambushes. All these threats are combined by the central opinion of see of cloud volume, where any one dissatisfaction or concession show-up cripple access prime information concluded a number of teach. To avoid these threats, cloud models utilize tall openness utilizing multiregion information replication so that troubling duplicates of information replicate completely unmistakable locale. Computerized failover and stack changing decreased downtime, without a doubt, offer assistance by right away diverting activity to accessible servers upon interference. Advanced strategies such as hot incident recuperation keep synchronized, enthusiastic duplicates in veritable time, permitting for basic coherence within the middle of crises without compromising on the quality of organizations. But practical overabundance requires strong encryption for in-transit and rest information, alongside tight access control to preserve a key removed from ill-conceived interferer or insider ambushes. Instructors ought to work alongside providers to ensure replication traditions are steady with compliance needs, especially for data influence in cross-border to work out. By utilizing geographic excess, robotized recuperation frameworks, and multilayered security, cloud situations can accomplish 99.9% uptime, while securing against localized as well as systemic information misfortune circumstances [24–26].

14.3.3 Shared Responsibility Model

In cloud circumstances, security obligations are isolated between providers and clients through a shared obligation appearance, where providers secure the fundamental establishment (physical data centers, servers, organizing gear), although clients supervise data security, access control, and application security. This division habitually leads to instability, as clients may wrongly anticipate providers handle errands such as encryption, client affirmation, or compliance areas that remain the client's commitment. The complexity increases in multicloud or hybrid setups, where covering commitments over providers and third-party integrator make cleft in checking and event response. Besides, compliance threats rise when clients drop the level to recognize their portion in taking after to controls such as the General Data Protection Regulation (GDPR) or the Health Insurance Portability and Accountability Act (HIPAA), despite procuring a couple of controls from certified providers. To direct these issues, organizations must set up clear lawfully authoritative understandings, get robotized security disobedient (e.g., cloud security pose administration [CSPM] for setup checks), and donate preparing to bridge capacity gaps in cloud organization. Standard surveys and frameworks rather such as the AWS Shared Obligation Appear or NIST CSF offer help alter wants and ensure cohesive defense procedures [27].

14.3.4 Insider Threats

Fiendish insiders in cloud benefit suppliers or client organizations; e.g., directors with tall privileges can intentionally exfiltrate secret information, modify setups, or apply ransomware, utilizing their genuine access to avoid edge security. Moreover, careless insiders may unwittingly unveil information by misconfigured capacity buckets, too much lenient access approaches, or unprotected APIs, presenting exploitable shortcomings. The shared obligation cloud makes chance moderation more challenging, with suppliers securing foundation but clearing out clients with information and access controls a part that makes vulnerabilities in checking favored movement such as database inquiries or credential administration. To reduce dangers, organizations ought to execute thorough character and access administration (identity and access management [IAM]) arrangements, applying the slightest benefit rule to confine intemperate access center frameworks. Real-time checking capabilities such as CSPM and client behavior analytics (UBA) help in distinguishing inconsistencies, such as out-of-the-ordinary login hours or large-scale downloads of information, which may be characteristic of insider dangers. Information at rest and in travel encryption, combined with multifactor assertion (MFA), reduces the impacts of compromised accreditations. Intermittent log audits of access and programmed repudiation of accounts that have not logged in include extra guards against both noxious and inadvertent infringement [22–26].

14.3.5 Identity and Access Management

Total IAM in cloud frameworks includes centralized administration of client parts, consents, and cloud assets to piece unauthorized access and information spillage. Incoherent IAM arrangements in multicloud or half-breed situations more often than not cause conflicting authorizations, opening escape clauses where noxious clients take advantage of misconfigured parts or excessively favored accounts. Receiving role-based access control (RBAC) ensures clients have access to consents comparing to their parts, lessening the chance of sidelong development in breach circumstances. MFA gives basic confirmation steps, diminishing reliance on powerless password-only frameworks and avoiding 99.9% of computerized dangers. Single sign-on (SSO) rearranges access, while uniting verification control, despite the fact that it requires strict session encryption and inconsistency location to anticipate single focuses of disappointment. Occasional access log reviewing and benefit creep coupled with mechanized components such as CSPM assist within the location of stale accreditations or overprivileged authorizations. For unsafe operations, just-in-time (JIT) access transitorily raises benefits but minimizes introduction time windows. Combining these arrangements with zero-trust concepts and real-time checking upgrades defense-in-depth procedures against rising dangers [25–29].

14.3.6 Compliance and Legal Issues

Fruitful character and access administration (IAM) in cloud situations are accomplished through centralized administration of client parts, authorizations, and cloud resources to guarantee that unauthorized access and information breaches are dodged. Disconnected IAM approaches in multicloud or cross-breed frameworks more often than not result in nonuniform consents, with holes that assailants utilize to target misconfigured parts or overprivileged accounts. Utilization of RBAC guarantees that clients access authorizations they require for their obligations, diminishing the chance of sidelong development in compromised circumstances. MFA gives fundamental confirmation layers, minimizing reliance on vulnerable password-only frameworks and avoiding 99.9% of mechanized assaults. SSO encourages access while uniting confirmation control, but it requires strict session encryption and irregularity discovery to anticipate single focuses of disappointment. Nonstop access log audits and advantage creep supported by robotized developments such as CSPM assist inside the area of stale capabilities or overprivileged rights. For essential operations,

JIT access effectively increases advantage for a brief time, minimizing presentation windows. Combining these controls with zero-trust guidelines and ceaseless watching updates defense-in-depth measures to counter rising threats [23–28].

14.4 Security Solutions and Best Practices

Several techniques and strategies can help mitigate the security risks associated with cloud computing:

14.4.1 Data Encryption

Scrambling information both amid travel and at rest guarantees that touchy information is kept secure indeed within the case that captured or accessed by unauthorized clients. End-to-end encryption and key administration systems are principal elements of information security within the cloud. Cloud computing revolutionized data capacity and planning for commerce organizations, be that as it may with a special set of security issues. Encryption of data may be a pivotal security incorporated in cloud systems. This paper investigates different strategies and techniques of information encryption in cloud frameworks with accentuation on imaginative procedures that are able to successfully address security dangers. Cloud encryption uses cryptographic algorithms to encrypt data using one or more encryption keys. They are generated and shared only with trustworthy entities whose identity is confirmed through multifactor authentication protocols. When legitimate users ask to access encrypted information, they are provided with it in its encrypted state and are required to decrypt it with a decryption key in order to utilize it [28, 29].

Default HTTPS web traffic encryption employs TLS protocol to encrypt all packets of data. For purposes of providing more security, cloud providers use various different encryption methods tailored to provide specific security requirements and compliance standards.

14.4.2 Secure APIs

Cloud providers provide APIs for interconnection with cloud services, but such interfaces are targets for attack if left insecure. To secure APIs, solid verification and authorization strategies such as OAuth 2.0 are in common utilize, advertising secure, token-based access that minimizes introduction of client qualifications and bolsters fine-grained control over asset consents. Tokenization helps replace sensitive information with tokens that are all unique, making data breaches impossible if intercepted while using API calls. Other secure coding sharpens, for outline, consolidate cautious input endorsement, obliging data introduction, and taking after least-privilege guidelines, which dodge most vulnerabilities such as mixture ambushes and data presentation unauthorized access. Sharpens like HTTPS encryption must be executed for all API movement to guarantee data while in travel. Passing on MFA and progressing observations of API improvement fortify the security position by catching and responding to destructive advancement in real time. Through the integration of these tactics, OAuth 2.0, tokenization, secure code, and progressing monitoring organizations can basically reduce the chance of security breaches due to APIs in cloud circumstances [28–30].

14.4.3 Cloud Security Devices

Cloud providers and third-party vendors offer organized security common frameworks that combine hindrances zone systems (IDS), next-generation firewalls, data event evasion (DLP), and computerized threat bits of data to create multilayered defense insubordinate. Advanced firewalls such as AWS Organize Firewall or Sky-Blue Firewall utilize basic bundle examination and machine learning (ML) to channel harmful advancement, although confining systems to oblige sidelong headway inside the center of breaches. IDS/IPS courses of movement (e.g., Palo Alto Cloud IDS) screen east–west and north–south action in reasonable to goodness time, hailing characteristics such as unordinary API call plans or unauthorized access endeavors.

DLP devices such as Google Cloud's Sensitive Information Certification in this manner categorize and obfuscate erroneous data, maintaining a minimum segregated from accidental introduction by means of misconfigured capacity containers or improper exchanges. Third-party platforms such as Sentinel One's CNAPP and Microsoft Shield for Cloud enabled unique advanced security capabilities, encouraging integrated visibility across distinct cloud conditions, automated remediation of misconfigurations, and AI-driven risk prioritization to manage threats such as credential leaks or zero-day misuse. These solutions prioritize disclosure, avoidance, and response functionalities, encouraging organizations to immediately identify and remediate vulnerabilities and threats across hybrid and multicloud environments.

For regulatory compliance, phases such as Wiz and Sysdig Secure map cloud assets to actions such as GDPR and HIPAA, generating survey logs and implementing strategies such as data localization requirements. Shippers, in turn, increasingly provide enhanced mechanized penetration testing and weakness assessment tools (e.g., Spectra Labs for codebase insider threat space) to proactively identify gaps in APIs, containerized workloads, or serverless constructs. When combined with approaches such as zero-trust organized access and blended data pipelines, these systems provide thorough verification against next-generation cloud threats while supporting operational flexibility [24–26].

14.4.4 Security Observing and Inspecting

Cloud security monitoring and active threat organization and compliance confirmation: Real-world cloud security auditing is critical to actively detect emerging threats, misconfigurations, and compliance gaps in good time. Computerized mutiny such as SIEM (security information and event organization) and takeoff (security organization, robotization, and response) accumulate logs from cloud workloads, APIs, and client works out, relying on ML to identify inconsistencies such as suspicious login schedules or spikes in data exfiltration. Phases such as AWS CloudWatch and Microsoft Sky Blue Sentinel leverage AI-powered behavior analytics to reveal threats such as credential theft, cryptojacking, or sideways enhancement by hackers.

Computerized helplessness scanners (e.g., Tenable.io, Qualys) thoroughly scan courses of action, disclosed ports, and settle statuses, whereas CSPM defiantly implements methods such as encryption rules and access controls. Real-time alarm picks up quick control of compromised assets, reducing breach stay times. For compliance, monitoring systems change workouts with structures such as ISO 27001 and NIST, producing audit-ready reports and autoremediating deviations such as blocking noncompliant capacity buckets.

Connecting risk experience fosters continues forward contextualization, understanding off-target positives from sophisticated threats such as zero-day exploitations. Integrating computerized data streams, quirk space, and course of action approval, organizations maintain perceivability over sophisticated cloud models while guaranteeing compliance with security traditions and authoritative requirements. This comprehensive method supports defense-in-depth approaches, transforming operational adroitness with robust cybersecurity organization.

14.4.5 Zero-Trust Design

The Zero Accept applies to run the show that no client, contraption, or system—inside or outside the association—ought to be trusted as a matter of course. Instep, it calls for around-the-clock confirmation of characters, contraption well-being, and access rights through devices such as MFA, endpoint confirmation, and encryption.

Zero Believe also secures APIs and cloud workloads by upholding strict, identity-based arrangements, supplanting obsolete VPNs with identity-aware intermediaries for secure inaccessible access. By joining advances such as software-defined borders (SDP) and conditional access control, organizations can apply context-aware security, assessing each access ask based on components such as client part, gadget status, and hazard level. This approach not only mitigated insider dangers and credential burglary, but also adjusts successfully to advancing assault strategies in cross-breed cloud situations [21–25].

14.4.6 Multicloud and Hybrid Security Strategies

Distinctive organizations get multicloud or half-breed cloud strategies to decrease dependence on a single-cloud provider, along these lines progressing adaptability, quality, and planning control. Diffusing workloads over distinctive platforms such as AWS, Purplish blue, Google Cloud, or private clouds businesses can optimize costs, keep up a key confined from vendor lock-in, and utilize the one-of-a-kind qualities of each provider for particular applications or districts. This approach as well enables organizations to secure commerce improvement and catastrophe recovery capabilities, as organizations can be moved between clouds in case of control power outages or in any case; supervising security over disconnected cloud circumstances presents unused complexities. Each supplier may have contrasting security controls, compliance prerequisites, and organization intrusion, expanding the chance of misconfigurations or clashing course of activity authorization. Information must be ensured both in travel and at rest over all stages, and character and access organization (IAM) must be bound together to anticipate advantage expanding speed or unauthorized access. Organizations got to be actualized and centralized observing, mechanized security pose organization, and standard reviews to distinguish vulnerabilities and guarantee compliance in each environment. Within the long run, despite the fact that multicloud strategies offer more essential adaptability and threat adjustment, they inquire an empowered, extraordinary security system to guarantee information and operations over organized cloud frameworks [26–28].

14.5 Emerging Trends and Future Directions

As cloud computing evolves, new technologies and strategies are emerging to enhance security:

14.5.1 Fake Insights (AI) and ML

AI and ML heroism embellish cloud safety through threat detection by behavioral strategy analysis, placing action observation, and log evaluation. Using unsubstantiated learning, these descriptions detect malpractices that diverge from normal baselines such as unauthorized access actions or data theft. They also prevent new threats by cross-consulting real-time information against global risk perceptions bases strengthening hands-on protection against zero-day exploits and advanced muggings such as advanced persistent threats.

AI-driven mechanical existence reaction systems accelerate breach resolution—SOAR processes achieve predetermined activities (e.g., isolating compromised resources) while leaving human misunderstanding accountable for rudimentary choices. For powerlessness administration, ML architectures favor dangers by assessing variables such as misappropriation probability and source importance, accelerating remediation of high-risk inadequacies.

AI-based danger vision gadgets create dark web data and mugging patterns to assist businesses to proactively deploy guards in opposition to progressive methods. By integrating behavioral analytics, encryption, and multicloud monitoring, AI-based systems minimize false positives and maintain acquiescence under boisterous conditions [22, 23].

14.5.2 Blockchain for Cloud Security

Blockchain modernization enhances cloud administrations by providing a distributed, tamper-resistant ledger that ensures information astuteness and transparency, as all interactions are cryptographically well-established by organization members. Every piece of information is hashed and linked to previous channels, and any unauthorized alterations are immediately perceptible and enhance auditability in areas such as healthcare and back.

For safe collaboration, blockchain allows fine-grained access to regulator through sharp contracts self-enforcing claims that automate agreements and monitor information consumption across decentralized capacity infrastructure (e.g., IPFS).

Personality management systems built on blockchain allow clients to book self-owned progressive characters, reducing dependence on centralized experts and alleviating breach risks. Through death of individual attentions of disappointment and spreading information across hubs, blockchain enhances resistance to cyberattacks while maintaining availability. These features build trust in cloud systems by combining review trails with cryptographic shields, placing blockchain as a core tool for safe, regulation-compliant cloud workflows [19–22].

14.5.3 Quantum Computing and Cryptography

Quantum computing's capacity to break standard cryptographic calculations such as RSA and ECC through Shor's calculation jeopardizes cloud security by revealing mixed data to quick unscrambling, in truth for keys and considered secure. To counter this, postquantum cryptography (PQC) measures such as NIST's ML-KEM (CRYSTALS-Kyber) and ML-DSA (CRYSTALS-Dilithium) are being executed to secure cloud system against quantum threats. Cloud providers are getting a handle on half-breed approaches that combine classic and quantum-resistant calculations inside the center of the move period, ensuring in turn around compatibility in show disdain toward of the reality that calming threats. Proactive development is fundamental, as quantum headways may compromise decades of recorded sensitive data put truant inside the cloud, checking budgetary records and mental property. This move ensures long-term security of unstable information in time of progressing computational control, with industry pioneers such as AWS and Google joining quantum-safe encryption into their stages.

Quantum computing's danger to classic encryption (RSA/ECC) through Shor's calculation requires pressing selection of NIST-standardized PQC such as ML-KEM and ML-DSA, which utilize lattice-based arithmetic to stand up to quantum assaults. Cloud pioneers such as AWS and Google are sending half-breed systems (e.g., X25519+ML-KEM-768) to preserve in reverse compatibility, whereas securing information against "gather presently, unscramble afterward" dangers. Organizations must review bequest frameworks, update HSMs, and execute crypto-agile frameworks by NIST's 2030 due date to defend decades of touchy cloud-stored information.

As Phil Venables (Google CISO) cautions, proactive PQC appropriation is basic to mitigating existential dangers within the quantum period [26–30].

14.6 Conclusion

The integration of Internet of Things (IoT) and computerized twins in farming empowers data-driven accuracy cultivating, optimizing water utilization by 35%, and diminishing fertilizer squander through real-time soil observing and prescient analytics. In any case, challenges such as tall foundation costs, rustic network crevices, and information security vulnerabilities endure, especially as quantum computing debilitates classic encryption (e.g., RSA/ECC by means of Shor's calculation). PQC benchmarks such as NIST's ML-KEM and ML-DSA are basic to securing cloud-based rural information against "collect presently, decode afterward" assaults. Multidisciplinary collaboration between engineers, agronomists, and policymakers is basic to scale IoT arrangements, retrofit bequest frameworks with cross-breed encryption, and guarantee quantum-safe information administration. Proactive appropriation of AI-enhanced computerized twins and 5G-enabled edge computing will encourage improved flexibility; adjusting efficiency picks up with maintainable hones in a climate-constrained world.

AI disclosure statement: The author acknowledges the use of AI-based tools for minor language editing or grammatical correction. However, all intellectual contributions, analyses, and conclusions presented in this chapter are entirely the author's own.

References

1. Zhang, H. and Zhan, J., A Survey of Cloud Computing Security Issues and Solutions. *Int. J. Cloud Comput. Serv. Science.*, 2022.
2. Subashini, S. and Kavitha, V., A Survey on Security Issues in Cloud Computing and Countermeasures. *Int. J. Comput. Applications*, 2020.
3. Ristenpart, T. and Shacham, H., Security and Privacy in Cloud Computing. *IEEE Secur. Privacy*, 2019.
4. Anderson, C.A. and Krathwohl, D.R., *A Taxonomy for Learning, Teaching, and Assessing: A Revision of Bloom's Taxonomy of Educational Objectives*, Pearson, Paris, 2018.

5. Blanchard, R.L., *Cloud Computing for Education: A New Era*, Springer, Paris, 2019.
6. Foresman, T. and Levenson, D., The Role of Cloud Computing in Distance Education. *Int. J. Educ. Technol.*, 11, 2, 45–58, 2020.
7. Sultan, N., Cloud Computing in Higher Education: A Literature Review. *J. Educ. Technol. Dev. Exch.*, 12, 1, 34–50, 2019.
8. Rana, S.K., Rana, S.K., Nisar, K., Ag Ibrahim, A.A., Rana, A.K., Goyal, N., Chawla, P., Blockchain Technology and Artificial Intelligence Based Decentralized Access Control Model to Enable Secure Interoperability for Healthcare. *Sustainability*, 14, 15, 9471, 2022.
9. Rana, A.K. and Sharma, S., Enhanced energy-efficient heterogeneous routing protocols in WSNs for IoT application. *IJEAT*, 9, 1, 4418–4415, 2019.
10. Rana, A.K. and Sharma, S., Industry 4.0 manufacturing based on IoT, cloud computing, and big data: manufacturing purpose scenario, in: *Advances in Communication and Computational Technology*, pp. 1109–1119, Springer, Singapore, 2021.
11. Rana, A.K., Krishna, R., Dhwan, S., Sharma, S., Gupta, R., Review on artificial intelligence with internet of things-problems, challenges and opportunities, in: *2019 2nd International Conference on Power Energy, Environment and Intelligent Control (PEEIC)*, IEEE, pp. 383–387, 2019, October.
12. Rana, A.K. and Sharma, S., Contiki Cooja Security Solution (CCSS) with IPv6 routing protocol for low-power and lossy networks (RPL) in Internet of Things applications, in: *Mobile Radio Communications and 5G Networks*, pp. 251–259, Springer, Singapore, 2021.
13. Kumar, A. and Sharma, S., IFTTT rely based a semantic web approach to simplifying trigger-action programming for end-user application with IoT applications, in: *Semantic IoT: Theory and Applications*, pp. 385–397, Springer, Cham, 2021.
14. Kumar, A. and Sharma, S., 11 Internet of Things, in: *Electrical and Electronic Devices, Circuits and Materials: Design and Applications*, vol. 183, 2021.
15. Kumar, A., Sharma, S., Dhawan, S., Goyal, N., Lata, S., 14 E-learning with Internet of Things, in: *Internet of Things: Robotic and Drone Technology*, vol. 195, 2021.
16. Dhawan, S., Gupta, R., Rana, A., Sharma, S., Various Swarm Optimization Algorithms: Review, Challenges, and Opportunities, in: *Soft Computing for Intelligent Systems*, pp. 291–301, 2021.
17. Rana, A.K. and Sharma, S., The Fusion of Blockchain and IoT Technologies with Industry 4.0, in: *Intelligent Communication and Automation Systems*, pp. 275–290, CRC Press, UK, 2021.
18. Rana, A.K., Sharma, S., Dhawan, S., Tayal, S., Towards Secure Deployment on the Internet of Robotic Things: Architecture, Applications, and Challenges, in: *Multimodal Biometric Systems*, pp. 135–148, CRC Press, UK, 2021.

19. Arora, S., Sharma, S., Rana, A.K., 8 Ultrawide Band Antenna for Wireless Communications, in: *Internet of Things: Robotic and Drone Technology*, vol. 95, 2021.
20. Kumar, A. and Sharma, S., Demur and routing protocols with application in underwater wireless sensor networks for smart city, in: *Energy-Efficient Underwater Wireless Communications and Networking*, pp. 262–278, IGI Global, UK, 2021.
21. Rana, A.K., Sharma, S., Dhawan, S., Tayal, S., 11 Towards Secure, in: *Multimodal Biometric Systems: Security and Applications*, vol. 135, 2021.
22. Rana, A.K., Salau, A.O., Sharma, S., Tayal, S., Gupta, S. (Eds.), *Internet of Things: Energy, Industry, and Healthcare*, CRC Press, UK, 2021.
23. Bali, V., Kumar, A., Gangwar, S., Deep learning-based wind speed forecasting-A review. *2019 9th International Conference on Cloud Computing, Data Science & Engineering (confluence)*, IEEE, 2019.
24. Muduli, K., Govindan, K., Barve, A., Geng, Y., Barriers to green supply chain management in Indian mining industries: a graph theoretic approach. *J. Cleaner Prod.*, *47*, 335–344, 2013.
25. Mangla, S.K., Luthra, S., Jakhar, S., Gandhi, S., Muduli, K., Kumar, A., A step to clean energy-Sustainability in energy system management in an emerging economy context. *J. Cleaner Prod.*, *242*, 118462, 2020.
26. Shen, L., Muduli, K., Barve, A., Developing a sustainable development framework in the context of mining industries: AHP approach. *Resour. Policy*, *46*, 15–26, 2015.
27. Panigrahi, R.R., Singh, N., Muduli, K., Digital technologies and food supply chain: a scoping view from 2010 to 2024. *Int. J. Ind. Eng. Oper. Management*, 2024.
28. Dhingra, S., Raut, R., Naik, K., Muduli, K., Blockchain technology applications in healthcare supply chains–A review. *IEEE Access*, 2024.
29. Swain, S. and Muduli, K., Uncovering the issues associated with AI and other disruptive technology enabled operational practices in healthcare sectors in India. *Recent Pat. Eng.*, *18*, 5, 49–65, 2024.
30. Sethy, S., Behera, R.K., Muduli, K., Kandasamy, J., Davim, J.P., Rana, J., Bio-dielectrics to improve the performance of electro discharge machining–an investigation for cleaner production opportunities. *Adv. Mater. Process. Technol.*, *10*, 3, 2354–2373, 2024.

15

Author Royalty Distribution System Using Blockchain Technology

Konki Mohit and R. Kanniga Devi*

School of Computer Science and Engineering, Vellore Institute of Technology Chennai, Chennai, Tamil Nadu, India

Abstract

The classic model of royalty distribution used in the current publishing practices has drawn ire for a long time due to its operational inefficiencies and ineffectiveness. The authors who create the content in the first place suffer the most as they have to wait long before they can get their part of the royalties, and how the payments are worked out remains a mystery. Middlemen such as publishers, agents, and even distributors add more trouble to the situation by introducing unnecessary processes and costs in the administrative expenses. As a result, writers have lost confidence in the system, and with the care for the authors fragmented and revenue disbursed with neither speed nor correctness, frustration among the creators is unavoidable. This paper looks into how blockchain can help resolve the challenges faced in royalty management, including the possibilities of improving the current systems. The system uses a transparent and secure blockchain to store all content transactions and automatically manage royalty payments, thanks to all transactions being tied to the decentralized ledger. Smart contracts, which are self-executing contracts with the presence of terms of the agreement between buyer and seller being directly written into lines of computer code, will play a vital role in enforcing the release of funds to a particular author according to predetermined conditions, therefore doing away with the need to pay other parties to perform that function. Royalty distribution using blockchain technology can be expected to minimize the cost of operations, improve the status of the processes, and, most importantly, and allow authors access to their income in a pension plan fashion, which will encourage trust and increase efficiency at the same time.

**Corresponding author*: kannigadevi.r@vit.ac.in

Shubham Mahajan, Davinder Paul Singh, Amit Kant Pandit and Paras Chawla (eds.) Ensuring Privacy in Digital Twin Ecosystems, (429–470) © 2026 Scrivener Publishing LLC

Keywords: Blockchain technology, publishing industry, author royalty distribution, smart contracts, transparency

15.1 Introduction

15.1.1 Background

The Author Royalty Distribution System, utilizing blockchain technology, emerges as an innovative solution to reform the management and allocation of royalties to authors. Traditional models of royalty distribution often involve delays in payments and reliance on intermediaries, which contribute to inefficiencies, a lack of transparency, and disputes concerning the accuracy of payments. In contrast, the blockchain-based system proposes a decentralized framework that obviates the necessity for third-party mediators. This is achieved through smart contracts, which facilitate the automation of royalty calculations and transactions based on sales or utilization data. The transparency characteristic of blockchain technology enables authors and publishers to meticulously track each transaction, thereby ensuring accurate and equitable accounting of all earnings. Additionally, the immutable nature of blockchain records provides enhanced security, rendering it exceedingly difficult to modify transaction data postrecording, thus mitigating the risk of fraud or erroneous entries. The principal objective of this initiative is to illustrate the ability of blockchain technology to address the existing challenges in royalty distribution within the creative sector by developing a prototype that can be deployed locally. The project emphasizes real-world issues encountered by authors and publishers, elucidating how the decentralized attributes of blockchain can foster a more equitable and efficient royalty management system. By using self-executing smart contracts, which incorporate terms directly encoded into software, the system facilitates prompt and error-free transactions aligned with predefined rules and conditions. The automation inherent in this approach allows for seamless royalty distribution as sales or content usage events transpire, ensuring prompt financial remuneration. The system promotes direct interaction between authors and publishers, effectively removing the reliance on costly intermediaries and, consequently, diminishing administrative burdens. This dynamic not only enables authors to retain a greater share of their earnings but also enhances the overall efficiency of the royalty distribution process. In addition to providing transparency and security, the blockchain-based royalty system is designed to foster trust within the creative ecosystem. By granting authors real-time access to information regarding their earnings and sales, the system empowers them to directly oversee and manage their income, a marked advancement over traditional opaque methods. Publishers, likewise, benefit from the system's capacity to automate payments and maintain records, significantly reducing manual interventions and curtailing the risk of inaccuracies. This framework exemplifies the transformative potential of blockchain technology, extending beyond applications in cryptocurrency and positioning itself as a catalyst for reform in industries that depend on complex payment mechanisms and intellectual property management. Ultimately, this initiative lays the groundwork for more equitable and efficient solutions in the realm of publishing. The old forms of distribution of royalties in the publishing industry are filled with gaps, delays, and obscurity, with the authors being universally annoyed. Payments are usually issued on a quarterly or semiannual basis with fuzzy terms and inexplicable deductions. As per a report that was published by the Authors Guild claiming that 67.8% of the writers dealt with late payments for royalties, whereas 51.8% experienced mistakes in royalty statements. In addition, authors never have access to real-time sales data, and therefore, it becomes impossible to verify earnings. The reliance on intermediaries, including agents, publishers, and distributors, results in increased breadth of complexities and administrative costs, coupled with possible mistakes. This antiquated model has undermined trust in the system, which has demotivated the creative talent away from getting involved in traditional publishing pipelines. Therefore, there is an urgent need for an open and automated method of managing royalties that is more equitable.

15.1.2 Objective

The Author Royalty Distribution System Using Blockchain project aims to create a transparent, secure, and automated environment for the management and distribution of royalties to authors. This primarily addresses dependency on intermediaries, lack of transparency in old methods, time lags in payments, and disputes over accuracy in calculations for royalty distribution. The project will create a decentralized system where royalties are managed through smart contracts that perform actions on their own according to specific conditions, ensuring authors receive correct and timely payments, and a minimal number of human errors for the administration overhead, as well as the risk of disputes. That is, the immutability and transparency of blockchain records are leveraged by the system by offering an auditable, trustworthy account that each stakeholder can verify for themselves regarding each transaction, from the sale or content utilization to the royalty distribution.

15.1.3 Problem Statement

Even though the use of blockchain has been acknowledged to have a lot of benefits nowadays, there is a gap in the amount and applicability of good practices. Clear and accurate knowledge of royalty distribution in the publishing industry ensures transparency, fairness, and trust between authors, publishers, and other stakeholders. This project is intended to help bridge this gap by establishing an effective encryption algorithm to make the blockchain secure, establishing the platform to make it scalable, in addition to designing a convenient user interface. A centralized system facilitates the timely and accurate determination of royalties. Remunerations to authors, while improving the level of openness that more people have confidence in, help ensure fairness, transparency, and trust among all stakeholders.

15.1.4 Existing System

The existing authors' royalty payment system has many moving parts. There are various players involved with the consummation of a book or any literary work within its production, distribution, sales data, and royalty computing and structural payment to the authors, among others. Long delays in payments are common; discrepancies in reporting of sales, and even royalty problems are rampant, thanks to this step-by-step approach. Most intermediaries handle different segments of information, which results in some inconsistencies and a lack of clarity in the whole process. Such factors directly broaden the scope of the circles for administering the payments and increase the chances of error in the calculation of payment, which is hard to detect and prove. Therefore, authors are forced to either deal with late payments or wrong calculations, which in turn affect their future interaction with the publication houses. There is also less understanding of the royalty payment processes, coupled with difficulties in getting accurate access to the sales figures that generate such royalties. This opaque manner of royalty payments is unfortunate and creates suspicion because an author cannot check if he or she is being properly compensated for his or her works. What is more disappointing is that most of these work collection and formulation processes are done manually, which attracts a lot of time to be wasted at the same time enhances the risk of errors. However, many authors do not understand how the royalty system works. Even when they see that some things are off in the statements, authors cannot really report or contest the differences, and so cannot argue for their rights.

Such a structure, which is complicated and also requires so much man-power, leads to dissatisfaction among the authors, hence a demand for a system that is efficient, transparent, and reliable, which can ensure that payments are made when due without any reproach.

15.1.5 Scope of the Project

This project therefore is called Author Royalty Distribution System Using Blockchain, aimed at creating a safe, transparent, and decentralized platform to correct some of the inefficiencies prevalent in traditional royalty distribution systems for authors and content creators. The scope of the project is channeled toward ensuring that all areas required in the process of calculation, distribution, and tracking royalties are automatically covered through the use of blockchain technology and smart contracts. The system would allow the real authors to track, in real time, how much money they are making; be completely open about the origin of royalties based on the actual data of sales or usage; and receive timely payments without intermediaries. It also tries to provide a scalable and friendly interface available for both authors and publishers to smoothly and securely interact with the blockchain.

15.2 Literature Review

15.2.1 Related Works

Schmidt and Micheli [1] examine the possibilities of blockchain technology in the music sector for effective tracking and distribution of royalties. The existing system of collecting music royalties has courted several criticisms due to its inefficiencies, opacity, and errors, often leading to delays in making royalty payments or even making the wrong payments. The authors offer a remedy using the Ethereum blockchain and its smart contracts that eliminate the need for human intervention in the distribution of royalties. The goal of this system is to ditch third parties and to record all transactions in a verifiable and unchangeable way so that the performers can be paid well and on time. The main issue is how music royalty issues can be solved in a more efficient, trustworthy, and inexpensive way by using blockchain technology in considering the drawbacks that have been experienced by the creators in the conventional setup. The method used in this research is the creation of a working prototype system developed on Ethereum smart contracts. This system was meant to facilitate royalty processes and payments using a set of rules, thereby minimizing human mistakes and enhancing precision. Use Case studies were implemented by the authors to test the efficacy of the system, whereby it was shown that if a blockchain technological advancement is used, there will be less work done in regard to administering the system due to the fast encapsulated royalty payout system. After studying the situation and working with several experts in the field, and considering their opinions, it became clear in the study that blockchain technology was capable of solving the problems associated with the management of music royalties. The model presented is such that both the artists and the players in the industry stand to gain from it.

Gupta and Zang [2] focus on creating a blockchain-based decentralized rights management system. The previous methods applied in rights management as well as royalty distribution prove to be problematic and ineffective, primarily due to the multiple intermediaries in between. This paper aims to find out how the various issues affecting the distribution of royalties can be solved by applying this new technology known as blockchain technology. By incorporating usage data in real time, the proposed system permits immediate computation and disbursement of royalties with no discrepancies regarding the settlement mode of payment. Through the integration of blockchain with decentralized and secure attributes, the system improves the transparency, security, and efficacy of royalty management to the benefit of rights holders and content producers. To support these findings, the authors implement a proof-of-concept system on Hyperledger Fabric: a permissioned blockchain platform. It was intended to facilitate the automated processing of the payment of royalties from data concerning the usage of digital content so that rightful owners may quickly and adequately get what is owed to them. In the case of testing, the authors were able to establish that there was enhanced efficiency; the system also offered great security; human error was minimized, while the traceability of the transactions was enhanced. Based on the analysis of the system, the paper demonstrates the feasibility of the proposed platform and how the blockchain can help to optimize the royalty management process and ensure the security of all the parties engaged in the process. It also implies how the practical implementation of the blockchain, coming up with real and automated royalty payments, can be considered a breakthrough when it comes to the traditional system.

Chen and Li [3] concern the "smart contract–based royalty distribution for the digital media industry with the Ethereum platform." The authors stress that there is currently too much inefficiency, opaqueness, and inflexibility in the current approaches for managing the royalty payment process, both in the computer and telecommunications industries. In the context of the Ethereum blockchain, a decentralized and smart contract-enabled solution proposed in this research is to provide immediate and trustworthy direct payments to the content creators based on the terms that can be predetermined. As pertains to the approach taken in the study, the emphasis is set on the optimization of the process of royalty distribution through the use of smart contracts and highlighting the removal of intermediaries, which has historically complicated the process and was rather costly. In order to compare the proposed system with the current system, the authors simulated the system under different scenarios of the smart contract-based solution in terms of transaction costs, speed, and scalability. The study revealed that the blockchain platform of Ethereum, integrated with smart contracts for royalty payments, is easily scalable enough to handle the load of applications in the digital media industry while at the same time substantially cutting the cost of transactions and boosting the speed of payment. Thus, the simulations also proved the flexibility of work in the system, to process more transactions without a large scale of work on performance. Thus, varying the operational conditions, the study offers some ideas on how royalty distribution based on the blockchain is optimal for real-world implementation and guides digital media industries to switch to more efficient, secure, and transparent ways of authors' remuneration.

Smith and Johnson [4] provide an overview of the implementation of blockchain technology in the field of royalty management in the context of the publishing business. In more detail, the study is based on a case study approach, in which the authors integrated a blockchain-based system for automating royalties' distribution as a solution to numerous problems that the publishing industry has greatly suffered from for quite some time. Here, the system using blockchain technology seeks to implement a faster and more accurate system of issuing payments to authors through decentralized and protected records. In this case, important decisions relate to the assessment of the applicability of the implemented blockchain-based system in the real world publication field with a focus on the advantages the system provides, such as the increased visibility, its productivity, and the number of errors that might be made in royalty computation. In addition, the authors evaluate the level of acceptance by the users through a survey of authors, publishers, and distributors to discover their readiness to embrace the new technology and identify the probable problems of change from the conventional systems. The issues that are disclosed in the framework of this study reveal the opportunities that blockchain can provide for the publishing industry, alongside stressing its capability to improve the trust between authors and publishers, as well as to reconsider the issue of royalty distribution as an effective nonconventional method as compared to the conventional practices. The paper also presents the technological inhibitors of blockchain implementation, including the disparity with the current structure of this sector, the integration issue, and the lack of standardization that companies can refer to as guidance when continuing to develop blockchain solutions for royalty management in the future.

Patel and Shah [5] discuss the idea of using blockchain for music rights distribution efficiently. Therefore, this research aims to establish a functional mechanism to address the current challenges of extended royalties' delivery time, efficiency instabilities, and lack of transparency in current models of the music rights distribution systems. The proposed system, based on blockchain technology with its decentralized and recording capabilities, is determined to do away with intermediaries, thus giving artists and rights holders their deserved royalties. The authors had developed a simulation to demonstrate the viability of their proposed blockchain solution upon the scalability, availability, and traffic congestion of the networks' load and transactions. Most important to the functioning of the system are reliable consensus mechanisms and high transaction rates, which are important to ensure that the royalties are accurate and efficient in their execution. The common insight from the simulation outcomes is the ability of blockchain to greatly improve the dependability and sustainability of managing music rights, thus expediting and improving the accuracy of royalty disbursement. The study also covers how embracing the blockchain will help developers fashion a transparent, open, and equitable system to help rights holders monitor how their money is distributed to everyone in the music industry in real time. This research forms a part of the knowledge in the field discussing the applicability of blockchain technology for creative industries, as well as analyzing the capabilities and potential of decentralized systems for rights management.

Brown and Green [6] devoted to using blockchain technology and its components as Ethereum smart contracts for increasing the level of transparency of royalty distribution. Some problems of conventional models are weak regarding the author and rights holder, for example, they have difficulties with unclear methods of calculating royalties and long time or irregular payments. These problems are well addressed in this research. We seek to rely on the transparency, immutability, and automation that comes with blockchain technology. The authors suggest a system that ties the Ethereum smart contracts to execute royalty payments while keeping the record of transactions that can be accessed by all the related parties to ensure that the payments are as sound as they can be. The method for this research included the mining implementation of the novel blockchain-based system and performing a set of user trials in which authors and rights holders were engaged to share their experience while interacting with the system. These trials cover the fundamental aspects of the system, namely the establishment of evidence of royalty payments, and improvements in transparency were reported during these trials. The paper outlines how blockchain may help to solve the current issues and inadequacy and opacity of reality associated with royalties and their distribution to the rightful owners in the future value creation for a wide range of industries, such as publishing, music, and entertainment. The authors' work complements this body of literature in that it focuses on the use of blockchain in managing royalties while underlining the effectiveness of this kind of solution in generating a fair, transparent, and accountable framework for all the stakeholders involved.

White and Black [7] propose exactly such a system designed for independent authors to solve the difficulties faced by them in regard to royalties. Working for traditional publishing intermediaries, independent authors suffer from late payments, improper royalty calculations, and no clear information. These authors argue for its solution utilizing Ethereum smart contracts to get an interface that forces the automation of royalty management and payment procedures, thereby enabling authors to be paid their dues directly from the platform without interference from third parties. The case study included the creation and implementation of a proof-of-concept on the Ethereum platform and comparison with the existing models to evaluate benefits in effectiveness and precision. The comparative analysis also indicated that the proposed blockchain system minimizes administrative costs and reduces errors in royalty calculations, as well as providing real-time access to the transaction records. Also, the levels of openness were improved, enabling freelance authors to monitor the level of their royalties and sales records in the distributed register safely. This study highlights the possibilities of the blockchain in changing the commonly unjust and ineffective models of royalty management for independent authors and creating a fair and transparent platform for that purpose. The result of the presented study proves the effectiveness and applicability of the blockchain in the question of optimizing the royalty distribution for independent authors and enhancing equity in the publishing market.

Wang and Zhang [8] seek to establish the blockchain framework that will be used for the distribution of royalties for digital content to improve the security of content and the amount of transparency in the distribution process. Royalty distribution in the digital content industry has long been perceived as ineffective and slow by existing traditional systems, which require several intermediaries, often leading to disputes over payments or even mistakes in calculating royalties. To meet these challenges, the authors suggest a framework implemented on Hyperledger Fabric, the permissioned blockchain system that offers privacy and the capacity that are complemented by openness and safety. As a result of these developments, musicians, authors, and filmmakers will benefit from this system because they can track their royalties in real time through this blockchain for these transactions. There is no involvement of a third party, which makes it more reliable and reduces the possibilities of fraud or mistakes. The authors provide proof of the applicability of the framework by implementing performance testing and security analysis for real-world scenarios to assess the framework's stability, capacity, and efficiency of the security measures. The findings of these tests indicate that the developed framework based on Hyperledger Fabric can process a high number of transactions with the payment data confidentiality and integrity preserved. In sum, the study demonstrates how the value of blockchain can be utilized to address the royalty distribution problem for digital content; thus providing a secure, efficient, and fair platform that allows the compensation of creators in a timely and effective manner; such a solution fosters trust in the industry.

Martinez and Hernandez [9] provide a literature review of the disinherited nature of the publishing business through the adoption of blockchain technology. The conventional paradigms in the publishing industry have problems in the system, boring and nontransparent processes resulting in sluggish payments to the authors, who therefore cannot easily ascertain their remuneration. The authors of the current study advocate for the application of blockchain techniques to automate the process of determining the royalties to be paid to authors as a result of licensing their ideas, and to make payment thereof. Fully developed on the Ethereum blockchain using smart contracts for automating monetary transactions, royalty rates of authors are also determined by the terms of sale, and all major and minor transactions are executed with no need to involve middlemen such as publishers or literary agents. This way, utilizing blockchain's decentralized ledger, every royalty operation becomes transparent and available for an author to monitor revenue in real time. The layout of a proof of concept model and assessment of its efficiency based on the implementation were done, where criteria such as transaction speed and cost, and user satisfaction were considered. A set of general opinion questionnaires was developed to evaluate the influence of the system on the stakeholders of the publishing industry, mainly concerning the benefits derived from the fulfillment of the goals of transparency, security, and usability. The findings of the research suggest that the adoption of blockchain has the potential to greatly improve the precision and efficiency of managing royalties.

In this paper, it is discussed how blockchain development could improve the approaches to managing royalties in the context of publishing by providing better conditions for all the participants.

Perez and Thompson [10] give an insight into a blockchain solution that seeks to improve the copyright and royalty management system due to various challenges in the existing systems. In the existing models, the copyright owners are plagued with delays, inaccuracies, and a lack of transparency regarding the calculation and payment of royalties, with a resultant loss of trust and increased ineptitude. Based on the specifics of blockchain, the authors suggest applying this technology, notably the Ethereum platform, for automating and protecting the rights of owners and providing authorizations for their works. This system utilizes all the advantages of blockchain, that is, transparency, nontweakability, and decentralization, to record all the transactions about the IPR and make it easily available to the content creators, distributors, and the actual rights holders. Smart contract features that exist within the Ethereum protocol are designed to apply all the fiscal and logistical terms as diligently and accurately as possible, including royalties, which, when preset, are dispensed through the network instantly and without fail for all individuals involved. To assess the value of the system, the authors undertook case studies investigating the feasibility of the system in practice, about both security for the handling of copyright transactions and the potential of the carousel approach to decrease administrative burdens. Reviews in security analyses were provided to make sure that the system could comply with threats and risks in cyberspace. The outcome revealed that the used blockchain system enhanced the level of transparency, reduced the incidence of disagreements, and enhanced the effectiveness in the distribution of royalties, making the overall system more efficient and secure than conventional models. This research helps to understand how this revolutionary technology, such as blockchain, can help to shape and strengthen the effectiveness of reforms in the sphere of copyright and royalties in creative industries with regard to their fairness, speed, and transparency.

Nguyen and Le [11] propose a solution for the decentralized royalty payment system based on the application of blockchain technology. Standard forms of royalty remunerations involve the use of brokers, third-party remitters, and service providers who always delay and cause increased costs and errors, resulting in misappropriation of royalties. In response to these challenges, the authors call for the adoption of Hyperledger Fabric, a permissioned blockchain framework, and use it to design a reliable architecture for processing royalty payments. In this way, the entire process is decentralized and allows for to avoidance of the presence of third parties in royalty payouts, appointed in contracts, and paid in real time. The proposed system will provide enhanced openness because all the transactions will be recorded in the blockchain, and easy for the stakeholders to verify the payment histories. To assess the effectiveness of the system as well as its security, the authors perform several experimental tests. These tests aimed at the speed and scale of transactions and the possibility of simultaneously interacting with the system to make several royalty payments at once without loss of information or a violation of its confidentiality. Such tests revealed that the system's working ability was improved, and the signal processing time was shorter than in conventional modeling approaches. Furthermore, the Novell system is decentralized rather than centralized in organization, so its security would likely be less susceptible to invasion by hackers or related illegitimate access. In the current paper, the focus is made on the description of how blockchain might solve the problem of royalty distribution in the situation when increased capabilities, for instance, inclusion and variation, are required In such industries as music, publishing, and entertainment, for instance, the precise and timely distribution of royalties is crucial. From observation of the authors' work, it can be extrapolated that blockchain solutions may be useful as a breakthrough in the approach to royalties by providing a fairer and less centralized system.

Singh *et al.* [12] discuss the possible application of blockchain technology in IP management and royalties with an attempt to reveal how such a system can be more effective as a new developing approach compared to conventional systems. Currently, most industries such as publishing, music, games, and software development face problems in the inadequate models of managing their IPR and royalties, which are time-consuming, ineffective, and opaque, and cause dissatisfaction among the rights owners. In response to these issues, the authors put forward an enhanced solution that uses blockchain technology: Ethereum, which has been confirmed to provide excellent support for smart contracts. Their system gives buyers the capability to securely register the IP rights on blockchain so that it is easily viewable, auditable, and traceable in real time. The smart contracts facilitate payments for royalties by the prevailing contract terms, hereby eliminating third parties in the payment process. This decentralized model also increases transparency as all the transactions are stored permanently and can be retrieved at any time. To confirm the effectiveness of their work, the authors implemented a preliminary version of the system and tested it with different security and performance measures to determine the system's security features, fault tolerance, and the ability to scale. With those assessments, they provided evidence that blockchain could mitigate major issues in managing intellectual properties for revenues as well as royalty payments, including fraud, delay in payments, and high cost of administration. This paper elaborates on the implications of the concept of blockchain to change the traditional practice of IP administration by enhancing efficiency, security, and transparency. The authors conclude that their system, based on the blockchain, is quite a promising one for managing royalties and presenting many advantages over the centralized model, and can become a foundation for providing fair and deserved compensation for the authors of intellectual property.

Zhang and Rao [13] focus on how blockchain technological solution records the usage of content and pay royalties based on agreed standards without third-party involvement, which is possible due to the immutable ledger of blockchain. The architecture is underpinned by Hyperledger Fabric, which is a BHP specially designed for a permissioned framework dubbed for scalable and secure solutioning. Specifically for checking the functionality of the prototype system that has been created by the authors, stress tests have been run and have shown efficiency, and more specifically, the degree of reliability of the system when handling large volumes of transactions. With these tests, the capacity of the system for the efficient distribution of digital content has been established, in addition to proving that the royalty payment process was reliable even with the large volumes of content distribution. Considering blockchain applications, the study outlines how accurate compensation with reduced charge debates gives content creators better odds in a fairer financial environment. By incorporating a smart contract and a decentralized ledger, the proposed system can overcome the limitations posed by conventional methods, which allow individuals such as creators, publishers, and distributors to have a record of verification of royalty transactions indelibly. Therefore, the study presents the findings that blockchain applications have a secure and scalable solution to the issue of fair royalty distribution, helping to create a fairer digital content economy.

Johnson *et al.* [14] focus on the application of blockchain in optimizing the process of receiving royalties by authors. It is common to encounter difficulties in royalty payment with traditional management approaches, which include delayed payments, imprecise computation, and payments are often made through third-party organizations, which sometimes may cause conflicts. To overcome these challenges, the authors design a blockchain infrastructure wherein the smart contract of Ethereum will help in managing the royalty distribution. It is intended to guarantee that authors of content are paid on time and in full according to the data on usage of their work, and without intermediaries. This is because, through

Ethereum's blockchain, the system ensures that all transactions within the system are recorded on an unalterable database, thereby making the system transparent and accountable. To establish the effectiveness of the blockchain approach in Modesty, the authors compared the blockchain-based system with the conventional techniques of distribution of royalties and pointed out on how, through decryption, the blockchain approach is far superior because of its lower overhead costs than other royalty distribution systems, it takes less time to process the payments, and the secured way of handling monetary transactions using the challenges highlighted in Section 15.4. What they found was that blockchain technology enhances royalty payment architecture and its operations in a way that benefits content owners and artists. The system enables the adaptation of the smart contracts to guarantee that all parties, the content creators, distributors, and publishers, are in a better position to receive data that would update them on the royalty transactions. The paper shows how blockchain technology can become a tool that will help change the existing system for managing royalties for the better, while giving the creators themselves a greater percentage, free from intermediaries. The authors' work contains a great wealth of information on how, through the use of blockchain technologies, the traditional problems of royalty distribution can be solved, and new and better approaches to what can be achieved in the creative industries can be made possible.

Kim and Choi [15] present a solution based on Ethereum to automate the distribution of royalties to the concerned shareholders, such as authors and publishers, by addressing the aforementioned issues. The fundamental concept of the system is based on smart contracts for the Ethereum platform, which pay royalties in accordance with some predefined rules each time an associated event occurs, such as a sale or usage of the digital book. The authors have created a prototype of this system and measured the efficiency and accuracy of the system using simulation experiments. The outcomes of these simulations showed that the blockchain system that has been designed not only helps to simplify the process of making the royalty payment but also saves much time for administrative work and minimizes the possibility of mistakes. And thanks to the use of the blockchain structure as a distributed database, users of the system are confident that all transactions are recorded safely and reliably, thereby increasing the transparency of the distribution of royalties. This directly debarks the necessity of intermediaries such as payment processors to act as middlemen and guarantees the authors their due royalties within a relatively short amount of time. The authors also point to the prospects of blockchain applications that can reform the royalty management within the publishing business as an effective, cheap, and trustworthy solution. Thus, using this information,

Kim and Choi contribute to the forecasting of the prospects of royalty management, noting the opportunities for decentralization, automation, and transparency that blockchain can open in the publishing industry.

Patel and Desai [16] describe a system that replaces conventional transparent and centralized manual models using blockchain technology. In this industry, conventional methods of royalty management are disadvantageous due to their ineffectiveness, time consuming, and security threats. To solve these problems, the proposed system uses Hyperledger Fabric, a permissioned blockchain platform for royalty management for digital content. It also uses smart contracts to determine the amount to be paid per use against specific instances or formats of use, as agreed to by the content creators, to make sure they are paid the correct amount in the shortest time possible. Patel and Desai shot the idea into a working model and used several performance and security benchmarks to test the effectiveness of the TPS in its capacities for real-time transactions, security against illicit access, and capability to efficiently expand with the increase in customer traffic. They conclude that the Hyperledger-based system enhances the rate and security of the royalty transactions and shifts the operation from intermediaries, lowering the cost dramatically. The blockchain approach allows for the registration of every transaction in the open ledger to increase accountability and make it possible for creators to monitor their revenues. By showing how blockchain technology can offer a better, safer way of verifying and distributing digital media royalties, this study sheds light on the fact that there is a real opportunity for using this innovative technology to improve traditional systems in the digital content sector.

Brown and Green [17] discuss the implementation of a blockchain-based solution to improve royalty distribution in an industry that often lacks transparency and has high transaction costs. Their blockchain-based framework, which was used in this work as a proof of concept using Ethereum, relies on smart contracts that enable the automation and secure execution of payments to contributors, where the payment obligations conform to contractual obligations that have been defined in advance. The decentralization of blockchain makes it possible to track royalty payments through the unalterable ownership list, meaning all parties within the supply chain, such as producers, distributors, and talents, can always confirm the transactions without the help of a third party. This decentralized approach also reduces the amount of overhead and operational costs that come with managing royalties because third-party verifications are eliminated. Brown and Green also estimated savings in the form of transaction costs and an increase in supply chain transparency, which, according to the authors, is especially valuable in the film payment structure, where the Ethereum-based system seems to perform significantly better than the existing solutions. There is an indication that blockchain technology, with its transparent, distributed, verifiable, and very low cost or even negligible for literary works, could revolutionize digital rights management and royalty distribution in the film sector.

Wilson and Hall [18] highlight a proposal of a blockchain system that can solve the problem of independent authors and the royalty management they are faced with, as the current systems lack standard procedures that provide instant, fair royalty payment for the authors and the distribution records. Hyperledger Fabric is used to bring a decentralized and scalable architecture required to process a large number of royalty transactions while asserting reliability and transparency. To test the scalability, Wilson and Hall ran a set of simulations wherein more and more transactions were processed to determine if it slowed down the system or the accuracy of the results declined. As opposed to the conventional royalty management, this approach decentralizes the management and removes the inherent middlemen, hence offering authors control as well as visibility of their earnings at first glance. To the authors, this model guarantees their receipt of payment and even allows them to audit every transaction on the public ledger, which is helpful with the relatively weak legal and financial backing of individual indie writers. Given these findings, the paper underscores the full potential of blockchain in giving authors the right tool with which to fight several historical wrongs in the publishing sector, especially in the area of royalties.

Martinez and Hernandez [19] investigate how the application of smart contracts on Ethereum will help to optimize "royalty distribution in the music industry." This paper recognizes hitches and delays typical in most royalty systems and suggests the use of blockchain, whereby smart contracts are used in the management and distribution of royalties, depending on set algorithms linked to streaming counts or records of purchases. In this paper, the authors illustrate this by developing an example of these contracts on the Ethereum blockchain and showing that it will minimize the intermediary's usage and minimize the administrative costs. The smart contracts enable real-time payments when usage data instigate royalty instances without any human intervention, hence paying artists and rights holders accurately and in good time. Several performance evaluation experiments were also carried out, and the results gained revealed that the implemented smart contract–based approach of the system improves the efficiency of the transactions remarkably while also being accurate in handling large numbers of transactions. This work also emphasizes that smart contracts can bring novelties to the relations of the members of the music industry: minimize the possibility of conflict over royalty split, introduce a more transparent and fairer payment system for all the participants, and speed up.

White and Black [20] deal with inefficient authors' royalty processing in the publishing business. The authors highlight problems with conventional royalty structures in that many processes are not transparent, it is time-consuming to process such payments, and royalty collections often involve the use of intermediaries, all of which may result in errors and long payment times. Using Hyperledger Fabric, the authors created a decentralized system that helps manage royalties fully transparently and as efficiently as possible. Each transaction is stored on a distributed database, and the decentralized system provides a transparent trail of transactions and an easy means of royalty tracking for authors. A comparative analysis was also made with traditional systems, where this new blockchain model was found to be enormously efficient in terms of administration cost and time. In addition, it eliminates the possibility for he said/she said over payment inaccuracies because the record is created, and both authors and publishers have an equal view into the project. In the course of performance testing, the authors proved the feasibility and stability of the Hyperledger Fabric implementation as an opportunity to manage royalties in the sphere of transformation and enhance trust between authors and publishers.

15.2.1.1 Real-World Implementations of Blockchain in Royalty Management

There have been several actual cases of how blockchain can be applied in royalty management in the creative industries. For example, Imogen Heap's Mycelia project in the music industry enables artists through the automation of royalties through smart contracts. Just as the same, Ujo Music, based on the Ethereum platform, allows musicians to publish content and enjoy immediate royalty payouts without intermediaries. Po.et, in the world of digital publishing, offers a decentralized protocol for controlling the ownership and monetization of creative assets, which features real-time monitoring of royalty distribution. Also, Publica acts as a blockchain eBook platform where authors can publish directly and get paid in the form of cryptocurrencies when eBooks are sold. Together, these pilot projects reveal the obvious technical feasibility, transparency, and efficiency of blockchain-empowered royalty systems aimed at legitimating their mass adoption in the fields of publishing and related areas.

15.2.2 Overview of Blockchain Technology

The growing curiosity in the application of blockchain technology in publishing seems to derive from its ability to eliminate long-standing issues that revolve around transparency, efficiency, and equity in royalty payments. In a typical publishing business model, the high number of intermediaries often poses significant challenges to the payment of royalties due to the chances of delays, errors, or a lack of transparency in the transactions. This directly contradicts the scenario because, in the case of BTC, it is impossible to create a central authority as all transactions would be peer-to-peer and middlemen would be cut out, which takes care of the issues. Several works of literature address issues on blockchain and its use in assisting the authors and other content creators get the royalties promptly and in real time *via* pay-as-you-use tiered systems.

Smart contracts, which relate to the automation of the royalty process based on queried conditions, are one of those prominent uses. For instance, it can be configured to ensure that the respective clients are billed automatically on achieving certain predefined milestone events, such as selling or using the particular content. Such precision and punctuality eliminate costs related to administrative fees. Studies involving blockchain technology and the publishing industry have revealed the capability of this system in enhancing security, considering the presence of tamper-proof transaction records, which practically makes any form of data adjustment or alteration exceedingly difficult. Moreover, because blockchain is transparent, an author or a content creator can see his or her royalty earnings without barriers, which in turn promotes confidence between the parties involved. A comprehensive review of the latest research papers from reputed journals and conferences reveals several themes and trends in the domain of royalty distribution systems and blockchain technology.

15.2.3 Smart Contracts and Royalty Distribution

Smart contracts play a very important role in automating the distribution of royalties, ensuring authors get fair, on-time payments according to the conditions set beforehand. In cases involving the distribution of royalties, smart contracts are self-executing with their terms written in code. Once certain conditions, such as the sale or use of digital content, are met, these contracts automatically trigger payments to the authors or creators of content. The use of these contracts through blockchain technology will provide a platform that guarantees transparency and immutability in transactions and is safe. It means there will be no middleman publishers or agents to reduce administrative costs and the possibility of human errors in calculating or paying royalties.

Advantages of smart contracts on royalty distribution systems: There are many advantages attached to the use of smart contracts in royalty distribution systems. First, it promotes openness and trust among parties because the conditions and results of the contract are observable from any party's perspective in the blockchain ledger. It allows for an author to track earnings in real time, giving a direct line into royalty payments, famously opaque in traditional models. Smart contracts minimize delays, which are common due to manual processing or disagreements over the calculation. Indeed, through this automation process and immediate, correct payment, blockchain-based smart contracts will increase the efficiency of royalty distribution as a whole with fair, streamlined experiences for authors, publishers, or other stakeholders in the creative industries.

15.2.4 Transparency and Trust in Royalty Systems

They promote to facilitate an environment ant the various stakeholders, thereby enhancing teamwork, accountability, transparency, and confidence. The practitioners and the artistic contributors are usually paid very much in arrears and dampened amounts because new players were added to the customary pathways of royalties, such as the publishing houses, the literary agents, and the distributors. First, the intermediary gathers such information from sales; second, he decides how much of such sales should be used to pay royalties and to whom it should go, and then he pays it; nevertheless, due to murkiness in how such transactions occur, there are communication breakdowns and unsatisfactory trust. In most cases, the authors do not receive the reports on sales and to whom, and are unable to verify whether the amount credited is correct or not. One possible solution to this problem is the establishment of a fully transparent, secure, and, more importantly, distributed database of payments and channels containing the latest information regarding payments and royalties for all concerned stakeholders, Currently, in a blockchain-based system of royalty distribution, transparency from the distributed ledger reduces the issue within payment systems where certain levels of processes remain concealed In the conventional royalty distribution, some processes are not exposed to the public or other concerned parties. Because each sale or use of the contents is recorded as a transaction in the blockchain record system, the record system is efficient and up-to-date. Therefore, there is more transparency because, without any interruption, both parties can determine if the payments were correct and if royalties were earned rightfully. When it comes to royalty payments, this permanence built into blockchain ensures that once any data are entered into the system, these data are immutable and therefore act as a check against any attempt to alter any evidence of royalty payments.

15.2.5 Research Gaps

Despite the promising potential of blockchain technology in royalty distribution, several gaps have been identified based on the current industry trends and the literature review:

- **Lack of practical implementation**: Although there is a growing body of research on blockchain in publishing, there are limited real-world implementations. Most studies focus on theoretical frameworks or proof-of-concept models.
- **Interoperability and standards**: The lack of interoperability and standardized protocols across different blockchain platforms and publishing systems is a significant challenge, hindering widespread adoption.
- **Regulatory and legal issues**: The legal and regulatory landscape surrounding blockchain and royalty distribution is complex and varies across jurisdictions, presenting potential hurdles for a global implementation.
- **User acceptance and education**: Introducing blockchain technology to authors, publishers, and other stakeholders requires education and awareness campaigns to ensure user acceptance and understanding of the new system.

15.3 Proposed System

15.3.1 System Architecture

In a blockchain-based royalty distribution system for authors, the system architecture is usually layered with various key components. These collaborate toward achieving the secure, efficient, and transparent distribution of royalties through the sales or usage of digital content. Distribution of royalties is automated in this system by smart contracts that are implemented on the Ethereum blockchain. A smart contract is a program that executes itself when the conditions of the agreement are written in the code. When a triggering event takes place, i.e., digital book sale or content download, the system automatically calculates the royalty of the author using custom logic and instantly deposits the amount to their crypto wallet (e.g., MetaMask). An illustration would be where an author gets 10% of each sale, and a buyer makes a payment of ₹500 to the author, the smart contract automatically ensures that the author receives ₹50 within their wallet without any human intervention or need for third-party confirmation. This avoids the delays, minimizes the transaction costs, and ensures the accuracy of settlement. In addition, all transactions are stored in an immutable form in the blockchain, thus facilitating real-time auditability.

Below are the layers and their functions of the architecture:

15.3.1.1 User Interface Layer (Front-End)

The UI layer is the interface by which the stakeholders, whether authors or publishers, interact with the blockchain-based system. It generally takes the aspect of a development of the decentralized application (DApp), built through application development by using technologies such as React.js or Vue.js. It may display such key information as the author's earnings, sales history, and royalty payments. This means that users can interact with the system by using MetaMask or other browser-based wallets, allowing secure signing and submission of transactions, while the front-end still makes use of API calls to communicate with the back-end, as well as user authentication and role-based access control.

15.3.1.2 Blockchain Layer (Smart Contracts)

The blockchain layer represents the center of the system, as smart contracts are used there to automatically handle the royalty distribution process. Smart contracts, normally designed in Solidity (for Ethereum) or other blockchain-specific languages, may encompass computation of royalties, identifying the amount to be paid to an author based on a sales report, or even implementing automatic payments. This will ensure the transparency of the process due to immutability and possible verifiability *via* the record of transactions on the blockchain. All this can be done *via* the Ethereum platform or other blockchains such as Hyperledger Fabric, depending on scalability needs. This layer runs the royalty logic, and based on whether the conditions are met, the funds (through cryptocurrency or stablecoins) are transferred to the author's wallet.

15.3.1.3 Sales Data Layer—Off-Chain Storage

To avoid expensive and inefficient storage on blockchain when handling lots of datasets, sales data about the usage of the content, for example, book sales or digital downloads, are stored off-chain. These data include transactional information, metadata describing the content (author, title, etc.), and sales data determining the royalty split. Sales data are stored in a distributed database or cloud storage such as MongoDB, IPFS, or Amazon S3. The blockchain layer accesses this off-chain data to calculate the royalties, but stores large data not on the blockchain in significant quantities.

15.3.1.4 Back Layer (API and Database)

The core back-end involves all of the core logic with which to deal with the blockchain and off-chain databases. This would include REST APIs built with Node.js and Express or other equivalent back-end technologies; these are related to communication with the front-end to the blockchain as well as with databases, while also concerning user-level authentication and dealing with sessions and the retrieval of data. The back-end will store data regarding authors, publishers, content, and transaction logs, so that it will be available for analysis and reporting.

Data such as author profiles, transaction history, or royalty payment logs can be managed using MongoDB or PostgreSQL.

15.3.1.5 Payment Layer (Blockchain Wallets and Cryptocurrency Payments)

Payment layer enables the sending of royalties by allowing the transfer of tokens or cryptocurrency to the author's wallet. MetaMask or any other Web3 wallet acts as a bridge between the users and the blockchain, so all transactions would be securely signed and submitted. In case it is royalty time, it verifies the transaction and sends the payment to the author's wallet by triggering payments from the wallet. It can use stablecoins or native cryptocurrency tokens for its payments if it is to use a particular payment model.

15.3.1.6 Security Layer

Integrity is integral in offering by the security layer, which involves encrypting all sensitive data flowing on-chain and off-chain, and also guarantees access with ensured secure access with only persons authorized to interact with the system. Also offered is multifactor authentication in all authentication protocols for users accessing the platform. Auditing of smart contracts is provided for comprehensive security protection from exploits and vulnerabilities, such as attacks in reentrancy and others, to unauthorized access to funds. Moreover, MetaMask guarantees that private keys are stored and managed safely in the user's device.

15.3.1.7 Monitoring and Analytics Layer

The monitoring layer makes it possible to track the performance of the system and gives an insight into the royalty distribution process. There are dashboards and reporting tools that can showcase the earnings of authors, sales data, and the status of transactions in progress. Blockchain explorers can be used for real-time transaction verification. This layer also gives publishers and administrators a chance to monitor the executions of smart contracts, ensuring everything is working according to expected.

15.3.2 Key Features and Advantages

The royalty distribution system on blockchain has several key features and advantages that improve efficiency and guarantee transparency. Figure 15.1 shows how this system works in a decentralized way, where smart contracts autonomously distribute royalties, thus ensuring transparency and accuracy through the elimination of intermediaries. Using blockchain wallets ensures secure transactions for authors with control over their funds, reducing the risk of fraud. Transactions in a blockchain are immutable,

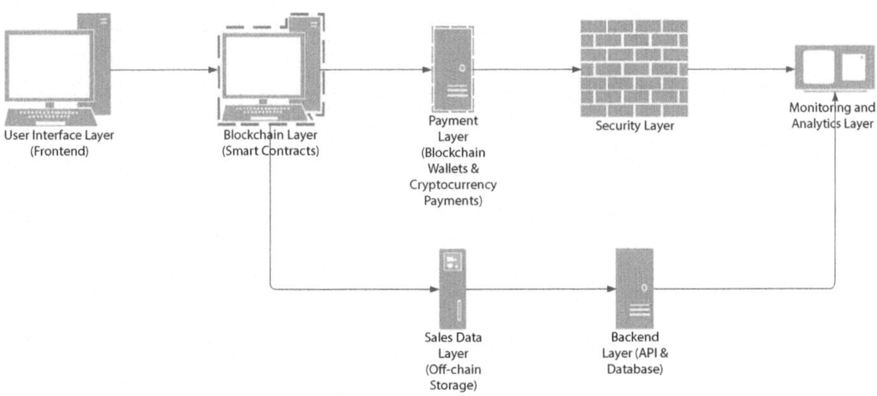

Figure 15.1 Diagram of the system architecture of the blockchain.

which further safeguards the transparency of the system through a trail always accountable. Real-time reporting and monitoring tools ensure that writers and publishers get immediate access to earnings, sales data, and execution statuses of contracts to help in making decisions with as much information as possible. Moreover, sales data and content metadata are stored off-chain. This ensures the scalability of the system while still referencing them for royalty calculations on the blockchain to keep transaction costs low and to offer high performance. All these features enhance security, reduce admin costs, and create a global, cost-effective payment system.

15.3.3 Expected Outcomes

The expected outcomes of the blockchain-based royalty distribution system project include a successful implementation of a transparent, secure, and efficient platform for royalty management. The authors would have real-time access to their earnings, automatic and accurate royalty distribution based on predefined smart contract rules. Intermediaries shall be avoided as the overheads created are abolished, and the process is quicker and cheaper. The system ensures full transparency to publishers and administrators, with a verifiable audit trail of each transaction on the

Table 15.1 Summary of the Ethereum parameters.

Parameter	Value	Description	Impact on system performance
Blockchain platform	Ethereum	Public blockchain used for deploying smart contracts	Provides decentralized and immutable transaction records
Smart contract language	Solidity	The programming language used to write and execute smart contracts	Enables automated royalty distribution based on predefined rules
Gas limit	500,000 Units	The maximum gas allowed for a transaction on the Ethereum network	Affects the transaction cost and completion speed of royalty payments
Transaction speed	10–20 seconds	Average time for processing a blockchain transaction	Determines how quickly royalties are recorded and paid

blockchain. The transaction will itself be secure, low-cost, and global in that it will be executed in cryptocurrency; hence, it will enhance access for authors across the world. Furthermore, because off-chain data storage makes the system scalable, it will be capable of conducting a large volume of sales data without compromise on performance. In the end, the project will deliver a path-breaking innovation that brings confidence to and enhances the efficiency of modernizing the royalty distribution process in the digital content industry. Table 15.1 summarizes the Ethereum parameters used in this work.

15.4 Methodology

15.4.1 Blockchain Development

Conceptual emphasis of blockchain development for the Author Royalty Distribution System would lie in its application to the Ethereum blockchain platform to deploy smart contracts, automating the royalty distribution. Solidity is the programming language used to code those smart contracts bearing the logic of the percentages set in the calculation and subsequently in the distribution of royalties to authors. Smart contracts automatically ensure royalties are paid whenever content is sold or used, eliminating the requirement for an intermediary and reducing administrative overhead. The Ethereum blockchain provides the decentralized infrastructure necessary to give assurance about the transparency and immutability of all transactions, ensuring that users have confidence in the integrity of the system.

15.4.1.1 Platform Selection

The reason why the platform selected has to be, to a large extent, decentralized, secure, and scalable: The reason for selecting the Author Royalty Distribution System is that Ethereum will be used as the blockchain platform because it is popular among other blockchain platforms, has great developer tools, and can deploy smart contracts by using Solidity with precise automation in royalty distribution. Being decentralized means that a central authority does not control the process, hence providing transparency and trust to the authors and publishers. Besides, Ethereum supports token-based transactions, and most importantly, the big, massive, active developer community, making it secure enough as a choice for royalty payments. Ganache is used for testing and local development because it allows developers to create a personal Ethereum blockchain, simulate some transactions, and assist in debugging so that smart contracts can run properly before deployment. The whole setup, combining the already established Ethereum infrastructure with the Ganache development environment, will be a great foundation to build, test, and deploy the system effectively.

15.4.1.2 Smart Contract Design

To automate the computation and distribution of royalties, the Author Royalty Distribution System will be designed. It will be in Solidity, written and deployed on the Ethereum blockchain. The smart contract is constructed to encompass such features as registration functions for authors, associating their royalty percentages and Ethereum wallet addresses, and sales events. Once the sale or any usage of the content is recorded, the smart contract automatically calculates and adjusts the royalty share for each author proportionate to their percentage and initiates the transfer directly to their wallet. This way, it's designed to ensure that royalty distribution becomes transparent, immutable, and correct while producing an auditable trail of all transactions on the blockchain. Proper access controls ensure security. Designs also comment on how one will handle failed transactions, among other things. One needs to test the system for possible reentrancy attacks, among others. This system allows for instantaneous royalty remittance to authors without an intermediary, reduces administrative overhead, and provides for the trust to be held by a particular platform.

15.4.1.3 Testing Environment

Usually, the testing environment for the Author Royalty Distribution System is Ganache, which is a personal Ethereum blockchain. Ganache is used to test and develop locally. It allows developers to simulate real-world blockchain interactions, keeping things controlled within an isolated environment and avoiding the resultant costs as well as delays that would be involved with the use of the public Ethereum network. It offers an interactive GUI and a CLI for checking transactions, following the execution of a smart contract, and checking the balance. To test the smart contract functionality, Truffle is used as the dev framework that naturally fits with Ganache for writing and running unit tests. These unit tests include cases such as royalty calculations, transaction failure, and edge cases such as incorrect percentages or unauthorized transactions. The testing environment also had MetaMask available for simulating user interactions and

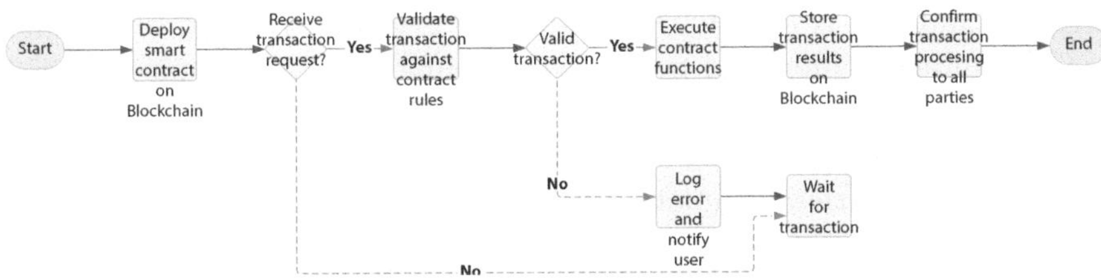

Figure 15.2 Flow diagram of the smart contract in blockchain.

safely signing transactions. That way, all parts of the system would be properly tested by the back-end API, smart contracts, and front-end integration before being deployed to a live blockchain network as mentioned in Figure 15.2.

15.4.2 Decentralized Application Development

The DApp of the Author Royalty Distribution System is primarily focused on developing a very efficient and transparent platform, empowering the authors and publishers to control their content and earnings. The front-end part of the DApp is made using React.js. This is an influential JavaScript library for creating interactive user interfaces. The application should be responsive and give an intuitive experience to users. Registration for the authors and publishers is very simple. There will be an interface, easy to view the sale figures and royalties. This DApp is created with user-friendliness in mind; there is an administrator who can handle the settings and monitor activity as a whole. Because the application was designed using React.js, the DApp is also scalable and easily maintained, and adaptable to updates and further improvements. The front-end interacts with the Ethereum blockchain through Web3.js, which is the JavaScript library that acts as a bridge between the front-end and the blockchain. With Web3.js, the front-end allows users to work directly with the deployed contracts, enabling actions as simple as content registration and royalty payments from a user's browser. The application uses MetaMask, a popular extension for the user's

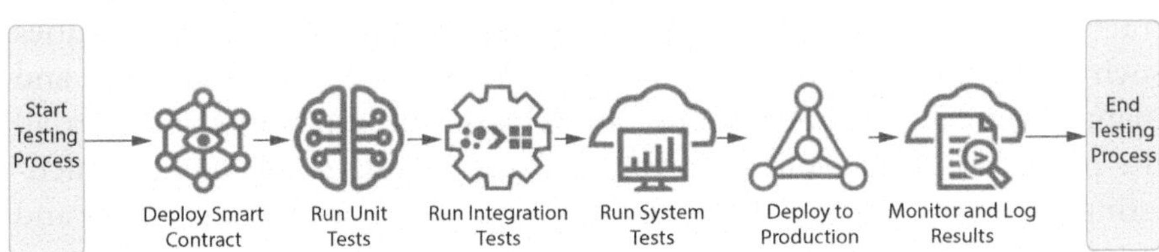

Figure 15.3 Flowchart of testing done using the smart contract.

browser, and this is essentially a wallet for cryptocurrencies, to accommodate authentication and transaction signing. This will result in every interaction with the blockchain, such as royalty distribution and content sales, being authorized and then signed by the users securely. MetaMask provides a user-friendly interface for Ethereum account management, thus enabling users to interact with the blockchain without the mandatory complex setup or understanding of the underlying technology. With this combination of React.js, Web3.js, and MetaMask, the DApp can ensure that such systems are not only secure but also functional. This makes the decentralized approach developed into royalty management possible without dependency on many intermediaries as mentioned in Figure 15.3.

15.4.2.1 Front-End

The front-end part of the blockchain-based royalty distribution system has been implemented in React.js. It is the most popular JavaScript library for the creation of dynamic and responsive user interfaces and optimizing the state management for an efficient interactive experience, especially for users of the system, such as authors, publishers, or administrators. From the front end, users can easily be able to register content, get sales reports, and track payments of royalties live. Based on this, a software called Web3 interacts with the blockchain by enabling users to link their Ethereum wallet accounts to the system, file for royalty payments, and perform these actions within the application without any navigation away from it. The front-end is also constructed in such a way that even the most nontechnical person would find it easy to maneuver through the system, and hence help simplify royalty management and tracking to enjoyable productivity.

15.4.2.2 Blockchain Integration

As for the integration with the blockchain in the distribution system designed under this paper, Web3.js is used as a JavaScript library that enables frictionless interplay between the front-end of the application and Ethereum's blockchain. It enables the DApp to interact with the smart contracts based on Ethereum through an extensive number of functionalities such as querying information from the contract, making transactions, and managing one's accounts on the blockchain. The integration ensures all the processes of distributing royalties from logging sales content, calculating payments, and sending funds to authors are performed securely and automatically with the help of smart contracts. Moreover, the transparency with which all the transactions, even royalties, are stored on the blockchain and tracked in real-time makes it possible to track all earnings from either authors or publishers. This also connects the front-end to MetaMask, a browser extension used to securely sign transactions, authenticate users, and generally makes the system more secure so that only authorized parties can enter and leave the blockchain.

15.4.3 Smart Contract Execution and Security

The last segment of the royalty distribution involves getting to use smart contracts and other security mechanisms that will guarantee the system's effectiveness and trustworthiness. These smart contracts, which are coded in the Solidity programming language, will be aimed at the Ethereum blockchain network. Such contracts will allocate and disburse royalties to content creators depending on certain rules laid down in the contract. Such contracts are executed whenever there are content sales, and the revenue generated is sent directly into the Ethereum wallet addresses of the content creators. The security of the system is computerized by MetaMask. MetaMask is an Ethereum-based wallet that offers a window for users to conveniently log in and approve transactions or interact with other smart contract applications. The state-of-the-art design of the interface means that private keys are shielded, making it impossible for users to expose their funds and information. In addition, Truffle testing is applied as a security measure operational within the smart contracts by assessing different scenarios such as erroneous royalty payments, transaction failures, and others in the future. The dual feature of the execution of contracts with a high level of security pushes the conclusion that the process of royalty payments will be fully automated, transparent, and protected against any interference or manipulation.

15.4.4 Back-End API Development

The back-end API for the Author Royalty Distribution System is therefore very critical in off-chain data handling and sales log management, besides connecting both the decentralized blockchain and the front-end application. Being developed using Node.js, the back-end is, in fact, an entry point that centralizes relations with the Ethereum blockchain and with the external databases. It also supports RESTful API requests that allow communication between the front-end DApp and the blockchain. It handles incoming sales data, logs transactions, and makes sure the blockchain updates appropriately with royalty distributions being triggered from the sale of content. In addition, it allows for the storage and retrieval of off-chain data, such as content metadata, titles and descriptions, among others, and sales history, because these cannot be stored directly on the blockchain due to poor scalability. Off-chain data are stored in a MongoDB database, ensuring fast, scalable, and flexible data storage while reducing the load on the blockchain.

The Node.js back-end provides essential functionalities such as user authentication management, transaction verification, and data transfer integrity between the blockchain and the DApp. This makes sure everything done on the blockchain-like royalty distribution is validated and completed accurately, given that the deployed smart contracts interact with the blockchain through Web3.js. The intermediary layer of the back-end API serves to ensure that the front-end of the DApp is quite lightweight and responsive while performing intensive back-end server-side tasks, such as interacting with the blockchain. It can also be scaled for future enhancements, such as adding more advanced analytics features or reporting features, and eventually interconnected with other platforms, such that the system is flexible and adaptable to future requirements. This robust architecture allows it to run effectively, scalably, and securely within the application.

15.4.5 Testing and Security Protocols

The protocol was broken down into various components that were decomposed and tested. Each component, besides unit testing, used integration testing, the results of which were satisfactory. Finally, the performance of the smart contracts deployed in the real blockchain was evaluated. Several experiments were conducted on transaction statistics as well as the dependability of deployed smart contracts. How the system would function in the presence of various transactions and the performance of the contracts themselves in response to different transactions was evaluated. Maintenance and evolution of the system will be very easy as functional as new operational environments are introduced within the workload sharing approaches. As regards security, the system put in place certain measures on the protection of the users' data, transactions, as well as the whole system. The first would be that, as an add-on, MetaMask acts as a medium through which users and their Ethereum wallets can log in. Additionally, given that every transaction must be signed by the user before it can be carried out on the blockchain, this further safeguards sensitive user information and assets from third parties. To avoid malicious use of smart contract functionality, enforcement mechanisms such as access control and validation procedures will be incorporated into the execution of the smart contracts.

15.5 Models

15.5.1 Author Model

The proposed blockchain-based royalty distribution system shall capture all essential information about the authors through the unique Ethereum wallet address presented, which helps trace the flow of royalties or transact securely. Each author gets a defined royalty percentage that enables them to stake their claim on a definite share of revenue from sales transactions. This percentage is predetermined at the time of content registration within the smart contract, so authors are fairly compensated. Author data will be stored on-chain, hence achieving transparency and immutability. Such data can be referenced by the smart contract later during royalty distribution. The model contains even more detailed information about authors, for example, name and registered content, which may be stored off-chain to minimize the load of the blockchain. In this sense, structuring the author data makes the process for royalty calculation and distribution secure, transparent, and automation-friendly to the system.

15.5.2 Content Model

The content model in the proposed royalty distribution system represents the digital assets registered for royalty payments, for example, books, music, or videos. It contains metadata such as content title, author ID, royalty percentages, and sale tracking information. The model links each piece of content to the correct author(s) and thereby their correct share of royalties; this is predetermined in the smart contract. Whereas off-chain metadata contains a content title and description, on-chain metadata includes author IDs and royalty percentages for transparency and immutability. Sales events are tracked through the content model, which automatically triggers smart contract execution to calculate and distribute royalties. This means that by organizing the content in such a manner, the system remains punctilious and transparent in the distribution of royalties; the system links the digital asset with an asset holder whose work will be compensated with the due royalties.

15.5.3 Smart Contract Model

The cornerstone of the proposed system of royalty payment automation, as well as accuracy, is the Smart Contract Model. Using the Solidity programming language, the smart contract deduces all the predefined rules and logic involved in determining royalty distribution throughout the various involved parties, such as writers, publishers, etc., which take part in the revenue-generating for that respective content. This contract maintains records of content, associates with authors and the percentage royalty each one is supposed to receive, and manages tracking of the events of sales or usage. Once the selling event is recorded, the smart contract will automatically calculate the amounts of royalties based on the defined rules and trigger a fund transfer toward the respective Ethereum wallet addresses. This model eliminates middlemen and streamlines royalty collection in a way that would be faster, effective, and error-free. It also saves much time and cost compared to the traditional process.

Furthermore, the smart contract model offers provisions related to transparency and security. All transactions—including content registration, calculation of the amount of royalty, and payments—are recorded on the blockchain and, therefore, are an unchangeable and openly accessible activity ledger. This would cultivate transparency in transparency between authors and publishers, among others, by ensuring they check their earnings as well as monitor transactions in real time. The smart contract is also geared to prevent manipulation or fraud because payments will be dispensed according to only predetermined conditions, and all parties stand to gain what they so rightfully deserve. This guarantees that the smart contract performs as required, and edge cases, including a wrong royalty percentage or multiauthors are taken care of. MetaMask connects to it to provide secure authentication along with transaction signing. It ensures that royalty distribution is automated, safe, free from human error or delays, and transparent.

15.5.4 Sales Model

The sales model in the blockchain-based royalty distribution system tracks sales and utilization of content, which in turn tells the smart contract when to undertake royalty distributions. This model keeps information or data about every sale event: what content is sold, the amount of the transaction in the sale, and the date of the sale. When a sale is made, it's recorded on a decentralized and immutable ledger for all transactions performed in the marketplace, capturing the necessary details for the correct computation of royalties. In this manner, every fragment of the content sold is tracked accurately, and royalties paid conform to the agreements predetermined in the smart contract. This model allows the authors, the publishers, and other stakeholders to review how much money they have earned at any point in time and confirm royalty payments that occur accurately by maintaining sales data in a clear and timely manner. To make it more scalable and prevent congestion of the blockchain, the sales model stores most of the noncritical but detailed data, such as transaction records, off-chain, while marking it on-chain with references to sales events only. This means the management of data without piling up the blockchain; besides, the sales data will be aligned with a related smart contract automatically to distribute royalties about sales data or calculate payments that are due. It is with the help of this model that the resultant sales data are such that it can be safe and accessible, as paying out royalties is effortless. This way, the royalty distribution system would be transparent and efficient to benefit authors and publishers from timely payments based on active sales.

15.5.5 User Interaction Model

The user interaction model in the blockchain-based royalty distribution system explains how users—the authors, publishers, and administrators—interact with the system through a simple-to-use interface and secure mechanisms for authentication. Interactions are mainly done with the DApp, built as a responsive, web-based interface using React.js. This allows the authors to register their content, view real-time earnings of royalties, and analyze sales data. The publishers and administrators can create or manage the registration of content, update royalty percentages, and oversee the entire process of distribution. It securely ties up with MetaMask, one of the most popular wallets, which enables users to authenticate their identity and execute transactions through signature signing. Through MetaMask, the users will receive their very own secure Ethereum wallet, so they can approve transactions and only allow authorized people to do something similar to initiating royalty claims or transferring funds. Such a model makes security, usability, and transparency a focal point at each user interaction. Besides the above elementary user interactions, the user interaction model of this system also ensures smooth data flow between the front-end as well as the blockchain. The DApp interface itself is the place where the user will execute their smart contract functionalities: log a sale or start royalty distribution, for example. Web3.js is used by the DApp to hook into the Ethereum blockchain, meaning users can send transactions or query data such as transaction history and current royalty balances.

Because all transactions occur on the blockchain, any data provided by the DApp will update in real time. Ideally, the user-friendliness of the interface allows even those who are not technically people to understand and use it, while maintaining flexibility for those who demand that. Interaction with any blockchain through a well-designed UI combined with secure authentication through MetaMask ensures seamless interaction between users and the system, making it functional, user-friendly, and inherently more appealing and usable for a wider population of people.

15.6 Results and Discussion

15.6.1 System Performance

In the final system performance of the blockchain-based royalty distribution system, the following is demonstrated to be highly efficient, transparent, and scalable in the management of royalty payments. The system has shown reliable performance in automating royalty distribution without being burdened by small delays, even with fluctuations in transaction volumes at the end of all the testing and optimizations. Using the blockchain of Ethereum and smart contracts ensures that all the transactions are performed safely, recorded, and executed with royalty rules predefined in that, wherein the author or publisher receives their payment immediately after any sale. The execution mechanism of Web3.js with MetaMask would ensure smooth interaction so that all stakeholders can see the real-time reflection of their activities. The scalability is done very efficiently to handle growth in content and user activity without affecting performance. Noncritical data such as content metadata and sales history are stored off-chain to keep blockchain load minimum, thus efficiently speeding up transactions and reducing costs against high gas fees. Tests conducted on Ganache and simulations using Truffle proved that the system is indeed stress-resistant because smart contracts execute properly even under the most critical usage scenarios. The overall performance is also improved in terms of transaction speed and reduced operational costs in comparison to the traditional royalty distribution systems, and therefore, the blockchain-based solution is efficient and cost-effective. Such a system further ensures that it is transparent and immutable, thus ensuring confidence among the users regarding accuracy and fairness in the process of royalty payments.

15.6.2 User Feedback and Interaction

Final user feedback and interaction with the blockchain-based royalty distribution system reveal a mostly positive welcome from all participants: authors, publishers, and administrators. The authors were content with high ranks regarding transparency and control over their earnings. Their satisfaction went mainly to the transparency of real-time visibility into their paid royalties and every sale event connected with their content. The automated royalty distribution, defined in a smart contract by predefined logic, was appreciated because it did not rely on the authors waiting for manual processing or, at least, being vulnerable to mismatched payments. The use of MetaMask with wallet management has proved secure and user-friendly; the initiation of transactions and managing funds is made hassle-free. In general, authors have commented that the system significantly improved the accuracy and efficiency of royalty tracking. Publishers also give thumbs up by indicating the impact on overhead reduction due to the operation. The distribution of royalties to authors was previously done manually. Sometimes, such distributions caused delays or errors due to the complexity of the process. With blockchain, the distribution of royalties is now automated and simplified, hence allowing it to free up resources for other business operations. This accounts for why the system was transparent, meaning publishers can issue verifiable transaction records to enhance mutual trust between parties. The system is further seen as flexible, which means royalty percentages and content management can easily be changeable according to specific principles of change within the publishing environment. The system is highly scalable, as reported in feedback. The back-end was found to be highly intuitive and easy to navigate by administrators for content, users, and sales logs management. The off-chain storage solution came in handy to keep the blockchain at the optimal operating state while allowing the system to maintain a growing number of users and increased content. Some of the users recommended changes in the user interface of the application to improve the accessibility of analytics and transaction history. Such proposals will have useful implications for future updates to further enhance the system. Overall, the actual user interaction of the system has been able to balance user-friendliness, security, as well as blockchain transparency in a successful manner, thus making this platform an exciting solution for the modern distribution of royalties.

15.6.2.1 Benefits to Authors

The most revolutionary effect of this blockchain-based royalty system is on authors, especially the independent or self-published writers, who are most hurt by systemic inefficiencies. Conventional royalty models usually leave income uncertain because the payments are delayed and obscure, and they depend on intermediaries. Contrarily, the proposed system makes instant payments after each sale is verified and minimizes errors because of automatic royalty computation, and at the same time implements complete transparency because authors can monitor their sales and income in real time. Authors can enjoy a larger amount of their earnings by reducing their dependence on third parties. Cumulatively, these strengths improve the financial stability and renew the trust in the publishing process.

15.6.3 System Demonstration

System demonstration culminates in the final visual representation of how the blockchain-based royalty distribution system works in real time. The demonstrations include several user interface elements, thus showing the seamless flow of interactions for authors, publishers, and administrators. Key screenshots are given below, which highlight the author dashboard where one can view the earnings, track sales data, and see all the detailed reports of royalties that are created based on transactions recorded on the blockchain. In turn, this interface allows members to view live updating royalties; they get to view their pay when the sales are updated, ensuring that the process is clear and reliable. Authors can now interact with their

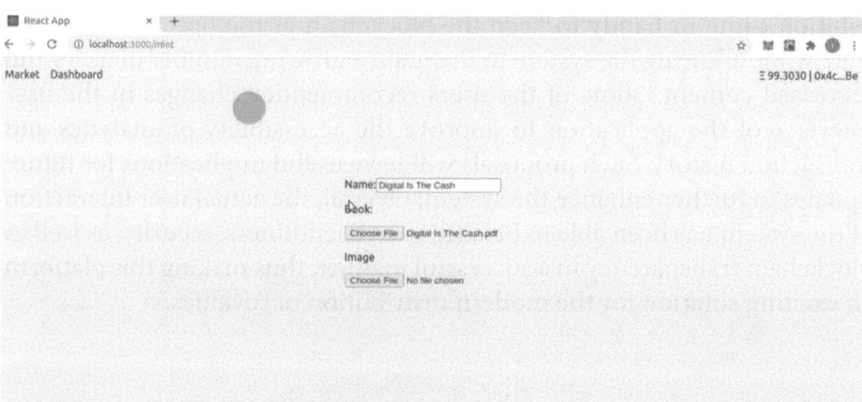

Figure 15.4 Author royalty distribution system user interface.

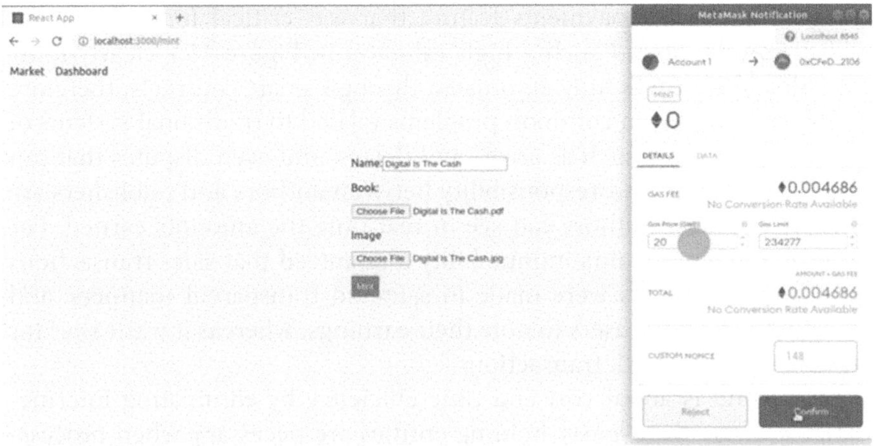

Figure 15.5 Connection with the MetaMask.

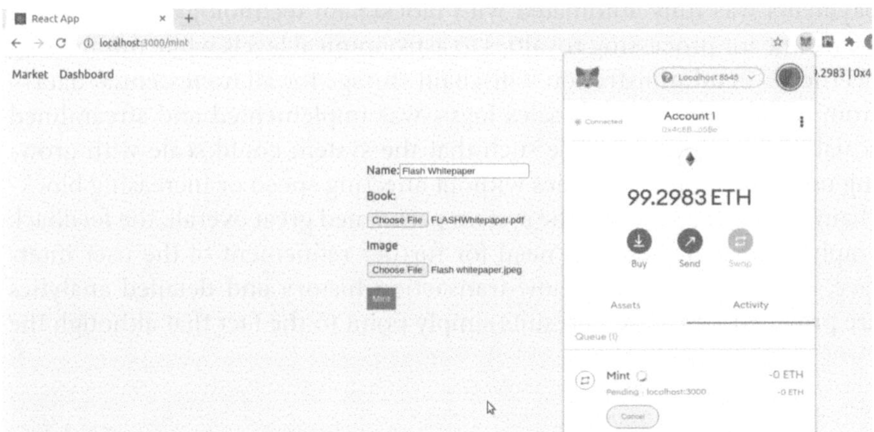

Figure 15.6 Ethereum transaction execution.

MetaMask wallet while directly being on the platform; this makes it easy to withdraw earnings or see the history of their transactions. Figures 15.4–15.6 illustrates the whole system demonstration.

15.6.4 Analysis of Key Findings

The final analysis of key findings about the blockchain-based royalty distribution system provides important insights into its effectiveness and efficiency and an opportunity for wide adoption. Among its findings, probably the most significant one is that the system can offer real-time transparency in regard to royalty payments feature that was critical for authors and publishers who placed such a high value on it. Figure 15.7 clearly illustrates this idea. It was fully automated through smart contracts, therefore totally liberating from common problems related to traditional systems of royalty distribution, such as errors and delays, and even disputes that can arise. Mutual trust and responsibility between authors and publishers are promoted because authors can see in real time the amounts earned. For instance, the blockchain's immutability guaranteed that sales transactions and royalty payments were made in safe and transparent manners, and this helped easily for users to note their earnings, whereas it was easier for auditors to cross-check transactions.

The second is about cost and time efficiency by eliminating intermediaries because third-party holding entities are necessary when processing payment in traditional royalty systems, which causes delay and errors and increases operational costs. In effect, the process of processing royalty payments was fully automated with blockchain technology, reducing the cycle time for processing royalties to astronomical levels while minimizing overheads in administration. Off-chain storage for all nonessential data—from content metadata to sales logs—was implemented and streamlined scalability and performance such that the system could scale with growing user and content volumes without affecting speed or increasing blockchain costs. Finally, while the system performed great overall, the feedback emphasized that there is a need for further refinement of the user interface, especially regarding how transaction history and detailed analytics are provided. Thus, these results simply point to the fact that although the

Figure 15.7 Number of books added by the author.

system fulfilled its prime objectives to automate, to provide transparency, and to reduce costs, still so much needs to be done in refining it to increase usability further and to appeal to a wider diversity of user preferences.

15.7 Conclusion and Future Work

15.7.1 Summary of Findings

The Author Royalty Distribution System integrated on the blockchain brings unprecedented benefits compared to the existing royalty distribution models in the context of decentralization, automation, and protection. The implementation of effective smart contracts means error-free transfer of royalties directly to the authors, thereby expunging the middlemen. An author is provided with the option of signing up, uploading content, and even checking royalties in real time, meaning they have authority and visibility over their fees. Due to decentralization of the system, fraud and dispute risks are eliminated as the transactions are stored on the blockchain database. Among other challenges that require to be solved for wide-scale adoption and implementation, there remain the following: for instance, scalability may involve many authors, content, and pieces, and transactions that may influence the performance of the system. The new system will also encounter some opposition from the industry players, including the traditional publishers and other stakeholders, who have been used to the old models of royalties. Also, the legal framework of blockchain and cryptocurrencies is not defined. Consequently, compliance problems will be a very challenging issue for the system. Based on all these factors, even though blockchain-based approach in royalty distribution has been tested and has been proven to bring a revolution in the current trend, it still requires a lot of work to be done, which should be complemented with the actual real life application of the system with the industry players to have most of these challenges factors worked out fully to guarantee success in the system. This research shows that there is vast potential that blockchain technology can be used to transform the way royalty in the publishing industry is managed. Using smart contracts, decentralized storage, and open transaction log, the proposed system ensures timely, secure, and verifiable revenues generated to authors. It attends to key aches, i.e., delayed payments, lack of transparency, and high administrative overhead that have been troubling the conventional system. Nonetheless, the issues of scalability and regulatory compliance, as well as the adoption from the users' side, must be resolved for wide deployment. Independently of the means of payment such as cryptocurrency, the legal ambiguities concerning cryptocurrency-based payment and data protection have to be navigated cautiously. Going forward, the system can be extended to accommodate multi-industry use cases, e.g., music, film, and digital art, as well as be integrated with the international payment gateways and tax modules. As blockchain grows up and acquires a mainstream trust, it can become a fundamental element of fair and efficient remuneration in the digital content economy.

15.7.2 Future Scope

The function of the Author Royalty Distribution System, which is founded on blockchain, shows through the analysis that there is great capacity for growth and improvement in the future. The first potential area to advance the system is to work on the scalability issue because it currently works only on a small scale with a few users and transactions. For extensive volumes of authors, content, and sales, the improvements in the blockchain infrastructure and transaction processing capability will be required. Options on Layer 2 solutions such as Optimism, Arbitrum, or even exploring other blockchains with a larger TPS could also be implemented to increase efficacy. As for the adoption, the system should be offered to other industries focused on IPR and royalties, for example, the music, film, and art industries. Such cross-industrial applicability could even further help drive the adoption of blockchain technology for royalty management. Further, it is also possible to connect more sophisticated functionalities to create even more benefit and comfort for authors and publishing companies, e.g., the computation of taxes or a link to worldwide payment systems. Additionally, the user interface and experience for the system could be designed to be even more user-friendly for the different client base, excluding the technical audience. Last but not least, pilot runs with various industry players are a prerequisite to assessing the system's efficiency and discovering operational realities. To achieve these goals, strategic partnerships with large publishing companies and content providers and cooperation with the official authorities to guarantee the sites' compliance with the currently effective laws will also be required. The future of this system is to make, consequently, a more efficient, transparent, and internationally accepted method of distribution of the royalties that will revolutionize how authors and creators of content are paid for their work.

AI disclosure statement: The author acknowledges the use of AI-based tools for minor language editing or grammatical correction. However, all intellectual contributions, analyses, and conclusions presented in this chapter are entirely the author's own.

References

1. Schmidt, K. and Micheli, P., Blockchain technology for royalty tracking in the music industry. *Int. J. Digital Innovation*, 12, 3, 45–60, 2019.
2. Gupta, M. and Zang, S., Decentralized rights management and royalty distribution using blockchain. *J. Media Blockchain Technol.*, 8, 1, 22–35, 2020.
3. Chen, L. and Li, X., Smart contract-based royalty distribution for the digital media industry with the Ethereum platform. *J. Emerging Technol. Content Manage.*, 6, 4, 71–85, 2021.
4. Smith, R. and Johnson, A., Blockchain for royalty management in publishing: A case study. *Publ. Technol. Rev.*, 14, 2, 55–68, 2018.
5. Patel, A. and Shah, R., A blockchain-based model for music rights distribution. *Int. J. Music Bus. Res.*, 11, 1, 33–48, 2019.
6. Brown, F. and Green, K., Enhancing transparency in royalty distribution with blockchain. *J. Blockchain Creative Economies*, 9, 2, 103–117, 2020.
7. White, M. and Black, T., Blockchain-enabled royalty management for independent authors. *Digital Publ. Blockchain Syst.*, 7, 3, 80–94, 2021.
8. Wang, H. and Zhang, Y., A blockchain framework for secure royalty distribution in digital content. *J. Secure Digital Media*, 5, 2, 60–75, 2019.
9. Martinez, J. and Hernandez, S.B., Royalty management in the publishing industry using blockchain. *J. Distrib. Publ. Technol.*, 3, 1, 44–59, 2018.
10. Perez, K. and Thompson, J., Blockchain-based copyright and royalty management system. *Creative Rights Technol. J.*, 6, 4, 25–39, 2019.
11. Nguyen, K. and Le, T., Decentralized royalty payment system using blockchain. *Int. J. Blockchain Appl.*, 10, 1, 91–105, 2020.
12. Singh, R., Mehta, A., Verma, P., Blockchain-based approach to intellectual property rights and royalty management. *J. Digital Rights Technol.*, 10, 2, 55–70, 2022.
13. Zhang, A. and Rao, L., Decentralized royalty payment system using Hyperledger Fabric for digital content distribution. *Int. J. Blockchain Appl.*, 8, 1, 44–58, 2021.
14. Johnson, M., Das, R., Banerjee, S., Enhancing author royalties using Ethereum smart contracts. *J. Emerging Tech. Publ.*, 7, 3, 60–74, 2022.
15. Kim, H. and Choi, Y., Automated smart contract-based royalty distribution using Ethereum. *J. Blockchain Solutions Publ.*, 9, 2, 85–98, 2022.
16. Patel, S. and Desai, K., Smart contract-enabled royalty management on Hyperledger Fabric. *Int. Rev. Digital Innovation*, 11, 4, 101–115, 2021.

17. Brown, R. and Green, D., Smart contracts for decentralized film royalty distribution: A proof of concept. *J. Digital Media Econ.*, 6, 4, 122–135, 2022.
18. Wilson, T. and Hall, M., Scalable blockchain-based solution for independent author royalty management. *J. Decentralized Content Syst.*, 8, 2, 92–106, 2023.
19. Martinez, J., Russo, F., Clark, A., Optimizing royalty payments in music using Ethereum smart contracts. *Blockchain Creative Ind. Rev.*, 5, 3, 70–84, 2022.
20. White, K., Moore, T., Gupta, S., Decentralized publishing royalties: A Hyperledger Fabric implementation. *J. Publ. Technol.*, 12, 1, 35–49, 2023.

16

LCR Circuit Analysis of Incident Angle Metamaterial Absorber for Double-Band Wi-Fi Applications in IoT-Based Sensors: A Mathematical Insight

Ram Krishna[1], Harendra Singh[1*], Arun Kumar Rana[2], Anurag Singh[3] and Avinash Kumar[1]

[1]*Department of Electronics & Communication Engineering, G. L. Bajaj Institute of Technology and Management, Greater Noida, Uttar Pradesh, India*
[2]*Department of Computer Science, Galgotias College of Engineering of Technology, Greater Noida, Uttar Pradesh, India*
[3]*Department of Electrical & Electronics Engineering, G. L. Bajaj Institute of Technology and Management, Greater Noida, Uttar Pradesh, India*

Abstract
The construction of a nonseparated electromagnetic metamaterial (MM) absorber with desirable gain and resonating recurrence (frequency) for double-band Wi-Fi signal absorption is described using an innovative and systematic approach. First, a schematic diagram with in-depth analysis has been developed to achieve the desired resonant frequency with expected *S* parameter values. Next, precise LCR elements are utilized in numerical simulation to enact the resonating frequencies into a frequency-selective MM absorber, which fulfilled the minimum unit cell cross-section (0.08), minimum substance width (0.01), and highest adequate medium ratio requirements (12.50). The optimum impact angle for straight and angled incidences during copolarization was computed for suggested absorber. With one negative value to verify MM properties, the absorptions at the necessary resonant frequency were detected to be at a realistic value by both simulations and experimentally measured. The equivalent circuit analysis method that is being suggested can aid in the development of copolarization-insensitive designs. Without lumped elements or multilayered substances, MM absorbers can produce

**Corresponding author*: harendramvn2010@gmail.com

Shubham Mahajan, Davinder Paul Singh, Amit Kant Pandit and Paras Chawla (eds.) Ensuring Privacy in Digital Twin Ecosystems, (471–498) © 2026 Scrivener Publishing LLC

the appropriate resonant frequency and output accuracy using conventional split-ring resonators. Other practical Wi-Fi–related uses for the suggested MM include Internet of Things–based crowd sensing and SAR reduction.

***Keywords*:** Metamaterial absorber, transmission line model, double-band absorber circuit, equivalent circuit of absorber, CRR

16.1 Introduction

Scientists and engineers have been much interested in metamaterials (MMs) during the last decade because simple metamaterial and periodic structure-based MMs have a lot of applications in real life such as electromagnetic (EM) clocking, EM interface, EM capability solutions, human body applications, super advance lenses, sound technological and sensor devices, etc. Among these applications, EM absorber is an important application of MM [1–3]. To minimize SAR to the human body, the developed framework can be used in laptops or mobile devices to absorb harmful EM radiation. This model can also be used for microwave energy harvesting tools in gadgets such as wireless headphones or smartwatches. At last, the unit cell engineering, as examined through analogous circuit analysis in this study, could potentially aid scientists in developing advanced EM absorbers for further relevant applications. Different types of EMEM wave absorbers have been configured recently. Negative permittivity and permeability, which results in positive/negative or refractive index and backward propagation, are surprising features that MM, a constructed structure, combines [4]. This unique phenomenon makes it possible for researchers to use MM for numerous applications, which includes consumption, detection, shape and construction of antenna, uses of mobile, military application, decrement in the area of radar, EM clock, filter, hallow sphere for transmitting of wave (also known as waveguide) [5], and many more. Sim *et al.* [11] were the first to introduce MPA. MPA was given the first priority at that time because it absorbs all the EM wave falls on it and reflected back nothing from the MPA surface. This allows wide applications, as energy harvesting, optical sensing, switching, unwanted frequency absorption, etc. Due to the location of the absorption range of frequency and absorption level, both are the same at distinct polarization phase, one of the crucial components of MPA is polarization insensitivity. High levels of structural symmetry are used to attain this characteristic. The suggested absorber's suitability for various applications is demonstrated by an investigation into its use with pressure and permittivity sensors. To show that the suggested structure can be used for applications in the K band, such as sensors, filters, intrusive clocks, etc., a comparison with previous research is also made.

In the current article we proposed a co–cross-polarization application based on EM wave absorber. The values of basic circuit parameters as resistor, inductor and capacitor have been its equivalent electrical circuit synthesis. This analysis also improves the results of GHz absorber that are used nowadays. MM absorbers are made up of certain type of material in which Fr-4 is the best material on account of its maximum absorption capacity [6–10]. But it has a drawback: with increment in absorption, its size and cost will increase. To overcome this drawback, a dielectric material with thickness equal to quarter wavelength ($\lambda/4$) and resistive sheet is used. This thickness is less than the wedge tapered absorber, so its cost is low. But this absorber is bulky because at lower absorption frequency, thicker absorber is required. That is why small thickness and minimum cost with excellent absorption are the necessary requirements for absorber [11–18]. Best absorber can be designed effortlessly at lower cost with requirement described above including resonating condition. As the wavelength of MM absorber is increased, its unit size also increases at low frequency. At a certain level of frequency, periodic structure of MM is widening rapidly. Reducing these types of drawbacks, recently a lot of MM absorbers are configured utilizing different methods such as including capacitor, multi-layer snake-shaped absorber can be designed [19, 20]. It can be provided by alluring rubber plate and hybrid resonator, grooved surface, and sandwich-shaped metal dielectric metal. It is difficult for small layer, small unit cell, and single layer. MM absorber is a quite interesting subject among the researchers and scientists on account of its broad application area. Lots of research have been conducted on it in the field of electromagnetism, sound optics, and mechanical engineering. During the last few decades, experimental analysis has been conducted on EM waves for accurate and reliable MM absorber design, which are present as the microwave MM absorber. Comparison with and without cross polarization is insensitive. Almost all absorbers are inaccurate due to the insensitive cross polarization caused by different designing structures [21–25]. It is the simplest among cut-ring resonator (CRR), cross CCR, and coupled and noncoupled CRR. The equivalent transmission line model of suggested MM absorber is presented in Figure 16.1.

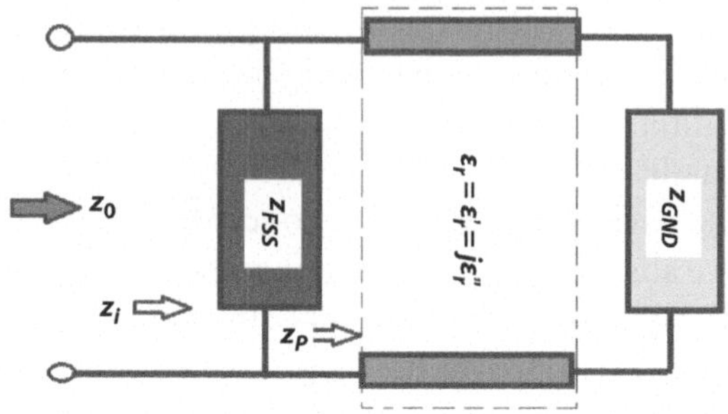

Figure 16.1 Equivalent transmission line model of proposed metamaterial absorber.

In research and a comprehensive analogous circuit study discuss the concept of a nonseparated insensitive MM absorber with suitable *S* constants and resonant frequencies for 2.40 and 5.00 GHz Wi-Fi signal absorption. The projected absorber's unit cell was created using an analogous circuit. In order to prevent unnecessary complications such as capacitive coupling caused by complex patch design and phase unmatching, typical arc-shaped CRR have now been used for optimal modeling of the absorber with approximated single cell dimension as well as mark size [26–28]. The proposed model describes a methodical process for designing a double-band absorber that operates at 2.4 and 5 GHz, perfect for Wi-Fi applications, using an analogous LCR circuit model. In order to ensure effective absorption with a small footprint, the design places a high priority on a high effective medium ratio (EMR = 12.5), a reduced substrate thickness, and a minimal unit cell size (0.081λ). Crucially, the absorber's polarization insensitivity up to 180° is a crucial characteristic for reliable operation. The usage of common arc-shaped cut-ring resonance devices (CRRs) avoids elaborate multilayer or bulk element designs. The absorber's broadband and angle-stable response enable practical applications such as SAR reduction, Internet of Things (IoT)–based crowd perception, and EM interference prevention in intelligent devices. This article has been split in subsections that each describe a different issue: the transmission line framework, the approximate circuit design, the evaluation of the resistances needed to achieve appropriate outcome of the *S* constants from equivalent circuit, the organization of the frequency selective surface for double-band consumption, the optimization techniques in a planned single cell, the quantification in case of fiction absorber, as well as consultation [29–32]. Crowd sensing in IoT-based systems depends on identifying and evaluating Wi-Fi signals sent by a large number of linked devices. The MM absorber's dual-band capabilities and high absorption capacity (up to 98%) enable it to effectively filter out undesired Wi-Fi noise or reflections. This lessens signal interference and increases the accuracy of data gathering and device localization in congested settings such as stadiums, shopping centers, and cities. The absorber is perfect for dynamic, multidirectional IoT situations because of its 180° polarization insensitivity, which guarantees steady performance regardless of the angle of incoming signals. The rate at which EM radiation from electronic gadgets is absorbed by the human body is known as SAR. When included into wearables, laptops, or smartphones, the MM absorber can drastically cut down on stray EM radiation by absorbing it before it reaches the user. It is simple to include into small consumer electronics due to its tiny profile (minimum unit cell cross-section and material thickness) and lack of large lumped components. Its capacity to precisely target and absorb hazardous Wi-Fi radiation is further enhanced by the virtual ground and circuit-analog design, which further guarantees exact control over the resonant frequency. Therefore, safer and more dependable applications in developing smart technologies are directly impacted by the absorber's small, accurate, and efficient design. The proposed architecture has been determined to be the best Wi-Fi absorber that encompasses the adequate equivalent circuit analysis for conclusion and comparison of the recommended absorber's execution standards with other Wi-Fi absorbers. Nowadays, there many applications of IoT-based sensors in the biomedical field such as telemedicine, remote surgery, tracking patient movement in biomedical field, continuous observation utilizing (RFID) wearable gadgets, and giving continuous therapy data and support for patients. The IoT technologies include 5G network, RFID, and sensor networks. The voice technology will soon be available to billions of people as speech recognition systems continue to develop and grow more advanced. According to experts, in the next 5 years, almost every app will use voice technology in some capacity.

16.2 Generalized Model of Transmission Line for the Nonseparated Absorber

Figure 16.1 below depicts transmission line and the right-side perspective of 3-layer MM structure (substance, patch and ground). In transmission line, "D" stands in for the structure's dielectric substance (of thickness *D*). The initial part of transmission line is linked with FSS (patch) impedance, Z_{FSS}, as well as another is attached to the lightly metallic ground of resistance, Z_{GND} [33–36]. To maximize both compactness and performance, it specifies a minimum unit cell cross-section of 0.08λ and a material width of 0.01λ. Effective Wi-Fi absorption at 2.4 and 5 GHz is supported by these exact figures. The comparable LCR circuit model uses precisely determined resistor, inductor, and capacitor values to simplify complex EM phenomena. Simulation and experimental data clearly demonstrate the high absorption efficiency (over 98%) and polarization insensitivity up to 180°, guaranteeing that the design's functionality is both comprehensible and practically verifiable. To behave as a remnant for impedance matching, the grounded metal will contain cut cross section in the middle that equalize exact value to the characteristic's impedance $Z_0 = \sqrt{\frac{L}{C}}$ of the MM. The transmission line model of proposed model is drawn in Figure 16.2.

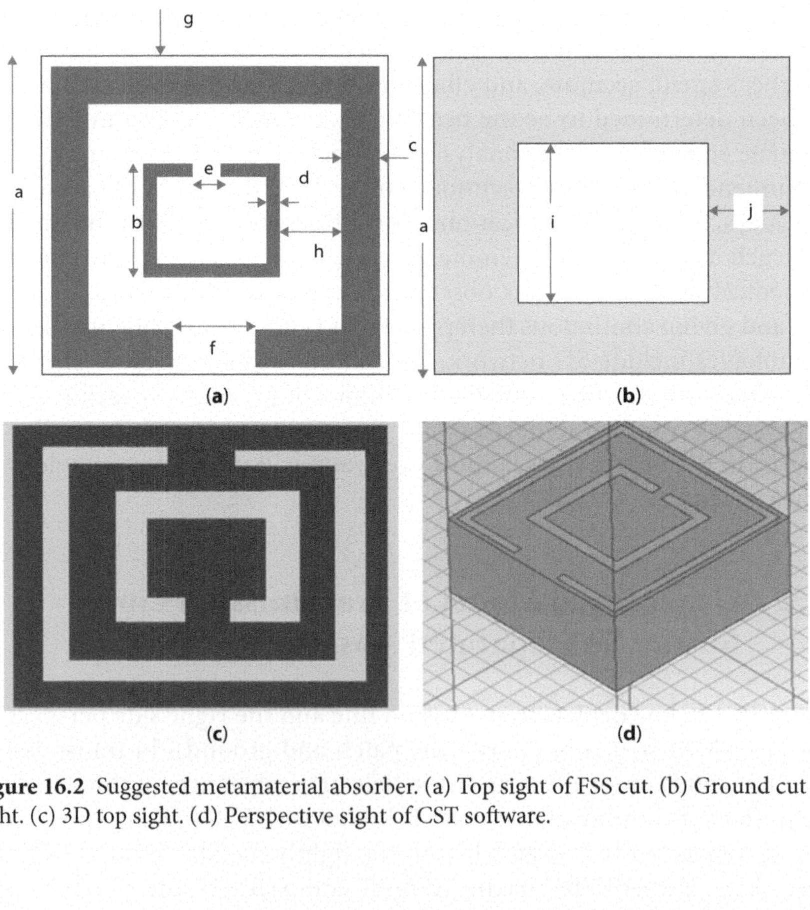

Figure 16.2 Suggested metamaterial absorber. (a) Top sight of FSS cut. (b) Ground cut sight. (c) 3D top sight. (d) Perspective sight of CST software.

The input side impedance of MM Z_i for the coupled transmission line at the grounded surface is written as:

$$z_p = J\frac{z_0}{\sqrt{\varepsilon_r}}tan(K_0\sqrt{\varepsilon_r}D) \tag{16.1}$$

where $\varepsilon_r = (\varepsilon_r^{'} - j\varepsilon_r^{''})$ permittivity of dielectric substance and k_0 = wave propagating constant.

To reduce the reflection and transmission of the injected MM EM wave, the net impedance Z_T of MM will coherent with the impedance of free space represented as Z_0.

$$z_T = z_{Fss}\left|\right|(z_D + z_{GND}) \tag{16.2}$$

So that $S_{11} = \frac{Z_T - Z_0}{Z_T + Z_0}$ and $S_{21} = \frac{2Z_T}{Z_T + Z_0}$. The framework's transmission coefficient and reflection coefficient must be zero in case of absorption. So, Z_T must follow (a) real (Z_T) ≈ Z_0, while (b) imaginary part (Z_T) with the flat transition from zero line [37, 38].

$z_c = Z_0\sqrt{\frac{\mu_r(\omega)}{\varepsilon_{r(\omega)}}}$ were characteristics impedance substrate

$S_{11} = \frac{z_{in}(\omega) - zc(\omega)}{z_{in}(\omega) + z_c(\omega)}$ reflection coefficient of absorber

$$\text{BW}(\%) = \frac{f_h - f_L}{f_C} \times 100$$

$$\text{Absorption} = 1 - \left|s_{11}\right|^2 - \left|s_{12}\right|^2 \tag{16.3}$$

16.3 Suggested Double-Band Absorber Circuit Model

The suggested equivalent circuit analysis approach uses a simplified LCR (inductor–capacitor–resistor) framework to develop a copolarization-insensitive MM absorber that accurately simulates EM behavior without the need for lumped components or intricate multilayer constructions. The design attains targeted resonance at 2.4 and 5 GHz with good absorption efficiency by precisely allocating *R*, *L*, and *C* values to each resonating component. This technique is perfect for real-world applications including SAR reduction, IoT-based crowd sensing, and EM shielding in wireless devices because it allows consistent performance under a range of polarization angles—up to 180°. The suggested double-band absorber circuit model is shown in Figure 16.3.

The input line impedance of individual DRA is calculated as:

$$Z_{in3} = Z_6\left[\frac{Z_0 - JZ_6\tan(K_z h1)}{Z_6 - JZ_0\tan(K_z h1)}\right];\; Z_{in2} = Z_5\left[\frac{Z_{P3} - JZ_6\tan(K_z h1)}{Z_6 - JZ_{P3}\tan(K_z h1)}\right];$$

$$Z_{in1} = Z_4\left[\frac{Z_{P2} - JZ_4\tan(K_z h1)}{Z_4 - JZ_{P2}\tan(K_z h1)}\right]$$ and $k_z = \sqrt{k_p^2 - k_0^2 \sin\theta}$ where Z_{D1}, Z_{D2}, and Z_{D3} are individual impedance of DRA.

$$Z_{D1} = R_1 + J\left(\omega L_1 - \frac{1}{\omega C_1}\right)$$

$$Z_{D2} = R_2 + J\left(\omega L_2 - \frac{1}{\omega C_2}\right)$$

$$Z_{D3} = R_3 + J\left(\omega L_3 - \frac{1}{\omega C_3}\right)$$

$$Z_{P3} = Z_{D3} \,||\, Z_{in3},\; Z_{P2} = Z_{D2} \,||\, Z_{in2} \text{ and } Z_{P1} = Z_{D1} \,||\, Z_{in1} = Z_T \tag{16.4}$$

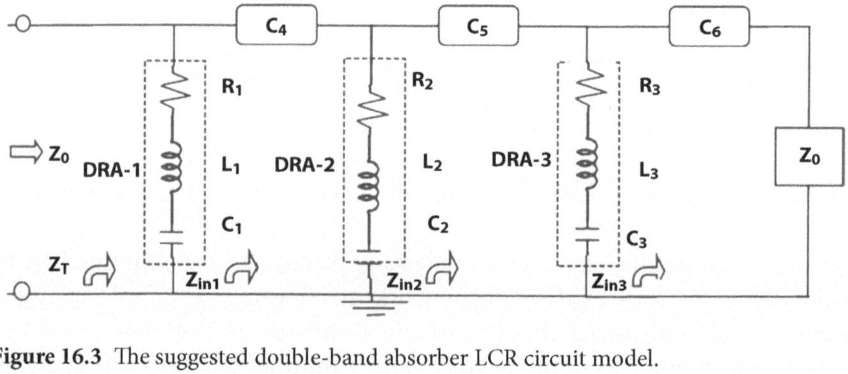

Figure 16.3 The suggested double-band absorber LCR circuit model.

Figure 16.3 illustrates the configuration of the double-band Wi-Fi signal absorber that has been suggested. To achieve the values of *R*, *L*, and *C* of the separate microstrip CRRs on the patch with accurate resonating frequency parameter is the first stage in design of an absorber unit cell with the required resonating conditions and *S* constants. The equivalent circuit diagram can be utilized to generate these precise readings. Same circuit can be generated by other software such as ADSs that are commercially available [39, 40].

Determination of *L* and *C* for resonant frequency: The inductive value of every resonator of the MM absorber single cell mark can be calculated by Eq. (16.5) as per Figure 16.2(d).

$$L_{ms} = 0.00508L\left[\ln\left(\frac{2l}{w+D}\right)+0\cdot5+0\cdot2235\left(\frac{\omega+D}{l}\right)\right] \quad (16.5)$$

where L_{ms} is per unit length inductance of microstrip (μH), *l* is strip length (inches), *W* is strip width (inches), and *D* is gap between the strip line and earth surface. Dimensions such as the length of microstrip CRR as well and the width of microstrip CRR can be calculated from Eq. (16.5).

At the preferred resonating frequency, the capacitance value may be attained from Eq. (16.6):

$$C = \frac{1}{4\pi^2 f^2 L_{ms}} \quad (16.6)$$

where *f* is the preferred resonating frequency.

The necessary values for *L* and *C* to be used in the circuit simulator can be found in Eqs. (16.5) and (16.6) for each desirable frequency. For 2.4 and 5 GHz, separately, the dimension *l* and w of the two-resonating cut-rings were chosen in accordance with Eq. (16.5). Following that, using Eq. (16.6), we can calculate the preferred values of capacitance (C_1 and C_3) at the resonant frequency, they were inserted in the patch by Eq. (16.5), in which capacitive gaps are computed as split gaps (Figure 16.2). For 2.4 GHz, the first or circumferential resonator's *l*, *w*, and split gap were set initially. For 5 GHz, the interior resonator's dimensions and the noncopper ground cut were established after taking into account nonmetal surface gaps that were constrained by other materials. When compared to optimum absorptions at resonant bandwidth, isolation is known as lesser or zero absorption. Capacitive components (C_4, C_5, and C_6) were put between

Table 16.1 Synthesize electrical parameters.

Frequency (GHz)	Synthesize electrical element value		
2.4 and 5 GHz Dual-band	R_1 (Ohm)	R_2 (Ohm)	R_3 (Ohm)
	30.786	45.925	47.75
	L_1 (nanoH)	L_2 (nanoH)	L_3 (nanoH)
	27.11	13.91	13.04
	C_1 (picoF)	C_2 (picoF)	C_3 ((picoF)
	0.162	0.0729	0.371
	C_4 (picoF)	C_5 (picoF)	C_6 (picoF)
	39	0.0645	0.146889

transmission lines and grounded transmission line in order to retain the isolation.

Because of capacitive gaps between the resonators, as represented in Figure 16.3, the measured values for L and C must be inputted on the ADS simulator as equidistant transmission lines coupled by capacitive elements [41, 42]. As no inductive devices can be substituted for capacitive gaps, a too high level of inductance would be necessary to shut off the main inductors (L_1 and L_2) because the connection between them is series and modifying resonating frequencies, the capacitive gaps resulting from the nonmetal region circumscribed as (16.5):

$$C = \varepsilon_0 \varepsilon_r \frac{A}{d} \tag{16.7}$$

where ε_0 is permittivity of air, ε_r is relative permittivity of a material, A is cross-sectional area of cutting strip of conductor, and d is h of outer resonator, $(b - 2d)$ of inner resonator and i of ground cut; Figure 16.3 shows the distance for the splits/gaps or the ground cut.

The unit cell in Figure 16.2 was made to accept in Wi-Fi signal at 2.40 and 5.00 GHz. For this, two standard square CRRs have been used. The inner CRR operates at larger resonant frequency than the outer CRR, which operates at lower resonating frequencies (2.4 GHz, 5 GHz). Each resonator has its impedance and inductance. The advanced design system circuit's capacitance and inductance values were adjusted as depicted in Figure 16.3. For resonating frequency 2.40 and 5.00 GHz, the computed values of inductance and capacitance are $L_1 = 2.711 \times 10^{-10}$ H, $C_1 = 1.62 \times 10^{-11}$ F, and $L_2 = 1.391 \times 10^{-10}$ H, $C_2 = 7.29 \times 10^{-10}$ F, individually. The matching values for ground are determined to be $L_3 = 1.304 \times 10^{-10}$ H, $C_3 = 3.71 \times 10^{-11}$ F.

According to Figure 16.3, the first TL (transmission line), circuit parameters, corresponds to the lesser resonant frequencies (2.4 GHz). With third TL (transmission line), circuit parameters, which protrudes from grounded surface, the second transmission line, L_2–C_3-R_2, functions for larger resonant frequencies (5 GHz). As there is some mutual coupling between them, these equidistant segmented transmission lines cannot guarantee different resonating at 2.4 and 5 GHz. The inductive element cannot be inserted between neighboring lines to lessen couplings because the new values will change the resonating frequencies. The capacitive gaps caused by nonmetal surfaces surrounded by split rings as illustrated in Figure 16.2 can be used to justify the insertion of series capacitive elements between parallel adjacent transmission lines. Between the first and second lines, C_4 was introduced, and between the second and third lines, C_5 (Figure 16.3). Because the MM absorbers are characterized as periodic structures, inductive and capacitive components in the circuit may cause EM coupling. These components can be removed on the addition of capacitances in series (such as C_6) to the circuit, as represented in Figure 16.3. The series connection of inductive elements and the grounded transmission line ($L_3/C_3/R_3$) and cannot be added to the circuit in place of C_6. Because the nonmetal area is confined by the outermost ring, C_4 is taken into consideration, and its value (=39 pF) was selected greater than that of C_5 (6.45×10^{-10} F) and C_6 (1.4668×10^{-11} F). The outer or initial split ring impacts the surrounding area up to the next unit cell and the interior area it borders. On the advanced design system circuit simulator, the values of C_4, C_5, and C_6 are adjusted until they provided the best isolation between resonating frequencies.

16.4 Estimated Value of Resistance of Each LCR by Equivalent Circuit Analysis

In the central area from 2.4 to 5 GHz as shown in Figure 16.4, mutual coupling in between second- and third-line pushes S_{11}'s constant in the domain of zero. The resonating peaks in Figure 16.4 are sharpened by capacitors C_4, C_5, and C_6 connected parallely, which are caused by plane

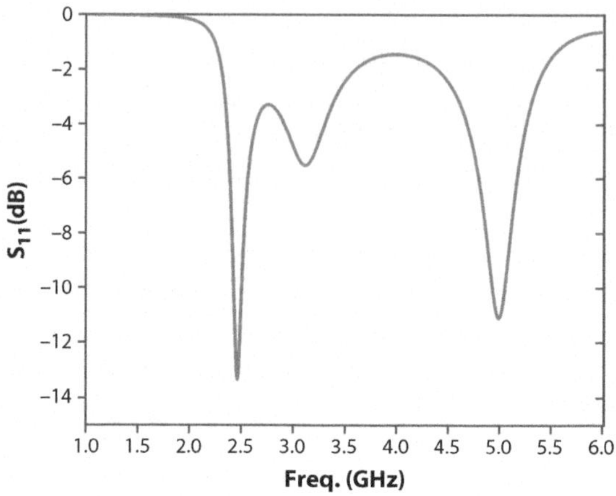

Figure 16.4 The suggested achievable dB *S* parameters' constant of double band absorber using CST software.

surfaces limited by resonators first, second, and the ground (illustrated in Figure 16.3). Each of the two waveguides ports input impedances was set by default to 50 ohms. Each LC transmission line has a series of resistances applied to it in order to get the necessary values of the S_{11} and S_{21} constants (in dB). Desired dB values of *S* parameters were attained by adjusting these resistances, as shown in.

R_o needs to be identified to assess the necessary input impedance of the unit cell structure, considering that the unit cell incurs losses due to the ohmic loss (R_o) within the area enclosed by CRRs and the dielectric loss (R_d) of the material.

$$R_0 = \frac{\text{cell area}}{\text{metallic area of CRR}} = \left(\frac{1}{\delta\sigma}\right) \tag{16.8}$$

Complex Poynting vector 33 predicts that energy will flow across the boundary surface as EM waves transition between different media. This energy flow can be calculated using the formula $\vec{P_c} = \frac{1}{2}\vec{E} \times \vec{H}$. As per the energy conservation law, the rate at which energy dissipated in the initial medium will equalize the energy flow rate in upcoming medium and same for reverse. The average power flow in complex media (where negative nonreal parts of permittivity, permeability, and refractive index) is determined by [43–45].

$$P_{av} = \frac{1}{2}\text{Re}\{\vec{E} \times \vec{H}\} = \frac{1}{2}\text{Re}(EH^*) = \frac{1}{2}\text{Re}(\eta HH^*)$$

If $1-1 = H_m e^{j\omega t}$ and $H^* = H_m e^{-j\omega t}$, then

$$P_{av} = \frac{1}{2} H_m^2 \,\text{Re}(\eta)$$

where Hm is maximum magnetic field, and $\eta\left[\sqrt{\frac{\mu}{\varepsilon}}\left(1 + J\frac{\sigma}{2\omega\varepsilon}\right)\right]$ is intrinsic impedance of second substance.

The impedance parameters of the suggested double-band absorber in dB are presented in Figure 16.5.

For FR4 substance (dielectric medium), the dissipation factor $\left(D_f = \frac{\sigma}{\omega\varepsilon}\right)$ is less than 1. To preserve EM energy in a complex medium, Chew states that the actual parts of ε and μ must be negative, whereas unreal parts must be positive and same for reverse. Furthermore, according to Eq. (16.8) and depending on the actual component of η, the mean power loss in medium 1 (in this case, the air medium the suggested absorber) will be equal to the power flow in medium 2 (the absorber). The suggested absorber adheres to the law of conservation of EM energy, as confirmed

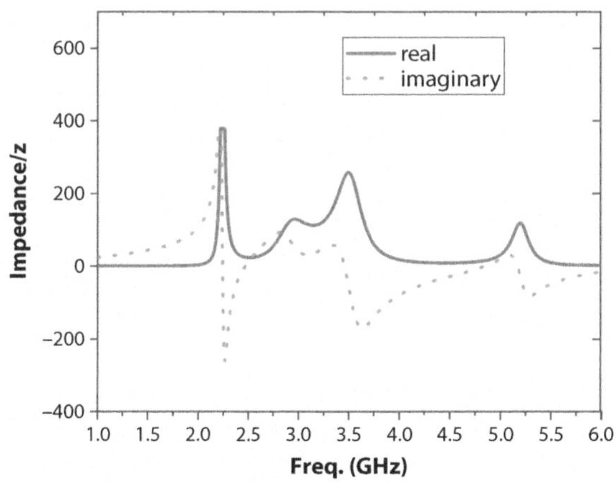

Figure 16.5 Suggested double-band absorber's impedance parameters.

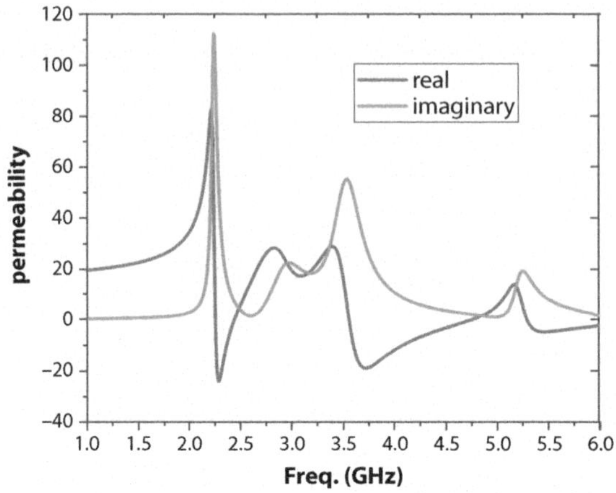

Figure 16.6 The permeability parameters of the suggested double-band absorber.

by the positive values of the actual parts of ε, μ, and refractive index at the resonant frequencies, along with negative corresponding unreal parts (Figure 16.6). According to the description above, the suggested absorber abides by the rule of (EM) energy conservation.

As shown in Figure 16.7, the unit cell was used with both straight and angled incidence of EM waves and represented identical absorptivity in both situations. The unit cell exhibits above 98% universal absorptivity at

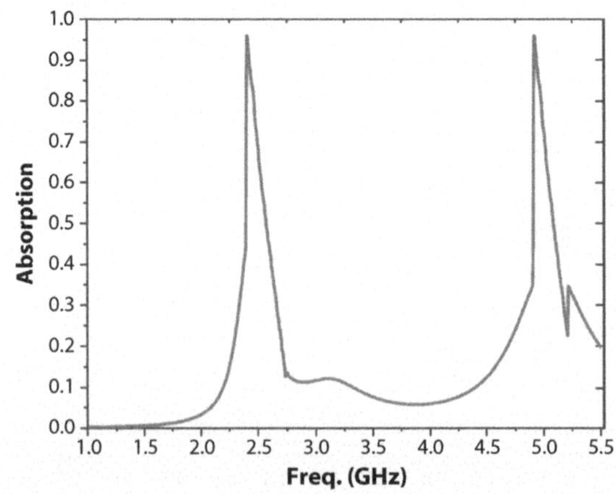

Figure 16.7 The absorption parameters of suggested double-band absorber.

2.4 and 5 GHz, which are specified for Wi-Fi signal, at all polarizing angles (nonseparated).

Absorption was calculated from S_{11} and S_{21} constants by the formula given below:

$$A = 1 - |s_{11}|^2 - |s_{21}|^2 \tag{16.9}$$

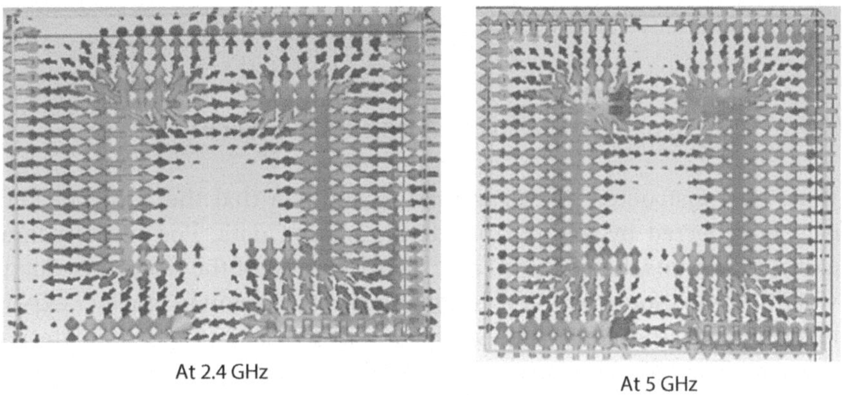

Figure 16.8 Electric field of suggested double-band metamaterial absorber at 2.4 and 5 GHz.

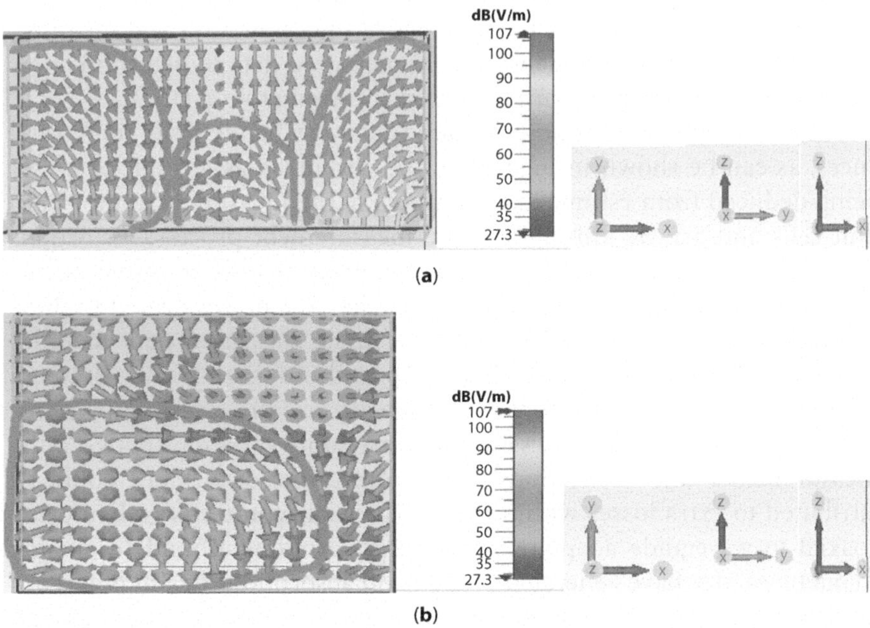

Figure 16.9 Double-band metamaterial absorber at 2.4 GHz. (a) Current distribution. (b) Electric field distribution in all coordinates.

All coordinates at the same frequency 2.4 GHz modes of the suggested absorber are the following:

The electric field of suggested double-band MM absorber at 2.4 and 5 GHz is shown in Figure 16.8.

Figure 16.8 illustrates the absorber proposed in this study, demonstrating complete absorption for both the unit cell and the array at the resonant frequencies of 2.4 and 5 GHz. Figure 16.9 illustrate, current distribution and corresponding electric field distribution in all coordinates of double-band metamaterial absorber at 2.4 GHz.

16.5 Computation of the Absorber's Size

It must be constructed and examined to confirm that the absorber performs as expected by theoretical and simulation data. For experimental measuring reasons, the unit cell and the formation of the necessary quantity of unit cells should be put through. The first criterion is a proper experimental setup without any undesirable interference coming from external EM waves. Therefore, the structure should be installed inside an anechoic chamber to ensure EM wave shielding externally. Figure 16.9 displays the experimental configuration utilized for examining the unit cell and structure using a vector network analyzer (VNA). The Methods section follows the conclusion and contains the specifics of the calibration and measurement. *S* characteristics were taken from measured data to determine how well the constructed absorber performed according to Eq. (16.9).

The observed results at nonresonant frequency bands show some variances, as can be shown in Figure 16.10. It occurred as a result of noises being deduced from estimated *S* constants of the measured data for both unit cells and arrays. Throughout the measurement process, distortions are evident at nonresonating frequencies, whereas only minimal distortions are discernible at resonating frequencies. The noises related to these aberrations were subtracted to reveal accurate measured data in order to achieve the best results, which are depicted in Figure 16.10. Although achieving absorptions at resonant frequencies was the measurement procedure' goal, and it was successful, there are some variations between the measurements' and simulations' bandwidths. This occurrence could be attributed to extra losses within the coaxial cable connectors when using coaxial-to-waveguide adapters. Spurious absorptions around resonating frequencies may have generated broad band absorptions due to poor connecting impedance. Similar to this, the advanced design system circuit, which is regarded as the comparable circuit, has demonstrated broad-band

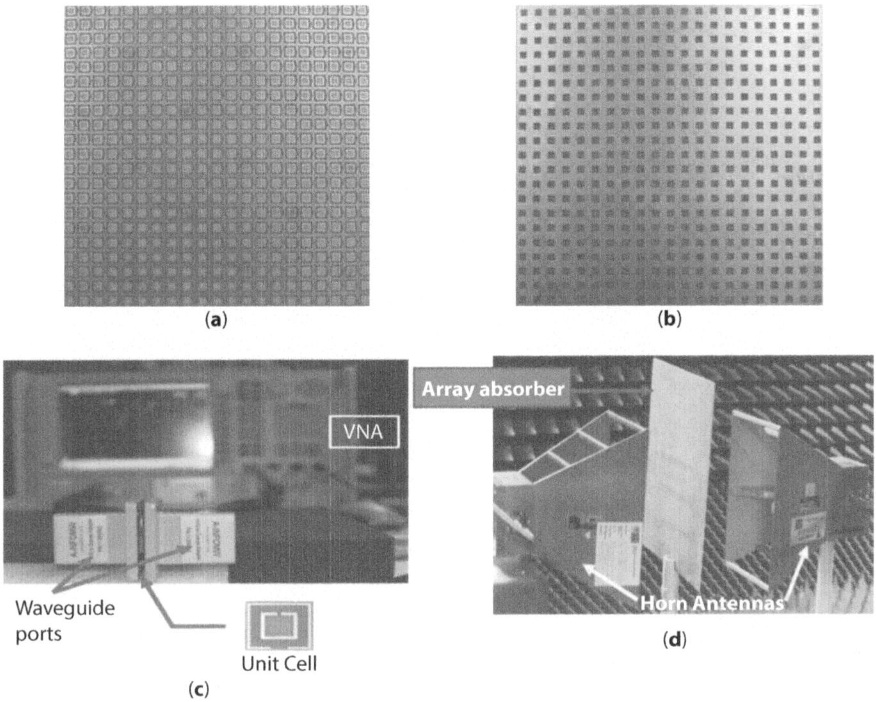

Figure 16.10 The investigational setup for measuring the single cell and array using a vector network analyzer (VNA).

absorption (unit cell designed on CST cannot be precisely replaced). Finally, Figure 16.10 illustrates the efficacy of the proposed equivalent circuit model and the ensuing methodology for crafting MM absorbers tailored to specific frequencies.

16.6 Discussion

To develop an MM unit cell that effectively blocks Wi-Fi signals regardless of polarization, the suggested technique stands as the sole viable approach, applicable to both 2.4- and 5-GHz frequencies. Based on classic square CRRs, the proposed unit cell incorporates computed dimensions for both the rings and their spacings. This design approach ensures precision and optimization in the unit cell's performance. By utilizing these calculated parameters, the unit cell can achieve desired characteristics for specific applications. The integration of computed dimensions allows

Table 16.2 Parameter analysis of proposed absorber with existing ones (maximum polarization angle insensitivity [MPAI] and electric circuit analysis [ECA]).

Ref.	Year	Resonance frequency (GHz)	Size of single cell (mm)	SNG/DNG values	Substrate and thickness (mm)	MPAI	ECA	EM radiation
[40]	2016	10.29	2.7 × 2.7 (0.56 mm)	Not reported	3-layer	90°	Simple analysis shown	Not shown
[41]	2014	2	12.2 × 12.2 (1.27 mm)	Not reported	3-layer	90°	Simple analysis shown	Not shown
[42]	2015	2.5	20 × 20 (2.4 mm)	Not reported	2-layer	90°	Not shown	Not shown
[43]	2001	0.45	40 × 40 (16 mm)	Not reported	3-layer	90°	Not shown	Not shown
[44]	2015	0.42	62.5 × 62.5 (14 mm)	Not reported	1-layer	90°	Not shown	Not shown
[45]	2018	2.4	4 × 4 (5.6 mm)	Not reported	1-layer	90°	Not shown	Not shown

(Continued)

Table 16.2 Parameter analysis of proposed absorber with existing ones (maximum polarization angle insensitivity [MPAI] and electric circuit analysis [ECA]). (*Continued*)

Ref.	Year	Resonance frequency (GHz)	Size of single cell (mm)	SNG/DNG values	Substrate and thickness (mm)	MPAI	ECA	EM radiation
[37]	2018	2.45 and 5	(34 mm) 0.271λ	NR	Double-layer FR4 (3.2 mm)	Not described	Not presented	3.67
[38]	2019	2.21 and 5.853	(40 mm) 0.291λ	NR	Polylayers ITO-PET (11 mm)	90°	Not shown	3.12
[39]	2020	2.45 and 5.12	(18 mm) 0.141λ	NR	Double-layer Rogers RO 3003 (1.75 mm)	90°	Simply analyzed	6.90
Suggested	2023	2.4 and 5	(10 mm) 00.81λ	SNG	1-layer FR4	180°	Extensive analysis shown	12.50

for customization and fine-tuning to meet various design requirements. Overall, this methodology enhances the efficiency and effectiveness of the unit cell in practical implementations. These dimensions are determined using the equations for resistance (R), inductance (L), and capacitance (C) through the analogous circuit theory presented in this study, which undergoes comprehensive analysis. In this proposed model, we analyzed S-parameters to ascertain absorption at 2.4 and 5-GHz resonant frequencies using a VNA in an anechoic chamber. For both frequencies, the results demonstrated absorptivity exceeding 98%, which was in good agreement with simulation results. The core resonant data stayed constant, whereas minor variations at nonresonant frequencies were ascribed to external noise and connector losses. The effectiveness of the absorber and the precision of the suggested equivalent circuit model are both validated by the strong agreement between the simulated and experimental findings.

Regarding the wavelength correlating to the minimum resonating frequency, the single cell size is the smallest (0.081λ). When compared to SNG values, it exhibits MM properties at lower resonating (Table 16.1).

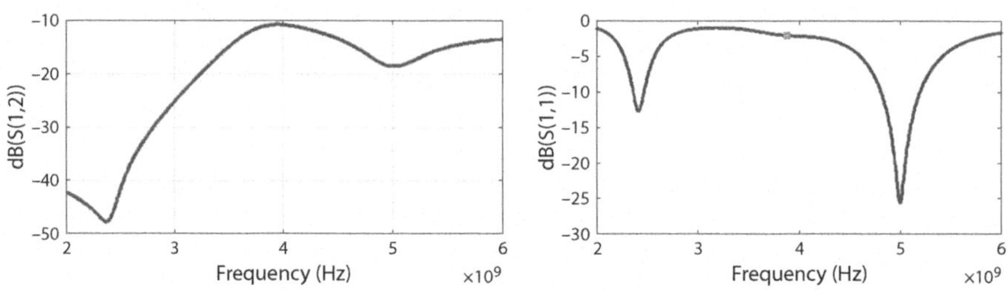

Figure 16.11 Transmission and reflection coefficient of proposed absorber using MATLAB software.

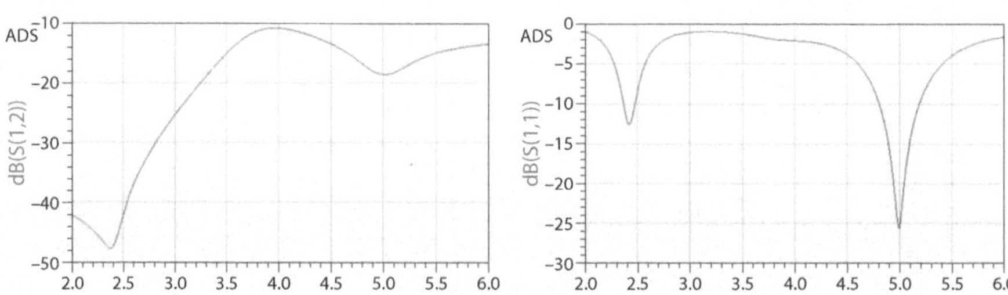

Figure 16.12 Transmission and reflection coefficient of proposed absorber using ADS software.

Furthermore, none of the concepts put out by other researchers for a similar objective include lumped elements or multilayer substances. Regarding the effective medium ratio (EMR = 0 L), the design exhibits modesty, registering a value of 12.49 at 2.4 GHz. The durability of the design was demonstrated by the laboratory results correlating with simulation on software. According to the given method, which is shown in Table 16.2 below, a comparative table can distinguish between the suggested accuracy of design and gain. The comparison in Table 16.2 has shown that designing MM absorbers with large EM radiation for required response at the desired resonating bandwidth is an effective way to use the equivalent circuit methodology. The proposed approach can be applied to precisely build a patch utilizing conventional CRRs. Furthermore, no combined element or polylayer substance will be required. The suggested absorber has number of Wi-Fi applications that includes RF energy trapping, SAR minimization for mobile gadgets, crowd sensor and estimation applications while under Wi-Fi coverage, Wi-Fi signal detecting, and RF coupling minimization in gadgets using Wi-Fi and LTE.

Figure 16.11, depicts the simulated transmission and reflection coefficients of the proposed absorber, derived using MATLAB. The transmission plot demonstrates considerable attenuation throughout the operating band, signifying diminished signal propagation through the structure. The reflection coefficient graph displays pronounced resonance nulls, indicating robust impedance matching and negligible reflected power. Collectively, these responses confirm the absorber's efficacy in trapping and dissipating incoming electromagnetic energy, thus illustrating strong absorption performance across the specified frequency range. Figure 16.12, illustrates the ADS-simulated transmission and reflection properties of the proposed absorber, effectively showcasing its electromagnetic performance. The transmission response demonstrates significant attenuation, signifying minimal wave propagation through the structure. The reflection coefficient exhibits pronounced resonance notches with significant minima, indicating superior impedance matching and negligible reflected power. These complementary responses collectively affirm the absorber's strong dual-band functionality, effective energy dissipation, and consistent performance throughout the specified GHz frequency range.

16.7 Conclusion

To create a perfect nonseparated MM absorber for Wi-Fi signal absorption having minimal possible of unit cell cross section and substance width, this paper discusses an effective equivalent circuit approach. This structure has demonstrated polarization insensitivity up to 180° of given EM waves' impact angle that is unequaled between comparable absorbers till now. Almost among all Wi-Fi absorbers, the suggested absorber attained highest of 98% absorptions with EMR 12.50. The suggested unit cell, which incorporates a virtual ground, introduces a novel approach to circuit design. This addition aligns seamlessly with the equivalent circuit analysis for resistance, inductance, and capacitance. The compatibility between the unit cell and its equivalent circuit analysis ensures accurate modeling and prediction of circuit behavior. Such integration enhances the efficiency and reliability of circuit design processes. Overall, the incorporation of a virtual ground represents a significant advancement in circuit design methodology. For the patch design to achieve the requisite surface resistance, R, which is less than 10 dB value of S constants, standard arc-shaped CRRs are selected for the calculation. This work introduces a new nonseparated MM absorber that uses an equivalent circuit technique to maximize the absorption of dual-band Wi-Fi signals. Important accomplishments include a high EMR (12.50), minimal unit cell dimensions (0.08), substance width (0.01), and 98% absorption efficiency. The absorber uses arc-shaped CRRs without lumped parts and is polarization-insensitive up to an incidence angle of 180°. The precision of circuit modeling and design is improved by a virtual ground. Applications include microwave energy harvesting and SAR reduction in electronics. Future studies can use improved circuit-analog techniques to investigate wider frequency ranges, IoT applications, and sophisticated absorber designs.

AI disclosure statement: The author acknowledges the use of AI-based tools for minor language editing or grammatical correction. However, all intellectual contributions, analyses, and conclusions presented in this chapter are entirely the author's own.

Bibliography

1. Wang, B.X., Xu, C., Duan, G., Xu, W., Pi, F., Review of broadband metamaterial absorbers: from principles, design strategies, and tunable properties to functional applications. *Adv. Funct. Mater.*, 33, 14, 2213818, 2023.
2. Jain, P., Singh, A.K., Pandey, J.K., Garg, S., Bansal, S., Agarwal, M., Kumar, S., Sardana, N., Gupta, N., Singh, A.K., Ultra-thin metamaterial perfect absorbers for single-/dual-/multi-band microwave applications. *IET Microwaves Antennas Propag.*, 14, 5, 390–396, 2020.

3. Berka, M., Özkaya, U., Islam, T., El Ghzaoui, M., Varakumari, S., Das, S., Mahdjoub, Z., A miniaturized folded square split ring resonator cell based dual band polarization insensitive metamaterial absorber for C-and Ku-band applications. *Opt. Quantum Electron.*, 55, 8, 699, 2023.
4. Wang, A.X., Qu, S.B., Yan, M.B., Wang, W.J., Wang, J.F., Zheng, L., Wang, J.L., Six-band polarization-insensitive perfect metamaterial absorber using L-shaped resonators. *Appl. Phys. A*, 125, 331, 2019.
5. Huang, Q., Wang, G., Zhou, M., Zheng, J., Tang, S., Ji, G., Metamaterial electromagnetic wave absorbers and devices: Design and 3D microarchitecture. *J. Mater. Sci. Technol.*, 108, 90–101, 2022.
6. Al-badri, K.S.L., Abdulkarim, Y., II, Alkurt, F.O., Karaaslan, M., Simulated and experimental verification of the microwave dual-band metamaterial perfect absorber based on square patch with a 45° diagonal slot structure. *J. Electromagn. Waves Appl.*, 35, 11, 1541–1552, 2021.
7. Fang, S., Deng, L., Zhang, P., Qiu, L., Xie, H., Du, J., Wang, H., Zhao, H., Dual-band metamaterial absorber with stable absorption performance based on fractal structure. *J. Phys. D: Appl. Phys.*, 55, 9, 095003, 2021.
8. Duan, G., Schalch, J., Zhao, X., Li, A., Chen, C., Averitt, R.D., Zhang, X., A survey of theoretical models for terahertz electromagnetic metamaterial absorbers. *Sens. Actuators, A*, 287, 21–28, 2019.
9. Wen, J., Wang, Y., Wang, Y., Advanced Engineering Design of the Metamaterial Absorbers, in: *Metamaterial Technology and Intelligent Metasurfaces for Wireless Communication Systems*, pp. 136–179, IGI Global, Hershey, PA, USA, 2023.
10. You, K.Y., Sim, M.S., Mutadza, H., Esa, F., Chan, Y.L., Free-space measurement using explicit, reference-plane and thickness-invariant method for permittivity determination of planar materials, in: *2017 Progress in Electromagnetics Research Symposium-Fall (PIERS-FALL)*, Singapore, pp. 222–228, 2017.
11. Sim, M.S., You, K.Y., Esa, F., Dimon, M.N., Khamis, N.H., Multiband metamaterial microwave absorbers using split ring and multiwidth slot structure. *Int. J. RF Microwave Comput. Aided Eng.*, 28, 7, e21473, 2018.
12. Valagiannopoulos, C.A., On smoothening the singular field developed in the vicinity of metallic edges. *Int. J. Appl. Electromagn. Mech.*, 31, 2, 67–77, 2009.
13. Zhou, J., Economon, E.N., Koschny, T., Soukoulis, C.M., Unifying approach to left-handed material design. *Opt. Lett.*, 31, 24, 3620–3622, 2006.
14. Stephen, L., Yogesh, N., Subramanian, V., Realization of bidirectional, bandwidth-enhanced metamaterial absorber for microwave applications. *Sci. Rep.*, 9, 1, 10058, 2019.
15. Xiong, H., Yang, Q., Huang, Z.C., Peng, W.X., Zhang, H.Q., Analyzing broadband tunable metamaterial absorbers by using the symmetry model. *Opt. Express*, 29, 25, 41475–41484, 2021.
16. Zhang, J., He, D., Wang, G., Wang, P., Qiao, L., Wang, T., Li, F., Equivalent electromagnetic parameters for microwave metamaterial absorber using a new symmetry model. *Chin. Phys. B*, 28, 5, 058401, 2019.

17. Valagiannopoulos, C.A. and Tretyakov, S.A., Symmetric absorbers realized as gratings of PEC cylinders covered by ordinary dielectrics. *IEEE Trans. Antennas Propag.*, 62, 10, 5089–5098, 2014.
18. Smith, D.R., Vier, D.C., Koschny, T., Soukoulis, C.M., Electromagnetic parameter retrieval from inhomogeneous metamaterials. *Phys. Rev. E*, 71, 3, 036617, 2005.
19. McKinley, A.F., White, T.P., Maksymov, I.S., Catchpole, K.R., The analytical basis for the resonances and anti-resonances of loop antennas and metamaterial ring resonators. *J. Appl. Phys.*, 112, 9, 094911, 2012.
20. Koschny, T., Markoš, P., Smith, D.R., Soukoulis, C.M., Resonant and antiresonant frequency dependence of the effective parameters of metamaterials. *Phys. Rev. E*, 68, 6, 065602, 2003.
21. Gao, X., Yu, F.L., Cai, C.L., Guan, C.Y., Shi, J.H., Hu, F., Terahertz metamaterial with broadband and low-dispersion high refractive index. *Opt. Lett.*, 45, 17, 4754–4757, 2020.
22. Urzhumov, Y.A., Shvets, G., Fan, J., Capasso, F., Brandl, D., Nordlander, P., Plasmonic nanoclusters: A path towards negative-index metafluids. *Opt. Express*, 15, 21, 14129–14145, 2007.
23. You, K.Y., Analytical modeling of bare monopole driven from coaxial line, in: *RF coaxial slot radiators: Modeling, measurements, and applications*, pp. 57–89, Artech House, London, England, 2016.
24. You, K.Y. and Sim, M.S., Precision permittivity measurement for low-loss thin planar materials using large coaxial probe from 1 to 400 MHz. *J. Manuf. Mater. Process.*, 2, 4, 81, 2018.
25. Tirkey, M.M. and Gupta, N., Te quest for perfect electromagnetic absorber: A review. *Int. J. Microw. Wirel. Technol*, 11, 151–167, 2019.
26. Hannan, S., *et al.*, Modifed-segmented split-ring based polarization and angle-insensitive multi-band metamaterial absorber for X, Ku and K band applications. *IEEE Access*, 8, 144051–144063, 2020.
27. Landy, N., II, Sajuyigbe, S., Mock, J.J., Smith, D.R., Padilla, W.J., Perfect metamaterial absorber. *Phys. Rev. Lett.*, 100, 207402, 2008.
28. Wu, Z., *et al.*, Broadband microwave absorber with a double-split ring structure. *Plasmonics*, 15, 1863–1867, 2020.
29. Landy, N., *et al.*, Design, theory, and measurement of a polarization-insensitive absorber for terahertz imaging. *Phys. Rev. B*, 79, 125104, 2009.
30. Zhang, K., *et al.*, Polarization-engineered noninterleaved metasurface for integer and fractional orbital angular momentum multiplexing. *Laser Photon. Rev*, 15, 2000351, 2021.
31. Bonache, J., Gil, M., Gil, I., García-García, J., Martín, F., On the electrical characteristics of complementary metamaterial resonators. *IEEE Microw. Wirel. Compon. Lett*, 16, 543–545, 2006.
32. Falcone, F., *et al.*, Babinet principle applied to the design of metasurfaces and metamaterials. *Phys. Rev. Let*, 93, 197401, 2004.

33. Zhang, K., Wang, Y., Burokur, S.N., Wu, Q., Generating dual-polarized vortex beam by detour phase: From phase gradient metasurfaces to metagratings. *IEEE Trans. Microw. Theory Techniq*, 2021, 1, 2021.
34. Sy Tuan, T., Hoa, T.Q., N., Defect induced co-polarization broadband metamaterial absorber. *AIP Adv.*, 9, 1, 2019.
35. Gao, X., *et al.*, Ultrawideband and high-efficiency linear polarization converter based on double V-shaped metasurface. *IEEE Trans. Antennas Propag.*, 63, 3522–3530, 2015.
36. Hannan, S., Islam, M.T., Almutairi, A.F., Faruque, M.R., II, Wide bandwidth angle-and polarization-insensitive symmetric metamaterial absorber for X and Ku band applications. *Sci. Rep.*, 10, 1–9, 2020.
37. Mendhe, S.E. and Kosta, Y.P., Metamaterial properties and applications. *Int. J. Inf. Technol. Knowl. Manag*, 4, 85–89, 2011.
38. Yuan, Y., *et al.*, Complementary transmissive ultra-thin meta-defectors for broadband polarization-independent refractions in the microwave region. *Photon. Res*, 7, 80–88, 2019.
39. De Araújo, B., *et al.*, An ultrathin and ultrawideband metamaterial absorber and an equivalent-circuit parameter retrieval method. *IEEE Trans. Antennas Propag.*, 99, 1, 2020.
40. Costa, F., Genovesi, S., Monorchio, A., Manara, G., A circuit-based model for the interpretation of perfect metamaterial absorbers. *IEEE Trans. Antennas Propag.*, 61, 1201–1209, 2012.
41. Xiong, H. and Ji, Q., Equivalent circuit analysis of metamaterial structure. *Plasmonics*, 1–6, 2020.
42. Borgese, M. and Costa, F., A simple equivalent circuit approach for anisotropic frequency-selective surfaces and metasurfaces. *IEEE Trans. Antennas Propag.*, 68, 7088–7098, 2020.
43. Wakatsuchi, H., Paul, J., Greedy, S., Christopoulos, C., Cut-wire metamaterial design based on simplifed equivalent circuit models. *IEEE Trans. Antennas Propag.*, 60, 3670–3678, 2012.
44. Wilbert, D.S., Hokmabadi, M.P., Kung, P., Kim, S.M., Equivalent-circuit interpretation of the polarization insensitive performance of THz metamaterial absorbers. *IEEE Trans. Terahertz Sci. Technol.*, 3, 846–850, 2013.
45. Mishra, R., Panwar, R., Singh, D., Equivalent circuit model for the design of frequency-selective, terahertz-band, graphene-based metamaterial absorbers. *IEEE Magn. Lett.*, 9, 1–5, 2018.
46. Chen, H., Ran, L., Huangfu, J., Grzegorczyk, T.M., Kong, J.A., Equivalent circuit model for lef-handed metamaterials. *J. Appl. Phys.*, 100, 024915, 2006.
47. Hossain, M., Nguyen-Trong, N., Sayidmarie, K., Abbosh, A., Equivalent circuit design method for wideband nonmagnetic absorbers at low microwave frequencies. *IEEE Trans. Antennas Propag.*, 68, 8215–8220, 2020.
48. Nemat-Abad, H.M., Zareian-Jahromi, E., Basiri, R., Design and equivalent circuit model extraction of a third-order band-pass frequency selective

surface flter for terahertz applications. *Eng. Sci. Technol. Int. J.*, 22, 862–868, 2019.
49. Pang, Y.-Q., Zhou, Y.-J., Wang, J., Equivalent circuit method analysis of the infuence of frequency selective surface resistance on the frequency response of metamaterial absorbers. *J. Appl. Phys.*, 110, 023704, 2011.
50. Xiong, H., Tang, M.-C., Li, M., Li, D., Jiang, Y.-N., Equivalent circuit method analysis of graphene-metamaterial (GM) absorber. *Plasmonics*, 13, 857–862, 2018.
51. Agarwal, M. and Meshram, M.K., An approach for circuit modeling of a multiband resonators based planar metamaterial absorber. *Microw. Opt. Technol. Lett*, 63, 181–187, 2021.
52. Yeom, K.-W., *Microwave circuit design: A practical approach using ADS*, Prentice Hall Press, London, 2015.
53. Lewis, R.M., *et al.*, Measuring changes in inductance with microstrip resonators. *IEEE Trans. Appl. Supercond.*, 29, 1–4, 2019.
54. Leferink, F.B., *Proceedings of International Symposium on Electromagnetic Compatibility*, IEEE, pp. 16–22, 1999.
55. Benedek, P. and Silvester, P., Equivalent capacitances for microstrip gaps and steps. *IEEE Trans. Microw. Teory Tech*, 20, 729–733, 1972.
56. Chen, T.-S., Determination of the capacitance, inductance, and characteristic impedance of rectangular lines. *IRE Trans. Microw. Teory Tech*, 8, 510–519, 1960.
57. Campos, I. and Jimenez, J., About Poynting's theorem. *Eur. J. Phys.*, 13, 117, 1992.
58. Chew, W.C., Some refections on double negative materials. *Prog. Electromagn. Res*, 51, 1–26, 2005.
59. Wang, Q. and Cheng, Y., Compact and low-frequency broadband microwave metamaterial absorber based on meander wire structure loaded resistors. *AEU Int. J. Electron. Commun.*, 120, 2020.
60. Bhati, A., Hiremath, K.R., Dixit, V., Bandwidth enhancement of triple layer microwave absorber using metallic square patch. *Appl. Phys. A*, 124, 798, 2018.
61. Alkurt, F.O., *et al.*, *AIP Conference Proceedings*, AIP Publishing LLC, p. 060001.
62. Wu, Y., Wang, J., Lai, S., Zhu, X., Gu, W., A transparent and fexible microwave absorber covering the whole WiFi waveband. *AIP Adv.*, 9, 9, 2019.
63. Tofgh, F., Amiri, M., Shariati, N., Lipman, J., Abolhasan, M., Polarization-insensitive metamaterial absorber for crowd estimation based on electromagnetic energy measurements. *IEEE Trans. Antennas Propag.*, 68, 1458–1467, 2019.
64. Yoo, M., Kim, H.K., Lim, S., Angular-and polarization-insensitive metamaterial absorber using subwavelength unit cell in multilayer technology. *IEEE Antennas Wire. Propag. Lett*, 15, 414, 2016.

65. Yoo, Y.J., *et al.*, Flexible and elastic metamaterial absorber for low frequency, based on small-size unit cell. *Appl. Phys. Lett.*, 105, 41902, 2014.
66. Cheng, Y., *et al.*, Complete Chloroplast Genome Sequence and Phylogenetic Analysis of the Medicinal Plant Artemisia annua. *Molecules*, 64902, 2015.
67. Mohammed, I.E. and Martin, S., Optical polymer thin films with isotropic and anisotropic nano-corrugated surface topologies. *Nature*, 410, 796–799, 2001.
68. Khuyen, B.X., *et al.*, Size-efficient metamaterial absorber at low frequencies: Design, fabrication, and characterization. *J. Appl. Phys.*, 117, 243105, 2015.
69. Lee, D., Kim, H.K., Lim, S., Textile Metamaterial Absorber using Screen Printed Chanel Logo. *Microwave Opt. Technol. Lett.*, 59, 1424–1427, 2018.

17

Digital Twin Technology in Education: Applications, Benefits, Challenges, Ethical Issues and Security Concerns

Ankur Nandi[1]*, Milan Barman[2], Sourav Sen[2], Tapash Das[2] and Tarini Halder[1]

[1]*Department of Education, Kalyani University, Kalyani, Nadia, West Bengal, India*
[2]*Department of Education, Kazi Nazrul University, Asansol, West Bengal, India*

Abstract
This study addresses the function of digital twin (DT) in the academic area, emphasizing its applications, benefits, implementation challenges, and associated ethical and security concerns. Using a qualitative, review-based methodology, the study highlighted that DT technology improves the quality of schooling through personalized instruction, immediate response, and realistic simulation. It helps in inclusive education and information-based decisions. However, high expenditure, limited digital literacy, the risk of data privacy, and moral challenges such as consent and transparency are obstructing its spread. This study emphasizes strict rules for safe and moral use, information governing policy, and the need for cooperation between partners.

***Keywords*:** Digital twin (DT) technology, ethical concerns, privacy, educational application, benefits, challenges

**Corresponding author*: ankurpalashdanga@gmail.com; ORCID: https://orcid.org/0009-0008-3459-3429
Milan Barman: ORCID: https://orcid.org/0009-0004-5290
Sourav Sen: ORCID: https://orcid.org/0009-0006-0431-9985
Tapash Das: ORCID: https://orcid.org/0000-0003-4619-0009
Tarini Halder: ORCID: https://orcid.org/0009-0007-8807-7182

Shubham Mahajan, Davinder Paul Singh, Amit Kant Pandit and Paras Chawla (eds.) Ensuring Privacy in Digital Twin Ecosystems, (499–520) © 2026 Scrivener Publishing LLC

17.1 Introduction

Globalization and technical growth are the base elements of the present-day corporate world, which digital twin (DT) technology supports by improving on the project front [44]. In today's very tech-based world, DTs have stepped forward as a revolutionary educational tool that brings a human-centered approach to teaching and learning. This is not only a technical step forward but also a shift in education [48], which presents a digital model of the real-world system or object. We have seen a transformation in education *via* the use of DT [46], and we note that many educational institutions have accepted that, through digital transformation, this technology does elevate the pedagogy and education process [32].

DT technology has seen great growth over the past decade, which has seen the academic and industrial world put forth many of its definitions. Although it is present and useful in manufacturing, healthcare, and agriculture, which are traditional domains for this tech, we are seeing it adopted in new areas also, which include education [1, 9]. In education, DTs must enact a large role in the progress of models for use in academic and professional training [1]. DT can enhance good life [22], while their educational applications promise several benefits [23]. Through quickening developments, technology has advanced new trends, which might create revolutions in different places, most evidently in DTs [1]. The DT technology industry is of tremendous significance for the Industry 4.0 era, which establishes an unbroken link between the world and the digital space [3, 45].

The application of digital twin (DT) in graduate studies signifies a paradigm shift — a lens change from the traditional DT of the physical laboratory to a more comprehensive digital replication encompassing equipment, teaching materials, field applications, campus infrastructure planning, curriculum development, and teacher professional development. Among the most important possible uses of DTs is to provide separate DT for each student, with which the learning experience could be modified, providing feedback, nurturing the professional readiness, plus the student's well-being [24]. Besides, DT systems (DTSs) are extensively used for educational experimental practices from classroom design to rocket engineering [11]. DT, Internet of Things (IoT), artificial intelligence (AI), data analytics, and cloud computing are in some ways pushing forward the IoT that can efficiently collect and process low data [9].

In the 21st century, innovation has evolved an important aspect of daily life, which is forcing professionals, academics, and students to think about using technology to reconstruct education and training [3]. Digital technology is also being adopted in the field of education to facilitate teaching, research, and administrative activity, and with the development of technology, its use in education is more likely to increase [9]. DT is imitating a physical system, process, or object in the digital world of objects, which simultaneously copies its actual replica for check, examination, and replication, so that improvement can be made [1]. Grieves and Vickers [2] specify a DT as a set of virtual information constructs that fully describe a potential or actual physical manufactured product from the microatomic level to the macrogeometrical level, allowing information extraction without physically inspecting the product.

The DT concept is increasingly gaining popularity in both academic and industrial domains [55]. In response, this paper presents the applications, benefits, and challenges of DT technology in education while addressing data security, privacy concerns, and ethical considerations. Furthermore, it proposes a privacy framework for secure implementation and strategies for integrating physical reality with DT to optimize its practical use.

17.2 Objectives

1. To highlight the applications of DT technology in the education sector.
2. To discuss the benefits of using DT technology in education.
3. To explore the challenges of using DT technology in education.
4. To discuss the ethical and security concerns associated with using DT technology.

17.3 Methodology

This research is documentary (review-based) research that constitutes qualitative research. Content analysis was used to analyze the data sources (web links, research articles). Major research databases such as Google Scholar, JSTOR, and ScienceDirect were searched with keywords such as "Digital Twins in Education," "Applications of Digital Twin Technology in Education," "Benefits of Digital Twins in Higher Education," "Challenges of Digital Twin Implementation in Education," "Ethical and Security Concerns in Digital Twin Technology." Web sources and relevant academic repositories were also examined to provide recent developments and industry insights to complement the study. Throughout the review process, data were systematically organized into thematic groups to determine key trends and findings. These thematic categorizations gave an overarching view of DT uses in education, highlighting opportunities and restrictions in their implementation.

17.4 Discussion

17.4.1 Applications of DT Technology in the Education Sector

- DTs can offer virtual laboratory environments mimicking actual ones. Even when physical laboratories could be limited or unavailable, this enables researchers to run experiments, observe things, and evaluate data in a simulated setting, therefore offering an important opportunity for active engagement. In scholastic fields such as engineering, physics, chemistry, and biology, scholars may also mimic and model sophisticated processes or systems [16–18].
- These digital models can replicate actual places, old sites, or natural landscapes. This lets learners go to these spots without leaving home, and they interact with the material better [9].
- DT learning should tackle the extra difficulty of offering isolated learning to a model of complicated physical or technical items and their depiction. Using several tools, teachers can remotely instruct their students/children while they are at home [43]. Using internet-connected devices, students should have access anywhere, anytime to virtual copies of systems of roads, farms, etc., tools, and help. DT learning will take forward the present power of contemporary open schooling, expand learning chances, and lower obstacles [1]. Particularly for pupils with impairments who may find it challenging to participate in conventional classroom environments, DTs can help education become more accessible [23]. Students from remote or resource-limited areas can

gain hands-on experience without geographical or financial barriers [31]. This change has the power to provide inclusive access to education, making it more accessible to learners from all walks of life, whether they are geographically distant, financially constrained, or otherwise marginalized. DTs' inclusive character lets people from many backgrounds participate in high-quality education, thereby inspiring hope for the next-generation of learning among parents, educators, pupils, and investors all together [48]. Powered by DTs, digital platforms improve accessibility and let kids' study on the go, outside of regular school time, therefore creating a surrounding where education may take place whenever and from any place [48].

- The virtual instructor can see the learner's outcome and action now. By looking at data such as how engaged students are, their progress, and their feelings, virtual teachers can spot initial indications of learning challenges or psychological trouble. This lets teachers step in early and help meet specific needs [19].
- Teachers can also use the DTs as tools for professional growth. They can offer teachers comments and recommendations, therefore helping them to hone their teaching approaches, test out new instructional strategies, and improve their pedagogical level. By simulating classroom scenarios, they enable teachers to practice and get direction on their performance [20].
- DT models of teachers for learning analysis and evaluation cover evaluating student data, tracking development, spotting learning gaps, and offering real-time comments to help students perform better [21].
- Digital teachers can create a virtual classroom or education environment that imitates the teaching situation in the real world. They can imitate different aspects of education, such as teaching, interacting with students, and managing classrooms. This imitation capacity provides the opportunity to do and hone their teaching mechanism in a safe and regulated setting for instructors.
- With the DT of the instructor, individualized teaching by examining facts on students and their learning profiles, pace, content, and instructional strategies could be adapted to suit the personalized demand, choice, and learning modalities of

each student. This personalization makes the learning experience more meaningful and helps learners connect better with the study material.

- Giving feedback and evaluating learners for their advancement in learning is another important factor of significance in academics. DTs can analyze student responses, identify misconceptions or areas of improvement, and provide tailored response immediately. This responsive input helps students progress by meeting personal difficulties and directing them toward skill [9].
- DTs can give instant feedback and information analysis, enabling educators to evaluate learners' growth and spot points where they need extra help [23].
- Data analytics may be used by online educators to offer insights and assist data-informed decision-making. They may examine trends in student performance, spot patterns, and create reports for educators, officials, and guardians; these insights help stakeholders make conscious choices regarding teaching methods, resource management, and learner care [9].
- DT can offer a personalized learning journey by examining learners' strengths, weaknesses, and styles of learning [23].
- DTs allow for sharing and joining by letting learners help in inexact worlds [23].
- Laboratories can adopt the use of DTs so that students will be able to study dangerous chemicals without physical contact in a real laboratory, more so if the chemicals have the possibility of releasing radioactive or radioactive elements or elements posing biohealth risk [26]. As far as resilience is concerned, in the case of DTs the former can be used at the time being when there is no scope to have a real exposure of tools/real scenario to learn that would need exposure of dangerous working conditions. For instance, one was able to learn how to manage risky civil construction site activities—specifically underground excavation and drilling—by simulating an excavator with its DT [4].
- DT technology allows to tailor education to different levels of understanding in a learner and let them use systems and equipment beyond the confines of a classroom so they can have extra practice and exploration, which occurs outside the designated time within a scheduling class. Learning activities

related to the DT can be designed in a personalized manner to give learners targeted resources and formative activities responsive to their learning needs and preferences [27]. The ability to create DTs of learners would build on this interest and expand the possibilities of harnessing the power of data to improve the learning experience for learners. At a micro level, DTs of learners could be used to provide individual learners get an immediate response to their studies. At a meso level, the aggregation of the DTs from a set of learners could help uncover behavioral patterns susceptible to being altered by an educator into a pedagogical strategy. At the macro level, a university could feed upon the data created by DTs to raise graduation rates, as well as to guide organizational decisions and development [28].

- DT can guide curriculum and pedagogical design, as well as professional learning for educators. The capability to predict, simulate in real time, and optimize the DT technology opens various avenues for learning designers, analytics professionals, instructors, and students [28].
- For trainees preparing for concurrent use of live equipment bearing a high risk if mishandled, DTs are used [25].
- The application of digital technologies may include just-in-time customized notifications to be delivered to learners regarding time management guidelines, such as reminders about lectures and assessments, or recommended learning materials [24].
- Data environments for the modeling of a learner DT can involve a whole range of educational systems and tools. More refined data gathering is also slowly becoming feasible: sound and sensory data (e.g., eye-tracking) for assessing learner emotional and attentional states [29].
- Moreover, DTs can be used for training purposes of medics, for better and more precise diagnosis of various cases and treatments in a safe environment [73].

17.4.2 Benefits of Using DT Technology in Education

- **Enhanced decision-making and efficiency**: Its impact could be game-changing for industries in the way decisions are made, the maintenance of systems is carried out, productivity is increased, and savings are achieved. Through a DT that mirrors the behavior and composition of its physical sibling, organizations can better understand slot through put understanding of their assets and processes, leading to improved operational efficiency and competitive advantage [1]. The aim of the DT tolls providing for decision-making, additionally implementing simulation and prediction capabilities [41, 42]. By taking over mundane administrative duties, such as grading, attendance, scheduling, and the like, the DTs would give teachers the freedom to focus on the real agenda of education: research, experimentation, and innovation [48].

- **Enables personalized learning**: Instructional content personalization is one of the most significant benefits that digital twin technology (DTT) can provide in education. [48]. The DT can make the student to access key management staff and explore its operation in a more personal way [39]. Personalized learning experiences also come about through DT. In this approach to pedagogy, what is presented is individualized to suit the student's demands, desires, and abilities. These virtual doppelgangers can be used to customize the content and rate of learning for each student [6]. Digitization in the classroom has been enhanced, but many digital services and digital content are present in the methodological and innovative arsenal to create personalized learning [40]; they include, among other tools, digital animation, video game development, AI, virtual and augmented reality, 2D/3D modeling, or DTs [39]. Combining interactive digital platforms, personalized learning paths, and immersive virtual environments makes lesson delivery lively and engaging, matching the requirements of different learning styles. Using DT technologies among the trends will deepen the student learning experience even more [1].
- **Facilitates collaborative learning**: DT is a tool that promotes cooperative learning through virtual cooperation among students. Peer pressure does not have to wane when students can work together on challenging projects, run virtual experiments, and debug one another, regardless of where they may reside. DT promotes immediacy of communication, sharing of information, and joint decision-making, thereby enhancing teamwork and collaboration [7]. Virtual

simulations promote cooperation among students where they can cooperate, communicate, and solve difficult problems as a team [47]. This collaborative learning approach prepares students for the collaborative nature of the modern workplace and encourages the exchange of ideas and perspectives [8].

- **Creates simulated learning environments**: A student-oriented perspective is therefore reflected in the studies of DTs that create classroom-simulated learning environments that offer one-on-one personalized learning experiences to students, are capable of assessing students and providing a record to teachers of their performance over time, and also support teacher professional development through ongoing feedback that pinpoints areas in need of improvement and resources for further development, connecting students virtually in collaborative learning environments, and adaptive instruction with a virtual laboratory and simulation in conducting experiments or scientific inquiry [10, 11].
- **Enhances teaching practices and teacher training**: DTs allow educators to refine and adapt their instructional methods, providing a more interactive and engaging learning environment [31]. Teachers can create a simulation model that is consistent with the educational purpose of the curriculum, so that students can be active participants, analyze the problem, and find its solution. Instead of the conventional teaching method, this method helps students become active partners in their education [47]. For teachers, the DTS is considered a way to improve the teaching system, to make education, and to ensure professional development [9]. In addition, the teacher's DT-based teaching method is helpful in the study of professional skills and design, which plays an effective role in the improvement of the learning process [29]. For example, the educational skills based on machine learning and DT technology have shown practical utility in determining the skills of the teacher and giving target-based recommendations [20]. Also, testing with new teaching methods or teaching equipment can be done in almost real time, where there is no disruption in the original curriculum or classroom—one of the most important aspects of the use of DT [28].

- **Real-time adaptive feedback**: Among the emerging factors enabling DT technology, one would certainly contemplate the IoT and the fact that one could also eliminate the real-time data collections [49]. DTs can be used for real-time analysis of the responses by students to identify misconceptions or areas in need of improvement, as well as giving feedback to students. This adaptive feedback supports student learning by addressing individual challenges and guiding them toward proficiency [9]. DTs can be used for conducting virtual laboratories on real equipment for educational purposes [51]. Creating DTs of laboratory equipment allows learners to use and experiment with such equipment within and outside the classroom, helping bridge the gap between theory and practice. Providing learners with the opportunity to test and try out different scenarios on this virtual equipment will allow them to learn from their errors deeper, thus enhancing their learning experience and situational awareness [11]. Access to laboratories has become limited due to the rise of distance learning and COVID-19 restrictions. To address the need for new competencies in remote education, universities and research centers must adopt innovative teaching and learning approaches [52, 53]. One of the possible approaches could be to construct a DT of the laboratory equipment. This way, students and researchers can virtually perform experiments and conduct them from a distance [54]. DTs offer a safety margin for people who are starting their learning curve on the operation of machines or equipment, as they enable to carry out simulations and assessments of situations without necessarily exposing individuals to risky environments [37, 38].
- **Improved virtual reality experiences**: With DTs, the realm of virtual reality may be enhanced; the enhancement allows learners to interact with realistic simulations related to different educational contexts [23]. Where AI meets DT technology, an emerging digital pedagogical instrument that offers sophisticated simulations and interactive learning experiences. This is due to the possibilities that DTs enable the replication of almost any laboratory equipment or test items available to those in the lab [31].
- **Practical and theoretical integration**: It is an alternative for ensuring students who could not engage in the physical

experimentation possible with the laboratory equipment through a DT that learning is not restricted to the absence of such facilities in laboratories, and for the pedagogue, it will learn to much better managed teaching strategies in which it will be able to integrate without problems theory and practice with full confidence [31].

- **Sustainability**: DTs can be advantageous, giving visibility and safety to ideas and virtually executing the experimentation process, with economies of time and cost [50]. The DT's ultimate purpose is to reduce overall costs, optimize maintenance, create new product and service opportunities, and improve existing results through optimizing parts or by eliminating waiting time between operations, linking different subsystems.
- **Tracks student progress and provides targeted feedback**: Both tracking and analysis of student progress through DTs will probably identify specific areas in which they excel as well as others in which they need to improve and provide tailored guidance and feedback. Also, adaptive learning programs could be incorporated within DT to adaptively direct the student's learning route according to his performance and his objectives, to maximize the learning outcomes [1].
- **Hands-on learning environment**: DT offers students an environment with hands-on experience by allowing them to interact with the virtual models, change variables, and see the development of the system in real time [4].
- **Fosters critical thinking and problem-solving**: Experiential learning cultivates deeper understanding, critical thinking, and problem-solving abilities [5].
- **Data-driven decision-making**: This makes it possible for organizations to simulate scenarios, put multiple strategic plans to the test, and evaluate the effects of changes or interventions before such plans or actions are executed in the real world and thereby minimize risk and uncertainties associated with decision processes [9].
- **Supports research and exploration**: The learning of different scenarios, analysis of data, and understanding of behaviors and interactions in complex systems can be supported by students and researchers [12, 13].
- **Enables virtual field trips**: There is the ability to put together simulated learning environments and analyze student data,

even when actual visits are not possible. Field trips promote active learning and understanding of diverse cultures, historical events, and natural phenomena [14, 15].

- **Encourages exploration and experimentation**: The learners appreciated their chance to use the DT to freely explore the system and vary its parameters to observe its impact on the overall system behavior.

17.4.3 Challenges of Using DT Technology in Education

- **Inconsistent data structure**: Due to the nonexistence of a unified data structure available, inconsistencies in building a DT might crop up in higher education, as learner data are siloed in different platforms—say portfolio systems, LMSs, and career development systems [29].
- **Lack of digital literacy and competency of educators**: Another burden in the relationship between DT technology and higher education is the digital literacy of educators to engage with this sophisticated technology. In addition, DTs incorporate from an array of disciplines including, among various others, computer science, psychology, statistics, and mathematics. The user does not have to be an expert in all these fields, but being familiar with some of the basic concepts from at least some of them will enable a more effective application of DTs in education [24].
- **Ethical issue**: Knowing that the second issue confronting the use of DTs in higher education rests on ensuring their ethical and legitimized uses, it is important to reflect on how data that propel DT technology are being collected, stored, and utilized to prevent any risk to learners. Learners have to understand what data are being utilized to power the DT, and designers/managers of DTs have to think about how the learners could be given some power over their data if possible [30].
- **Challenges in digital transformation:** For universities, the most pressing challenge in becoming an intelligent environment is putting together an educational model that effectively responds to trends set in place by the fourth industrial revolution whose hallmark is the total transformation of universities themselves into intelligent environments [33]. Digital transformation presupposes always introducing that

into the broader so-called fourth industrial revolution context [34–36]. The other class of challenges facing successful model building of DTs comprises model accuracy and associated pitfalls, connected issues related to transferring data or codes between the DT and the real systems, difficulties with data acquisition and validation, accuracy of data fusion, the process of computation, and the time available for analysis of data and sending responses to the physical twin [50].

- **Lack of accessibility**: However, the main disadvantage concerning this digitization of learning environments is the fact that appropriate tools are not available to obtain it, open to all users, free of charge, and with software students find comprehensible and recognized so that they can develop them without much hassle [42].
- **Excessive cost**: According to Torres [42], one of the limitations that make it difficult to use DT technology lies in the large technological infrastructure, the processes of which are economically prohibitive for some organizations.
- **Job displacement**: A major concern revolves around job displacement by the automation of certain educational processes. With an increase in automation, traditional education roles may not see as much demand in the distant future, leading to speculation on where that leaves teaching jobs eventually [48].
- **Lack of privacy**: Student data protection will be another concern. DTs generate very much information on students and their behavior, interests, and performance, and this information must be protected. Educational institutions have to care for privacy and data protection for personal information to be captured and used ethically [48].

17.4.4 Ethical and Security Concerns Associated with Using DT Technology

17.4.4.1 Ethical Concerns Associated with Using DT Technology

Eight ethical principles that deal with salient issues, such as privacy and control and ownership of data, transparency and consent, nonmaleficence and beneficence, data security and management, and even access [74].

Not providing the opportunity to give meaningful consent in situations involving data processing in a smart city context, where DTs constitute an important factor, is one of the significant impediments to privacy protection [60]. Privacy protection means securing that a particular piece of information is kept secret and not disclosed to an unauthorized party [61]. Privacy protection is the act of limiting correspondence between a personal datum and other information to prevent identity fraud and theft [62].

DT has raised a new social–ethical problem, as they can be unreal or cause widespread data discrimination and injustice and concern about control and autonomy loss [63].

Various moral problems have been identified on the use of Big Data, especially regarding security and privacy. Creating a Big Data governance structure can be solved by solving these problems, which will help the organizations to determine the principles and criteria for information management [64].

Information consent, ownership of information, and patient autonomy—all of these are vital to ensure ethical and responsible use of DT technology [65].

Relevant information needs to be evaluated about information ownership, access, and security [66]. Therefore, the information that pertains to the DT model needs to be guaranteed [67].

Will security, strong privacy, and moral responsibility overstep legal boundaries? Such powerful privacy will need to be addressed [68].

Different privacy-preserving models for the DTS will provide assurance of confidence and legal satisfaction.

17.4.4.2 Security Concerns Associated with Using DT Technology

This can mean potential threats such as the stealing of information through the internet or the modification of information on the computer. The private information related to students, civilians, and workers should be kept private, ensuring their privacy and safety [1, 56].

So, the findings are in the eye of the beholder of the DT concept because security and privacy are the key issues in the design process and the realization of DT [58]. Another survey finding is that DTs can pose privacy risks if they store sensitive data. So, they open new doors for cybercriminals to reach sensitive data and use it. Such growing concerns over privacy in the context of DT technology show how much need there is in exercising good data responsibility and regulatory compliance [57]. In the case of personal information, it is essential to be honest and transparent about the purpose of collecting information and the methods of protecting the information collected.

It is essential to take appropriate security measures and adhere to the applicable restrictions and criteria when collecting, preserving, and using information. Ignoring these concerns can lead to data theft, intellectual property damage, and other security risks [59].

INCIBE [69] has rementioned that taking powerful cybersecurity steps such as surveillance, secure communication systems, additional backup systems, and resource management to protect DTSs in the field of education. The proper governance requires awareness and active participation of all stakeholders, including teachers and administrators, so that the changing threats can be effectively dealt with.

The security of DT is not only the cybersecurity team, but also the participation of the entire company, which should also include senior management, management workers, suppliers, and maintenance workers [69].

In addition, the DT network naturally increases the area of attacks, thus making strict authenticity and entry control essential [70].

Companies will have to react more actively to events and implement penetration testing so that stability can be ensured [71].

17.5 Conclusion

DT is transforming the education field, which is creating individual-centered teaching, immediate response, inclusive education, and cooperative teaching opportunities. Through realistic simulation, adapted teaching method, and remote access, this technology helps to eliminate the gap between theoretical and practically and practical education. This study highlights the extensive use of DT technology, including virtual laboratories, teachers' training, and evaluation of students, indicating its impact on educational results and administrative skills. However, there are some challenges in applying this technology widely in the field of education. The expense of high implementation, lack of digital literacy among teachers, chaos management, and insufficient infrastructure are obstructing the widespread adoption. Information privacy, conscious consent, and transparency moral anxiety also require an urgent solution on an urgent basis. The research highlights the importance of the development of strong data governance, moral criteria, and cyber protection protocols. Combined efforts of policymakers, technicians, teachers, and students will help ensure the moral, safe, and inclusive implementation of DT technology.

AI disclosure statement: The author acknowledges the use of AI-based tools for minor language editing or grammatical correction. However, all intellectual contributions, analyses, and conclusions presented in this chapter are entirely the author's own.

Bibliography

1. Jankovskis, D., Cirule, I., Carbone, A., Digital twins and e-learning: Navigating challenges and opportunities, in: *Online Higher Education Learning Methodologies and Technologies. HELMeTO 2023*, vol. 2076, G. Casalino, *et al.*, (Eds.), pp. 169–179, Springer, Switzerland, 2024, [Online]. Available: https://doi.org/10.1007/978-3-031-67351-1_12.
2. Grieves, M. and Vickers, J., Origins of the digital twin concept. *Fla. Inst. Technol.*, 8, 3–20, 2016, [Online]. Available: https://www.researchgate.net/publication/307509727_Origins_of_the_Digital_Twin_Concept.
3. Basak, S.K., Wotto, M., Belanger, P., E-learning, m-learning, and d-learning: Conceptual definition and comparative analysis. *E-Learning Digital Media*, 15, 4, 191–216, 2018, [Online]. Available: https://doi.org/10.1177/2042753018785180.
4. Sepasgozar, S.M., Digital twin and web-based virtual gaming technologies for online education: A case of construction management and engineering. *Appl. Sci.*, 10, 13, 4678, 2020, [Online]. Available: https://doi.org/10.3390/app10134678.
5. Tagliabue, L.C., Cecconi, F.R., Maltese, S., Rinaldi, S., Ciribini, A.L., Flammini, A., Leveraging digital twin for sustainability assessment of an educational building. *Sustainability*, 13, 2, 480, 2021, [Online]. Available: https://doi.org/10.3390/su13020480.
6. Bucchiarone, A., Gamification and virtual reality for digital twin learning and training: Architecture and challenges. *Virtual Real. Intell. Hardw.*, 4, 6, 471–486, 2022, [Online]. Available: https://doi.org/10.1016/j.vrih.2022.10.002.
7. Georgakopoulos, I., Piromalis, D., Ntanos, S., Zakopoulos, V., Makrygiannis, P., A prediction model for remote lab courses designed upon the principles of education for sustainable development. *Sustainability*, 15, 6, 5473, 2023, [Online]. Available: https://doi.org/10.3390/su15065473.
8. Dembski, F., Wossner, U., Letzgus, M., The digital twin tackling urban challenges with models, spatial analysis, and numerical simulations in immersive virtual environments, in: *Proc. 23rd Int. Conf. Computer-Aided Architectural Design Research in Asia (CAADRIA)/Doctoral Students Track*, pp. 334–343, 2019.
9. Chande, S.V., An exploratory view of application of digital twin technology in education. *Int. J. Adv. Trends Comput. Sci. Eng.*, 13, 2, 53–58, 2024, [Online]. Available: https://doi.org/10.30534/ijatcse/2024/031322024.

10. Vikhman, V.V. and Romm, M.V., Digital twins in education: Prospects and reality. *Vysshee Obrazovanie v Rossii (Higher Educ. Russia)*, 30, 2, 22–32, 2021, [Online]. Available: https://doi.org/10.31992/0869-3617-2021-30-2-22-32.
11. David, J., Lobov, A., Lanz, M., Learning experiences involving digital twins, in: *Proc. IECON 2018 - 44th Annu. Conf. IEEE Industrial Electron. Soc*, pp. 3681–3686, 2018, [Online]. Available: https://doi.org/10.1109/IECON.2018.8591460.
12. Brylina, O.G., Kuzmina, N.N., Osintsev, K.V., Modeling as the foundation of digital twins, in: *Proc. 2020 Global Smart Industry Conf. (GloSIC)*, pp. 276–280, 2020, [Online]. Available: https://doi.org/10.1109/GloSIC50886.2020.9267835.
13. Guc, F., Viola, J., Chen, Y., Digital twins enabled remote laboratory learning experience for mechatronics education, in: *Proc. 2021 IEEE 1st Int. Conf. Digital Twins Parallel Intell. (DTPI)*, pp. 242–245, 2021, [Online]. Available: https://doi.org/10.1109/DTPI52997.2021.00052.
14. Klippel, A., Sajjadi, P., Zhao, J., Wallgrun, J.O., Huang, J., Bagher, M.M., Embodied digital twins for environmental applications. *ISPRS Ann. Photogramm. Remote Sens. Spatial Inf. Sci.*, V-4, 193–202, 2021, [Online]. Available: https://doi.org/10.5194/isprs-annals-V-4-2021-193-2021.
15. Zhao, J. and Klippel, A., Scale-unexplored opportunities for immersive technologies in place-based learning, in: *Proc. IEEE Conf. Virtual Reality and 3D User Interfaces (VR)*, Osaka, Japan, pp. 155–162, 2019, [Online]. Available: https://doi.org/10.1109/VR.2019.8797867.
16. Dietz, M., Meissner, B., Goppelt, F., Schmidt-Vollus, R., On the development of virtual labs using digital twins and a proposal for didactic optimization using design-based research, in: *Proc. 2021 Fifth World Conf. Smart Trends Syst. Security Sustainability (WorldS4)*, pp. 186–191, 2021, [Online]. Available: https://doi.org/10.1109/WorldS451998.2021.9514044.
17. Alsaleh, S., Tepljakov, A., Kose, A., Belikov, J., Petlenkov, E., ReImagine Lab: Bridging the gap between hands-on, virtual and remote control engineering laboratories using digital twins and extended reality. *IEEE Access*, 10, 89924–89943, 2022.
18. Mingshi, L.I., Yue, M.A., Zhenyu, Y.I.N., Chunxiao, W.A.N.G., Structural design of digital twin laboratory model based on instruments sharing platform, in: *Proc. 2020 Chinese Control and Decision Conf. (CCDC)*, Aug. 2020, pp. 797–802, [Online]. Available: https://doi.org/10.1109/CCDC49329.2020.9164813.
19. Song, L., Lu, Z., Petsangsri, S., Reconstruction of smart learning space based on digital twin (DT) technology, in: *Proc. 2020 7th Int. Conf. Dependable Syst. Their Appl. (DSA)*, pp. 398–406, 2020, [Online]. Available: https://doi.org/10.1109/DSA51864.2020.00070.
20. Siyan, C., Tinghuai, W., Xiaomei, L., Liu, Z., Danying, W., Research on the improvement of teachers' teaching ability based on machine learning and

digital twin technology. *J. Intell. Fuzzy Syst.*, 40, 4, 7323–7334, 2021, [Online]. Available: https://doi.org/10.3233/JIFS-189557.
21. Kouvara, T., Tsoni, R., Verykios, V.S., Openness is not enough without inclusiveness: The learning analytics parable, in: *Innovating Higher Education Conf. 2022*, [Online]. Available: https://www.academia.edu/92170099/Openness_Is_not_Enough_Without_Inclusiveness_The_Learning_Analytics_Parable?uc-sb-sw=22266962.
22. El Saddik, A., Digital twins: The convergence of multimedia technologies. *IEEE Multimedia*, 25, 2, 87–92, 2018, [Online]. Available: https://doi.org/10.1109/MMUL.2018.023121167.
23. Hawkinson, E., Automation in education with digital twins: Trends and issues. *Int. J. Open Distance e-Learning (IJODeL)*, 8, 2, 1–9, 2022, [Online]. Available: https://ijodel.upou.edu.ph/index.php/ijodel/article/view/229/239.
24. Addanki, K. and Corrin, L., Unveiling the potential of Digital Twin technology for higher education, in: *Proc. ASCILITE 2023 Conf*, pp. 1–10, 2023, [Online]. Available: https://doi.org/10.14742/apubs.2023.635.
25. Maksimovic, M. and Davidovic, N., The role of Digital Twin technology in transforming engineering education, in: *9th Int. Sci. Conf. Technics and Informatics in Education*, pp. 264–270, 2022, [Online]. Available: https://doi.org/10.46793/TIE22.264M.
26. Klami, A., Damoulas, T., Engkvist, O., Rinke, P., Kaski, S., Virtual Laboratories: Transforming research with AI (Version 1), TechRxiv, 2022, [Online]. Available: https://doi.org/10.36227/techrxiv.20412540.v1.
27. Walkington, C. and Bernacki, M.L., Appraising research on personalized learning: Definitions, theoretical alignment, advancements, and future directions. *J. Res. Technol. Educ.*, 52, 3, 235–252, 2020, [Online]. Available: https://doi.org/10.1080/15391523.2020.1747757.
28. Sylvester, A., Mines, R., David, R., Campbell-Meier, J., Conceptualization of Digital Twins in an Education Services Environment: A Straw Man Proposal, in: *Proc. 56th Hawaii Int. Conf. Syst. Sci*, pp. 5643–5652, 2023, [Online]. Available: https://hdl.handle.net/10125/103321.
29. Martynov, V., Filosova, E., Egorova, Y., Information architecture to support engineering education in the era of industry 4.0, in: *2022 VI Int. Conf. on Information Technologies in Engineering Education (Inforino)*, pp. 1–5, 2022, [Online]. Available: https://doi.org/10.1109/Inforino53888.2022.9782999.
30. Berisha-Gawlowski, A., Caruso, C., Harteis, C., M., The concept of a Digital Twin and its potential for learning organizations, in: *Digital Transformation of Learning Organizations*, D. Ifenthaler, S. Hofhues, Egloffstein, C. Helbig (Eds.), pp. 95–114, Springer, Cham, 2021, [Online]. Available: https://doi.org/10.1007/978-3-030-55878-9_6.
31. Chamorro-Atalaya, O., *et al.*, Use of digital twin technology in the teaching-learning process, in the field of university education: A bibliometric review. *Int. J. Learn. Teach. Educ. Res.*, 23, 2, 313–329, 2024, [Online]. Available: https://doi.org/10.26803/ijlter.23.2.15.

32. Lopez-Gracia, A., Gonzalez-Ramirez, T., Pablos-Pons, J.D., Key factors in the educational digital transformation of educational organizations. *Profesorado Sci. J.*, 26, 2, 75–101, 2022, [Online]. Available: https://doi.org/10.30827/profesorado.v26i2.21222.
33. Carvajal, C.A.R. and Arenas, N.A.G., Approach to digital transformation in higher education institutions through the theory of change. *En Contexto J.*, 10, 17, 229–263, 2022.
34. Camacho, J.P.C. and Loayza, L.M.H., Development of a digital twin of the handling and sorting stations of the Festo MPS 500 modular production system, Bachelor's thesis, Electronic Engineering Career, Salesian Polytechnic University, Cuenca, Ecuador, 2023, [Online]. Available: https://dspace.ups.edu.ec/handle/123456789/24619.
35. Lin, J., Development of digital twins of simple linear elastic structures, Bachelor's thesis, Barcelona School of Engineering, Universitat Politècnica de Catalunya, Barcelona, Spain, 2022, [Online]. Available: https://upcommons.upc.edu/handle/2117/389759.
36. Trujillo, V.G., Rodriguez, A.L., Mejia, A.D., Lopez, P.R., Digital transformation in Latin America: a systematic review. *Venez. Manag. J.*, 27, 100, 1519–1536, 2022, [Online]. Available: https://doi.org/10.52080/rvgluz.27.100.15.
37. Anez, R.J., Modeling and virtual commissioning of the digital twin of a Flowpack machine with the Melsoft Gemini tool, M.S. thesis, Univ. Pais Vasco, Bilbao, Spain, 2023, [Online]. Available: https://addi.ehu.es/handle/10810/62801.
38. Grisales, G.A.D.J., Prospects for appropriation of digital twins in learning factories for decision-making. *EDUTEC 2022, Palma XXV Int. Cong*, pp. 73–77, 2022, [Online]. Available: https://dspace.uib.es/xmlui/handle/11201/160460?show=full.
39. Garcia, D.S.E., Digital twin in AR of the Automation Plant of the Santo Tomas University, Thesis, Univ. Santo Tomas, Bucaramanga, Colombia, 2023, [Online]. Available: https://repository.usta.edu.co/handle/11634/53052.
40. Grau, F.G., Bautista, C.V., Cantabrana, J.L.L., Strategies for the digital transformation of an educational center: a systematic review. *RiiTE*, 13, 1, 157–172, 2022, [Online]. Available: https://doi.org/10.6018/riite.533971.
41. Clarke, H.A., Urban digital twins, Thesis, Polytechnic Univ. Cartagena, Cartagena, Colombia, 2023, [Online]. Available: https://repositorio.upct.es/handle/10317/12665.
42. Torres, R.B., FMS200 flexible manufacturing cell station 3 digital twin, Thesis, Jaen Univ., Spain, 2022, [Online]. Available: https://crea.ujaen.es/bitstream/10953.1/19855/1/MEMORIA-GEMELODIGITAL-ESTACION-8-CELULA-DE-FABRICACION-FLEXIBLE-FMS200-firmado%20-%20Oscar%20Espejo%20Quesada.pdf.
43. Kartashova, L., Gurzhii, A., Zaichuk, V., Sorochan, T., Zhuravlev, F., Digital twin of an educational institution: An innovative concept of blended learning, in: *Proc. 1st Symp. Advances Educational Technol.*

(AET 2020), vol. 2, pp. 300–310, 2022, [Online]. Available: https://doi.org/10.5220/0010931100003364.

44. Selim, A., Ali, I., Saracevic, M., Ristevski, B., Application of the digital twin model in higher education. *Multimedia Tools Appl.*, 2024, [Online]. Available: https://doi.org/10.1007/s11042-024-20014-3.
45. Hermann, M., Pentek, T., Otto, B., Design principles for Industrie 4.0 scenarios, in: *Proc. 49th Hawaii Int. Conf. Syst. Sci. (HICSS)*, pp. 3928–3937, 2016, [Online]. Available: https://doi.org/10.1109/HICSS.2016.488.
46. Sekione, R.J., Laurence, T.Y., Jong, H.P., Digital twin-assisted resource allocation framework based on edge collaboration for vehicular edge computing. *Future Gener. Comput. Syst.*, 150, 243–254, 2023, [Online]. Available: https://doi.org/10.1016/j.future.2023.09.001.
47. Reddy, M., Applications of AI-powered digital twins in education: Simulating campus operations for sustainable growth, Express Computer, Nov. 11, 2024, [Online]. Available: https://www.expresscomputer.in/guest-blogs/applications-of-ai-powered-digital-twins-in-education-simulating-campus-operations-for-sustainable-g.
48. Jha, R., Are digital twins seen as a threat or an opportunity in the education sector?, Blog Site of KSOM, Sep. 25, 2024, [Online]. Available: https://blog.ksom.ac.in/2024/09/are-digital-twins-seen-as-a-threat-or-an-opportunity-in-the-education-sector/.
49. Parmar, R., Leiponen, A., Tomas, L.D., Building an organizational digital twin. *Bus. Horiz.*, 63, 6, 725–736, 2020, [Online]. Available: https://doi.org/10.1016/j.bushor.2020.08.001.
50. Lu, Y., Liu, C., Wang, K.I.K., Huang, H., Xu, X., Digital twin-driven smart manufacturing: Connotation, reference model, applications, and research issues. *Robot. Comput.-Integr. Manuf.*, 61, 2019, [Online]. Available: https://doi.org/10.1016/j.rcim.2019.101837.
51. Maddikunta, P.K.R., *et al.*, Industry 5.0: A survey on enabling technologies and potential applications. *J. Ind. Inf. Integr.*, 2021, [Online]. Available: https://doi.org/10.1016/j.jii.2021.100257.
52. Hattinger, M. and Eriksson, K., Mind the gap: A collaborative competence e-learning model evolving between university and industry. *J. Strategic Innov. Sustain.*, 15, 5, 1–15, 2020, [Online]. Available: https://doi.org/10.33423/jsis.v15i5.3582.
53. Eriksson, K., Branneby, E., Hagelin, M., An educational model for competence development within simulation and technologies for Industry 4.0, in: *Proc. Winter Simulation Conf*, 2021, [Online]. Available: https://doi.org/10.1109/WSC52266.2021.9715395.
54. Eriksson, K., Alsaleh, A., Far, S.B., Stjern, D., Applying digital twin technology in higher education: An automation line case study, in: *Proc. SPS2022*, IOS Press, pp. 461–468, 2022, [Online]. Available: https://doi.org/10.3233/ATDE220165.

55. Jones, D., Snider, C., Nassehi, A., Yon, J., Hicks, B., Characterising the digital twin: A systematic literature review. *CIRP J. Manuf. Sci. Technol.*, 29, A, 36–52, 2020, [Online]. Available: https://doi.org/10.1016/j.cirpj.2020.02.002.
56. Elnakib, A.A., *et al.*, Privacy and security challenges of the digital twin: Systematic literature review. *Multimedia Tools Appl.*, 82, 34527–34561, 2023, [Online]. Available: https://doi.org/10.1007/s11042-023-14636-w.
57. de Magalhaes, S.T., The European Union's General Data Protection Regulation (GDPR), in: *Cyber Security Practitioner's Guide*, pp. 529–558, Mar. 2020, [Online]. Available: https://doi.org/10.1142/9789811204463_0015.
58. Wang, Y., *et al.*, A survey on digital twins: Architecture, enabling technologies, security and privacy, and future prospects. *IEEE Internet Things J.*, 2023, [Online]. Available: https://doi.org/10.1109/JIOT.2023.3244205.
59. Crawford, M., Five ways to protect digital twins that probably lack cyber protection, ASME, 2021, [Online]. Available: https://www.asme.org/topics-resources/content/five-ways-to-cyber-protect-your-digital-twin.
60. Wernick, A., Banzuzi, E., Mörelius-Wulff, A., Do European smart city developers dream of GDPR-free countries? *Internet Policy Rev.*, 12, 1, 1–45, 2023, [Online]. Available: https://doi.org/10.14763/2023.1.1660.
61. Lohr, K.N. and Donaldson, M.S. (Eds.), *Health data in the information age: Use, disclosure, and privacy*, National Academies Press, Washington, DC, 1994.
62. Sweeney, L., Achieving k-anonymity privacy protection using generalization and suppression. *Int. J. Uncertainty Fuzziness Knowl.-Based Syst.*, 10, 5, 571–588, 2002, [Online]. Available: https://doi.org/10.1142/S021848850200165X.
63. Winter, P.D. and Chico, T.J., Using the NASSS framework to identify barriers and facilitators for the implementation of digital twins in cardiovascular medicine. *Sensors*, 23, 14, 6333, 2023, [Online]. Available: https://doi.org/10.3390/s23146333.
64. Rahmadian, E., Feitosa, D., Virantina, Y., Digital twins, big data governance, and sustainable tourism. *Ethics Inf. Technol.*, 25, 4, 61, 2023, [Online]. Available: https://doi.org/10.1007/s10676-023-09730-w.
65. Turab, M. and Jamil, S., A comprehensive survey of digital twins in healthcare in the era of metaverse. *BioMedInformatics*, 3, 3, 563–584, 2023, [Online]. Available: https://doi.org/10.3390/biomedinformatics3030039.
66. Afzal, M., *et al.*, Delving into the digital twin developments and applications in the construction industry: A PRISMA approach. *Sustainability*, 15, 23, 16436, 2023, [Online]. Available: https://doi.org/10.3390/su152316436.
67. Pervez, Z., Khan, Z., Ghafoor, A., Soomro, K., SIGNED: Smart city digital twin verifiable data framework. *IEEE Access*, 11, 29430–29446, 2023, [Online]. Available: https://doi.org/10.1109/ACCESS.2023.3263651.
68. Naikwadi, A.S. and Shrivastav, S.J., Privacy and ethical issues in digital twins. *Int. Res. J. Modernization Eng. Technol. Sci.*, 7, 2, 3258–3261, 2025, [Online]. Available: https://www.irjmets.com/uploadedfiles/paper//issue_2_february_2025/67559/final/fin_irjmets1739855171.pdf.

69. INCIBE, Cybersecurity challenges of digital twins: Threats and security measures, INCIBE-CERT, Sep. 5, 2024, [Online]. Available: https://www.incibe.es/en/incibe-cert/blog/cybersecurity-challenges-digital-twins-threats-and-security-measures.
70. Enzoic, Twin to win: Security pros and cons of digital twins, 2025, [Online]. Available: https://www.enzoic.com/blog/pros-and-cons-of-digital-twins.
71. Simpson, I., The security implications of a digital twin, Netskope, Jan. 24, 2023, [Online]. Available: https://www.netskope.com/blog/the-security-implications-of-a-digital-twin.
72. Arantes, J., Digital twins and the terminology of 'personalization' or 'personalized learning' in educational policy: A discussion paper. *Policy Futures Educ.*, 22, 4, 524–543, 2023, [Online]. Available: https://doi.org/10.1177/14782103231176357.
73. Toofaninejad, E., Rezapour, S.M., Kalantarion, M., Utilizing Digital Twins for the Transformation of Medical Education. *J. Adv. Med. Educ. Prof.*, 12, 2, 132–133, Apr. 2024. Available: https://doi.org/10.30476/JAMP.2023.100264.1883.
74. Corrin, L., Colvin, C., de Barba, P., Fisher, J., Mirriahi, N., Bakharia, A., Enhancing the ethical use of learning analytics in Australian higher education, in: *Proc. ASCILITE 2019: Shaping the Future of Learning with Artificial Intelligence: Enhance · Change · Transformation*, pp. 631–639, Singapore, Nov. 2019.

18

Navigating the Future: Cloud Computing's Progress and Challenges in Healthcare

Arun Kumar Rana[1*], Sumit Kumar Rana[2], Deepak Kumar[3], Ram Krishna[3], Anurag Singh[4] and Harendra Singh[3]

[1]*Galgotias College of Engineering of Technology, Greater Noida, Uttar Pradesh, India*
[2]*University Institute of Engineering, Chandigarh University, Mohali, Punjab, India*
[3]*Department of Electrical & Electronics Engineering, G. L. Bajaj Institute of Technology and Management, Greater Noida, Uttar Pradesh, India*
[4]*ITS Engineering College, Greater Noida, India*

Abstract

Cloud computing has radically changed multiple industries including healthcare by providing flexible cost-effective and scalable solution for handling large amount of data. This paper explores the role of cloud computing in healthcare, its advantages, challenges, and its potential to enhance healthcare delivery. This paper explores the role of cloud computing in healthcare, focusing on its benefits, challenges, and transformative potential for improving healthcare delivery. It discusses various cloud computing models and technologies, highlights case studies, and examines the regulatory and security concerns that must be addressed. It discusses different cloud computing technologies and models. It highlights case studies, regulatory requirements and compliance frameworks, and security concern that must be addressed. By giving a comprehensive understanding of current and future state of cloud computing in healthcare, this paper purpose is to enhance the ongoing research in this vital area.

Keywords: Cloud computing, healthcare, cost scalability, infrastructure as a service, platform as a service, software as a service, scalability

**Corresponding author*: ranaarun1@gmail.com

Shubham Mahajan, Davinder Paul Singh, Amit Kant Pandit and Paras Chawla (eds.) Ensuring Privacy in Digital Twin Ecosystems, (521–534) © 2026 Scrivener Publishing LLC

Introduction

Healthcare is a data-intensive sector that gives the result of huge amount of data from patient record to medical images. The growing challenge is to manage and store huge amount of data security by ensuring efficient access. Traditionally data storage system is having a loop of challenges such as maintenance cost scalability and data accessibility. Cloud computing is giving a solution to these problems by giving virtualized resource through internet enabling the storage processing and sharing of large datasets [1–6].

Cloud computing has the capability to revolutionize healthcare by enhancing efficiency, decreasing costs, and enabling innovative solutions such as personalized treatment, report monitoring, and telemedicine. This paper gives an insight of cloud computing's importance in healthcare, detailing its advantages implementation strategies security concerns and real-time usage [7–12]. Figure 18.1 shows cloud computing in healthcare.

18.1 What is Cloud Computing?

Cloud computing denotes to the transfer of computing amenities—such as storage, processing power, software, and networking over the internet [13–20].

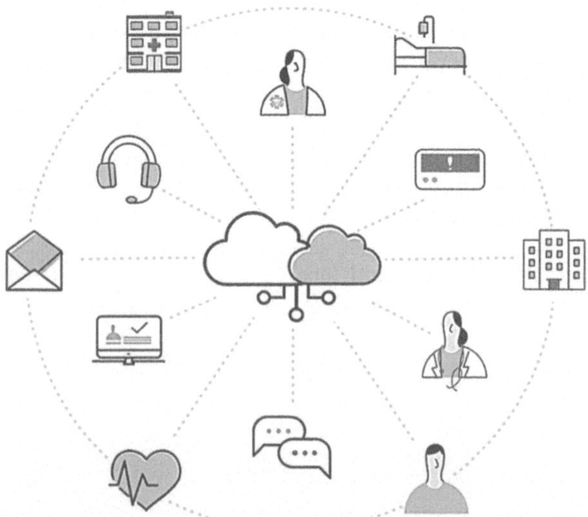

Figure 18.1 Cloud computing in healthcare.

These services are typically provided by third-party cloud service providers; third-party cloud service providers are providing these services that work on huge data centers that host and handle the infrastructure. Cloud computing is generally divided into several service models:

1. **Infrastructure as a service (IaaS):** IaaS is providing virtualized computing resources such as on demand networking virtual machines and storage.
2. **Platform as a service (PaaS):** PaaS is providing a platform for developing managing application and running without the complexity of managing the given hardware.
3. **Software as a service (SaaS):** SaaS provides software application over the Internet and removing the need for customer to install and maintain them on local devices.

Healthcare organizations are increasingly adopting these models to manage patient data, support clinical workflows, and improve collaboration among healthcare professionals [21–28].

18.2 Advantages of Cloud Computing in Healthcare

18.2.1 Scalability

Cloud computing provides flexible scalability, which enables healthcare organizations to scale up or down, depending on the needs. This is important as it considers the varying amounts of healthcare data that may be generated, such as during outbreak periods of disease or seasonal changes in volumes of patients.

18.2.2 Cost Efficiency

Through a transition to cloud infrastructure, healthcare organizations are able to minimize capital expenses on hardware and software. Further, the pay-as-you-go model that comes with cloud services guarantees that healthcare providers will only be required to pay for resources consumed, thereby making budgeting easier.

18.2.3 Improved Collaboration

Cloud computing underpins real-time collaboration between well-being laborers independent of their area. It is especially valuable for multidisciplinary groups, telemedicine meetings, and inaccessible persistent observing. It makes it simple to share electronic well-being records (electronic health records [EHRs]), restorative pictures, and other understanding information, coming about in more facilitated care.

18.2.4 Data Accessibility

Cloud stages encourage secure, on-demand access to quiet data from nearly anyplace, progressing persistent care. Specialists are able to get to understanding histories and therapeutic records indeed when exterior to the clinic, ensuring that treatment choices are based on current information.

18.2.5 Resource Optimization

Cloud computing decreases the requirement for overwhelming forthright speculation in information technology framework, moving costs to a pay-as-you-go demonstration. This adaptability permits healthcare organizations to scale assets in reaction to fluctuating requests, such as amid malady episodes or regular surges.

18.2.6 Automated Workflows

Characteristic dialect preparing (NLP) and artificial intelligence (AI)–powered computerization streamline authoritative assignments, such as EHR documentation and understanding triage. For illustration, computerized colleagues can cut charting time by half, liberating clinicians to center more on understanding care.

18.2.7 Disaster Recovery and Business Continuity

Cloud computing provides high-capacity backup and disaster recovery capabilities that maintain continuity of care even when the system or nature itself suffers from disasters. Cloud providers commonly provide data redundancy in multiple sites, which helps protect healthcare organizations against data loss.

18.3 Challenges of Cloud Computing in Healthcare

18.3.1 Security and Privacy

Healthcare information is extremely sensitive, and security for it is of utmost concern in the use of cloud computing. HIPAA (Health Insurance Portability and Accountability Act) compliance in America and other local laws mandate that healthcare organizations institute tight data security standards.

Data security challenges are there with the rise in healthcare data breaches; robust security is paramount. Essential measures include the following:

- Encryption for data at rest and in transit
- Identity and access management with multifactor authentication
- Network security tools such as firewalls and intrusion detection/prevention systems
- Compliance monitoring for regulations such as HIPAA and General Data Protection Regulation (GDPR)
- Backup and disaster recovery with geodistributed storage for resilience

Cloud service providers should ensure that data are encrypted in transit and at rest, that there are proper access controls, and that security audits are regularly performed. Nevertheless, even with these measures, data breaches and cyberattacks are still a threat in the healthcare sector [29–31].

18.3.2 Data Interoperability

Interoperability—the capacity of various systems to send and utilize information seamlessly—is a big challenge in healthcare. Most healthcare organizations have distinct EHR systems, which are not necessarily compatible with the cloud. Data need to be transferred in standardized and secure fashion across heterogeneous systems in order to fully take advantage of cloud computing. A persistent challenge in healthcare is interoperability—seamless data exchange between disparate EHR systems and cloud platforms. Standards such as HL7 FHIR (Fast Healthcare Interoperability Resources) are being adopted to facilitate secure, standardized data sharing, improving coordinated care and enabling cross-institutional research.

18.3.3 Regulatory Compliance

Healthcare information is directed by strict laws that cover capacity, access, and transmission. Cloud providers got to meet directions such as HIPAA, the Common Data Affirmation Heading (GDPR) inside the European Union (EU), and neighborhood laws. It incorporates complexity to educate that must fulfill understanding through affirmation cloud organizations. Cloud providers must back compliance with frameworks such as HIPAA (US), GDPR (EU), and adjacent laws. This incorporates standard security surveys, strict access controls, and direct data taking care of approaches.

18.3.4 Reliability and Downtime

Whereas cloud providers do pledge tall availability, there is no outline that is totally faultless when it comes to downtime. Cloud dealers signed-on benefit level assertions for uptime and unwavering quality can guarantee healthcare organizations that they have. Downtime in well-being frameworks can put off treatment, imperil understanding security, and make systemic operational disturbance.

18.3.5 Blockchain Integration

Blockchain is developing as a key innovation for upgrading information astuteness and auditability in healthcare. Its decentralized record guarantees tamper-evident records and straightforward get to logs, which is particularly profitable for therapeutic records and clinical trials. Coordination blockchain with cloud stages reinforces compliance and understanding beliefs.

18.4 Cloud Computing Models in Healthcare

18.4.1 Public Cloud

In a third-party public cloud model, the operation and the infrastructure are owned and managed by the third-party provider and shared among a number of organizations. Public cloud services are adaptive and economical but can be challenging in regulatory compliance as well as data security.

18.4.2 Private Cloud

Private clouds provide committed resources to one healthcare organization, either on site or by a third-party vendor. This option provides more data security and compliance management but is generally more costly than public cloud options.

18.4.3 Hybrid Cloud

Hybrid cloud is a mix of public and private cloud infrastructure, enabling healthcare organizations to hold private data on a private cloud while using public cloud services for less sensitive applications. This setup gives them more flexibility and enables them to manage cost and security based on their needs.

18.5 Use Cases of Cloud Computing in Healthcare

18.5.1 EHR Management

Cloud-based electronic well-being record frameworks offer healthcare suppliers a secure store in which to keep persistent records, see them over the Web, and send them to other suppliers. Cloud-based EHR systems have the capability to enhance patient care by enhancing coordination of care among healthcare providers and a complete picture of a patient's medical history.

18.5.2 Telemedicine

Cloud computing empowers farther healthcare administrations such as telemedicine interviews over video conferencing and farther checking computer program. Cloud computing also empowers the capacity and examination of quiet information to help in real-time persistent checking and opportune mediations by healthcare experts. Cloud computing has fueled the explosive growth of telemedicine, especially since 2020. Beyond virtual consultations, cloud platforms now support sophisticated remote monitoring, where IoT-enabled devices continuously transmit patient vitals and health trends to clinicians. This enables proactive care for chronic disease management and postoperative recovery, improving outcomes while reducing hospital visits. For example, cloud-based platforms allow real-time monitoring of cardiac arrhythmias *via* wearable devices, with automated alerts for clinicians.

18.5.3 Medical Imaging

Cloud imaging medicine solutions enable medical images, such as X-rays, magnetic resonance imaging, and computed tomography (CT) scans, to be saved, shared, and interpreted by medical practitioners. Cloud platforms have enormous storage and advanced analytics capabilities, which can improve the accuracy of diagnosis and minimize the use of physical storage. AI algorithms, particularly convolutional neural networks, outperform radiologists in detecting conditions such as pneumonia from chest X-rays and identifying metastatic lymph nodes in pathology slides. For instance, DeepMind Health's retinal scan analysis detects early diabetic retinopathy with 94% accuracy, enabling timely interventions.

18.5.4 Big Data Analytics

Cloud computing enables the acquisition, storage, and examination of massive healthcare datasets. With cloud-based analytics, healthcare organizations can inform choices, enhance decision-making, and tailor treatments. Large datasets such as these can be analyzed by machine learning (ML) and AI models to foretell the outcome of patients and optimize the allocation of resources.

18.5.5 Drug Discovery and Personalized Medicine

ML accelerates drug development by screening chemical compounds for target interactions. Deep learning models at MD Anderson predict radiation toxicity in cancer patients, optimizing treatment plans. Precision therapeutics is integrating multi-omic data (genomic, proteomic) with AI tailors' therapies for conditions such as cancer. For example, IBM Watson for Oncology recommends personalized regimens based on tumor profiles.

18.5.6 Operational Efficiency

NLP automates EHR documentation, reducing administrative burdens. Nuance's Dragon Ambient experience cuts charting time by 50%. AI-powered chatbots (e.g., Babylon Health) triage symptoms, reducing unnecessary clinic visits.

18.5.7 Remote Patient Monitoring

Wearables with edge analytics (e.g., cardiac screens) recognize arrhythmias in veritable time, actuating alerts without cloud dependence. Intel's edge contraptions engage attack pumps to auto-adjust measurements based on glucose levels. In COVID-19 response, edge contraptions took care of lung ultrasound data at point of care, diminishing delays in diagnosing essential cases.

18.5.8 Telemedicine and Surgical Robotics

Edge-based video preprocessing decreases inertia in telehealth interviews, ensuring smooth 4K video spilling in low-bandwidth areas. Mechanical surgery systems similar to the da Vinci Xi utilize edge center points for real-time haptic feedback, minimizing procedural danger.

18.5.9 Digital Healthcare Platforms and Collaboration

Computerized healthcare stages (DHPs), built on cloud-native plans, encouraged information surfaces, prebuilt trade capabilities, and composition contraptions to make comprehensive applications. These stages engage clinical collaboration, understanding engagement, and unfaltering information trade, supporting multidisciplinary care bunches and virtual healthcare communities.

18.6 Future Trends and Opportunities

18.6.1 AI and ML Integration

Cloud-based AI/ML stages are revolutionizing diagnostics and treatment by analyzing ceaseless datasets from helpful imaging, genomics, and EHRs. For occasion, DeepMind's AI wraps up 94% precision in recognizing diabetic retinopathy through retinal looks, whereas IBM Watson for Oncology businesses tumor profiles to support personalized cancer solutions. Integration with NLP robotizes EHR documentation, reducing authoritative burdens by 50%, and AI-driven chatbots streamline constant triage. Be that since it may, challenges connect guaranteeing outline straightforwardness and tending to inclines in arranging information.

18.6.2 Edge Computing

Edge computing shapes information locally on contraptions such as wearables or bedside screens, lessening torpidity for basic applications. For layout, Medtronic's glucose screens anticipate hypoglycemia in legitimate to goodness time, whereas edge-enabled ambulances analyze CT checks en course to clinics, cutting stroke treatment times. This approach minimizes dependence on cloud organize, guaranteeing esteem within the middle of organize control blackouts. In telemedicine, edge centers preprocess 4K video streams for smooth interviews in low-bandwidth areas.

18.6.3 Blockchain for Healthcare Data Security

Blockchain's decentralized record ensures tamper-proof records and direct survey trails, tending to vulnerabilities in centralized systems. Cryptographic calculations such as AES and ECC scramble tireless data, whereas smart contracts robotize access controls. For outline, blockchain-powered EHRs engage secure, consent-based data sharing over teach, and stages such as Medwave utilize it to expect charging blackmail [32–37].

18.6.4 Personalized and Precision Medicine

Cloud stages facilitated multi-omic data (genomic, proteomic) with AI to tailor medications. IBM Watson for Genomics recognizes critical changes in cancer, although organizations such as Google Cloud-Quantiphi enliven steady revelation utilizing AI-driven genomic examination. AWS Wellbeing Lake engages Tufts Pharmaceutical to personalize sepsis medications by collecting data from wearables and EHRs. These systems diminish trial-and-error support, but impediments join data standardization and ethical concerns over genetic security.

18.6.5 Global Health and Accessibility

Cloud-based telemedicine and EHRs bridge gaps in underserved regions, enabling remote consultations and diagnostic support. For example, edge computing in low-resource areas processes lung ultrasound data for COVID-19 diagnostics, whereas blockchain-secured platforms in India improve rural care coordination. Scalable cloud infrastructure reduces costs for clinics, and AI-powered tools such as Nuance's Dragon Ambient experience automate clinical documentation. Challenges include internet accessibility and training healthcare workers in digital tools.

18.6.6 Internet of Medical Things Integration

A significant future prospect for cloud computing in healthcare, highlighted in recent research, is the integration of the Internet of Medical Things (IoMT). IoMT refers to a network of connected medical devices—such as wearables, remote monitors, and smart implants—which collect, transmit, and analyze patient data in real time. When combined with cloud computing platforms, IoMT enables continuous patient monitoring, early detection of health anomalies, and rapid intervention by healthcare providers. For case, cloud-connected cardiac screens can right away caution clinicians to arrhythmias or other basic occasions, progressing persistent security and results. The cloud's versatility underpins the accumulation and investigation of gigantic, heterogeneous information streams from differing IoMT gadgets, encouraging populace well-being analytics and personalized care. As IoMT appropriation develops, cloud stages will be central to overseeing gadget interoperability, guaranteeing information security, and supporting administrative compliance, in this manner driving another wave of advancement in computerized healthcare conveyance.

Conclusion

Cloud computing holds progressive potential for the healthcare industry, with arrangements that move forward information administration, bolster real-time collaboration, and speed up quiet care. Be that as it may, information security, privacy, and administrative compliance concerns must be legitimately tended to guarantee the fruitful usage of cloud advances. With the headway of cloud foundation, the consolidation of AI, ML, and blockchain innovations will improve the esteem and usefulness of cloud computing for healthcare assistance, opening entryways to unused openings and upgrading persistent results. The merging of AI, edge computing, and blockchain is making a worldview move from receptive to proactive healthcare. Whereas AI improves symptomatic exactness, edge computing empowers real-time intercessions, and blockchain guarantees belief in information sharing. Overcoming specialized and administrative challenges will require collaboration between tech designers, clinicians, and policymakers. Emerging standards such as IEEE P2801 for clinical AI and HL7's FHIR blockchain extensions are critical to scaling these technologies.

AI disclosure statement: The author acknowledges the use of AI-based tools for minor language editing or grammatical correction. However, all intellectual contributions, analyses, and conclusions presented in this chapter are entirely the author's own.

References

1. Agarwal, R. and Dhar, V., Cloud computing in healthcare: Opportunities and challenges. *Healthcare Technol. Lett.*, 10, 2, 50–61, 2023.
2. Chien, H. and Chang, Y., Data security and privacy in cloud-based health-care systems. *J. Med. Syst.*, 48, 6, 1001–1014, 2024.
3. Jones, S.A. and Lee, T.H., The future of telemedicine and cloud computing in healthcare. *Telemed. e-Health*, 31, 3, 123–131, 2025.
4. Rana, A., Sharma, S., Nisar, K., Ibrahim, A., Ag, A., Dhawan, S., Goyal, N., The Rise of Blockchain Internet of Things (BIoT): Secured, Device-to-Device Architecture and Simulation Scenarios. *Appl. Sci.*, 12, 15, 7694, 2022.
5. Dewan, R., Nagpal, T., Rana, A.K., Iot based efficient and secure building architecture with constrained application protocol (coap). *J. Electr. Syst.*, 20, 7s, 1456–1467, 2024.
6. Jha, R., Singh, A., Rana, A.K., Convergence of AR, VR, IoT with Artificial Intelligence to Train Surgeons for Medical Surgeries, in: *Evolution of Machine Learning and Internet of Things Applications in Biomedical Engineering*, pp. 218–224, CRC Press, UK, 2025.
7. Singh, I., Singh, B., Rana, A.K., Role and Impact of Blockchain–IoT-Enabled Supply Chain Management Model for Medical Supply, in: *Convergence of Blockchain and Internet of Things in Healthcare*, pp. 54–67, p. CRC Press, 2024.
8. Negi, A.S., Gupta, P., Srivastava, R., Rana, A.K., COVID-19 Detection and Pandemic Prevention System Using Data Science, in: *Convergence of Blockchain and Internet of Things in Healthcare*, pp. 210–222, CRC Press, UK, 2024.
9. Dewan, R., Rana, A.K., Nagpal, T., 5 Impact of Big Data, in: *Internet of Things and Big Data Analytics-Based Manufacturing*, p. 93, 2024.
10. Dewan, R., Rana, A.K., Nagpal, T., Rana, S.K., Singh, S., Impact of Big Data and Internet of Things in Manufacturing: Next Level of Revolution, in: *Internet of Things and Big Data Analytics-Based Manufacturing*, pp. 93–101, CRC Press, UK, 2025.
11. Chahal, N., Rana, A.K., Bansal, P., Kaur, S., Sachan, H., Modi, S., Kesarwani, A.K., Role of IoT and Big Data in Evolving Smartness in Manufacturing and

Lifestyle, in: *Internet of Things and Big Data Analytics-Based Manufacturing*, pp. 117–142, CRC Press, UK, 2025.
12. Gulati, V. and Rana, A.K., Research Applications in Healthcare with Machine Learning Approaches, in: *Internet of Things and Big Data Analytics-Based Manufacturing*, pp. 195–206.
13. Kumar, A., Sharma, S., Goyal, N., Singh, A., Cheng, X., Singh, P., Secure and energy-efficient smart building architecture with emerging technology IoT. *Comput. Commun.*, 176, 207–217, 2021.
14. Kumar, A., Sharma, S., Singh, A., Alwadain, A., Choi, B.J., Manual-Brenosa, J., Goyal, N., Revolutionary Strategies Analysis and Proposed System for Future Infrastructure in Internet of Things. *Sustainability*, 14, 1, 71, 2021.
15. Rana, A., Chakraborty, C., Sharma, S., Dhawan, S., Pani, S.K., Ashraf, I., Internet of Medical Things-Based Secure and Energy-Efficient Framework for Health Care. *Big Data*, 10, 1, 18–33, 2022.
16. Kumar, A. and Sharma, S., Internet of robotic things: Design and develop the quality of service framework for the healthcare sector using CoAP. *IAES Int. J. Robot. Autom.*, 10, 4, 289, 2021.
17. Dhawan, S., Chakraborty, C., Frnda, J., Gupta, R., Rana, A.K., Pani, S.K., SSII: secured and high-quality steganography using intelligent hybrid optimization algorithms for IoT. *IEEE Access*, 9, 87563–87578, 2021.
18. Rana, S.K., Kim, H.C., Pani, S.K., Rana, S.K., Joo, M.I., Rana, A.K., Aich, S., Blockchain-Based Model to Improve the Performance of the Next-Generation Digital Supply Chain. *Sustainability*, 13, 18, 10008, 2021.
19. Rana, A.K. and Sharma, S., Internet of Things Based Stable Increased-throughput Multi-Hop Protocol for Link Efficiency (IoT-SIMPLE) For Health Monitoring Using Wireless Body Area Networks. *Int. J. Sens. Wirel. Commun. Control*, 11, 7, 789–798, 2021.
20. Kumar, A., Sharma, S., Goyal, N., Gupta, S.K., Kumari, S., Kumar, S., Energy-Efficient fog Computing in Internet of Things based on Routing Protocol for Low-Power and Lossy Network with Contiki. *Int. J. Commun. Syst.*, 35, 4, e5049, 2022.
21. Pandit, M., Gupta, D., Anand, D., Goyal, N., Aljahdali, H.M., Mansilla, A.O., Kumar, A., Towards Design and Feasibility Analysis of DePaaS: AI Based Global Unified Software Defect Prediction Framework. *Appl. Sci.*, 12, 1, 493, 2022.
22. Lilhore, U.K., Imoize, A.L., Lee, C.C., Simaiya, S., Pani, S.K., Goyal, N., Li, C.T., Enhanced Convolutional Neural Network Model for Cassava Leaf Disease Identification and Classification. *Mathematics*, 10, 4, 580, 2022.
23. Rana, S.K., Rana, S.K., Nisar, K., Ag Ibrahim, A.A., Rana, A.K., Goyal, N., Chawla, P., Blockchain Technology and Artificial Intelligence Based Decentralized Access Control Model to Enable Secure Interoperability for Healthcare. *Sustainability*, 14, 15, 9471, 2022.
24. Rana, A.K. and Sharma, S., Enhanced energy-efficient heterogeneous routing protocols in WSNs for IoT application. *IJEAT*, 9, 1, 4418–4415, 2019.

25. Rana, A.K. and Sharma, S., Industry 4.0 manufacturing based on IoT, cloud computing, and big data: Manufacturing purpose scenario, in: *Advances in Communication and Computational Technology*, pp. 1109–1119, Springer, Singapore, 2021.
26. Rana, A.K., Krishna, R., Dhwan, S., Sharma, S., Gupta, R., Review on artificial intelligence with internet of things-problems, challenges and opportunities, in: *2019 2nd International Conference on Power Energy, Environment and Intelligent Control (PEEIC)*, pp. 383–387, IEEE, 2019, October.
27. Rana, A.K. and Sharma, S., Contiki Cooja Security Solution (CCSS) with IPv6 routing protocol for low-power and lossy networks (RPL) in Internet of Things applications, in: *Mobile Radio Communications and 5G Networks*, pp. 251–259, Springer, Singapore, 2021.
28. Kumar, A. and Sharma, S., IFTTT rely based a semantic web approach to simplifying trigger-action programming for end-user application with IoT applications, in: *Semantic IoT: Theory and Applications*, pp. 385–397, Springer, Cham, 2021.
29. Kumar, A. and Sharma, S., 11 Internet of Things, in: *Electrical and Electronic Devices, Circuits and Materials: Design and Applications*, p. 183, 2021.
30. Kumar, A., Sharma, S., Dhawan, S., Goyal, N., Lata, S., 14 E-learning with Internet of Things, in: *Internet of Things: Robotic and Drone Technology*, p. 195, 2021.
31. Dhawan, S., Gupta, R., Rana, A., Sharma, S., Various Swarm Optimization Algorithms: Review, Challenges, and Opportunities. *Soft Computing for Intelligent Systems*, pp. 291–301, 2021.
32. Mangla, S.K., Luthra, S., Jakhar, S., Gandhi, S., Muduli, K., Kumar, A., A step to clean energy-sustainability in energy system management in an emerging economy context. *J. Cleaner Prod.*, *242*, 118462, 2020.
33. Shen, L., Muduli, K., Barve, A., Developing a sustainable development framework in the context of mining industries: AHP approach. *Resour. Policy*, *46*, 15–26, 2015.
34. Panigrahi, R.R., Singh, N., Muduli, K., Digital technologies and food supply chain: A scoping view from 2010 to 2024. *Int. J. Ind. Eng. Oper. Manag.*, 2024.
35. Dhingra, S., Raut, R., Naik, K., Muduli, K., Blockchain technology applications in healthcare supply chains–A review. *IEEE Access*, 2024.
36. Swain, S. and Muduli, K., Uncovering the issues associated with AI and other disruptive technology enabled operational practices in healthcare sectors in India. *Recent Pat. Eng.*, *18*, 5, 49–65, 2024.
37. Sethy, S., Behera, R.K., Muduli, K., Kandasamy, J., Davim, J.P., Rana, J., Bio-dielectrics to improve the performance of electro discharge machining–an investigation for cleaner production opportunities. *Adv. Mater. Process. Technol.*, *10*, 3, 2354–2373, 2024.

Index

Also of Interest

Check out these other related titles from Scrivener Publishing

Blockchain Solutions for Securing Internet of Things Networks, Edited by Swati Vashisht, Santosh Kumar Srivastava, Praveen Kumar, and Shubhi Gupta, ISBN: 9781394417100. Bridge the gap between theoretical blockchain concepts and real-world IoT security with this indispensable guide to building decentralized, tamper-proof ecosystems that eliminate data tampering and unauthorized access.

Secure Blockchain and Quantum Technologies for 6G-Enabled IoT, Edited by T. Perarsi, M. Karthiga, S. Sountharrajan, E. Suganya, and Balamurugan Balusamy, ISBN: 9781394310678. Future-proof your hyper-connected infrastructure against the looming quantum threat bwith this guide to mastering blockchain-driven security frameworks and quantum-resistant architectures essential for safeguarding data integrity in the 6G-powered era.

Attacks and Defenses in Explainable Artificial Intelligence, Edited by Aml Dattatraya Vibhute, Rajesh Kumar Dhanaraj, Malathy Sathyamoorthy, and Paramasivam A. ISBN: 9781394305582. Bridge the critical gap between AI transparency and security with this essential guide to the systematic defense frameworks and ethical strategies needed to protect explainable AI (XAI) systems from sophisticated adversarial attacks.

Generative Artificial Intelligence for Next-Generation Security Paradigms, Edited by Santosh Kumar Srivastava, Durgesh Srivastava, Manoj Kumar Mahto, Ben Othman Soufiane, and Praveen Kantha, ISBN: 9781394305643. Fortify your digital defenses with this essential book, which provides a roadmap for moving beyond the limitations of traditional encryption by leveraging generative AI algorithms to proactively anticipate, detect, and mitigate the next generation of cyber threats in real-time.

Security and Privacy in 6G Communication Technology, Edited by Parita Jain, Puneet Kumar Aggarwal, Mandeep Singh, Sushil Kumar Singh, and Amit Singhal, ISBN: 9781394311002. Future-proof your knowledge and expertise in telecommunications with this essential guide, which provides a comprehensive analysis of the critical security and privacy challenges in the transition to 6G communication.

Development of 6G Networks and Technology, Edited by Suman Lata Tripathi, Mufti Mahmood, C. Narmadha, and S. Albert Alexander, ISBN: 9781394230655. *Development of 6G Networks and Technology* provides an in-depth exploration of the potential impact of 6G networks on various industries, including healthcare, agriculture, transport, and national security, making it an essential resource for researchers, scholars, and students working in the field of wireless networks and high-speed data processing systems.

Quantum Machine Learning for 6G Networks, Edited by Pallavi Sapkale, Shilpa Mehta and S. Balamurugan, ISBN: 9781394238088.

Virtual Reality and Augmented Reality with 6G Communication, Edited by B. Sundaravadivazhagan, N. Gnanasankaran, C. Pethuru Raj, and A. Saleem Raja, ISBN:9781394336050. Stay ahead of the technological curve with this essential book, which provides a comprehensive guide to the transformative convergence of Virtual Reality (VR), Augmented Reality (AR), and 6G communication.

INTEGRATED DEVICES FOR ARTIFICIAL INTELLIGENCE AND VLSI: VLSI Design, Simulation and Applications, Edited by Balwinder Raj, Suman Lata Tripathi, Tarun Chaudhary, K. Srinivasa Rao, and Mandeep Singh, ISBN: 9781394204359. With its in-depth exploration of the close connection between microelectronics, AI, and VLSI technology, this book offers valuable insights into the cutting-edge techniques and tools used in VLSI design automation, making it an essential resource for anyone seeking to stay ahead in the rapidly evolving field of VLSI design.

DECENTRALIZED SYSTEMS AND DISTRIBUTED COMPUTING, Edited by Sandhya Avasthi, Suman Lata Tripathi, Namrata Dhanda, and Satya Bhushan Verma, ISBN: 978139420436. This book provides a comprehensive exploration of next-generation internet, distributed systems, and distributed computing, offering valuable insights into their impact on society and the future of technology.

ELECTRIC VEHICLE DESIGN: Design, Simulation and Applications, Edited by Krishan Arora, Suman Lata Tripathi, and Himashu Sharma, ISBN: 9781394204373. This book will serve as a definitive guide to conceptual and practical knowledge about the design of hybrid electrical vehicles (HEV), battery electrical vehicles (BEV), fuel cell electrical vehicles (FCEV), plug-in hybrid electrical vehicles (PHEV), and efficient EV charging techniques with advanced tools and methodologies for students, engineers, and academics alike.

INDUSTRIAL CONTROL SYSTEMS, Edited by Vipin Chandra Pal, Suman Lata Tripathi, and Souvik Ganguli, ISBN: 9781119829256. This volume serves as a comprehensive guide in the journey of industrial control systems with a multidisciplinary approach to the key engineering problems in the 21st century.

MODERN AUTOMOTIVE ELECTRICAL SYSTEMS: Theory and Applications, Edited by Pedram Asef, Sanjeevikumar Padmanaban, and Andrew Lapthorn, ISBN: 1119801047. Presenting the concepts and advances of modern automotive electrical systems, this volume, written and edited by a global team of experts, also goes into the practical applications for the engineer, student, and other industry professionals.

NANODEVICES FOR INTEGRATED CIRCUIT DESIGN, Edited by Suman Lata Tripathi, Abhishek Kumar, K. Srinivasa Rao, and Prasantha R. Mudimela, ISBN: 9781394185788. Written and edited by a team of experts in the field, this important new volume broadly covers the design of nano-devices and their integrated applications in digital and analog integrated circuits (IC) design.

EXPLAINABLE MACHINE LEARNING MODELS AND ARCHITECTURES: Real-Time System Implementation, Edited by Suman Lata Tripathi and Mufti Mahmud, ISBN: 9781394185849. This cutting-edge new volume covers the hardware architecture implementation, the software implementation approach, and the efficient hardware of machine learning applications.

MACHINE LEARNING TECHNIQUES FOR VLSI CHIP DESIGN, Edited by Abhishek Kumar, Suman Lata Tripathi, and K. Srinivasa Rao, ISBN: 9781119910398. This cutting-edge new volume covers the hardware architecture implementation, the software implementation approach, and the efficient hardware of machine learning applications with FPGA or CMOS circuits, and many other aspects and applications of machine learning techniques for VLSI chip design.

INTELLIGENT GREEN TECHNOLOGIES FOR SMART CITIES, Edited by Suman Lata Tripathi, Souvik Ganguli, Abhishek Kumar, and Tengiz Magradze, ISBN: 9781119816065. Presenting the concepts and fundamentals of smart cities and developing "green" technologies, this volume, written and edited by a global team of experts, also goes into the practical applications that can be utilized across multiple disciplines and industries, for both the engineer and the student.

DESIGN AND DEVELOPMENT OF EFFICIENT ENERGY SYSTEMS, edited by Suman Lata Tripathi, Dushyant Kumar Singh, Sanjeevikumar Padmanaban, and P. Raja, ISBN 9781119761631. Covering the concepts and fundamentals of efficient energy systems, this volume, written and edited by a global team of experts, also goes into the practical applications that can be utilized across multiple industries, for both the engineer and the student.

Electrical and Electronic Devices, Circuits, and Materials: Technical Challenges and Solutions, edited by Suman Lata Tripathi, Parvej Ahmad Alvi, and Umashankar Subramaniam, ISBN 9781119750369. Covering every aspect of the design and improvement needed for solid-state electronic devices and circuit and their reliability issues, this new volume also includes overall system design for all kinds of analog and digital applications and developments in power systems.

Wiley The manufacturer's authorized representative according to the EU General Product Safety Regulation is Wiley-VCH GmbH, Boschstr. 12, 69469 Weinheim, Germany, e-mail: Product_Safety@wiley.com.

Printed and bound by CPI Group (UK) Ltd, Croydon, CR0 4YY
15/07/2026
02167956-0001